# Range Rover Owners Workshop Manual

## P. Methuen and I. Coomber

**Models covered**
All standard production models of the Range Rover,
including special limited edition variants; 3528 cc

*Does not cover specialist conversions*
*Partially covers optional equipment*

**ISBN 1 85010 189 2**

© Haynes Publishing Group 1982, 1985

ABCDE
FGHIJ
K

All rights reserved. No part of this book may be reproduced or transmitted in any form or by any
means, electronic or mechanical, including photocopying, recording or by any information storage
or retrieval system, without permission in writing from the copyright holder.

Printed in England *(606–7L1)*

**Haynes Publishing Group**
Sparkford Nr Yeovil
Somerset BA22 7JJ England

**Haynes Publications, Inc**
861 Lawrence Drive
Newbury Park
California 91320 USA

| British Library Cataloguing in Publication Data |
| --- |
| Methuen, P.M. |
| Range Rover owners workshop manual.–2nd ed. |
| (Owners Workshop Manuals) |
| 1. Range Rover |
| I. Title  II. Coomber, Ian  III.Series |
| 629.28'722  TL230.5.R3 |
| ISBN 1-85010-189-2 |

# Acknowledgements

Thanks are due to Land Rover Limited for the provision of technical information and for the use of certain illustrations. The Champion Sparking Plug Company supplied the illustrations showing the various spark plug conditions. Castrol Limited suppled the lubrication data.

Special thanks are due to Mr. Dick Robathan of Camel Cross Motors who kindly loaned us the Range Rover used as the project vehicle for this manual.

Finally, thanks to the staff at Sparkford who assisted in the production of this manual.

# About this manual

## Its aim

The aim of this manual is to help you get the best value from your car. It can do so in several ways. It can help you decide what work must be done (even should you choose to get it done by a garage), provide information on routine maintenance and servicing, and give a logical course of action and diagnosis when random faults occur. However, it is hoped that you will use the manual by tackling the work yourself. On simpler jobs it may even be quicker than booking the car into a garage and going there twice to leave and collect it. Perhaps most important, a lot of money can be saved by avoiding the costs the garage must charge to cover its labour and overheads.

The manual has drawings and descriptions to show the function of the various components so that their layout can be understood. Then the tasks are described and photographed, in a step-by-step sequence so that even a novice can do the work.

## Its arrangement

The manual is divided into thirteen Chapters, each covering a logical sub-division of the vehicle. The Chapters are each divided into Sections numbered with single figures, eg 5; and the Section into paragraphs (or sub-sections), with decimal numbers following on from the Section they are in, eg 5.1, 5.2, 5.3 etc.

It is freely illustrated, especially in those parts where there is a detailed sequence of operations to be carried out. There are two forms of illustration: figures and photographs. The figures are numbered in sequence with decimal numbers, according to their position in the Chapter: eg Fig. 6.4 is the 4th drawing/illustration in Chapter 6. Photographs are numbered (either individually or in related groups) as the Section or sub-section to which they relate.

There is an alphabetical index at the back of the manual as well as a contents list at the front.

References to the 'left' or 'right' of the vehicle are in the sense of a person in the driver's seat facing forwards.

Unless otherwise stated nuts and bolts are removed by turning anti-clockwise, and tightened by turning clockwise.

Vehicle manufacturers continually make changes to specifications and recommendations, and these, when notified, are incorporated into our manuals at the earliest opportunity.

**Whilst every care is taken to ensure that the information in this manual is correct, no liability can be accepted by the authors or publishers for loss, damage or injury caused by any errors in, or omissions, from the information given.**

# Introduction to the Range Rover

The Range Rover was first introduced in 1970 and has not looked back since, as it has been a remarkable success both at home and abroad. Production has never been able to keep up with demand even though output has been considerably increased. The introduction of the Range Rover was not intended to eclipse the success story of the more basic Land-Rover but to complement it and widen the scope of Land-Rover capability.

Powered by the well proven all alloy Rover $3\frac{1}{2}$ litre V8 engine and with permanent 4-wheel drive, the Range Rover set totally new standards in the field of both on and off-road performance and comfort. The engine is fitted with low compression cylinder heads to enable it to work happily on 2-star (91 octane rating) petrol. This may be some compensation for its thirst (around 12 to 14 mpg on average).

Transmission is by an all-synchromesh four-speed gearbox and transfer box to both front and rear axles simultaneously, but this is a different gearbox to the Land-Rover itself.

Not only can the Range Rover perform as a rugged workhorse in much the same way as the Land-Rover, but it also has an amazing main road performance, when it is considered that the top speed is around 95 mph. Also the luggage area is cavernous, and it is good as a towing vehicle.

Like the Land-Rover it features a rigid box section chassis and most of the body panels are aluminium, although the tailgate is not, and this rusts very quickly. In really tough going the differential unit in the transfer gearbox can be locked up to provide maximum traction at all four wheels. Unlike the Land-Rover however braking is by disc brakes on all four wheels.

Throughout the ten years of Range Rover production there have been minor additions and modifications, but the basic vehicle has remained the same. The 1980 model has been given a facelift externally and internally to bring it up to modern motoring standards.

Not only has the Range Rover been a huge success as a vehicle in its own right, but it has also become a status symbol both here and in Europe.

# Contents

1980 Range Rover in unusually clean condition

1980 Range Rover in use

# General dimensions, weights and capacities

*For modifications, and information applicable to later models, see Supplement at end of manual*

## Dimensions

|  | m | in |
|---|---|---|
| Overal length | 4.470 | 176 |
| Overall width | 1.780 | 70 |
| Overall height (maximum) | 1.800 | 71 |
| Wheelbase | 2.540 | 100 |
| Track – front and rear | 1.490 | 58.5 |
| Ground clearance: |  |  |
|     Under differential | 0.190 | 7.5 |
|     Under centre of vehicle | 0.317 | 12.5 |
| Turning circle | 11.280 | 444 |
| Tailgate opening – width | 1.400 | 55.25 |
| Loading platform height | 0.660 | 26 |

## Weights

|  | kg | lb |
|---|---|---|
| Kerb weight (includes oil, water and 5 gallons fuel) | 1723 | 3800 |
| Maximum vehicle weight (GVW): |  |  |
|     Front axle | 998 | 2200 |
|     Rear axle | 1506 | 3320 |
|     Total GVW | 2504 | 5520 |
| Maximum payload | 780 | 1720 |

**Note**: *Included in these figures are 100 kg (220 lb) for fitting auxiliaries (eg winches) which must only be fitted to the front of the vehicle*

## Towing capacities

|  | kg | lb |
|---|---|---|
| 4-wheel road trailer with power braking: |  |  |
|     Trailer weight | 4000 | 8816 |
|     Trailer and vehicle weight (GTW) | 6504 | 14 336 |
| 'Off-road' trailer: |  |  |
|     Trailer weight | 1000 | 2204 |
|     Trailer and vehicle weight (GTW) | 3504 | 7724 |
| Emergency use *only* – maximum road speed 18 mph (30 km/h): |  |  |
|     Trailer weight | 6000 | 13 224 |
|     Trailer and vehicle weight (GTW) | 8504 | 18 744 |
| Roof rack load – maximum | 50 | 112 |

## Capacities

|  | litres | pints |
|---|---|---|
| Engine oil: |  |  |
|     Sump | 5.1 | 9 |
|     Oil filter | 0.56 | 1 |
| Main gearbox | 2.6 | 4.5 |
| Transfer gearbox | 3.1 | 5.5 |
| Front differential: |  |  |
|     Early models | 2.5 | 4.5 |
|     Later models | 1.7 | 3.0 |
| Rear differential | 1.7 | 3.0 |
| Swivel housing | 0.26 | 0.5 |
| Steering box (not power-assisted) | 0.40 | 0.75 |

|  | litres | gallons |
|---|---|---|
| Fuel tank: |  |  |
|     Early models | 86 | 19 |
|     Later models | 81.5 | 18 |
| Cooling system | 11.3 | 2.5 |

# Buying spare parts and vehicle identification numbers

## Buying spare parts

Spare parts are available from many sources, for example: Range Rover garages, other garages and accessory shops, and motor factors. Our advice regarding spare part source is as follows:

*Officially appointed Range Rover garages* – This is the best source of parts which are peculiar to your vehicle and are otherwise not generally available (eg complete cylinder heads, internal gearbox components, badges, interior trim etc). It is also the only place at which you should buy parts if your vehicle is still under warranty – non-Range Rover components may invalidate the warranty. To be sure of obtaining the correct parts it will always be necessary to give the storeman your vehicle's engine and chassis number, and if possible, to take the old part along for positive identification. Remember that many parts are available on a factory exchange scheme – any parts returned should always be clean! It obviously makes good sense to go straight to the specialists on your vehicle for this type of part, for they are best equipped to supply you.

*Other garages and accessory shops* – These are often very good places to buy materials and components needed for the maintenance of your vehicle (eg oil filters, bulbs, fan belts, oil and greases, touch-up paint, filler paste etc). They also sell general accessories, usually have convenient opening hours, charge lower prices and can often be found not far from home.

*Motor factors* – Good factors will stock all of the more important components which wear out relatively quickly (eg clutch components, pistons, valves, exhaust systems, brake cylinders/pipes/hoses/seals/pads etc). Motor factors will often provide new or reconditioned components on a part exchange basis – this can save a considerable amount of money.

## Vehicle identification numbers

*The chassis number* will be found on a plate attached to the front body crossmember above the radiator grille (photo).

*The engine number* is stamped on the cylinder block on the left-hand top face in the centre (photo).

*The gearbox number* is stamped on the front of the gearbox in early models (photo) and on the lower rear face of the transfer box in later models.

*The front axle number* is stamped on the front of the axle casing on the left-hand side (photo) and the rear axle number is on the rear of the axle casing, also on the left-hand side.

Chassis number plate

Engine number location between the manifold branches

Gearbox number (arrowed) – early models

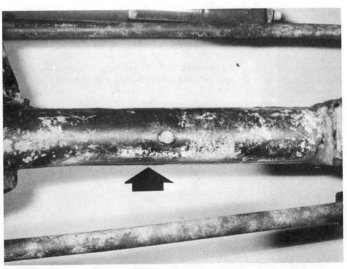

Front axle number (arrowed)

# Tools and working facilities

## Introduction

A selection of good tools is a fundamental requirement for anyone contemplating the maintenance and repair of a motor vehicle. For the owner who does not possess any, their purchase will prove a considerable expense, offsetting some of the savings made by doing-it-yourself. However, provided that the tools purchased are of good quality, they will last for many years and prove an extremely worthwhile investment.

To help the average owner to decide which tools are needed to carry out the various tasks detailed in this manual, we have compiled three lists of tools under the following headings: *Maintenance and minor repair, Repair and overhaul,* and *Special.* The newcomer to practical mechanics should start off with the *Maintenance and minor repair* tool kit and confine himself to the simpler jobs around the vehicle. Then, as his confidence and experience grow, he can undertake more difficult tasks, buying extra tools as, and when, they are needed. In this way, a *Maintenance and minor repair* tool kit can be built-up into a *Repair and overhaul* tool kit over a considerable period of time without any major cash outlays. The experienced do-it-yourselfer will have a tool kit good enough for most repair and overhaul procedures and will add tools from the *Special* category when he feels the expense is justified by the amount of use these tools will be put to.

It is obviously not possible to cover the subject of tools fully here. For those who wish to learn more about tools and their use there is a book entitled *How to Choose and Use Car Tools* available from the publishers of this manual.

## Maintenance and minor repair tool kit

The tools given in this list should be considered as a minimum requirement if routine maintenance, servicing and minor repair operations are to be undertaken. We recommend the purchase of combination spanners (ring one end, open-ended the other); although more expensive than open-ended ones, they do give the advantages of both types of spanner. The fixings used in the Range Rover are a mixture of metric, UNF and UNC sizes. For this reason, start nuts, bolts and screws with the fingers to ensure thread compatibility.

AF Combination spanners - $\frac{7}{16}$, $\frac{1}{2}$, $\frac{9}{16}$, $\frac{5}{8}$, $\frac{11}{16}$, $\frac{3}{4}$, $\frac{3}{16}$, $\frac{15}{16}$ in
Combination spanners - 10, 13, 17, 19, 22 mm
Adjustable spanner - 9 inch
Engine sump/gearbox/differential drain plug key
Spark plug spanner (with rubber insert)
Spark plug gap adjustment tool
Set of feeler gauges
Brake bleed nipple spanner
Screwdriver - 4 in long x $\frac{1}{4}$ in dia (flat blade)
Screwdriver - 4 in long x $\frac{1}{4}$ in dia (cross blade)
Combination pliers - 6 inch
Hacksaw (junior)
Tyre pump

Tyre pressure gauge
Grease gun
Oil can
Fine emery cloth (1 sheet)
Wire brush (small)
Funnel (medium size)

## Repair and overhaul tool kit

These tools are virtually essential for anyone undertaking any major repairs to a motor vehicle, and are additional to those given in the *Maintenance and minor repair* list. Included in this list is a comprehensive set of sockets. Although these are expensive they will be found invaluable as they are so versatile - particularly if various drives are included in the set. We recommend the $\frac{1}{2}$ in square-drive type, as this can be used with most proprietary torque spanners. If you cannot afford a socket set, even bought piecemeal, then inexpensive tubular box wrenches are a useful alternative.

The tools in this list will occasionally need to be supplemented by tools from the *Special* list.

Sockets (or box spanners) to cover range in previous list
Special socket or box spanner $1\frac{5}{16}$ in AF for removing and refitting the crankshaft pulley bolt and starter handle dog
Reversible ratchet drive (for use with sockets)
Extension piece, 10 inch (for use with sockets)
Universal joint (for use with sockets)
Torque wrench (for use with sockets)
Self-grip wrench - 8 inch
Ball pein hammer
Soft-faced hammer, plastic or rubber
Screwdriver - 6 in long x $\frac{5}{16}$ in dia (flat blade)
Screwdriver - 2 in long x $\frac{5}{16}$ in square (flat blade)
Screwdriver - 1$\frac{1}{2}$ in long x $\frac{1}{4}$ in dia (cross blade)
Screwdriver - 3 in long x $\frac{1}{8}$ in dia (electricians)
Pliers - electricians side cutters
Pliers - needle nosed
Pliers - circlip (internal and external)
Cold chisel - $\frac{1}{2}$ inch
Scriber (this can be made by grinding the end of a broken hacksaw blade)
Scraper (this can be made by flattening and sharpening one end of a piece of copper pipe)
Centre punch
Pin punch
Hacksaw
Valve grinding tool
Steel rule/straight-edge
Allen keys
Selection of files
Wire brush (large)
Axle-stands
Jack

## Special tools

The tools in this list are those which are not used regularly, are expensive to buy, or which need to be used in accordance with their manufacturers' instructions. Unless relatively difficult mechanical jobs are undertaken frequently, it will not be economic to buy many of these tools. Where this is the case, you could consider clubbing together with friends (or joining a motorists' club) to make a joint purchase, or borrowing the tools against a deposit from a local garage or tool hire specialist.

The following list contains only those tools and instruments freely available to the public, and not those special tools produced by the vehicle manufacturer specifically for its dealer network. You will find occasional references to these manufacturers' special tools in the text of this manual. Generally, an alternative method of doing the job without the vehicle manufacturer's special tool is given. However, sometimes, there is no alternative to using them. Where this is the case and the relevant tool cannot be bought or borrowed you will have to entrust the work to a franchised garage.

> Valve spring compressor
> Piston ring compressor
> Balljoint separator
> Universal hub/bearing puller
> Impact screwdriver
> Micrometer and/or vernier gauge
> Carburettor flow balancing device (where applicable)
> Dial gauge
> Stroboscopic timing light
> Dwell angle meter/tachometer
> Universal electrical multi-meter
> Cylinder compression gauge
> Lifting tackle
> Light with extension lead

## Buying tools

For practically all tools, a tool dealer is the best source since he will have a very comprehensive range compared with the average garage or accessory shop. Having said that, accessory shops often offer excellent quality tools at discount prices, so it pays to shop around.

Remember, you don't have to buy the most expensive items on the shelf, but it is always advisable to steer clear of the very cheap tools. There are plenty of good tools around at reasonable prices, so ask the proprietor or manager of the shop for advice before making a purchase.

## Care and maintenance of tools

Having purchased a reasonable tool kit, it is necessary to keep the tools in a clean serviceable condition. After use, always wipe off any dirt, grease and metal particles using a clean, dry cloth, before putting the tools away. Never leave them lying around after they have been used. A simple tool rack on the garage or workshop wall, for items such as screwdrivers and pliers is a good idea. Store all normal spanners and sockets in a metal box. Any measuring instruments, gauges, meters, etc, must be carefully stored where they cannot be damaged or become rusty.

Take a little care when tools are used. Hammer heads inevitably become marked and screwdrivers lose the keen edge on their blades from time to time. A little timely attention with emery cloth or a file will soon restore items like this to a good serviceable finish.

## Working facilities

Not to be forgotten when discussing tools, is the workshop itself. If anything more than routine maintenance is to be carried out, some form of suitable working area becomes essential.

It is appreciated that many an owner mechanic is forced by circumstances to remove an engine or similar item, without the benefit of a garage or workshop. Having done this, any repairs should always be done under the cover of a roof.

Wherever possible, any dismantling should be done on a clean flat workbench or table at a suitable working height.

Any workbench needs a vice: one with a jaw opening of 4 in (100 mm) is suitable for most jobs. As mentioned previously, some clean dry storage space is also required for tools, as well as the lubricants, cleaning fluids, touch-up paints and so on which become necessary.

Another item which may be required, and which has a much more general usage, is an electric drill with a chuck capacity of at least $\frac{5}{16}$ in (8 mm). This, together with a good range of twist drills, is virtually essential for fitting accessories such as wing mirrors and reversing lights.

Last, but not least, always keep a supply of old newspapers and clean, lint-free rags available, and try to keep any working area as clean as possible.

## Spanner jaw gap comparison table

| Jaw gap (in) | Spanner size |
|---|---|
| 0.250 | $\frac{1}{4}$ in AF |
| 0.276 | 7 mm |
| 0.313 | $\frac{5}{16}$ in AF |
| 0.315 | 8 mm |
| 0.344 | $\frac{11}{32}$ in AF; $\frac{1}{8}$ in Whitworth |
| 0.354 | 9 mm |
| 0.375 | $\frac{3}{8}$ in AF |
| 0.394 | 10 mm |
| 0.433 | 11 mm |
| 0.438 | $\frac{7}{16}$ in AF |
| 0.445 | $\frac{3}{16}$ in Whitworth; $\frac{1}{4}$ in BSF |
| 0.472 | 12 mm |
| 0.500 | $\frac{1}{2}$ in AF |
| 0.512 | 13 mm |
| 0.525 | $\frac{1}{4}$ in Whitworth; $\frac{5}{16}$ in BSF |
| 0.551 | 14 mm |
| 0.563 | $\frac{9}{16}$ in AF |
| 0.591 | 15 mm |
| 0.600 | $\frac{5}{16}$ in Whitworth; $\frac{3}{8}$ in BSF |
| 0.625 | $\frac{5}{8}$ in AF |
| 0.630 | 16 mm |
| 0.669 | 17 mm |
| 0.686 | $\frac{11}{16}$ in AF |
| 0.709 | 18 mm |
| 0.710 | $\frac{3}{8}$ in Whitworth, $\frac{7}{16}$ in BSF |
| 0.748 | 19 mm |
| 0.750 | $\frac{3}{4}$ in AF |
| 0.813 | $\frac{13}{16}$ in AF |
| 0.820 | $\frac{7}{16}$ in Whitworth; $\frac{1}{2}$ in BSF |
| 0.866 | 22 mm |
| 0.875 | $\frac{7}{8}$ in AF |
| 0.920 | $\frac{1}{2}$ in Whitworth; $\frac{9}{16}$ in BSF |
| 0.938 | $\frac{15}{16}$ in AF |
| 0.945 | 24 mm |
| 1.000 | 1 in AF |
| 1.010 | $\frac{9}{16}$ in Whitworth; $\frac{5}{8}$ in BSF |
| 1.024 | 26 mm |
| 1.063 | $1\frac{1}{16}$ in AF; 27 mm |
| 1.100 | $\frac{5}{8}$ in Whitworth; $\frac{11}{16}$ in BSF |
| 1.125 | $1\frac{1}{8}$ in AF |
| 1.181 | 30 mm |
| 1.200 | $\frac{11}{16}$ in Whitworth; $\frac{3}{4}$ in BSF |
| 1.250 | $1\frac{1}{4}$ in AF |
| 1.260 | 32 mm |
| 1.300 | $\frac{3}{4}$ in Whitworth; $\frac{7}{8}$ in BSF |
| 1.313 | $1\frac{5}{16}$ in AF |
| 1.390 | $\frac{13}{16}$ in Whitworth; $\frac{15}{16}$ in BSF |
| 1.417 | 36 mm |
| 1.438 | $1\frac{7}{16}$ in AF |
| 1.480 | $\frac{7}{8}$ in Whitworth; 1 in BSF |
| 1.500 | $1\frac{1}{2}$ in AF |
| 1.575 | 40 mm; $\frac{15}{16}$ in Whitworth |
| 1.614 | 41 mm |
| 1.625 | $1\frac{5}{8}$ in AF |
| 1.670 | 1 in Whitworth; $1\frac{1}{8}$ in BSF |
| 1.688 | $1\frac{11}{16}$ in AF |
| 1.811 | 46 mm |
| 1.813 | $1\frac{13}{16}$ in AF |
| 1.860 | $1\frac{1}{8}$ in Whitworth; $1\frac{1}{4}$ in BSF |
| 1.875 | $1\frac{7}{8}$ in AF |
| 1.969 | 50 mm |
| 2.000 | 2 in AF |
| 2.050 | $1\frac{1}{4}$ in Whitworth; $1\frac{3}{8}$ in BSF |
| 2.165 | 55 mm |
| 2.362 | 60 mm |

# Jacking and towing

## Jacking

It is vital that the correct procedure is always followed when changing a roadwheel, or the results could hazard the operator and damage the vehicle. Because the Range Rover is fitted with a transmission-mounted handbrake it is imperative that the main gearbox is engaged in bottom gear (1st) and that the gearbox differential lock is engaged before the vehicle is jacked up. It is also better if low range is selected in the transfer box. *The handbrake alone will not be effective if one or both of the rear wheels are jacked up while either the main or transfer gearbox is in the neutral position, without the differential lock being engaged.* Also, because of the amount of backlash in the transmission, and therefore potential fore-and-aft movement when the vehicle is jacked up, especially on sloping ground, the wheels, except the one to be removed, must always be chocked.

If the vehicle has been standing for some time (eg overnight) and has a flat tyre that needs to be changed, it will be necessary first to start the engine to build up a vacuum in order to operate the gearbox differential lock. This is engaged only when the warning light in the top of the switch (early models) or on the dashboard (later models) is illuminated· when the ignition is switched on. Once engaged, the engine can then be switched off.

Here is a summary of the jacking procedure:

(a)  Engage bottom gear and low transfer gear
(b)  Engage the differential lock and switch off engine
(c)  Apply the handbrake
(d)  Chock the roadwheels
(e)  Position the jack under the appropriate axle
(f)  Loosen the wheel nuts
(g)  Raise the jack
(h)  Change the roadwheel
(j)  Lower the jack
(k)  Tighten the wheel nuts

Remember to disengage the differential lock and low transfer gear after completing the wheel change and before continuing on the road.

Jack positioning – the jack must be placed under the axle casing adjacent to the wheel to be removed and directly below the coil spring. On the front axle it should be located between the flange on the outer end of the axle casing and the suspension arm mounting bracket. On the rear axle it should be located as near the shock absorber mounting brackets as possible.

When working under the vehicle never rely solely on the vehicle jack. Always use axle stands or blocks to adequately support the vehicle before attempting to work underneath it.

## Towing

When towing a trailer or another vehicle, the specified maximum weights must not be exceeded. Remember also that it is the driver's responsibility to ensure that all current regulations with regard to towing are complied with.

In the event of the Range Rover being on the receiving end of a tow-rope, towing eyes are provided on the front bumper mountings (photo).

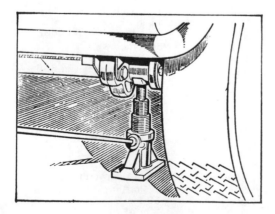

**Correct position for jack at the front of the vehicle**

**Front towing eye**

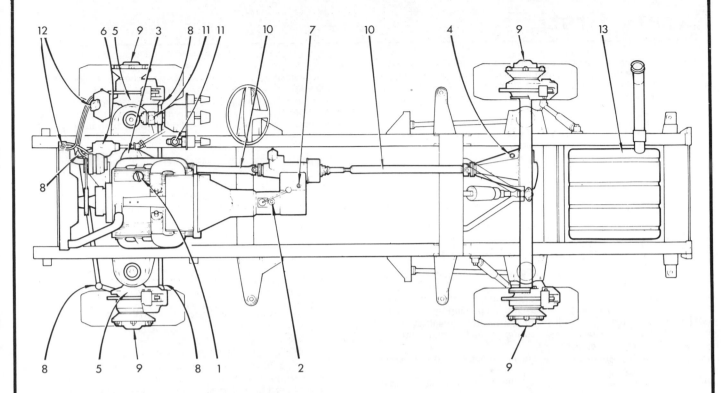

# Recommended lubricants and fluids

These recommendations apply to climates where operation temperatures are above 10°C (14°F). Information on recommended lubricants for use under extreme winter conditions can be obtained from Land Rover Ltd, Technical Service Department, or a Range Rover distributor or dealer.

| Component or system | Lubricant type or specification |
| --- | --- |
| 1 Engine | Multigrade engine oil SAE 20W/50 |
| 2 Main gearbox* | Multigrade engine oil SAE 20W/50 (see Supplement) |
| 3 Front differential | Hypoid gear oil SAE 90EP |
| 4 Rear differential | Hypoid gear oil SAE 90EP |
| 5 Swivel housing | Hypoid gear oil SAE 90EP |
| 6 Steering box (manual) | Hypoid gear oil SEA 90EP |
| Power steering (if fitted) | Automatic transmission fluid type F |
| 7 Transfer gearbox* | Multigrade engine oil SAE 20W/50 (see Supplement) |
| 8 Balljoints | Multi-purpose grease |
| 9 Front and rear hubs | Multi-purpose grease |
| 10 Propeller shafts | Multi-purpose grease |
| 11 Brake and clutch hydraulic reservoirs | Hydraulic fluid to SAE J1703 |
| 12 Cooling system | Antifreeze to BS3150 |
| 13 Fuel tank | Petrol 91 to 93 RON (UK 2-star) |

*Note: The first hundred gearboxes were fitted with a limited slip differential and the recommended lubricant was hypoid gear oil SAE 80EP for the main gearbox and SAE 90EP for the transfer box. Unless the vehicle is fitted with an early model gearbox use engine oil (as above) throughout the gearbox.

# Safety first!

Professional motor mechanics are trained in safe working procedures. However enthusiastic you may be about getting on with the job in hand, do take the time to ensure that your safety is not put at risk. A moment's lack of attention can result in an accident, as can failure to observe certain elementary precautions.

There will always be new ways of having accidents, and the following points do not pretend to be a comprehensive list of all dangers; they are intended rather to make you aware of the risks and to encourage a safety-conscious approach to all work you carry out on your vehicle.

## Essential DOs and DON'Ts

**DON'T** rely on a single jack when working underneath the vehicle. Always use reliable additional means of support, such as axle stands, securely placed under a part of the vehicle that you know will not give way.

**DON'T** attempt to loosen or tighten high-torque nuts (e.g. wheel hub nuts) while the vehicle is on a jack; it may be pulled off.

**DON'T** start the engine without first ascertaining that the transmission is in neutral (or 'Park' where applicable) and the parking brake applied.

**DON'T** suddenly remove the filler cap from a hot cooling system – cover it with a cloth and release the pressure gradually first, or you may get scalded by escaping coolant.

**DON'T** attempt to drain oil until you are sure it has cooled sufficiently to avoid scalding you.

**DON'T** grasp any part of the engine, exhaust or catalytic converter without first ascertaining that it is sufficiently cool to avoid burning you.

**DON'T** allow brake fluid or antifreeze to contact vehicle paintwork.

**DON'T** syphon toxic liquids such as fuel, brake fluid or antifreeze by mouth, or allow them to remain on your skin.

**DON'T** inhale dust – it may be injurious to health (see *Asbestos* below).

**DON'T** allow any spilt oil or grease to remain on the floor – wipe it up straight away, before someone slips on it.

**DON'T** use ill-fitting spanners or other tools which may slip and cause injury.

**DON'T** attempt to lift a heavy component which may be beyond your capability – get assistance.

**DON'T** rush to finish a job, or take unverified short cuts.

**DON'T** allow children or animals in or around an unattended vehicle.

**DO** wear eye protection when using power tools such as drill, sander, bench grinder etc, and when working under the vehicle.

**DO** use a barrier cream on your hands prior to undertaking dirty jobs – it will protect your skin from infection as well as making the dirt easier to remove afterwards; but make sure your hands aren't left slippery.

**DO** keep loose clothing (cuffs, tie etc) and long hair well out of the way of moving mechanical parts.

**DO** remove rings, wristwatch etc, before working on the vehicle – especially the electrical system.

**DO** ensure that any lifting tackle used has a safe working load rating adequate for the job.

**DO** keep your work area tidy – it is only too easy to fall over articles left lying around.

**DO** get someone to check periodically that all is well, when working alone on the vehicle.

**DO** carry out work in a logical sequence and check that everything is correctly assembled and tightened afterwards.

**DO** remember that your vehicle's safety affects that of yourself and others. If in doubt on any point, get specialist advice.

**IF**, in spite of following these precautions, you are unfortunate enough to injure yourself, seek medical attention as soon as possible.

## Asbestos

Certain friction, insulating, sealing, and other products – such as brake linings, brake bands, clutch linings, torque converters, gaskets, etc – contain asbestos. *Extreme care must be taken to avoid inhalation of dust from such products since it is hazardous to health.* If in doubt, assume that they *do* contain asbestos.

## Fire

Remember at all times that petrol (gasoline) is highly flammable. Never smoke, or have any kind of naked flame around, when working on the vehicle. But the risk does not end there – a spark caused by an electrical short-circuit, by two metal surfaces contacting each other, by careless use of tools, or even by static electricity built up in your body under certain conditions, can ignite petrol vapour, which in a confined space is highly explosive.

Always disconnect the battery earth (ground) terminal before working on any part of the fuel or electrical system, and never risk spilling fuel on to a hot engine or exhaust.

It is recommended that a fire extinguisher of a type suitable for fuel and electrical fires is kept handy in the garage or workplace at all times. Never try to extinguish a fuel or electrical fire with water.

## Fumes

Certain fumes are highly toxic and can quickly cause unconsciousness and even death if inhaled to any extent. Petrol (gasoline) vapour comes into this category, as do the vapours from certain solvents such as trichloroethylene. Any draining or pouring of such volatile fluids should be done in a well ventilated area.

When using cleaning fluids and solvents, read the instructions carefully. Never use materials from unmarked containers – they may give off poisonous vapours.

Never run the engine of a motor vehicle in an enclosed space such as a garage. Exhaust fumes contain carbon monoxide which is extremely poisonous; if you need to run the engine, always do so in the open air or at least have the rear of the vehicle outside the workplace.

If you are fortunate enough to have the use of an inspection pit, never drain or pour petrol, and never run the engine, while the vehicle is standing over it; the fumes, being heavier than air, will concentrate in the pit with possibly lethal results.

## The battery

Never cause a spark, or allow a naked light, near the vehicle's battery. It will normally be giving off a certain amount of hydrogen gas, which is highly explosive.

Always disconnect the battery earth (ground) terminal before working on the fuel or electrical systems.

If possible, loosen the filler plugs or cover when charging the battery from an external source. Do not charge at an excessive rate or the battery may burst.

Take care when topping up and when carrying the battery. The acid electrolyte, even when diluted, is very corrosive and should not be allowed to contact the eyes or skin.

If you ever need to prepare electrolyte yourself, always add the acid slowly to the water, and never the other way round. Protect against splashes by wearing rubber gloves and goggles.

When jump starting a car using a booster battery, for negative earth (ground) vehicles, connect the jump leads in the following sequence: First connect one jump lead between the positive ( + ) terminals of the two batteries. Then connect the other jump lead first to the negative (–) terminal of the booster battery, and then to a good earthing (ground) point on the vehicle to be started, at least 18 in (45 cm) from the battery if possible. Ensure that hands and jump leads are clear of any moving parts, and that the two vehicles do not touch. Disconnect the leads in the reverse order.

## Mains electricity

When using an electric power tool, inspection light etc, which works from the mains, always ensure that the appliance is correctly connected to its plug and that, where necessary, it is properly earthed (grounded). Do not use such appliances in damp conditions and, again, beware of creating a spark or applying excessive heat in the vicinity of fuel or fuel vapour.

## Ignition HT voltage

A severe electric shock can result from touching certain parts of the ignition system, such as the HT leads, when the engine is running or being cranked, particularly if components are damp or the insulation is defective. Where an electronic ignition system is fitted, the HT voltage is much higher and could prove fatal.

# Routine maintenance

The maintenance schedules listed in this Section are based on those recommended by the makers and apply to a Range Rover that is being used in the conventional manner, ie, normal roadwork, trailer towing and light cross-country duties.

If the vehicle is used in rough terrain and is constantly working in mud and dust, the oil should be changed more frequently and the air cleaner should be checked more frequently than would be usual. In exceptionally harsh conditions or if the vehicle is used for deep wading, the engine oil should also be checked daily, as should the gearbox and transfer box oils.

The gearbox, transfer box, differential and swivel pin oils should also be changed more frequently if the vehicle is being used in the conditions described in the previous paragraph. In particular the propeller shaft sliding joints should be lubricated frequently if driving through sand. The main gearbox and transfer box oils should be changed at least monthly under deep wading conditions.

When the vehicle is being used for very muddy work or where any form of wading is involved the flywheel housing can be completely sealed by means of a plug, which is located in the bellhousing flange during normal use (photo). This plug must be removed after the job has been completed and before roadwork is resumed. If constant wading is being undertaken, or if severe conditions prevail, then the plug must be removed periodically to allow any accumulated oil to drain out, before it is refitted.

**Every 250 miles (400 km), weekly, or before a long journey**

Check the engine oil level and top up if necessary (photos)
Check the brake fluid level and top up if necessary (photo)
Check the battery electrolyte level and top up if necessary (photo)

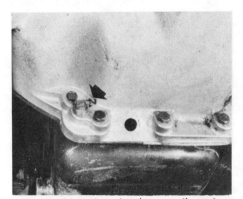

Flywheel housing plug (arrowed) can be screwed into hole at right to prevent entry of water or mud

Checking the engine oil level on the dipstick

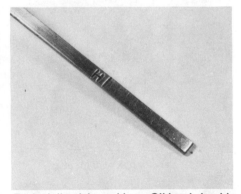

Typical dipstick markings. Oil level should be kept up to mark

Topping up the engine oil

Brake fluid reservoir must be kept full

Topping up the battery

Topping up the windscreen washer reservoir

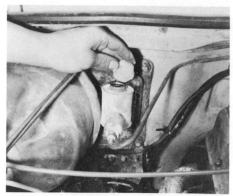

Clutch hydraulic reservoir

Topping up a carburettor damper

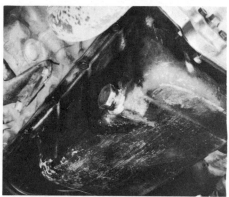

Engine sump drain plug

Transfer box oil filler plug

Swivel pin filler plug (arrowed, top) and level plug (arrowed, bottom)

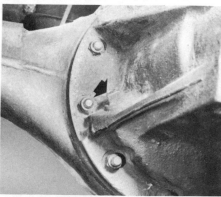

Rear differential filler/level plug (arrowed)

Main gearbox oil dipstick. Some models have level plug instead

Main gearbox oil filler hole

Propeller shaft lubrication point. Further grease nipples are fitted to the universal joints

Check the coolant level in the expansion tank and top up if necessary
Check the tyre pressures including the spare
Check and top up the windscreen and tailgate washer reservoirs (photo)
Check the horn operation
Check the washer and wiper operation
Check that all the lights work correctly

---

**Every 3000 miles (5000 km) or 3 months, whichever occurs first**

---

*In addition to the weekly checks*
## Engine compartment
Check for oil, fuel or coolant leaks
Check the heater and coolant hoses for condition
Check the brake servo hose for condition and tightness
Check the clutch fluid reservoir (photo) and top up as necessary
Check and adjust the fan-belt tension
Check the power steering fluid reservoir (where fitted) and top up as necessary
Check the power steering system (where fitted) for leaks

## Under the vehicle
Check for any oil leaks
Check the condition of steering joints and gaiters
Check the shock absorbers for fluid leaks
Check the self-levelling unit for fluid leaks
Check the brake and clutch hydraulic pipes for leaks and corrosion
Check the fuel pipes for chafing and leaks
Check the exhaust system for tightness and leaks
Remove flywheel housing drain plug if in use, and allow to drain

## Exterior
Check the headlamp alignment
Check the wiper blades and renew if necessary
Check the condition and wear of the brake pads
Check the condition of the brake discs
Check the tyres for tread depth, cuts, lumps or bulges (don't forget the spare)
Check the tightness of the roadwheel nuts

## Interior
Check the steering wheel for play
Check the footbrake for correct operation
Check the handbrake operation and adjust as necessary
Check the correct functioning of all electrical equipment
Check the safety belts for condition and the mountings for security
Check the rear view mirrors for condition

---

**Every 6000 miles (10 000 km) or 6 months, whichever occurs first**

---

*In addition to the servicing operations listed under the 3000 mile (5000 km) heading*
## Engine compartment
Clean and adjust the spark plugs
Lubricate the distributor
Clean and adjust the ignition contact breaker points
Check the ignition timing and reset if necessary
Check the condition of the crankcase breathing hoses
Lubricate the accelerator linkage and check its operation
Top up the carburettor piston dampers (photo)
Clean the battery terminals and smear them with petroleum jelly

## Under the vehicle
Drain the engine oil when hot (photo) and refill with fresh oil
Renew the oil filter
Lubricate the handbrake linkage
Check the transmission handbrake and adjust if necessary (Chapter 9)
Check and top up the transfer box oil as necessary (photo)
Check and top up the front axle differential oil as necessary
Check and top up the front axle swivel pin housings with oil as necessary (photo)

Check the propeller shaft flange coupling bolts and nuts for tightness
Lubricate the propellor shaft internal joints
Check and top up the rear axle differential oil as necessary (photo)

## Exterior
Check the front wheel alignment and adjust as necessary
Lubricate all locks and hinges (except the steering lock)

## Interior
Check the oil level in the main gearbox and top up as necessary (photos)
Check that all the doors open and close correctly (including the tailgate)
Check that the bonnet lock operates correctly
Check that all the windows work correctly
Lubricate the accelerator pedal pivot

---

**Every 12 000 miles (20 000 km) or every 12 months, whichever occurs first**

---

*In addition to the servicing operations listed under the 3000 mile (5000 km) and 6000 mile (10 000 km) headings*
## Engine compartment
Renew the spark plugs
Renew the distributor contact breaker points
Check the condition of the HT leads
Clean the alternator moulded cover and slip ring end bracket
Renew the main fuel filter element and in-line filter (if fitted)
Renew the engine flame traps
Check the air intake flap valve for correct operation (where fitted – later models)
Renew the air cleaner elements
Renew the engine breather filter on rear of crankcase
Check the manual steering box and top up as necessary

## Under the vehicle
Check all the suspension mountings for security

---

**Every 18 000 miles (30 000 km) or 18 months, whichever occurs first**

---

*In addition to the items listed previously*
Renew the hydraulic fluid in the braking system

---

**Every 24 000 miles (40 000 km) or 24 months, whichever occurs first**

---

*In addition to those items listed previously*
Drain, flush and refill the cooling system
Renew the main gearbox oil
Renew the transfer box oil
Renew the front axle oil
Renew the front axle swivel pin housings oil
Renew the rear axle oil
Renew power steering reservoir filter (if applicable)
Lubricate the propeller shaft sealed sliding joint (photo)

---

**Every 36 000 miles (60 000 km) or 36 months, whichever occurs first**

---

*In addition to those items listed previously*
Renew all the rubber seals in the braking system

---

**Every 48 000 miles (80 000 km) or 4 years, whichever occurs first**

---

*In addition to all the items listed previously*
Renew all the cooling and heater hoses
Clean the filter in the electric fuel pump (later models)

# Fault diagnosis

## Introduction

The car owner who does his or her own maintenance according to the recommended schedules should not have to use this section of the manual very often. Modern component reliability is such that, provided those items subject to wear or deterioration are inspected or renewed at the specified intervals, sudden failure is comparatively rare. Faults do not usually just happen as a result of sudden failure, but develop over a period of time. Major mechanical failures in particular are usually preceded by characteristic symptoms over hundreds or even thousands of miles. Those components which do occasionally fail without warning are often small and easily carried in the car.

With any fault finding, the first step is to decide where to begin investigations. Sometimes this is obvious, but on other occasions a little detective work will be necessary. The owner who makes half a dozen haphazard adjustments or replacements may be successful in curing a fault (or its symptoms), but he will be none the wiser if the fault recurs and he may well have spent more time and money than was necessary. A calm and logical approach will be found to be more satisfactory in the long run. Always take into account any warning signs or abnormalities that may have been noticed in the period preceding the fault – power loss, high or low gauge readings, unusual noises or smells, etc – and remember that failure of components such as fuses or spark plugs may only be pointers to some underlying fault.

The pages which follow here are intended to help in cases of failure to start or breakdown on the road. There is also a Fault Diagnosis Section at the end of each Chapter which should be consulted if the preliminary checks prove unfruitful. Whatever the fault, certain basic principles apply. These are as follows:

**Verify the fault.** This is simply a matter of being sure that you know what the symptoms are before starting work. This is particularly important if you are investigating a fault for someone else who may not have described it very accurately.

**Don't overlook the obvious.** For example, if the car won't start, is there petrol in the tank? (Don't take anyone else's word on this particular point, and don't trust the fuel gauge either!) If an electrical fault is indicated, look for loose or broken wires before digging out the test gear.

**Cure the disease, not the symptom.** Substituting a flat battery with a fully charged one will get you off the hard shoulder, but if the underlying cause is not attended to, the new battery will go the same way. Similarly, changing oil-fouled spark plugs for a new set will get you moving again, but remember that the reason for the fouling (if it wasn't simply an incorrect grade of plug) will have to be established and corrected.

**Don't take anything for granted.** Particularly, don't forget that a 'new' component may itself be defective (especially if it's been rattling round in the boot for months), and don't leave components out of a fault diagnosis sequence just because they are new or recently fitted. When you do finally diagnose a difficult fault, you'll probably realise that all the evidence was there from the start.

## Electrical faults

Electrical faults can be more puzzling than straightforward mechanical failures, but they are no less susceptible to logical analysis if the basic principles of operation are understood. Car electrical wiring exists in extremely unfavourable conditions – heat, vibration and chemical attack – and the first things to look for are loose or corroded connections and broken or chafed wires, especially where the wires

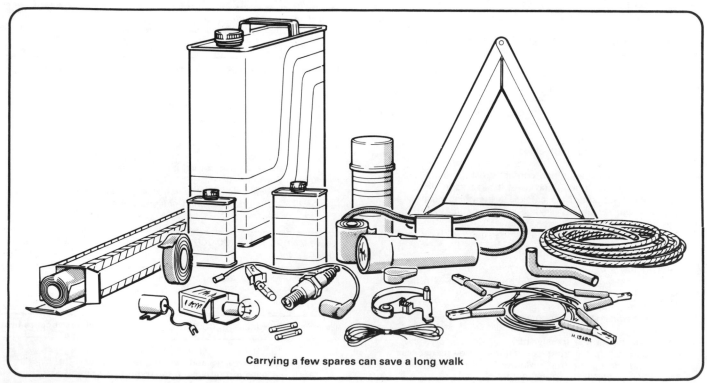

**Carrying a few spares can save a long walk**

pass through holes in the bodywork or are subject to vibration.

All metal-bodied cars in current production have one pole of the battery 'earthed', ie connected to the car bodywork, and in nearly all modern cars it is the negative (−) terminal. The various electrical components' motors, bulb holders etc − are also connected to earth, either by means of a lead or directly by their mountings. Electric current flows through the component and then back to the battery via the car bodywork. If the component mounting is loose or corroded, or if a good path back to the battery is not available, the circuit will be incomplete and malfunction will result. The engine and/or gearbox are also earthed by means of flexible metal straps to the body or subframe; if these straps are loose or missing, starter motor, generator and ignition trouble may result.

Assuming the earth return to be satisfactory, electrical faults will be due either to component malfunction or to defects in the current supply. Individual components are dealt with in Chapter 10. If supply wires are broken or cracked internally this results in an open-circuit, and the easiest way to check for this is to bypass the suspect wire temporarily with a length of wire having a crocodile clip or suitable connector at each end. Alternatively, a 12V test lamp can be used to verify the presence of supply voltage at various points along the wire and the break can be thus isolated.

If a bare portion of a live wire touches the car bodywork or other earthed metal part, the electricity will take the low-resistance path thus formed back to the battery: this is known as a short-circuit. Hopefully a short-circuit will blow a fuse, but otherwise it may cause burning of the insulation (and possibly further short-circuits) or even a fire. This is why it is inadvisable to bypass persistently blowing fuses with silver foil or wire.

## Spares and tool kit

Most cars are only supplied with sufficient tools for wheel changing; the *Maintenance and minor repair* tool kit detailed in *Tools and working facilities,* with the addition of a hammer, is probably sufficient for those repairs that most motorists would consider attempting at the roadside. In addition a few items which can be fitted without too much trouble in the event of a breakdown should be carried. Experience and available space will modify the list below, but the following may save having to call on professional assistance:

*Spark plugs, clean and correctly gapped*
*HT lead and plug cap − long enough to reach the plug furthest from the distributor*
*Distributor rotor, condenser and contact breaker points*
*Drivebelt − emergency type may suffice*
*Spare fuses*
*Set of principal light bulbs*
*Tin of radiator sealer and hose bandage*
*Exhaust bandage*
*Roll of insulating tape*
*Length of soft iron wire*
*Length of electrical flex*
*Torch or inspection lamp (can double as test lamp)*
*Battery jump leads*
*Tow-rope*
*Ignition waterproofing aerosol*
*Litre of engine oil*
*Sealed can of hydraulic fluid*
*Emergency windscreen*
*Worm drive hose clips*
*Tube of filler paste*
*Tyre valve core*

If spare fuel is carried, a can designed for the purpose should be used to minimise risks of leakage and collision damage. A first aid kit and a warning triangle, whilst not at present compulsory in the UK, are obviously sensible items to carry in addition to the above.

When touring abroad it may be advisable to carry additional spares which, even if you cannot fit them yourself, could save having to wait while parts are obtained. The items below may be worth considering:

*Throttle cable*
*Cylinder head gasket*
*Alternator brushes*

One of the motoring organisations will be able to advise on availability of fuel etc in foreign countries.

### Engine will not start

## Engine fails to turn when starter operated
Flat battery (recharge, use jump leads, or starting handle)
Battery terminals loose or corroded
Battery earth to body defective
Engine earth strap loose or broken
Starter motor (or solenoid) wiring loose or broken
Ignition/starter switch faulty
Major mechanical failure (seizure) or long disuse (piston rings rusted to bores)
Starter or solenoid internal fault (see Chapter 10)

## Starter motor turns engine slowly
Partially discharged battery (recharge, use jump leads, or starting handle)
Battery terminals loose or corroded
Battery earth to body defective
Engine earth strap loose
Starter motor (or solenoid) wiring loose
Starter motor internal fault (see Chapter 10)

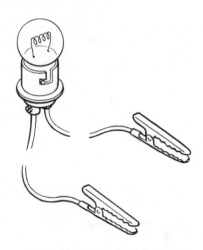

**A simple test lamp is useful for diagnosing electrical faults**

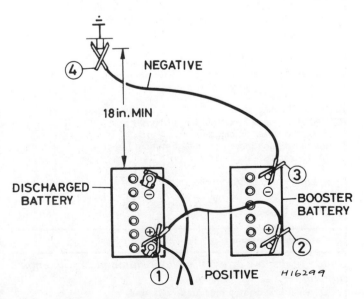

**Jump start lead connections for negative earth − connect leads in order shown**

*Starter motor spins without turning engine*
    Flywheel gear teeth damaged or worn
    Starter motor mounting bolts loose

*Engine turns normally but fails to start*
    Damp or dirty HT leads and distributor cap (crank engine and check for spark)
    Dirty or incorrectly gapped contact breaker points
    No fuel in tank (check for delivery at carburettor)
    Excessive choke (hot engine) or insufficient choke (cold engine)
    Fouled or incorrectly gapped spark plugs (remove, clean and regap)
    Other ignition system fault (see Chapter 4)
    Other fuel system fault (see Chapter 3)
    Poor compression (see Chapter 1)
    Major mechanical failure (eg camshaft drive)

*Engine fires but will not run*
    Insufficient choke (cold engine)
    Air leaks at carburettor or inlet manifold
    Fuel starvation (see Chapter 3)
    Ballast resistor defective, or other ignition fault (see Chapter 4)

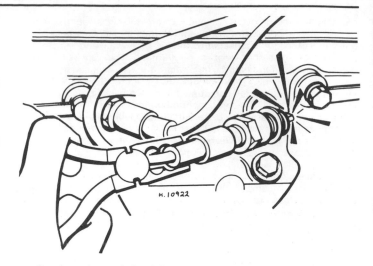

**Crank engine and check for spark. Note use of insulated tool**

---

**Engine cuts out and will not restart**

*Engine cuts out suddenly – ignition fault*
    Loose or disconnected LT wires
    Wet HT leads or distributor cap (after transversing water splash)
    Coil or condenser failure (check for spark)
    Other ignition fault (see Chapter 4)

*Engine misfires before cutting out – fuel fault*
    Fuel tank empty
    Fuel pump defective or filter blocked (check for delivery)
    Fuel tank filler vent blocked (suction will be evident on releasing cap)
    Carburettor needle valve sticking
    Carburettor jets blocked (fuel contaminated)
    Other fuel system fault (see Chapter 3)

*Engine cuts out – other causes*
    Serious overheating
    Major mechanical failure (eg camshaft drive)

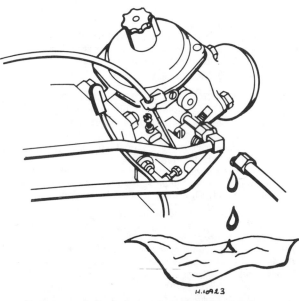

**Remove main fuel pipe and check for fuel delivery**

*Mechanical fuel pump – disable ignition and crank engine*
*Electric fuel pump – switch on ignition briefly*

---

**Engine overheats**

*Ignition (no-charge) warning light illuminated*
    Slack or broken drivebelt (photo) – retension or renew (Chapter 2)

*Ignition warning light not illuminated*
    Coolant loss due to internal or external leakage (see Chapter 2)
    Thermostat defective
    Low oil level
    Brakes binding
    Radiator clogged externally or internally
    Engine waterways clogged
    Ignition timing incorrect or automatic advance malfunctioning
    Mixture too weak

**Note**: *Do not add cold water to an overheated engine or damage may result*

**A slack drivebelt can cause overheating and battery charging problems**

---

**Low engine oil pressure**

*Gauge reads low or warning light illuminated with engine running*
    Oil level low or incorrect grade
    Defective gauge or sender unit
    Wire to sender unit earthed

Engine overheating
Oil filter clogged or bypass valve defective
Oil pressure relief valve defective
Oil pick-up strainer clogged
Oil pump worn or mountings loose
Worn main or big-end bearings

**Note**: *Low oil pressure in a high-mileage engine at tickover is not ncessarily a cause for concern. Sudden pressure loss at speed is far more significant. In any event, check the gauge or warning light sender before condemning the engine.*

## Engine noises

### Pre-ignition (pinking) on acceleration

Incorrect grade of fuel
Ignition timing incorrect
Distributor faulty or worn
Worn or maladjusted carburettor
Excessive carbon build-up in engine

### Whistling or wheezing noises

Leaking vacuum hose
Leaking carburettor or manifold gasket
Blowing head gasket

### Tapping or rattling

Incorrect valve clearances
Worn valve gear
Worn timing chain
Broken piston ring (ticking noise)

### Knocking or thumping

Unintentional mechanical contact (eg fan blades)
Worn fanbelt
Peripheral component fault (generator, water pump etc)
Worn big-end bearings (regular heavy knocking, perhaps less under load)
Worn main bearings (rumbling and knocking, perhaps worsening under load)
Piston slap (most noticeable when cold)

# Chapter 1 Engine

*For modifications, and information applicable to later models, see Supplement at end of manual*

## Contents

## Specifications

### General

| | |
|---|---|
| Engine type | V8, 4-stroke, water-cooled, ohv |
| Cubic capacity | 3528 cc (215 cu in) |
| Bore | 88.90 mm (3.50 in) |
| Stroke | 71.12 mm (2.80 in) |
| Compression ratio: | |
|     Pre-1974 models | 8.5 : 1 |
|     1974 to 1979 | 8.25 : 1 |
|     1979 onwards | 8.13 : 1 |
|     Certain export models | 7.1 : 1 |
| Power output (DIN): | |
|     Up to 1979 | 130 BHP (98 kW) at 5000 rpm |
|     1979 onwards | 156 BHP (116 kW) at 5000 rpm |
| Maximum torque (DIN): | |
|     Up to 1979 | 25.6 kgf m (185 lbf ft) at 2500 rpm |
|     1979 onwards | 28.3 kgf m (205 lbf ft) at 3000 rpm |
| Firing order | 1–8–4–3–6–5–7–2 |
| Cylinder numbering (front to rear): | |
|     Left-hand bank | 1–3–5–7 |
|     Right-hand bank | 2–4–6–8 |
| Compression pressure at cranking speed | 9.5 kgf/cm² (135 lbf/in²) minimum |

### Cylinder block

| | |
|---|---|
| Material | Aluminium alloy |
| Cylinder liner type | Dry, cast integrally with block |
| Liner material | Cast iron |

## Cylinder heads

| | |
|---|---|
| Material | Aluminium alloy |
| Type | Two separate heads, in-line valves, separate inlet manifold |
| Valve seat material | Piston ring iron |
| Valve seat angle | 46° ± ¼° |
| Oversize inserts available | + 0.25 and 0.50 mm (0.010 and 0.020 in) |
| Inlet valve seat diameter: | |
|     Early models | 35.25 mm (1.388 in) |
|     Later models | 37.03 mm (1.458 in) |
| Exhaust valve seat diameter: | |
|     Early models | 30.48 mm (1.200 in) |
|     Later models | 31.50 mm (1.240 in) |

## Valves

| | |
|---|---|
| Overall length | 116.58 to 117.34 mm (4.590 to 4.620 in) |
| Angle of face | 45° |
| Stem height above spring seat when fitted | 47.63 mm (1.875 in) minimum |
| Valve lift | 9.9 mm (0.39 in) |
| Valve clearance | Not adjustable (hydraulic self-adjusting tappets) |

| | Inlet | Exhaust |
|---|---|---|
| Valve head diameter: | | |
|   Early models | 37.97 to 38.22 mm (1.495 to 1.505 in) | 33.215 to 33.466 mm (1.3075 to 1.3175 in) |
|   Later models | 39.75 to 40.00 mm (1.565 to 1.575 in) | 34.341 to 34.595 mm (1.3475 to 1.3575 in) |
| Valve stem diameter: | | |
|   At valve head | 8.640 to 8.666 mm (0.3402 to 0.3412 in) | 8.628 to 8.654 mm (0.3397 to 0.3407 in) |
|   Increasing to | 8.653 to 8.679 mm (0.3407 to 0.3417 in) | 8.640 to 8.666 mm (0.3402 to 0.3412 in) |
| Stem-to-guide clearance: | | |
|   Top | 0.02 to 0.07 mm (0.001 to 0.003 in) | 0.038 to 0.088 mm (0.0015 to 0.0035 in) |
|   Bottom | 0.013 to 0.063 mm (0.0005 to 0.0025 in) | 0.05 to 0.10 mm (0.002 to 0.004 in) |

## Valve springs

| | |
|---|---|
| Number per valve | 2 on early engines, 1 on later engines |
| Spring length under given load: | |
|   Early models, outer | 40.6 mm (1.60 in)/17.6 to 20.4 kgf (39 to 45 lbf) |
|   Early models, inner | 41.2 mm (1.63 in)/9.7 to 12.0 kgf (21.5 to 26.5 lbf) |
|   Later models (single spring) | 40.0 mm (1.577 in)/30 to 33 kgf (66.5 to 73.5 lbf) |

## Valve gear

| | |
|---|---|
| Type | Overhead, alloy rockers operated by pushrods |
| Tappets (cam followers) | Self-adjusting hydraulic |

## Valve timing

| | Inlet | Exhaust |
|---|---|---|
| Valve opens | 30° BTDC | 68° BBDC |
| Valve closes | 75° ABDC | 37° ATDC |
| Duration | 285° | 285° |
| Peak opening | 112° 30' ATDC | 105° 30' BTDC |

## Camshaft

| | |
|---|---|
| Material | Cast iron |
| Location | Central, in vee of cylinder block |
| Drive | Inverted tooth chain (54 links) |
| Bearings: | |
|   Number | 5 |
|   Type | Steel-backed, babbit lined |

## Crankshaft and bearings

| | |
|---|---|
| Material | Iron, spheroidal graphite |
| Number of main bearings | 5 |
| Main bearing journal diameter (standard) | 58.400 to 58.413 mm (2.2992 to 2.2997 in) |
| Main bearing clearance | 0.023 to 0.061 mm (0.0009 to 0.0024 in) |
| Undersizes available | 0.25, 0.50, 0.76 and 1.02 mm (0.010, 0.020, 0.030 and 0.040 in) |
| Big-end bearing journal diameter (standard) | 50.800 to 50.812 mm (2.0000 to 2.0005 in) |
| Big-end bearing clearance | 0.015 to 0.055 mm (0.0006 to 0.0022 in) |
| Undersizes available | As for main bearings |
| Journal ovality | 0.04 mm (0.0015 in) maximum |
| Crankshaft endthrust | Taken on centre (No 3) main bearing shell flanges |
| Crankshaft endfloat | 0.10 to 0.20 mm (0.004 to 0.008 in) |

## Connecting rods

Type ................................................................... Horizontally split big-end, solid small-end
Length between centres ........................................ 143.71 to 143.81 mm (5.658 to 5.662 in)
Endfloat on crankpin ........................................... 0.15 to 0.37 mm (0.006 to 0.014 in)

## Gudgeon pins

Length ................................................................ 72.67 to 72.79 mm (2.861 to 2.866 in)
Diameter ............................................................. 22.215 to 22.220 mm (0.8746 to 0.8749 in)
Fit in connecting rod ........................................... Press fit
Fit in piston ....................................................... Sliding fit
Clearance in piston ............................................. 0.002 to 0.007 mm (0.0001 to 0.0003 in)

## Pistons

Type ................................................................... Aluminium alloy, with flat or concave crown depending on year of manufacture. The two types are not interchangeable

Clearance in bore:
    Top land ...................................................... 0.647 to 0.812 mm (0.0255 to 0.0320 in)
    Skirt top ..................................................... 0.0178 to 0.0330 mm (0.0007 to 0.0013 in)
    Skirt bottom ................................................ 0.008 to 0.043 mm (0.0003 to 0.0017 in)
Ring groove depth ............................................... 4.930 to 5.118 mm (0.1940 to 0.2015 in)
Piston grades:
    Standard (Grade Z) ....................................... Nominal size to + 0.0075 mm (0.0003 in)
    Grade A ...................................................... + 0.0075 to 0.0150 mm (0.0003 to 0.0006 in)
    Grade B ...................................................... + 0.0150 to 0.0225 mm (0.0006 to 0.0009 in)
    Grade C ...................................................... + 0.0225 to 0.0300 mm (0.0009 to 0.0012 in)
    Grade D ...................................................... + 0.0300 to 0.0375 mm (0.0012 to 0.0015 in)
Grade letter location ........................................... Piston crown and cylinder block face
Oversize pistons available after rebore (ungraded) ..... + 0.25 and 0.50 mm (0.010 and 0.020 in)

## Piston rings

Number of compression rings ................................ 2
Number of oil rings ............................................. 1
Number one compression ring ............................... Chrome faced
Number two compression ring ............................... Stepped, L-shaped and marked TOP or T
Compression ring end gap in bore .......................... 0.44 to 0.57 mm (0.017 to 0.022 in)
Compression ring clearance in groove ..................... 0.05 to 0.10 mm (0.002 to 0.004 in)
Oil control ring type ............................................ Expander ring with top and bottom rails
Oil control ring gap in bore ................................... 0.38 to 1.40 mm (0.015 to 0.055 in)

## Flywheel

Ring gear thickness:
    Early models ............................................... 9.52 to 9.65 mm (0.375 to 0.380 in)
    Later models ............................................... 10.97 to 11.22 mm (0.432 to 0.442 in)
Minimum flywheel overall thickness for refacing:
    Early models ............................................... 38.35 mm (1.510 in)
    Later models ............................................... 39.93 mm (1.572 in)

## Lubrication system

Oil filter type:
    Early models ............................................... Full flow, disposable cartridge, nut on end of canister for easy removal
    Later models ............................................... Full flow, disposable cartridge, plain canister with relief valve incorporated
Oil pump type .................................................... Gear
Oil pump drive ................................................... From bottom end of distributor driveshaft, off camshaft gear
Clearance between pump gears and front cover ......... 0.05 mm (0.0018 in)
Bypass valve seat location (early models only) .......... 0.5 to 1.0 mm (0.020 to 0.040 in) below surface of casing
Oil pressure at 2400 rpm (50 mph in top gear) with engine warm ..... 2.11 to 2.81 kgf/cm² (30 to 40 lbf/in²)

## Torque wrench settings

| | lbf ft | kgf m |
|---|---|---|
| Main bearing cap bolts (1 to 4) | 50 to 55 | 7.0 to 7.6 |
| Rear (No 5) main bearing cap bolts | 65 to 70 | 9.0 to 9.6 |
| Connecting rod cap nuts | 30 to 35 | 4.0 to 4.9 |
| Flywheel bolts | 50 to 60 | 7.0 to 8.5 |
| Oil pump cover bolts | 10 to 15 | 1.4 to 2.0 |
| Oil pressure relief valve | 30 to 35 | 4.0 to 4.9 |
| Cylinder head bolts | 65 to 70 | 9.0 to 9.6 |
| Rocker shaft bolts | 25 to 30 | 3.5 to 4.0 |
| Timing chain cover bolts | 20 to 25 | 2.8 to 3.5 |
| Crankshaft pulley/starter dog bolt | 140 to 160 | 19.3 to 22.3 |
| Water pump retaining bolts: | | |
| $\frac{1}{4}$ inch | 7 to 10 | 0.9 to 1.4 |
| $\frac{5}{16}$ inch | 16 to 20 | 2.2 to 2.7 |
| Distributor drivegear-to-camshaft front end bolt | 40 to 45 | 5.5 to 6.2 |
| Engine mounting rubbers - nuts | 13 to 16 | 1.8 to 2.2 |
| Inlet manifold bolts | 25 to 30 | 3.5 to 4.0 |
| Inlet manifold gasket clamp bolts | 10 to 15 | 1.4 to 2.0 |
| Exhaust manifold bolts | 10 to 15 | 1.4 to 2.0 |
| Clutch cover bolts | 35 to 38 | 4.9 to 5.2 |

## 1 General description

The engine is an overhead valve high performance V8. The cylinder block and cylinder heads are aluminium alloy castings and the two banks of four cylinders are set at 90° to each other. The cylinder liners are of cast iron and are integral with the block so they can be rebored within certain tolerances. The valve guides and seats are also of iron and can be renewed. A large one-piece aluminium alloy inlet manifold is mounted between the cylinder heads and is fitted with two Stromberg carburettors. Separate cast iron exhaust manifolds are fitted to the outside of each bank of cylinders. The camshaft is mounted centrally at the bottom of the Vee of the engine and is driven by a chain from the crankshaft. There is no chain tensioner.

The valves are operated by pushrods and hydraulic tappets which are self-adjusting to ensure quiet engine operation. The pistons are made in special lightweight alloy and are of full skirt design. Depending upon the model year they will have either a flat crown or a crown with a shallow circular depression. This is because of the changes that have occurred in the compression ratio since 1970.

The crankshaft runs in five main bearings and is fitted with a torsional vibration damper. The thrust of the crankshaft is taken on the centre main bearing.

Lubrication is by a gear-driven oil pump at the front of the engine, which delivers oil under pressure to all the main, big-end and camshaft bearings, the valve gear, distributor driveshaft and cylinder bores. A full flow cartridge type of disposable oil filter is fitted at the front of the engine.

*IMPORTANT:* Because the engine is of aluminium construction, it is vital when tightening bolts related to the engine, that the correct torque settings specified should be strictly observed. It is also of equal importance that bolt lengths are noted and bolts refitted in the same location from which they were removed. Where specified, always use thread lubricant and sealer.

Because of the weight and bulk of this unit it is essential that substantial lifting tackle is available, otherwise the removal of the engine is undesirable and impractical for the average home mechanic. It is fully realised that any major overhaul tasks could be greatly facilitated if the unit were out of the frame and supported on an engine stand or strong workbench. For those who are determined, or find it really necessary to remove the unit, the procedure is outlined in the following text. In the following section all the items that can be tackled with the engine in position are progressively listed, and the owner must fully assess the amount of work entailed before starting the task.

## 2 Major operations which can be performed with the engine in the car

It is possible to remove the following components for inspection and/or overhaul without having to lift the engine out of the vehicle:

(a) *Radiator and cooling fan*
(b) *Water pump*
(c) *Carburettors*
(d) *Inlet manifold*
(e) *Distributor*
(f) *Alternator*
(g) *Starter motor*
(h) *Cylinder heads and valve assembly*

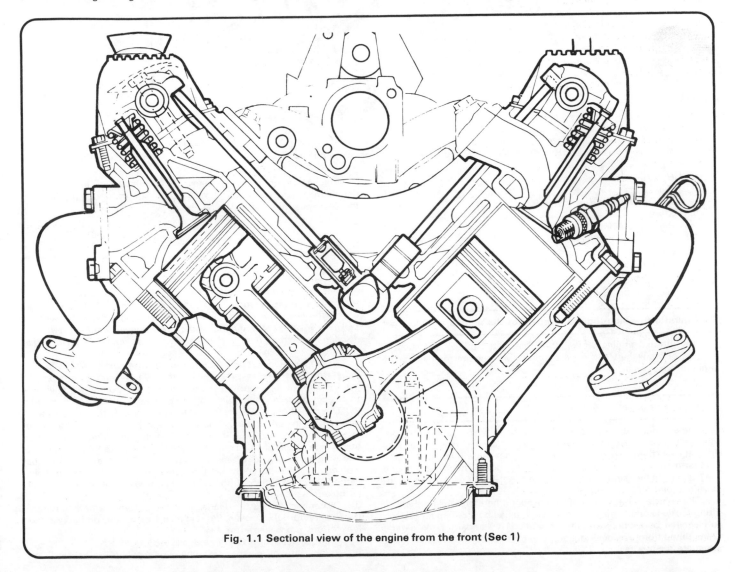

**Fig. 1.1 Sectional view of the engine from the front (Sec 1)**

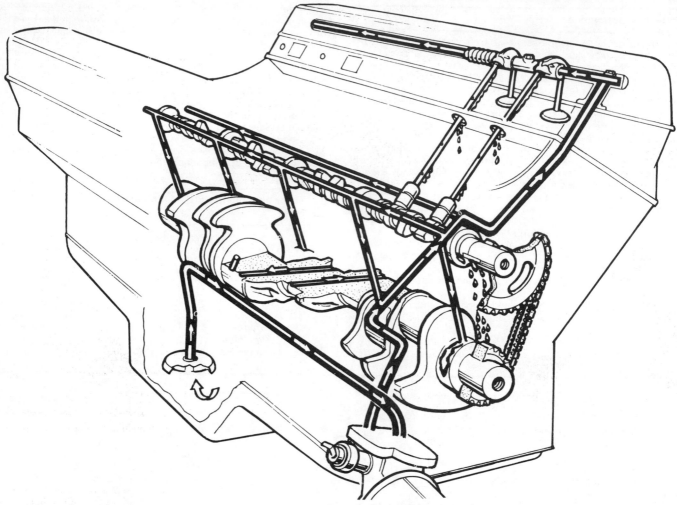

Fig. 1.2 Lubrication system (Sec 1)

(j)   Hydraulic tappets
(k)   Camshaft
(l)   Timing chain and gearwheels
(m)  Sump
(n)   Big-end bearings
(p)   Pistons and connecting rods
(q)   Oil pump
(r)   Timing chain cover
(s)   Gearbox

## 3   Operations which require removal of the engine from the car

Any internal engine work (other than listed previously) such as refitting of crankshaft and main bearings, will require removal of the engine from the car.

## 4   Engine removal – general

The engine of the Range Rover must be removed separately from the gearbox. Because of the size of the vehicle the task is not very difficult, as there is generally enough space within the engine compartment to reach most of the retaining bolts. The exceptions are the upper bellhousing bolts and the right-hand exhaust pipe-to-manifold joint.

The vehicle is quite high off the ground, therefore ensure that the lifting tackle is adequate so that the engine can be lifted up far enough to clear the bodywork when it is removed. A standard $\frac{1}{2}$ ton garage crane (hired from the local tool and equipment hire centre) is perfectly adequate for this task.

This operation is a two-man task. Remember that at no time during the lifting operation should either person be directly beneath the suspended weight of the engine.

## 5   Engine – removal

*The sequence of operations listed in this Section is not critical as the position of the person undertaking the work, or the tool in his hand, will determine to a certain extent the order in which the work is tackled. Obviously the engine cannot be removed until everything is disconnected from it and the following sequence will ensure that nothing is forgotten.*

*Assemble a collection of containers for the small parts, nuts and bolts etc that are removed and keep them in convenient groups.*
1   Because of the height of the vehicle off the ground it is advisable to protect the wings when leaning over into the engine compartment.
2   Open the bonnet and, with the help of your assistant, place a thick pad against the upper part of the windscreen in the centre. The bonnet can then be lifted up until it rests against the pad. We found that an empty one gallon plastic container was the ideal size for this purpose. The bonnet is very heavy and this saves a lot of time and effort that would otherwise be spent in removing it. Unless the task is being carried out in conditions with very low headroom, this should normally be quite practical (photo).
3   Disconnect the battery leads, undo the battery clamp and remove the battery from the vehicle. Put it in a safe place. It is probably a good idea to put it on charge for a while.
4   Drain the cooling system as described in Chapter 2.
5   Remove the air cleaner assembly as described in Chapter 3.

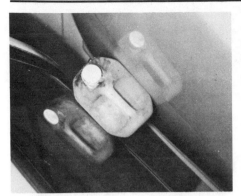

5.2 The bonnet can be propped open like this

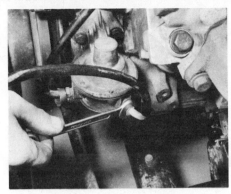

5.8 Disconnecting the fuel supply to the fuel pump (early models)

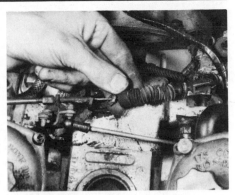

5.10 Disconnecting the throttle cable

5.11 Disconnecting the fuel return pipe

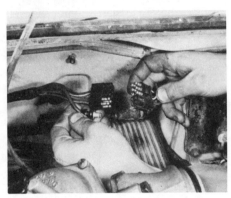

5.15 Disconnecting the wiring loom and electrical supply

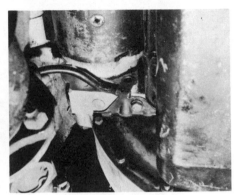

5.20 Disconnecting the earthing strap

6　Remove the radiator, fan cowl, fan and drivebelt(s) as described in Chapter 2.

7　Disconnect the HT and LT leads from the coil to the distributor.

8　On models with a mechanical fuel pump, disconnect and plug the fuel line from the tank to the pump.

9　On models with an electric fuel pump, disconnect and plug the fuel line at the in-line filter.

10　On all models, disconnect the throttle and choke cables (as applicable) from the left-hand carburettor (photo). Refer to Chapter 3 if necessary.

11　Disconnect the fuel return pipe from the right-hand carburettor, and tuck it out of the way (photo).

12　Disconnect the brake servo vacuum pipe from the inlet manifold and tuck it out of the way.

13　Similarly disconnect the differential lock actuator vacuum pipe.

14　The electrical connections may be tackled in two ways. Either remove all the connections first and leave the loom in the vehicle, or unplug the wiring loom for the engine from the main loom and remove it with the engine. The second method is easier in many ways and it means that there are fewer loose ends to snag the engine assembly as it is lifted out. The procedure below covers the second way.

15　Disconnect the engine wiring loom from the main loom and also the main electrical supply connectors at the rear of the left-hand rocker cover (photo).

16　Disconnect the engine wiring loom from the wiring clips of the engine compartment rear bulkhead.

17　Disconnect the handbrake warning light switch cable from the loom.

18　Disconnect the oil pressure warning light switch cable.

19　Disconnect the power cable from the starter solenoid; that is, the heavy black cable.

20　Disconnect the engine earthing strap from the starter to the right-hand side of the body (photo).

21　Undo the hose clips and disconnect the heater flow and return hoses from the inlet manifold (photo).

22　Working underneath the car undo the two exhaust pipe-to-exhaust manifold connections. There are three brass nuts per side. Because of

the heat shield on the right-hand side, the nuts are some of the most difficult to undo in the whole engine removal operation (photo).

23　Undo the upper and lower nuts on both engine mountings (photo).

24　Undo the bellhousing lower cover plate and stiffening plate nuts and bolts and remove the plates (photo).

25　Undo the bellhousing to engine retaining bolts. Some are accessible from under the car, the others from inside the engine compartment. However it must be said that the latter are very difficult to reach and this is probably the worst part of the operation.

26　The engine is now ready to be lifted out, if an overhead lifting system is being employed. However, if an ordinary floor crane is being used then the front grille and top panel will have to be removed to allow the necessary space and reduce the lifting height.

27　To remove the grille, undo the four self-tapping screws in the top and the two in the lower edge, outer corners.

28　The top panel is secured by four bolts on each side, and the two bolts in the centre which retain the locking plate also retain the two bracing bars. With all the bolts removed, release the wiring loom from the clips on the underside of the panel and the panel can be lifted away and placed on the inner left-hand wing with the locking cable still attached to it. Note that the two horizontal bolts on each side retain the horn mounting brackets. Disconnect the wiring to the horns and place them to one side (photos).

29　Remove the two bracing bars, which are now retained by one nut and bolt each.

30　On models with power steering, undo the power steering pump mounting bolts and free the pump from its mounting. Remove the belt from the pulleys.

31　Tie the pump up so that the fluid lines are not stretched.

32　Release the wiring loom from the clips on the outer front panels behind the wings. Push the wiring down so that it rests on the chassis front crossmember out of the way.

33　Attach lifting chains or slings to the engine lifting eyes. Ensure that they are securely attached before attempting to remove the engine.

34　Take the weight of the engine and lift it just enough to remove the engine mounting rubbers (photo).

35　Pull the engine forward to disengage the bellhousing dowels, and

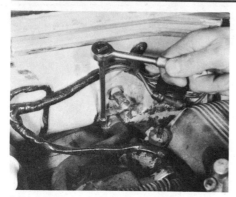

5.21 Disconnecting the heater hoses

5.22 Undoing the left-hand exhaust pipe-to-manifold connection

5.23 Undoing the left-hand engine mounting lower nut

5.24 Withdrawing the bellhousing lower cover plate

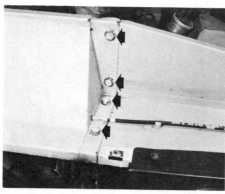

5.28a Undo the four bolts (arrowed) on each side to remove the panel

5.28b The diagonal bracing bars can be removed when the panel is out of the way. (Note the horns on either side)

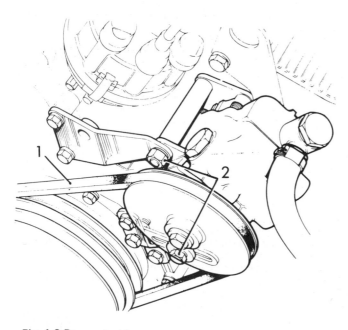

**Fig. 1.3 Power steering pump arrangement (if fitted) (Sec 5)**

1  Drivebelt        2  Adjuster and mounting bolts

the input shaft from the clutch. Do not allow the weight of the engine to rest on the input shaft.

36  Lift the engine upwards and forwards in stages. Ensure that all cables, pipes and wires have been disconnected and removed from retaining clips. As the engine is removed check carefully that no wires, pipes etc become snagged (photo).

37  Lift the engine high enough to clear the front body panel, then pull it clear of the vehicle.

---

## 6  Engine dismantling – general

1  It is best to mount the engine on a dismantling stand but if one is not available, then stand the engine on a strong bench so it is at a comfortable working height. Failing this, the engine can be stripped down on the floor.

2  During the dismantling process the greatest care should be taken to keep the exposed parts free from dirt. As an aid to achieving this, if is sound advice to thoroughly clean the outside of the engine, removing all traces of oil and congealed dirt.

3  Use paraffin or a good grease solvent. The latter will make the job much easier, after the solvent has been applied and allowed to stand for a time, a vigorous jet of water will wash off the solvent and all the grease and filth. If the dirt is thick and deeply embedded, work the solvent into it with a wire brush.

4  Finally wipe down the exterior of the engine with a rag and only then, when it is quite clean, should the dismantling process begin. As the engine is stripped, clean each part in a bath of paraffin or petrol.

5  Never immerse parts with oilways in paraffin, eg, the crankshaft, but to clean, wipe down carefully with a petrol-dampened rag. Oilways can be cleaned out with wire. If an air line is present, all parts can be blown dry and the oilways blown through as an added precaution.

6  Re-use of old engine gaskets is false economy and can give rise to oil and water leaks, if nothing worse. To avoid the possibility of trouble after the engine has been reassembled, **always** use new gaskets throughout.

7  Do not throw away old gaskets as it sometimes happens that an immediate replacement cannot be found and the old gasket is then very useful as a template. Hang up the old gaskets as they are removed on a suitable hook or nail.

8  To strip the engine it is best to work from the top down. The sump provides a firm base on which the engine can be supported in an upright position. When the stage is reached where the sump must be

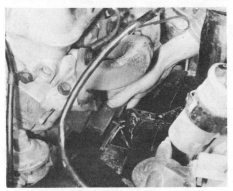
5.34 Removing the engine left-hand mounting rubber

5.36 Lifting the engine out

7.1a The plug leads are all numbered

7.1b The coolant temperature transmitter wire is at the front

7.1c The inlet manifold transmitter is on top

7.1d The oil dipstick tube is retained by a plate and bolt

removed, the engine can be turned on its side and all other work carried out with it in this position.

9   Wherever possible, refit nuts, bolts and washers fingertight from wherever they were removed. This helps avoid later loss and muddle. If they cannot be refitted then lay them out in such a fashion that it is clear from where they came.

## 7   Ancillary components – removal prior to engine overhaul

1   With the engine out of the vehicle and thoroughly cleaned, the externally mounted components should now be removed as follows:

  (a)  *Alternator – as described in Chapter 10*
  (b)  *Distributor cap and plug leads. Unclip the distributor cap spring clips, disconnect the plug leads from the plugs and remove the cap and leads complete*
  (c)  *Wiring loom. Disconnect the temperature gauge transmitter wire, the inlet manifold transmitter wire, and the oil transmitter wires (photos)*
  (d)  *Wiring loom retaining brackets*
  (e)  *Distributor – as described in Chapter 4*
  (f)  *Starter motor – as described in Chapter 10*
  (g)  *Fuel pump (mechanical) – as described in Chapter 3 (early models only)*
  (h)  *Clutch assembly – as described in Chapter 5*
  (j)  *Oil filter – as described in Section 19*
  (k)  *Spark plugs*
  (l)  *Exhaust manifolds – as described in Chapter 3*
  (m)  *Retaining plate for oil dipstick tube. This is secured to the left-hand cylinder head by one bolt (photo)*

## 8   Ancillary components – removal (engine in situ)

1   If the inlet manifold, cylinder heads, rocker assembly, valves, pistons, timing chain etc are to be removed with the engine in the vehicle, a different procedure is called for.

2   Begin by draining the radiator and cylinder block, as described in Chapter 2, and remove the top hose.

3   Disconnect the battery negative terminal.

4   Remove the air cleaner assembly as described in Chapter 3.

5   Disconnect the HT lead to the coil, unclip the distributor cap spring clips, pull off the plug leads from the plugs, unclip the leads from the rocker cover brackets and remove them as one assembly.

6   Disconnect the throttle and choke cables (as applicable) from the left-hand carburettor as described in Chapter 3.

7   Disconnect and remove the fuel feed pipe between the left-hand carburettor and the fuel pump. On later models the fuel pipe to the in-line fuel filter attached to the engine lifting eye needs to be detached.

8   Disconnect the fuel return pipe from the right-hand carburettor.

9   Disconnect and remove the engine breather hoses between the carburettors and rocker covers.

10  Disconnect the brake servo and differential lock actuator vacuum hoses from the inlet manifold.

11  Detach the distributor advance/retard vacuum pipe from the left-hand carburettor.

12  Disconnect the wiring to the transmitters on the inlet manifold, noting which wires fit where.

13  Disconnect the water inlet hoses to the front of the manifold and the two heater hoses from the rear of the inlet manifold.

14  If the overhaul involves removal of the timing cover (ie camshaft removal or timing gear/chain renewal) then the radiator bottom hose, bypass hose, cooling fan (Chapter 2) and the alternator (Chapter 10) will also have to be removed. In addition, remove the power steering pump (if fitted), where applicable the mechanical fuel pump (Chapter 3) and the oil filter.

15  If the cylinder heads are to be removed, the exhaust manifolds (Chapter 3), the alternator (Chapter 10) and the oil dipstick tube retaining plate and bolt must first be removed.

## 9   Inlet manifold – removal

1   With the ancillary components removed it is now possible to

remove the inlet manifold. For engine overhaul purposes, the carburettors need not be disturbed.

2    Disconnect the following items first if they have not already been removed:

(a)   *Distributor advance/retard vacuum pipe. This can be disconnected from the left-hand carburettor and its retaining bracket from the inlet manifold, or from the distributor*

(b)   *The differential lock actuator vacuum pipe from the inlet manifold union*

(c)   *The engine breather hoses and flame traps from between the carburettors and rocker covers*

(d)   *The crankcase breather filter retaining bracket from the rear of the inlet manifold (photo)*

(e)   *The various transmitter leads, and the EGR valve connections where fitted (see Chapter 3)*

(f)   *The bypass hoses from the front of the inlet manifold to the water pump and the heater hoses (photo)*

3    There are twelve bolts securing the inlet manifold to the cylinder heads. These should be eased off progressively and then removed. The bolts are of differing length so take note of their exact locations.

**Note**: *Any bolts removed from the cylinder heads or block should have their threads cleaned with a wire brush dipped in paraffin or clean petrol.*

*If this cleaning cannot be carried out immediately, it is vital that they are stored in petrol or paraffin as the sealant used when the bolts were originally fitted will tend to harden on exposure to the air making its removal difficult.*

4    Move aside the heater hoses and the hose from the water pump, and ease the manifold away from the cylinder head (photo).

5    Before removing the gasket clamps ensure that there is no coolant lying on top of the gasket. Remove the clamps and lift away the gasket followed by the rubber gasket seals (photos). Although tempting, do not think that you can re-use the gasket, as it is certain to leak.

## 10  Valve gear – removal

1    This operation covers the removal of the rocker arms and shaft assembly, the pushrods and hydraulic tappets for one cylinder head. Repeat the procedure, if necessary, for the other one. First drain the cooling system, remove the air cleaner and the inlet manifold as already described.

2    Remove the rocker cover, which is retained by four cross-head screws (photo).

3    Undo the four rocker shaft assembly retaining bolts in stages so that the assembly rises evenly on the pressure of the valve springs (photo).

4    Lift out the assembly complete with bolts and place it to one side. Note that the baffle plate will be at the rear of the assembly on the right-hand side and at the front on the left-hand side.

5    Make up a piece of card with 8 numbered holes punched in it. Then remove the pushrods and place them in order through the holes in the card (photo).

6    Take a box and section it into eight compartments. An alternative container is a section of an old egg-tray. Number the sections 1 to 8.

7    Carefully withdraw each tappet and place it in the appropriate section in the container. This operation can be performed in conjunction with the pushrod removal sequence provided the card for the pushrods and the container for the tappets are to hand, as the tappets will usually lift up as the pushrod is carefully pulled upwards and can then be removed more easily (photo).

8    If a tappet is difficult to remove, and the engine is being completely stripped, leave it until the camshaft has been withdrawn and then push it downwards to remove it.

## 11  Cylinder heads – removal

1    With the inlet manifold and valve gear removed, slacken off the cylinder head bolts by stages and in the reverse sequence to that used for tightening down (see Fig. 1.25).

2    Remove the cylinder head bolts, noting where the three different length bolts fit.

3    Lift the cylinder head straight off and place it to one side. Remove and discard the gasket.

4    Repeat the operation for the other cylinder head if that is also to be removed. If the alternator mounting bracket is left attached to the right-hand head, there is no danger of mixing up the two cylinder heads when both are removed for a complete overhaul.

## 12  Valves – removal

1    Before starting to remove the valves from the cylinder head, take a piece of cardboard and pierce 8 numbered holes in it. If both cylinder heads are being done together then make two such cards and mark one LEFT and the other RIGHT.

2    The procedure for each cylinder head is the same. Start at the front of the head and arrange a valve spring compressor tool over the first valve.

3    Clamp the tool and remove the two split collets, then release the tool (photo).

4    Remove the upper cup, valve springs (or spring in later models which only have single valve springs) and valve from the cylinder head (photos).

5    Place the valve in the No 1 hole in the card and the spring(s), collets and upper cup in a suitable container.

6    Remove the rest of the valves in turn in each cylinder head, making sure that they are put into the correct holes in the card for their particular head.

## 13  Timing cover, chain and gears – removal

1    Having removed all the ancillary components as described in Sections 7 and 8, do not forget to remove the wires from the oil pressure switch if the job is being done with the engine in situ.

2    Begin by removing the starter dog and crankshaft pulley retaining bolt. This requires a deep $1\frac{5}{16}$ inch socket or box spanner. If the engine is in the vehicle, engage bottom low range gear to stop the engine rotating whilst the bolt is undone. If the job is being tackled on the workbench, a plate will have to be made up to lock the flywheel to stop the crankshaft rotating (photo).

3    If the task is being done with the engine in the car without removing the cylinder heads, set the engine so that No 1 piston (front of left-hand bank) is at TDC on the firing stroke. Rotate the engine and observe the rotor arm of the distributor. When it points to the No 1 cylinder HT lead position the engine is firing on No 1 cylinder. This can be verified by the timing pointer (bracket) which should be in line with the TDC mark on the crankshaft pulley.

4    If the vehicle is fitted with power steering, slacken the power steering pump adjuster bolt, release the tension on the drivebelt and remove it. Remove the power steering pump from its mounting bracket and support it securely within the engine compartment. There is no need to disconnect the hoses from the pump.

5    Pull off the crankshaft pulley. This may require a three-legged puller, but should slide off quite easily by hand (photo).

6    Mark the relationship of the distributor to the timing gear cover, undo the clamp bolt and remove the clamp and the distributor.

7    Undo and remove the two sump bolts which locate in the bottom of the timing cover.

8    Undo and remove the nine bolts which retain the timing cover and remove the complete assembly which includes the water and oil pumps. Be careful not to damage the oil sump gasket. Place the power steering pump mounting brackets to one side, noting where they fit.

9    Remove the old timing cover gasket.

10   Check that the timing marks on the two timing gears are in line.

11   Undo the retaining bolt for the distributor drivegear and remove it and the washer, gear and fuel pump cam (or spacer in later models) from the front end of the camshaft. Make sure that the camshaft does not turn when the bolt is undone (photo).

12   The chain and both chainwheels can now be slid off together from their respective shafts.

13   If the rocker assemblies are to remain in place, **do not** on any account allow the crankshaft or camshaft to be rotated, otherwise damage will be caused by the pistons and valves coming into contact with each other.

9.2a A single screw retains the crankcase breather filter

9.2b Disconnect the bypass and heater hoses from the water pump

9.4 Lifting the inlet manifold off

9.5a There is one clamp at each end of the engine

9.5b Removing the rear seal

10.2 Each rocker cover is retained by four cross-head screws

10.3 Each rocker shaft is retained by four bolts (arrowed)

10.5 Removing a pushrod

10.7 Removing a tappet

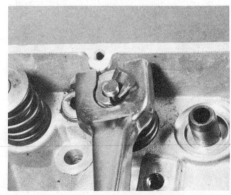

12.3 Clamp the compressor and remove the collets

12.4a Remove the upper cup ...

12.4b ... and the valve springs ...

12.4c ... followed by the valve

13.2 Removing the starter dog and crankshaft pulley bolt

13.5 Removing the crankshaft pulley. Note alignment of timing marks

13.11 The distributor drivegear and mechanical fuel pump cam are retained by the bolt and washer to the front of the camshaft

14.2 Withdrawing the camshaft

16.2 Removing the oil pick-up and strainer

16.6 Withdrawing No 1 cylinder connecting rod cap

16.8 Protect the connecting rod bolts to avoid damage to the bores

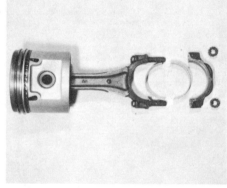
16.11 One complete assembly should contain all these parts

17.4 The flywheel is secured by six bolts

17.7 Insert a wedge (arrowed) to stop the flywheel rotating

18.4 Removing the centre main bearing cap with special flanged bearing shell

## 14 Camshaft – removal

1 To remove the camshaft first remove the following engine sub-assemblies as already described:

    (a) Ancillary components (Section 7 or 8)
    (b) Inlet manifold (Section 9)
    (c) Valve gear (Section 10)
    (d) Timing cover, chain and gears (Section 13)

2 Withdraw the camshaft from the cylinder block. Take care when doing so that the bearings are not damaged (photo). The bearings cannot be renewed; if they are damaged, a new block will be required.

## 15 Sump – removal

1 Drain the engine oil into a suitable container, having first raised the front of the vehicle if this task is being done with the engine in the vehicle. Make sure that it is adequately supported.
2 Undo the sump retaining bolts either from beneath the car, or tilt the engine onto first one side of the block and then the other to reach all the bolts (engine on the bench).
3 Prise off the sump, but do not use excessive force.
4 Place the sump to one side.
5 Remove the two bolts and withdraw the oil pick-up pipe and strainer if necessary.

## 16 Pistons and connecting rods – removal

1 To remove the piston and connecting rod assemblies first remove the ancillary components, inlet manifold, valve gear, cylinder heads and sump as already described.
2 Remove the oil pick-up pipe and strainer with the engine lying on one side if the engine is out of the vehicle. Alternatively this operation can be performed from underneath with the engine still in the vehicle (photo).
3 Before the removal operation commences note that the cylinders are numbered from front to rear, even numbers on the right-hand bank and odd numbers on the left-hand bank. The big-end caps for the odd numbered assemblies are on the front of the shared crankshaft journals and the even numbered assemblies fit on the rear of the journals. The big-end caps and con-rods are *not* marked, so great care must be taken and each connecting rod and cap must be scribed with its appropriate number as it is removed. So that no confusion can arise, make up two boxes big enough to each take four piston and connecting rod assemblies. Mark one box 2–4–6–8 and the other one 1–3–5–7. Place each assembly in order in its correct box as it is removed.
4 If the operation is being carried out with the engine in the vehicle, the assemblies can be removed from front to rear, starting at No 1 and working through to No 8, since it is easy to withdraw the pistons through the tops of both banks of cylinders with the engine upright.
5 With the engine on the workbench it is easier to work down one side, removing the odd or even numbered assemblies first, and then to turn the cylinder block over onto the other side and repeat the operation for the other cylinder bank. Because of the design of the block it is easier to do one side at a time.
6 Rotate the crankshaft so that the connecting rod cap nuts for No 1 cylinder are easily accessible. Undo and remove the nuts and withdraw the cap (photo).
7 Mark the cap with the appropriate cylinder number.
8 Cut two short lengths of plastic tubing and fit them over the connecting rod bolts so that when the assembly is withdrawn the bolt threads do not damage the journals or cylinder walls (photo).
9 Push the connecting rod and piston assembly up the bore; if necessary tap the end of the connecting rod bolts with the wooden handle of a hammer.
10 Withdraw the piston and connecting rod through the top of the bore, and remove the protective tubing from the bolts.
11 Scribe the connecting rod with the cylinder number and then refit the connecting rod cap and nuts to the assembly (photo). Note that the rib on the bearing cap faces in the same direction as the boss on the connecting rod.
12 Place the assembly in the appropriate box in its correct place.

13 Rotate the crankshaft to reach the next pair of connecting rod cap nuts and repeat the operation as already described for all the other piston and connecting rod assemblies.

## 17 Flywheel – removal and refitting

1 The flywheel can only be removed with the engine out of the vehicle.
2 If a major engine overhaul is being undertaken, leave the flywheel in position as long as possible as it can be used for stopping the engine rotating whilst the crankshaft pulley bolt is removed, and for rotating the crankshaft to remove the piston and connecting rod assemblies. However, before the starter dog is undone, slightly slacken the flywheel retaining bolts.
3 If the main task, having removed the engine, is to remove the flywheel, then first remove the clutch assembly as described in Chapter 5.
4 Undo and remove the 6 retaining bolts and then remove the flywheel (photo). Be careful, it is heavy!
5 When refitting the flywheel it will be found that the bolt holes are offset so that it cannot be fitted incorrectly.
6 Offer the flywheel to the spigot end of the crankshaft with the starter ring gear towards the engine and align the holes.
7 Fit all the 6 bolts and screw them in. Before finally tightening them to the specified torque, take up any clearance by rotating the flywheel against the direction of rotation of the engine. Make up a wedge or bracket to stop the assembly rotating when the bolts are tightened (photo).

## 18 Crankshaft – removal

1 This task can only be performed with the engine out of the vehicle.
2 Strip the engine completely as described in the previous Sections so that only the crankshaft remains in the cylinder block.
3 Undo the main bearing cap retaining bolts.
4 Remove the bearing caps and bolts together with the lower bearing shells. Note that the first four caps are numbered from the front 1–2–3–4. The rear one, which is larger and easily identified, is not marked. The caps also have arrows on them which point to the front of the engine (photo).
5 The rear cap will have to be eased out as it also forms part of the rear oil seal construction.
6 Hold the crankshaft at both ends and lift it out carefully. The later lip type rear oil seal will come out with it (photo).
7 Remove the upper bearing shells from the bearing seats. Note that the centre bearing (No 3) has a flanged shell as this bearing takes the endthrust of the crankshaft (photo). Identify the shells if they are to be re-used.
8 Remove the lower bearing shells from the bearing caps only if they are to be renewed (photo).

## 19 Oil pump and oil filter – removal and refitting

1 In the course of a major engine overhaul the oil pump will be removed as part of the timing cover assembly and can then be removed and overhauled on the bench. This procedure covers the removal and refitting of the oil filter and oil pump independently during servicing or overhaul.

### Oil filter

2 Two types of oil filter are fitted. The early type has a hexagonal nut on the end and the later one is plain, but it also has an internal relief valve. The two types are **not** interchangeable.
3 Unscrew the oil filter. The early type with the nut can be undone by a spanner, whereas the later type will require a filter wrench.
4 Take care when removing the filter as it will be full of oil.
5 Remove the sealing ring and discard it.
6 Do not delay in fitting a new filter, as the oil may drain out of the pump which will then have to be removed and primed as described below.
7 Fit a new sealing ring to the new oil filter and screw it on by hand until the filter and sealing ring touch the oil pump mating face. Screw

18.6 Lift the crankshaft straight out

18.7 Removing the centre main bearing upper shell

18.8 Lower main bearing shell freed from its cap

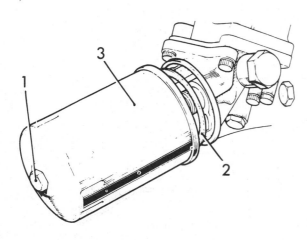

**Fig. 1.4 Oil filter – early type (Sec 19)**

*1   Hexagonal nut        2   Sealing ring        3   Filter*

it on another half turn **only** by hand. It is extremely important not to overtighten the oil filter. The nut on the end of the early type of filter is for **removing** only (photo).
8   If the oil in the sump has not been changed, then check the level on the dipstick after the engine is next run and top up as necessary.

*Oil pump*

9   Remove the oil filter as described above. If the same filter is to be reused, do not allow it to drain.
10   Disconnect the electrical connector from the pressure switch.
11   Release the special bolts securing the pump cover. Place an oil tray underneath. Remove the bolts and cover (photo).

12   Remove and discard the old cover gasket.
13   Slide out the pump gears (photo).
14   When refitting use a new gasket, placing it on the pump cover.
15   Pack the pump housing with petroleum jelly (no other type of grease will do).
16   Locate the pump gears into their correct positions, ensuring that the petroleum jelly is filling every visible cavity. If the pump is not completely packed with jelly then the pump may not prime itself when the engine is restarted (photo).
17   Offer up the pump cover to the body and locate it in position. Have the special fixing bolts handy, refit them and finger tighten.
18   Finally tighten all the securing bolts evenly, working in alternate sequence to a final torque figure as given in the Specifications.
19   Check the oil level in the sump and top up as necessary.

## 20   Engine components – examination for wear

When the engine has been stripped down and all parts properly cleaned, decisions have to be made as to what needs renewal and the following sections tell the examiner what to look for. In any borderline case it is always best to decide in favour of a new part. Even if a part may be serviceable its life will have been reduced by wear and the degree of trouble needed to replace it in the future must be taken into consideration. However, these things are relative and it depends on whether a quick 'survival' job is being done or whether the vehicle as a whole is being regarded as having many thousands of miles of useful and economical life remaining.

The Sections which follow consider the examination and renovation of the various components.

## 21   Rocker shaft assemblies – inspection and overhaul

1   With the rocker shaft assemblies removed from the vehicle the first job is to inspect the rockers and shafts for wear, in order to determine whether the assemblies need to be stripped and overhauled.

19.7 Fitting a new oil filter (later type)

19.11 The oil pump cover is retained by 6 special bolts (4 of them arrowed here)

19.13 Sliding out the pump gears

19.16 Packing the pump housing with petroleum jelly

21.3 New rocker (left) compared with old one (right). Note damage to cup

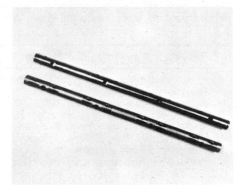

21.4 Worn (bottom) and new (top) rocker shafts being compared

21.6a Refit split pin, plain washer and wave washer – notch uppermost

21.6b Then refit two rockers with pedestal between – note relationship of valve bearing faces away from pedestal

21.9 Rocker shaft assembly laid out prior to refitting to engine

2    Take one assembly at a time and do not mix up left and right-hand assemblies. The shafts are handed and can only fit one way.

3    First examine the rockers. The rockers themselves are alloy but they have hardened inserts at each end. The pads bear on the ends of the valve stems and the cups fit over the upper ends of the pushrods. With high mileage or hard wear the hardened cup inserts tend to crack up and wear badly. If bad wear is evident in a cup then the pushrod will be badly worn as well. Similarly the pads will wear and if this is noticeable the rockers need renewing (photo).

4    Check the amount of lateral movement of the rockers on the shafts. If play is evident then look further. Slide the rockers along the shaft against their springs and examine the rocker shaft itself. If this is done from above only, the wear pattern on the rocker shaft may be missed as the wear occurs on the underside of the shaft; the rockers cut into the shaft under pressure from the valves and pushrods below. With high mileage engines or those which have been used for hard work, or where there has been a lack of oil being fed to the top of the engine, the amount of wear can be quite severe (photo).

5    Remove the pedestal bolts and slide the pedestals along the shaft. Check for wear in the pedestal/shaft contact areas.

6    To overhaul the rocker shaft assembly proceed as follows. Remove the split pin from one end of the rocker shaft and slide off the components carefully retaining them in the correct order of sequence for reassembly, as follows: split pin, plain washer, wave washer, rocker arm, pedestal, rocker and spring (photos).

7    If new rocker arms are being fitted ensure that the protective coating material used in storage is removed from the oil holes, and the new rocker given a smearing of clean oil before fitting to the shaft. **Note:** *Two different types of rocker arm are used; they must be fitted ensuring that the valve ends slope away from the pedestals.*

8    The rocker shafts are notched. This is to ensure that the oil feed holes line up correctly. The notch in each case should be uppermost. On the right-hand bank it should be located facing forwards, and on the left-hand bank it must be located to the rear of the engine. Use a new split pin.

9    Refit the baffle plate and pedestal bolts to the shaft. Note that the plate fits at the opposite end of the shaft to the notch (photo).

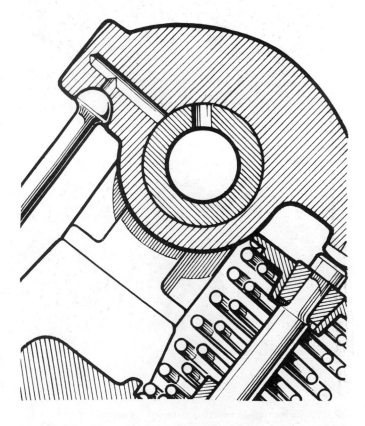

Fig. 1.5 Rocker relationship to pushrod and valve stem (Sec 21)

10 The rocker shaft assembly is now ready for refitting. Carry out the same inspection and overhaul procedure for the other assembly.

## 22 Tappets and pushrods – inspection

1 If an hydraulic tappet has to be removed downwards then there is a good chance that the lower end has become belled or rimmed. Inspect and renew if wear is bad.
2 If there is a prominent wear pattern just above the lower end of the body, this should only merit renewal of the tappet if it is badly grooved or scored. This condition is caused by the side thrust of the cam against the body whilst the tappet moves vertically in its guide.
3 Inspect the tappet inner and outer surfaces for blow holes and scoring. Renew the tappet if the body is roughly grooved or scored, or has a blow hole extending through the wall.
4 Inspect the tappet/camshaft lobe contact area. Fit a new tappet if the surface is badly worn or damaged. The tappet must rotate as it moves up and down and should produce an even circular wear pattern.

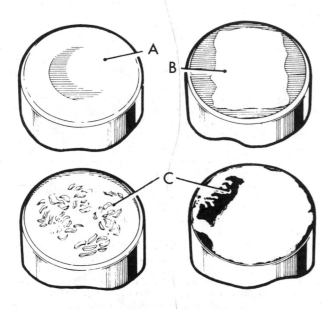

**Fig. 1.6 Tappet wear patterns (Sec 22)**

A    *Correct rotating wear pattern*
B    *Wear pattern for non-rotating tappet*
C    *Typical examples of excessive wear*

If the tappet has not been rotating the wear pattern will be square with a dip in the centre. Non-rotating tappets must be renewed. Check the wear on the camshaft lobe if there is a non-rotating tappet. When renewing a tappet check that it moves freely in the guide in the cylinder block.
5 Check the pushrod contact end of the tappet for roughness or damage. If either sorts of wear are apparent then the tappet must be renewed (photo).
6 Check the pushrods. Firstly ensure that they are all straight. If any one is bent or distorted, renew it.
7 Check the ends of each pushrod. If the ball end or seat is rough, damaged or badly worn, it must be renewed. If one pushrod is discovered that is badly worn and you have not rejected either the rocker or tappet for that rod, then check the tappet and/or rocker again (photo).

## 23 Camshaft – inspection

1 Thoroughly clean the camshaft and dry off, handling with care.
2 Examine all the bearing surfaces for obvious defects, wear, score marks etc.
3 Similarly inspect the cam lobes for excessive wear.
4 Ensure that the key or keyway is not damaged or burred and that the key is a tight fit in its keyway.
5 If in doubt seek professional advice and/or replace with a new component.
6 The camshaft bearings in the cylinder block are not renewable. If they are badly worn or damaged, a new block will be required.

## 24 Cylinder heads – inspection and overhaul

1 This section covers the cleaning/decarbonising of the cylinder heads and valves, the examination and recutting of valve seats, and valve seat insert renewal. Tackle one cylinder head at a time.

### Cylinder head

2 Thoroughly clean the cylinder heads using paraffin, or a mixture of paraffin and petrol, and dry off.
3 Clean the combustion chambers and ports using a brass wire brush. Draw clean rag through each valve guide bore.
4 Wash or, using a tyre pump, blow away all loose carbon particles.
5 Check the fit of the valves in their guides. If appreciable lateral movement of the valve in the guide is possible, new valves and/or guides are required. (New valves can be fitted without renewing the guides, but not vice versa). The fitting of new valve guides should be left to your Rover dealer.

22.5 Check the pushrod seat in the top of the tappet

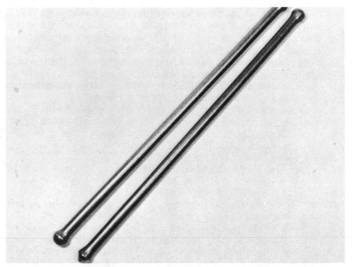

22.7 Comparing the badly worn end of the old pushrod (right) with a new one

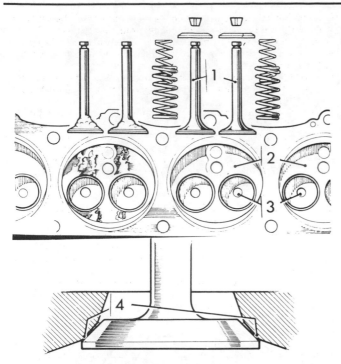

Fig. 1.7 Cylinder heads and valves – inspection and cleaning (Sec 24)

1   Valves
2   Combustion chambers
3   Valve guide bores
4   Valve and seat should meet
    at the outer edge

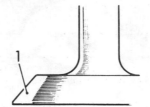
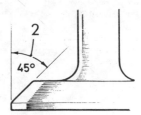

Fig. 1.8 Valve grinding and valve faces (Sec 25)

1   If a valve has to be reground like this – renew it
2   Valve face correct angle

### Valve seats – recutting and valve seat insert fitting

6   Having examined the valves and valve seats and discovered that the seats are badly worn or pitted then the seats will have to be recut. If, however, the valve seats are so worn that they cannot be recut then it will be necessary to fit new valve seat inserts. These latter two jobs should be entrusted to the local Rover agent. In practice it is seldom that the seats are so badly worn that they require renewal. Normally, it is the exhaust valve that is too badly worn, and the owner can easily purchase a new set of valves and match them to the seats by valve grinding.

### Valve cleaning

7   Clean the valves. Remove all the hard carbon deposit from the tops and underside using a blunt knife blade. Care should be taken not to mark or score the valve seating faces. Finish off the valve cleaning with a soft wire brush, again exercising care not to touch the seat face or valve stems.

### 25  Valves – examination and grinding-in

### Examination

1   Examine the heads of the valves for pitting and burning especially the heads of the exhaust valves. The valve seating should be examined at the same time. If the pitting on valve and seat is very slight, the marks can be removed by grinding the seats and valves together with coarse, and then fine grading paste. Where bad pitting has occurred to the valve seats it will be necessary to recut them and fit new valves as described in the last Section. If however the valves and valve seats require grinding-in to remove pitting or slight wear, or if new valves are being fitted to the original seats, then follow the instructions below.

### Grinding-in

2   Support the head on wooden blocks and start with No 1 valve.
3   Smear a trace of coarse or medium carborundum paste on the seat face and apply a suction grinder tool to the valve head. With a semi-rotary motion, grind the valve head to its seat, lifting the valve occasionally to redistribute the grinding paste. When a dull matt even surface finish is produced on both the valve seat and the valve, then

wipe off the paste and repeat the process with fine carborundum paste, lifting and turning the valve to redistribute the paste as before. A light spring placed under the valve head will greatly ease this operation. When a smooth unbroken ring of light grey matt finish is produced, on both valve and valve seat faces, the grinding operation is completed. Carefully clean away every trace of grinding compound, taking great care to leave none in the ports or in the valve guides. Clean the valves and valve seats with a paraffin soaked rag then with a clean rag. If an air line is available, blow the valves, valve guides and valve parts clean.
4   Finally give the cylinder head a rinse in clean paraffin to remove any remaining traces of valve grinding paste. Discard this paraffin, and dry the head with a clean non-fluffy rag.
5   Draw clean rag through each guide bore.

### 26  Timing cover oil seal – renewal

1   The timing cover casing need not be removed in order to remove and insert the oil seal of the later 'lip' type. For the earlier type the timing cover must be removed first. Refer to Section 42 for details of renewing the earlier type of seal.
2   If the later type seal is to be renewed with the cover in situ, then take care to prevent damaging the cover when extracting the old seal.
3   Follow the instructions given in Section 13 for removal of the crankshaft pulley. Then undo the ring of self-tapping screws and withdraw the mud shield from the front of the cover (photo).
4   Drill two small holes on opposite sides of the front face of the seal and screw in two self-tapping screws, leaving enough of each screw sticking out so that it can be gripped with a pair of pliers. The seal can then be worked out of the front cover.
5   Where the timing cover has to be removed then drive the seal out from the cover squarely, having removed the mud shield.

26.3 Undo the screws and remove the mud shield

26.7 Offer up a new seal

26.8 Using a suitable piece of tube to drive the seal into position

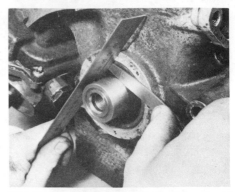

26.9 Checking the seating depth of the oil seal

6    After extracting the old seal, clean the housing and remove any burrs on the front edge.

7    Lubricate the new seal and fit it squarely with the lip face leading (photo).

8    Drive the seal carefully into position with a suitable drift. A flat block of wood and a hammer are ideal if the cover has been removed. Otherwise a large socket or similar object can be used (photo).

9    Check that the seal is seated to the correct depth and is square with the casing using a straight-edge as a guide. It should be 1.5 mm (0.062 in) below the front edge of the cover (photo).

10 Refit the mud shield and secure it with the ring of self-tapping screws.

## 27 Timing gears and chain – inspection

1    Examine the teeth on the camshaft and crankshaft gearwheels. If they are worn they should be renewed.

2    Inspect the camshaft wheel for signs of cracking.

3    Inspect the chain for wear, and the links for slackness. There should be no undue slackness in the chain. When the timing cover is removed during the overhaul procedure the chain should not have any 'sag' in it. There are no chain tensioners, and a slack chain could jump off the gearwheels. Renew the chain if necessary.

## 28 Pistons and connecting rods – inspection and overhaul

1    The condition of the pistons, rings, and the big-end bearings and small end bushes will be governed by many factors, but principally:

 (a)  *The total mileage covered by the vehicle*
 (b)  *The maintenance of oil level and regular oil and filter changes and usage to which the vehicle has been subjected*

2    The home mechanic is advised that to assess the true condition of these components, he must be in possession of, or have access to, certain professional equipment and tools. For instance, the gudgeon pin has to be removed by means of an hydraulic press or ram that will exert a pressure of not less than 8 tons (8128 kg). A micrometer especially constructed for measurement of cylinder bore wear and ovality and a normal micrometer capable of encircling a piston to assess the degree of piston wear will also be required.

3    'Standard' size pistons are available in five grades (see Specifications). The grade originally fitted is marked by matching letters stamped on the piston crown and cylinder block face.

4    If fitting new pistons to a standard size bore, select the appropriate grade of piston to give the specified piston-to-bore clearance. Note that the wear ridge at the top of the bore must be removed, or the top piston ring must be stepped, in order to avoid the top piston ring hitting the wear ridge and breaking.

5    Where the same pistons are to be refitted, then they must be marked to correspond with their respective connecting rods, and cylinder bore positions.

6    If new rings are to be fitted, this can be achieved without removing the pistons from their connecting rods.

7    Carefully remove the piston rings and retain in sequence.

8    Clean all the carbon deposits from the piston head. Clean out the

**Fig. 1.9 Checking the piston diameter using a micrometer (Sec 28)**

ring grooves using a piece of a broken piston ring as a scraper. Protect your fingers – piston rings are sharp! Take care not to scratch the piston during this operation.

9    Examine the piston carefully for any scoring of the bearing surfaces, cracking or chipping particularly at the skirt. Examine the crown for dents or marks caused by foreign objects in the combustion chamber or broken rings, plug electrodes etc. Rings that have been broken in the bore during running will have caused damage to the grooves in the piston, making the rings sloppy through having excessive clearance in the grooves. Damaged or faulty pistons of this nature should be renewed. It is also possible that broken rings will have scratched the cylinder wall – in bad cases this will necessitate a rebore. Refer to Section 32.

10 If the engine has been rebored then oversize pistons of 0.010 in (0.25 mm) and 0.020 in (0.50 mm) are available.

11 Examine the connecting rods carefully. They are not subject to wear, but in extreme cases such as partial engine seizure they could be distorted. Such conditions may be visually apparent, but if doubt exists they should be changed or checked for alignment by engine reconditioning specialists.

## 29 Piston rings – fitting

**Note:** *If fitting new piston rings in worn bores, either the top ring must be stepped or the wear ridge at the top of the cylinder bore must be removed. If one of these conditions is not met, the new ring may hit the wear ridge and break.*

1    When fitting new rings it is advisable to remove the glaze from the cylinder bores. It is strongly advised that the deglazed bore should have a cross hatch finish (diamond pattern) and should be carried out in such a way as not to increase the bore size in any way. This cross hatch finish provides the cylinder walls with good oil retention properties.

2    The top compression ring on early models must be fitted with the *T* or *Top* marking facing uppermost (inner bevel downwards). Later models have a plain top compression ring which is unmarked and can be fitted either way up. The second compression ring is of the stepped type and must only be fitted from the top of the piston. The second compression ring is marked *T* or *Top* and it is this side of the ring which must face uppermost.

3    The special oil control ring needs no gapping, but care must be taken to ensure that the ends of the expander, (fitted first), do not overlap but just abut each other. Fit the rails, one at a time, making sure that they locate snugly within the piston groove.

4    Fit the rings by holding them open, using both hands, thumbs at the gaps with fingers around the outer edges, easing them open enough to slip over the piston top and straight to the groove in which they belong. Use feeler gauges or strips of tin as guides to prevent the rings dropping into the wrong groove. Do not twist the rings whilst doing this or they will snap.

5    Before fitting however, a word on gapping. Push a compression ring down the cylinder bore using a piston to position it squarely at about 1 in (25 mm) below the top of the block and measure the piston ring gap with a feeler gauge (photo). The gap should be within the limits given in the Specifications. If required, file the gap using a flat fine cut file. Exercise care and judgement not to overdo it. Refit the ring, square off with the piston as before and re-measure. Repeat the process until correct. If the gap is too big initially then a new ring will be required.

6    Once the rings have been fitted to the piston, then the vertical

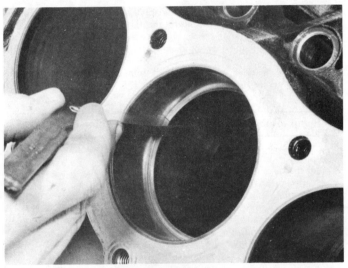

29.5 Checking the piston ring gap in the cylinder bore

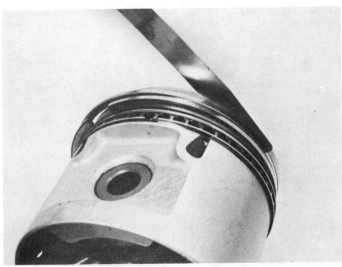

29.6 Checking the piston ring gap in the groove

clearance in the groove should be checked (photo). The correct clearance is given in the Specifications.

7    Fit the compression rings so that the gap in each ring is diametrically opposite, and the oil control ring so that its gap appears on the same side between gudgeon pin and the piston thrust face but staggered. Locate the rail ring gaps approximately 1 in (25 mm) either side of the expander join. This will ensure good compression.

## 30  Crankshaft – inspection

1    With the crankshaft suitably mounted on V blocks at No 1 and 5 main bearing journals, give a thorough visual check for scoring of, or white metal sticking to, the journals. Heavy scoring indicates that the crankshaft should be reground.

2    Check using a dial test indicator (Fig. 1.10) as follows:

   *(a)  The run-out at main journals 2, 3 and 4*
   *(b)  Note the relative eccentricity of each journal to the others*
   *(c)  The maximum indication should come at nearly the same angular location on all journals*

3    With an engineer's micrometer check each journal for ovality. If this proves to be in excess of the specified maximum, the crankshaft must be reground.

4    Undersize bearings are available in four sizes as listed in the Specifications.

## 31  Crankshaft main and big-end bearing clearances

*Crankshaft bearings (big-end and main) should only be re-used if they are known to have done a very low mileage only (less than 15 000 miles). As replacement bearings are relatively cheap it is false economy to refit the old ones. Where the condition of the bearings and journals was so bad that the crankshaft has to be reground, new bearings of the correct undersize will be provided by the firm which carried out the regrinding.*

*If new bearings of standard size are being fitted, or if for some reason you do not know which undersize bearings should be used – the following paragraphs detail a method of establishing bearing clearance, and therefore correct bearing size.*

1    Use Plastigage to measure the bearing clearances.

2    Before using Plastigage, all the parts to be measured must be clean, dry and free from oil.

3    With a piece of the Plastigage laid on the top of each main bearing journal, (Fig. 1.11), refit the bearing caps as though reassembling. The inner bearing shells must be in position as well.

4    The crankshaft rear oil seals should not be fitted during this operation.

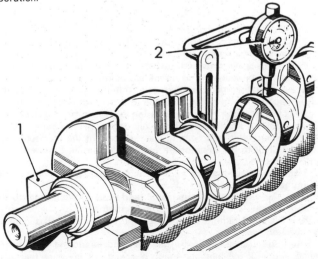

Fig. 1.10 Checking the crankshaft for straightness (Sec 30)

*1    Vee block          2    Dial gauge*

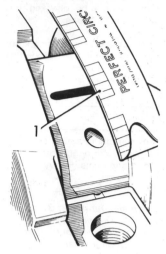

**Fig. 1.11 Use Plastigage (1) to check the bearing clearances (Sec 31)**

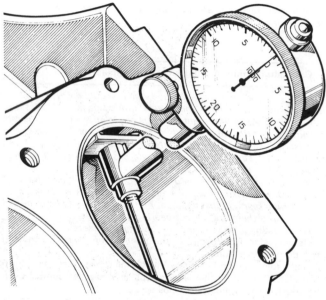

**Fig. 1.12 Measuring the cylinder bore with a micrometer (Sec 32)**

5    Tighten all bolts to the correct torque as listed in the Specifications. **Do not** rotate the crankshaft.
6    Remove the main bearing caps – the Plastigage will be found sticking to either the journal or the shell face. *Do not remove it.*
7    With the scale provided, measure the compressed piece of Plastigage on each bearing at its widest point.
8    The graduation number that most closely corresponds to this width indicates the bearing clearance in thousandths of an inch.
9    The clearance of a new main bearing is given in the Specifications.
10   Wipe off the Plastigage with an oily rag. **Do not** scrape it off.
11   To check the big-end bearing clearances, refit the connecting rod and inner shell to the appropriate crankshaft journal. Ensure it is the right way round.
12   Place a piece of Plastigage over the centre of the exposed half of the journal.
13   Refit the bearing cap, outer shell and nuts. Tighten them to the specified torque. **Do not** rotate the crankshaft.
14   Remove the bearing cap and shell and measure the Plastigage as described above.
15   The correct clearance for a new big-end bearing is given in the Specifications. If the bearings being checked are the ones that were removed earlier, they must be renewed if the clearance is greater than 0.003 in (0.08 mm).
16   Wipe off the Plastigage using an oily rag. It must not be scraped off.

## 32 Cylinder block and crankcase – inspection

1    The cylinder bores must be examined for taper, ovality, scoring and scratches. Start by carefully examining the top of the cylinder bores. If they are at all worn a very slight ridge will be found on the thrust side. This marks the top of the piston ring travel. The owner will have a good indication of the bore wear prior to dismantling the engine, or removing the cylinder head. Excessive oil consumption accompanied by blue smoke from the exhaust is a sure sign of worn cylinder bores and piston rings.
2    Measure the bore diameter just under the ridge with a bore micrometer, at right-angles to the gudgeon pin and about $1\frac{1}{2}$ to 2 in (40 to 50 mm) below the top of the block face.
3    Measure the dimension of the piston, also at right-angles to the gudgeon pin, at the top of the skirt.
4    The piston must be smaller than the bore diameter by the amount given in the Specifications for piston skirt clearance in the bore.
5    If the bores are slightly worn but not so badly worn as to justify reboring them, then special oil control rings and pistons can be fitted which will restore compression and stop the engine burning oil. Several different types are available and the manufacturer's instructions concerning their fitting must be followed closely.
6    Deglaze the bores with a hone or abrasive paper if reboring is not being carried out. See Section 29 for details.
7    If the engine is rebored, the crankshaft main bearing caps must be in position and tightened to the specified torque during the reboring process.
8    Examine the crankcase for cracks and leaking core plugs. To renew a core plug, drill a hole in its centre and tap a thread in it. Screw in a bolt and using a distance piece, tighten the bolt and extract the core plug. When fitting the new plug, smear its outer edge with gasket cement.
9    Probe oil galleries and waterways with a piece of wire to make sure that they are quite clear.

## 33 Sump – overhaul

1    Thoroughly clean the exterior, removing all traces of encrusted road dirt.
2    Wash the sump interior with paraffin, brushing out any sludge which may be there.
3    With the sump now perfectly clean, carefully scrape off the remains of the sump gasket.
4    Similarly clean the mating surface of the crankcase, paying particular attention to the joints between the timing cover and cylinder block.
5    Renew the sump if it is cracked or badly dented.

## 34 Oil pump – inspection and overhaul

*If the car has covered a high mileage then be prepared to renew all the working parts contained in the oil pump.*
1    First clean all the components as they are dismantled.
2    Visually check the gears for obvious scoring or chipping of the teeth. Renew if they are in poor condition (photo).
3    Now work on the components contained within the cover.
4    Dismantle the pressure relief valve and inspect it for excessive wear and/or scoring (photo).
5    Pay special attention to the pressure relief valve spring. Note whether it shows signs of wear on its sides or whether it is on the point of collapse, if not collapsed.
6    Thoroughly clean the gauze filter housed within the relief valve bore.
7    Test the valve in its bore in the cover; it should have no more clearance than to make it an easy sliding fit. If any side movement is obviously apparent, then the valve and/or the cover will have to be renewed.
8    With earlier engines, inspect the oil filter bypass valve located in the pump cover. Prise out the seat and withdraw the valve and spring. Check the valve for cracks, nicks or scoring.
9    Wash the stripped casting in clean paraffin or petrol. Dry with a clean rag. Smear parts with clean engine oil before reassembly.
10   With the gears refitted in the pump housing, check the pump gear

34.2 Visually check the condition of the gears

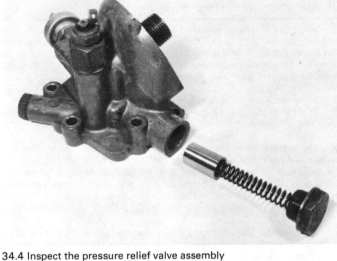

34.4 Inspect the pressure relief valve assembly

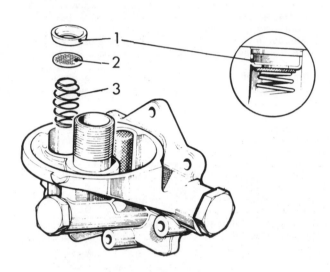

Fig. 1.13 Oil filter bypass valve (early engines) (Sec 34)

1   Seat          2   Valve          3   Spring

34.10 Checking the pump gear endfloat

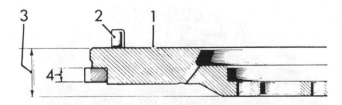

Fig. 1.14 Flywheel sectional view (Sec 35)

1   Mating surface      3   Overall flywheel thickness
2   Dowel               4   Starter ring gear thickness

endfloat (photo). Lay a straight-edge across the two gear wheels and with a feeler gauge, measure the clearance between the straight-edge and the surface of the front cover. The clearance should be within the specified limits. If the measurement is less than the minimum specified, inspect the front cover recess for signs of wear.

11   Reassemble the relief valve components, and the bypass valve assembly on earlier models.

12   Lubricate the relief valve and fit it into its bore, then insert the relief valve spring. Fit the washer to the plug and screw it home. Tighten it to the specified torque.

13   Insert the bypass spring into its bore, place the valve on the spring and press in the valve seat with its concave face outwards. The outer rim should be located 0.020 to 0.040 in (0.5 to 1.0 mm) below the surface of the bore.

## 35 Flywheel – inspection and refacing

1   Remove the flywheel as described in Section 17.
2   Two different types of flywheel are fitted to the Range Rover. They are identified by the thickness of the starter ring gear – see Specifications.
3   Examine the surface of the flywheel which mates with the clutch

driven plate. If this is scored or shows signs of many small cracks then it must be refaced or renewed.

4   To determine whether the flywheel can be refaced, check its overall thickness. If it is less than the minimum specified, it is not possible to reface it.

5   If the flywheel is thicker than the above dimensions then it can be refaced. The dowels must be removed and it must be refaced over the complete surface.

6   When the refacing has been carried out, check the flywheel thickness once more. If the refacing has taken the overall thickness below the minimum specified, then it must be renewed.

## 36 Starter ring gear – renewal

1 With the flywheel removed from the engine, drill a small hole approximately 0.375 in (10 mm) laterally across the starter ring gear. Take care not to allow the drill to enter or score the flywheel or flange. The hole should be made between the root of any gear teeth. This will weaken the ring gear and facilitate removal by breaking with a cold chisel (Fig. 1.15).
2 Hold the flywheel in a soft jawed vice.
3 **Warning**: *Beware of flying fragments. A piece of cloth draped over the whole assembly will protect the operator from possible injury.*
4 Split the starter ring gear with a hammer and chisel.
5 The new starter ring gear must be heated uniformly. The expansion of the metal permits it to fit over the flywheel and against the flange. Heat to between 338 degrees and 347 degrees Fahrenheit (170 and 175 degrees Centigrade). **Do not exceed the specified temperature.**
6 Place the flywheel on a flat surface with the flanged side downwards.
7 Offer up the heated ring to the flywheel with the chamfered inner diameter downwards, pressing it firmly against the flange until the ring contracts sufficiently to grip the flywheel. Allow cooling to take place naturally and do not attempt to hasten cooling in any way as this could cause weakening by setting up internal stresses in the ring gear,

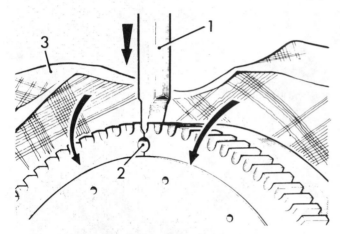

**Fig. 1.15 Starter ring gear renewal (Sec 36)**

1   Cold chisel
2   Drilled hole
3   Protective cloth

36.7 Starter ring gear in position on flywheel

leading to later break-up. Where the ring gear is chamfered on both sides it may be fitted either way round (photo).

## 37 Crankshaft spigot bearing – renewal

1 The spigot bearing, which is located in the rear end of the crankshaft and carries the front end of the gearbox input shaft, can only be removed when the engine is out of the vehicle.
2 With the engine removed from the vehicle, first remove the clutch assembly as described in Chapter 5.
3 Remove the old bearing which is a push fit into the crankshaft end flange.
4 Push in the new bearing which should finish flush with the end face of the crankshaft. Below this level is acceptable provided it does not recess more than 0.063 in (1.6 mm). (See Fig. 1.16).
5 The inside diameter of the spigot bearing should be 0.7504 + 0.001 in (19.177 + 0.025 mm). Reamer out if necessary.

## 38 Engine reassembly – general

To ensure maximum life with minimum trouble from a rebuilt engine, not only must everything be correctly assembled, but everything must be spotlessly clean, all the oilways must be clear, locking washers and spring washers must always be fitted where indicated and all bearing and other working surfaces must be thoroughly lubricated during assembly.

Before assembly begins renew any bolts or studs, the threads of which are in any way damaged, and whenever possible use new spring washers.

Gather together a torque wrench, oil can and clean rag, also a set of engine gaskets, crankshaft front and rear oil seals and a new oil filter element.

## 39 Crankshaft, main bearings and rear oil seal – refitting

1 Fit the upper main bearing shells to the crankcase. The inner shells have oil holes and grooves. Make sure that the tongue locates in the slot in the crankcase (photo).
2 The centre main bearing (No 3) has a special flanged bearing shell as it takes the crankshaft endthrust.
3 There are two different types of rear oil seal fitted to the Range Rover engine. The earlier type consists of a rubber strip in two halves;

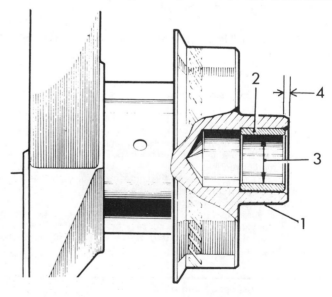

**Fig. 1.16 Spigot bearing location (Sec 37)**

1   End of crankshaft
2   Spigot bearing
3   Inside diameter of bearing
4   Maximum seating position below end face of crankshaft

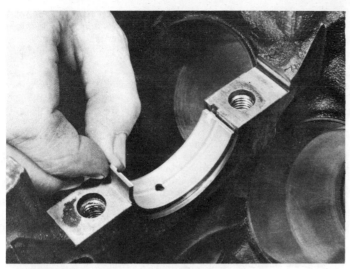

39.1 Refitting a main bearing upper shell

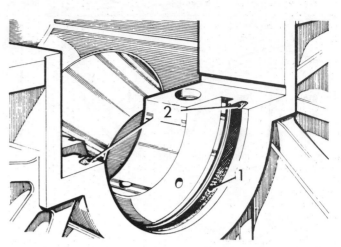

**Fig. 1.17 A new half oil seal (early type) fitted to the crankcase (Sec 39)**

1   *Oil seal*          2   *Seal ends trimmed off*

39.8 Lubricate the main bearing shells generously

39.10 The tags must locate in the grooves. This is the flanged shell for No 3 bearing

one half is embedded into a groove in the crankcase (behind the rear main bearing location) and the other half is embedded into a groove in the combined oil seal carrier and rear main bearing cap. Later models have a standard round lip type oil seal which is clamped in place by the rear main bearing cap. Both types also incorporate rubber strip seals in the side faces of the rear main bearing cap, although they are of different design. The early type have a single straight strip whereas the later ones are of a cruciform pattern.

4   In the earlier type engines the oil seal has by its design to be fitted in two operations, one before the crankshaft is refitted and one after. The later type is fitted after the crankshaft has been refitted.

*Early models*

5   Fit a new half oil seal to the crankcase groove. The ends should project above the mating face. Force the seal into the groove using a hammer handle to rub it down. The seal should not project more than 0.031 in (1.5 mm) above the groove.

6   When the seal has been forced right into the groove, cut off the ends level with the packing face.

7   Apply heavy engine oil to the oil seal.

*All models*

8   Lubricate the upper shell bearings and main bearing journals with engine oil. Inject some into the oilways too (photo).

9   Lift the crankshaft and lower it evenly into position in the inner bearing shells.

10   Fit the lower bearing shells, which are plain, to the main bearing caps, ensuring that the tags locate correctly in the grooves in the caps (photo).

11   Lubricate the shells in the caps for numbers 1 to 4 main bearings and refit them in the correct order. The caps are marked 1 to 4 from front to rear and the arrows on them should all point the same way — to the front of the engine.

12   Refit the retaining bolts but only do them up finger tight at this stage.

13   The next task is to refit the rear main bearing cap and oil seal carrier. As already described the rear oil seals differ, so here again the procedure varies.

*Early models*

14   Fit the other half seal to the groove in the rear main bearing cap as described in paragraphs 5 and 6.

15   Fit new seals to the side of the bearing cap. Do not cut them as they must protrude $\frac{1}{16}$ in (1.5 mm) above the packing face of the cap.

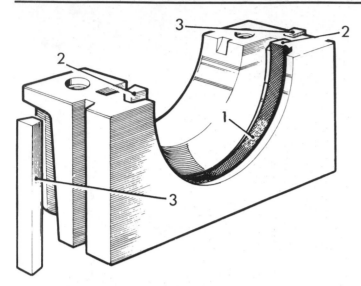

**Fig. 1.18 Early type rear main bearing cap and oil seal carrier (Sec 39)**

| 1 | Seal | 3 | Side strip seals |
|---|------|---|------------------|
| 2 | Seal ends | | |

16  Lubricate the rear oil seal strip with heavy engine oil and the side seals with light engine oil.

17  Fit and lubricate the lower bearing shell in the bearing cap and then fit the assembly to the crankcase. Refit the bolts finger tight.

18  Use a blunt instrument to drive the side seals into the bearing cap channels as far as they will go.

19  Use a mallet to tap the crankshaft first as far to the rear and then as far forward as it will travel. This is to align the centre main bearing thrust faces.

20  Tighten the main bearing caps numbers 1 to 4 to the specified torque.

21  Tighten the rear main bearing cap to its specified torque, and trim any of the side seals protruding from the cap.

22  Check that the crankshaft endfloat does not exceed that specified (photo). If it is not correct, check the assembly procedure or the components for faults.

*Later models*

23  In order to align the thrust faces of the centre main bearing tap the end of the crankshaft with a mallet, forward and rearward.

24  The securing bolts of the main bearing caps can now be tightened down evenly to the recommended torque setting (see Specifications) (photo).

25  Fit the new cruciform side seals to the grooves at the sides of the rear main bearing cap (photo).

26  Do not cut the cruiciform seals at this stage as they must project above the bearing cap mating faces approximately 0.062 in (1.5 mm).

27  Apply a coating of jointing compound to the rear half of the rear main bearing cap mating face, or alternatively apply the jointing compound to the equivalent area on the cylinder block (photo).

28  Lubricate the bearing shell and the cruciform side seals with clean engine oil and refit the bearing cap.

29  Do not fully tighten the two retaining bolts at this stage, but make sure that the cap is both fully home and squarely seated on the cylinder block.

30  Tighten the retaining bolts equally by one quarter of a turn from finger tight to settle the cap. Now back off the bolts by one complete turn.

31  The crankshaft rear oil seal can now be fitted, but it is strongly recommended that the Rover service tool (RO.1014), which is a seal guide, be used when fitting the oil seal (Fig. 1.19).

32  If however the tool is unobtainable, it is possible to fit the seal provided that the greatest possible care is taken. Lightly oil the outer edge of the flange, ensuring that no oil is deposited on the seal housing surfaces, or the seal will not stay in position when clamped down. Lubricate the inner circumference of the seal, making sure that the outer edge remains absolutely dry and clean, or again it will not stay in position (photo).

33  Offer the seal to the flange, locating the lower edge in position and feeding the lip round under the flange. Then press the upper edge into position very gently. Push the seal home (photo).

34  If the tool can be obtained proceed as follows.

35  First make sure that the oil seal guide and the crankshaft journal are scrupulously clean and then coat the seal guide and crankshaft journal with clean engine oil. **Note:** *The lubricant must totally coat the outer surface of the oil seal guide to prevent the possibility of turning back the lip of the oil seal when fitting it.*

36  In respect of handling the oil seal, avoid touching the seal lip at any time. Visually inspect the seal for damage and make sure that the outer diameter of the seal remains clean and dry at all times.

37  Position the oil seal, onto the seal guide tool, with the lip of the oil seal facing towards the engine.

38  Position the seal guide tool on the end of the crankshaft and push the seal, by hand, into the recess formed in the main bearing cap and cylinder block. The seal must fit squarely and abut the machined step in the recess.

39  With the seal so held in position, carefully withdraw the guide tool.

40  Once the seal is home in the recess, the rear main bearing cap bolts can be tightened to the specified torque.

41  Check the crankshaft endfloat as described in paragraph 22.

42  Observe the rear main bearing seal whilst the piston assemblies are being refitted and before the flywheel is refitted. It has an unhappy knack of popping out under pressure if there is any trace of oil on the outer edge of the seal or the seal recess.

**40  Pistons and connecting rods – refitting**

1  As with removing the piston assemblies, the same comments apply on refitting. Refit each one in sequence and make sure the correct assembly is fitted to the appropriate bore, unless new pistons are being fitted. Place the engine on one cylinder block and refit the four piston assemblies to the other side, then turn the block over and refit the other four. If the task is being done with the engine in the car,

39.22 Checking the crankshaft endfloat at the centre bearing

39.24 Tightening the main bearing cap bolts

39.25 Fitting new side seals to the rear main bearing cap (later model)

39.27 Applying jointing compound to the rear half of the cap mating face

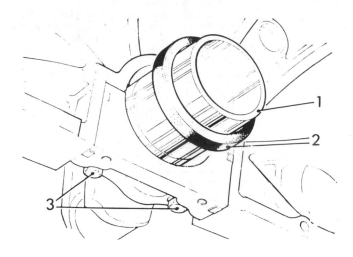

Fig. 1.19 Rover service tool RO.1014 – seal guide (Sec 39)

1   Seal guide                    3   Main bearing cap bolts
2   Seal

it is easier to work from front to rear, starting at No 1 cylinder.
2   Lubricate the bores and crankshaft big-end journals with oil.
3   Fit the upper big-end bearing shell to the connecting rod, ensuring that the tag slots into the groove (photo).
4   Fit the two plastic tubing pieces to the connecting rod bolts so they will not damage the bores or the journal (photo).
5   Lubricate the piston and rings. Using a piston ring compressor, clamp the piston rings, having checked tht they are spaced correctly.
6   Lubricate the upper bearing shell and the piston and offer the assembly to its appropriate cylinder.
7   Remember that the domed boss on the connecting rod must face

forwards for the right-hand bank of cylinders (2–4–6–8) and rearwards for the left bank (1–3–5–7). When the assemblies are refitted, the domed bosses should face each other on the crankshaft journals.
8   Push the piston into the bore as far as the ring compressor will allow. Then tap the piston into the bore using the wooden handle of a hammer (photo).
9   Guide the protected connecting rod bolts over the journal and then push the connecting rod and piston into position (photo).
10   Remove the protective plastic tubing from the bolts.
11   Refit the lower bearing shell to the bearing cap and ensure that the

39.32 Carefully lubricate the flange outer diameter

39.33 Feed the seal very carefully over the flange edge

40.3 Fitting a new bearing shell to the connecting rod big-end

40.4 Don't forget to protect the connecting rod bolts

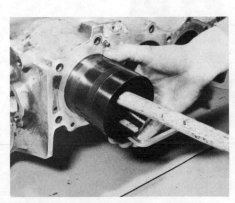

40.8 Using a hammer handle to push the piston into the bore

40.9 Lubricate the crankshaft journal as the connecting rod is drawn onto it

tag engages in the groove (photo). Lubricate the shell.

12 Refit the big-end bearing cap to the connecting rod (photo). Note that the rib on the edge of the cap faces in the same direction as the domed boss on the connecting rod, so that when the two connecting rods and caps are refitted to each of the four journals the ribs face each other.

13 Tighten the connecting rod cap nuts to the specified torque (photo).

14 Rotate the crankshaft so that the next journal is in the most convenient position and then refit the next assembly. Repeat the operation for the other piston and connecting rod assemblies.

## 41 Camshaft – refitting

1    Having inspected the camshaft it may now be refitted.
2    Take care when inserting the camshaft that the bearings are not damaged.
3    Check that the key is correctly located in the keyway (photo). It must be seated to its full depth and the key must be parallel with the shaft. The overall measurement of shaft and key must not exceed 1.187 in (30.16 mm) (Fig. 1.20). The reason for strict observance of the parallel attitude and seating of the key is that the remainder of the keyway in the camshaft gear acts as an oilway to feed the gears and chain. If it becomes blocked the results could be serious.

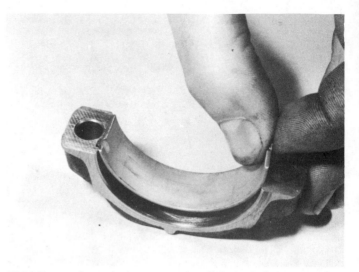

40.11 Engage the tag in the groove when fitting a shell to a cap

40.12 Refitting the big-end cap – note the rib on the cap

40.13 Tightening the big-end bearing cap nuts

41.3 Check that the key is correctly refitted to the camshaft keyway

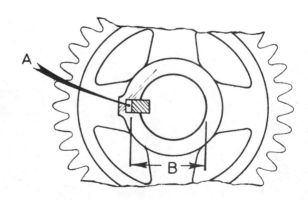

Fig. 1.20 Camshaft key location and clearances (Sec 41)

A   Clearance that must exist as an oilway   B   1.187 in (30.16 mm)

4   Two types of camshaft can be fitted. Make sure if the camshaft has been renewed that the correct one has been fitted. The early type has a spacer or cam which fits between the chainwheel and distributor drivegear to operate the mechanical fuel pump if one is fitted.

5   Refit the components and sub-assemblies that were removed for access to the camshaft in the reverse order to that described in Section 14.

## 42  Timing cover, chain and gears – refitting

**Note**: *This operation includes the renewal of the early type of oil seal.*

1   Rotate the crankshaft if the engine has been the subject of a full overhaul, so that No 1 piston is at top dead centre. If the engine has only been the subject of a partial strip-down it should have been left in this position.

2   Where the camshaft is not already aligned, refit the camshaft chainwheel temporarily with the FRONT marking facing outwards and rotate the camshaft so that the pointer on the chainwheel is at the 6 o'clock position with the engine vertical. (ie it is pointing directly at the crankshaft). If a full engine overhaul is being undertaken then the engine will probably still be upside-down on the bench, as this is the easiest method of reassembly. In this case the pointer will be at 12 o'clock, as shown in the photographs.

3   To check the correct alignment of the two shafts, temporarily refit the timing cover without its oil seal. Locate it on the crankcase dowels. Then refit the crankshaft pulley. Check the alignment of the TDC mark on the pulley with the pointer on the timing cover (photo). Rotate the crankshaft if necessary by rotating the flywheel, as it is possible to be several degrees out by visual checking of the No 1 for TDC.

4   Remove the crankshaft pulley and timing cover.

5   Fit the chain to the chainwheels with the timing marks aligned on both chainwheels. Remember the FRONT marking faces out.

6   Offer up the chainwheels and chain to both the camshaft and crankshaft simultaneously, ensuring that the timing marks stay in line.

7   Fit the chainwheels over the keys on both shafts and push them home. Check that the alignment is still correct (photo).

8   Check that the camshaft key is still parallel with the shaft and that the oilway is clear as described in the previous Section. Then refit the oil thrower (dished side out) to the crankshaft. This is only fitted to very early models.

9   Fit the fuel pump cam or spacer to the early type of camshaft, and ensure that the F marking faces outward (photo). The keyway oilway again must be clear.

10   Refit the distributor drivegear, washer and bolt (photo).

11   Tighten the bolt to the specified torque.

12   Fit a new timing cover oil seal. For the later 'lip' type of oil seal, this is covered in Section 26. For the earlier type follow these instructions.

### Oil seal renewal (early type)

13   Drive the oil seal and oil thrower out of the casing to the rear. Both seal and thrower should then be discarded (Fig. 1.22).

14   Coil a new seal into a new oil thrower and fit the assembly into the cover from the rear, with the oil seal ends at the top (Fig. 1.23).

15   Stake the oil thrower in position at four opposite and equal points.

16   Run a hammer handle around the inside of the seal to seat it, until

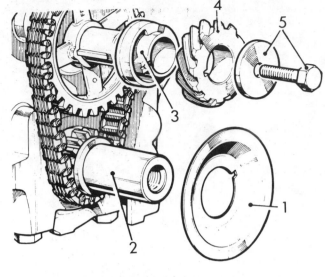

**Fig. 1.21 Timing chain and gears assembly (Sec 42)**

1   *Oil thrower (very early models only)*
2   *Crankshaft*
3   *Fuel pump cam (mechanical fuel pump models)*
4   *Distributor drivegear*
5   *Retaining bolt and washer*

the crankshaft pulley can be inserted. The seal is now fitted.

### Timing cover refitting

17   Fit a new gasket to the cylinder block mating face. Apply jointing compound to the gasket first to retain it in position. If the mating faces are as rough as those on our project vehicle, apply jointing compound to both sides.

18   If the job is being done with the engine in the vehicle, prime the oil pump with engine oil by injecting it through the suction port. Also apply jointing compound to the exposed part of the sump gasket.

19   Offer up the cover to the cylinder block and locate it on the dowels (photo).

20   If the bolt threads have not been cleaned, clean them and apply 3MEC776 thread lubricant/sealant to them.

21   Fit the bolts and tighten to secure the cover. Ensure the correct bolts are in the correct holes, as they were removed. Tighten the bolts to the specified torque.

22   Refit the two sump bolts into the bottom face of the timing cover and tighten them (engine in the vehicle).

23   Refit the remainder of the components which were removed to reach the timing cover, in the reverse order to that described in Section 13, if the job is being done with the engine in the vehicle.

24   Check and adjust the ignition timing if necessary.

42.3 Check the alignment of the pointer and TDC mark on the pulley

42.7 Camshaft and crankshaft chainwheel alignment marks. Note FRONT marking on camshaft chainwheel

42.9 Refit the fuel pump cam – F marking faces out (early models)

42.10 The distributor drivegear, washer and bolt refitted

42.19 Locate the timing cover on the dowels

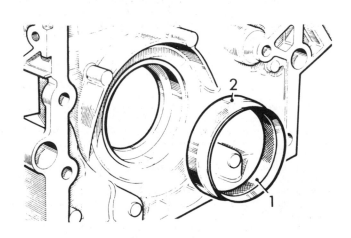

**Fig. 1.22 Early type of timing cover oil seal and thrower (Sec 42)**

1   *Seal*                        2   *Thrower*

43.4 Refit the sump using a new gasket

### 43 Sump – refitting

1   Refit the oil pick-up pipe and strainer. There is a small gasket between the flange and the crankcase. The flange is retained by two bolts.
2   Ensure that both the crankcase and sump mating surfaces are clean and free from old gasket or jointing compound.
3   Apply jointing compound to the area of the joint between the crankcase and timing cover.
4   Grease the crankcase or the sump mating face depending on whether the engine is on the bench or in the vehicle, and place the new sump gasket in position (photo).
5   Refit the sump and secure with 16 bolts and washers.
6   Do not overtighten the bolts. Check that the sump drain plug has been refitted.
7   If the task is being done with the engine in the vehicle, refill the sump in the normal manner. Check for leaks after running the engine.

**Fig. 1.23 Fitting an early type of oil seal (Sec 42)**

1   *Seal – ends at top*          3   *Hammer*
2   *Staking points*

### 44 Cylinder heads – reassembly and refitting

1   Place the cylinder head on its side.
2   Fit each valve in turn into the guide from which it was removed, unless the valves are new ones.

3 Check the height of the valve stems above the valve spring seat surface. This distance **must not** exceed 47.63 mm (1.875 in). If necessary, grind the end of the valve stem to reduce the height. However, if this is going to entail too much grinding, new valves or even valve seat grinding may be required.

4 Remove the valves and lubricate both the valve stems and valve guides with engine oil, then refit them to their respective positions.

5 Refit the valve spring(s). Make sure that the bottom of the single valve spring (on later models) locates correctly in the recess in the cylinder head.

6 Refit the valve spring caps, compress the spring using a valve spring compressor and refit the split collets.

7 When all the valves and springs have been fitted, place the head face down on the bench and give each valve stem end a light tap with the butt end of a hammer handle or with a plastic-headed mallet to ensure that the collets are well seated into their respective caps (photo).

8 Refit the oil dipstick tube to the left-hand cylinder block top face if it has been removed during overhaul.

9 Fit a new gasket to the cylinder block and engage it on the two small dowels. Note that the gasket is marked TOP to show which way up it should fit (photo). Do not use any sealant.

10 Lift up the cylinder head and lower it into position on the two dowels which ensure that it is aligned correctly (photo).

11 Clean the cylinder head bolts of all old sealant, if this has not already been done.

12 Apply thread sealant to each bolt in turn and refit it to its appropriate position. Rover recommend 3MEC776 thread lubricant and sealant for this purpose.

13 There are 3 long bolts, 7 medium length bolts, and 4 short ones. The long bolts fit in the three central holes in the cylinder head main section, the medium length bolts fit in the two outer holes on either side of the long bolts and the row immediately below the spark plugs, and the short bolts fit in the outer (lower edge) row – see Fig. 1.25. Note that there is a special short bolt which fits in the left-hand cylinder head immediately adjacent to the oil dipstick tube. This has a threaded head insert. The dipstick tube retaining clip bolt is screwed into it.

14 Tighten the cylinder head bolts gradually in the correct sequence until they are at the specified torque (photo).

15 Repeat the procedure for the other cylinder head where it has been removed and overhauled.

16 Refit the rest of the components as they were removed.

## 45 Valve gear – refitting

1 This operation covers the refitting of the tappets, pushrods and rocker shaft assemblies, all of which have been inspected and overhauled or renewed as necessary.

2 Refit the tappets the right way up to the positions from which they were removed. New tappets must be fitted to the positions where tappets have been discarded for reasons of wear etc. Check the tappet oilways before refitting.

3 Similarly refit the pushrods to their correct positions.

4 Refit the rocker shaft assemblies. Note that they are handed and must be fitted the correct way round to align the oilways. On the right-hand cylinder head the notch in the end of the shaft faces upwards and towards the front of the engine. On the left it faces upwards and towards the rear (photo).

5 As with the rocker shafts themselves, so the baffle plates are handed and fit on the opposite ends of the assemblies to the notches in the shaft (ie at the front on the left-hand bank and at the rear on the right-hand bank).

6 Offer up the assembly complete with the retaining bolts in position through the pedestals.

7 Locate the pushrod ends in the rocker arm cups, then check the rocker pad alignment with the valves and ensure that they are correct. Gradually tighten the pedestal bolts in an even pattern. This must be done carefully as the varying tensions on the rockers must be taken up gradually.

8 Tighten the bolts finally to the specified torque (photo).

9 Rotate the crankshaft to ensure that all the valves, rockers and tappets function correctly.

10 Refit the rocker covers and secure them with the four cross-head screws.

11 Should the rocker cover gasket need renewing, note that it is stuck to the cover mating face using Bostik 1775 impact adhesive. Any old gasket and adhesive must be cleaned off before a new one is fitted. Before applying adhesive to the new gasket and cover check which way round it fits. It can only fit one way. Don't try to fit it in one go. Start at one end and push it firmly into the recessed face in the cover, then work the rest of the gasket into place. The gasket and cover should be left for fifteen minutes between applying the adhesive and fitting the gasket to the cover. Once fitted allow the gasket and cover

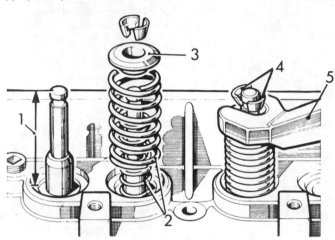

**Fig. 1.24 Valve refitting sequence (Sec 44)**

1 Height of valve stem above valve spring seat
2 Inner and outer valve springs (earlier models)
3 Cap
4 Collets
5 Valve spring compressor

44.7 Valve and springs assembly with collets correctly seated

44.9 Fit a new gasket and locate it on the dowels

44.10 Lowering a cylinder head into position

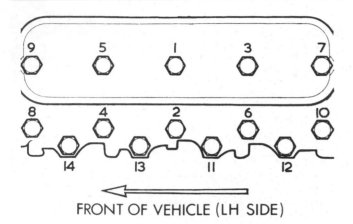

**Fig. 1.25 Cylinder head retaining bolts loosening/tightening sequence (Sec 44)**

*Short bolts – sequence numbers 11, 12, 13 and 14*
*Medium bolts – sequence numbers 2, 4, 6, 7, 8, 9 and 10*
*Long bolts – sequence numbers 1, 3 and 5*

44.14 Tightening the cylinder head bolts – note special bolt (arrowed) for dipstick tube retaining clip

45.4 Left-hand rocker shaft refitted – notch to rear, baffle at front (viewed from rear of engine)

45.8 Tightening the rocker pedestal bolts

45.11 Rocker cover, with new gasket fitted, being offered up to the engine

to stand for about thirty minutes before refitting it to the engine (photo).

12   In the meantime refit the inlet manifold.

### 46   Inlet manifold – refitting

1   As the inlet manifold also serves to cover the pushrod cavities of the cylinder block, a single manifold gasket is fitted. Made from sheet metal, this gasket extends downwards over the inlet port face of each cylinder head and over each of the respective pushrod cavities. Rubber seals are fitted at each end to seal the manifold to the timing chest and rear flange. It is important that the gasket and seals are carefully fitted or oil leaks may develop.

2   Locate the new seals to the front and rear walls of the engine. The seals must be smeared on both sides with silicone grease and their ends must locate in the notches between the cylinder head and cylinder block joints.

3   Apply gasket sealing compound to the joints between the seals and cylinder heads, and around the manifold gasket cylinder head and inlet manifold water passages.

4   Fit the new gasket with the word FRONT at the front. The open notch should be at the right-hand side front (photo).

5   Refit the two gasket clamps but do not tighten the bolts fully. Note that the two clamps are different and can only fit at one end or the other (photo).

46.4 Lining up the inlet manifold gasket – note the seals at each end

46.5 Refit the two gasket clamps

46.8 Tightening the inlet manifold bolts

47.3a Tightening the starter dog/crankshaft pulley bolt ...

47.3b ... with a wedge in position to stop the flywheel rotating

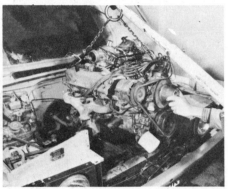
48.2 Clearing the front bodywork as the engine is refitted

6 Refit the inlet manifold. Note that the open bolt hole aligns with the open hole in the gasket.
7 Refit the bolts. Again they should be cleaned and coated in 3MEC776 lubricant/sealant.
8 Tighten the bolts evenly and gradually, working on alternate sides from the centre to the ends. Do not exceed the specified torque (photo).
9 Finally tighten the gasket clamps front and rear.
10 Refit the remainder of the components removed to perform this operation.
11 When all the components are refitted, start the engine and check for oil and water leaks.

## 47 Ancillary components – refitting (engine out of car)

1 With the major components and sub-assemblies refitted to the engine, the ancillary components can now be refitted.
2 Always use new gaskets when refitting previously removed components and refer to the Chapter or Section concerned for the detailed instructions relating to any individual component.
3 The ancillary components listed below can be refitted in the order given:

(a) Flywheel (Section 17) – unless it has already been refitted to rotate the crankshaft when refitting the timing gear or piston and connecting rod assemblies
(b) Crankshaft pulley and starter dog: engage the pulley on the crankshaft key. Screw in the starter dog bolt. Lock the flywheel to stop the crankshaft turning and tighten the starter dog to the specified torque. Remove the wedge or bracket from the flywheel (photos)
(c) Oil pump and oil filter (Section 19)
(d) Distributor and advance/retard vacuum pipe (Chapter 4)
(e) Rocker covers (Section 45)
(f) Fuel pump (mechanical type - early models) (Chapter 3)
(g) Exhaust manifolds (Chapter 3)
(h) Clutch (Chapter 5)
(j) Spark plugs (Chapter 4)
(k) Crankcase breather valve (Chapter 3)
(l) Rocker breather pipes and flame traps (Chapter 3)
(m) Distributor cap and plug leads (Chapter 4)
(n) Starter motor (Chapter 10)
(p) Alternator and drivebelt (Chapter 10)
(q) Wiring loom and retaining brackets

## 48 Engine – refitting

Note: This is a 2-man operation.
Basically the installation of the engine is the reverse procedure to the removal operation; however, mating the engine to the gearbox can be difficult unless the following method is used.
1 Make sure the clutch is centralised on the flywheel as described in Chapter 5.
2 Carefully lower the engine into the engine compartment using a suitable hoist until the flywheel housing is straight and level with the clutch housing. This can be tricky as the exhaust pipes tend to get in the way. Make sure the cables and wires do not snag (photo).
3 Push the engine rearwards, ensuring the gearbox input shaft enters the clutch assembly in a straight line and not at an angle.
4 If the engine begins to mate up and then stops with a couple of inches still to go, fit a spanner onto the crankshaft starter dog and turn it slowly while pushing the engine rearwards.
5 As soon as the flywheel and clutch housings touch, line up and engage the bellhousing dowels. Insert a bolt finger tight to hold them together, and then refit and tighten all the bolts except the one that retains the clutch slave cylinder pipe joint brackets.
6 Raise the engine on the hoist sufficiently for the engine mounting rubbers to be inserted. Then lower the engine onto the mountings, ensuring that the exhaust pipes are in line with their manifolds.
7 Finally, lower the hoist completely and remove the engine slings and the jack or blocks from beneath the transmission. Reconnect all the controls, electrical leads, fuel pipes, exhaust pipe etc, checking

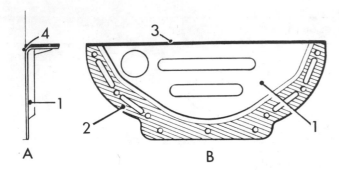

Fig. 1.26 Bellhousing cover plate gasket and sealant application points (Sec 48)

1  Cover plate
2  Apply gasket sealant to shaded area
3  New gasket fits on top face
4  Apply a fillet of sealing compound along angled face
A  Side-on view of plate
B  Rear view of plate

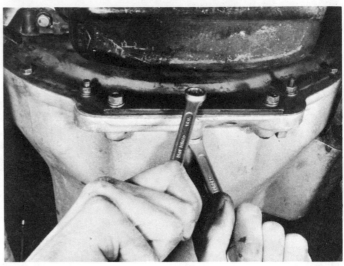

48.8 Tightening the bellhousing cover plate nuts and bolts – note stiffening plate

each item against the sequence given in Section 5.

8   When refitting the bellhousing cover plate, ensure that gasket sealing compound is applied to the vertical face and a new gasket is placed on the top horizontal face. The angled section across the top of the plate should have a good fillet of compound laid across it (Fig. 1.26). Do not forget the stiffening plate across the bottom of the cover plate (photo).

9   Do not forget to refill the cooling system, and refill the engine with the recommended grade and quantity of oil.

## 49 Engine – initial start-up after overhaul or major repair

1   Make sure that the battery is fully charged and that the oil, water and fuel are replenished.

2   If the fuel system has been dismantled it will require several revolutions of the engine on the starter motor to get the petrol up to the carburettor (models with mechanical fuel pump).

3   As soon as the engine fires and runs, keep it going at a fast tickover only (not faster) and bring it up to normal working temperature. **Do not** exceed 1000 rpm initially, or the crankshaft rear oil seal may be damaged.

4   Tappet noise will be experienced initially on starting up after an overhaul or major repair. This noise should vanish quite quickly as the tappets fill with oil. If excessive noise is apparent, run the engine at around 2500 rpm which should eliminate any tappet noise.

5   As the engine warms up there will be odd smells and some smoke from parts getting hot and burning off oil deposits. The signs to look for are leaks of oil or water which will be obvious, if serious. Check also the connections of the exhaust pipes to the manifolds as these do not always 'find' their exact gas-tight position until the warmth and vibration have acted on them and it is almost certain that they will need tightening further. This should be done, of course, with the engine stopped.

6   When normal running temperature has been reached adjust the idling speed as described in Chapter 3.

7   Stop the engine and wait a few minutes to see if any lubricant or coolant is dripping out when the engine is stationary.

8   Road test the car to check that the timing is correct and giving the necessary smoothness and power. Do not race the engine – when new bearings and/or pistons and rings have been fitted it should be treated as a new engine and run in at reduced revolutions for the first 500 miles. Change the engine oil and oil filter after the first 500 miles in order to get rid of the metallic particles which will have been created during the running-in process.

## 50 Fault diagnosis – engine

| Symptom | Reason(s) |
| --- | --- |
| Engine will not turn when starter switch is operated | Flat battery<br>Bad battery connections<br>Bad connections at solenoid and/or starter motor<br>Defective starter motor |
| Engine turns normally but fails to start | No spark at plugs<br>No fuel reaching engine<br>Too much fuel reaching the engine (flooding) |
| Engine starts but runs unevenly and misfires | Ignition and/or fuel system faults<br>Sticking or leaking valves<br>Burnt out valves<br>Worn out piston rings |
| Lack of power | Ignition and/or fuel system faults<br>Burnt out valves<br>Worn out piston rings |
| Excessive oil consumption | Oil leaks from crankshaft oil seals, timing cover gasket, rocker cover gasket, oil filter gasket, sump gasket, sump plug<br>Worn piston rings or cylinder bores resulting in oil being burnt by engine<br>Worn valve guides and/or defective inlet valve stem seals |
| Excessive mechanical noise from engine | Worn crankshaft bearings<br>Worn cylinders (piston slap)<br>Slack or worn timing chain and sprockets |

**Note**: *When investigating starting and uneven running faults do not be tempted into snap diagnosis. Start from the beginning of the check procedure and follow it through. It will take less time in the long run. Poor performance from the engine in terms of power and economy is not normally diagnosed quickly. In any event the ignition and fuel systems must be checked first before assuming any further investigation needs to be made.*

# Chapter 2 Cooling system

*For modifications, and information applicable to later models, see Supplement at end of manual*

## Contents

## Specifications

### General
| | |
|---|---|
| System type | Pressurised, spill return, thermostatically controlled, pump and fan assisted |
| System pressure | 15 lbf/in$^2$ (1.05 kgf/cm$^2$) maximum |

### Coolant pump
| | |
|---|---|
| Type | Centrifugal |
| Location | In timing cover |

### Thermostat
| | |
|---|---|
| Type | Wax pellet |
| Location | Front of inlet manifold |
| Jiggle pin position | 12 o'clock |
| Opening temperature | 173° to 182°F (78° to 83°C) |

### Coolant capacity
20 Imp pints (11.3 litres)

### Drivebelt tension
0.437 to 0.562 in (11 to 14 mm) deflection midway between alternator and crankshaft pulleys

### Torque wrench settings
Water pump cover bolts:

| | lbf ft | kgf m |
|---|---|---|
| Long | 20 to 25 | 2.8 to 3.5 |
| Short | 6 to 8 | 0.8 to 1.0 |

## 1  General description

The engine cooling system is conventional, acting on the thermosyphon pump-assisted principle. The coolant flow is controlled by a thermostat which is fitted at the forward end of the inlet manifold casting and behind the outlet elbow. The purpose of this thermostat is to prevent the full flow of the coolant around the system before the most efficient operating temperature is reached.

The purpose of pressurising the cooling system is to prevent premature boiling in adverse conditions and also to allow the engine to operate at its most efficient running temperature.

The overflow pipe from the radiator is connected to an expansion tank which makes topping-up unnecessary. The coolant expands when hot, and instead of beng forced down an overflow pipe and lost, it flows into the expansion tank. As the engine cools the coolant contracts and, because of the pressure differential, flows back into the top tank of the radiator. Excess pressure is vented to the atmosphere via a pressure relief valve fitted to the expansion tank filler cap.

The cooling system comprises the radiator, water pump, thermostat, interconnecting hoses and waterways in the cylinder block and heads. The water pump is driven from the engine crankshaft pulley by a V-belt.

On early models a five-bladed metal fan is fitted directly to the water pump pulley. Later models are fitted with a multi-bladed plastic fan which is connected to a Holset viscous coupling which limits the fan speed at high engine revolutions. This works in a similar manner to a torque converter, and provides a 'slipping clutch' effect; its aim is to reduce noise and engine loading.

## 2  Cooling system – draining

**Warning**: *Do not remove the expansion tank cap when the engine is hot, or the water will scald you.*

*With the car on level ground, and the system cold, proceed as follows:*

1  Move the heater control lever to the *Hot* position.
2  Depress and remove slowly the expansion tank filler cap.
3  Unscrew and remove the hexagon radiator filler plug (photo).
4  If antifreeze is used in the cooling system, and has been in use for less than two years, drain the coolant into a container of suitable capacity for re-use.
5  Remove the radiator drain plug from the bottom left-hand corner of the radiator.
6  Drain taps are provided in each of the cylinder banks and positioned directly beneath the exhaust manifolds (photo). Turn the taps in an anti-clockwise direction to drain the coolant.

2.3 The radiator filler plug removed

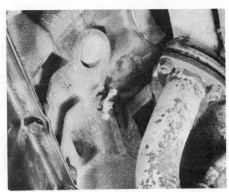

2.6 Left-hand cylinder block drain tap

4.6 Half-fill the expansion tank with coolant mixture

## 3  Cooling system – flushing

1    With the passing of time, the cooling system will gradually lose its efficiency as the radiator becomes choked with rust, scale deposits from water and other sediment. To clear the system out, initially drain the system as described previously, then detach the lower radiator hose.
2    Using a garden hose, allow water to enter the radiator via the radiator filler plug. It will be necessary to close the cylinder block drain taps during this operation.
3    Allow the water from the hose to run through the radiator for several minutes until it emerges clean, then refit the lower hose.
4    When it is desired to flush the cylinder block, simply remove the radiator filler plug and the cylinder block drain taps. The removal of the cylinder block drain taps will permit speedy clearance of the sediment and scale deposits. The garden hose can be inserted in the radiator filler plug hole as described in paragraph 2.
5    If when flushing the radiator the sediment and scale deposits are very dirty then it will be found desirable to remove the radiator and reverse flush it. Reverse flushing simply means feeding the clean flushing water into the lower radiator connection and expelling the sediment from the top radiator connection.
6    The alternative to the reverse flushing method, described in paragraph 5, is the use of a proprietary brand of radiator descaler available at most motor accessory shops or garages. The correct usage of the descaler compound is described on the container, but generally necessitates leaving it in the cooling system for a short period to free the deposits which can then be flushed out as described in paragraphs 3 and 4. Make sure that such a descaler is suitable for mixed metal (iron and aluminium) engines.

## 4  Cooling system – filling

1    The importance of refilling with the correct mixture of anti-freeze/inhibitor and water, or inhibitor only with water, cannot be over-emphasised. Antifreeze solution conforming to British Standard No 3150 or 3151 should be used. Alternatively, where applicable, a Rover approved cooling corrosion inhibitor should be used. Antifreeze mixture can remain in the system for two years, provided that the specific gravity of the coolant is checked regularly, especially before the beginning of the second winter. If necessary it must be topped up with new antifreeze. After the second winter the system must be drained and flushed as described in Sections 2 and 3.
2    Before filling the system, check all hoses, clips and joints to make sure that they are in sound order. Renew any that are defective or cracked even if they are not actually leaking. This is a form of insurance and is in your best interest. Antifreeze has a very searching effect on hoses and joints.
3    When mixing water with the antifreeze inhibitor, or just inhibitor, it is better to use soft tap water or rain water, the mixture being carried out in a plastic bucket. It is not necessary to mix the whole amount required to fill the system, as further topping-up can be done once the initial coolant mix has been poured into the system.
4    Use the following table to ensure adequate protection according

to the local climatic conditions:

| Amount of antifreeze | Protection provided down to |
|---|---|
| 7 pints (4 litres) (33%) | –25°F (–32°C) |
| 10 pints (6 litres) (50%) | –33°F (–36°C) |

5    Fill the system with the mixture through the radiator filler plug orifice then refit the filler plug.
6    Save a little of the mixture and half-fill the expansion tank and refit the cap (photo). There is a water level plate inside the tank.
7    Run the engine until the normal operating temperature is reached (ie the thermostat is open) and then switch off. Allow the system to cool, then check the coolant level. Top up as necessary.

## 5  Radiator – removal and refitting

1    For safety reasons disconnect the battery negative terminal.
2    Drain the cooling system as described in Section 2.
3    Disconnect the following hoses at the radiator (photos):

   *Top hose*
   *Bottom hose*
   *Manifold vent hose*
   *Expansion tank bottom hose*

4    Undo the two nuts and washers which retain the cowl to the top of the radiator brackets, as described in Section 6.
5    Lift the cowl straight up to release the lower edge from the clips on the bottom of the radiator. Then move the cowl back over the fan (photo).
6    Undo the two nuts and bolts which retain the radiator to the front body panels (photo).
7    Lift the radiator straight out to withdraw the pegs at the bottom corners from the grommets in the mounting brackets beneath. Take care that the fan does not catch the radiator matrix as it is removed, as the matrix is easily damaged (photo).
8    Refitting is the reverse procedure to removal. Check before refitting the radiator that the grommets into which the pegs fit are in good condition and that the rubber mounting bushes for the radiator main fixing bolts are also in good order (photo).
9    After refitting, refill the cooling system as described in Section 4.

## 6  Fan cowl, blades, viscous coupling and pulley – removal and refitting

1    Undo the cowl retaining nuts and washers from the brackets on top of the radiator (photo).
2    Lift the cowl straight up to release the lower edge from the clips on the bottom edge of the radiator (photo).
3    Carefully lift the cowl out, taking care that it does not catch on one of the fan blades and thereby damage the radiator matrix as it twists. The clearance is very limited for this.
4    Slacken the alternator adjusting bolt, push the alternator towards the engine and slip the belt from the pulley.
5    To remove the fan on early models, undo the four bolts and remove the fan (photo). Undo the four nuts and bolts which retain the

5.3a Disconnect the top hose at the radiator ...

5.3b ... the bottom hose and the two small hoses at the top of the photograph

5.5 Move the cowl back over the fan out of the way

5.6 Undoing the radiator right-hand retaining nut and bolt

5.7 The radiator removed – note the locating pegs and the cowl clips at the bottom

5.8 Check the grommets and bushes (arrowed) – left-hand side shown

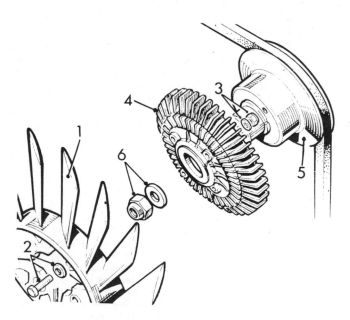

Fig. 2.1 Multi-bladed fan and viscous coupling assembly (later models) (Sec 6)

1  Fan
2  Fan-to-coupling bolt and washer
3  Fan-to-coupling nut and washer
4  Viscous coupling
5  Pump/fan pulley
6  Coupling and pulley retaining nut and washer

fan to the viscous coupling (Fig. 2.1).
6   To remove the water pump pulley on early models, undo the three bolts which retain it to the hub and remove it (photo). On later models remove the viscous coupling retaining nut from the pump shaft. The viscous coupling and pulley can now be pulled off the shaft in turn.
7   Refitting is the reverse procedure to removal. Note that the metal fan has a locating dowel on the pulley hub mounting face and the plastic fan has large diameter bosses on one side, which face forward to ensure that it is fitted the right way round.
8   Adjust the fanbelt when the belt has been refitted as described in Section 7.

## 7  Fan/alternator drivebelt – removal, refitting and adjustment

1   Loosen the alternator mounting and adjuster nuts and bolts (photo). If air conditioning is fitted, the alternator will be mounted on the left-hand side of the engine.
2   Tip the alternator towards the engine, slip the belt from the pulleys, and feed it over the fan blades to remove it.
3   Refitting of the drivebelt is the reverse of removal, but it is important to tension the belt correctly.
4   Pull the alternator away from the engine until the tension of the drivebelt is such that it can only be deflected by the specified amount at a point midway between the alternator and crankshaft pulleys.
5   With the alternator so held, tighten the mounting and adjuster nuts and bolts, then recheck the tension (photo).
6   If a new drivebelt has been fitted then it will need to be retensioned after approximately 250 miles (400 km) owing to the fact that a certain amount of stretching occurs during the bedding-in stage.

## 8  Water pump – removal and refitting

1   Disconnect the battery negative terminal.
2   Drain the cooling system and remove the radiator as described in the previous Sections.

6.1 Undo the cowl retaining nuts (right-hand nut arrowed)

6.2 The cowl is retained by two clips at the bottom like the one arrowed (radiator and cowl out of the car for clarity)

6.5 Undo the four bolts to remove the fan (early models)

6.6 The pulley is secured to the fan hub by three bolts

7.1 Slacken the alternator adjuster bolt

7.5 Checking the fanbelt tension

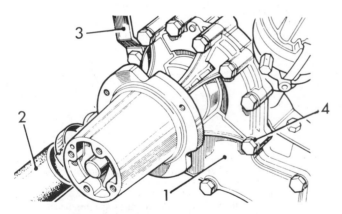

Fig. 2.2 Water pump assembly (Sec 8)

1  *Pump housing*
2  *Water inlet hose*
3  *Alternator adjuster link*

4  *Water pump housing retaining bolt*

3  Remove the cooling fan blades, cowl, fan hub or viscous coupling and water pump pulley as described in Section 6.
4  Remove the bottom hose from the water pump inlet pipe.
5  Free the inner end of the alternator adjuster link from the water pump.
6  On later models with power steering, slacken the power steering pump mounting bolts, slip the belt off the pump pulley and then remove the mounting bolts and support the pump out of the way without straining the hoses.
7  Remove the water pump retaining bolts, noting that four of them are much longer than the others. Note where those four fit. Note also where the power steering pump mounting brackets fit as they are removed (if applicable).
8  Pull the pump away from the locating dowels in the main casing

section which is part of the timing cover.
9  Clean the threads of the pump securing bolts ready for re-assembly. The threads of these bolts have a coating of thread lubricant sealant which will harden if left in contact with air.
10  It is in most cases cheaper and less frustrating to replace worn assemblies with an exchange unit. The water pump is no exception to this rule and though it is possible to renew bearings, shafts and seals, it is advised that the former course is adopted, since special tools including a press are required.
11  Refitting is mainly a matter of reversing the removal procedure. However, there are one or two points to note during the operation.
12  Ensure that the mating surfaces of pump and engine front cover are scrupulously clean.
13  Using a smear of light grease, secure the new gasket to the pump body.
14  Apply a light smear of grease to the other gasket surface and offer the unit to the engine taking care to ensure the dowels locate in the pump body holes (photo).
15  The pump securing bolts should be cleaned, and treated with lubricant sealant 3M EC776 or equivalent.
16  Refit the bolts to their correct locations. Also ensure that the alternator adjuster link and the power steering pump mounting brackets (where fitted) are located in the correct positions.
17  Tighten the pump mounting bolts to the specified torque settings.
18  Do not forget to adjust the fanbelt and power steering pump drivebelt tensions, and refill the system with coolant as already described.
19  Run the engine and check for water leaks.

## 9  Thermostat – removal, testing and refitting

1  If the engine tends to overheat, the cause is most likely to be a faulty thermostat that is failing to open at a predetermined temperature setting.
2  Conversely, where the thermostat is stuck permanently open, it will be found that the engine takes a long time to warm up. In cold

8.14 Refit the water pump using a new gasket

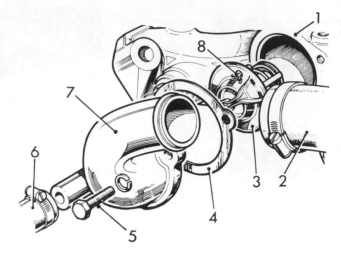

Fig. 2.3 Thermostat and water elbow assembly (Sec 9)

| 1 | Inlet manifold | 5 | Bolt |
|---|---|---|---|
| 2 | Top hose | 6 | Thermostat bypass hose |
| 3 | Thermostat | 7 | Water elbow |
| 4 | Gasket | 8 | Jiggle pin |

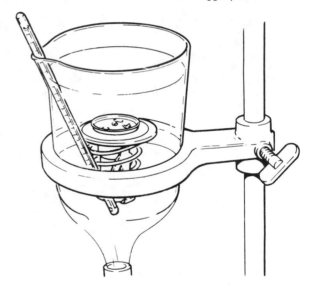

Fig. 2.4 Testing the thermostat (Sec 9)

weather, this results in having to drive considerable distances using the choke. If in doubt take out the thermostat and test it.

3  There is no need to drain the whole system, but simply drain enough so that the inlet manifold is empty. Then refit the drain plug.

4  Disconnect the thermostat bypass hose and the radiator top hose from the water elbow.

5  There are two bolts securing the thermostat housing elbow to the front of the engine. These should be removed, and the housing elbow lifted off (Fig. 2.3).

6  Remember to have a new gasket available for reassembly.

7  Carefully remove the thermostat, which should just lift out.

8  With the engine cold examine carefully to ascertain whether or not it is stuck open. If so, there is no point in making further tests; it should be renewed.

9  If the thermostat looks normal then proceed as follows.

10  Place the unit in a saucepan of cold water. Do not allow it to touch the bottom. Suspend it or support it with a piece of wire or string (Fig. 2.4).

11  Heat the saucepan and raise the temperature to that at which the thermostat is specified to open. The specified opening temperature is stamped on either the upper or lower face of the thermostat.

12  Should the thermostat fail to operate correctly, renew it with one of the correct type.

13  If it happens that you do not have a spare, the car will run quite well for a day or so without a thermostat until a replacement can be obtained, but the engine will take much longer to reach operating temperature.

14  Refit the elbow and thermostat housing cover using a new gasket.

15  When fittting the new thermostat, make sure that the small split pin, called a jiggle pin, which pokes through the valve face, is placed at the 12 o'clock position in the housing. This will prevent airlocks occurring in this area.

16  Finally reconnect the radiator and bypass hoses, top up the cooling system and check for leaks.

## 10 Fault diagnosis – cooling system

| Symptom | Reason(s) |
|---|---|
| Overheating | Insufficient water in cooling system<br>Fanbelt slipping (accompanied by a shrieking noise on rapid engine acceleration)<br>Radiator core blocked or radiator grille restricted<br>Thermostat not opening properly<br>Ignition timing incorrectly set (accompanied by loss of power, and perhaps misfiring)<br>Carburettors incorrectly adjusted (mixture too weak)<br>Exhaust system partially blocked<br>Oil level in sump too low<br>Blown cylinder head gasket (water/steam being forced down the radiator overflow pipe under pressure)<br>Engine not yet run-in<br>Brakes binding |
| Overcooling | Thermostat jammed on<br>Incorrect thermostat fitted allowing premature opening of valve<br>Thermostat missing |
| Loss of cooling water | Loose clips of water hoses<br>Top, bottom, or bypass water hoses perished and leaking<br>Radiator core leaking<br>Expansion tank pressure cap spring worn or seal ineffective<br>Blown cylinder head gasket (pressure in system forcing water/steam down overflow pipe)<br>Cylinder wall or head cracked |

# Chapter 3
# Fuel, exhaust and emission control systems

*For modifications, and information applicable to later models, see Supplement at end of manual*

## Contents

## Specifications

### Fuel pump
Type:
- Early models ............ AC mechanical
- Later models ............ AC or Bendix electrical

Location:
- Mechanical pump ............ Left-hand side of engine at front
- Electrical pump ............ Front chassis outrigger bracket on left-hand side, or beneath rear seat

### Fuel filters
Main filter:
- Type ............ AC, renewable paper element
- Location ............ Left-hand chassis member in engine compartment

Auxiliary filter (where fitted):
- Type ............ In-line, disposable
- Location ............ Front of left-hand rocker cover

### Carburettors
- Number ............ Two
- Make ............ Zenith/Stromberg

Type:
- Early models ............ 175 CD2S
- Later models ............ 175 CDSE
- Emission control models ............ 175 CDSET
- Spring colour (all models) ............ Red
- Jet orifice (all models) ............ 1.75 mm with 2 mm washer

Metering valve
- 175 CD2S ............ B2AQ
- 175 CDSE ............ B2AS, B1DW or B1EJ
- 175 CDSET ............ B1EN
- Float height (all models) ............ 0.67 to 0.71 in (16 to 17 mm)

### Carburettor tuning data
Dashpot oil:
- Type ............ SAE 20 engine oil
- Level ............ 0.25 in (6 mm) below top of dashpot

Engine idling speeds (rpm):

| | Idle | Fast idle |
|---|---|---|
| Pre-1972 models | 600 to 650 | 1000 to 1200 |
| 1972 to 1976 models | 650 to 750 | 1100 to 1300 |
| 1976 onwards | 750 to 850 | 1100 to 1300 |
| Full emission control models | 850 to 950 | 1400 to 1500 |

Exhaust gas CO level ............ 4% maximum at idle speed

**Fuel tank capacity** ......................................................... 18 gallons (81.5 litres)

**Fuel octane rating**
With normal ignition timing ............................................ 91 to 93 RON (UK 2-star)
With retarded ignition timing (see Chapter 4) ................... 85 RON

**Emission control equipment**
Equipment fitted ............................................................ Closed crankcase ventilation system (all models); thermostatically controlled air cleaner, air injection, exhaust gas recirculation system, fuel evaporative control system (according to model and market)

Air pump drivebelt tension ............................................. 0.016 in (0.4 mm) deflection per inch (25 mm) of belt run between pulley centres

**Torque wrench settings**

|  | lbf ft | kgf m |
|---|---|---|
| Exhaust manifold bolts | 10 to 15 | 1.4 to 2.0 |
| Inlet manifold bolts | 20 to 25 | 3.5 to 4.0 |
| Inlet manifold gasket clamp | 10 to 15 | 1.4 to 2.0 |
| Auto choke-to-carburettor screws | 3.5 | 0.5 |

## 1  General description

### Fuel system

The fuel system in the Range Rover varies depending on the age of the vehicle. Early vehicles have a mechanical fuel pump driven off the camshaft with an in-line fuel filter as well as a main fuel filter fitted with a renewable paper element. Later vehicles have an electric fuel pump located on the left hand side of the chassis or under the rear seat and retain the main fuel filter. The fuel tank in all cases is mounted at the rear of the vehicle with the filler cap on the right-hand side.

The carburettors, twin Zenith Strombergs, vary also. Early ones have a mechanical choke whereas the later models, fitted with emission control equipment, have an automatic choke.

### Exhaust system

The exhaust system is a straightforward, rugged assembly. Twin downpipes take the gases from the exhaust manifolds on either side of the engine and join together behind the gearbox to feed one main silencer box. A single pipe carries the exhaust gas to the left-hand side rear of the vehicle via a tail silencer on early models. Later vehicles have a similar arrangement but with twin pipes running all the way from the main silencer to the rear.

### Emission control systems

All models have a crankcase breather valve and rocker cover breather pipes, providing crankcase emission control. Clean air is taken from the air cleaner and fed to the crankcase via the filter. Crankcase fumes rise via the hoses and flame traps.

Later models are fitted with an air intake temperature control system to warm up the engine quickly and reduce noxious gas output, while at the same time improving petrol consumption.

Vehicles with full emission control equipment are fitted with special twin air cleaners, air injection system (AIS), charcoal filter canister for absorbing petrol fumes, and an exhaust gas recirculation (EGR) system.

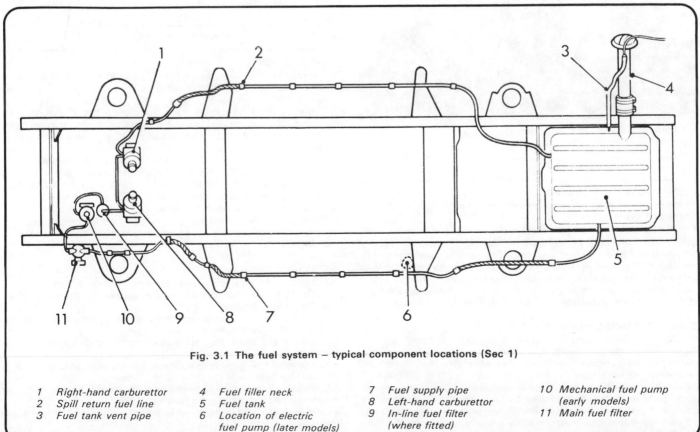

**Fig. 3.1 The fuel system – typical component locations (Sec 1)**

| | | | |
|---|---|---|---|
| 1  Right-hand carburettor | 4  Fuel filler neck | 7  Fuel supply pipe | 10  Mechanical fuel pump (early models) |
| 2  Spill return fuel line | 5  Fuel tank | 8  Left-hand carburettor | 11  Main fuel filter |
| 3  Fuel tank vent pipe | 6  Location of electric fuel pump (later models) | 9  In-line fuel filter (where fitted) | |

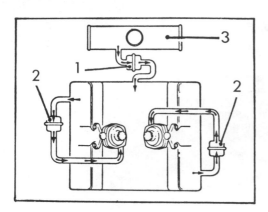

Fig. 3.2 Crankcase emission control system (Sec 1)

1   Crankcase breather valve
2   Breather hoses and flame traps
3   Air cleaner

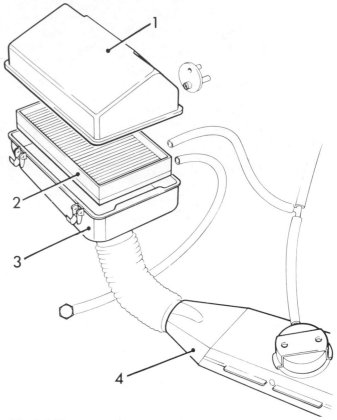

Fig. 3.3 Thermostatically controlled air cleaner components
(Sec 2)

1   Air cleaner top half       3   Air cleaner bottom half
2   Air filter element         4   Air intake and valve

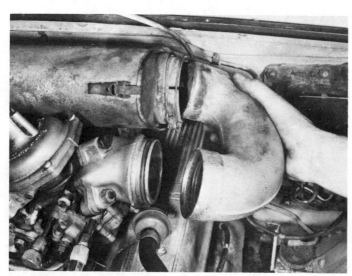

3.1 Removing the left-hand air intake elbow

## 2  Air cleaners – description

### Standard type

1   The air cleaner is an oval metal cylinder. A paper disposable air filter is fitted into each end, and alloy elbows feed the air to the twin carburettors. The air cleaner is located on mounting pegs attached to the rear of the inlet manifold and the air intake protrudes forward between the carburettors. On early models it is open-ended, but later vehicles have an air temperature control device mounted on the front of the intake pipe and attached to it by a short section of flexible hose.

### Emission control equipment type

2   Some emission control equipment models are fitted with air cleaners of a different type to the standard one. These models have two separate air cleaners which are large rectangular containers with four clips, which retain the top to the bottom. One container is mounted onto each carburettor. Each container houses a flat element, rectangular in shape. The two air cleaners are linked together by balance pipes and each air cleaner has a separate air intake temperature control system attached to its intake connection at the front (Fig. 3.3). The temperature sensor is in the right-hand air cleaner.

## 3  Air cleaners – removal and refitting

### Standard type

1   Undo the hose clips on each inlet pipe on either side of the air cleaner housing, then pull off the elbows. They are only retained by an O-ring to the carburettor (photo).
2   Release the choke cable from the clip on the air cleaner, and disconnect the two small pipes to the temperature sensor in the right-hand end of the air cleaner on models with air intake temperature control.
3   Lift the air cleaner assembly up to free it from the mounting pegs and detach the hose from the crankcase breather valve attached to the underside of the air cleaner as it is lifted. Release the air temperature intake valve flexible hose from the intake pipe (if applicable).
4   Place the air cleaner to one side.
5   Refitting is the reverse procedure to removal. Smear the carburettor intake O-rings with molybdenum disulphide grease before refitting the elbows.

### Emission control type

6   Disconnect the balance pipe between the two air cleaners.
7   Disconnect the rocker cover breather pipe and crankcase breather pipe from the right-hand air cleaner.
8   Slacken the hose clips and release both intake temperature control system flexible hooses from the air cleaner intakes.
9   Release the spark plug HT leads from the clips on the two air cleaners.
10  Disconnect the two pipes connected to the temperature sensor in the front inside face of the right-hand air cleaner.
11  Undo the four nuts which retain the air cleaner housings to their respective carburettor adaptor flanges.
12  Remove the air cleaners and gaskets from the carburettor adaptors.
13  Refitting is the reverse procedure to removal.

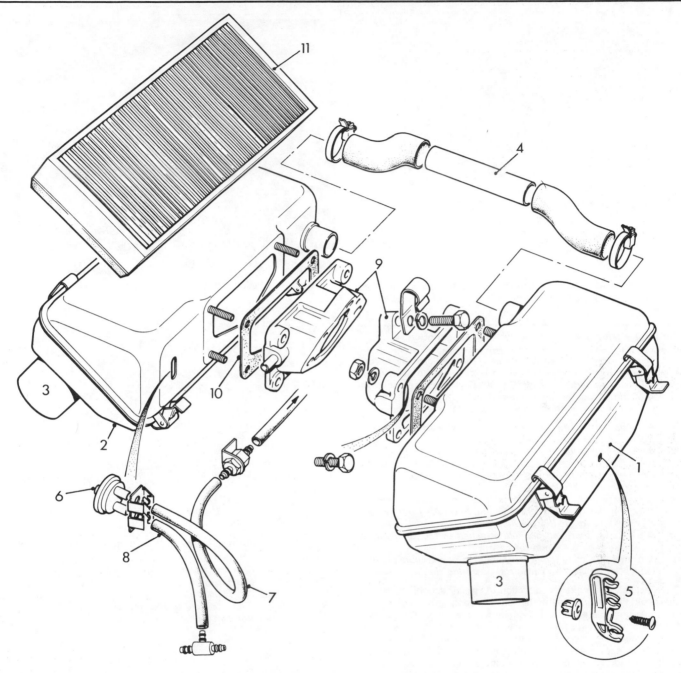

**Fig. 3.4 Thermostatically controlled air cleaner layout (Sec 3)**

| | | | |
|---|---|---|---|
| 1 | Air cleaner container – left-hand | 3 Air intakes | 6 Temperature sensor | 9 Carburettor adaptors |
| 2 | Air cleaner container – right-hand | 4 Balance pipe<br>5 Spark plug lead clip assembly | 7 Pipe to sensor from inlet manifold<br>8 Pipe to vacuum capsules | 10 Gasket<br>11 Air cleaner element |

---

## 4 Air filter elements – renewal

### Standard type air cleaner

1  Slacken the hose clips on either end of the air cleaner and pull off the elbows.
2  Release the clips on each end of the air cleaner canister in turn and withdraw the endplate and air filter element from both ends (photo). Note that the air intake temperature control sensor pipes (if fitted) are attached to the right-hand assembly.
3  Remove the wing nut and retaining plate from the inner end of each assembly and remove the elements.
4  Fit a new element to each assembly and refit the retaining plate and wing nut. Check that the sealing washers on the end plate and retaining plate are in good condition, otherwise they must be renewed. Wipe clean the element housing.
5  Refit one assembly into the end of the housing and secure it with the spring clips. Refit the elbows and secure the hose clips.

### Emission control type (rectangular) air cleaners

6  Undo the four spring clips which retain the two halves of the air cleaner housing together, release the spark plug leads from the clip on the air cleaner and separate the air cleaner halves.
7  Lift the element out of the housing and place it to one side.
8  Fit a new element to the air cleaner. Note that the chamfered edge faces downwards.

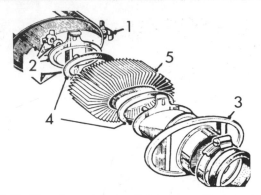

Fig. 3.5 Air filter element and endplate assembly (standard type)
(Sec 4)

| | | | |
|---|---|---|---|
| 1 | Canister clips | 4 | Sealing washers |
| 2 | Wing nut and washer | 5 | Element |
| 3 | Endplate | | |

9   Refit the two halves together and secure with the four spring clips. Refit the spark plug leads to the clip in the lower half of the air cleaner.

4.2 Removing the left-hand air filter element assembly

## 5   Air intake temperature control system – description

1   In order that the engine can operate at its most efficient air-to-fuel ratio, later vehicles have a system which is designed to achieve an optimum running temperature of 38°C (100°F) as quickly as possible regardless of the outside air temperature.

2   The system comprises the following elements:

(a)   *A vacuum-operated thermostatically controlled flap valve in the air cleaner intake pipe(s)*

(b)   *A hot box over the right-hand exhaust manifold connected to the air intake pipe by a flexible hose. Models with two air cleaners have a hot box over each exhaust manifold feeding their own air cleaners*

(c)   *A temperature sensing device situated in the air cleaner on the clean side of the air filter element. In vehicles with two air cleaners it is located in the right-hand one*

(d)   *A pipe from the inlet manifold attached to the temperature sensing device via a non-return valve*

(e)   *A further pipe from the other side of the temperature sensing device to the vacuum capsule(s) operating the flap valve(s)*

3   The flap valve controls the direction of the air supply. When the engine is cold the flap will cut off the cold air supply and will only draw air from the 'hot box' area. As the engine warms up, so the flap will gradually alter its setting so that a mixture of cold and hot air is drawn into the engine. When the engine is fully warmed up the flap will close off the hot air supply and allow only cold air to be drawn in. This, however, depends on the outside air temperature.

4   The optimum operating temperature is maintained by the sensing device in the air cleaner. The sensor allows the vacuum created in the inlet manifold to operate the flap valve. If the vacuum effect is changed suddenly (eg by depressing the accelerator hard to overtake), there will no effect on the flap valve because of the one-way valve that is fitted into the system.

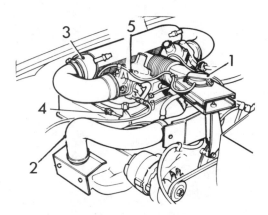

Fig. 3.6 The air intake temperature control system (Sec 5)

| | |
|---|---|
| 1 | Flap valve and vacuum capsule |
| 2 | Hot box and flexible pipe to air intake |
| 3 | Air cleaner |
| 4 | Inlet manifold-to-sensor pipe |
| 5 | Vacuum pipe to vacuum capsule |

## 6   Air intake temperature control system – operational check

1   Check the correct operation of the flap valve(s) in the air intake(s) by observing the valve(s) after starting the engine from cold.

2   The flap valve(s) should start to open slowly within a few minutes of starting up. They should continue to open until a steady position is reached. This position will be dependent on the outside air temperature.

3   If the valve(s) do not open at all then the fault can lie in two places. Either the vacuum capsule which operates the flap valve or the temperature sending device has failed, or both can be defective.

4   Failure of the temperature sensor or valve can be checked by

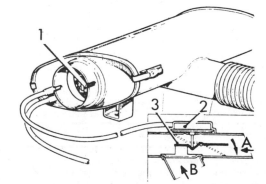

Fig. 3.7 Air cleaner sensor and flap valve assembly (Sec 5)

| | | | |
|---|---|---|---|
| 1 | Temperature sensor located inside air cleaner | 3 | Flap valve |
| 2 | Vacuum capsule | A | Cold air intake |
| | | B | Hot air intake |

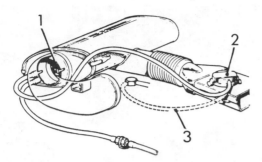

Fig. 3.8 Checking the temperature sensor or vacuum capsule
(Sec 6)

1   Temperature sensor
2   Vacuum capsule and flap valve
3   Temporary pipe connected directly to the inlet manifold

9.2 The crankcase breather valve

connecting a pipe directly from the flap valve to the inlet manifold. If
the flap valve now opens then the sensor is faulty. If the flap valve still
does not move then the vacuum capsule operating the flap valve is at
fault.
5   Renew the faulty part. The vacuum capsule and flap valve form an
integral part of the air intake assembly.

## 7   Flap valve – renewal

### Non-emission controlled models

1   The flap valve is an integral part of the front section of the air
intake assembly, together with the vacuum capsule. The whole
assembly has to be renewed if the valve becomes faulty or the vacuum
capsule is defective.
2   Disconnect the vacuum pipe to the vacuum capsule.
3   Undo the two self-tapping screws on the top of the air intake box.
One has a clip which retains the vacuum pipe and the other has a
double clip which retains the carburettor-to-distributor vacuum pipe.
The two screws also retain the front section of the air intake to the rear
section.
4   Lift the air intake section upwards and release the rubber
mounting from the pin. Release the pipe from the hot air box from the
underneath of the air intake and remove the assembly.
5   Fit a new unit following the reverse procedure.

### Emission controlled models

6   Disconnect the vacuum pipe from the vacuum capsule.
7   Slacken the hose clip which retains the air intake box to the hot
box flexible pipe connector from the exhaust manifold.
8   Remove the two self-tapping screws which retain the intake box
to the connector and withdraw the assembly.
9   Fitting the new unit follows the reverse procedure.

## 8   Temperature sensor – renewal

1   The temperature sensor for the air intake flap valve(s) is located in
the right-hand end of the air cleaner in conventional systems, or in the
inside face of the right-hand air cleaner where full emission control
equipment is fitted.
2   If the standard air cleaner is fitted, remove the right-hand air filter
element assembly as already described in Section 4. Disconnect the
two tubes which run to and from the sensor.
3   With the assembly on the workbench, remove the sensor from the
endplate.
4   With the rectangular air cleaner, remove the right-hand air cleaner
as described in Section 3. Separate the two halves to remove the
element. The sensor can then be extracted from the side of the air
cleaner housing.
5   Fit a new sensor to the air cleaner and follow the reverse
procedure to removal.

## 9   Crankcase breather valve – renewal

### Vehicles with standard air cleaner

1   Remove the air cleaner as described in Section 3.
2   Undo the single self-tapping screw and slide the valve out of the
retaining clamp (photo).
3   Pull the valve carefully out of the hose from the crankcase. Equally
carefully pull off the short length of hose from the valve outlet end.
With age the material from which the valve is made goes brittle and
it is very easy to break off the two ends.
4   Fit a new filter with the end marked 'IN' facing forwards. If the
filter is marked with arrows, they must point to the rear.
5   Clamp the retaining screw and fit the filter hoses.
6   Refit the air cleaner.

### Vehicles with twin air cleaners

7   If the vehicle has full emission control equipment and two air
cleaners, the valve can be renewed by simply disconnecting the tubes
at either end of the valve which is easily reached. The points in
paragraph 4 still apply. The location of the valve may vary according
to equipment fitted.

## 10   Flame traps – removal, cleaning and refitting

1   Two flame traps are fitted. One is located on each side of the
engine between the rocker cover and the carburettor in the rocker
breather pipe.
2   Disconnect the pipe from the rocker cover and carburettor at
either end and remove it. Separate the flame trap from the pipes
(photo).
3   Place the flame trap and pipes in a petrol bath and clean them.
Allow the flame trap to dry. Pull dry rag through the pipes.
4   Refitting is the reverse procedure to removal.

## 11   Throttle cable – removal, refitting and adjusting

1   Remove the air cleaner as described in Section 3.
2   Remove the split pin and clevis pin and disconnect the cable end
from the carburettor linkage (photo).
3   Slide back the rubber cover and undo the adjuster nut so that the
adjuster can be removed from the bracket (photo).
4   Inside the vehicle, remove the right-hand lower dash panel to
reach the top of the accelerator pedal.
5   Remove the split pin and clevis pin so that the cable is freed from
the pedal (photo).
6   Undo the outer cable retaining nut and withdraw the cable and
grommet into the engine compartment. The complete cable can now
be removed.

10.2 Disconnecting the breather pipe from the carburettor

11.2 The throttle cable is connected to the linkage by a clevis pin

11.3 Undo the adjuster nut to free the cable from the bracket

11.5 The cable is attached to the top of the pedal by a clevis pin (arrowed)

7    Adjust the cable with the throttle pedal fully released. The adjustment should be such that the linkage moves with slight pressure on the pedal and not before. At the pedal end connection check that the cable yoke and clevis pin are not too tight a fit, and that the yoke can pivot freely.

## 12  Choke cable – removal and refitting

1    The choke cable is fitted to all vehicles which do not have an automatic choke.
2    The choke cable is attached to the trunnion at the front of the left-hand carburettor. Undo the screw to release it.
3    Disconnect the outer cable from the cable clip by the carburettor and the clip on the air cleaner housing.
4    Disconnect the choke warning light switch cables from the choke control assembly below the dashboard on the right-hand side of the steering column.
5    Undo the outer cable retaining nut and then withdraw the choke control knob and cable complete.
6    Refitting is the reverse procedure to removal. Ensure that the spring washer and nut are fitted over the cable before feeding it through the dashboard panel.
7    There should be approximately 1.5 mm (0.05 in) free play when the cable has been reconnected to the trunnion.
8    Run the engine and check the choke for correct operation.

## 13  Carburettors – general description

The carburettors are of the variable choke type. The fuel, which is drawn into the air passage through a jet orifice, is metered by a tapered needle which moves in and out of the jet, thus varying the effective size of the orifice. This needle is attached to, and moves with, the air valve piston which controls the variable choke opening.
At rest, the air valve piston is right down, choking off the air supply, and the tapered needle is fully home with the jet virtually cutting off the fuel outlet from the jet.
For starting, the choke control is used except for the SET model which has an automatic starting device. The standard carburettor incorporates a disc valve for cold starting which allows additional fuel to flow into the mixture stream. The disc valve itself incorporates several orifices which are progressively uncovered as the disc is moved when the choke control is pulled. The throttle butterfly is also opened a small amount. Also included is a temperature controlled valve which weakens the mixture under light load and idling conditions when the engine is hot. The choke on SET models is operated automatically by a bi-metallic spring arrangement which is heated by water from the engine cooling system.
As soon as the engine fires, the suction from the engine (or manifold depression) is partially diverted to the upper side of the chamber in which the diaphragm attached to the air valve piston is positioned. This causes the valve to rise and provides sufficient airflow

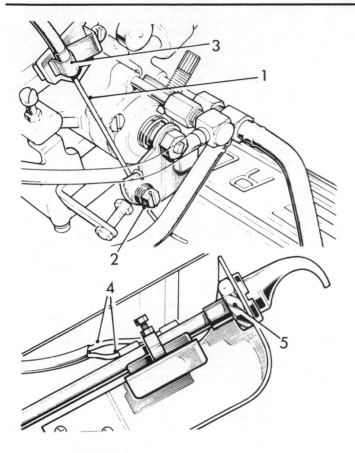

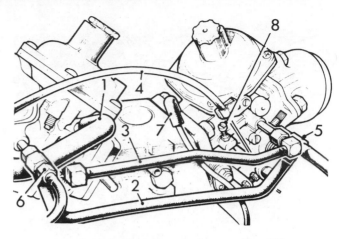

**Fig. 3.10 Carburettor attachments (Sec 14)**

1 Rocker breather pipe
2 Main fuel supply pipe
3 Choke fuel pipe
4 Choke cable
5 Main fuel supply union
6 Fuel spill return union
7 Vacuum pipe to distributor
8 Idle speed (throttle stop) screw

**Fig. 3.9 Choke cable connections (Sec 12)**

1 Choke inner cable
2 Trunnion retaining screw
3 Cable retaining clip
4 Warning light wires
5 Retaining nut

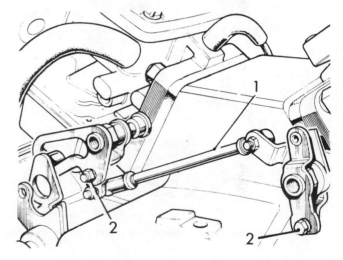

**Fig. 3.11 Carburettor linkage connection (Sec 14)**

1 Adjustable link
2 Throttle lever securing nuts

to enable the engine to run. As the throttle is opened further, manifold depression is reduced and now it is the speed of air through the venturi which causes the depression in the upper chamber, thus causing the piston to rise further. If the throttle is opened suddenly, the natural tendency of the air valve piston to rise – causing a weak mixture when it is least required (ie during acceleration) – is prevented by a hydraulic damper which delays the piston in its upward travel. The air intake is thus restricted and a proportionately larger quantity of fuel to air is drawn through.

The later types of carburettors with automatic choke (SET models) are fitted to enable the vehicle to conform to the prevailing emission control regulations, which vary from country to country. Tamperproof seals are also fitted to many carburettors so that adjustment, and therefore CO emissions, can be controlled. The object is to prevent adjustment by unqualified mechanics. Satisfy yourself before removing a tamperproof seal that you are not breaking any local or national regulations by so doing.

## 14 Carburettors – removal and refitting

1 Remove the air cleaner(s) as described in Section 3.
2 Remove the air intake pipe(s), disconnecting the vacuum hoses (if applicable) first. Slacken the hose clip and separate the hose from the hot air box as the assembly is lifted away.
3 Disconnect the rocker breather pipes from the carburettors.
4 Disconnect the main fuel supply pipe which runs between the carburettors.
5 Disconnect the choke fuel supply pipe which runs between the carburettors.

6 To remove the left-hand carburettor, disconnect the following:

(a) Throttle cable (Section 11)
(b) Choke cable (Section 12) or auto choke coolant pipes (as applicable)
(c) Fuel supply pipe at the front of the carburettor
(d) Throttle linkage between the carburettors
(e) Vacuum pipe to the distributor

7 To remove the right-hand carburettor, disconnect the following:

(a) Fuel return pipe, from the union in front of the carburettor
(b) Throttle linkage between the carburettors
(c) Coolant pipes to automatic choke housing (where fitted)
(d) Brake vacuum servo hose from inlet manifold (for convenience)

8 Undo the four retaining nuts and washers for each carburettor and lift it away.
9 The gaskets and insulator can then be removed if necessary. Note

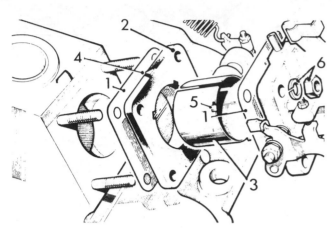

**Fig. 3.12 Gaskets, insulator and liner assembly (Sec 14)**

| | |
|---|---|
| 1  Gaskets | 4  Arrow |
| 2  Insulator | 5  Lug |
| 3  Liner | 6  Carburettor retaining nuts and washers |

**Fig. 3.13 Carburettor mixture adjustment (early models) (Sec 15)**

| | |
|---|---|
| 1  Piston lifting pin | 2  Jet adjusting screw |

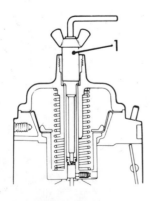

**Fig. 3.14 Mixture adjustment, later models (Sec 15)**

1  Special tool S.353

that there is a liner fitted inside the insulator on some models.

10 Refitting of the carburettors is the reverse of the removal procedure, but the following points should be noted.

11 Clean the mating faces of the carburettor and the inlet manifold.

12 Fit the inner gasket, followed by the insulator, making sure that the arrow points towards the centre of the manifold.

13 Refit the liner taking care to ensure that the lugs locate properly in the insulator recesses and do not stand proud. **Note:** *The liner can only be fitted one way round, that is with the tabs engaged in the slots.*

14 The remainder of the fitting procedure is a direct reversal of the removal sequence.

15 After installation it will be found necessary to tune and adjust the carburettors as described in Section 15.

## 15 Carburettors – tuning and adjusting

Before attempting to tune and adjust the carburettors, it is important to realise that certain items of equipment will be required. If these are not available, the job should not be attempted, but should be carried out by a suitably equipped Rover dealer. For those motorists intending to do the job themselves, it is essential that service tool number 'S.353' or a similar item is purchased beforehand to enable the later type of jet needle to be repositioned. An airflow balancing meter is also a very useful device for tuning and balancing, although listening carefully at the end of a rubber or plastic tube of about $\frac{1}{4}$ in (6mm) diameter may be sufficient. It is also highly desirable that an exhaust gas analyser is used to check the CO content of the exhaust gas.

Before any attempt is made to adjust the carburettors, the ignition timing, spark plugs and distributor dwell angle should be checked and adjusted as necessary.

### Manual choke carburettors

1 Check the throttle cable adjustment as described in Section 11. Also check that the linkage and cable move freely without any tendency to stick.

2 Start the engine and run it until warm. The thermostat must be open (indicated by the radiator becoming warm) before switching off.

4 Slacken off the throttle adjusting lever securing nuts on both carburettors.

5 Start the engine and check that the idling speed is as specified. If necessary, adjust the throttle stop screws. On some models a tamperproof sleeve is fitted and this setting can only be adjusted by an authorized dealer with special tools.

6 Check the mixture in each carburettor in turn. Raise the piston very slightly (0.8 mm/0.031 in) using a long thin screwdriver, or by means of the piston lifting pin on early models. If the engine speed immediately increases, the mixture is too rich. If the engine speed immediately decreases, the mixture is too weak. No change, or a very slight fall in engine speed, indicates a correct mixture.

7 To correct the mixture strength, screw the jet adjusting screw (below the carburettor) into the carburettor to weaken or out of the carburettor to enrich the mixture.

8 In later models tool S.353 has to be employed to adjust the mixture. Remove the piston damper from each carburettor in turn (Fig. 3.14).

9 Carefully insert the special tool S.353 into the dashpot until the outer part engages in the air valve, and the inner part engages in the hexagon of the needle adjuster plug.

10 Whilst preventing the outer part of the tool from moving (to prevent the diaphragm from rupturing) rotate the inner part either clockwise to enrichen the mixture or anti-clockwise to weaken the mixture.

11 When the mixture is correctly adjusted the engine speed will remain steady, or may drop very slightly, when the piston is lifted slightly.

12 Repeat this on the second carburettor, ensuring that the adjustment is made by the same amount. Remove the special tool.

13 The next stage is to balance the carburettors. The easiest way to do this is with an airflow balancing meter, although the rubber tube method can give a fairly accurate setting, depending on the experience of the person carrying out the task. Various proprietary balancing meters are available. The procedure described below relates to the Rover balancer, tool No 605330.

14 Zero the gauge on the meter and fit it to the carburettor adaptors.

Fig. 3.15 Balancing meter in position (Sec 15)

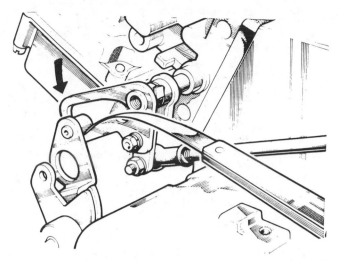

Fig. 3.16 Adjusting the left-hand throttle lever. Press in direction arrowed (Sec 15)

Ensure that there are no air leaks. If the engine speed falls or if the engine stalls when the gauge is fitted, the mixture is too rich. If the engine speed rises noticeably, the mixture is too weak.

15  If necessary, remove the meter, adjust the mixture and then refit the meter. When correctly balanced the gauge should read in the central (zero) sector.

16  If the pointer moves to the left sector of the gauge, decrease the amount of airflow through the right-hand carburettor or increase the amount flowing through the left-hand one. Unscrew the idle speed (throttle stop) screw to decrease the airflow, or screw it in to increase it. If the pointer moves to the right reverse the procedure above.

17  If the idling speed rises too high or drops during these checks, adjust to the correct idle speed, maintaining the gauge needle in the zero area.

18  The difference in engine speeds set with and/or without the balancer in position will be negligible, being in the region of plus or minus 25 rpm. However, a wide variation in speeds would indicate a basic carburettor fault that may only be remedied by an overhaul, or replacement units.

19  Balancing the carburettors using a piece of rubber tubing is done by comparing the hiss in one carburettor intake with the hiss in the other (stick one end of the tubing in your ear). The noise is caused by the airflow through the carburettors and this is what you are trying to equalize.

20  Using a recognised type of CO meter, check the exhaust gas CO content.

21  Insert the probe into the end of the exhaust pipe. The reading should not exceed the maximum given in the Specifications. Adjust the mixture if necessary to correct.

22  The next stage is to adjust and secure the throttle adjusting levers. Insert a 0.006 in (0.15 mm) feeler gauge between the throttle lever and the underneath of the roller on the countershaft lever. Apply pressure to the throttle lever to hold the feeler gauge and tighten the securing screw (Fig. 3.16).

23  Fit the feeler gauge between the pin on the right-hand throttle lever and the left leg of the fork on the adjusting lever on the right-hand carburettor. Apply light pressure to the linkage to hold the feeler gauge and tighten the screw. Withdraw the feeler gauge (Fig. 3.17).

24  Refit the air cleaner as described in Section 3.

25  To set the fast idle adjustment, which is pre-set on the left-hand carburettor and should not normally require adjustment, set the fast idle adjustment screw against the cam to give a fast idle speed within the specified limits when the choke warning light just goes out. On some carburettors this can only be adjusted by an authorised dealer with special tools.

26  The final step is to set the cold start adjuster screw. Where the vehicle is being used with an ambient temperature of -18°C (0°F) and above, push the cold start adjuster screw fully inwards and turn it through 90° to lock it in position. Should the vehicle be subjected to ambient temperatures below -18°C (0°F), the adjuster must be positioned fully outward.

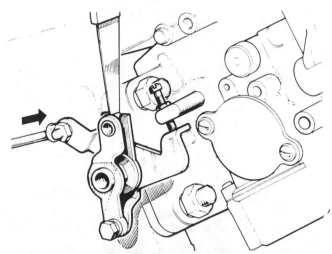

Fig. 3.17 Adjusting the right-hand throttle lever. Press in direction arrowed (Sec 15)

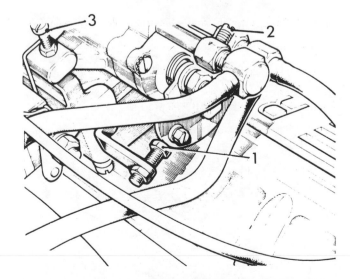

Fig. 3.18 Fast idle and cold start adjustment (Sec 15)

1  *Fast idle adjustment screw*
2  *Cold start adjustment screw*
3  *Idle speed throttle stop screw*

*Automatic choke carburettors*

27 The following components must not be changed or modified in any way, or compliance with legal requirements relating to exhaust emissions may not be fulfilled.

- (a) *The fuel jet assembly*
- (b) *The piston assembly*
- (c) *The depression cover*
- (d) *The temperature compensator*
- (e) *The piston assembly return spring*

The last two items if faulty must be replaced by new factory set components.

**Note**: *During the following procedure do not allow the engine to idle for longer than three minutes without purging for one minute's duration at 2000 rpm.*

28 Run the engine until the normal operating temperature is attained, then remove the air cleaner(s) (refer to Section 3 if necessary).

29 Disconnect the throttle linkage so that each carburettor operates independently.

30 Ensure that the fast idle screw is clear of the fast idle cam, then check the balance of the carburettor inlet air flow using an airflow meter. If this is not available, listen to the airflow hiss using the small bore tube referred to in the introduction to this Section.

31 The procedure for adjusting the airflow balance is the same as that described for manual choke vehicles. But note that the adjustment screws are different. On auto choke carburettors the fast idle adjusting screw is in the place occupied by the idle speed (throttle stop) adjusting screw on manual choke types. The idle speed screw is adjacent.

32 Increase the engine speed to 1600 rpm and check the airflow balance. If necessary, turn the idle speed adjusting screws by equal amounts to achieve the balance.

33 Recheck the balance at idling speed.

34 Disconnect and plug the air pump outlet hose (if fitted).

35 With the engine still at normal operating temperature, check that the idle speed is as specified, then use an exhaust gas analyser to check that the CO content is within the specified maximum, or in accordance with the engine compartment emission control decal.

36 If slight adjustment is required, the idle trim screw on each carburettor may be rotated by equal amounts until the correct CO reading is obtained (Fig. 3.19).

37 If further adjustment is required, remove the piston damper from each carburettor and adjust the mixture as described in paragraphs 9 to 12.

38 Top up the carburettor piston dampers using SAE 20 engine oil. Fully raise each piston using a finger, and add oil until it is $\frac{1}{4}$ in (6 mm)

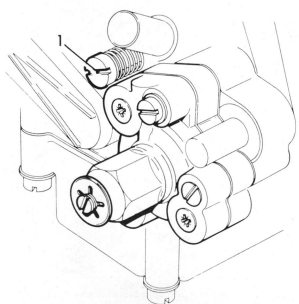

Fig. 3.19 CO content adjustment – auto choke carburettors
(Sec 15)

1   *Idle trim screw*

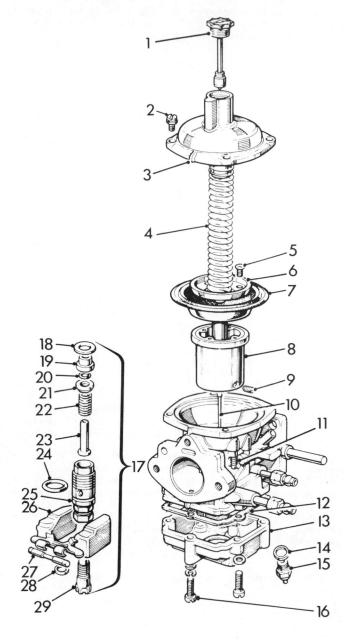

**Fig. 3.20 Zenith Stromberg 175 CD carburettor – exploded view**
**(Sec 16)**

| | | | |
|---|---|---|---|
| 1 | *Oil cap and damper* | 16 | *Float chamber screw* |
| 2 | *Cover retaining screw* | 17 | *Jet and float assembly* |
| 3 | *Top cover* | 18 | *Washer* |
| 4 | *Spring* | 19 | *Top bush* |
| 5 | *Screw* | 20 | *O-ring* |
| 6 | *Retaining plate* | 21 | *Guide bush* |
| 7 | *Diaphragm* | 22 | *Spring* |
| 8 | *Piston* | 23 | *Jet orifice* |
| 9 | *Grub screw* | 24 | *O-ring* |
| 10 | *Needle* | 25 | *Jet carrier* |
| 11 | *Piston lifting pin* | 26 | *Float* |
| 12 | *Float chamber gasket* | 27 | *Float spindle* |
| 13 | *Float chamber* | 28 | *O-ring* |
| 14 | *Washer* | 29 | *Jet adjusting screw* |
| 15 | *Needle valve* | | |

below the top of the damper tube. Release the piston and refit the damper. Screw down the plug, then raise and lower the piston to ensure correct location of the oil retaining cup in the damper tube.

39  Recheck the CO content and idle speed as already described, then switch off the ignition. Unplug the air injection hose and reconnect it to the pump (if applicable).

40  Remove the auto choke housing and adjust the fast idle setting as described in Section 17.

41  All that remains is to adjust the throttle linkage. With the throttle lever clamp bolt slackened, disconnect the ball end link.

42  Unscrew both idle speed (throttle stop) screws away from the stops.

43  Adjust each screw until the lever and fast idle screw meet, then screw in a further three turns.

44  Check the airflow balance again and adjust if necessary.

45  Set the throttle link to a length of 3.452 in (77.68 mm).

46  Refit the ball end link. This will cause the left-hand carburettor throttle to open slightly.

47  Whilst holding the left-hand carburettor throttle lever in the fully closed position, take up the clearance with the spring lever screw.

48  Tighten the lever clamp bolt. Check and adjust the idle speed by turning the adjustment screws equal amounts on each carburettor.

## 16  Carburettors – overhaul

### Diaphragm, piston assembly and metering needle

1  Unscrew and remove the oil cap and damper plunger.

2  Mark the installed position of the top cover, then remove the four screws and spring washers (photo).

3  Carefully lift off the cover, then remove the spring, retaining plate, diaphragm and piston, together with the metering needle (photos).

4  The diaphragm is retained to the top of the piston by a retaining plate and four small cross-head screws. Remove these and lift the diaphragm away. Fit a new diaphragm in the reverse order (photo).

5  To remove the needle from the base of the piston in early models, undo the locking screw in the side of the piston and remove it (photo).

Refit the needle in the reverse order, but ensure that the shoulder of the needle is level with the face of the piston before locking the grub screw. The needle must be checked for centralisation during refitting.

6  Installation is the reverse of the removal procedure, but ensure that the inner and outer tags of the diaphragm locate in the air valve and body recesses respectively.

7  To centralise the metering needle in the jet orifice, refit the spring and top cover with the piston and diaphragm in position.

8  Lift the piston up and tighten the jet assembly fully. Then slacken it off half a turn. Release the piston and allow it to fall. This will automatically centralise the jet orifice. Slowly tighten the jet assembly, making sure that the needle is still free. Check by lifting the piston 6 mm ($\frac{1}{4}$ in) and letting it fall. The piston should stop firmly on the bridge.

9  Refill the dashpot with SAE 20 engine oil to within 6 mm ($\frac{1}{4}$ in) of the top (photo). Refit the damper plunger and screw in the cap.

10  Later model carburettors have fixed jets and sprung needles which cannot be removed or adjusted.

### Float chamber needle valve – removal and installation

11  Remove the carburettors as described in Section 14.

12  Remove the jet assembly on earlier models only. Later models have a one-piece jet pressed into the body.

13  Remove the six screws and spring washers, and take off the float chamber and gasket.

14  Prise the spindle out of the locating clips, then remove the needle valve and washer.

15  Installation is the reverse of the removal procedure. Use a new washer on the float needle valve and ensure that the spindle is firmly secured in the locating clips. It is recommended that the float level is checked as described in the following paragraphs before fitting the float chamber.

### Float level – checking and adjustment

16  Remove the carburettors as described in Section 14.

17  Remove the float chamber as described above.

18  With the carburettor in the inverted position, measure the distance between the carburettor body face to the highest point on the float.

16.2 Undo the screws

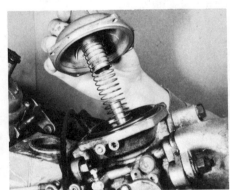

16.3a Lift off the cover and spring ...

16.3b ... then lift out the diaphragm and piston

16.4 The diaphragm retaining plate is retained by four screws

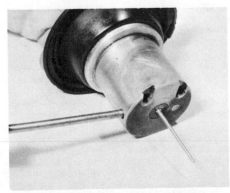

16.5 Undo the grub screw to remove the needle on early models

16.9 Refilling the dashpot with engine oil

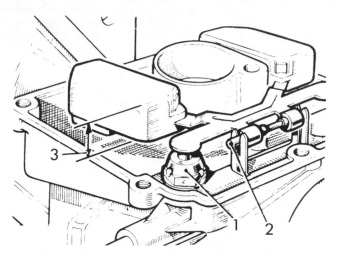

**Fig. 3.21 Float level setting (Sec 16)**

| | | | |
|---|---|---|---|
| 1 | Float needle valve | 3 | Float height – 0.67 to |
| 2 | Spindle | | 0.71 in (17 to 18 mm) |

Bend the tab that contacts the needle valve, if necessary, to obtain a float height as given in the Specifications. Ensure that the tab remains at right angles to the valve for satisfactory operation.

19  Install the float chamber using a new gasket. With early models, do not fully tighten the screws yet.

20  Refit the jet assembly to earlier models. One O-ring fits into the guide bush. Another O-ring fits over the jet carrier, and a third O-ring fits over the jet adjusting screw. Place the spring over the jet orifice and fit the guide bush onto it. Then fit the top bush to the jet orifice as well, with a plain washer on top. The jet assembly fits into the carrier. With the jet and carrier assembly together, insert it through the bottom of the float chamber and tighten it fully. Then tighten the float chamber retaining screws.

*Temperature compensator – removal and installation*

21  Remove the air cleaner (refer to Section 3 if necessary).

22  Remove the two screws and shakeproof washers, and detach the compensator. No repairs can be carried out; if defective, a new unit must be obtained (Fig. 3.22).

23  Installation is the reverse of the removal procedure. Ensure that the mating faces are clean and use new O-rings if the existing ones are hardened, distorted or cracked.

*Deceleration bypass valve – removal and installation*

24  Remove the carburettors as described in Section 14.

25  Remove the two cheesehead screws and the single countersunk head slotted screw. Do not touch the countersunk head cross-slotted screws (Fig. 3.23).

26  Withdraw the valve assembly and remove the gasket. No repairs can be carried out; if defective, a new unit must be obtained.

27  Installation is the reverse of the removal procedure. Ensure that the mating faces are clean and use a new gasket. Before the air cleaner is fitted, check the deceleration bypass valve(s) as follows.

28  With the engine idling at normal operating temperature, disconnect the vacuum pipe from the distributor.

29  Plug the end of the pipe with the finger and check that the idle speed increases to around 1300 rpm.

30  Should the speed increase to 2000 to 2500 rpm, it indicates that one or both of the deceleration bypass valves is floating off its seat. In this condition, if the throttle is momentarily opened; the additional increase in rpm will be slow to fall.

31  If adjustment is required, screw the bypass valve adjusting screw fully anti-clockwise onto its seat **on the carburettor not being adjusted.** (This procedure will not need to be repeated when adjusting the second carburettor).

32  With the vacuum pipe still plugged, turn the bypass valve adjusting screw clockwise until the speed increases abruptly to 2000 to 2500 rpm.

33  Turn the screw anti-clockwise until the engine speed falls to

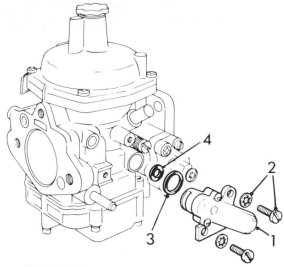

**Fig. 3.22 Temperature compensator (Sec 16)**

| | | | |
|---|---|---|---|
| 1 | Compensator assembly | 3 | O-ring |
| 2 | Retaining screw and washer | 4 | O-ring |

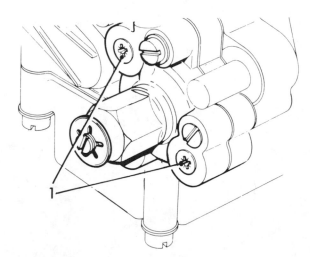

**Fig. 3.23 Deceleration bypass valve (Sec 16)**

1    Countersunk cross-head
screws must not be touched

around 1300 rpm.

34  Momentarily open, then release, the throttle. The engine speed should increase then fall to around 1300 rpm. If this does not occur, repeat the adjusting sequence.

35  Repeat the adjustment for the second carburettor, then turn each bypass adjusting screw ½ turn anti-clockwise to seat the valves.

36  Reconnect the vacuum pipe and refit the air cleaner.

---

**17  Automatic choke – removal, installation and setting-up**

---

1    Remove the air cleaner from the carburettor.

2    Remove the carburettor from the engine.

3    Hold the throttle in the open position by inserting a suitable wooden plug between the throttle bore and butterfly.

4    Remove the three retaining screws and lift off the automatic choke and gasket. No repairs can be carried out; if defective, a new unit must be obtained.

5    Clean the carburettor and choke mating faces.

6    Remove the bolt and washer, and take off the water jacket and rubber sealing ring.

7    Remove the clamp ring (three screws and washers).

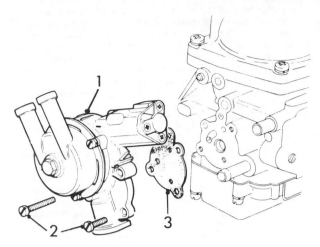

**Fig. 3.24 Automatic choke assembly (Sec 17)**

1  Automatic choke unit      3  Gasket
2  Screws

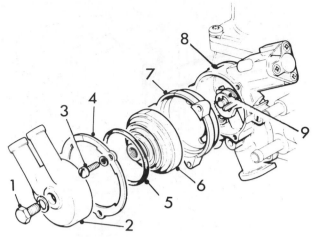

**Fig. 3.25 Automatic choke – exploded view (Sec 17)**

| 1  Centre bolt | 6  Heat mass |
| 2  Water jacket | 7  Heat insulator |
| 3  Screw | 8  Choke body |
| 4  Clamp ring | 9  Bi-metallic spring |
| 5  Rubber sealing ring | |

8    Carefully remove the heat mass, ensuring that the bi-metal coil is not strained.
9    Take off the heat insulator.
10 Using a new gasket, fit the choke body to the carburettor. Progressively and evenly tighten the screws to the specified torque; note that the lower screw is the shortest.
11 Adjust the fast idle screw to obtain a gap of 0.035 in (0.889 mm) between the base circle of the cam and the fast idle pin (dimension A in Fig. 3.26).
12 Position the heat insulator so that the bi-metal lever protrudes through the slot. Provided that the choke is in the ON position, the insulator can only be fitted in one position; the back of it locates in the choke body when the three holes are aligned.
13 Position the heat mass with the ribs facing outwards so that the bi-metal rectangular loop fits over the bi-metal lever.
14 Without lifting the heat mass, rotate it 30° to 40° only, in each direction, and check that it returns to the static position under spring action. If this does not occur, repeat paragraph 13.
15 Loosely fit the clamp ring, screws and spring washers.
16 Rotate the heat mass anti-clockwise 30° to 40° to align the scribed line on its edge with the datum mark on the insulator and choke body. Hold it in this position while tightening the clamp ring screws.
17 Fit the sealing ring and water jacket, but do not fully tighten the screw and washer.
18 Refit the carburettor to the engine. After connecting the water pipes, tighten the water jacket screw.
19 Top up the damper oil level as described in Section 16.
20 Operate the throttle before attempting to start the engine. This must be done in order to rest the auto choke.
21 Fit the air cleaner, then run the engine up to normal operating temperature and adjust the idle speed to the specified value by means of the throttle adjusting screw.
22 Stop the engine, allow it to cool, then top up the cooling system as necessary.

## 18 Mechanical fuel pump – removal, overhaul and refitting

1    Remove the inlet and outlet pipe connections at the fuel pump. Plug the ends of the pipes to prevent fuel leaking out and dirt getting in (photo).
2    Undo the two bolts securing the fuel pump to the timing cover.
3    Withdraw the fuel pump and remove the gasket (photo).
4    Undo the single screw from the bottom cover. Remove the cover and pulsator diaphragm (photo).
5    Scribe the two halves of the pump body and remove the retaining screws.
6    Separate the two halves of the pump. The diaphragm will still be

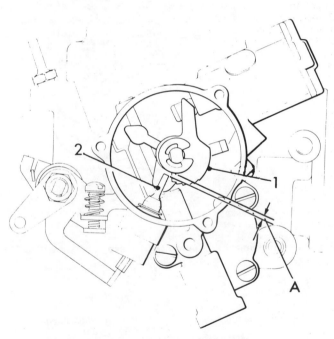

**Fig. 3.26 Automatic choke adjustment (Sec 17)**

1  Cam                    A = 0.035 in (0.9 mm)
2  Fast idle pin

attached to the upper half with the operating lever.
7    Remove the operating bar return spring and hold the lever down.
8    Push the diaphragm into the body and tilt it to release the diaphragm operating rod from the link on the end of the operating lever.
9    Withdraw the diaphragm, spring and oil seal.
10 If the operating lever needs to be removed, use a parallel pin punch to drive the pivot pin and its end caps out. The lever and link can then be withdrawn.
11 If the valves need renewing, smooth out the staking marks and prise out the valve gaskets.
12 Clean all the parts to be re-used in petrol and blow out all the passages with an air line.
13 Inspect the body of the pump and cover for cracks or damage.

Examine screw holes and unions for worn or stripped threads.

14  Inspect the operating lever contact surface at the end for wear, and the lever and link for lateral play on the pivot pin.

15  If the unit is suspect then it is advisable to fit a replacement unit on an exchange basis, especially if the pivot pin is loose.

16  Reassembly and refitting are the reverse procedures to dismantling and removal, but note the following points.

17  When fitting the pivot pin, smear jointing compound on the end caps before refitting them.

18  When fitting the new diaphragm, make sure the spring and oil seal are located over the pull-rod before engaging the end of the pull-rod on the link hook.

19  Make sure that the valves are fitted the correct way round (Fig. 3.28). Stake them into place at four points evenly spaced around the valve.

20  Fit a new pulsator diaphragm as well as a new main diaphragm when overhauling a fuel pump.

21  Keep the operating lever fully depressed whilst tightening the fuel cover screws alternately and evenly. Make sure the holes in the diaphragm are correctly lined up before refitting the other half of the pump body, and line up the marks previously scribed.

22  When refitting the pump to the vehicle, remember that the operating lever fits under the operating cam on the end of the camshaft.

23  Use a new gasket when refitting the pump to the vehicle.

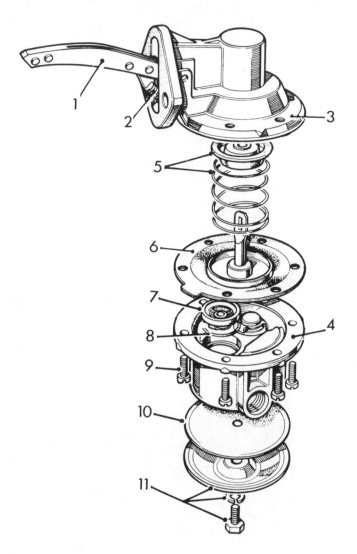

**Fig. 3.27 Mechanical fuel pump (AC) – exploded view (Sec 18)**

| | | | |
|---|---|---|---|
| 1 | Operating lever | 6 | Diaphragm |
| 2 | Spring | 7 | Valve |
| 3 | Top half of pump | 8 | Gasket |
| 4 | Bottom half of pump | 9 | Screw |
| 5 | Diaphragm spring and oil seal | 10 | Pulsator diaphragm |
| | | 11 | Cover, screw and washer |

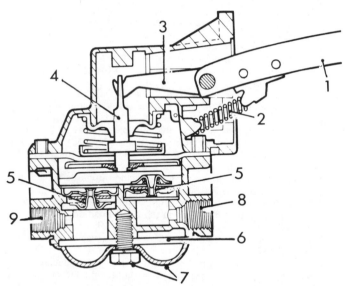

**Fig. 3.28 Sectional view of mechanical fuel pump (Sec 18)**

| | | | |
|---|---|---|---|
| 1 | Operating lever | 6 | Pulsator diaphragm |
| 2 | Lever return spring | 7 | Cover and screw |
| 3 | Link | 8 | Inlet connection |
| 4 | Diaphragm operating rod | 9 | Outlet connection |
| 5 | Valves | | |

18.1 Fuel pump *in situ* – inlet pipe removed

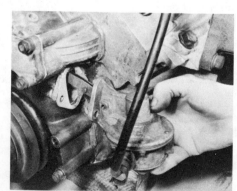

18.3 Withdrawing the fuel pump

18.4 Screw, cover and pulsator diaphragm removed

## 19 Electric fuel pump – removal, overhaul and refitting

1 The electric type of fuel pump is fitted to later vehicles and may be found in one of two places. It is located either on the chassis outrigger on the left-hand side of the car in front of the rear wheel, or beneath the rear passenger seat under the car.
2 The pump may be mounted either vertically or horizontally and may or may not have a protective cover.
3 Disconnect the battery negative lead before starting work.
4 Remove the protective cover (where fitted).
5 Disconnect the electrical leads at the pump.
6 Undo the fuel pipe unions at the pump and plug the ends to prevent loss of fuel and ingress of dirt.
7 Undo the fuel pump mounting bracket nuts and washers and remove the pump and bracket together.
8 Remove the bracket from the pump, if necessary.
9 Only very limited overhauling is possible with an electrical fuel pump.
10 Remove the end cap (twist and pull off).
11 Withdraw the filter and gasket. Remove the magnet from the end of the cap and clean it.
12 Renew the filter and gasket and refit the end cap, having refitted the magnet in the centre of the cap.

13 Refit the pump in the reverse order to removal. Do not forget to reconnect the battery lead.
14 No further overhaul of the electrical fuel pump is possible. If cleaning as described fails to remedy any malfunction, the pump must be renewed.

## 20 Fuel main filter – element renewal

1 Unscrew the centre bolt which retains the filter bowl. Withdraw the bowl complete with filter, bolt, spring and seals.
2 Remove the small and large sealing rings from underneath the mounting bracket.
3 Remove the paper element from the bowl. Empty any petrol from the bowl and clean out any sediment.
4 Withdraw the seals and spring from the retaining bolt.
5 Fit a new element, small hole downward, to the filter bowl over the bolt with spring and new seals fitted.
6 Fit a new small sealing ring to the top of the element and a new large sealing ring to the mounting face.
7 Refit the filter bowl and tighten the bolt.

## 21 Fuel in-line filter – renewal

1 The in-line fuel filter is fitted to some models at the front of the left-hand rocker cover in the feed pipe from the fuel pump to the left-hand carburettor.
2 Undo the unions at the top and bottom of the filter and remove it from the engine front lifting eye after undoing the two small cross-head screws.
3 Fit a new filter with the end marked IN downwards. Alternatively, if marked with arrows they must point upwards.
4 Connect the fuel lines top and bottom, and connect the filter bracket to the lifting eye.

## 22 Fuel tank and tank gauge unit – removal and refitting

WARNING: *This operation must be carried out in a well ventilated area.*
1 Disconnect the battery negative lead for safety.
2 Remove the drain plug on the front right-hand side of the fuel tank and drain the petrol into a suitable (non-plastic) sealed container.
3 Disconnect the wires from the tank gauge unit (photo).
4 Undo the fuel outlet pipe union on the tank gauge unit.
5 Release the breather pipe from the fuel tank next to the filler neck.
6 Undo the hose clips and release the filler neck from the tank.
7 Undo the pipe union and release the spill return pipe from the front

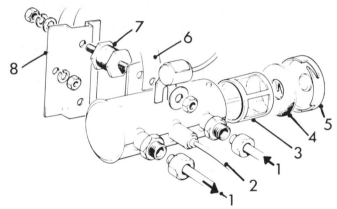

**Fig. 3.29 Electric fuel pump – horizontally mounted model (Sec 19)**

| | |
|---|---|
| 1 Fuel pipes | 5 End cap |
| 2 Electrical feed from ignition | 6 Earth strap |
| 3 Filter | 7 Rubber mounting |
| 4 Gasket | 8 Pump mounting bracket |

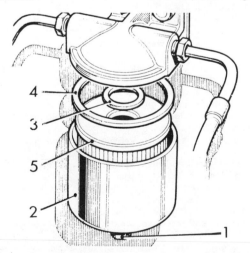

**Fig. 3.30 Main fuel filter assembly (Sec 20)**

| | |
|---|---|
| 1 Centre bolt | 4 Large sealing ring |
| 2 Bowl | 5 Paper element |
| 3 Small sealing ring | |

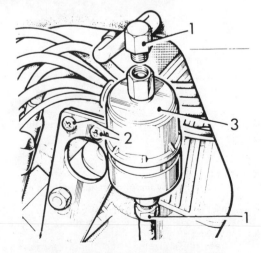

**Fig. 3.31 In-line fuel filter (Sec 21)**

| | |
|---|---|
| 1 Fuel pipe unions | 3 Filter |
| 2 Retaining screws | |

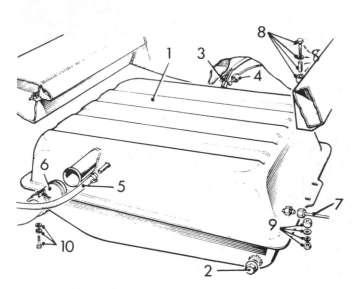

**Fig. 3.32 Fuel tank installation (Sec 22)**

1   Fuel tank
2   Drain plug
3   Gauge sender unit electrical leads
4   Fuel supply pipe
5   Vent pipe
6   Filler pipe flexible connector
7   Spill return fuel pipe
8   Tank retaining bolt, washer, sleeve and bush
9   Tank retaining nut, washers, and bush
10  Mounting bolt

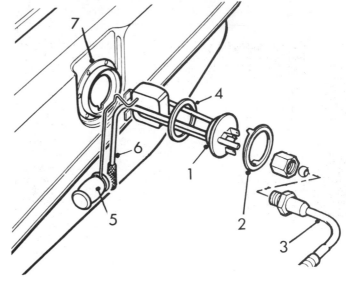

**Fig. 3.33 Fuel gauge sender unit (Sec 22)**

1   Gauge sender unit
2   Locking ring
3   Petrol pipe
4   Sealing ring
5   Float
6   Petrol pick-up filter
7   Mounting plate

15  Reconnect the battery lead.
16  Never be tempted to solder or weld a leaking fuel tank unless it has been thoroughly steamed out beforehand. This work should be left to the professionals. Temporary repairs are seldom satisfactory for long.

**23 Exhaust manifolds – removal and refitting**

**Note:** *The exhaust manifolds are handed. Check that any replacement parts are correct.*
1   Allow the exhaust system to cool down sufficiently if the engine has just been running.
2   Undo the hose clip and pull off the hot air intake/hose from the hot air box (where fitted).
3   Remove the bolts and washers, and lift away the hot air box (where fitted).
4   Bend back the ends of the locking tabs on the eight manifold retaining bolts (photo).
5   Raise the front of the vehicle and undo the three nuts securing the downpipe to the manifold flange (photo).
6   Lower the vehicle, undo the eight manifold retaining bolts and lift the manifold away (photo).
7   Refitting is the reverse of removal, but the following points should be noted.
8   Clean the cylinder head and manifold faces scrupulously, as no gasket is used between the two parts.
9   Discard the two copper O-rings fitted to the downpipe flange and use new O-rings on reassembly.
10  Discard the old locking tabs and use new ones.
11  Fit the manifold and reconnect the downpipe, but do not turn back the ends of the tab washers at this stage, or refit the hot air box.
12  Start the engine, allow it to warm up and check for exhaust gas leakage.
13  Stop the engine and allow the exhaust system to cool down. Now check the tightness of the exhaust manifold bolts and the downpipe flange nuts.
14  Turn back the ends of the locking tabs on to the bolt heads.
15  The hot air box can now be refitted and the hot air hose reconnected to it (if applicable).

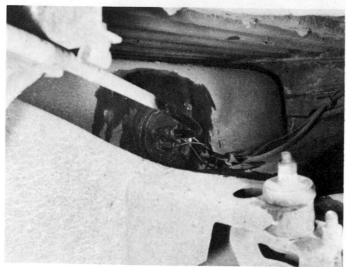

22.3 Tank gauge unit wiring and fuel feed pipe viewed through wheel arch

of the tank.
8   Support the fuel tank and undo the tank mounting nuts and bolts front and rear.
9   Withdraw the fuel tank from under the vehicle.
10  With the tank removed from the vehicle the tank gauge unit can be removed.
11  Undo the locking ring and remove it. Withdraw the tank gauge unit with float, fuel pick-up strainer and seal.
12  Refit the assembly using a new seal and secure the locking ring tightly.
13  Refit the tank in the reverse order to removal.
14  Fill the tank with petrol and check for leaks.

23.4 The manifold bolts have locking tabs or plates

23.5 The downpipe is secured by three nuts to the manifold

23.6 Lifting the right-hand exhaust manifold away

24.3 Flanged pipe joint and U-bolt mounting bracket

## 24 Exhaust system – renewal

1 The exhaust system is of conventional design and comes in five sections:

(a) *Right-hand downpipe*
(b) *Left-hand downpipe*
(c) *Front Y-section*
(d) *Main silencer box*
(e) *Tailpipe and silencer*

2 Early systems have a single pipe running from the main silencer box to the rear, later systems have twin pipes.
3 All the main pipe joints are flanged connections with three bolt locking collars, except for the two front downpipes (photo).
4 The system is supported by tough brackets with rubber bushes to allow flexing and U-bolt clamps.
5 When removing any section, apply penetrating oil liberally to the flange nuts and bolts before unscrewing them, and obtain new joint gaskets before reassembly.
6 When assembling the exhaust system do not tighten the flange coupling bolts any more than finger tight until the whole system has been connected.
7 Commencing at the manifold flange, proceed to secure the

exhaust system, but take care that undue strain is not placed on any part of the system due to misalignment. Incorrect fitting will shorten the life of the system by causing fractures at the connecting points.
8 After fitting the system start the engine and check for exhaust gas leakages from the couplings and flanges.
9 Allow the system to cool down, then recheck the security of the entire system as some settling is bound to have occurred due to expansion and contraction.

## 25 Emission control systems – general description

1 The standard emission control systems include the crankcase breather valve, rocker cover breather pipes and air intake temperature control systems.
2 This Section deals with the components which are fitted to vehicles with full emission control equipment.

### Air injection system

3 This system is used to reduce the emission of hydrocarbons, nitric oxide and carbon monoxide in the exhaust gases, and comprises an air pump, a combined diverter and relief valve, a check valve and an air manifold.
4 The rotary vane type pump is belt-driven from the engine and

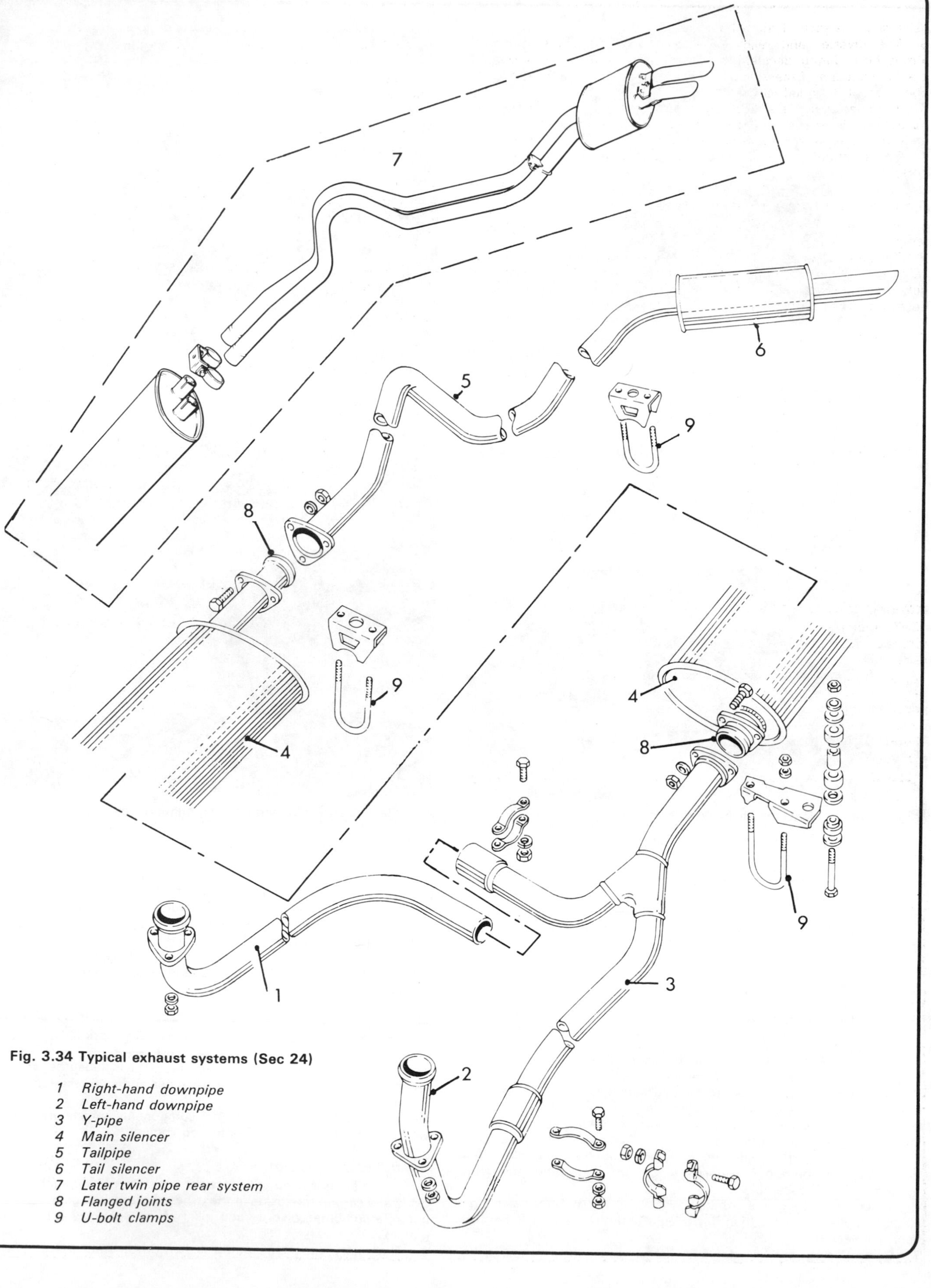

Fig. 3.34 Typical exhaust systems (Sec 24)

1   Right-hand downpipe
2   Left-hand downpipe
3   Y-pipe
4   Main silencer
5   Tailpipe
6   Tail silencer
7   Later twin pipe rear system
8   Flanged joints
9   U-bolt clamps

delivers air to each of the exhaust ports.

5   The diverter and relief valve diverts air from the pump to atmosphere during deceleration, being controlled in this mode by manifold vacuum. Excessive pressure is discharged to atmosphere by operation of the relief valve.

6   The check valve is a diaphragm-spring operated non-return valve. Its purpose is to protect the pump from exhaust gas pressure both under normal operation and in the event of the drivebelt failing.

7   The air manifold is used to direct the air into the engine exhaust ports.

## Air intake control air cleaner

8   Refer to Section 2 for further information on the air cleaner and temperature sensor.

9   The control system for the air cleaner incorporates a one-way valve so that full vacuum influence on the flap valve is maintained during sudden acceleration when the manifold vacuum is temporarily destroyed. The valve is installed in the vacuum line.

## Evaporative control system

10  This system uses an activated absorption canister through which the fuel tank is vented, and incorporates the following features:

   (a)  The carburettor float chambers are vented to the engine when the throttle is open, and to the absorption canister when the throttle is closed

   (b)  The carburettor constant depression is used to induce a purge condition through the canister. The crankcase breathing is also coupled into this system

   (c)  A separator tool is used to prevent fuel surges from reaching the canister which could otherwise saturate the system

   (d)  A sealed filler cap is used to prevent loss by evaporation

   (e)  The fuel filler tube extends into the fuel tank to prevent complete filling; this permits the fuel to expand in hot weather

## Exhaust gas recirculation (EGR) system

11  To minimise nitric oxide exhaust emission, the peak combustion temperatures are lowered by recirculating a metered quantity of exhaust gas through the inlet manifold.

12  A control signal is taken from the throttle edge tapping of the left-hand carburettor. At idle or full load no recirculation is provided, but under part load conditions a controlled amount of recirculation is provided according to the vacuum signal profile of the metering valve. The EGR valve is mounted on the rear end of the left-hand exhaust manifold.

## 26 Emission control systems – repair and maintenance

1   This Section is similar to the previous one in that it covers only that equipment found on vehicles with full emission control systems.

### Air pump – removal and installation

2   Detach the battery earth lead.
3   Disconnect the air pump hoses.
4   Remove the adjusting nut and bolt, and the pivot nut and bolt.
5   Remove the pump.
6   Installation is the reverse of the removal procedure. Refer to the following paragraphs for belt tensioning.

### Air pump drivebelt – removal, installation and tensioning

7   Detach the battery earth lead.
8   Remove the alternator drivebelt, power steering pump drivebelt and air conditioning pump drivebelt (as applicable) in order to reach the air pump drivebelt.
9   Slacken the idler pulley mountings.
10  Push the idler pulley towards the engine and free the belt from the pulleys.
11  Fit a new belt and apply leverage to the idler pulley; then tighten the mounting nuts.
12  Check that the tension is correct (see Specifications).
13  Connect the battery earth lead.

### Air distribution manifold – removal and installation

14  Remove the air cleaners as described in Section 3.
15  Uncouple the manifold pipework at the check valve union.
16  Unscrew the four union nuts, one on each manifold, and withdraw the complete manifold. Alternatively the centre branches and the two outer unions can be released.
17  Refitting is the reverse of the removal procedure.

### Check valve – removal, testing and installation

18  Disconnect the air hose at the check valve.
19  Using two open-ended spanners, unscrew the check valve whilst preventing strain on the air manifold.
20  If necessary the valve can be checked by blowing air (by mouth only) through the valve. Air should pass through from the hose connection end but not from the manifold end. Renew a defective valve.
21  Installation is the reverse of the removal procedure.

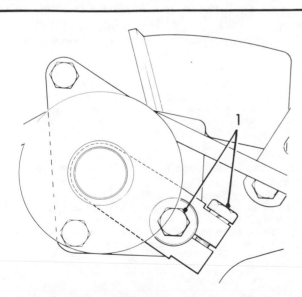

**Fig. 3.35 Air pump drivebelt idler pulley (Sec 26)**

*1   Idler pivot and pinch-bolts*

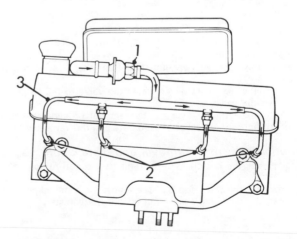

**Fig. 3.36 Air distribution manifold – right-hand side (Sec 26)**

*1   Check valve*
*2   Manifold union nuts*
*3   Air distribution manifold*

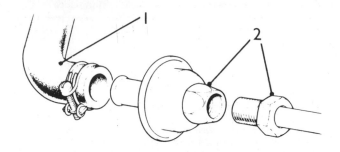

**Fig. 3.37 Check valve installation (Sec 26)**

1   Air hose
2   Air manifold/check valve union

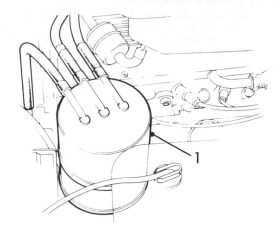

**Fig. 3.39 Absorption canister (1) (Sec 26)**

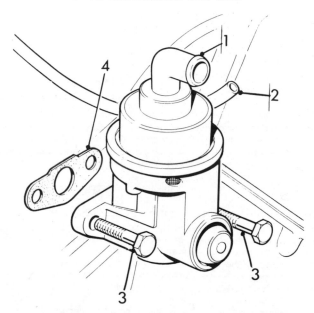

**Fig. 3.38 Diverter and relief valve installation (Sec 26)**

1   Air hose connection       3   Retaining bolts
2   Vacuum line               4   Gasket

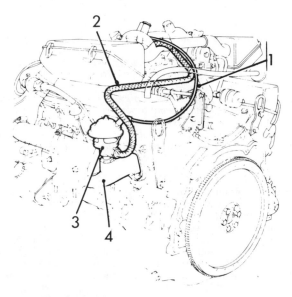

**Fig. 3.40 EGR valve installation (Sec 26)**

1   Vacuum pipe               3   EGR valve
2   Asbestos lagged pipe      4   Left-hand exhaust manifold

### Diverter and relief valve – removal and installation

22 Detach the battery earth lead.
23 Detach the hose and vacuum line from the diverter and relief valve.
24 Remove the two bolts which retain the valve to the air pump.
25 Remove the valve.
26 Installation is the reverse of the removal procedure; it is recommended that a new gasket is used between the valve and bracket.

### Absorption canister – removal and installation

27 Disconnect the bottom pipe leading to the anti-run-on valve (if fitted).
28 Disconnect the three top pipes, noting their installed positions.
29 Loosen the clamping screw and lift out the canister.

30 Installation is the reverse of the removal procedure.
**WARNING**: *Do not use compressed air to clean out the absorption canister, or clear a blockage. Explosive gas in the canister could be ignited by the heat generated by the compressed air passing through the canister.*

### Exhaust gas recirulation (EGR) valve – removal and installation

31 Disconnect the vacuum pipe from the valve.
32 Disconnect the asbestos-lagged pipe from the valve.
33 Unscrew the valve from the exhaust manifold.
34 Refitting is the reverse of the removal procedure. Ensure that the valve is securely sealed to the exhaust manifold.

## 27 Fault diagnosis – fuel system

*Unsatisfactory engine performance and excessive fuel consumption are not necessarily the fault of the fuel system or carburettor(s). In fact they more commonly occur as a result of ignition faults. Before acting on the fuel system it is necessary to check the ignition system first. Even though a fault may lie in the fuel system it will be difficult to trace unless the ignition is correct.*

*The table below, therefore, assumes that the ignition system is in order.*

| Symptom | Reason(s) |
| --- | --- |
| Smell of petrol when engine is stopped | Leaking fuel lines or unions<br>Leaking fuel tank |
| Smell of petrol when engine is idling | Leaking fuel line unions between pump and carburettor(s)<br>Overflow of fuel from float chamber due to wrong level settings, ineffective needle valve or punctured float |
| Excessive fuel consumption for reasons not covered by leaks or float chamber faults | Worn needle<br>Sticking needle |
| Difficult starting, uneven running, lack of power, cutting out | Incorrectly adjusted carburettor(s)<br>Float chamber fuel level too low or needle sticking<br>Fuel pump not delivering sufficient fuel<br>Intake manifold gasket leaking, or manifold fractured<br>Carburettor diaphragm split |

## 28 Fault diagnosis – emission control systems

| Symptom | Reason(s) |
| --- | --- |
| Low CO content of exhaust gases (weak or lean mixture) | Fuel level incorrect in carburettor(s)<br>Incorrectly adjusted carburettor(s)<br>Induction air leak |
| High CO content of exhaust gases (rich mixture) | Incorrectly adjusted carburettor(s)<br>Choke sticking<br>Absorption canister blocked<br>Fuel level incorrect in carburettor(s)<br>Air injection system fault |
| Noisy air injection pump | Belt tension incorrect<br>Relief valve faulty<br>Diverter faulty<br>Check valve faulty |

# Chapter 4  Ignition system

*For modifications, and information applicable to later models, see Supplement at end of manual*

## Contents

## Specifications

### General

System type ................................................................... Contact breaker and coil with ballast resistor
Firing order .................................................................. 1-8-4-3-6-5-7-2
Location of No 1 cylinder ............................................. Front of left-hand bank
Cylinder numbering (from front):
    Left-hand bank .................................................... 1-3-5-7
    Right-hand bank .................................................. 2-4-6-8

### Distributor

Make and type .............................................................. Lucas 35D8
Serial number:
    Pre-1972 ............................................................. 41325
    1972 to 1976 ...................................................... 41487
1976 onwards ............................................................... 41680A
    Full emission control models ............................. 41681A
Direction of rotation .................................................... Clockwise viewed from above
Contact breaker points gap (initial setting only) ......... 0.014 to 0.016 in (0.35 to 0.40 mm)
Dwell:
    Angle ................................................................... 26 to 28°
    Percentage ........................................................... 58 to 62%
Condenser capacity ...................................................... 0.18 to 0.25 microfarad

### Ignition coil

Make and type .............................................................. Lucas 16C6 and BA 16C6 with ballast resistor
Primary resistance ....................................................... 1.2 to 1.4 ohms at 20°C (68°F)
Consumption at 2000 rpm ............................................ 1 amp approximately

### Spark plugs

Make and type:
    Early models (pre-1976) ..................................... Champion L87Y, L92Y or equivalent
    Later models (1976 on) ...................................... Champion N12Y or equivalent
Electrolyte gap:
    Early models ........................................................ 0.025 in (0.60 mm)
    Late models .......................................................... 0.030 in (0.75 mm)

### Ignition timing

| | 41325 | 41487 | 41680A | 41681A |
|---|---|---|---|---|
| Distributor serial number | | | | |
| Static timing, and dynamic at idle speed: | | | | |
|   For 91 to 93 octane fuel | 3° BTDC | 5° ATDC | 7° BTDC | 5° ATDC |
|   For 85 octane fuel | 0° (TDC) | 8° ATDC | 5° BTDC | — |
| Centrifugal advance (decelerating check, vacuum pipe disconnected, initial advance/retard not included): | | | | |
|   4800 rpm | 27° to 31° | 23° to 27° | 24° to 28° | 22° to 26° |
|   1800 rpm | 15° to 19° | 10° to 14° | 12° to 16° | 2.5° tp 6.5° |
|   1000 rpm | 5° to 9° | 0° to 5° | 1° to 5° | No advance |

## 1  General description

In order that the engine may run correctly, it is necessary for an electrical spark to ignite the fuel/air charge in the combustion chamber at exactly the right moment in relation to engine speed and load. The ignition system is based on supplying the low tension voltage from the battery to the ignition coil where it is converted to high tension voltage by virtue of contact breaker operation. The high tension voltage is powerful enough to jump the spark plug gap in the cylinder many times a second under high compression pressure, providing that the ignition system is in good working order and that all adjustments are correct.

The ignition system comprises two individual circuits, known as the low tension circuit and the high tension circuit.

The low tension (or primary) circuit comprises the lead from the positive terminal of the 12 volt battery, the ignition/starter switch, a ballast resistor wire, the primary winding of the 6 volt ignition coil, the contact breaker points of the distributor (which are bridged by the condenser) and an earth connection. Since the negative terminal of the battery is also earthed, current will flow in the low tension circuit when the distributor contacts are closed and a magnetic field will be set up in the primary winding of the coil.

The high tension (or secondary) circuit comprises the secondary winding of the ignition coil (one end of which is connected internally to the output terminal of the primary winding), the heavily insulated ignition lead from the centre of the coil to the centre of the distributor cap, the rotor arm, the spark plug leads and the spark plugs.

When the contacts open, the magnetic field in the primary coil winding collapses rapidly and induces a voltage in the secondary winding. At this instant, the distributor rotor is bridging the coil output terminal and one of the spark plug connections in the distributor caps, and a spark therefore jumps the electrode gap. The condenser across the contacts serves the dual puspose of assisting the rapid collapse of the magnetic field in the primary winding and acting as a spark suppressor for the contacts.

The whole cycle is repeated when the contacts open again which will be when the distributor shaft has turned through 45°, but this time the next spark plug in the ignition sequence will fire.

During the starting sequence, the ballast resistor or resistor wire in series with the coil primary winding is bypassed so that the full battery voltage (which will be low anyway due to the high current drawn by the starter motor) is passed to the 6 volt coil. In this way a bigger secondary voltage will be induced and therefore a bigger spark will result.

Whilst the above sequence is apparently satisfactory, in that the distributor can be physically set to provide a spark when it is needed, some variation of ignition timing is required to obtain optimum efficiency under varying conditions of engine load and speed. A centrifugal advance mechanism is used inside the distributor body which will give an increasing amount of spark advancement (ie, firing earlier in the cycle) as the engine speed increases. Additionally, a vacuum device is fitted, which is operated by the depression in the inlet manifold and will give additional spark advancement at low and moderate throttle openings, eg when the car is cruising. At wide throttle openings, eg when hill climbing, there is less suction in the inlet manifold and hence there will be little or no additional advancement. The combination of the two devices will provide a wide range of ignition advancement or retardation according to the engine requirements at any particular time.

## 2  Condenser – removal, testing and refitting

1    The purpose of the condenser (sometimes known as the capacitor)

is to ensure that when the contact breaker points open, there is no sparking across them which would waste voltage and cause wear. It also boosts the HT voltage.

2    The condenser is fitted in parallel with the points. If it develops a short circuit, ignition failure will result as the points will be prevented from interrupting the low tension circuit.

3    If the engine becomes very difficult to start or begins to 'miss' after several miles running and the points show sign of excessive wear or burning, then the condition of the condenser must be suspect.

4    Without special equipment the only way to check whether the condenser is faulty is to fit a new one and observe the results.

5    To remove the condenser from the distributor, take off the distributor cap and rotor arm. Now remove the condenser locating screw and lead connection (photo).

6    Refitting the condenser is the reverse of the removal procedure, but take care that the lead cannot contact the moving parts or become trapped when the cap is refitted.

## 3  Contact breaker points – checking and adjustment

1    At the intervals specified in Routine Maintenance, or whenever new contact breaker points have been fitted, the points should be checked and adjusted as described below. For best results the use of a dwell meter is indispensable, but if one is not available, setting the contact breaker gap with feeler gauges will enable the engine to run until the dwell angle can be checked professionally.

### Points gap adjustment

2    The contact breaker points gap should be adjusted as follows when fitting new points to enable the engine to be run.

3    With the distributor cap and rotor arm removed, turn the engine on the starting handle until the heel of the contact breaker is on a cam peak, ie, points opened by the cam as far as they will go.

4    Insert a clean feeler gauge between the point faces and check the gap. The correct gap is given in the Specifications. Take care not to contaminate the point faces with oil from the feeler gauge.

5    If adjustment is necessary, turn the adjusting nut on the side of the distributor clockwise to increase the gap or anti-clockwise to reduce it (photo). If much adjustment is required, it may be necessary to loosen the points retaining screw.

6    If no external adjuster is fitted, slacken the points retaining screw and move the fixed contact plate as necessary until the correct gap is achieved. Tighten the screw on completion.

7    Refit the rotor arm and distributor cap, then check the dwell angle as described below.

### Dwell angle adjustment

8    Dwell angle is the angle through which the distributor cam turns between the instants of closure and opening of the contact breaker

2.5 Removing the condenser (points removed)

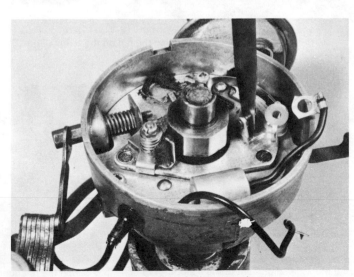
3.5 Insert a feeler gauge and adjust the hexagonal nut

points. Reducing the points gap increases the dwell angle; increasing the gap reduces the dwell angle. The correct dwell angle is given in the Specifications.

9  Various proprietary instruments are available to measure dwell angle. Some operate with the engine running at idle speed, others require the engine to be cranked on the starter motor.

10  Connect the dwell meter to the engine in accordance with the maker's instructions. It may be necessary to zero it first.

11  Start the engine or crank it on the starter motor, as applicable, and read the dwell angle on the meter. (If an 8-cylinder scale is not provided, use the 4-cylinder scale and double the specified angle). If adjustment is necessary, turn the adjuster screw on the outside of the distributor clockwise to reduce the dwell angle or anti-clockwise to increase it. If no adjustment screw is fitted, adjust the points gap as described in paragraph 6.

12  Check the ignition timing as described in Section 8 and adjust if necessary.

## 4  Contact breaker points – removal, cleaning and refitting

1  At the intervals specified in Routine Maintenance, or if ignition trouble is suspected, the points should be removed for cleaning or renewal as described below.

2  Unclip and remove the distributor cap.

3  Remove the rotor arm.

4  Remove the nut on the contact breaker terminal post (photo) and the fixed contact securing screw (photo).

5  Remove the plastic washer, LT lead and condenser lead, and lift off the spring and moving contact. Recover the other plastic washer if it is not attached to the top one.

6  Remove the fixed contact.

7  On models with 'Quickfit' contact breaker points, remove the securing screw, relieve the spring tension at the terminal connection, unclip the leads and remove the contact set. Note the arrangement of any spacers, insulators etc.

8  If the points are to be cleaned and re-used, then rub the faces of the contacts on fine emery cloth or fine carborundum paper (400 grade wet and dry). It is important that the faces are kept flat and parallel otherwise they will not meet properly when refitted and ingition problems may easily recur.

9  Refitting of the now cleaned set of points or the fitting of a new set, is simply the reverse procedure to removal. Remember to clean any preservative off a new set of points before fitting them, and apply a smear of grease to the heel of the moving contact.

10  Set the points gap and then check the dwell angle, as described in Section 3. (If new points have been fitted it is necessary to check the dwell angle again after 1000 miles (1600 km) have been covered).

11  Check the ignition timing as described in Section 8.

## 5  Distributor – removal and refitting

1  Disconnect the battery negative lead.

2  Disconnect the vacuum pipe from the vacuum unit.

3  Undo the two clips and remove the distributor cap.

4  Disconnect the low tension lead from the coil.

5  It is not necessary to set the engine to TDC on No 1 cylinder (on compression stroke) to remove the distributor, unless the engine is to be rotated whilst the distributor is off the engine. Instead, mark the alignment of the rotor arm to the distributor body (photo).

6  Scribe the body of the distributor to show its relationship to the timing cover (photo).

7  Undo the clamp plate bolt and remove the plate (photo).

8  Withdraw the distributor from the timing cover.

9  Refitting is a straightforward procedure as long as the engine has remained static. If however it has been turned, follow the procedure from paragraph 15.

10  Fit a new O-ring to the distributor shaft casing.

11  Rotate the distributor driveshaft until the rotor arm is 30° anti-clockwise from the mark scribed on the body. This will allow the distributor drivegear to engage correctly as the distributor is refitted. As the distributor is pushed home, so the gear will rotate and the marks will be correctly aligned.

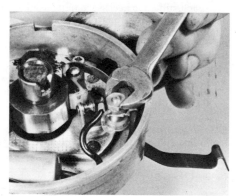

4.4a Removing the nut on the terminal post ...

4.4b ... and the fixed contact screw

5.5 Mark the alignment of the distributor rotor arm to the body

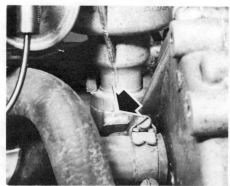

5.6 Scribe the relationship of the distributor body to the timing cover (arrowed)

5.7 Removing the clamp plate bolt

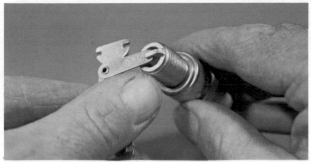

**Measuring plug gap.** A feeler gauge of the correct size (see ignition system specifications) should have a slight 'drag' when slid between the electrodes. Adjust gap if necessary

**Adjusting plug gap.** The plug gap is adjusted by bending the earth electrode inwards, or outwards, as necessary until the correct clearance is obtained. Note the use of the correct tool

**Normal.** Grey-brown deposits, lightly coated core nose. Gap increasing by around 0.001 in (0.025 mm) per 1000 miles (1600 km). Plugs ideally suited to engine, and engine in good condition

**Carbon fouling.** Dry, black, sooty deposits. Will cause weak spark and eventually misfire. Fault: over-rich fuel mixture. Check: carburettor mixture settings, float level and jet sizes; choke operation and cleanliness of air filter. Plugs can be re-used after cleaning

**Oil fouling.** Wet, oily deposits. Will cause weak spark and eventually misfire. Fault: worn bores/piston rings or valve guides; sometimes occurs (temporarily) during running-in period. Plugs can be re-used after thorough cleaning

**Overheating.** Electrodes have glazed appearance, core nose very white – few deposits. Fault: plug overheating. Check: plug value, ignition timing, fuel octane rating (too low) and fuel mixture (too weak). Discard plugs and cure fault immediately

**Electrode damage.** Electrodes burned away; core nose has burned, glazed appearance. Fault: pre-ignition. Check: as for 'Overheating' but may be more severe. Discard plugs and remedy fault before piston or valve damage occurs

**Split core nose (may appear initially as a crack).** Damage is self-evident, but cracks will only show after cleaning. Fault: pre-ignition or wrong gap-setting technique. Check: ignition timing, cooling system, fuel octane rating (too low) and fuel mixture (too weak). Discard plugs, rectify fault immediately

12  Refit the distributor with the marks scribed on the body and timing cover correctly aligned. Check as the distributor is offered up, that the oil pump driveshaft slot is correctly lined up to accept the end of the distributor driveshaft. If it is not in alignment, insert a screwdriver and set it to the correct position (photo).

13  Fit the clamp plate and bolt and secure the distributor in its original location.

14  Reconnect the low tension lead to the coil and the vacuum pipe to the vacuum unit. Refit the distributor cap. Reconnect the battery and set the dwell angle and ignition timing as described in Sections 3 and 8 respectively.

15  If the timing has been lost completely (eg after engine rebuild), first set the engine so that No 1 piston (front, left-hand) is at TDC on its compression stroke.

16  Turn the distributor driveshaft so that the rotor arm position is 30° anti-clockwise from the No 1 cylinder HT lead position in the distributor cap (Fig. 4.1).

17  Fit the distributor to the engine, ensuring that the oil pump driveshaft slot engages in the end of the distributor driveshaft.

18  Check that the rotor arm is now aligned to the No 1 cylinder HT lead position in the distributor cap. If necessary rotate the body of the distributor to align it correctly so that the contact breaker points are just about to open.

19  Push the distributor fully home and refit the clamp plate and bolt, but do not tighten them yet.

5.12 Aligning the oil pump driveshaft

20  Check the static timing as described in Section 8.

21  Reconnect the low tension lead to the coil and the vacuum pipe to the distributor. Refit the distributor cap.

22  Reconnect the battery negative lead.

23  Set the dwell angle and then the ignition timing dynamically, as described in Sections 3 and 8 respectively.

---

### 6   Distributor – dismantling, overhaul and reassembly

*Check that spares are available before deciding to overhaul the distributor.*

1  Although the distributors fitted to the Range Rover vary through the years of manufacture, the same basic instructions apply to all models, except where a different or alternative procedure is indicated. All photographs are of the earlier type of distributor.

2  Remove the distributor as described in the previous Section.

3  Remove the rotor arm (photo).

4  Remove the contact breaker points as described in Section 4.

5  Remove the condenser.

6  Release the nut, spring and washer from the pivot pin on the contact breaker baseplate on early models (photos).

7  Unscrew and remove the dwell angle adjuster screw and spring. Note its relationship before removing it.

8  Disconnect the earthing lead from the centrifugal advance mechanism cover plate (photo).

9  Remove the contact breaker base plate. Then remove the vacuum unit and grommet. Note that this operation has to be reversed for later models (photos).

10  Remove the centrifugal advance mechanism cover plate (photo).

11  Withdraw the two springs very carefully so as not to stretch or damage them.

12  Remove the felt lubricating pad and undo the screw inside the top of the distributor cam shaft. The cam and foot can be lifted away (photo).

13  Remove the centrifugal advance weights if necessary.

14  To remove the drivegear from the end of the shaft, drive out the roll pin using a pin punch and remove the gear and tab washer (photo).

15  Remove the O-ring from the distributor body.

16  Clean the mechanical parts carefully in petrol, then examine them for wear as described in the following paragraphs.

17  Check the fit of the balance weights on the distributor shaft. If the pivots are loose or the holes excessively worn, the relevant parts must be renewed. The springs are best renewed anyway (if available).

18  Examine the drivegear teeth for wear and renew if necessary.

19  Check the fit of the driveshaft in the housing. If excessive wear is present, the parts must be renewed.

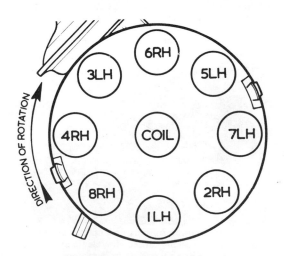

Fig. 4.1 Plan view of distributor from above showing spark plug lead positions (Sec 5)

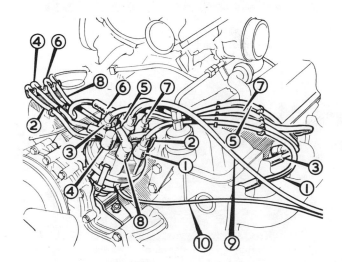

Fig. 4.2 Distributor cap and HT leads layout (Sec 5)

1 to 8 HT leads
9   HT lead to coil
10  LT lead to coil

20 Check that the vacuum unit is working correctly by sucking through the tube and checking that the linkage moves.

21 Check the metal contact on the distributor rotor for security of fixing and burning. Small burning marks can be removed with a smooth file or very fine emery paper, but if anything else is wrong the rotor should be renewed. Look also for cracks in the plastic moulding.

22 Check the distributor cap in a similar manner, renewing it if necessary.

23 Reassembly is essentially the reverse of the dismantling procedure, but the following points should be noted:

(a) Lubricate the weight assembly with a dry lubricant
(b) Lubricate the shaft with a dry lubricant
(c) Lubricate the moving plate pin with a dry lubricant

(d) Don't stretch the centrifugal weight springs
(e) With later types of distributor it helps if the vacuum advance lever is located to the baseplate by the 'Quick fit' contact set before the vacuum unit is secured to the body of the distributor
(f) Screw in the dwell angle adjuster screw halfway. Any further adjustment can be made once the contact breaker points have been refitted.

24 With the distributor reassembled, set the points gap as described in Section 3.

25 Once the distributor has been refitted to the vehicle, check the static ignition timing, then check the dwell angle and the dynamic ignition timing as described in Sections 3 and 8 respectively.

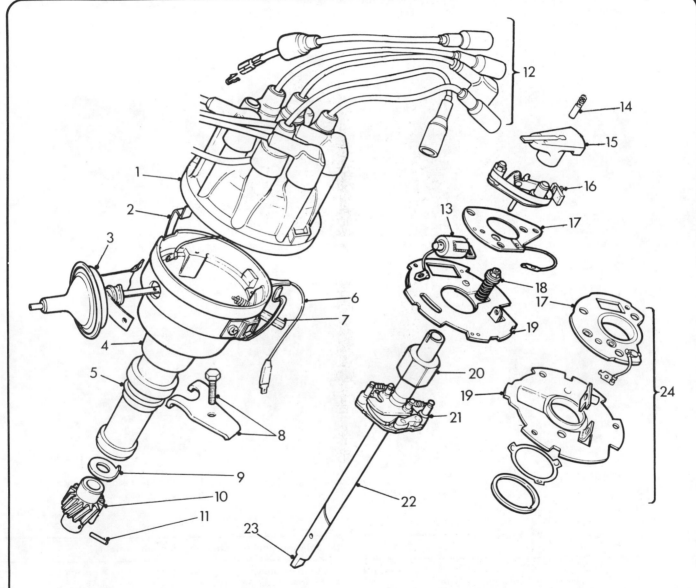

**Fig. 4.3 Distributor – exploded view (Sec 6)**

| | | | |
|---|---|---|---|
| 1  Distributor cap | 8  Clamp plate and bolt | 16  Contact breaker set | 21  Centrifugal advance |
| 2  Clip | 9  Locking hub washer | 17  Contact breaker | weights and springs |
| 3  Vacuum unit | 10  Driving gear | baseplate | assembly |
| 4  Distributor body | 11  Roll pin | 18  Pivot pin with nut, | 22  Distributor driveshaft |
| 5  O-ring | 12  HT leads | spring and washer | 23  Oil pump driving end |
| 6  Low tension (LT) lead | 13  Condenser | 19  Centrifugal advance | 24  Central section of |
| 7  Dwell angle adjuster | 14  Carbon brush and spring | mechanism cover plate | distributor for later |
| screw | 15  Rotor arm | 20  Cam | models |

6.3 Remove the rotor arm

6.6a Undo the nut ...

6.6b ... and remove the washer and spring

6.8 Disconnecting the earthing lead

6.9a Removing the contact breaker baseplate

6.9b Unhook and withdraw the vacuum unit

6.10 Removing the centrifugal advance mechanism cover plate

6.12 Removing the felt lubricating pad to reveal the screw

6.14 The drivegear is retained by a roll pin. Note the O-ring (arrowed)

## 7 Distributor – lubrication

1 During routine maintenance and where otherwise stated in this Chapter, the distributor should be lubricated as follows.
2 Remove the distributor cap and rotor arm.
3 Apply a few drops of engine oil to the felt pad to lubricate the cam spindle bearing.
4 Squirt a few drops of engine oil through the lubrication holes to oil the centrifugal timing control.
5 Lubricate the contact plate bearing by putting one drop of engine oil in each of the oil holes in the plate.
6 Grease the cam with a light smear of general purpose grease.
7 The contact post may be lubricated in the same manner.
8 Wipe up any excess lubricant and take care not to get any on the contact breaker point faces. Oil contamination of the point faces will cause burning, misfiring or total ignition failure.

## 8 Ignition timing – checking and adjustment

1 Correct ignition timing is vital for the proper running of the engine. If the ignition is over-advanced, pre-ignition (pinking), and possible piston damage, will result; if the ignition is retarded, there will be loss of power, overheating and high fuel consumption.
2 Methods are given below for both static and dynamic timing. Static timing should be regarded only as a basic method for getting the engine running, and should be followed as soon as possible by a dynamic check. If the engine is known to be running reasonably well, dynamic timing is all that is necessary.

### Static timing
3 Remove the distributor cap and rotor arm.
4 Connect a test lamp (12 volts, up to 5 watts – a sidelight or panel light bulb will do) between the contact breaker points LT terminal and

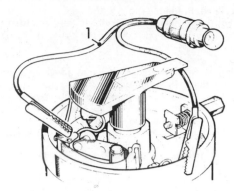

Fig. 4.4 Timing light (1) connected (Sec 8)

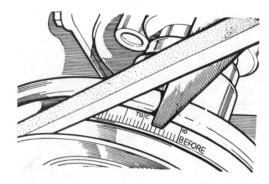

Fig. 4.5 Check that the scale and pointer are correctly aligned
(Sec 8)

if the timing is correct, the specified mark on the scale will be aligned with the pointer. Take care not to let the lamp or its leads come into contact with moving parts of the engine.
14  If the timing is incorrect, stop the engine, slacken the distributor clamp bolt and move the distributor in the required direction (clockwise to retard, anti-clockwise to advance) to correct the timing. Tighten the clamp bolt and recheck the timing.
15  Note that if the engine idle speed is too high, it will be impossible to set the timing correctly since the centrifugal advance mechanism in the distributor will have started to operate. Connect a tachometer to the engine if in doubt. Refer to Chapter 3 for the specified idle speeds.
16  If it is wished to check the operation of the centrifugal advance mechanism, connect a tachometer to the engine and refer to the Specifications for centrifugal advance data. As the engine speed is increased, the timing scale will appear to drift relative to the pointer in the advanced (BTDC) direction. Accurate checking is difficult without special equipment, but any jerkiness or sticking in the movement of the scale should be regarded with suspicion.

### Timing for low octane fuels

17  Suggested ignition timing settings for 85 octane fuel are given in the Specifications. Where fuel of even lower, or unknown, octane rating is to be used, the ignition should be retarded to the point where pinking on acceleration just disappears. Engine power and efficiency will be reduced, and the standard ignition timing should be restored when normal fuel is again available.

### 9  Spark plugs and HT leads

**Note:** *There is very little clearance between the body of the spark plug and the cylinder head. The best tool is the box spanner and tommy-bar supplied in the vehicle tool kit as this is thin enough to fit.*
   *Take care when fitting spark plugs that they are not cross-threaded. It is all too easy with alloy cylinder heads, and although thread inserts can be fitted it can be quite a costly business, since the cylinder head will require removal.*
1  The correct functioning of the spark plugs is vital for the correct running and efficiency of the engine.
2  At intervals of 6000 miles (10 000 km) the plugs should be removed, examined, cleaned and if the electrodes are worn, renewed. The spark plugs should be renewed in any event every 12 000 miles (20 000 km).
3  The condition of the spark plugs will also tell much about the overall condition of the engine.
4  If the insulator nose of the spark plug is clean and white, with no deposits, this is indicative of a weak mixture, or too hot a plug (a hot plug transfers heat away from the electrode slowly, a cold plug transfers heat away quickly).
5  If the top and insulator nose is covered with hard black deposits, then this is indicative that the mixture is too rich. Should the plug be black and oily, then it is likely that the engine is fairly worn, as well as the mixture being too rich.
6  If the insulator nose is covered with light tan to greyish brown deposits, then the mixture is correct and it is likely that the engine is in good condition.
7  If there are any traces of long brown tapering stains on the outside of the white portion of the plug, then the plug will have to be renewed. This shows that there is a faulty joint between the plug body and the insulator allowing compression to leak away.
8  Plugs should be cleaned by a sand blasting machine, which will free them from carbon more thoroughly than cleaning by hand with a wire brush. The machine will also test the condition of the plugs under compression. Any plug that fails to spark at the recommended pressure should be renewed.
9  The spark plug gap is of considerable importance, as, if it is too large or too small, the size of the spark and its efficiency will be seriously impaired. Refer to the Specifications for the correct gap.
10  To set it, measure the gap with a feeler gauge, and then bend open, or close, the outer plug electrode until the correct gap is achieved. The centre electrode should never be bent as this may crack the insulation and cause plug failure, if nothing worse.
11  Replace the distributor HT leads in the correct firing order, which is given in the Specifications.
12  The plug leads require no routine maintenance other than being kept clean and wiped over regularly.

earth (Fig. 4.4). Switch on the ignition. When the points are open, the lamp will light.
5  Turn the engine on the starting handle, observing the timing scale on the crankshaft pulley (Fig. 4.5). When the correct number of degrees before or after TDC is aligned with the pointer, the test lamp should just come on. Refer to Specifications for the correct static timing value for your model.
6  If the lamp lights too soon, the ignition timing is advanced. If the lamp does not come on when the relevant marks are aligned, the timing is retarded. In either case, slacken the distributor clamp bolt and rotate the distributor body slightly in the appropriate direction to correct the timing (clockwise to retard, anti-clockwise to advance).
7  Turn the engine 360° and recheck the timing.
8  Switch off the ignition, disconnect the test lamp and refit the rotor arm and distributor cap.

### Dynamic timing

9  If not already done, check and adjust the dwell angle as described in Section 3.
10  The engine must be at normal operating temperature. Disconnect and plug the distributor vacuum hose.
11  Connect a timing light (strobe) into the ignition system in accordance with the manufacturer's instructions – usually to the No 1 HT lead. Some lights also require a connection to be made to the battery or to a mains power supply.
12  Depending on the brightness of the timing light and the ambient light level, it may be necessary to highlight the specified timing mark (on the scale on the pulley) and the pointer with quick-drying white paint. Typist's correcting fluid is ideal.
13  Start the engine and allow it to idle. Point the timing light at the timing marks and pointer. The timing marks will appear stationary, and

## 10 Fault diagnosis – ignition system

### Engine fails to start

1    If the engine fails to start and the car was running normally when it was last used, first check there is fuel in the fuel tank. If the engine turns over normally on the starter motor and the battery is evidently well charged, then the fault may be in either the high or low tension circuits. **Note**: *If the battery is known to be fully charged, the ignition light comes on and the starter motor fails to turn the engine, check the tightness of the leads on the battery terminal and also the secureness of the earth lead to its connection to the body. It is quite common for the leads to have worked loose, even if they look and feel secure. If one of the battery terminal posts gets very hot when trying to work the starter motor this is a sure indication of a faulty connection to that terminal.*

2    One of the commonest reasons for bad starting is wet or damp spark plug leads and distributor. Remove the distributor cap; if condensation is visible internally, dry the cap with a rag and also wipe the leads. Refit the cap.

3    If the engine still fails to start, check that current is reaching the plugs by disconnecting each plug lead in turn at the spark plug end and holding the end of the cable with an insulated tool or rubber glove about $\frac{1}{8}$ in (3 mm) away from the cylinder block. Spin the engine on the starter motor.

4    Sparking between the end of the cable and the block should be fairly strong with a regular blue spark. If current is reaching the plugs, remove, clean and regap them. The engine should now start.

5    If there is no spark at the plug leads, take off the HT lead from the centre of the distributor cap and hold it to the block as before. Spin the engine on the starter once more. A rapid succession of blue sparks between the end of the lead and block indicates that the coil is in order and that the distributor cap is cracked, the rotor arm faulty, or the carbon brush in the top of the distributor cap is not making good contact with the spring on the rotor arm.

6    If there are no sparks from the end of the lead from the coil, check the connections at the coil end of the lead. If it is in order, start checking the low tension circuit. First check the contact breaker points for correct gap and cleanliness (Sections 3 and 4)

7    Use a 12 volt voltmeter, or a 12 volt bulb and two lengths of wire. With the ignition switched on and the points open, test between the low tension wire to the coil connection (+ ve) and earth. No reading indicates a break in the supply from the ignition switch. Check the connections at the switch to see if any are loose. Refit these and the engine should run. A reading shows that electricity is reaching the coil.

8    Take the condenser wire off the points assembly and with the points open, test between the moving points and earth. If there now is a reading, the fault is in the condenser. Fit a new one and the fault should be cleared.

9    With no reading from the moving point to earth, take a reading between earth and the negative (–ve) terminal of the coil. A reading here shows a broken wire (which will need to be renewed) between the coil and distributor. No reading confirms that the coil has failed and

must be renewed. Remember to refit the condenser wire to the points assembly. For these tests it is sufficient to separate the points with a piece of dry paper whilst testing with the points open.

### Engine misfires

10    If the engine misfires regularly, run it at a fast idling speed. Pull off each of the plug caps in turn and listen to the note of the engine. Hold the plug cap in a dry cloth or with a rubber glove as additional protection against a shock from the HT supply.

11    No difference in engine running will be noticed when the lead from the defective circuit is removed. Removing the lead from one of the good cylinders will accentuate the misfire.

12    Remove the plug lead from the end of the defective plug and hold it with an insulated tool or rubber glove about $\frac{1}{8}$ in (3 mm) away from the block. Restart the engine. If the sparking is fairly strong and regular, the fault must lie in the spark plug.

13    The plug may be loose, the insulation may be cracked, or the electrodes may have burnt away, giving too wide a gap for the spark to jump. Worse still, one of the electrodes may have broken off. Either renew the plug or clean it; reset the gap, and then test it.

14    If there is no spark at the end of the plug lead, or it is weak and intermittent, check the ignition lead from the distributor to the plug. If the insulation is cracked or perished, renew the lead. Check the connections at the distributor cap.

15    If there is still no spark, examine the distributor cap carefully for tracking. This can be recognised by a very thin black line running between two or more electrodes or between an electrode and some other part of the distributor. These lines are paths which conduct electricity across the cap thus letting it run to earth. The only remedy is a new distributor cap.

16    Apart from the ignition timing being incorrect, other causes of misfiring have already been dealt with under the section dealing with the failure of the engine to start. To recap – these are that:

(a)    the coil may be faulty giving an intermittent misfire
(b)    there may be a damaged wire or loose connection in the low tension circuit
(c)    there may be a mechanical fault in the distributor

17    If the ignition timing is too far retarded, it should be noted that the engine will tend to overheat and there will be a quite noticeable drop in power. If the engine is overheating and the power is down and the ignition timing is correct, then the carburettors should be checked, as it is likely that this is where the fault lies.

### Engine fires but will not run

18    If the engine fires when the starter motor is cranking but cuts out as soon as the starter switch is released, the ballast resistor or resistance wire must be suspect, since this is bypassed only when the starter motor is operating (See Section 1).

19    Do not be tempted by bypass a failed ballast resistor or resistance wire with ordinary wire, or coil overheating and possible failure may result.

# Chapter 5  Clutch

## Contents

## Specifications

### General

| | |
|---|---|
| Make ......................................................................................... | Borg and Beck |
| Type .......................................................................................... | Diaphragm |
| Clutch plate diameter ........................................................... | 10.5 in (266.5 mm) |
| Actuation ................................................................................. | Hydraulic |

### Torque wrench settings

| | lbf ft | kgf m |
|---|---|---|
| Clutch cover bolts ....................................................... | 35 to 38 | 4.9 to 5.2 |

## 1  General description

The clutch which is fitted to the Range Rover is a single dry plate diaphragm spring type and is hydraulically operated.

The unit comprises a steel cover which is dowelled and bolted to the rear face of the flywheel and contains the pressure plate, diaphragm spring and fulcrum rings.

The clutch disc is free to slide along the splined input (primary) shaft and is held in position between the flywheel and the pressure plate by the pressure of the pressure plate spring. Friction lining material is riveted to the clutch disc and it has a spring cushioned hub to absorb transmission shocks and to help ensure a smooth take-off.

The circular diaphragm spring is mounted on shoulder pins and held in place in the cover by two fulcrum rings. The spring is also held to the pressure plate by three spring steel clips which are riveted in position.

The clutch release mechanism consists of a hydraulic master cylinder and slave cylinder and the interconnecting pipework, a release arm and sealed ball type release bearing – the latter being in permanent contact with the fingers of the pressure plate assembly.

As the friction linings on the clutch driven plate wear, the pressure plate automatically moves closer to the driven plate to compensate. This makes the centre of the diaphragm spring move nearer to the release bearing, so decreasing the release bearing clearance. Depressing the clutch pedal actuates the clutch release arm by means of hydraulic pressure. The release arm pushes the release bearing forwards to bear against the release fingers, so moving the centre of the diaphragm spring inwards. The spring is sandwiched between two annular rings which act as fulcrum points. As the centre of the spring is pushed in, the outside of the spring is pushed out, so moving the pressure plate backwards and disengaging the pressure plate from the clutch disc.

When the clutch pedal is released, the diaphragm spring forces the pressure plate into contact with the friction linings on the clutch disc and at the same time pushes the clutch disc a fraction of an inch forwards on its splines so engaging the clutch disc with the flywheel. The clutch disc is now firmly sandwiched between the pressure plate and the flywheel so the drive is taken up.

## 2  Maintenance

1  This consists of occasionally checking the security of the bolts which retain the master and slave cylinders and applying a little engine oil to the operating rod clevis joints.
2  Periodically check the hydraulic pipes and unions for leaks, corrosion or deterioration.
3  At weekly intervals remove the clutch master cylinder cap and check the fluid level. Before unscrewing the cap wipe it clean to prevent the ingress of dirt. Use only the recommended type of clutch fluid. If topping-up becomes a common occurrence, then carry out a visual inspection of the clutch hydraulic system. Any leakage of fluid would then be evident.
4  The clutch is self-adjusting, so periodic adjustment is not required.

## 3  Master cylinder – removal and refitting

1  From within the car remove the pivot bolt and bushes securing the clutch master cylinder pushrod to the clutch pedal.
2  From the engine compartment disconnect the metal hydraulic pipe at the master cylinder union. Plug the end of the pipe and the hole in the master cylinder to prevent the escape of the fluid. Remember that the fluid is corrosive and will have a detrimental effect on paintwork. If you should spill any fluid wipe it up immediately (photo).
3  Remove the two bolts, spring washers and plain washers securing the master cylinder to the scuttle/pedal assembly.
4  The master cylinder can now be withdrawn.
5  Refitting is the reverse of the removal procedure, but the following points should be noted.
6  Check the brake pedal setting as described in Chapter 9.
7  Unscrew the upper and lower stop bolts for the clutch pedal.
8  Refit the master cylinder to the bulkhead and refit the pivot bolt but do not tighten it.
9  Set the clutch pedal to the same level as the brake pedal. This is achieved by rotating the pivot bolt with its integral cam.
10  Tighten the pivot bolt and nut.
11  Adjust the upper stop bolt by screwing it until it is just touching

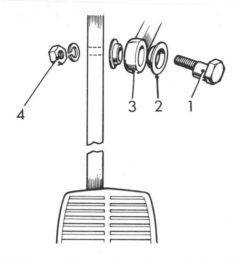

**Fig. 5.1 Master cylinder pushrod-to-pedal linkage (Sec 3)**

| 1 | Pivot bolt | 3 | Pushrod |
|---|------------|---|---------|
| 2 | Bush       | 4 | Nut     |

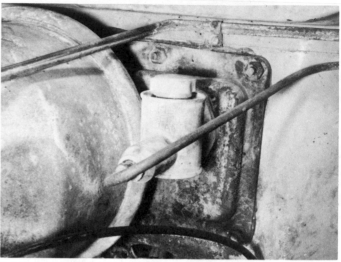

3.2 The clutch fluid pipe is attached to the front of the unit

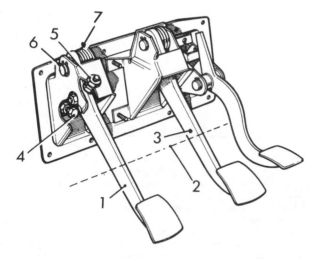

**Fig. 5.2 Clutch pedal adjustment (Sec 3)**

| 1 | Clutch pedal | 5 | Upper stop bolt |
|---|--------------|---|-----------------|
| 2 | Clutch and brake pedal alignment | 6 | Pedal spindle and circlip |
| 3 | Brake pedal | 7 | Clutch pedal return spring |
| 4 | Lower stop bolt | | |

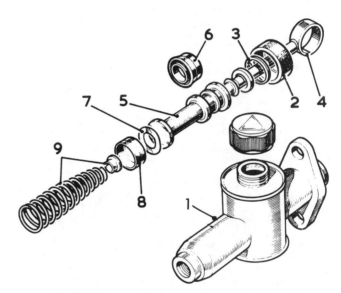

**Fig. 5.3 Master cylinder – exploded view (Sec 4)**

| 1 | Body and reservoir | 6 | Piston seal |
|---|--------------------|---|-------------|
| 2 | Rubber boot | 7 | Piston washer |
| 3 | Circlip | 8 | Main seal |
| 4 | Pushrod | 9 | Spring and seat |
| 5 | Piston | | |

the pedal arm, then continue another $\frac{1}{2}$ turn.

12  Depress the clutch pedal fully, and then adjust the lower stop bolt. This time continue for a full turn after touching the pedal. The lower stop bolt should protrude from the pedal box by a distance of 1.75 to 2.00 in (45 to 50 mm).

13  Refill the hydraulic system and bleed it as described in Section 8.

### 4  Master cylinder – overhaul

1  Remove the master cylinder as described in the previous Section.

2  Unscrew the reservoir cap and drain out the fluid.

3  Refer to Fig. 5.3, slide the rubber boot off the master cylinder and ease it down the pushrod.

4  From the pushrod end of the master cylinder extract the circlip retaining the pushrod.

5  Withdraw the pushrod assembly. The rubber boot can now be removed from the inner end of the pushrod.

6  Invert the master cylinder and bump the pushrod end into the palm of your hand to dislodge the piston assembly, or alternatively

apply air supplied from a tyre foot pump to the outlet port.

7  Remove the piston seal.

8  Withdraw the piston washer.

9  Remove the main seal using a low pressure air jet.

10  Invert the master cylinder and tip out the spring and seat.

11  Discard all the old seals as they must not be used again.

12  Examine all the components for scores or 'bright' wear areas and if evident, renew the complete master cylinder. Wash all components in methylated spirit or clean hydraulic fluid.

13  If the master cylinder is serviceable, obtain a repair kit which includes new seals and other components.

14  Use Castrol Girling rubber grease to coat the new seals. The remaining parts should be smeared with Castrol Girling Brake and Clutch fluid.

15  Reassembly is the reverse procedure to removal. Note that care must be taken to ensure that the main seal lip does not fold over when inserted into the cylinder bore.

16  The convex face of the piston washer faces the piston.

17  Fill the rubber boot with rubber grease before refitting it to the end

of the master cylinder.

18 Having rechecked that all the operations have been correctly carried out and there are no components left on the workbench, the unit can now be refitted to the car.

## 5 Slave cylinder – removal and refitting

1 Unscrew the clutch master cylinder reservoir cap and place a thin sheet of polythene over the reservoir then refit the cap. This measure prevents the fluid syphoning out when the slave cylinder is removed.
2 Raise the car and support it securely.
3 Clean the external surface of the slave cylinder, especially in the region of the fluid pipe and union nut.
4 Undo the union nut, pull aside the fluid pipe and plug the end.
5 Remove the two bolts and spring washers securing the slave cylinder to the bellhousing (photo).
6 Withdraw the slave cylinder and pushrod (photo).
7 Fully extend the pushrod before refitting the unit.
8 Apply gasket jointing compound to the slave cylinder and bellhousing mating surfaces.
9 Position the plate (if fitted) and locate the end of the pushrod into the release arm seat.
10 Make sure that the bleed nipple is located above the fluid pipe union nut as it is possible to install the slave cylinder in an upside-down position.
11 After refitting it will be necessary to bleed the clutch hydraulic system as described in Section 8.

## 6 Slave cylinder – overhaul

1 Remove the slave cylinder as detailed in Section 5.
2 Clean the exterior of the unit, prior to dismantling, using clean brake fluid or methylated spirit.
3 Obtain the necessary servicing kit of spares which will include the required seal and dust cover. In the case of a high mileage vehicle, the piston return spring should also be renewed.
4 Remove the dust cover from the end of the pushrod.
5 Remove the circlip from the cylinder bore and remove the piston and seal from the cylinder.
6 Withdraw the spring and seat.
7 Unscrew the bleed valve from the cylinder.
8 Clean all the components in methylated spirit or clean brake and clutch fluid, then allow them to dry.
9 Examine the cylinder bore for wear or ridging. Renew the cylinder complete if evident.
10 All seals must be discarded and new ones used.
11 When reassembling, lubricate all the seals using rubber grease, and lubricate all the other components using brake and clutch fluid.
12 Fit a new seal, flat side first, to the piston.
13 Fit the smaller end of the spring into the seat and assemble it to the piston.
14 Offer the complete assembly to the cylinder bore, spring first.

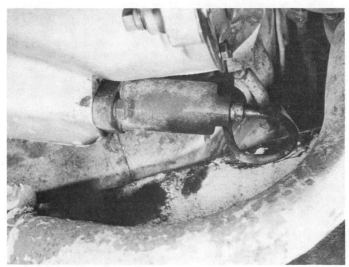

5.5 The clutch slave cylinder in position (viewed from beneath)

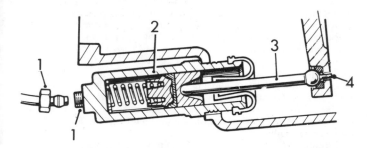

**Fig. 5.4 Slave cylinder installation (Sec 5)**

| | | |
|---|---|---|
| 1 | Hydraulic pipe and union | 3 Pushrod |
| 2 | Slave cylinder | 4 Release arm seat |

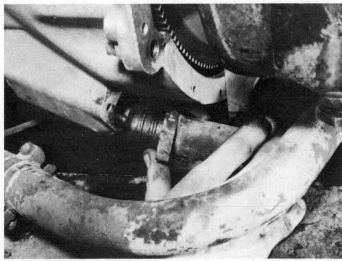

5.6 Withdrawing the slave cylinder (viewed from beneath)

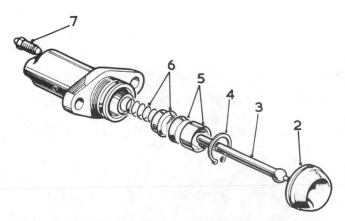

**Fig. 5.5 Slave cylinder – exploded view (Sec 6)**

| | | |
|---|---|---|
| 2 | Dust cover | 5 Piston and seal |
| 3 | Pushrod | 6 Spring and seat |
| 4 | Circlip | 7 Bleed nipple |

Make sure that the seal lip does not fall back.

15  Secure the assembly in position with the circlip.

16  Fill the dust cover with rubber grease before refitting it to the end of the slave cylinder.

17  Refit the pushrod and then refit the cylinder to the car as described in Section 5.

## 7  Clutch pedal assembly – removal and refitting

1  Remove the lower facia panel from inside the cab.

2  Undo the pivot nut and bolt and withdraw the bushes which connect the clutch master cylinder pushrod to the pedal arm.

3  Remove the right-hand pedal spindle circlip and push out the spindle. Reclaim the return spring.

4  Remove the pedal.

5  Refit in the reverse order. Refer to Section 3 for aligning and setting the clutch pedal.

## 8  Bleeding the hydraulic system

*Whenever the clutch hydraulic system has been overhauled, a part is renewed, or the level in the reservoir is too low, air will have entered the system necessitating its bleeding. During this operation the level of hydraulic fluid in the reservoir should not be allowed to fall below half full, otherwise air will be drawn in again.*

1  Obtain a clean, dry, glass jar, a length of plastic or rubber tubing which will fit the bleed nipple of the clutch slave cylinder and which is about 12 in (300 mm) long, a supply of the correct type of fluid and the services of an assistant.

2  Check that the master cylinder reservoir is full and, if not, fill it to within $\frac{1}{4}$ in (6.5 mm) of the top. Also add about one inch of fluid to the jar.

3  Remove the rubber dust cap from the slave cylinder bleed nipple, wipe the nipple clean then attach the bleed tube.

4  With the other end of the tube immersed in the fluid in the jar and the assistant ready inside the car, unscrew the bleed nipple one full turn.

5  The assistant should now pump the clutch pedal up and down until the air bubbles cease to emerge from the end of the tubing. Tighten the bleed nipple at the end of each downstroke. Check the reservoir frequently to ensure that the hydraulic fluid does not drop too far, so letting air into the system.

6  When no more air bubbles appear, tighten the bleed nipple at the bottom of a downstroke.

7  Fit the rubber dust cap over the bleed nipple.

8  If a one-man bleeding kit is available, refer to Chapter 9 for details of its use.

9  Discard hydraulic fluid from the system as it is likely to be contaminated and unfit for re-use.

## 9  Clutch – removal, inspection and refitting

1  Remove the engine, as described in Chapter 1, unless the gearbox is to be removed anyway, in which case the clutch can be removed once the gearbox has been withdrawn. There is no easy way to tackle the task of clutch renewal with the Range Rover.

2  The clutch cover is secured to the flywheel by a peripheral ring of bolts. Mark the position of the clutch cover in relation to the flywheel.

3  Unscrew the securing bolts evenly, a turn at a time in diametrically opposite sequence, to avoid distortion. The three bolts located in the deep recesses of the cover should not be disturbed.

4  When the bolts are finally removed, withdraw the pressure plate assembly from the flywheel and catch the driven plate as it is released from the face of the flywheel. Note which way round the plate is fitted.

5  The pressure plate assembly should not be dismantled but if worn, cracked or distorted, it should be renewed on an exchange basis.

6  Examine the driven plate for wear. If the linings are worn almost down to the rivets then a factory reconditioned unit should be obtained on an exchange basis – do not waste your time trying to reline the plate, it seldom proves satisfactory.

7  If there is evidence of oil staining, find and rectify the cause which will probably be a faulty gearbox input shaft oil seal or a crankshaft rear oil seal.

8  Check the machined surfaces of the flywheel and pressure plate; if grooved or scored then the flywheel should be machined (within the specified limits – see Chapter 1), and the pressure plate assembly renewed.

9  Check the release bearing for smooth operation. There should be no harshness or slackness in it and it should spin reasonably freely bearing in mind that it is grease sealed (Refer to next Section). Renew the release bearing as a matter of course at time of major overhaul.

10  It is important that no oil or grease gets on the clutch plate friction linings of the pressure plate and flywheel. It is advisable to refit the clutch with clean hands and to wipe down the pressure plate and the flywheel faces with a clean rag before assembly begins.

11  Place the clutch plate against the flywheel, ensuring that it is the correct way round. The flywheel side of the driven plate is marked accordingly (photos).

12  Refit the clutch cover assembly loosely on the dowels. Refit the six bolts and spring washers and tighten them finger tight so that the clutch plate is gripped but can still be moved. The clutch disc must now be centralised so that the engine and gearbox are mated, the gearbox input shaft splines will pass through the splines in the centre of the driven plate (photo).

13  Centralisation can be carried out quite easily by inserting a round bar or long screwdriver through the hole in the centre of the clutch, so that the end of the bar rests in the small hole in the end of the crankshaft containing the spigot bush. Ideally a mandrel should be used.

14  Using the input shaft spigot bush as a fulcrum, moving the tool sideways or up and down will move the clutch disc in whichever direction is necessary to achieve centralisation.

15  Centralisation is easily judged by removing the tool and viewing the driven plate hub in relation to the hole in the centre of the clutch cover plate diaphragm spring. When the hub appears exactly in the centre of the hole, all is correct.

16  Tighten the clutch bolts firmly in a diagonal sequence to ensure that the cover plate is pulled down evenly and without distortion of the flange. Finally tighten the bolts to the recommended torque setting (photo).

9.11a Ensure that the driven plate markings are the right way round

9.11b Using a mandrel, the driven plate can be located easily

9.12 Refitting the clutch cover plate with centralising tool in position

9.16 Tightening the clutch cover bolts

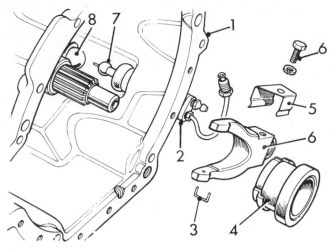

**Fig. 5.6 Clutch release mechanism components (Sec 10)**

1   Bellhousing
2   Slave cylinder
3   Staple
4   Release bearing and sleeve
5   Spring clip

6   Clip retaining bolt
7   Slave cylinder pushrod
    end
8   Pivot post

10.4 Withdrawing the staple

## 10  Clutch release mechanism – removal and refitting

1   The clutch release mechanism, which is operated by the slave cylinder and pushrod, consists of the release arm and pivot and the release bearing and sleeve assembly (Fig. 5.6).

2   Should the fault diagnosis indicates that the release bearing needs renewal then the engine or gearbox will have to be removed first. The easiest task is to remove the engine, unless the gearbox is being removed anyway.

3   With the engine removed as described in Chapter 1 work can proceed.

4   Withdraw the staple which links the release bearing sleeve to the release arm (photo).

5   Withdraw the bearing and sleeve assembly from the input shaft (photo).

6   Remove the spring clip retaining bolt and then remove the clip (photo).

7   The release arm can now be slid off the pivot post (photo).

8   Inspect the bearing and sleeve. The bearing should rotate smoothly. It is packed with grease and sealed for life. Renew the

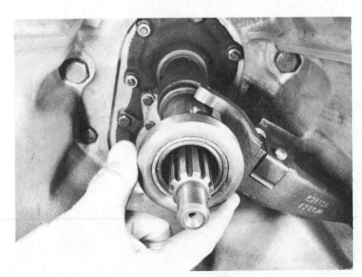

10.5 Withdrawing the release bearing and sleeve

10.6 Undo the bolt

10.7 Withdrawing the release arm

assembly if necessary. If in doubt, consider the work which will be entailed if the bearing fails in a relatively short time.
9   Grease the pivot post bolt and refit the release arm. Engage the pushrod into its seat at the outer end.
10 Refit the spring clip and secure it in position. The clip fits over the washer behind the pivot ball.
11 Lubricate the release bearing sleeve inner surface with a thin film

of molybdenum disulphide based grease and fit it to the front cover sleeve.
12 Line up the holes in the release arm and sleeve and refit the staple.
13 Check that the release bearing and sleeve slide smoothly on the input shaft assembly.
14 Refit the engine or transmission to the vehicle as applicable.

## 11  Fault diagnosis – clutch

| Symptom | Reason(s) |
| --- | --- |
| Judder when taking up drive | Loose engine mountings<br>Worn or oil-contaminated driven plate friction linings<br>Worn splines on driven plate hub or first input (primary) shaft<br>Worn crankshaft spigot bush (pilot bearing) |
| Clutch slip | Damaged or distorted pressure plate assembly<br>Driven plate linings worn or oil-contaminated |
| Noise on depressing clutch pedal | Dry, worn or damaged clutch release bearing<br>Excessive play in input (primary) shaft splines |
| Noise as clutch pedal is released | Distorted driven plate<br>Broken or weak driven plate hub cushion coil springs<br>Distorted or worn input (primary) shaft<br>Release bearing loose |
| Difficulty in disengaging clutch for gearchange | Fault in master cylinder or slave cylinder<br>Air in hydraulic system<br>Driven plate hub splines rusted on shaft |

# Chapter 6 Transmission

*For modifications, and information applicable to later models, see Supplement at end of manual*

## Contents

## Specifications

### Main gearbox
Type ................................................................................................ Four forward speeds and one reverse with synchromesh on all forward gears

Ratios:
4th .................................................................................................. 1.00 to 1
3rd .................................................................................................. 1.50 to 1
2nd .................................................................................................. 2.44 to 1
1st ................................................................................................... 4.06 to 1
Reverse ........................................................................................... 3.66 to 1

### Transfer gearbox
Type ................................................................................................ 2-speed on main gearbox output (high or low ratio)

| | Early models | Later models |
|---|---|---|
| Ratios: | | |
| High | 1.174 to 1 | 1.113 to 1 |
| Low | 3.321 to 1 | 3.321 to 1 |

### Overall ratios

| | High Transfer | | Low Transfer |
|---|---|---|---|
| | Early models | Later models | |
| 4th | 4.16 to 1 | 3.94 to 1 | 11.76 to 1 |
| 3rd | 6.25 to 1 | 5.93 to 1 | 17.69 to 1 |
| 2nd | 10.17 to 1 | 9.64 to 1 | 28.78 to 1 |
| 1st | 16.91 to 1 | 16.03 to 1 | 47.83 to 1 |
| Reverse | 15.23 to 1 | 14.43 to 1 | 43.07 to 1 |

### Oil capacities
Main gearbox .................................................................................. 4.5 Imp pints (5.5 US pints) (2.6 litres)
Transfer gearbox ............................................................................ 5.5 Imp pints (6.5 US pints (3.1 litres)

### Main gearbox tolerances
Primary pinion endfloat (maximum) ............................................... 0.002 in (0.05 mm)
Layshaft rolling resistance ............................................................. 6.0 to 8.5 lb (3.0 to 3.8 kg)
Transfer gear endfloat (maximum) ................................................. 0.002 in (0.05 mm)
Mainshaft transfer gear endfloat (maximum) ................................ 0.002 in (0.05 mm)
Mainshaft gears endfloat ................................................................ 0.001 to 0.006 in (0.025 to 0.150 mm)

### Transfer gear tolerances
Selectors clearance ........................................................................ 0.010 in (0.25 mm)
Intermediate gears endfloat ........................................................... 0.006 to 0.009 in (0.15 to 0.23 mm)

## Torque wrench settings

|  | lbf ft | kgf m |
| --- | --- | --- |
| Main gear lever securing bolts | 11 | 1.5 |
| Output flange nut (front) | 85 | 11.7 |
| Output flange nut (rear) | 85 | 11.7 |
| Gearbox case-to-bellhousing studs/bolts: |  |  |
| Large diameter | 120 | 16.6 |
| Small diameter | 70 | 9.6 |
| Reversing light switch | 15 to 20 | 1.4 to 2.0 |

### 1  General description

The Range Rover transmission gives four forward speeds and one reverse in either high or low ratio gearing, thus giving a total selection of eight forward and two reverse speeds. Where the situation demands it, the two ranges can be used progressively when changing up.

The transmission unit houses three main assemblies, these being the main gears, the intermediate gears and the transfer gears. The main gearbox section provides the normal road use gears which are fitted with synchromesh units. The rear end of the mainshaft carries a transfer gear which is meshed with the intermediate transfer gears, which are in turn meshed with the output shaft differential gears.

The differential unit enables the vehicle to have a permanent four-wheel drive and prevents the possibility of transmission 'wind-up' under certain conditions. The differential can be locked to provide a positive four-wheel drive motion whereby all roadwheels rotate at the same speed. This is only normally used to provide the maximum traction when operating in severe conditions. The differential is locked by means of a switch mounted on the floor next to the main gear lever. The differential lock can only be operated when the engine is running and should only be engaged when the vehicle is being driven in the straight-ahead position, or the differential unit could suffer damage.

The gear assemblies and shafts run in ball or roller bearings, and the endthrusts are adjusted by means of shim washers which are available in varying thicknesses to suit.

The main gearbox and transfer gearbox each have their own oil supply and are therefore individually drained and topped up as and when necessary.

The main gearbox components are lubricated by means of a gear-driven oil pump attached to the front of the unit within the clutch bellhousing. The oil pump drive is direct from the end of the layshaft. The transfer gearbox components are splash fed with lubricant.

Although an overdrive unit has been available as an optional fitting to the Range Rover since 1978, at the time of writing no maintenance or overhaul procedures are available and this is not therefore included.

### 2  Transmission removal – special notes

1   As the transmission unit is removed upwards through the interior of the vehicle, the seats, flooring and heater unit must be removed to allow access and clearance for lifting the unit out.

2   Although no special Rover tools or equipment are required to perform the removal, you will need to have a suitable mobile hoist and this is most probably available from a tool hire dealer.

3   The removal and refitting procedures are more time-consuming than difficult, and therefore plenty of time should be allowed when starting. The aid of an assistant will not only help to speed things up but is almost essential during the actual removal and refitting procedures.

4   Some items of the transmission can be withdrawn without having to completely remove the transmission and these are mainly in the transfer gearbox. If a fault is suspected to be in the transfer gearbox, refer to Section 11, which lists those items which can be removed with the transmission in position.

### 3  Transmission – removal and refitting

1   Raise and support the bonnet and then disconnect the battery earth lead.

2   Remove the front seats and floor panel as described in Chapter 12 (photo).

3   Position a suitable container of sufficient capacity under the gearbox drain plugs and drain the oils from the gearboxes.

4   Unbolt and detach the front propeller shaft universal joint at the gearbox drive flange. Mark the shaft mating flanges for correct realignment on assembly.

5   Unbolt and detach the rear propeller shaft joint in a similar manner.

6   Disconnect the two wires at the reversing light switch, noting their respective positions (photo).

7   Disconnect the differential lock actuator wires, noting their respective positions. Also detach the handbrake warning light switch wire. Early models have only one wire to the differential lock actuator.

8   Undo the right-hand front bolt from the gearbox top cover and detach the cable bracket.

9   Detach the speedometer cable retaining clips, one on the left-hand chassis and one on the rear end of the gearbox. Withdraw the cable from the gearbox (photo).

10   Undo the exhaust pipe clamp mounting bolt and detach the

3.2 General view of transmission with vehicle seats and floor panels removed

3.6 Detach the reversing light switch wires

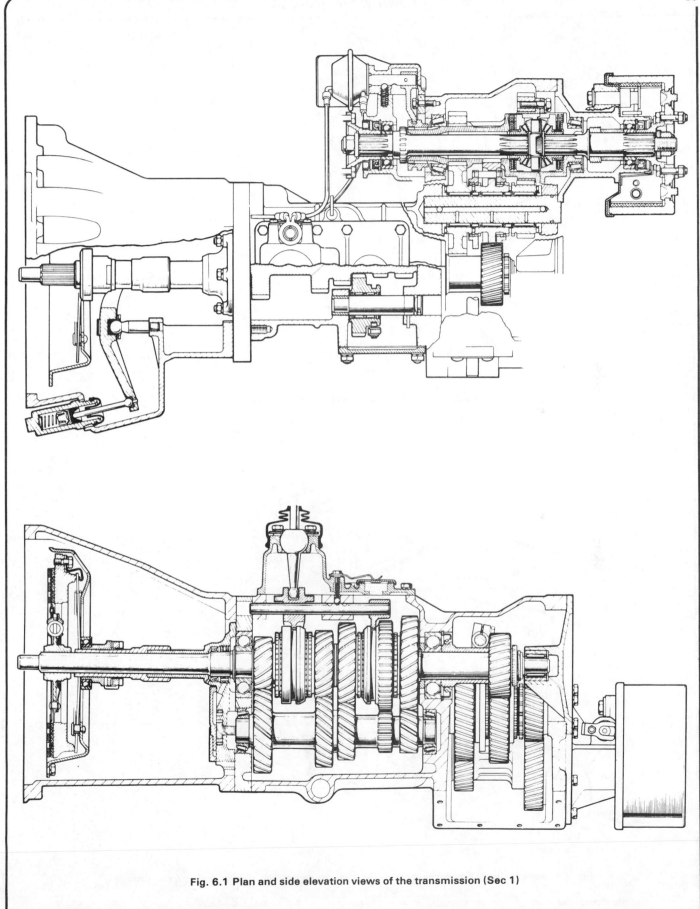

Fig. 6.1 Plan and side elevation views of the transmission (Sec 1)

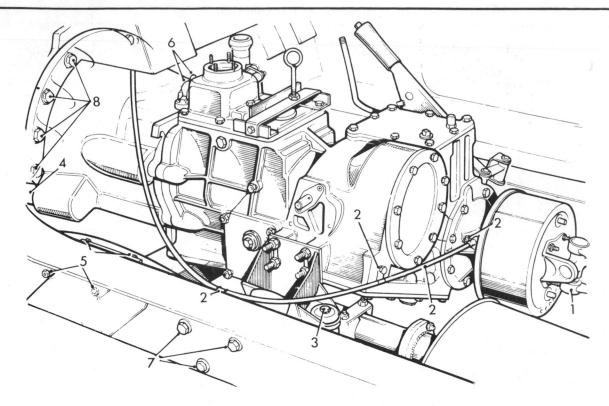

**Fig. 6.2 Items to be disconnected – left side (Sec 3)**

1   Rear propeller shaft
2   Speedometer cable and
    location clips

3   Exhaust mounting
4   Clutch slave cylinder

5   Crossmember-to-chassis
    side-member bolts
6   Reversing light switch
    wires

7   Mounting bolts
8   Bellhousing bolts

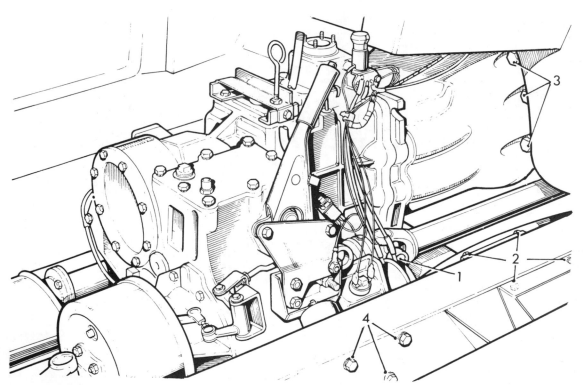

**Fig. 6.3 Items to be disconnected – right side. Note lifting bracket and eye on top cover (Sec 3)**

1   Front propeller shaft

2   Crossmember-to-chassis
    side-member bolts

3   Bellhousing bolts

4   Mounting bolts

3.9 Disconnect the speedometer cable

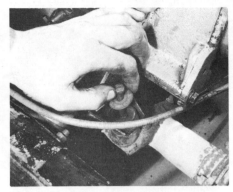
3.10 Remove the exhaust pipe clamp bolt

3.11 Remove the left-hand mounting bolts and bracket nut

3.13 Remove the bellhousing cover plate underneath

3.16 Lifting sling in position

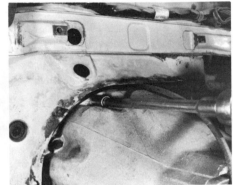
3.18 Remove the bellhousing-to-engine bolts

mounting bracket, noting the rubber bushes. If the bushes are worn, damaged or perished they must be renewed on assembly (photo).

11 Support the gearbox with a jack and then undo and remove the three left-hand mounting bolts (photo).

12 Undo and remove the right-hand mounting bolts and nuts of which there are also three, mounted through the chassis.

13 Working underneath the vehicle, remove the bellhousing cover plate and stiffening plate (photo).

14 Disconnect the clutch hydraulic hose at the slave cylinder. Plug the end of the hose to prevent leakage and dirt ingress.

15 Position a jack under the engine and raise to support it.

16 To lift the gearbox out, either arrange a lifting sling around it (photo) or fabricate a lift bracket similar to that shown in Figs. 6.2 and 6.3, attached to the top cover.

17 Insert the jib of the hoist through the passenger side doorway. (If working from the driver's side, the steering wheel must be removed before lifting the gearbox out).

18 With the hoist attached to the sling or lifting bracket eye, raise to support the gearbox and then remove the gearbox bellhousing-to-engine retaining bolts (photo).

19 Check that all gearbox attachments are disconnected, then carefully pull the gearbox rearwards to disengage it from the engine. When the primary (input) shaft is clear of the clutch unit, lift the gearbox, pushing the front end down in order that the bellhousing can clear the bulkhead and crossmember. Assist by lifting at the rear end. An assistant will be required during this operation to ensure that the gearbox is manouevred as required and to avoid it damaging the surrounding fittings.

20 Once clear of its location aperture, level the gearbox and carefully withdraw it through the side doorway. Transport it to the work area.

21 Refitting the transmission unit is a reversal of the removal sequence. In order to engage the primary pinion with the clutch splines it will probably be necessary to select a gear and then turn the transmission brake drum whilst pushing on the rear face of the gearbox. When the splines are in alignment the gearbox will slide forwards over the shafts.

22 Smear the vertical joint face of the bellhousing cover plate with jointing compound before fitting. The cover plate and seal fillet must also be fitted with sealing compound.

23 After refitting, check that all fastenings are tightened to the specified torque wrench settings and then top up the gearbox and transfer box oil levels.

## 4  Transmission dismantling – special notes

1  When viewed as a complete assembly, the transmission may appear to be a rather complex mechanism. However, providing the three basic units are dealt with separately as described, the DIY mechanic with a well equipped workshop, and a reasonable engineering knowledge, should not experience any major problems in overhauling part, or all of the transmission assembly.

2  Before deciding to dismantle the transmission, an assessment should be made of the possible cause of the fault in question that has necessitated its removal. Removal of the top cover, end cover, side and bottom covers will enable you to make an initial inspection of the various sub-assemblies and you will then be able to assess the extent of any damage or wear that has occurred. If there is major damage or extensive wear in all components, serious consideration should be given to getting a replacement transmission unit complete, as the cost of individual parts, not to mention your time, could well be prohibitive. If you choose to dismantle the transmission, you will require a bearing puller, circlip pliers and a selection of tube drifts apart from your normal workshop tools.

## 5  Gearbox (main) – dismantling

### Clutch bellhousing and bearing endplate

1  Extract the clutch release sleeve and release lever locating staple and then withdraw the sleeve and bearing assembly.

2  Unscrew and remove the bellhousing retaining nuts and bolts from within the housing using a suitable socket and extension (photo).

3  The bellhousing can now be detached from the gearbox front face. Support the gearbox and withdraw the bellhousing complete with the

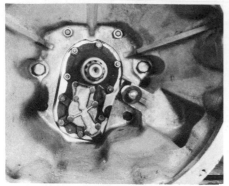

5.2 The bellhousing retaining nuts and bolts

5.4a Withdraw the oil pump cover ...

5.4b ... and drivegear

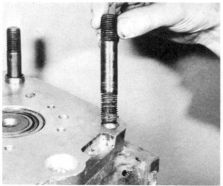

5.5 Remove the bellhousing studs

5.11 Remove the detent springs and balls

5.13a Remove the selector fork shafts ...

5.13b ... and selector forks

5.15 The reverse gear engagement lever pivot bolt, showing lockwire to cover bolt

release lever. If necessary, lightly tap the housing to ease it from the location dowels in the gearbox front face using a soft-headed mallet.

4    Position and support the gearbox on its tail end. Unbolt and remove the oil pump cover and gasket from the front face of the bearing plate. Withdraw the pump drivegear (photos).

5    Use a stud extractor or lock two nuts together on each of the bellhousing studs in turn and unscrew them from the gearbox (photo).

6    The bearing plate assembly can now be lifted from the gearbox and the two locating dowels extracted.

7    Separate the layshaft from the bearing plate and remove the gasket from the flange face.

8    The front cover can be removed from the bearing plate by unscrewing the retaining nuts and then withdrawing the cover and oil pump assembly. As it is removed, recover the shim washer which is located between the cover and the layshaft front bearing.

## Selector mechanism

9    Unscrew and remove the reversing light switch from its location in front of the top cover. Note and retain the shim washers under the switch.

10 Select neutral and then unbolt and remove the top cover retaining bolts. Lift clear the cover and remote its gasket.

11 Extract the three detent springs and balls from the central bridge piece. Use a magnetic rod or a suitable rod with grease applied to its end to withdraw the balls (photo).

12 To disengage the selector shafts from the selectors, use a suitable pin punch and drive out the location pins from the selectors. On later models the selector shafts and selectors are secured by means of clamp bolts which are unscrewed and removed to release them.

13 Drive out each selector shaft in turn and withdraw the selector jaws and forks, noting their respective locations (photos).

14 Extract the interlock plungers from the cross drilling by removing the bolt in the side of the housing and tilting the gearbox to allow the plungers to slide out.

15 Snip the lockwire free and remove the reverse gear engagement lever pivot bolt from the side of the casing. Withdraw the reverse gear selector lever (photo).

## Mainshaft

16 Next to be removed is the mainshaft assembly. Unbolt and remove the rear bearing housing and gasket and withdraw the needle roller bearing nut (Fig. 6.4).

17 Unbolt and detach the bottom cover from the transfer gearbox.

18 From the rear end of the mainshaft, prise free the snap-ring and withdraw the shim washer and transfer gear (photo).

19 The use of a suitable puller, or if available special extractor RO.1004 is now required to withdraw the spacer along the mainshaft to the point where the spacer large diameter is aligned with the transfer gear lever cross-shaft. The mainshaft should be driven forward as the spacer is withdrawn.

20 The mainshaft can now be removed but as it is withdrawn, leave 1st speed gear in position so that it does not foul the casing. When the mainshaft is removed the 1st gear can be lifted out and refitted to the mainshaft.

21 Also refit the scalloped thrust washer, needle bearing unit and stepped thrust washer (with the step face outwards).

22 Extract the mainshaft spacer.

## Reverse idler gear and shaft

23 Unscrew and remove the four retaining bolts and withdraw the side cover. Note the lockwire attached to one of the bolts, which locks the reverse idler gear lever pivot bolt.

24 If not already removed, unbolt and detach the gearbox bottom cover.

25 Before removing the idler gear shaft retaining pin on the earlier models, fit a short length of rod to the retaining pin to prevent it from collapsing when being removed. Later models are fitted with a bolt.

26 Extract the retaining pin or undo the bolt, as applicable.

27 Using the extractor thread, withdraw the idler gear shaft, by inserting a suitable bolt into the end of the shaft and then clamping a self-grip wrench onto the bolt head to enable the shaft to be pulled free (photo).

28 Prise free and remove the O-ring from its groove in the shaft.

29 Lift the reverse idler gear unit from the gearbox. To extract the needle roller bearings from the gear, extract the snap-ring and plain washer. On removing the bearings note that there is a further plain washer which abuts against the inner snap-ring (Fig. 6.5).

30 The shaft support bush in the gearbox can be removed but will not normally have worn to any extent to necessitate this.

## Primary pinion (input shaft)

31 To remove the input shaft from the front bearing plate, expand and remove the circlip and withdraw the shim washer.

32 Press or drift out the primary pinion (input shaft), ensuring that the gearbox is suitably supported.

33 The bearing can be removed only after the retaining plates have been withdrawn. The plates are retained in position by their studs which in turn are located in the place by serrated sections. Drift the bolts and plates out and withdraw from their location holes, then press or drift out the ball-bearing (photo).

## Layshaft bearings

34 The layshaft gear unit is supported by and runs in taper roller

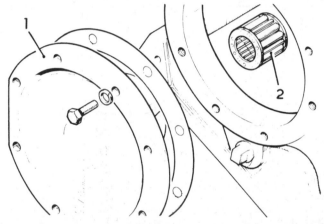

**Fig. 6.4 Remove the bearing housing (1), gasket and roller bearing (2) (Sec 5)**

5.18 Remove the transfer gear

5.27 Idler gear shaft removal method

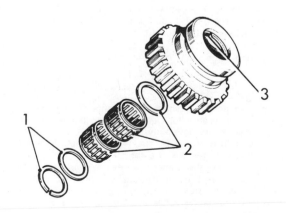

**Fig. 6.5 Reverse idler gear assembly (Sec 5)**

| | |
|---|---|
| 1   Snap-ring and washer | 3   Inner snap-ring |
| 2   Bearings and inner washer | |

5.33 Remove the bearing retaining plates

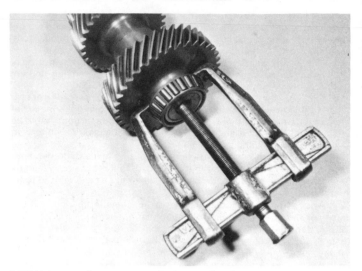

5.35 Using a puller to remove the laygear bearing cones

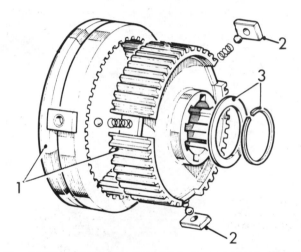

**Fig. 6.6 The 3rd/4th synchromesh hub components (Sec 5)**

1    *Synchro hubs – inner and outer*
2    *Sliding blocks and balls*
3    *Snap-ring and shim washer*

bearings at each end. The bearing cups can be pressed or driven from their housings in the gearbox and front plate using suitable diameter tube drifts, but ensure that the front plate and gearbox are suitably supported during removal.
35  The bearing cones can be removed using a suitable puller as shown (photo).

*Mainshaft gears*
36  As the respective mainshaft components are removed, lay them out in order of appearance for cleaning and inspection. Keeping them in order will reduce the possibility of confusion on assembly.
37  Start by withdrawing the 1st speed gear, thrust washers and roller bearings from the rear end of the shaft.
38  At the front end of the shaft, prise free the snap-ring, withdraw the shim washer and then the 3rd/4th gear synchromesh hub unit.
39  Now remove the 3rd and 2nd speed gears together with their thrust washers and needle roller bearings (keeping them in order of fitting).
40  Extract the oil seal from its location in the mainshaft front end.
41  To dismantle the 3rd/4th gear and 1st/2nd gear synchromesh unit, compress the sliding blocks to release the synchromesh balls from the outer hub groove. As the assembly is separated, cup it with the hands or wrap it in a cloth to prevent the balls and sliding blocks flying apart under spring pressure.

42  With the respective gearbox components removed, they can be cleaned and laid out for careful inspection as given in the following Section.

## 6   Gearbox (main) – inspection of components

1    Examine the mainshaft and the respective gears for signs of excessive wear and/or damage. Unless the gears are very badly worn or possibly damaged, it is not advisable to renew them, as, apart from the cost factor, meshing new mainshaft gears with worn layshaft gears usually gives a very noisy operation when engaged.
2    Examine the synchromesh units for wear and damage. The synchro cones are the most likely items to be worn and unless they are known to be fairly new they should be renewed. Where the vehicle is known to have covered a high mileage, renew the synchromesh hub assemblies complete.
3    Examine all bearings for signs of wear and if suspect renew as necessary.
4    Inspect the various selector components and renew any found to be excessively worn or damaged.
5    All oil seals and gaskets must always be renewed on reassembly. Check that all traces of the old gaskets are removed from the mating flanges and that the respective mating surfaces of the gearbox and associated covers etc are perfectly clean.
6    Thoroughly clean the oil pump components and inspect for wear. Again, if a high mileage has been covered this is best renewed as a unit. To renew the oil seal housed in the front cover, refer to Section 9.
7    If the transfer gearbox components are also being removed and overhauled, keep the major assemblies separate during inspection and list the replacement items separately to avoid confusion. For general information concerning the transfer gearbox refer to Section 11.
8    Having compiled your list of requirements, you will also need to have the gearbox type (early or late) identity number to ensure getting the correct replacements. The gearbox number is stamped into the casing in one of two places, depending on whether it is an early or later type gearbox (Fig. 6.7).
9    Note that any bearings and thrust washers should not be degreased prior to assembly.

## 7   Gearbox (main) – reassembly

*Mainshaft – reassembly*
1    First insert the oil seal into its housing in the end of the mainshaft (photo).
2    Reassemble the 1st/2nd gear synchromesh hub assembly by inserting the detent balls with springs and blocks (rounded sides facing outwards) and slide the outer gear onto the hub with the groove

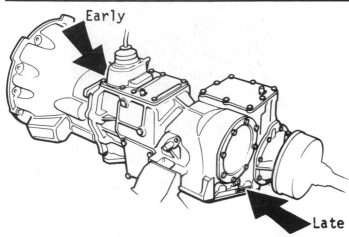

Fig. 6.7 The early and late gearbox identification number locations (Sec 6)

towards the front of the shaft. This is best achieved by standing the shaft on end and with the aid of an assistant, holding the balls and springs in position whilst sliding the sleeve upwards to engage over the detent assemblies. Slide the sleeve up until the balls locate in the groove in the outer gear unit (photos).

3    Locate the synchromesh cone against the hub assembly (photo).
4    Slide the chamfered thrust washer (chamfer to rear), needle thrust bearing and scalloped thrust washer into position (photo).
5    Lubricate the radial needle roller bearing and slide this onto the shaft, then fit 2nd gear as shown (photo).
6    Now slide the needle thrust bearing, with a scalloped thrust washer on each side, onto the shaft against 2nd gear (photo).
7    Lubricate and slide the radial needle bearing into position on the shaft, followed by the 3rd gear which is located on the bearing (photo).
8    Locate the needle roller bearing and scalloped thrust washers onto

the shaft against 3rd gear (photo).
9    Locate the synchromesh cone onto 3rd gear (photo).
10  Reassemble the 3rd/4th synchromesh hub in a similar manner to that described for the 1st/2nd synchro hub and then slide it into position on the shaft with the cone face rearwards (photo). The baulk ring lugs must be aligned with the hub grooves for full engagement.
11  The gear endfloat must now be checked. Locate a thrust washer into position against the synchromesh hub, then stand the mainshaft on end (with 3rd gear uppermost) and push down and rotate the gears to take up any slack. Insert the snap-ring into its shaft location groove as shown and insert a feeler gauge between the snap-ring and washer to determine the clearance (photo). Select a thrust washer of suitable thickness to give the correct clearance (endfloat) as given in the Specifications. Various washer thicknesses are available.
12  With the selected washer in position, locate the snap-ring into the groove on the shaft and recheck the endfloat (photo).
13  Although the synchromesh cone and roller bearing still have to be fitted to complete the assembly at the front end of the mainshaft (photo), their fitting is best left until later when they can be retained by engagement with the primary (input) shaft.
14  The remaining components can now be fitted to the rear end of the mainshaft. Start by sliding the chamfered thrust washer (chamfered face to front) onto the shaft, followed by the needle thrust bearing and scalloped washer (photo).
15  Locate the synchromesh cone as shown (photo), followed by the needle radial bearing, which must be lubricated, and 1st gear (photo).
16  Slide the scalloped washer, needle thrust bearing and stepped thrust washer into position on the shaft in that order. The stepped face of the outer washer faces away from the bearing (rearwards) (photo).
17  The spacer, transfer gear, shim washer and retaining snap-ring are fitted to the mainshaft later when fitting to the gearbox.

*Layshaft – preparation*

18  If the bearing cones have been removed from the layshaft, the new bearings must be pressed or drifted into position. It is then ready for fitment to the gearbox and for the bearing preload to be checked (photo).

7.1 Renew oil seals and gaskets. This is the mainshaft seal (arrowed)

7.2a Locate the detent balls, springs and blocks into position in the inner hub ...

7.2b ... compress them and slide the outer gear sleeve into position

7.3 Locate the synchromesh cone

7.4 Fit the needle thrust bearing and thrust washers

7.5 Fit 2nd gear onto radial bearing

7.6 Locate needle thrust bearing and thrust washers against 2nd gear

7.7 Fit 3rd gear and needle bearing

7.8 Locate needle thrust bearing and thrust washers against 3rd gear

7.9 Fit the synchromesh cone

7.10 Locate the 3rd/4th synchromesh hub

7.11 Check the gear endfloat to assess shim washer thickness requirement

7.12 Recheck the gear endfloat with selected washer and snap-ring fitted

7.13 Fit bearing and synchro cone to front end of mainshaft

7.14 Slide thrust washers and thrust bearing onto rear of shaft

7.15a Locate the synchromesh cone ...

7.15b ... followed by the radial bearing and 1st gear

7.16 Fit scalloped washer, thrust bearing and stepped thrust washer

7.18 The layshaft and bearings ready for fitment

7.20 The reverse idler gear with radial bearings fitted

7.22 The reverse idler gear-to-shaft orientation

7.23 Idler gear shaft retaining bolt in position

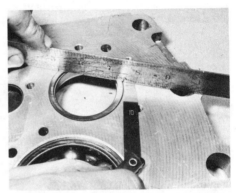

7.29 Layshaft bearing preload check method (front plate not fitted for clarity)

## Reverse idler gear – reassembly and refitting

19  If the idler shaft bush in the gearbox was removed, smear the new bush with locking compound before fitting. Press or drive the bush into position.

20  To refit the radial bearing assemblies into the reverse idler gear, first insert the inner circlip followed by a plain washer and the bearing assemblies. Locate the plain washer and outer circlip to secure (photo).

21  Lower the reverse idler gear into its location in the gearbox.

22  Fit the new O-ring seal into position on the shaft, lubricate the shaft and insert it through the end face of the gearbox, tapping it lightly through using a soft-headed mallet. The shaft is fitted with the O-ring end trailing. As it passes through, engage the idler gear in the direction shown (photo). Do not forget to engage the selector fork foot into its location in the idler gear groove during assembly.

23  Check that the retaining pin holes in the casing and shaft are aligned and then drive in a new retaining pin. On later models a bolt is fitted instead of the pin, in which case smear the bolt threads with thread locking compound before fitting and tightening (photo).

24  Lubricate the shaft and rotate the gear to ensure that it spins freely.

## Primary pinion, layshaft and front bearing plate – reassembly

25  Before fitting the primary (input) pinion unit to the endplate, the layshaft bearing preload must be checked.

26  If the layshaft bearings are being renewed, press or drive the respective bearing cups into their housings in the gearbox and bearing plate (ensuring that their housings are perfectly clean first). The bearing fitted to the gearbox can be fully inserted. The bearing fitted to the front plate should not be fully located at this stage, but only partially inserted into its housing. Lubricate the bearing.

27  If the primary pinion is in position in the plate this must be removed as given in Section 5, paragraphs 31 and 32.

28  Stand the gearbox on end and then lower the layshaft into position. Locate the new gasket onto the front face of the gearbox, followed by the bearing plate.

29  The layshaft front bearing cup should now be pressed towards its

Fig. 6.8 Check the layshaft rotational resistance (Sec 7)

bearing to take up any endfloat in the shaft and give no bearing end load. Now select a shim washer of suitable thickness to allow a 0.010 in (0.25 mm) protrusion measured from the washer outer face to the bearing plate front face. This can be measured using a feeler gauge and rule as shown (photo).

30  Leaving the shim washer in position, temporarily locate the oil pump top cover with a new gasket to the bearing plate and tighten the retaining nuts.

31  The rotational resistance of the layshaft must now be checked and this can be achieved by coiling a length of cord around the shaft and attaching the loose end to a spring balance as shown (Fig. 6.8). Pull the balance and measure the resistance required to turn the layshaft. It should be within the limits given in the Specifications. If a spring balance is not available, turn the shaft by hand to ensure that it does

not bind or have too much slack in its movement.

32  Should further adjustment be necessary, change the layshaft shim washer for one of a suitable thickness. With the bearing preload satisfactory, remove the oil pump cover and the front bearing plate and withdraw the layshaft unit.

33  The primary (input) pinion can now be fitted to the front plate.

34  If the pinion ball-bearing has been removed, this can be pressed or drifted into position in its housing so that it is fitted flush with the plate face. Before fitting, ensure that the oilway hole is clear.

35  Relocate the bearing retaining plates, pressing or driving them carefully into position whilst supporting the plate.

36  Press or drive the primary pinion into position (photo). The bearing will have to be supported underneath, or it will be pushed out of its housing in the endplate.

37  Slide a shim washer down the pinion shaft so that it is flush against the inner bearing race, then locate the circlip into its groove as shown (photo) and check the circlip-to-washer clearance using feeler gauges. Select a washer of the required thickness to give an endfloat within the specified limits.

38  Fit the selected washer into position and then fully locate the circlip to secure the primary pinion. Recheck the endfloat.

### Mainshaft – installation

39  The mainshaft can now be lowered into position in the gearbox (photo). If not already fitted, locate the 3rd gear synchromesh cone

and the radial roller bearing to the front end of the shaft. Lubricate the bearing. As the mainshaft is fitted, the 1st gear will have to be temporarily moved rearwards along the shaft so that it can be manoeuvred past the reverse idler gear. When the mainshaft is engaged into its bearing, mesh the 1st/2nd gear synchro outer gear with the reverse idler gear, press the mainshaft home and locate the spacer on its rear end (photo). The shouldered section of the spacer is fitted forwards (past the transfer gear lever cross-shaft).

40  Relocate 1st gear with the thrust washers and needle bearing, ensuring that they are correctly fitted against the gear.

41  Slide the spacer along the mainshaft and push it into the oil seal so that it is flush against the ball-bearing inner race. The oil seal lips should be lubricated prior to inserting the spacer to ease assembly and avoid distortion (Fig. 6.9).

42  Slide the transfer gear into position on the mainshaft and fit a thrust washer. Locate the snap-ring into its groove in the shaft and check the clearance between the washer and snap-ring using feeler gauges (photo). Select a thrust washer to give a transfer gear endfloat within the specified limits.

43  Having calculated the required washer thickness, remove the snap-ring, washer and transfer gear then pull the mainshaft spacer as far back as possible (to the gear lever cross-shaft) so that a thin coating of locking compound can be applied to the exposed section of mainshaft.

44  Push home the spacer, refit the transfer gear and the selected

7.36 Driving the primary pinion into position – note the protective block

7.37 Check the pinion endfloat

7.39a Locate the mainshaft assembly in the gearbox

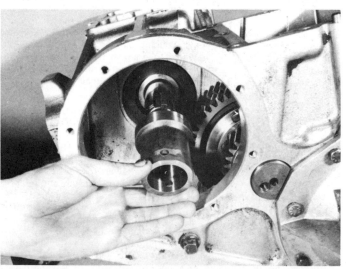

7.39b Fit the spacer onto the shaft rear end. If transfer selector lever cross-shaft is fitted, spacer must be fitted to shaft as it is fed through into housing

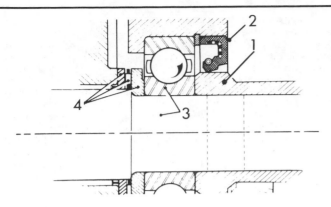

**Fig. 6.9 Sectional view of the mainshaft rear bearing assembly (Sec 7)**

| | | | |
|---|---|---|---|
| 1 | Spacer | 3 | Bearing |
| 2 | Seal | 4 | Thrust washers and needle bearing assembly |

thrust washer, and then engage the snap-ring into its groove in the shaft to secure.

### Primary pinion, layshaft and front bearing plate – refitting

45 Stand the gearbox on its rear face. If the speedometer drive housing is fitted, pack and support the base of the assembly to protect it during the following operations.
46 Smear the endplate gasket with grease and locate it in position on the gearbox front face (photo).
47 Engage the layshaft with the primary shaft as shown (photo), and carefully lower the combined endplate, primary shaft and layshaft assembly into position on the gearbox (photo). As the assembly is being lowered into position, the laygears and mainshaft gears will have to be re-meshed; this may require some patience.

48 With the bearing endplate in position, the location dowels can be driven into position (photo).
49 Refit the studs, having smeared the threads with locking compound. If the bellhousing is not to be refitted at this stage, the bearing plate assembly can be secured to the gearbox by means of spacers and nuts fitted to the studs.

### Front cover and oil pump – refitting

50 If the oil pump components in the front cover have been dismantled, reassemble them as given in Section 9.
51 Smear the cover gasket with grease and locate it in position on the bearing plate. Insert the layshaft bearing preload washer into its recess.
52 Lubricate the layshaft front bearing and the primary shaft bearing with gearbox oil, and smear the lip of the oil seal houses in the front cover with lubricant.
53 Lower the front cover into position over the primary shaft, the location studs of the bearing retainer plate and the location dowel (photo). Loosely locate the retaining nuts and insert the bolts, then check that the cover is centralised on the input shaft.
54 Insert the pump drivegears (engaging with the layshaft), lubricate with gearbox oil (photo) and then locate the cover gasket smeared with grease. Locate the cover and secure with bolts fitted with spring washers.
55 Tighten the cover nuts and bolts to secure.

### Gearbox final assembly

56 The selector rods and forks are now refitted to the gearbox. Details of this are given in Section 8.
57 With the selector assemblies fitted, the side and top covers can be relocated (photo). Check that the mating flanges are clean and use new gaskets smeared with grease. Secure the covers with their retaining bolts, remembering the lockwire between the crossover lever bolt and a top cover bolt.
58 Refit the reversing light switch together with its shim washers as given in Section 20.
59 The rear cover can be fitted together with a new gasket. Check that the roller bearing is in position on the rear end of the mainshaft

7.42 Measuring the transfer gear washer thickness requirement to give correct endfloat

7.46 Locate the bearing plate gasket onto the gearbox front face

7.47a Engage the layshaft with the primary shaft and ...

7.47b ... carefully lower it into the gearbox

7.48 Refit the location dowels

7.53 Fit the front cover

7.54 Fit the pump gears and lubricate to prime the pump

7.57 Refit the side cover – note the new gasket

7.59 Refit the rear cover

7.61 Refit the oil drain plug (later model shown). Filler/level plug is arrowed

8.8 Tighten the reverse gear crossover lever pivot bolt

8.11 Drift 3rd/4th gear selector fork retaining pin into position to secure

8.12 Insert the interlock pins

8.13 Insert the reverse gear selector shaft into position and locate the hinge spring

8.14a Locate the reverse crossover lever selector finger and ...

8.14b ... tighten the retaining bolt (or insert pin as applicable) to secure

8.15a Locate 1st/2nd selector jaw onto shaft ...

8.15b ... and secure with retaining pin (or clamp bolts)

and that it is well lubricated before fitting the cover (photo).
60 Relocate and secure the bellhousing after fitment of the oil pump assembly and the selector mechanism components.
61 Insert the oil drain and filler/level plugs. Tighten the drain plug, but do not tighten the filler plug until after the gearbox is refitted to the vehicle and the oil replenished (photo).

## 8 Gearbox selector mechanism – removal, inspection and refitting

1 If problems are experienced in changing gears the problem is most likely to be caused by a worn or defective clutch, information on which is given in Chapter 5.
2 If it is found that only one or two gears are difficult to select, the problem is most likely to be a worn or defective synchromesh unit or defective selectors.
3 Since removal of the selectors (and the mainshaft) necessitates gearbox removal, and in the case of the selectors, partial dismantling, reference should be made to Section 2 in this Chapter for general information and advice on gearbox removal. If you intend to remove the gearbox for access to the selectors, refer to Section 3 (for transmission removal) and Section 5, paragraphs 1 to 3 and 9 to 15 inclusive, for removal of the selectors. When the selectors are removed, proceed as follows for inspection and reassembly. Note that the removal and refitting of the transfer gearbox gear lever, selectors and selector shaft are dealt with separately in Sections 14 and 15 respectively.
4 Clean and lay out in order of fitting the selector rods, forks and associated components for inspection.
5 Check the detent springs and balls for signs of wear and the springs for distortion. Check the selector rods, jaws and forks for damage or excessive wear. Renew any worn, defective or suspect components and when ordering replacements, get a new set of roll pins (where applicable) for securing the selectors and shafts.
6 Before commencing assembly, ensure that the respective shaft, detent and interlock pin ports in the gearbox are clear and perfectly clean. Lubricate all parts as they are fitted with gearbox oil.
7 Locate the reverse gear crossover lever into position and engage the lever foot into the reverse idler gear groove.
8 Refit the pivot bolt in position in the side of the casing, having lightly smeared the threads with thread locking compound. Do not allow the compound to enter the casing or run on the exposed bolt threads (photo).
9 Locate the 1st/2nd gear selector fork into position (with its offset boss to the right) in the outer gear hub groove. On later models, grease and locate the fork-to-groove shoes.
10 Position the 3rd/4th selector fork into its synchro hub groove so that its retaining pin entry hole is on the top right-hand side.
11 Now slide the 3rd/4th gear selector shaft into position, locating the loose collar (where applicable) and the interlock pin, and secure the fork in position on the shaft by driving in the retaining pin (photo).
12 Insert an interlock pin and engage with the cutaway sections in the shaft on each side (photo).
13 Locate the reverse gear stop hinge plate with the selector jaw into position (next to 3rd/4th gear) and slide the selector shaft through to

engage with it. Ensure that the spring location lug faces towards the central bridge and as the shaft is passed through, locate the coil spring with its small hook end facing out (photo).
14 As the reverse gear shaft is passed through the bridge, locate the reverse crossover lever selector finger as shown (photo) and secure with the retaining pin or bolt as applicable (photo).
15 Slide the 1st/2nd gear selector shaft into position, engaging the selector jaw (photo) and push through to engage with the fork. Insert the retaining pins (front first) or tighten the clamp bolts as applicable (photo).
16 Operate the reverse gear selector to ensure that its action is satisfactory and also check that there is a clearance between the selector finger and crossover lever, otherwise they may snag during operation.
17 Secure the crossover lever pivot bolt by wiring it in conjunction with a side cover bolt as shown in photo 5.15.
18 Insert the detent balls and springs into their location holes in the bridge piece (photos).
19 Smear the top cover gasket with grease and carefully locate into position on the mating flange of the gearbox (photo). The top cover can now be lowered into position and secured with the retaining bolts.
20 Refit the reversing light switch as given in Section 20.
21 Refit the gearbox bellhousing, smearing the three selector shaft holes in its rear face with a jointing solution. With the housing located on the dowels, refit the retaining nut and bolts to secure.
22 Refer to Chapter 5 and refit the clutch withdrawal mechanism.
23 Refer to Section 3 and refit the transmission.

## 9 Front cover and oil pump – removal and refitting

1 The front cover and the oil pump unit are located within the bellhousing and attached to the gearbox front bearing plate. The front cover houses the primary shaft bearing seal to prevent oil running down the shaft (from the gearbox) into the clutch assembly. The primary shaft extension sleeve is an interference fit on the front of the cover.
2 The lower half of the cover houses the gearbox oil pump and this is driven by means of its central gear, the shaft of which engages with and is driven by the layshaft.
3 The two main reasons for removal of the front cover and oil pump unit are to renew the primary shaft seal or to inspect and overhaul the oil pump.
4 Although no special tools are required to remove or refit the pump and/or cover unit, access to them is only available after removing either the engine or transmission units. Refer to Chapter 1 or to Sections 2 and 3 of this Chapter for information on their respective removal.
5 With the engine or transmission removed, refer to Chapter 5 and remove the clutch withdrawal mechanism and release lever.
6 The front cover can now be withdrawn having removed its retaining nuts and bolts. As the cover is withdrawn from the bearing plate, recover the shim washer which is housed in the layshaft recess. This washer is of a selected thickness to adjust the bearing endplay and must therefore be refitted on reassembly.

8.18a Insert detent balls and springs

8.18b The completed selector mechanism assembly

8.19 Refit the top cover and gasket

9.7 Extractor in position for withdrawal of the oil feed ring

9.10 Align the oil holes (arrowed) when fitting the feed ring

9.11a Withdraw the inner ...

9.11b ... and outer gears for inspection

9.11c Removing the relief valve screw, spring ...

9.11d .. and relief valve ball

7   If the primary shaft oil seal is to be removed for replacement, you will need to fabricate or have the use of a suitable extractor with which to withdraw the oil feed ring (photo).

8   With the oil feed ring removed, the oil seal may be extracted in a similar manner.

9   Press or drift the new seal into position with its plain side inwards.

10  When refitting the oil feed ring, first align the centre hole in the ring with the oil feed hole in the cover, then press it into position (photo).

11  The oil pump assembly comprises an inner and outer gear, both of which can be removed from the front face of the cover, having removed the pump cover (photos). A relief valve unit is fitted into its rear face. To remove the relief valve, spring and ball, unscrew and remove the retaining screw (photos).

12  Inspect the oil pump components for signs of excessive wear and/or damage and renew any defective components (Fig. 6.10).

13  Reassemble in the reverse order to dismantling, and lubricate the components with gearbox oil. When the oil pressure ball and spring are inserted (in that order), tighten the retaining screw so that it is flush with, or not more than 0.010 in (0.25 mm) below, the face of the cover.

14  The cover gasket must be renewed and all traces of the old gasket removed from the mating faces of the cover and endplate. Smear the gasket surfaces with grease and locate it onto the endplate. Reinsert the layshaft bearing thrust washer into its recess. Do not refit the oil pump gear cover yet.

15  Reposition the cover assembly into position on the front endplate, taking care not to damage the primary shaft oil seal as it is slid down the shaft. With the cover in position loosely fit the retaining nuts and bolts (with spring washers).

16  Insert the oil pump drivegears, engaging the inner gear shaft square section wth the laygear.

17  Refit the oil pump cover with a new gasket and tighten its retaining bolts.

18  Prior to tightening the front cover retaining bolts and nuts, the front cover position should be checked to ensure that it is concentric with the primary pinion. As the pinion is liable to a small amount of

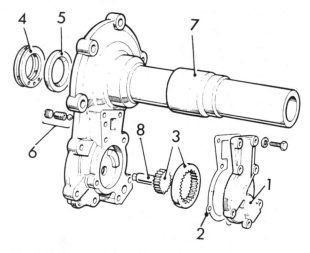

Fig. 6.10 The front cover and oil pump components (Sec 9)

1   Pump cover
2   Cover gasket
3   Pump gears
4   Oil feed ring
5   Seal
6   Relief valve ball, spring and plug
7   Front cover
8   Inner pump gear shaft

radial movement, it should be aligned with the bellhousing using the Rover special tool number RO.1005 if this is available (Fig. 6.11). If necessary adjust the cover position and then tighten the cover retaining nuts and bolts to secure.

19  The clutch withdrawal mechanism and engine or transmission unit can now be refitted in the reverse sequence to removal as given in the respective Chapters.

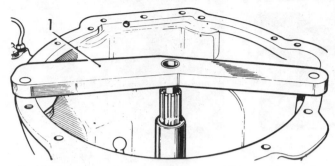

Fig. 6.11 Primary shaft centralising tool (1) in position on the bellhousing (Sec 9)

## 10 Speedometer drive housing – removal, overhaul and refitting

1   Remove the transfer gearbox drain plug and drain the oil into a suitable container.
2   Disconnect the rear propeller shaft from the transmission brake attachment as described in Chapter 7.
3   Extract the split pin and withdraw the handbrake linkage clevis pin at its transmission brake connection.
4   Detach the speedometer drive cable from the drive housing and move the cable back out of the way.
5   Unscrew the speedometer housing-to-gearbox retaining bolts and supporting the housing and transmission brake assembly, withdraw and lower it.
6   Clean the exterior of the housing, but do not allow any cleaning fluid used to enter the transmission brake assembly.
7   Extract the speedometer cable/spindle housing followed by the driven gear and spindle. Prise free the O-ring seal and on later models observe which way round the seal lip is. Withdraw the thrust washer and the small oil seal from the spindle housing.
8   Unscrew and remove the output coupling flange-to-shaft retaining locknut and washer, then withdraw the brake drum and coupling flange complete.
9   The new output shaft can now be withdrawn by pressing or driving out (use a hide mallet) forwards through the housing.
10  The spacer collar and speedometer worm can now be withdrawn along the shaft (if required).
11  Unbolt and remove the oil catcher and the oil shield and then withdraw the oil seal.
12  To remove the ball-bearing, extract the retaining clip and press or drift the bearing out using a suitable tube drift.
13  Clean and carefully inspect the housing components and renew any found to be worn or defective. If a new speedometer drive housing is to be fitted then the differential bearing preload should be checked as follows. **Note:** *This check should also be made if the gearbox, differential unit (transmission) or differential bearings are being renewed.*
14  Position the speedometer housing against the gearbox, but do not fit the gasket at this stage. The differential shaft taper roller bearing cone and cup should be in contact. Measure the clearance between the gearbox and the drive housing joint faces using feeler gauges to establish the gasket thickness requirement (Fig. 6.12). When assembled, the gasket will be compressed a given amount (under the retaining nut torque) to give the correct bearing preload of 0.002 to 0.004 in (0.050 to 0.100 mm).
15  The joint face clearance is adjusted by fitting the required thickness of shim behind the rear bearing cup. The bearing cup must be removed using a suitable puller, then with the shim adjustment made to allow the correct joint face clearance, press or drive the bearing cup back into its housing and recheck the clearance.
16  To reassemble the housing, press or drive the ballbearing into its housing recess so that it is flush with the shoulder inside, then make secure by refitting the circlip.
17  Carefully insert the coupling oil seal, with its cavity section inwards, to the point where its plain face is just clear of the chamfer in the housing bore (Fig. 6.13).
18  Relocate the oil shield so that is a close fit on the housing, then fit the oil catcher, smeared with sealant, to seal between the catcher and brake backplate (photo).

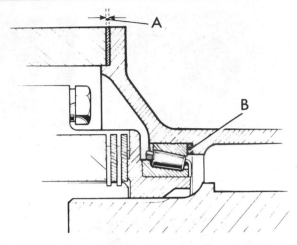

Fig. 6.12 Check the drive housing-to-gearbox flange faces clearance (A) to select gasket of the required thickness. Adjust joint face clearance by shimming behind the bearing at (B) (Sec 10)

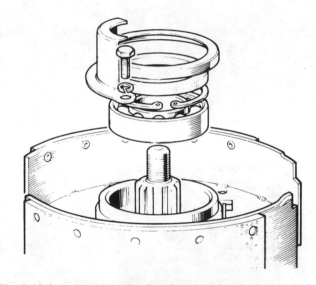

Fig. 6.13 Speedometer drive housing showing the bearing, circlip, oil seal and oil shield (Sec 10)

10.18 Speedometer housing oil seal, oil shield and catcher fitted to the housing

10.19 Insert the shaft fitted with speedometer drivegear and spacer

12.2 Remove bottom cover for access to transfer gears

12.11 Locate the thrust washer with spigot downwards

12.12a Locate the thrust bearing washer ...

12.12b ... and the inner ring

12.13 Fit the roller bearing and high gear

12.14a Locate the thrust washer ...

12.14b ... followed by the spacer

12.15 Insert the needle roller bearing

12.16a Fit the spacer ...

12.16b ... and thrust washer

12.17 Assemble the low gear components before fitting

19 Refit the speedometer worm gear and spacer onto the shaft, then insert the shaft into the housing (photo).
20 Refit the brake drum and coupling flange.
21 Fit the plain washer and locknut onto the output shaft and tighten the nut to the specified torque.
22 Lubricate and reassemble the speedometer driven gear seals and housing in the reverse sequence to dismantling and then refit it into the main housing.
23 Refit the speedometer housing, reversing the procedures given in paragraphs 1 to 5. Refit the drain plug and top up the transfer gearbox with the recommended grade and quantity of oil.

## 11 Transfer gearbox – dismantling and repairs (general)

1 Complete dismantling of the transfer gearbox can only be achieved with the transmission unit removed from the vehicle as described in Section 3.
2 The following sub-assemblies can however be removed and refitted from the transfer gearbox without having to remove the transmission unit:

(a) *Gear lever and cross-shaft – see Section 14*
(b) *Gear selectors and shaft – see Section 15*
(c) *Differential lock actuator – see Section 16*
(d) *Differential unit – see Section 17*
(e) *Front output shaft and housing – see Section 19*
(f) *Transmission output shaft oil seals – see Section 13*

3 The intermediate shaft gear assembly can only be removed with the transmission out of the vehicle. To remove and overhaul the intermediate gear assembly refer to Section 12.

## 12 Intermediate transfer gears – removal, inspection and re-assembly

*Access to the intermediate gears for removal and overhaul is only available on removal of the transmission unit from the vehicle and this is detailed in Section 3. However, an initial inspection of gears can be made by draining off the transfer gearbox oil and removing the bottom cover. If the gears are to be removed, proceed as follows.*
1 With the transmission unit removed from the vehicle, position and support it with the transmission brake upwards, and referring to Section 10, remove the speedometer drive housing.
2 Unbolt and remove the gearbox bottom cover with its gasket (photo).
3 Screw a suitable slave bolt into the end of the intermediate gear shaft and withdraw it from the gearbox. Remove the O-ring seal.
4 To keep the intermediate gears together during removal, insert a suitable slave shaft through them – use Rover special tool number R0.1003 if available. Lift the intermediate gears clear.
5 The thrust washers, bearings and gears can now be withdrawn from the slave shaft, but note their order of fitting.
6 On inspection it will be noted that the input gear and outer member are rivetted together. Under no circumstances should they be separated. If worn, broken or defective in any way the complete unit must be renewed.

7 Clean and inspect the respective components and renew any that show signs of excessive wear or damage.
8 To reassemble the gears, if a slave shaft is available, the gears can be preassembled before inserting into the gearbox in the reverse order to removal. Once the gear assembly is inserted into the gearbox and the intermediate shaft is refitted, the upper thrust washer-to-casing clearance must be checked and if necessary adjusted as given in paragraph 21.
9 Where a slave shaft is not available, the gears can be reassembled into position in the gearbox in the following manner.
10 Position and support the gearbox on its front end and assemble the gears from front to rear.
11 Locate the thrust washer with its spigot downwards (photo).
12 Locate the thrust bearing washer (photo) and the inner ring with its grooves side downwards (photo) into position.
13 Lubricate the roller bearing and then insert it together with the high gear into the gearbox (photo).
14 Fit the thrust washer (photo) and spacer (photo).
15 Lubricate the needle roller bearing, insert it into the input gear and fit them into position (photo).
16 Fit the spacer and thrust washer (photos).
17 Assemble the low gear unit prior to fitting. Lubricate and insert the roller bearing and then locate the thrust ring, inner ring and end thrust washer (photo). The inner ring must be fitted with its grooved face upwards.
18 Insert the assembled low gear unit into position (photo).
19 Temporarily refit the speedometer housing and mark the housing-to-intermediate shaft cutaway section location so that the shaft can be correctly located when in position. Remove the speedometer housing.
20 Insert the intermediate shaft. Lubricate it before fitting and also locate the O-ring seal into its groove on the shaft. Ensure that all gears and washer assemblies are centralised prior to pushing the shaft into position. Use a wooden block or a hide mallet to drift the shaft into its fully fitted position (photo) and align the shaft end face shoulder with the scribed line (of the speedometer housing) on the gearbox end face (photo).
21 Check the upper thrust washer-to-gearcase clearance using a feeler gauge (photo). This dimension represents the intermediate gears endfloat – refer to Specifications for the correct value. Should adjustment be necessary, change the thrust washer for one of a suitable alternative thickness.
22 Refit the speedometer drive housing as described in Section 10.
23 Refit the gearbox bottom cover together with a new gasket. Ensure that the mating faces are clean.
24 Refit the transmission unit to the vehicle as described in Section 3.

## 13 Transmission shaft oil seals – renewal

### Rear seal

1 Raise and support the vehicle at the rear using strong axle stands. Chock the front wheels.
2 Refer to Chapter 7 and disconnect the rear propeller shaft at the transmission brake coupling.
3 Unscrew the central locknut and remove it together with its

12.18 Low gear assembly in position

12.20a Drive home the intermediate shaft ...

12.20b ... with end face shoulder correctly aligned with marks made on gearbox end face

12.21 Check the upper thrust washer-to-gearbox clearance using feeler gauges

14.4 Top cover removed, showing clamp bolt of selector finger (A) and lever retaining pin position (B)

14.6 Remove the endplates and extract the seal rings

washer and (on later models) the felt/rubber oil seal.

4    Remove the transmission brake drum retaining screws and withdraw the brake drum. If necessary further information on its removal is given in Chapter 9.

5    Withdraw the oil catcher, prise free the oil shield and withdraw the oil seal.

6    The new seal is pressed or drifted into position with its cavity face leading. When in position the plain face must be just clear of the seal housing bore chamfer.

7    Refit the oil shield so that it fits closely to the speedometer housing and then insert the oil catcher, which should be smeared with a suitable sealant so that when fitted it is sealed against the brake backplate.

8    Other reassembly procedures are a direct reversal of the removal sequence. Tighten the locknut to the specified torque and ensure that the propeller shaft is correctly realigned with its coupling flange.

### Front seal

9    Raise the vehicle at the front end, support with axle stands and chock the rear wheels.

10   Refer to Chapter 7 and detach the front propeller shaft at the transmission coupling.

11   Unscrew and remove the coupling shaft locknut and remove it with its washer.

12   Withdraw the coupling flange together with its mud shield.

13   Prise free and extract the oil seal.

14   The new seal is fitted with its cavity side inwards (towards the transmission). Drift or press it into position using a suitable size tube.

15   Refit the coupling and attach the propeller shaft in the reverse order to removal. Tighten the coupling nut to the specified torque and be sure to correctly align the propeller shaft with the coupling flange.

---

### 14 Gear lever and cross-shaft (transfer gearbox) – removal and refitting

1    Refer to Chapter 12 and remove the front floor.

2    Refer to Chapter 9 and remove the transmission brake lever and its linkage.

3    Unbolt and remove the top cover from the transfer gearbox. Care must now be taken not to drop tools and fittings into the transfer gearbox, or the gearbox will have to be drained and the bottom cover removed as well.

4    Loosen the clamp bolt of the selector finger and then drive out the cross-shaft-to-gear lever retaining pin using a suitable diameter drift. Remove the gear lever from the end of the shaft (photo).

5    Support the distance collar and selector finger within the gearbox and then withdraw the cross-shaft. Lift out the collar and selector finger.

6    Remove the retaining screws, detach the endplates and extract the seal rings (photo).

7    On early models the damper is removed by unscrewing the knob and removing it with its rubber sleeve. Unscrew the upper rod and withdraw the metal and rubber sleeve assembly. Note the rubber spacer which can be withdrawn (Fig. 6.14).

8    Examine the various components for signs of wear and renew as

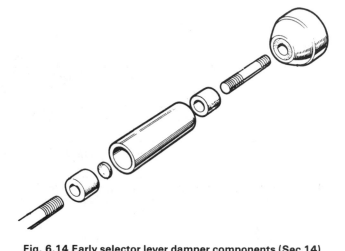

Fig. 6.14 Early selector lever damper components (Sec 14)

necessary. The shaft seals and the top cover gasket should always be renewed.

9    Commence reassembly by locating the selector finger into position in the gearbox, engaging with the fork.

10   Insert the cross-shaft and locate the spacer collar onto it as it is pushed through, then slide the shaft through the selector finger and into its opposing location housing.

11   Lubricate and fit the right-hand seal ring and its retaining plate, securing with the cross-head screws.

12   Refit the gear lever and make secure on the shaft by drifting the retaining pin through the lever and shaft location holes.

13   Lubricate and fit the opposing seal ring and retaining plate.

14   Tighten the selector finger clamp bolt with the gear lever positioned 10° forward of its vertical position (photo).

15   Refit the top cover using a new gasket (photo) and secure.

16   The gear lever damper unit of the early models is reassembled in the reverse order to removal.

17   Refit the transmission brake lever and linkage as given in Chapter 9.

18   Refit the floor as given in Chapter 12.

---

### 15 Gear selectors and shaft (transfer gearbox) – removal and refitting

1    Refer to Chapter 12 and remove the front floor section.

2    Refer to Section 10 and remove the speedometer drive housing.

3    Unbolt and remove the transfer gearbox top cover and gasket. Care must be taken not to drop tools or fittings into the transfer gearbox once the cover is removed.

4    Select transfer gear low range, then drive out the front selector fork retaining pin just sufficiently to enable the fork to slide along the shaft when required.

14.14 Tighten the selector finger clamp bolt with lever positioned 10° forwards of vertical

14.15 Refit the top cover

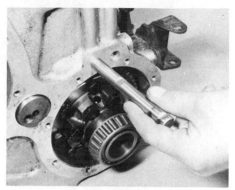

15.8a Remove the selector rod ...

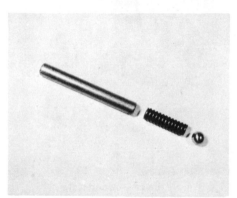

15.8b ... spacer rod, spring and ball

15.13 Inserting the spacer rod into the vertical port

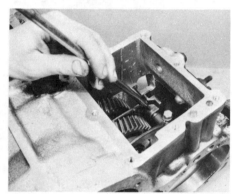

15.15 Drive the retaining pin into position to secure the front fork

5   Pull the differential unit rearwards.
6   Press the front selector fork forwards and pull the rear selector fork rearwards to enable the selector shaft to be disengaged from the detent balls located in the gearbox rear face.
7   Remove the rear selector fork clamp bolt, then withdraw the selector shaft sufficiently to allow the two selector forks to be lifted out of their locations in the gearbox.
8   If the shaft is to be withdrawn completely from the gearbox, seal the housing aperture as the shaft is extracted to prevent the detent balls from dropping down into the gearbox (photo). With the shaft removed, extract the balls and then withdraw the spacer rod and spring (photo).
9   Unscrew and remove the side plug and extract the detent spring from the cross port.
10  Clean and examine the components for excessive wear and renew as necessary. Clean the detent ball and spring ports using a pipe cleaner if they are sludged up. A new top cover gasket should be fitted on reassembly and all traces of the old gasket cleaned off the mating faces.
11  Commence reassembly by inserting the cross port inner detent spring into position, followed by its ball. Lubricate them with grease to prevent them from rolling out.
12  Insert the selector shaft and compress the selector ball against its spring to enable the shaft to pass through.
13  Locate the detent ball, sping and spacer rod into the vertical port (photo).
14  Lower the rear selector fork into position with its plain face rearwards, then insert the front fork with its extended boss rearwards.
15  Push the shaft through to engage in the selector forks and align the retaining pin holes. Drive the front fork retaining pin into position to secure (photo).
16  Engage the transfer gears in the neutral position, then adjust the rear fork to allow 0.010 in (0.25 mm) clearance between the input gear inner member rear face and the front face of the fork. Tighten the fork retaining bolt to secure in this position (photo).

17  Refit and tighten the detent cross port end plug.
18  Refit the top cover using a new gasket and secure with retaining bolts.
19  Refit the spedometer drive housing as given in Section 10.
20  Refit the front floor panels and seats to complete.

## 16  Differential lock actuator (transfer gearbox) – removal and refitting

Note: To remove the differential lock valve, refer to Chapter 10, Section 22
1   Referring to Chapter 12, remove the front seats and floor panels, then proceed as follows.
2   Take a note of the fitted position of the vacuum supply hoses and detach the hoses from the actuator unit. Detach the wiring connection from the warning switch.
3   Unscrew and remove the actuator unit retaining nuts and bolts, or screws, and withdraw it from the transmission. On later models, remove the heat shield as well.
4   Extract the detent spring and ball from the flange port.
5   To dismantle the actuator unit, unscrew and remove the differential lock warning switch. Retain any shims fitted.
6   Drive out and extract the actuator fork-to-shaft retaining pin (photo).
7   Unscrew and remove the retaining bolts securing the actuator valve unit to the main housing and separate the two. Remove the O-ring seal and gasket.
8   Renew any excessively worn or defective components and then reassemble in the reverse order to dismantling. Smear the vacuum unit and main housing joint faces with a suitable sealant prior to fitting.
9   Refit the actuator unit in the reverse order to removal (photo). Smear the gasket faces with sealant before fitting. When in position reconnect the vacuum tubes, ensuring their correct fitting.
10  Refit the floor panels and seats in the reverse order to removal.

15.16 Check the rear selector fork-to-input gear clearance

16.6 The actuator removed, showing the actuating fork and spring locations

16.9 Refitting the actuator. Note spring location (arrowed)

17.5 Removing the differential unit

18.1 The differential lock actuator switch (arrowed)

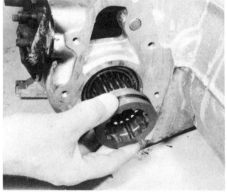

19.6 Remove the lock-up dog clutch

19.9 Bearing and retaining circlip position in housing

19.11a Insert the oil seal and lubricate the lips, then ...

19.11b ... insert the shaft

19.12a Location dowel position (arrowed)

19.12b Tighten the housing retaining bolts

19.13 Temporary plate attached to prevent coupling from turning

## 17 Differential unit (transfer gearbox) – removal and refitting

1 Refer to Chapter 12 and remove the front seats and floor panels, then proceed as follows.
2 Refer to the previous Section and remove (do not dismantle) the differential lock actuator unit.
3 Disconnect and remove the front output shaft and housing as given in Section 19.
4 Remove the speedometer drive housing as given in Section 10.
5 The differential unit can now be extracted from the housing (photo).
6 The dismantling, overhaul and reassembly of the transmission differential unit is a specialised operation and is therefore not recommended as a DIY task. If the differential is known to be faulty, or is suspected of malfunction, have it checked and if possible repaired by your Range Rover dealer, or renew the unit complete. Two different types have ben fitted, the earlier models being equipped with a Salisbury unit.
7 Refitting is a reversal of the removal procedure, but note that if the differential unit, its bearings, the gearbox housing or speedometer drive housing have been renewed, then a differential bearing preload check must be made. This is described in Section 10 and is made before fully refitting the speedometer housing.

## 18 Differential lock actuator switch – removal and refitting

1 Located on the differential lock actuator housing, the switch is removed by detaching the wires and unscrewing the switch unit together with the shim washers (photo).
2 Correct setting is important during refitting and the following procedure should be taken.
3 Start the engine and locate the differential lock vacuum control valve in the 'up' position. Now reconnect the wires to the switch and screw the switch into its housing without the shim washers. As soon as switch contact is made, screw the switch in a further half turn.
4 Now measure the switch-to-housing flange face clearance using feeler gauges. Remove the switch and fit washers of the measured thickness. Reinsert the switch and tighten to secure.
5 Locate the differential lock vacuum control valve in the down position and switch off the engine to complete.

## 19 Front output shaft and housing – removal, overhaul and refitting

1 Remove the transfer gearbox drain plug and drain the oil into a suitable container.
2 Whilst the oil is being drained, refer to Chapter 12 and remove the front seats and floor panel.
3 Unbolt and detach the front propeller shaft from the gearbox coupling. Scribe a line across the coupling flange and the propeller shaft for correct reassembly.
4 Refer to Section 16 and remove the differential lock actuator unit, but do not detach the vacuum lines or wires to the switch.
5 Unscrew and remove the housing retaining bolts and detach the housing from the gearbox.
6 Withdraw the lock-up dog clutch unit (photo).
7 To dismantle the housing, support the shaft and unscrew the retaining nut at the front end. Remove the nut and washer and then withdraw the coupling flange with its mud shield.
8 Support the housing and press or drift the shaft out rearwards, then withdraw the oil seal.
9 Using circlip pliers, contract and remove the bearing retaining circlip. Press or drift the bearing out of the housing (photo).
10 Inspect the respective components and renew any excessively worn or damaged parts as required. The mud shield can be pressed free from the coupling if required.
11 Reassembly is a reversal of the removal sequence. Grease the bearing when fitted and ensure that the circlip is fully located. Lubricate the lips of the oil seal before inserting the shaft (photos).
12 When refitting the housing to the gearbox, ensure that the location dowel is in position (photo) for correct housing alignment. Do not forget to fit and tighten the housing retaining bolt located within the actuator location aperture (photo).
13 Tighten the coupling locknut to the specified torque. This can be achieved by temporarily attaching a plate to one of the coupling studs as shown (photo) which will prevent the shaft from turning as the nut is tightened. Remove the plate when the nut has been tightened.

## 20 Reversing light switch – removal and refitting

1 Disconnect the battery earth lead.
2 Peel back and remove the main gear lever rubber grommet from its retaining flange on the floor.
3 The reversing light switch is now accessible. Disconnect the lead(s), unscrew the switch unit using a suitable box spanner and lift it clear (photo). Note the shim washers.
4 Engage reverse gear and refit the switch, without the shim washers, with the leads connected. With the ignition switched on and the battery reconnected, screw the switch down until switch contact is made. Screw the switch in a further half turn and then using a feeler gauge, measure the switch lower flange-to-gearbox clearance.
5 Remove the switch, fit shim washers of the measured thickness, then refit the switch and tighten it to the specified torque.
6 Recheck the switch operation and then refit the rubber grommet, engaging with the floor plate flange to secure in position.

20.3 Reversing light switch location in front of the main gear lever turret. It is not necessary to remove the lever

**21 Fault diagnosis – transmission**

| Symptom | Reason(s) |
| --- | --- |
| Difficult engagement of gears | Clutch fault (see Chapter 5)<br>Worn or damaged synchromesh units |
| Jumps out of gear (on overrun or drive) | Weak detent springs, worn selector forks or worn synchro sleeves |
| Gear lever engages reverse gear instead of 1st too easily | Reverse stop hinge plate spring weak or broken |
| Noisy gearbox | Low oil level or incorrect oil grade<br>Worn bearings and/or gears<br>Gear trains/bearing endfloats incorrectly set (after rebuild) |
| Difficult disengagement of gears | Worn synchromesh<br>Damaged or distorted splines or gear dogs |
| Oil leaks | Defective input or output oil seals<br>Defective gasket or gearbox/transfer box cover plates<br>Loose drain or level plug<br>Cracked or broken casing |

**Note**: *It is sometimes difficult to decide whether it is worthwhile removing and dismantling the gearbox for a fault which may be nothing more than a minor irritant. Gearboxes which howl, or where the synchromesh is worn but double declutching can overcome the problem, may continue to perform for a long time in this stage. A worn gearbox usually needs a complete rebuild to eliminate noise because the various gears, if re-aligned on new bearings, will continue to howl when different wearing surfaces are presented to each other.*

*The decision to overhaul therefore, must be considered with regard to time and money available, relative to the degree of noise or malfunction that the driver can tolerate.*

# Chapter 7 Propeller shafts

## Contents

## Specifications

### General

Propeller shaft type .................................................... Tubular, splined joint
End joints .................................................................... Hardy Spicer universal joint couplings with needle bearings

### Dimensions

Shaft diameter .............................................................. 2.0 in (50.8 mm)
Shaft lengths (overall – flange face-to-flange
face with splined joint midway):
    Front shaft .......................................................... 25.33 in (643,4 mm)
    Rear shaft ............................................................ 34.937 in (887,4 mm)

### Torque wrench setting

| | lbf ft | kgf m |
|---|---|---|
| Drive flange bolts and nuts ....................................... | 35 | 4.8 |

---

## 1 General description

The drive from the transmission assembly to the front and rear axles is transmitted by two tubular propeller shafts fitted with a universal joint at each end. The universal joints cater for the varying angle between the axle and transmission, caused by road spring deflection, while any fore-or-aft variation is taken care of by means of

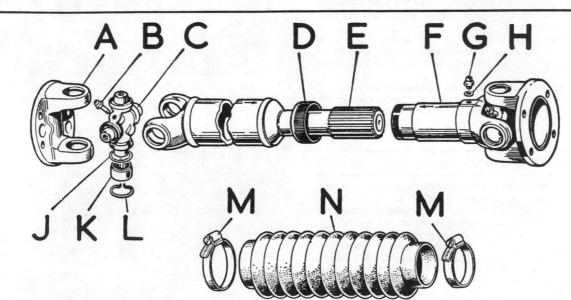

Fig. 7.1 Propeller shaft components (Sec 1)

| | | | | | | | |
|---|---|---|---|---|---|---|---|
| A | Flanged yoke | E | Splined shaft | J | Seal for spider | M | Clips fixing rubber bellows (front shaft only) |
| B | Grease nipple for universal joint | F | Splined sleeve | K | Needle roller bearing assembly | N | Rubber bellows for sliding joint (front shaft only |
| C | Spider for bearings | G | Grease nipple for splined joint | L | Circlip retaining bearing | | |
| D | Dust cap | H | Washer for nipple | | | | |

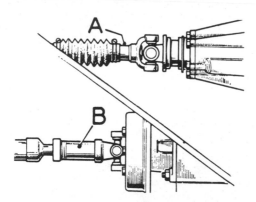

**Fig. 7.2 Propeller shaft splined sleeve locations (Sec 1)**

A    Sleeve end of front propeller shaft
B    Sleeve end of rear propeller shaft

a splined sleeve in each shaft.

Although of different lengths, the front and rear propeller shafts are virtually identical in construction with the exception of the position of the splined sleeve which is on the transmission end of the rear shaft and the axle end of the front shaft.

## 2   Propeller shafts – removal and refitting

1   The method of removing either the front or rear propeller shaft is almost the same. Any differences in procedure will be mentioned where necessary.
2   Depending on the shaft to be removed, jack up the appropriate end of the vehicle until the wheels are just clear of the ground. Place heavy duty axle stands beneath the chassis.
3   Scribe a line across the side of the axle coupling flange and the propeller shaft, remove the four nuts and bolts and lower the end of the shaft to the ground (photo).
4   If the rear propeller shaft is being removed, undo the four nuts securing the shaft flange to the brake drum. Pull the shaft rearwards to clear the studs and remove the complete shaft assembly from beneath the vehicle (photo).
5   In the case of the front propeller shaft, remove the four nuts and bolts securing the rear end of the shaft to the front output shaft flange on the transfer box and remove the shaft assembly from the vehicle (photo).
6   Refitting the propeller shafts is the reverse sequence to removal. Note that the splined sleeve on the front shaft must be towards the front axle while the sleeve on the rear shaft must be adjacent to the transmission brake.

## 3   Universal joints – inspection and repair

1   Wear in the universal joint needle roller bearings is characterised by vibration in the transmission, 'clonks' on taking up the drive and in extreme cases of lack of lubrication, metallic squeaking and ultimately grating and shrieking sounds as the bearings break up.
2   To test the universal joints for wear prior to removing the propeller shaft(s) from the vehicle, apply the handbrake and chock the wheels. Working under the vehicle, apply leverage between the yokes using a large screwdriver or flat metal bar. Wear is indicated by movement between the shaft yoke and coupling flange yoke. Check all four universal joints in this way.
3   To check the splined sleeve on the front of both shafts, attempt to push the shafts from side to side and note any excessive movement between the sleeve and shaft. A further check can be made by gripping the shaft and sleeve and turning them in opposite directions, noting any excessive movement.
4   If the universal joint is worn, a repair kit comprising a new spider, bearings, cups and seals should be purchased prior to removing the affected shaft.
5   If excessive wear is apparent on the propeller shaft splined sleeve, a new shaft will have to be obtained.

2.3 The rear axle/rear propeller shaft coupling flange

2.4 The rear propeller shaft front coupling to the transmission brake drum

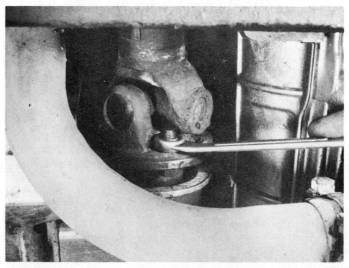

2.5 Undoing the front shaft coupling flange bolts at the transfer box from underneath

## 4 Universal joints and sleeve — dismantling and inspection

1 Remove the propeller shaft from the vehicle as described in Section 2.

2 If a protective rubber boot is fitted over the sleeve section, slacken the securing clips and slide the boot rearwards. A rubber boot should be fitted to the front shaft but not the rear.

3 Check that alignment marks are visible on the sleeve and shaft (two arrows). If no marks can be found, scribe a line along the sleeve and shaft to ensure the splined shaft and sleeve are reassembled in the original position. This is most important.

4 Unscrew the dust cap and withdraw the front universal joint and sleeve assembly from the splined end of the shaft.

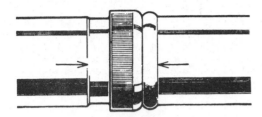

Fig. 7.3 Alignment marks on shaft and splined sleeve (Sec 4)

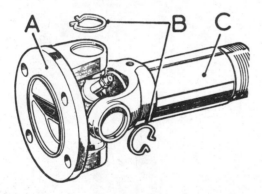

Fig. 7.4 Universal joint (Sec 4)

A  Yoke flange          C  Shaft yoke
B  Circlips

5 Clean away all the traces of dirt and grease from the circlips located on the ends of the spiders, and using a pair of circlip pliers compress their open ends and hook them out with the aid of a screwdriver. If they are difficult to remove, place a drift between the circlip and tap the top of the bearing cup to ease the pressure on the circlip. Remove the grease nipple.

6 Support the shaft in a vice with the yoke in a vertical plane. Using a hammer and drift of suitable diameter, tap the uppermost bearing cup until the bearing cup at the bottom protrudes from the yoke by approximately $\frac{1}{4}$ in (6 mm) (photo). Remove the shaft and securely grip the protruding bearing cup in the vice jaws. Turn the shaft from side to side while at the same time lifting the shaft until it comes free of the bearing cup.

7 Replace the shaft in the vice with the exposed spider uppermost. Tap the spider with the hammer and drift until the lower bearing cup protrudes and then remove the cup as previously described.

8 The flange and spider can now be removed from the shaft and the remaining two bearing cups dismantled in the previously described manner.

9 With the universal joint dismantled, carefully examine the needle rollers, bearings cups and spider for wear, scoring and pitting of the surface finish. If any wear is detected the joint must be renewed (photo).

10 Temporarily fit the splined end of the shaft into the sleeve with the alignment marks adjacent. Grip the sleeve in a soft-jawed vice and ascertain the amount of spline wear by turning the shaft in either direction. The maximum permissible movement is 0.004 in (0.10 mm) and this can only be accurately checked using a dial indicator. As a rough guide, if you can *see* any movement as the shaft is turned then it is worn and should be renewed.

11 If there is any sign of ovality in any one of the eight yoke holes in any one propeller shaft assembly, then a new complete propeller shaft assembly must be fitted.

## 5 Universal joints and sleeve — reassembly

1 Before fitting the new bearing caps and spider, check that the bearing caps are half full of fresh lubricant, and that all the needle rollers are present and properly positioned. If necessary use a smear of grease to keep them in place during the refitting operation.

2 Insert the new spider complete with seals into the flange yoke. Ensure that the grease nipple hole faces away from the flange.

3 Partially insert one of the bearing cups into the yoke and enter the spider trunnion into the bearing cup, being careful not to dislodge the needle rollers.

4 Partially insert the other bearing cup into the flange yoke. Using a vice carefully press both cups into place, but ensure that the spider trunnion does not dislodge any of the needle rollers (photo).

5 Using a socket which is small enough to fit inside the yoke press

4.6 Tap the uppermost bearing cup

4.9 Universal joint bearing components

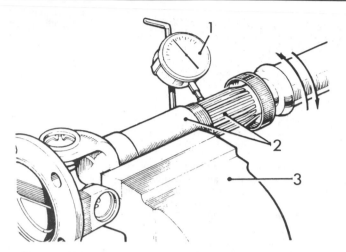

**Fig. 7.5 Checking spline wear using a dial indicator (Sec 4)**

1   Dial indicator                    3   Vice
2   Sleeve and shaft splined
    sections

one of the bearing cups in *just* far enough to allow the circlip to be fitted (photo). Repeat this operation with the other bearing cup.

6   Insert the spider into the yokes of the propeller shaft. Partially insert both bearing cups, being careful to ensure that the spider trunnions do not dislodge any of the needle rollers (photo).

7   Using a vice carefully press both bearing cups into place but ensure that none of the bearing rollers are dislodged. Repeat the operation given in paragraph 5 (photo).

8   Fit the grease nipple to the spider.

9   Smear the splines on the end of the shaft with grease. Carefully match up the alignment mark and slide the shaft into the sleeve. Tighten the dust cap. **Note:** *Do not pack grease into the sleeve prior to fitting the shaft as it may prevent the shaft being pushed fully home.*

10   If the front propeller shaft is being serviced, pull the rubber boot over the sleeve and tighten the clips. Ensure that the worm drives on the clips are 180° apart from each other to retain the balance of the shaft.

11   Refit the shaft to the vehicle as described in Section 2 and lubricate the bearings using a grease gun applied to the universal joint and sleeve nipples. **Note:** *If the sleeve is fitted with a plug instead of a grease nipple, replace it with a nipple to enable lubrication of the sleeve splines. Do not overfill the sleeve splines with grease. These should be sufficient to lubricate the splines only.*

5.4 Press the cups into place using a vice and socket

5.5 Refitting a circlip

5.6 Inserting the bearing cups with the spider in position in the shaft yoke

5.7 Using a vice and socket to press the bearing cups into place

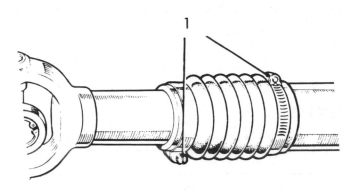

Fig. 7.6 Refit the rubber boot to the shaft with worm drives (1)
180° apart (Sec 5)

## 6  Propeller shaft sliding sleeves – lubrication

1    The rear propeller shaft splined sleeve is fitted with a grease nipple
and this should be greased every 6000 miles (10 000 Km) with the
specified lubricant (photo).
2    The front propeller shaft does not have a grease nipple fitted to its
splined sleeve because of its exposed location. A plug is fitted instead.
Every 24 000 miles (40 000 Km) or 2 years, the splined sleeve
should be lubricated as follows.
3    Undo the front end of the propeller shaft as directed in Section 2.
4    Remove the plug from the splined sleeve greasing point and fit a

6.1 The rear shaft grease nipple for the splined section

grease nipple.
5    Compress the sliding joint as far as possible and then lubricate it
with the specified grease. Compressing the joint first will ensure that
too much grease is not injected.
6    Remove the grease nipple and refit the plug.
7    Refit the propeller shaft as directed in Section 2.

## 7  Fault diagnosis – propeller shafts

| Symptom | Reason(s) |
| --- | --- |
| Vibration | Wear in sliding sleeve splines |
| | Worn universal joint bearings |
| | Propeller shaft out of balance |
| | Distorted propeller shaft |
| Knock or 'clunk' when taking up drive | Worn universal joint bearings |
| | Worn axle drive pinion splines |
| | Loose drive flange bolts |
| | Excessive backlash in axle gears |

# Chapter 8  Front and rear axles

*For modifications, and information applicable to later models, see Supplement at end of manual*

## Contents

## Specifications

### Axle type
Front ........................................................................................ Spiral bevel with enclosed CV joint
Rear ........................................................................................ Spiral bevel with fully floating halfshafts
Final drive ratio .................................................................... 3.54 : 1

### Adjustment data
Hub-to-stub axle endfloat(front and rear) ....................... 0.002 to 0.004 in (0.05 to 0.10 mm)
Endfloat on CV joint ............................................................ 0.025 in (0.64 mm) maximum
Swivel pin adjustment shims available .............................. 0.003, 0.005, 0.010 and 0.030 in (0.076, 0.127, 0.254 and 0.762 mm)
Differential pinion pre-load ................................................ 7 to 12 lb (3.2 to 4.5 kg) measured at flange
Crownwheel-to-bevel gear backlash .................................. 0.008 to 0.010 in (.20 to 0.25 mm)

### Lubricant capacity
Differentials .......................................................................... 3 Imp pints (1,7 litres)
Swivel pin housings ............................................................ 0.5 Imp pints (0.25 litres)

### Torque wrench settings

| | lbf ft | kgf m |
|---|---|---|
| Differential carrier-to-axle casing ........................................... | 28 | 3.8 |
| Propeller shaft flanges ............................................................ | 25 | 3.5 |
| Halfshaft and hub cap ............................................................ | 38 | 5.2 |
| Drive flange – differential pinion .......................................... | 85 | 11.7 |
| Crownwheel retaining bolts: | | |
|    Early models – cross-shaft with pin fixing ................. | 35 | 4.8 |
|    Later models – cross-shaft retained by circlips ......... | 45 | 6.2 |
| Crownwheel bearing cap bolts ............................................... | 60 | 8.3 |
| Self-levelling load adjuster – pivot bracket ......................... | 30 | 4.0 |
| Track rod end balljoint retaining nut ................................... | 30 | 4.0 |
| Brake caliper-to-front swivel ................................................. | 60 | 8.5 |
| Front axle swivel housing-to-axle casing bolts .................. | 44 | 6.0 |
| Stub axle-to-swivel housing (front) ..................................... | 44 | 6.0 |
| Stub axle-to-axle casing (rear) ............................................ | 44 | 6.0 |
| Front axle swivel pin retaining bolts ................................... | 60 | 8.5 |
| Front swivel-to-housing oil seal retainer plate bolts ........ | 10 | 1.4 |

## 1  General description

Both the front and rear axles of the Range Rover are of a similar design, comprising a one-piece steel casing housing the differential assembly and two driveshafts (halfshafts). The rear shafts are of solid steel construction, the inner ends of which are splined into the differential assembly, while the outer ends are attached to integral limbs.

To enable the front wheels to turn from lock-to-lock while being driven, the front halfshafts incorporate a CV joint on the outer end. The CV joint runs inside an oil-filled swivel pin housing, the swivel pins being located in tapered roller bearings.

Both the front and rear axle assemblies are attached to the chassis via coil springs and telescopic shock absorbers. Other methods of location are also employed; radius arms and a Panhard rod at the front, with the rear also incorporating a self-levelling ride unit in the centre of the axle and trailing lower links beneath.

**2   Rear axle halfshaft – removal and refitting**

1   Chock the front wheels securely, jack up the rear of the vehicle and remove the roadwheels. **Note:** *The handbrake will be ineffective once a halfshaft has been removed.*

2   Undo and remove the 5 bolts securing the halfshaft hub to the wheel hub and place a container beneath the hub to catch any oil.

3   Withdraw the hub and halfshaft from the wheel hub as a complete assembly. If the hub is initially tight, gently tap its circumference with a soft-faced mallet.

4   The halfshaft and hub are a one-piece assembly and cannot be separated.

5   Refitting the halfshafts is the reverse sequence to removal, noting the following additional points:

(a)  *Fit a new gasket between the halfshaft nut and the wheel hub, lightly coated on both sides with medium grease*

(b)  *Check and if necessary top up the rear axle oil*

(c)  *Tighten the halfshaft hub retaining bolts to the specified torque*

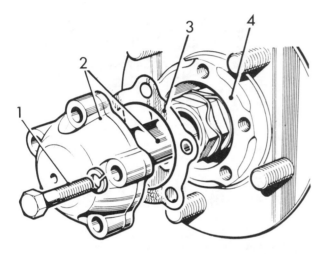

**Fig. 8.1 Rear axle halfshaft assembly (Sec 2)**

| | |
|---|---|
| 1   Bolt | 3   Gasket |
| 2   Halfshaft and hub | 4   Wheel hub |

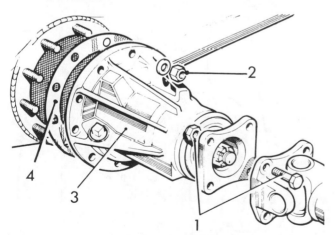

**Fig. 8.2 Rear axle differential unit (Sec 3)**

| | |
|---|---|
| 1   Rear propeller shaft nut and bolt | 3   Differential unit |
| 2   Differential unit retaining nut | 4   Gasket |

**3   Rear axle differential assembly – removal and refitting**

1   The task of overhauling the differential assembly is a highly skilled operation requiring a considerable number of special tools. Taking into consideration the cost and non-availability of many of the parts involved, overhaul of a worn unit is not really an economical proposition.

2   Often the best course of action is to replace the complete differential with a new or reconditioned assembly or carefully selected unit from a breaker's yard.

3   Jack up the rear of the vehicle and support the axle on heavy duty stands. Check the remaining roadwheels.

4   Drain the axle lubricating oil into a suitable container as described in Section 14.

5   Undo and remove the four bolts and locknuts securing the propeller shaft flange to the rear differential pinion flange and lower the propeller shaft to the ground.

6   Withdraw the rear halfshafts as described in Section 2. It is only necessary to withdraw the shafts sufficiently to disengage from the differential unit.

7   Undo and remove the nuts and washer securing the differential to the axle casing. Support the unit with both hands and carefully withdraw the complete housing from the axle casing. Remove the gasket. Note that the brake pipe distribution bracket is mounted on one of the upper mounting studs. Hold it out of the way when withdrawing the differential unit (photo).

8   Refitting the differential is the reverse sequence to removal. Use a new gasket smeared on both sides with jointing compound when refitting the housing to the axle casing and refill the axle with the correct oil.

9   Tighten all retaining nuts and bolts to the specified torques.

**4   Rear axle – removal and refitting**

1   Chock the front roadwheels, slacken the rear roadwheel nuts, jack up the rear of the vehicle and support it on strong axle stands.

2   Place a jack under the rear axle to take the weight off the suspension.

3   Remove the rear roadwheels.

4   Undo the lower rear shock absorber retaining nuts and remove the washer, the outer bush and the cone.

5   Remove the top of the brake fluid reservoir and place a piece of polythene over the top before refitting the cap. This will prevent loss of fluid when the brake pipes are disconnected.

6   Undo the flexible brake hose union at the three-way junction on top of the rear axle. Plug the end of the pipe to prevent ingress of dirt and loss of fluid.

7   Undo the nuts and drive out the bolts to release the trailing lower suspension links from the rear axle brackets.

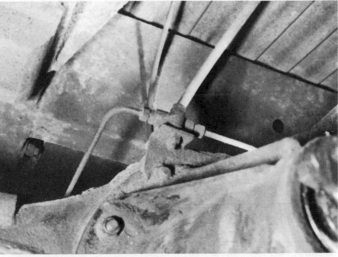

3.7 Rear brake pipe 3-way junction and bracket are secured to the rear axle casing

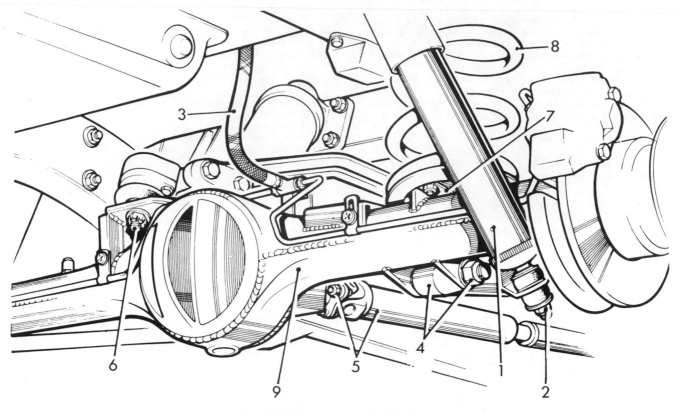

**Fig. 8.3 Rear axle assembly (Sec 4)**

| | | | | | |
|---|---|---|---|---|---|
| 1 | Rear shock absorber | 4 | Lower suspension link | 6 | Self-levelling unit |
| 2 | Shock absorber lower | | and nut | | balljoint and nut |
| | retaining nut | 5 | Propeller shaft and | 7 | Retaining plate |
| 3 | Flexible brake pipe | | retaining nut | | |

| | |
|---|---|
| 8 | Coil spring |
| 9 | Rear axle |

8   Undo the bolts and nuts and separate the propeller shaft from the pinion drive flange, as described in Chapter 7.

9   Undo the nut which retains the self-levelling unit pivot bracket balljoint to the bracket on the top of the rear axle casing.

10   Undo the two bolts which retain the bottom endplates for each coil spring.

11   Lower the axle carefully on the jack and withdraw both coil springs when there is adequate clearance.

12   Lower the jack further so that the complete axle assembly can be removed from the vehicle.

13   Refitting is a straightforward procedure, but not quite the same as for removal.

14   Begin by lining up the axle beneath the vehicle with the weight on the jack, raise the axle so that the lower suspension links can be refitted to their mounting brackets.

15   Refit the coil springs and lock them in place with their respective retaining plates.

16   Jack the axle up into position, locating the top of the coil springs in their seats.

17   Reconnect the balljoint on the end of the pivot bracket and tighten it to the specified torque.

18   Refit the shock absorber lower ends to their mounting points. Refit the cone, bush and washer, and tighten the nut.

19   Refit the propeller shaft flange to the drive pinion as described in Chapter 7.

20   Reconnect the brake flexible hose to the three-way junction and then bleed the rear brakes as described in Chapter 9.

21   Refit the roadwheels and remove the axle jack and the chassis stands. Remove the wheel chocks and tighten the roadwheel nuts.

---

## 5   Front and rear wheel hubs and bearings – renewal

1   If the front hub bearings are to be renewed, first drain the oil from the swivel pin housing and from the front differential casing as

described in Sections 13 and 14. Then remove the front stub driveshaft and integral hub as described in Section 8.

2   If the rear hub bearings are to be renewed, remove the appropriate halfshaft from the rear axle as described in Section 2.

3   Remove the brake caliper assembly as described in Chapter 9 and tie it up out of the way without straining the brake pipes.

4   Undo the wheel hub central locking nut, having first knocked back the locking plate, and remove them both (photo).

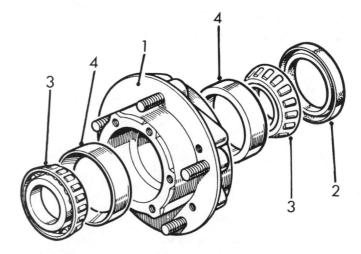

**Fig. 8.4 Hub and bearing assembly (exploded view) (Sec 5)**

| | | | |
|---|---|---|---|
| 1 | Hub | 3 | Roller bearing races |
| 2 | Oil seal | 4 | Outer bearing tracks |

5.4 Knock back the locking plate and remove nut and plate

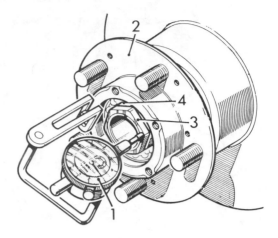

Fig. 8.5 Checking the hub bearing endfloat (Sec 5)

| | | | |
|---|---|---|---|
| 1 | Dial gauge | 3 | Inner nut |
| 2 | Hub | 4 | Keyed washer |

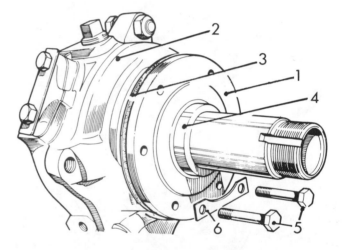

Fig. 8.6 Front wheel hub stub axle (Sec 6)

| | | | |
|---|---|---|---|
| 1 | Stub axle | 4 | Distance piece |
| 2 | Steering swivel hub | 5 | Retaining bolts |
| 3 | Gasket | 6 | Locking plate |

5    Remove the inner hub nut and keyed washer.
6    The wheel hub and brake disc can now be slid off the stub axle as a complete assembly with the hub bearings.
7    Hold one hand over the end of the hub to prevent the outer bearing from falling out and withdraw the hub and bearings from the stub axle.
8    Withdraw the outer roller bearings from the hub. Carefully prise out the oil seal from the rear of the hub and remove the inner roller bearing.
9    Examine the bearings for wear. If there is any sign of scoring or pitting of the rollers or roughness of the bearings generally they must be renewed. If badly damaged or broken up, then examine also the stub axle sleeve.
10   If new bearings are being fitted, support the hub in a vice or on wooden blocks and drive out the bearing outer track using a hammer and suitable drift.
11   Clean all the old grease out of the casing and wash it out with paraffin. Dry it thoroughly before reassembly.
12   Carefully tap the new outer bearing track into the hub with the smaller inside diameter toward the centre of the hub. Ensure that the track is kept square to the hub during fitting. If it jams do not force it. Tap it out from the other end of the hub and start again.
13   Pack the inner bearing with medium grease and place it in position on the hub. Smear the outside diameter of a new oil seal with jointing compound and gently tap it into position using a flat block of wood. Ensure that the seal is fitted with the lip facing towards the bearing. The outer flat face of the oil seal should be flush with the edge of the hub when fitted.
14   Fill the hub to half its capacity with medium grease and pack the outer bearing. Place the outer bearing in position on the hub.
15   Holding the outer roller bearing in position, slide the hub assembly onto the stub axle.
16   Refit the keyed washer and inner hub nut. Tighten the hub nut securely until there is no endfloat of the hub assembly. Rotate the hub several times to settle the bearings. Back off the hub nut until it is just possible to detect a trace of endfloat in the hub assembly. If a dial gauge is available set the endfloat to between the limits given in the Specifications. Rotate the hub and ensure that it turns freely with no harshness.
17   When the hub is adjusted correctly, fit the lockwasher and outer nut and tighten the outer nut. Recheck that the hub turns freely. Bend over an edge of the lockwasher to secure the hub nut.
18   Refit the hub and driveshaft, referring to the Section(s) used when removing them.
19   Refit the brake caliper assembly as described in Chapter 9.
20   Refill the front swivel pin housing and front differential with oil of the specified grade to the correct level, as described in Sections 13 and 14 (if applicable).

## 6    Front and rear stub axles – removal, overhaul and refitting

1    When renewing the wheel hub bearings as described in the last Section, it may be found that not only are the bearings in need of renewal but that damage has been caused to the stub axle itself and that it too requires replacement.
2    Remove the hub as described in the previous Section.
3    Remove the six retaining bolts and the locking plates and then withdraw the stub axle and gasket from the end of the rear axle casing, or from the front steering swivel in the case of the front stub axle.
4    If a new stub axle is to be fitted, or if the old one is serviceable but is being overhauled, the distance piece on the inner end of the stub axle will have to be renewed, or a new one fitted to the new stub axle.
5    To renew the distance piece on an existing stub axle, secure the stub axle in a vice with protected jaws. Split the distance piece using a cold chisel and then remove it from the shaft (Fig. 8.7).
6    To fit a new distance piece, apply sealing compound to the seating face of the distance piece. Drive it onto the stub axle so that it seats against the flange. Remove any excess sealant from the shaft or flange.
7    The front stub axle has a bush fitted into the rear of the sleeve. On a new stub axle, press a new bush into the rear of the sleeve with the stub axle firmly supported in a vice with protected jaws (Fig. 8.8). If the

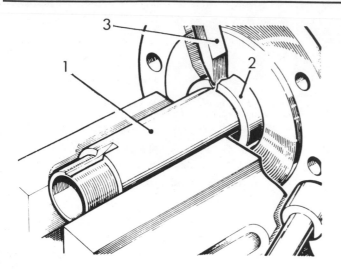

**Fig. 8.7 Renewing the distance piece (Sec 6)**

1   Stub axle              3   Cold chisel
2   Distance piece

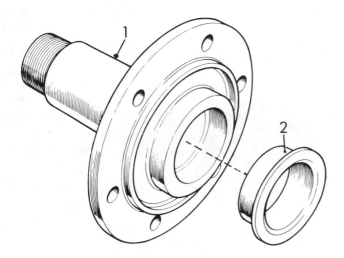

**Fig. 8.8 Front stub axle and bush (Sec 6)**

1   Stub axle                    2   Bush

original stub axle is to be used then the old bush must first be removed and then a new one can be fitted as above.

8   Fit the new gasket to the mating surface of the stub axle, having smeared it with grease on both sides.

9   Offer up the stub axle to the swivel housing or rear axle casing, line up the bolt holes and refit the bolts and locking plates.

10  Tighten the bolts evenly in diagonal sequence to the specified torque.

## 7   Differential pinion oil seal – renewal

1   This procedure covers the renewal of the differential pinion oil seal for both front and rear differential units.

2   Remove the plugs and drain the oil from the differential casing into a container, as described in Section 14.

3   Detach the propeller shaft from the pinion drive flange as described in Chapter 7.

4   Remove the split pin and make up a bracket to stop the pinion drive flange rotating so that its retaining nut can be undone. Alternatively use the help of an assistant to apply the footbrake to lock the axle.

5   Remove the retaining nut and washer and use a soft-faced mallet to tap the drive flange off the pinion shaft.

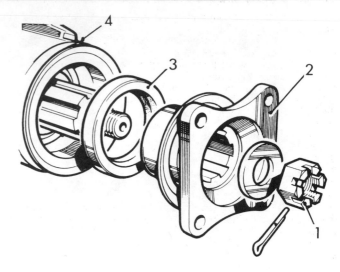

**Fig. 8.9 Differential pinion oil seal renewal (exploded view) (Sec 7)**

1   Castellated nut          4   Differential pinion
2   Pinion drive flange           housing
3   Oil seal

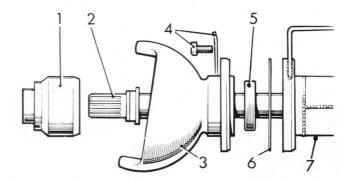

**Fig. 8.10 Front axle halfshaft, constant velocity joint and axle casing oil seal assembly (exploded view) (Sec 8)**

1   Constant velocity joint      5   Oil seal
2   Inner section halfshaft      6   Gasket
3   Swivel housing               7   Axle casing
4   Bolt and lockplate

6   Prise the oil seal from the housing front end using a screwdriver or a similar pointed tool. Take care not to damage the seal housing.

7   Smear the outside diameter of the new oil seal with the jointing compound, and the inside diameter with oil and tap it into position in the housing with the lips facing inwards.

8   Smear the outside diameter of the pinion drive flange sleeve with oil, checking it for any roughness or damage which may have damaged the last oil seal. Engage it on the splines of the shaft and push it carefully into position, taking care not to damage the new seal.

9   Refit the washer and castellated nut and tighten the nut to the specified torque. Insert a new split pin.

10  Refit the propeller shaft and secure with the bolts and locknuts.

11  Refill the axle with the correct grade of oil and check that the axle breather is clear. Remove the axle stands and lower the vehicle to the ground.

## 8   Front axle halfshafts and constant velocity joints – removal and refitting

1   Apply the handbrake and chock the rear wheels.

2   Slacken the front roadwheel nuts, jack up the front of the vehicle and remove the roadwheels.

3    Drain the oil from the swivel pin housing as described in Section 13.

4    Undo the five bolts which retain the front stub driveshaft and its integral hub to the wheel hub.

5    Tap the integral hub loose and withdraw it and the stub driveshaft from the constant velocity joint in the swivel housing (photo). This is the outer section of the jointed driveshaft. The constant velocity joint is located in the swivel housing and is jointed to the main section of the halfshaft in the front axle casing. The left-hand inner driveshaft is larger than the right-hand one due to the location of the differential housing on the axle.

6    Remove the front wheel hub and bearing assembly as described in Section 5.

7    Remove the front wheel stub axle as described in Section 6.

8    Remove the constant velocity joint from the end of the inner section of the halfshaft assembly.

9    Withdraw the inner section halfshaft, taking care not to damage the oil seal in the outer end of the axle casing with the splined inner end of the halfshaft.

10   Lubricate the halfshaft inner section with oil and carefully feed the splined inner end through the oil seal, taking care not to damage it.

11   Engage the splined inner end in the differential side gear and push it right home.

12   Check the condition of the constant velocity joint and fit a new one if in any doubt.

13   Refit the stub axle as described in Section 6.

14   Refit the front wheel hub and bearing assembly as described in Section 5.

15   Fit a new gasket to the mating face of the stub driveshaft hub and offer the driveshaft to the stub axle sleeve. Engage the splines into the constant velocity joint and align the holes in the shaft hub with the holes in the wheel hub.

16   Refit and tighten the hub bolts to the specified torque.

17   Refill the swivel pin housing with oil to the correct level and refit the plug.

18   Refit the roadwheel, lower and remove the jack and tighten the roadwheel nuts.

## 9    Front axle casing oil seals – removal and refitting

1    Remove the roadwheel, front hub, stub axle and the front axle halfshaft assembly as described in the previous Sections. Then clean off all the mud and road dirt from the swivel assembly and axle end.

2    Separate the track rod balljoint from the front swivel.

3    In the case of the left-hand swivel, disconnect the drag link balljoint as well from the swivel front arm (Fig. 8.11).

4    Knock back the locking tabs, undo the swivel housing retaining bolts and remove the swivel and housing assembly from the axle casing.

5    Remove the gasket and withdraw the oil seal from the inner end of the swivel housing.

6    Fit a new seal to the swivel housing with the lipped face outwards.

7    Fit the swivel housing assembly and a new gasket to the axle casing. Tighten the bolts to the specified torque evenly and diagonally. Then knock down the tabs to secure them.

8    Reconnect the steering arm balljoint(s) to the swivel and tighten the nut(s) to the specified torque.

9    Refit the front axle halfshaft assembly, stub axle, front hub and roadwheel as directed in the previous Sections.

## 10   Front steering swivel and housing assembly – removal, overhaul, adjustment and refitting

1    Remove the front axle halfshaft assembly, front wheel hub and

8.5 Withdrawing the front stub driveshaft and hub

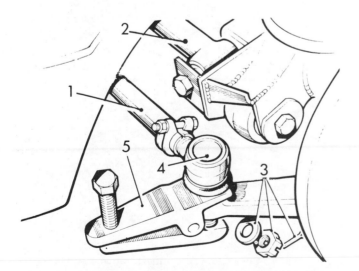

**Fig. 8.11 Drag link removal from left-hand steering swivel (Sec 9)**

1   Drag link
2   Panhard rod
3   Split pin, nut and washer
    from balljoint
4   Balljoint
5   Balljoint extractor

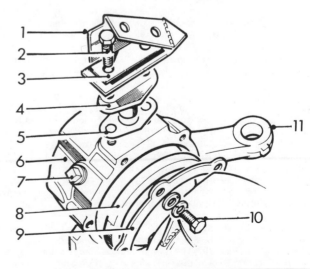

**Fig. 8.12 Front steering swivel and housing assembly (Sec 10)**

1   Brake pipe bracket
2   Swivel pin retaining
    bolt
3   Locking plate
4   Swivel pin
5   Shim
6   Steering swivel
7   Filler plug
8   Oil seal
9   Oil seal retainer plate
10  Retainer plate bolt
11  Steering arm

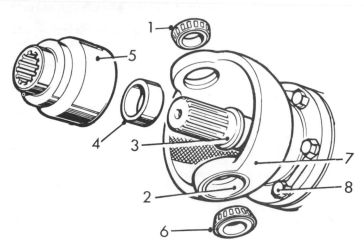

**Fig. 8.13 Swivel housing assembly (exploded view) (Sec 10)**

| | |
|---|---|
| 1   Roller bearing race – top | 5   CV joint |
| 2   Outer bearing track | 6   Roller bearing race – bottom |
| 3   Inner halfshaft section | 7   Swivel housing |
| 4   Bush | 8   Housing retaining bolt |

bearing assembly and stub axle as described in Sections 5, 6 and 8.

2   Remove the complete steering swivel and housing assembly and oil seal as described in Section 9. Clean the outside of the assembly thoroughly using a proprietary degreasing agent before dismantling begins.

3   Undo the bolts which retain the swivel and housing oil seal retainer plate.

4   Withdraw the retainer plate and the large oil seal.

5   Knock back the locking plate and undo the two bolts which retain the upper swivel pin and shim(s). Remove the complete swivel pin assembly.

6   Undo the two lower swivel pin assembly retaining bolts and remove the lower pin assembly in the same way.

7   Separate the steering swivel from the housing.

8   Remove the swivel bearing races from the top and bottom bearing positions in the swivel housing.

9   Examine the general condition of the steering swivel and swivel housing surfaces. The swivel surface of the housing must be free from corrosion, pitting and damage, otherwise the main swivel oil seal will become damaged and begin to leak.

10   Examine the roller bearing races for wear, damage and fit on the swivel pins. They should be a light push fit onto the pins. If necessary renew the bearings, as follows.

11   Drive the outer bearing tracks from the swivel housing using a hammer and suitable drift from inside the housing.

12   Fit a new bearing track to each bearing location in turn. Drive the track in squarely using a block of hardwood. Make sure that the swivel housing is adequately supported.

13   Reassemble the swivel housing assembly as follows. Fit the lower swivel pin to the steering swivel and position the bearing race on the pin. Fit the other bearing race to the upper bearing track in the housing. Secure the housing flange in a vice with projected jaws with the bearings in a vertical plane, so that the swivel area is clear of the vice.

14   Offer the steering swivel to the swivel housing and engage the lower swivel pin and bearing into the lower bearing track. As the bearing enters the location, tilt the steering swivel so that the upper swivel pin location is over the upper bearing position.

15   Refit the upper swivel pin and shim(s).

16   Check that the swivel pin bolts are tightened to the correct torque.

17   Connect a spring balance to the balljoint eye of the steering arm on the rear of the steering swivel in order to measure the resistance of the swivel to rotation in a horizontal plane. After overcoming the initial inertia, it should require a steady pull of 2.5 to 3 lb (1.2 to 1.3 kg) to turn the steering swivel on its pins.

18   To adjust the resistance where necessary, the shims beneath the

top swivel pin can be changed. Shims range from 0.003 to 0.030 in (0.076 to 0.762 mm) as shown in the Specifications.

19   If adjustments have been made to the shims, refit the swivel pin bolts and tighten them. Then recheck that the rotational resistance is acceptable. Knock over the locktabs when it is satisfactory.

20   Pack the new large oil seal with heavy grease and fit it to the assembly with the flat face to the rear.

21   Refit the seal retainer plate and refit the retaining bolts, flat and spring washers. Tighten the bolts to the specified torque.

22   Refit the steering swivel and housing assembly to the front axle using a new gasket, having renewed the axle casing oil seal, as described in Section 9.

23   Rotate the steering swivel before reconnecting the track rod balljoint, and the drag link balljoint in the case of the left-hand swivel, and check that the oil seal wipes evenly over the surface of the swivel housing.

24   Refit the remainder of the removed assemblies in the reverse order to removal as described in Sections 5, 6 and 8.

25   Check the front wheel alignment and the setting of the steering stop bolts as described in Chapter 11.

## 11   Front axle differential assembly – removal and refitting

**Note:** *Refer to paragraphs 1 and 2 of Section 3 as they apply equally here.*

1   Slacken the front roadwheel nuts, jack the vehicle up, place strong axle stands under the chassis side-members and remove the road-wheels. Chock the rear roadwheels.

2   Remove the drain plug from the front differential casing and drain the oil into a suitable container.

3   Remove the steering track rod by undoing the balljoints at each end and use a separator to free them from the swivel arms. Note which way round the track rod fits before placing it to one side.

4   Remove the steering telescopic damper as decribed in Chapter 11.

5   Detach the drag link balljoint from the left-hand steering swivel.

6   Remove the cap from the brake fluid reservoir. Place a sheet of polythene over the neck and then refit the cap to help prevent loss of fluid when the brake hoses are undone.

7   Undo the flexible brake hoses to the front calipers at the wing valance brackets, and cover the open ends of the hoses to prevent the ingress of dirt.

8   Undo the steering swivel housing retaining bolts from the front

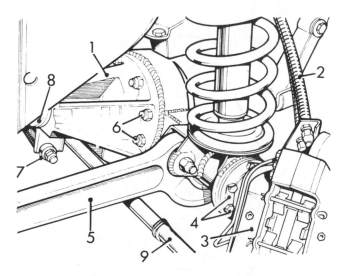

**Fig. 8.14 Front axle differential location (Sec 11)**

| | |
|---|---|
| 1   Differential unit | 6   Differential housing nuts |
| 2   Flexible brake pipes | 7   Steering damper retaining nut |
| 3   Front steering swivel | |
| 4   Swivel housing bolt and locking plate | 8   Pinion drive flange |
| 5   Radius arm | 9   Track rod |

axle casing, having knocked down the locktabs.
9  Pull the wheel hubs gently outwards just far enough to disengage the inner halfshaft sections from the differential unit side gears.
10  Remove the front propeller shaft from the front pinion drive flange as described in Chapter 7. Move the shaft to one side out of the way.
11  Undo the differential unit retaining nuts and washers while supporting the unit using a jack (photo).
12  Remove the unit carefully from the axle casing using both hands. Recover the gasket.
13  Refitting the differential unit is the reverse of the removal procedure. Note that the braking system will have to be bled when the brake hoses have been connected. Details are given in Chapter 9.
14  Refit the differential drain plug and fill the casing with the correct grade of oil to the correct level.
15  Tighten all nuts and bolts to the specified torque settings.

## 12  Front axle – removal and refitting

1  Should it be necessary, the complete front axle assembly with

11.11 The front differential unit viewed from above with the engine removed

steering swivels, track rod and differential unit can be removed in one operation.
2  Slacken the front roadwheel nuts, jack up the front of the vehicle, and support it securely with axle stands under the chassis side-members.
3  Support the weight of the front axle and remove the front roadwheels. Chock the rear roadwheels.
4  Remove the front radius arms and front shock absorber lower mounting nuts as described in Chapter 11.
5  Knock back the locking tabs and remove the brake pipe bracket retaining bolts from the steering swivel.
6  Move the bracket ot one side and refit the bolts.
7  Remove the front brake caliper as described in Chapter 9 and tie it up out of the way. Do not strain the brake pipes.
8  Separate the drag link balljoint from the left-hand steering swivel front arm using a balljoint separator. Move the drag link out of the way.
9  Disconnect the Panhard rod from the bracket on the axle casing as described in Chapter 11.
10  Disconnect the front propeller shaft from the pinion drive flange as described in Chapter 7.
11  Lower the axle carefully on the jack and withdraw the two front coil springs.
12  Lower the axle and remove it from under the vehicle.
13  Refitting is straightforward. With the axle in position under the vehicle, reconnect the Panhard rod to it.
14  Place the coil springs over the shock absorbers, then raise the axle and support the left hand-side on a jack. Reconnect the radius arms to the axle and chassis.
15  Reconnect the shock absorber lower mountings as described in Chapter 11.
16  Reconnect the propeller shaft to the front pinion drive flange and the drag link to the left-hand steering swivel front arm. Tighten the bolts and nuts.
17  Refit the brake calipers and brake pipe brackets. Tighten the mounting bolts to the specified torque.
18  Remove the jack from beneath the axle.
19  Refit the roadwheels, jack up and remove the axle stands supporting the chassis, and lower the vehicle to the ground. Remove the jack.
20  Tighten the roadwheel nuts and remove the chocks from the rear wheels.

## 13  Steering swivel pin housing – oil changing and level checking

1  The front wheel drive CV joints and the swivel pins are lubricated by oil in the swivel housings.
2  To check the level, remove the recessed level plug (Fig. 8.16) or the square-headed plug at the front of the swivel (photo), as

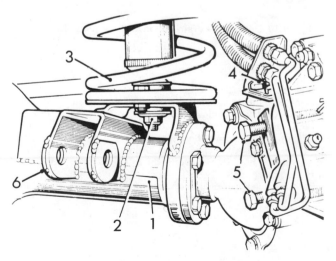

Fig. 8.15 Front axle removal (Sec 12)

1  Front axle
2  Shock absorber lower retaining nut
3  Coil spring
4  Brake pipe bracket/swivel pin bolt
5  Brake caliper bolts
6  Radius arm mounting bracket

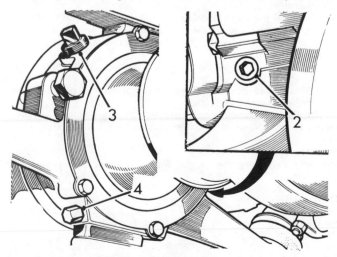

Fig. 8.16 Steering swivel pin housing – drain, level and filler plugs (Sec 13)

2  Level plug
3  Filler plug
4  Drain plug

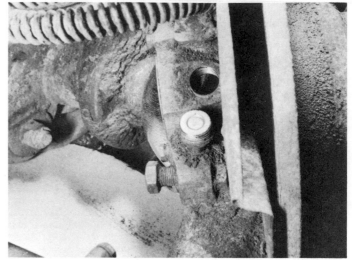

13.2 Check the steering swivel oil level by removing the front plug (this is too full)

13.3 Remove the filler plug

applicable. The oil should be level with the bottom of the hole. Do not overfill, or the oil seals may be damaged and start to leak.

3    To top up the oil, remove the filler plug from the top of the steering swivel at the front (photo). If considerable amounts of oil are required, check the oil seals and gaskets for leakage. Also check that the level and drain plugs are screwed in tightly.

4    To renew the oil in the swivel housings, remove the level and filler plugs as above and remove the drain plug from the housings at the lower front side of the steering swivels, preferably after a run when the oil is warm. Drain the oil, approx half a pint (one quarter of a litre), into a container.

5    Refit the drain plugs tightly.

6    Fill the housings with fresh gear oil, as specified, to the bottom of the level plug and no higher.

7    Refit the level plug and filler plug tightly.

8    Wipe off any excess oil from the steering swivel and housing.

---

## 14  Front and rear axle oil – changing and level checking

1    Both differential units have the same lubricant type and capacity. The filler level and drain plugs are also similar.

### Checking

2    Remove the combined filler and level plug from the differential casing. This is located on the right-hand side of the differential at the rear, and on the left-hand side of the differential at the front, since the positions are reversed.

3    The plug fitted in the front axle casing at the front can be disregarded.

4    The oil level should be at the bottom of the level plug hole and no higher, or oil seals may suffer.

5    If significant topping-up is required, check the oil seals (pinion and axle casing ends) drain plug and gaskets for signs of leakage.

### Oil changing

6    When changing the oil, do so after a run when it is warm as it

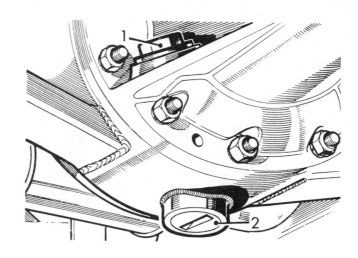

Fig. 8.17 Differential drain and level/filler plugs (Sec 14)

1    Filler and level plug          2    Drain plug

flows better.

7    Remove the filler/level plug.

8    Place a container beneath the differential, large enough to hold 3 pints (1.7 litres), and remove the drain plug from the bottom of the differential housing.

9    Allow the axle to drain thoroughly, then refit the drain plug tightly.

10  Fill the axle with the specified quantity of fresh oil, to the bottom of the level plug hole. Do not overfill the axle or damage to the oil seals will result.

11  Refit the level/filler plug and wipe off any excess oil from the axle and casing.

## 15 Fault diagnosis – front and rear axles

| Symptom | Reason(s) |
| --- | --- |
| Vibration | Out of balance propeller shaft<br>Worn hub bearings<br>Wheels out of balance<br>Universal joints or constant velocity joints worn<br>See also Fault diagnosis – suspension and steering |
| Noise on drive and overrun | Worn crownwheel and pinion gears<br>Worn differential bearings<br>Lack of lubrication in axle or swivel pin housings<br>See also Fault diagnosis – transmission |
| Noise consistent with road speed | Worn hub bearings<br>Worn differential bearings<br>Lack of lubricant in axle or swivel pin housings<br>See also Fault diagnosis – transmission |
| 'Clonk' on drive or overrun | Excessive crownwheel and pinion backlash<br>Worn propeller shaft or halfshaft universal joints<br>Worn halfshaft splines<br>Hub flange or roadwheel securing bolts loose<br>Broken, damaged or worn suspension or axle fittings<br>See also Fault diagnosis – transmission |
| Oil leakage | Faulty differential pinion or halfshaft oil seals<br>Blocked axle breather valve<br>Damaged swivel housing or oil seal |

# Chapter 9  Braking system

*For modifications, and information applicable to later models, see Supplement at end of manual*

## Contents

## Specifications

### System type

| | |
|---|---|
| Footbrake | Disc brakes front and rear, dual hydraulic system, servo-assisted |
| Handbrake | Mechanically-operated drum brake transmission rear output shaft |

### Front brakes

| | |
|---|---|
| Disc diameter | 11.75 in (298.17 mm) |
| Disc thickness | 0.510 in (13.0 mm) minimum |
| Disc run-out | 0.006 in (0.15 mm) maximum |
| Pad minimum thickness | 0.125 in (3.0 mm) |
| Number of caliper pistons | 4 (2 per circuit) |

### Rear brakes

| | |
|---|---|
| Disc diameter | 11.42 in (290.0 mm) |
| Disc thickness | 0.460 in (12.0 mm) minimum |
| Disc run-out | 0.006 in (0.15 mm) maximum |
| Pad minimum thickness | 0.062 in (1.5 mm) |
| Number of caliper pistons | 2 |

### Handbrake (transmission brake)

| | |
|---|---|
| Lining width | 3.0 in (76.2 mm) |
| Drum internal diameter | 7.25 in (184.05 mm) |
| Refinishing limit | +0.030 in (0.76 mm) |

### Torque wrench settings

| | lbf ft | kgf m |
|---|---|---|
| Brake disc retaining bolts | 38 | 5.0 |
| Brake caliper retaining bolts | 60 | 8.3 |
| Brake caliper halves retaining bolts | 60 | 8.3 |
| Transmission output flange | 120 | 16.6 |
| Transmission brake backplate bolts | 25 | 3.5 |
| Transmission brake pivot bolt | 43 | 5.9 |
| Brake failure warning switch end plug | 16 | 2.2 |

## 1  General description

The Range Rover is equipped with self-adjusting servo-assisted disc brakes at the front and rear. A dual-line hydraulic system is employed. This has primary and secondary circuits. The primary circuit is connected to all four disc brake calipers whereas the secondary circuit is connected to the front brakes alone. A brake failure warning switch is incorporated in the system so that in the event of failure of either circuit, a warning light will be illuminated on the dashboard.

In order that there is no connection between the primary and secondary circuits in the front brakes, each front caliper has four pistons. The primary circuit is connected to the upper pair of pistons and the secondary circuit to the lower pair. The rear brake calipers have only two pistons each.

The brake fluid reservoir is divided with an internal partition so that the rear section feeds the primary circuit and the front section feeds the secondary circuit.

In the event of a failure in the primary system, the secondary system will still function and will operate the front brakes. Although this will still stop the vehicle adequately, it will inevitably take longer to do so.

Should the vacuum servo unit fail, the brakes will still function, although greater effort will be required to push the brake pedal down. The purpose of the vacuum unit is to reduce the effort required by the driver to operate the brakes.

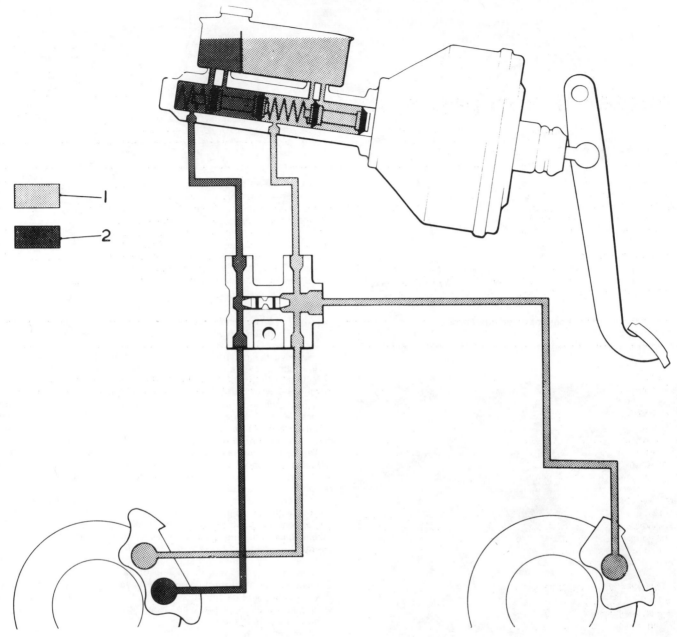

**Fig. 9.1 Hydraulic system layout (Sec 1)**

*1   Primary circuit*                              *2   Secondary circuit*

The handbrake operates independently of the footbrake. A central lever operates a drum brake, which is mounted on the rear end of the transfer gearbox output shaft, via a mechanical linkage. Since the effect of operating the handbrake is to lock the rear propeller shaft, the Range Rover being a four-wheel drive vehicle has effectively a handbrake which operates on all four wheels. There is however a certain amount of slack in the system and before any work is done under the car the wheels should be chocked.

The handbrake, or transmission brake, has two brake shoes and is adjustable externally. Since it is mounted high up under the vehicle it is in a well-protected position from flying dirt and water, unless deep wading is being undertaken.

## 2   Brake hydraulic system – bleeding

1   If any of the hydraulic components in the braking system have been removed or disconnected, or if the fluid level in the master cylinder has been allowed to fall appreciably, it is inevitable that air will

have been introduced into the system. The removal of all this air from the hydraulic system is essential if the brakes are to function correctly, and the process of removing it is known as bleeding.

2   There are a number of one-man, do-it-yourself, brake bleeding kits currently available from motor accessory shops. It is recommended that one of these kits should be used whenever possible as they greatly simplify the bleeding operation and also reduce the risk of expelled air and fluid being drawn back into the system.

3   If one of these kits is not available, then it will be necessary to gather together a clean jar and suitable length of clear plastic tubing which is a tight fit over the bleed screw, and also to engage the help of an assistant. If the complete system is to be bled, two lengths of tubing will be required.

4   Before commencing the bleeding operation, check that all rigid pipes and flexible hoses are in good condition and that all hydraulic unions are tight. Take great care not to allow hydraulic fluid to come into contact with the vehicle paintwork, otherwise the finish will be seriously damaged. Wash off any spilled fluid immediately with cold water.

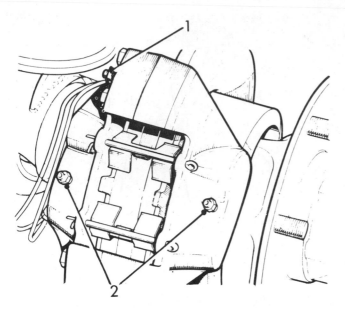

Fig. 9.2 Front caliper bleed nipples (Sec 2)

*1   Primary circuit bleed nipple     2   Secondary circuit bleed nipples*

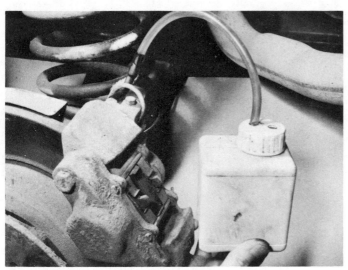

2.10 Connecting the one-man bleeding kit to the rear caliper

5    If hydraulic fluid has been lost from the master cylinder, due to a leak in the system, ensure that the cause is traced and rectified before proceeding further or a serious malfunction of the braking system may occur.
6    To bleed the system, clean the area around the bleed screw at the wheel cylinder to be bled. If the hydraulic system has only been partially disconnected and suitable precautions were taken to prevent further loss of fluid, it should only be necessary to bleed that part of the system. However, if the entire system is to be bled, start at the wheel furthest away from the master cylinder.
7    If the secondary circuit only is being bled, start at the caliper furthest from the master cylinder, first bleeding the screw on the same side as the fluid pipes. Then bleed from the other secondary bleed screw on the same caliper. Repeat on the other front caliper.
8    If the entire system is being bled, the primary and secondary bleed screws on the same side of the front caliper must be bled simultaneously, followed by the secondary bleed screw on the other side of the caliper. Obviously two lengths of bleed tubing will be required for this, and a T-piece adaptor if a one-man bleeding kit is being used.

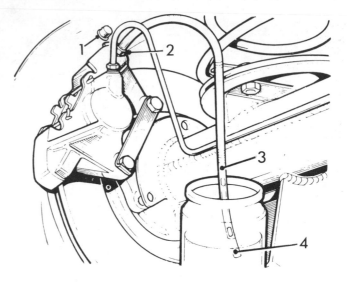

Fig. 9.3 Brake bleeding – the traditional method (Sec 2)

*1   Bleed nipple dust cap          3   Tube*
*2   Bleed nipple                   4   Jar*

9    Remove the master cylinder filler cap and top up the reservoir. Periodically check the fluid level during the bleeding operation and top up as necessary.
10   If a one-man brake bleeding kit is being used, connect the outlet tube to the bleed screw (photo) and then open the screw half a turn. If possible position the unit so that it can be viewed from the car, then depress the brake pedal to the floor (or as far as it will go) and slowly release it. The one-way valve in the kit will prevent dispelled air from returning to the system for 5 seconds, between each stroke. Repeat this operation until clean hydraulic fluid, free from air bubbles, can be seen coming through the tube. Now tighten the bleed screw and remove the outlet tube.
11   If a one-man brake bleeding kit is not available, connect one end of the plastic tubing to the bleed screw and immerse the other end in the jar containing sufficient clean hydraulic fluid to keep the end of the tube submerged. Open the bleed screw half a turn and have your assistant depress the brake pedal to the floor (or as far as it will go) and then slowly release it. Pause for 5 seconds between each stroke. Tighten the bleed screw at the end of each downstroke to prevent expelled air and fluid from being drawn back into the system. Repeat this operation until clean hydraulic fluid, free from air bubbles, can be seen coming through the tube. Now tighten the bleed screw and remove the plastic tube.
12   If the entire system is being bled the procedures described above should now be repeated at each wheel, finishing at the wheel nearest the master cylinder. Do not forget to recheck the fluid level in the master cylinder at regular intervals and top up as necessary. See also paragraph 8.
13   When completed, recheck the fluid level in the master cylinder, top up if necessary and refit the cap. Check the 'feel' of the brake pedal which should be firm and free from any 'sponginess' which would indicate air still present in the system.
14   Discard any expelled hydraulic fluid as it is likely to be contaminated with moisture, air and dirt which makes it unsuitable for further use.

## 3   Brake pads – removal and refitting

1    Apply the handbrake, slacken the appropriate roadwheel nuts and jack up the front or rear of the vehicle. Chock the roadwheels still on the ground.
2    Remove the roadwheel.
3    Withdraw the split pins from the caliper (photo).
4    Lift the pad retaining springs away.
5    Withdraw the pads, and the shims as well at the rear. Note which way the shims fit (photo).

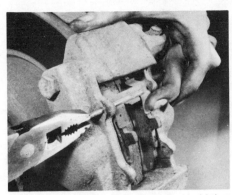

3.3 Withdraw the upper split pin and hold the retaining spring

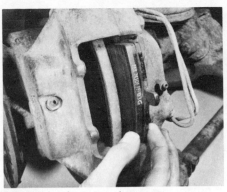

3.5 Withdrawing a front brake pad

3.6 When the pads have been withdrawn the pistons must be pushed back

3.7 Use new split pins when refitting the pads

6    Carefully press the caliper pistons back into their bores (photo). **Note**: *This will cause the reservoir fluid level to rise. Prevent it from overflowing by loosening the caliper bleed nipple as the piston is being moved, then close it when movement is complete.*

7    Refitting is the reverse of the removal procedure, but the following points should be noted:

 (a)  *Ensure that the pad location area in the caliper is free from dust and dirt. Smear a little disc brake lubricant on the metal-to-metal contact arms*

 (b)  *If the shims are corroded, obtain new ones; they should be inserted with the D-shaped cut-out downwards (rear brakes only)*

 (c)  *Use new split pins. Fold back one leg of each split pin (photo)*

 (d)  *Depress the brake pedal several times on completion to correctly locate the pads*

 (e)  *Check the reservoir fluid level on completion*

8    If new brake pads are being fitted remember that the pads in *both* calipers on any one axle must be renewed at the same time, otherwise unbalanced braking will be the result.

## 4    Brake caliper – removal and refitting

**Note**: *The brake caliper can be unbolted from the axle casing and tied up out of the way without undoing the brake pipes, but the pipes must not be strained. On the rear axle undo the brake pipe clips to ease the strain.*

1    Slacken the roadwheel nuts, jack up the front or rear of the vehicle and remove the appropriate roadwheel(s). Chock the roadwheels still on the ground. Place axle stands beneath the raised axle to support it.

2    Clean off the road dirt from the caliper, hub and disc assembly.

3    Place a film of polythene over the neck of the brake fluid reservoir and refit the cap to reduce the fluid loss when the brake pipes are disconnected at the calipers.

4    Disconnect the brake pipe(s) from the caliper at the connector(s). There are two pipes feeding each of the front calipers and one pipe

feeding each of the rear calipers. Wipe up any spilled fluid that cannot be collected in a container.

5    On early models knock back the locking plates used to retain the caliper mounting bolts. Later models have spring washers instead.

6    Undo the two mounting bolts and withdraw them so that the caliper can be lifted away. Note that the later types have splash guards

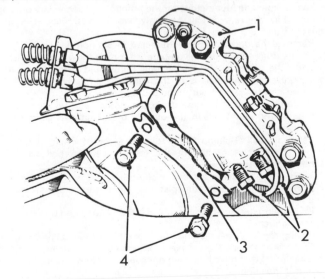

**Fig. 9.4 Front brake caliper (Sec 4)**

 1    *Caliper assembly*
 2    *Primary and secondary circuit brake fluid pipes*
 3    *Locking plate (early models only)*
 4    *Caliper mounting bolts (and spring washers - later models)*

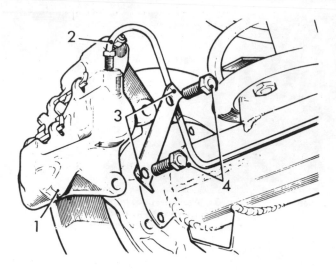

Fig. 9.5 Rear brake caliper assembly (Sec 4)

1   Caliper assembly          3   Locking plate
2   Brake fluid pipe          4   Caliper mounting bolts

on the rear brake calipers and these can be lifted away with the caliper.
7    Remove the brake pads from the calipers, referring to Section 3 if necessary.
8    Refitting is the reverse procedure. Do not fit the pads until after the calipers have been refitted.
9    Tighten the caliper mounting bolts to the specified torque. Knock up the locking plates (where fitted).
10   Refit the brake pads as described in Section 3.
11   Connect the brake fluid pipes and bleed the brakes in accordance with the instructions given in Section 2. Refit the roadwheels and lower the vehicle. Check the brakes for correct operation.

## 5   Brake caliper – overhaul

1    The overhaul procedure for both front and rear brake calipers is basically the same. The differences that occur are due to the fact that the front caliper has four pistons for the primary and secondary braking circuits while the rear caliper has only two pistons, since it is only connected to the primary circuit.
2    Remove the brake caliper as directed in Section 4.
3    The overhaul procedure given here is for the renewal of the piston seals and the inspection of the pistons, bores, and seal grooves. **Do not** separate the two halves of the caliper, as the whole overhaul procedure can be carried out without doing so.
4    Having removed the caliper from the vehicle and withdrawn the brake pads, thoroughly clean the outside of the caliper using methylated spirits.
5    Using a small G-clamp and a thin flat piece of wood, clamp the piston(s) on the inside half of the caliper (i.e. the half with the mounting bracket).
6    Apply a low pressure air line or alternatively a tyre foot pump to the fluid port(s) and eject the piston(s) from the outer half of the caliper.
7    Take great care when doing this that the pistons and bores do not become scratched.
8    Having removed the piston(s) from one half of the caliper, remove the G-clamp and place the flat piece of wood over the hole(s) vacated by the piston(s) that have just been removed. Carefully clamp the piece of wood in position.
9    Apply the low pressure air source to the fluid port and eject the other piston(s), then remove the G-clamp.
10   Note the exact positions of the pistons. Under no circumstances change their caliper positions. Should one of the pistons be seized in the caliper, the whole caliper must be renewed.
11   Using a blunt screwdriver, carefully prise out the wiper seal retainers. Do not scratch any metal parts.
12   Extract the wiper dust seals and fluid seals from the bores.

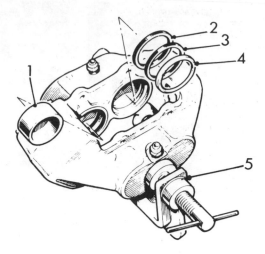

Fig. 9.6 Front brake caliper overhaul (Sec 5)

1   Piston            4   Retainer
2   Fluid seal        5   Clamp
3   Wiper seal

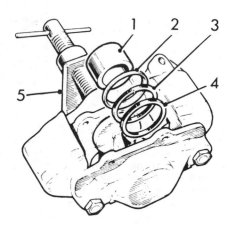

Fig. 9.7 Rear brake caliper overhaul (Sec 5)

1   Piston            4   Fluid seal
2   Retainer          5   Clamp
3   Wiper seal

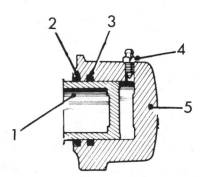

Fig. 9.8 Sectional view of caliper and piston assembly (Sec 5)

1   Piston            4   Bleed nipple
2   Wiper seal        5   Caliper housing
3   Fluid seal

13 Thoroughly clean the metal parts using clean brake fluid, methylated spirit or isopropyl alchohol. Inspect the caliper bores and pistons for wear, scoring and corrosion, renew parts as necessary. *Do not attempt to separate the two halves of the calipers.*

14 To reassemble the caliper and pistons, first coat the fluid seal with clean brake fluid or disc brake lubricant. Then using your fingers only, position new fluid seals in the caliper bores, ensuring that they are properly located. They will stand proud of the bore at the edge furthest away from the mouth of the bore.

15 Lubricate the bores with new brake fluid and squarely insert the pistons in their original positions. Leave about $\frac{5}{16}$ in (8 mm) of each piston projecting. It is easier if the bleed nipples are slackened off when this operation is carried out; the pistons will then slide in more easily as there is no counter pressure.

16 Smear the wiper seal with disc brake lubricator brake fluid. Fit a new wiper seal into each seal retainer, and slide an assembly into each bore, seal side first. Use the piston as a guide.

17 Press the seals and pistons fully home, using the G-clamp if necessary.

18 Refitting of the caliper is now the reverse of the removal procedure. Fit the remaining bolts only finger tight at first and reconnect the fluid pipe(s).

19 Tighten the retaining bolts to the recommended torque setting and, where fitted on earlier models, bend back the ends of the tab washers. The fluid coupling can now be fully tightened.

20 On completion of this installation the brakes will have to be bled as described in Section 2. Fitting of the brake pads is covered in Section 3.

## 6  Brake disc – removal and refitting

1  Remove the brake caliper as described in Section 4.
2  Remove the wheel hub assembly as described in Chapter 8.
3  Undo and remove the bolts which retain the brake disc to the wheel hub.
4  Using a soft-faced mallet tap the disc off the wheel hub.
5  Refit the disc to the wheel hub and secure it with the retaining bolts. Tighten them to the specified torque.
6  Use a dial gauge to check the disc run-out. This must not exceed that specified. If necessary undo the bolts, remove the disc and fit it with the holes aligned differently. Tighten the bolts and recheck the run-out, until correct. If the run-out is excessive with the disc in all possible positions, renew the disc.
7  Refit the wheel hub assembly as described in Chapter 8 and the brake caliper as described in Section 4.

## 7  Brake disc – inspection and refacing

1  Remove the roadwheel.
2  Check the surfaces of the disc for wear, scoring, ridging or breaking up. As a vehicle gets older there is a tendency for the disc to break up from the outer edge. Less of the effective braking area is left and the rough edges quickly ruin the brake pads. A disc in this condition must be renewed.
3  If however the disc is slightly scored or ridged it may be refaced, provided that in so doing the thickness of the disc is not reduced below that specified.
4  Refacing of the disc is done by machining equal amounts off both sides of the disc. This is a specialist job and must be done properly, or there is a good chance that the braking efficiency of the vehicle will be worse than before. Check the cost of refacing against the cost of a new disc before deciding to go ahead.
5  The disc original thickness is marked on the disc boss. Using this value, the amount that can be removed before the minimum thickness is reached can be worked out.
6  Also check the disc for run-out as described in Section 6. If the disc is in the vehicle, be sure that excessive run-out is not due to worn hub bearings.

## 8  Brake failure warning valve and switch – removal, overhaul and refitting

1  The brake failure warning valve and switch are located beneath the brake master cylinder in the engine compartment.
2  Unplug the electrical connector at the switch (photo).
3  Remove the brake fluid reservoir cap, place a piece of polythene film over the filler opening and refit the cap, to reduce the loss of fluid when the brake fluid pipes are disconnected from the switch.
4  Undo the five brake pipe connectors and plug the ends of the pipes to prevent ingress of dirt or foreign matter.
5  Undo the single central bolt and remove the switch and valve unit from the inner wing panel.
6  To overhaul the unit, first clean the outside with methylated spirit.
7  Remove the end plug and copper washer. The washer should be discarded.
8  Unscrew and remove the switch itself.
9  The shuttle valve can now be removed. Use a low pressure air line or tyre pump if necessary.
10  Remove the O-rings from the shuttle valve.
11  Clean all the components in brake fluid or methylated spirit and

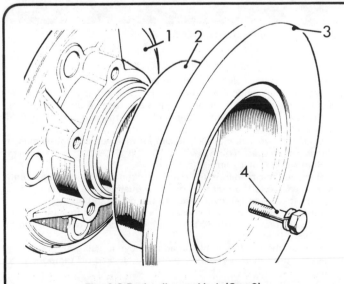

**Fig. 9.9 Brake disc and hub (Sec 6)**

| | | | |
|---|---|---|---|
| 1 | Wheel hub | 3 | Disc |
| 2 | Boss | 4 | Retaining bolt |

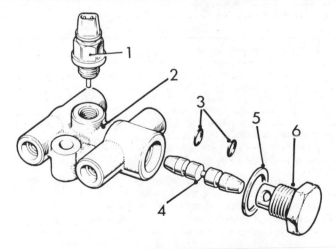

**Fig. 9.10 Brake failure warning valve and switch assembly (exploded view) (Sec 8)**

| | | | |
|---|---|---|---|
| 1 | Switch | 4 | Shuttle valve |
| 2 | Valve body | 5 | Copper washer |
| 3 | O-rings | 6 | Plug |

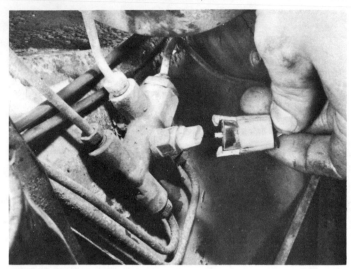

8.2 Unplug the electrical connector

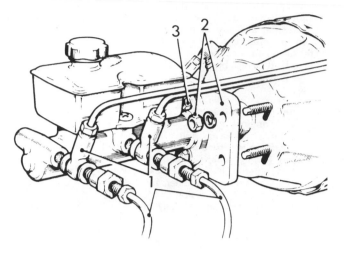

Fig. 9.11 Early type of master cylinder (Sec 9)

1   Brake pipes              3    Master cylinder-to-adaptor nut
2   Adaptor and retaining nut

inspect the valve and its bore for any signs of scratching, corrosion, or wear. They must be in perfect condition. If they are not, fit a new complete assembly.

12   Check the operation of the warning light switch by reconnecting the leads to the switch. Press the switch plunger against any earthing point on the vehicle and the warning light should be illuminated (ignition on). If not, then check the warning light bulb and renew it if necessary; alternatively renew the switch, having checked the circuit for continuity first.

13   To reassemble the valve and switch unit, first fit two new O-rings to the shuttle. Lubricate them with disc brake lubricant or clean brake fluid.

14   Lubricate the shuttle bore with brake fluid and refit the shuttle.

15   Refit the end plug using a new copper washer. Tighten the plug to the specified torque.

16   Screw in the warning switch tightly.

17   Refit the unit to the inner wing with the plug facing to the rear. Secure it with the single bolt.

18   Unplug and refit the five brake pipes to the unit. Make sure that they are fitted to their correct locations.

19   Refit the warning light switch lead.

20   Bleed the complete braking system, both primary and secondary circuits, as described in Section 2.

## 9  Master cylinder and servo unit – general

1   There are two different types of master cylinder and servo unit assemblies fitted to the Range Rover. On the early type the master cylinder is secured to an adaptor plate, which is then attached to the servo unit by four nuts. On the later models the master cylinder is attached directly to the servo unit with two nuts. In both cases a tandem master cylinder is fitted.

2   Individual components are not interchangeable between the two different types, nor can the later master cylinder be fitted to the early servo unit.

3   If either the master cylinder or servo unit of the early pattern requires renewal, then it will be necessary to replace both with a complete master cylinder and servo unit of the later type.

4   With the later type, individual components or assemblies can be renewed.

## 10  Master cylinder – removal, overhaul and refitting

Note: Read Section 9 before overhauling the master cylinder.

1   Disconnect the brake pipes from the master cylinder. Note their installed positions. Plug the ports and cover the ends of the pipes to prevent the ingress of dirt or foreign matter and loss of fluid.

2   Early models: undo the master cylinder and adaptor plate nuts and

10.3 The later type of master cylinder

remove the master cylinder from the servo unit.

3   Later models: undo the two units which secure the master cylinder directly to the servo unit on later models and remove the unit (photo).

4   Remove the fluid reservoir cap and invert the unit. Drain the fluid into a container.

5   Undo the two screws which secure the reservoir unit to the master cylinder. Lift the reservoir away.

6   Remove the inlet port seals.

7   Remove the circlip from the rear end of the cylinder bore and apply low air pressure to the rear fluid outlet to push out the primary piston.

8   With the piston removed, recover the guide and spring.

9   Push the secondary piston down the bore against its spring using a copper or brass rod so that the locating pin can be withdrawn from the forward inlet port.

10   Release the secondary piston and remove it, using air pressure if necessary. Both inlet ports will have to be blocked off temporarily to do this.

11   Withdraw the secondary piston spring and guide.

12   Separate the seals and shim washers from the two pistons. Note which type fits where and how it fits.

13   Wash all components in methylated spirit, isopropyl alcohol or clean fluid, and examine the surfaces of the pistons and cylinder bore for scoring or 'bright' wear areas. Where these are evident renew the

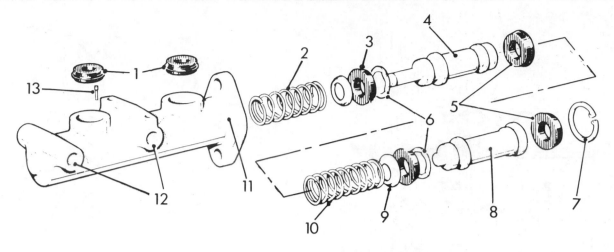

**Fig. 9.12 Brake master cylinder – exploded view (Sec 10)**

| | | | |
|---|---|---|---|
| 1 | Inlet port seals | 5 | Seals | 8 | Primary piston | 11 | Master cylinder housing |
| 2 | Piston spring | 6 | Shim washers | 9 | Guide | 12 | Brake pipe connections |
| 3 | Seal | 7 | Circlip | 10 | Piston spring | 13 | Locating pin |
| 4 | Secondary piston | | | | | | |

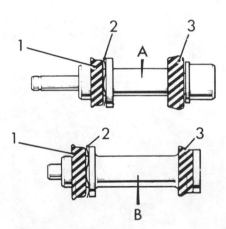

**Fig. 9.13 Master cylinder piston seal assembly (Sec 10)**

| | | | |
|---|---|---|---|
| A | Secondary piston | 2 | Shim washer |
| B | Primary piston | 3 | Rear seal |
| 1 | Front seal | | |

complete master cylinder.
14  If the components are in good condition, discard all seals and obtain the appropriate repair kit.
15  Install a shim washer to the primary and secondary pistons, with the concave face towards the seal.
16  Using the fingers only, manipulate the two identical piston seals into place on the primary and secondary piston (lips facing away from the washers).
17  Of the two remaining seals contained in the repair kit, fit one to the primary piston (lip towards primary spring seat). Fit the other to the secondary piston (lip towards rear).
18  Fit the shorter return spring and cup to the secondary piston, dip the assembly into clean hydraulic fluid and insert it into the master cylinder body. Take care not to turn back the lip of the seal.
19  Depress the secondary piston and insert the stop pin after the head of the piston has been seen to pass the feed port.
20  Fit the return spring and cup to the primary piston, dip the assembly into clean hydraulic fluid and insert it into the master cylinder body. Take care not to turn back the seal lips. Refit the retaining circlip.
21  Fit new seals to the inlet ports.
22  Refit the reservoir and secure it with the two screws.

23  Refit the master cylinder to the servo unit and secure it with four nuts (early models with adaptor plate) or two nuts (later models).
24  Reconnect the brake pipes to their correct locations on the master cylinder.
25  Refit the brake fluid reservoir with brake fluid of the specified type.
26  Bleed the complete braking system as described in Section 2.

## 11  Servo unit – removal, filter renewal and refitting

Note: *Read Section 9 before removing the servo unit.*
1    The vacuum servo unit on early models cannot be repaired. If it has to be renewed then the master cylinder will have to be renewed as well.
2    Remove the master cylinder as described in Section 10, unless the complete early type assembly is being replaced by the complete later type.
3    Disconnect the servo vacuum pipe from the servo valve.
4    On later models (1979 on), disconnect the vacuum loss warning switch lead.
5    Separate the servo operating rod from the brake pedal, undo the servo and brake pedal mounting bracket nuts and release the stop-light switch wiring from the brake pedal bracket as described in Section 12.
6    Withdraw the servo unit from the engine compartment.
7    To renew the servo air filter, slide the rubber boot and end cap along the operating rod.
8    Prise the old filter from the diaphragm housing neck.
9    Cut the filter from the outside to the inside diameter to remove it from the rod.
10  Cut the new filter obliquely from the outer edge to the centre to fit it over the operating rod.
11  Fit the new filter into the neck of the diaphragm housing.
12  Refit the seal end cap and rubber boot.
13  Refitting is the reverse procedure to removal. Note that the servo pushrod should be reconnected to the brake pedal with the cam on the bolt facing forward. Do not tighten it immediately.
14  On the early type of servo there should be some free play in the pedal action. Adjust the sleeve and locknut if necessary to achieve this.
15  Rotate the pivot bolt to pull the brake pedal back until it just touches the rubber buffer. Then tighten the nut.
16  Reconnect the brake pipes to the master cylinder and the vacuum servo hose to the unit. Reconnect the vacuum loss switch lead and brake failure switch lead, (as applicable).
17  Bleed the complete braking system as described in Section 2.

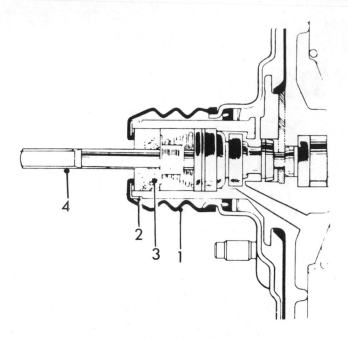

**Fig. 9.14 Brake servo air filter assembly (Sec 11)**

| | |
|---|---|
| 1   *Rubber boot* | 3   *Filter* |
| 2   *End cap* | 4   *Operating rod* |

## 12  Brake pedal assembly – removal, overhaul and refitting

1    Remove the trim panel below the dashboard on the driver's side of the car (photo).
2    Undo the nut and remove the pivot bolt which attaches the servo operating rod to the brake pedal.
3    Disconnect the two wires from the stop-light switch on the brake pedal box.
4    Undo and remove the four nuts and washers which attach the brake pedal box and servo unit to the bulkhead.
5    Withdraw the brake pedal and box assembly from the car.
6    To remove the brake pedal from the pedal box, unhook the pedal return spring from the pedal and remove the circlip from the flattened end of the pedal pivot shaft. Withdraw the shaft, and the pedal and return spring can be separated from the pedal box.
7    Remove the pivot bushes from the pedal.
8    Fit new bushes to the pedal pivot. Press them in squarely and evenly.
9    Offer the pedal and return spring to the pedal box and refit the pivot shaft. Secure the shaft with the circlip.
10   The assembly can now be refitted to the car, the procedure being the reversal of the removal sequence. Refer to Section 11 for servo pushrod adjustment (early models) and pivot bolt adjustment.

## 13  Brake pipes and hoses – inspection, removal and refitting

1    Inspection of the braking system hydraulic pipes and flexible hoses is part of the maintenance schedule. Carefully check the rigid pipes along the rear axle, underbody and in the engine compartment, not forgetting the short runs to the front wheel calipers. Any pipes showing signs of corrosion or damage should be renewed, following which it will be necessary to bleed the system as described in Section 2.
2    Carefully inspect the flexible hoses. There is one flexible pipe to the rear axle and two to each of the front calipers. Look for any signs of swelling, cracking and/or chafing. If any of these maladies is evident, renew the hoses straight away. Remember that your life could depend on it.
3    Where flexible hoses are to be renewed, unscrew the metal pipe union nut from its connection to the hose, and then holding the

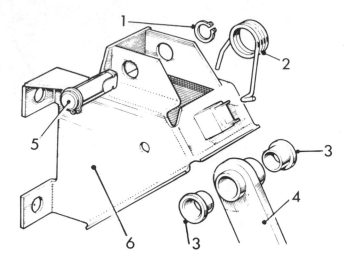

**Fig. 9.15 Brake pedal mounting – exploded view (Sec 12)**

| | |
|---|---|
| 1   *Circlip* | 4   *Pedal* |
| 2   *Pedal return spring* | 5   *Pivot pin* |
| 3   *Bushes* | 6   *Pedal box* |

12.1 View of brake pedal assembly with trim removed

hexagon on the hose with a spanner, unscrew the attachment nut and washer.
4    The body end of the flexible hose can now be withdrawn from the chassis mounting bracket and will be quite free.
5    Refitting is the reverse of the removal procedure, following which it will be necessary to bleed the appropriate part of the system, as described in Section 2.

## 14  Handbrake lever and linkage – removal and refitting

**Note:** *This operation is complicated by the location of the linkage, which is attached to the right-hand side of the transfer gearbox and requires the removal of the front section of the floor of the vehicle in order to reach and remove it. The rear end of the linkage which is connected to the handbrake lever can be reached from underneath the vehicle in the normal way.*

1    Remove the carpet or rubber matting from the front of the vehicle and remove the floor as described in Chapter 12.
2    The linkage is in two parts. The main section consists of a mounting bracket for the handbrake lever and ratchet assembly, and to

6 Lift the assembly away, disconnecting the warning light switch wiring as this is done.
7 Refitting is the reverse procedure to removal. Once the linkage has been reconnected at the pivot end, the slack in the linkage can be taken up in the screw adjuster to the rear of the handbrake lever.

## 15 Transmission brake (handbrake) assembly – dismantling, overhaul, brake shoe renewal and reassembly

1 Jack the rear of the vehicle up and support it securely on strong axle stands. If the front of the vehicle is not jacked up, chock the front wheels.
2 Disconnect the propeller shaft from the transmission brake as described in Chapter 7 (photo).
3 Remove the clevis pin at the rear of the handbrake linkage pivot (photo).
4 Remove the two countersunk cross-head screws in the rear face of the brake drum and pull off the drum (photo).
5 If the drum is difficult to remove, slacken the shoe adjuster as described in Section 16.
6 Note the positions of the brake shoes and springs. Remove the steady cups and springs from the shoes and withdraw the steady pins from the rear of the backplate (photo).
7 Slacken the adjuster completely to relieve the tension on the brake shoes and springs, and withdraw the adjuster (photo).
8 Unhook the tensioner spring (lower one) and remove it.
9 Unhook and remove the upper spring (photo).
10 Remove the left-hand (leading) shoe and the right-hand (trailing) shoe, which has to be freed from the actuating lever (photo).
11 Remove the actuating lever and shim by withdrawing them through the backplate towards the rear of the vehicle, should this be necessary.
12 To remove the transmission backplate, have an assistant apply the footbrake and engage a low gear to stop the output flange rotating, and remove the output flange retaining nut. Withdraw the flange.
13 Undo and remove the brake shoe pivot bolt (photo).

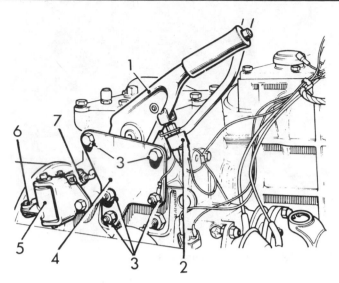

**Fig. 9.16 Handbrake, mounting bracket and linkage (Sec 14)**

1 Handbrake lever
2 Warning light switch
3 Mounting bracket retaining nuts and bolts
4 Mounting bracket
5 Main pivot
6 Clevis pin
7 Adjuster

the rear of this is the bracket which holds the main pivoting part of the handbrake linkage.
3 Remove the split pins and clevis pins from the main linkage pivot arms.
4 Remove the split pin from the main pivot pin and withdraw the pivot pin. The main pivot can now be removed from its bracket (photo).
5 Undo and remove the retaining nuts and bolts for the handbrake mounting bracket (photo).

14.4 Withdrawing the pivot pin

14.5 Undoing the handbrake mounting bracket (gearbox removed)

15.2 Disconnecting the propeller shaft

15.3 Removing the linkage clevis pin

15.4 Pull off the brake drum

15.6 Removing the steady cup and spring for the trailing shoe

15.7 Pull the brake shoes apart to remove the adjuster

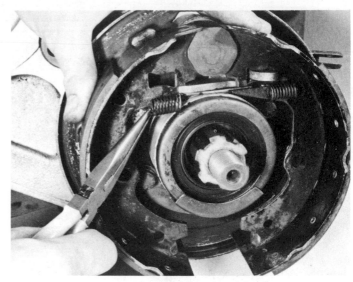

15.9 Unhook and remove the upper spring

15.10 Disconnect the actuating lever from the trailing shoe as it is removed

15.13 Removing the pivot bolt

15.14 Undo the oil catcher and backplate bolts

15.15 Lifting the backplate away

14 Undo the backplate and oil catcher retaining bolts and remove them. Lift the oil catcher away (photo).

15 Carefully remove any brake lining dust from the backplate, taking care not to inhale it as it can be injurious to health. Remove the backplate (photo).

16 Examine the brake shoes for wear. If the linings are worn down to or near the rivets they must be renewed, or new brake shoes must be fitted.

17 Check that the brake shoes are not contaminated with oil. Renew them if necessary and correct the leakage.

18 Examine the brake drum for scoring, uneven wear or cracks. If the drum is scored then it can be skimmed to the maximum oversize listed in the Specifications.

19 Reassembly is basically the reverse procedure to dismantling.

20 Refit the backplate and oil catcher, but do not tighten the bolts until the pivot bolt has been refitted and the backplate aligned. The threads of the pivot bolt should be coated with sealant.

21 Tighten the pivot bolt and backplate/oil catcher bolts to the specified torques.

22 Refit the actuator lever and the sealing shim together if they were removed.

23 Refit the trailing (right-hand) shoe first and engage the actuator lever in the slot in the shoe.

24 Refit the steady pin, spring and cup for that shoe.

25 Refit the other shoe, steady pin, spring and cup.

26 Refit the upper spring and then the lower spring.

27 Pull the shoes apart to refit the adjuster with the wheel facing to the left.

28 Refit the coupling flange and tighten its retaining nut to the specified torque (photo).

29 Refit the brake drum and secure it.

30 Adjust the brake shoes as described in Section 16.

31 Reconnect the handbrake linkage.

32 Operate the handbrake several times to centralise the brake shoes.

33 Recheck the handbrake shoe adjustment.

34 Refit the rubber bungs to the brake drum, reconnect the propeller shaft and remove the axle stands and chocks.

## 16 Transmission brake (handbrake) – adjustment

1 The transmission brake is located beneath the vehicle and is attached to the rear output end of the transfer gearbox shaft. Because of the high ground clearance the brake can be reached by sliding underneath the vehicle.

2 Chock the front and rear road wheels, having positioned the vehicle on level ground.

3 Release the handbrake fully.

4 Remove the rubber bungs from the face of the brake drum.

5 Rotate the drum if necessary so that one of the adjuster holes is at the bottom. The easiest way to do this is to move aside the wheel chocks and move the vehicle forwards or backwards the small amount required.

6 Put the chocks back in position.

7 Insert a screwdriver through the hole in the brake drum and engage it in the notches of the adjuster (photo).

8 Lever the screwdriver downwards to tighten the shoes, or upwards to slacken them off.

9 If new shoes have just been fitted, or if taking up the slack due to normal wear, turn the adjuster wheel until the brake shoes are touching the drum.

10 Slacken the adjuster by two notches.

11 With new brake shoes it will be necessary to centralise the brake shoes by operating the handbrake lever several times. Then recheck the adjustment.

12 Refit the rubber bungs.

13 Check the operation of the handbrake lever. Remove the chocks and check that it holds the vehicle.

15.28 Refitting the coupling flange

16.7 Insert a screwdriver to rotate the adjuster notched wheel

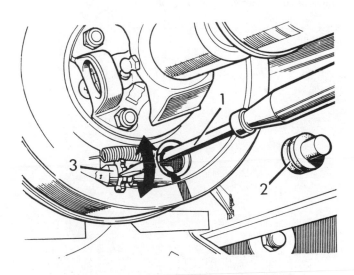

**Fig. 9.17 Handbrake adjustment (Sec 16)**

1   Screwdriver                    3   Adjuster
2   Rubber bung

## 17 Fault diagnosis – braking system

| Symptom | Reason(s) |
|---|---|
| Pedal travels almost to floorboards before brakes operate | Brake fluid too low<br>Caliper leaking<br>Master cylinder leaking (bubbles in master cylinder fluid)<br>Brake flexible hose leaking<br>Brake line fractured<br>Brake system unions loose |
| Brake pedal feels springy | New pads not yet bedded-in<br>Brake discs badly worn or cracked<br>Master cylinder securing nuts loose |
| Brake feels spongy and soggy | Caliper piston seals leaking<br>Master cylinder leaking (bubbles in master cylinder reservoir)<br>Brake pipe line or flexible hose leaking<br>Unions in brake system loose<br>Air in hydraulic system |
| Excessive effort required to brake car | Pads badly worn<br>New pads recently fitted – not yet bedded-in<br>Harder pads fitted than standard causing increase in pedal pressure<br>Pads and discs contaminated with oil, grease<br>or hydraulic fluid<br>Servo unit inoperative or faulty<br>One half of dual brake system inoperative |
| Brakes uneven and pulling to one side | Pads and discs contaminated with oil, grease<br>or hydraulic fluid<br>Tyre pressures unequal<br>Brake caliper loose<br>Brake pads fitted incorrectly<br>Different type of pads fitted at each wheel<br>Anchorages for front suspension or rear suspension loose<br>Brake discs badly worn, cracked or distorted |
| Brakes tend to bind, drag or lock-on | Air in hydraulic system<br>Wheel cylinders seized |
| Handbrake will not hold vehicle | Shoes worn or need adjustment<br>Linkage too slack<br>Shoes and drum contaminated with oil |
| Transmission judder when moving off | Brake shoes too tight, need adjustment<br>Brakes shoes sticking in 'on' position |

# Chapter 10 Electrical system

*For modifications, and information applicable to later models, see Supplement at end of manual*

## Contents

## Specifications

### General

| | |
|---|---|
| System type | 12 volt, negative earth |
| Battery capacity (typical) | 60 Ah at 20-hour rate |

### Alternator

Type:

| | |
|---|---|
| Early models | Lucas 16ACR |
| 1975 to 1979 models | Lucas 18ACR |
| 1980 models | Lucas 20ACR or 25ACR |

Test data:

| | 16ACR | 18ACR | 20/25ACR |
|---|---|---|---|
| Maximum output (nominal) | 34A | 45A | 66A |
| Regulating voltage | 14.1 to 14.5 | 13.6 to 14.4 | 13.5 to 14.4 |
| Field resistance (ohms) | 4.33 | 3.2 | 3.6 |
| Minimum brush length | 0.2 in (5 mm) | 0.3 in (8 mm) | 0.3 in (8 mm) |

| | |
|---|---|
| Drivebelt tension | 0.4 to 0.5 in (11 to 14 mm) deflection under firm thumb pressure at mid-point of longest run |

### Starter motor

| | |
|---|---|
| Make | Lucas M45 or 3M100PE |
| Type | Pre-engaged |

| Repair data: | M45 | 3M100PE |
|---|---|---|
| Minimum brush length | 0.3 in (8 mm) | 0.375 in (9.5 mm) |
| Armature endfloat | 0.005 to 0.015 in (0.12 to 0.40 mm) | 0.010 in (0.25 mm) |
| Minimum copper thickness on commutator after refinishing | – | 0.14 in (3.5 mm) |

## Wiper motors

Make and type:
| | |
|---|---|
|     Windscreen | Lucas 17W 2-speed |
|     Tailgate and headlamps (as applicable) | Lucas 14W single speed |
| Armature endfloat | 0.002 to 0.008 in (0.05 to 0.20 mm) |
| Minimum brush length | 0.187 in (4.8 mm) |

## Horns

| | |
|---|---|
| Number | 2 |
| Make and type | Lucas 6H or Mixo TR89 |

## Bulbs

| | Wattage | Type |
|---|---|---|
| Headlamps: | | |
|     Tungsten | 75/50 | Butlers 1967/4 DE |
|     Quartz halogen | 60/55 | – |
| Sidelamps | 4 | Lucas 233 |
| Stop/tail lamps | 21/6 | Lucas 380 |
| Reversing lamps | 21 | Lucas 382 |
| Direction indicator lamps | 21 | Lucas 382 |
| Number plate lamps | 4 | Lucas 233 |
| Instrument illumination and warning lamps | 2.2 | Smiths capless |
| Hazard warning switch illumination | 2 | Lucas 281 |
| Clock illumination | 2 | Lucas 281 |
| Interior lamp | 10 | Lucas 585 (festoon) |

## Fuses

Location:
| | |
|---|---|
|     Main fuse box | Under bonnet, on left-hand bulkhead |
|     In-line fuses | Heated rear window, heater blower motor |

Rating:
| | |
|---|---|
|     Main fuse box | 35 amp |
|     Heater rear window | 50 amp |
|     Heater blower motor | 10 amp |

## Torque wrench settings

| | lbf ft | kgf m |
|---|---|---|
| Starter motor securing bolts | 30 to 35 | 4.0 to 4.4 |
| Alternator pulley nut | 25 to 30 | 3.5 to 4.2 |
| Wiper motor yoke bolt | 12 to 16 | 1.6 to 2.2 |

## 1 General description

The electrical system is of the 12 volt type and the major components comprise a 12 volt battery, of which the negative terminal is earthed. A Lucas alternator is fitted to the front right-hand side of the engine and is driven from the engine crankshaft pulley. A pre-engaged Lucas starter motor is mounted on the rear right-hand side of the engine.

The battery supplies current for the ignition, lighting and other electrical circuits, and provides a reserve of electricity when the current consumed by the electrical equipment exceeds that being produced by the alternator. Normally, the alternator is able to meet any demand placed upon it. In later models there is an option available to provide a split charging facility. With this option, two batteries can be fitted instead of the normal single unit. When equipment such as an electric winch is being used the power will be provided by the second battery leaving the main one untouched for normal usage.

When fitting electrical accessories to cars with a negative earth system, it is important, if they contain silicon diodes or transistors, that they are connected correctly, otherwise damage may result to the components concerned. Before purchasing any electrical accessory check that it has or can be adjusted to the correct polarity to suit the car.

It is important that the battery leads are always disconnected if the battery is to be boost charged, or if any body or mechanical repairs are to be carried out using electric arc welding equipment, otherwise serious damage can be caused to the more delicate instruments, especially those containing semi-conductors.

Apart from carrying spare fuses in the vehicle as a normal precaution, it is wise to carry space bulbs as well. In many countries this is required by law. One of the most important bulbs is the ignition (charge) warning light bulb. This is connected into the charging circuit and if it fails, no charge will be made by the alternator. If this bulb fails it must therefore be renewed immediately.

## 2 Battery – removal and refitting

1 Detach the nagative battery lead followed by the positive battery lead from the battery terminal lugs. Disconnecting the leads in this order reduces the possibility of 'shorting' the battery (photo).
2 Remove the wing nuts and lift off the frame.
3 Lift out the battery.
4 Before refitting the battery, clean the battery tray thoroughly.

2.1 The battery in position. Negative (earth) lead Is the one connected to the strap

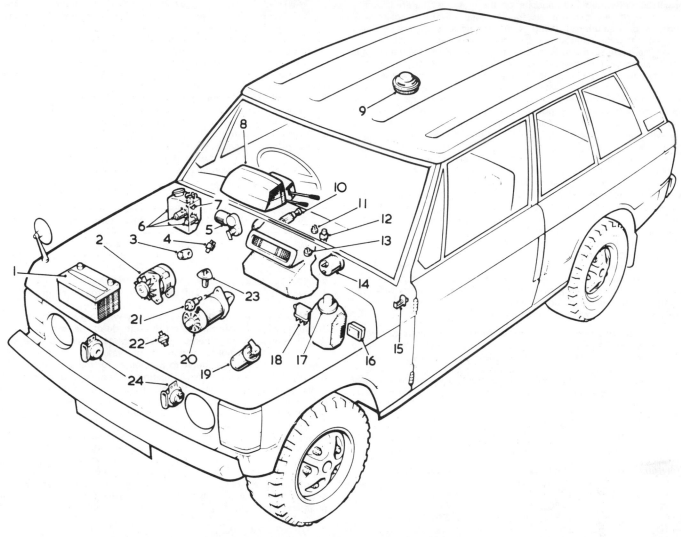

**Fig. 10.1 Location of electrical equipment (Sec 1)**

| | |
|---|---|
| 1 | Battery |
| 2 | Alternator |
| 3 | Brake warning switch (circuit failure) |
| 4 | Stop-light switch |
| 5 | Windscreen wiper motor |
| 6 | Windscreen/tailgate washer reservoir and motors (later models) |
| 7 | Starter relay |
| 8 | Instrument housing |
| 9 | Roof lamp |
| 10 | Hazard warning switch |
| 11 | Reversing light switch |
| 12 | Differential lock switch |
| 13 | Handbrake switch |
| 14 | Clock |
| 15 | Door pillar switch |
| 16 | Fuse box |
| 17 | Windscreen washer reservoir and motor (earlier models) |
| 18 | Starter relay |
| 19 | Ignition coil |
| 20 | Starter motor |
| 21 | Thermostat |
| 22 | Oil pressure switch |
| 23 | Thermostat switch |
| 24 | Horns |

5   Fit the battery, then connect the terminal leads, positive first. Do not hammer them on. They may jam or at worst the battery will crack.

6   Finally, smear the battery terminals and lead ends with a little petroleum jelly or a proprietary brand of battery corrosion inhibitor. **Do not** use regular lubricating grease as a substitute.

7   Never disconnect the battery while the engine is running or the alternator semi conductors will be damaged.

## 3   Battery – maintenance and inspection

1   Normal battery maintenance consists of checking the electrolyte level of each cell to ensure that the separators are covered by $\frac{1}{4}$ in (6 mm) of electrolyte. If the level has fallen, top up the battery using distilled water only. Do not overfill. If a battery is overfilled or any electrolyte spilled, immediately wipe away the excess as electrolyte attacks and corrodes any metal it comes into contact with very rapidly.

2   If the battery has the 'Auto-fill' device fitted, a special topping-up sequence is required. The white balls in the 'Auto-fill' battery are part of the automatic topping-up device which ensures correct electrolyte level. The vent chamber should remain in position at all times except when topping-up or taking specific gravity readings. If the electrolyte level in any of the cells is below the bottom of the filling tube, top up as follows:

(a)  Lift off the vent chamber cover
(b)  With the battery level, pour distilled water into the trough until all the filling tubes and trough are full
(c)  Immediately refit the cover to allow the water in the trough and tubes to flow into the cells. Each cell will automatically receive the correct amount of water.

3   As well as keeping the terminals clean and covered with petroleum jelly, the top of the battery, and especially the top of the cells, should be kept clean and dry. This helps prevent corrosion and ensures that the battery does not become partially discharged by leakage through dampness and dirt.

4   Once every three months remove the battery and inspect the battery securing bolts, the battery clamp plate, tray and battery leads

for corrosion (white fluffy deposits, on the metal, which are brittle to the touch). If any corrosion is found, clean off the deposits with ammonia or a solution of bicarbonate of soda and warm water, and paint over the clean metal with anti-rust and anti-acid paint.

5   At the same time inspect the battery case for cracks. If a crack is found, clean and plug it with one of the proprietary compounds marketed for this purpose. If leakage through the crack has been excessive then it will be necessary to refill the appropriate cell with fresh electrolyte as detailed later. Cracks are frequently caused to the top of the battery case by pouring in distilled water in the middle of winter *after* instead of *before* a run. This gives the water no chance to mix with the electrolyte and so the former freezes and splits the battery case.

6   If topping-up the battery becomes too frequent and the case has been inspected for cracks that could cause leakage, but none are found, the battery is being overcharged and the alternator will have to be checked. Generally, this indicates that the regulator (housed within the alternator end cover) is at fault thus allowing the alternator to operate uncontrolled, delivering full ouput even when the battery is fully charged. A fairly basic check can be carried out (See Section 7), but as a general principle this sort of job is best left to a competent auto-electrician or your Rover dealer.

7   With the battery on the bench at the three-monthly interval check, measure the specific gravity with a hydrometer to determine the state of charge and condition of the electrolyte. There should be very little variation between the different cells, and, if a variation in excess of 0.025 is present, it will be due to either:-

(a)  *Loss of electrolyte from the battery at some time caused by spillage or a leak, resulting in a drop in the specific gravity of the electrolyte when the deficiency was replaced with distilled water instead of fresh electrolye.*

(b)  *An internal short-circuit caused by buckling of the plates or similar malady, pointing to the likelihood of total battery failure in the near future.*

8   The specific gravity of the electrolyte for fully charged and fully discharged conditions at the electrolyte temperature indicated, is listed below.

| Fully discharged | Electrolyte temperature | Fully charged |
|---|---|---|
| 1.098 | 38°C (100°F) | 1.268 |
| 1.102 | 32°C (90°F) | 1.272 |
| 1.106 | 27°C (80°F) | 1.276 |
| 1.110 | 21°C (70°F) | 1.280 |
| 1.114 | 16°C (60°F) | 1.284 |
| 1.118 | 10°C (50°F) | 1.288 |
| 1.122 | 4°C (40°F) | 1.292 |
| 1.126 | −1.5°C (30°F) | 1.296 |

## 4   Battery electrolyte – replenishment

1   With the battery fully charged, check the specific gravity of the electrolyte in each of the cells. If one or more of the cells reads 0.025, or more, below the others, it is likely that some electrolyte has been lost. Check each cell for short-circuits with a voltage meter. A four to seven second test should give a steady reading of between 1.2 and 1.8 volts. (This test is only possible if the cell connectors are exposed on the top of the battery).

2   Top up the cell with a solution of 1 part sulphuric acid to 2.5 parts of water. If the cell is already fully topped up draw some electrolyte out of it with a pipette.

3   When mixing the sulphuric acid and water, *NEVER ADD WATER TO SULPHURIC ACID* – always pour the acid slowly onto the water in a glass container. *IF WATER IS ADDED TO SULPHURIC ACID IT WILL EXPLODE.*

4   Continue to top up the cell with the freshly made electrolyte and then recharge the battery and check the hydrometer readings.

## 5   Battery – charging

**Note:** *Before charging the battery disconnect the terminal leads, check the electrolyte level and if possible, remove the battery from the car.*

1   In winter time when heavy demand is placed upon the battery, such as when starting from cold and much electrical equipment is continually in use, it is a good idea to occasionally have the battery fully charged from an external source at the rate of 3.5 to 4 amps.

2   Continue to charge the battery at this rate until no further rise in specific gravity is noted over a four-hour period.

3   Alternatively, a trickle charger, charging at the rate of 1.5 amps, can be safely used overnight.

4   Specially rapid 'boost' charges which are claimed to restore the power of the battery in 1 to 2 hours are most dangerous as they can cause serious damage to the battery plates through overheating.

5   Whilst charging the battery note that the temperature of the electrolyte should never exceed 100°F (38°C).

6   Always disconnect both battery cables before the external charger is connected, otherwise serious damage to the alternator may occur.

## 6   Alternator – general description, maintenance and precautions

1   Briefly, the alternator comprises a rotor and stator. Voltage is induced in the coils of the stator as soon as the rotor revolves. This is a 3-phase alternating voltage which is then rectified by diodes to provide the necessary current for the electrical system. The level of the voltage required to maintain the battery charge is controlled by a regulator unit.

2   Maintenance consists of occasionally wiping away any oil or dirt which may have accumulated on the outside of the unit.

3   No lubrication is required as the bearings are sealed for life.

4   Check the drivebelt tension at intervals given in the 'Routine Maintenenace' Section. Refer to Section 8, for the procedure.

5   Due to the need for special testing equipment and the possibility of damage being caused to the alternator diodes if incorrect testing methods are adopted, it is recommended that overhaul or major repair is entrusted to a Lucas or Rover dealer. Alternatively, a service exchange unit should be obtained.

6   Alternator brush renewal is dealt with in Section 9.

7   Take extreme care when connecting the battery to ensure that the polarity is correct, and never run the engine with a battery charger connected. Do not stop the engine by removing a battery lead as the alternator will almost certainly be damaged. When boost starting from another battery ensure that it is connected positive to positive and negative to negative.

## 7   Alternator – testing in situ

*If the alternator is suspected of being faulty, a test can be carried out which can help in isolating any such fault. A dc voltmeter (range 0 to 15V) and a dc ammeter (suitable for the nominal output current – see Specifications) will be required.*

1   Check the alternator drivebelt tension and adjust if necessary – see Section 8.

2   Disconnect the brown cable which runs from the alternator at the starter motor solenoid. Connect the ammeter between this cable and the starter motor solenoid terminal.

3   Connect the voltmeter across the battery terminals.

4   Run the engine at 3300 rpm (6000 rpm of the alternator); the ammeter reading should stabilize.

5   If the ammeter reads zero, an internal fault in the alternator is indicated.

6   If less than 10 amps is indicated, and the voltmeter shows 13.6 to 14.4 volts, where it is known that the battery is in a low state of charge, the alternator is suspect and should be checked by an auto-electrician. The nominal output is given in the Specifications. (If the battery is fully charged, a low current reading is normal).

7   If the ammeter reads less than 10 amps and the voltmeter reads less than 13.6 volts, a fault in the alternator internal regulator is indicated. A fault in the regulator is also indicated when the voltage exceeds 14.4 volts.

8   On 18ACR models a surge protection unit is fitted. This can be checked by removing the rear cover from the alternator and then disconnecting the device from the terminal marked IND. Reassemble and test the unit. If the alternator functions correctly when run, renew the surge protection unit.

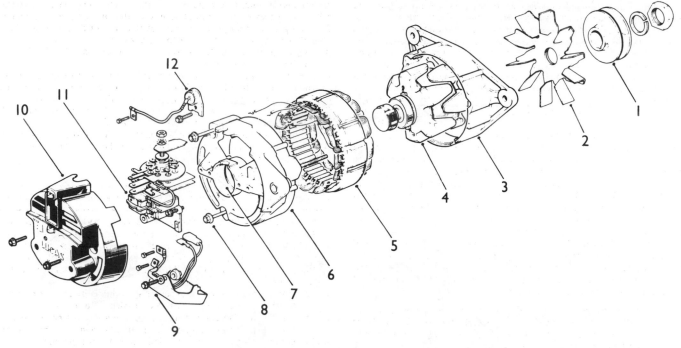

Fig. 10.2 Lucas 16 ACR alternator – exploded view (Sec 6)

| | | | | | | |
|---|---|---|---|---|---|---|
| 1 | Pulley | 5 | Stator | 8 | Retaining bolts | 11 Rectifier |
| 2 | Fan | 6 | End bracket | 9 | Regulator | 12 Anti-surge protection |
| 3 | Drive end bracket | 7 | O-ring | 10 | Cover | device |
| 4 | Rotor | | | | | |

## 8  Alternator – removal, refitting and drivebelt adjustment

1   Detach the battery earth lead.
2   Disconnect the plug-in connector(s) and wiring from the rear of the alternator (photo).
3   Slacken the adjustment bolt and the mounting bolts in that order.
4   Push the alternator towards the engine so that the drivebelt can be removed.
5   Remove the adjustment bolt and washer, and the main mounting bolts, nuts and washers.

6   Support the alternator and withdraw the main mounting bolts and washers. The alternator can now be lifted clear.
7   Refitting is basically the reverse of the removal procedure, but do not tighten the nuts and bolts until the drivebelt tension has been checked as described below.
8   Where necessary, slacken the adjustment bolt, and the mounting bolts (Fig. 10.3).

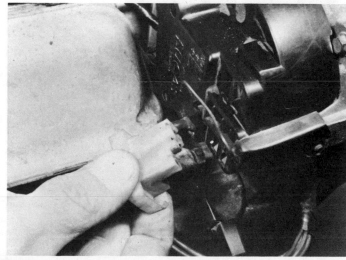

8.2 Disconnecting the alternator plug

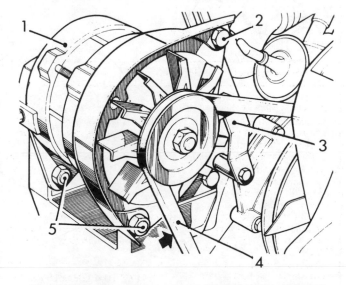

Fig. 10.3 Alternator fixing and drivebelt tensioning (Sec 8)

| | | | |
|---|---|---|---|
| 1 | Alternator | 4 | Drivebelt |
| 2 | Adjustment bolt | 5 | Pivot bolts |
| 3 | Adjustment bracket | | |

9    Pull the alternator away from the engine and tighten the adjustment bolt. Check the total movement of the belt (see Specifications)
under firm thumb pressure at the midpoint of the longest belt run,
between the alternator and crankshaft. Re-adjust, if necessary. **Note:**
*It is permissible to apply leverage at the drive end bracket, if necessary
to obtain the correct tension, but only a softwood lever or similar item
may be used.*
10   Tighten the mounting bolts on completion.
11   If a new belt has been fitted, the belt tension should be rechecked
after about 150 miles (250 km) of travelling.

12   On later vehicles which are fitted with air conditioning systems,
the alternator is located beneath the vehicle on the left-hand side of
the engine. Access to the alternator, adjustment bracket and mounting
bolts is from underneath the vehicle. Otherwise the main instructions
still apply.

### 9    Alternator – brush renewal

1    With the alternator removed from the car, remove the two

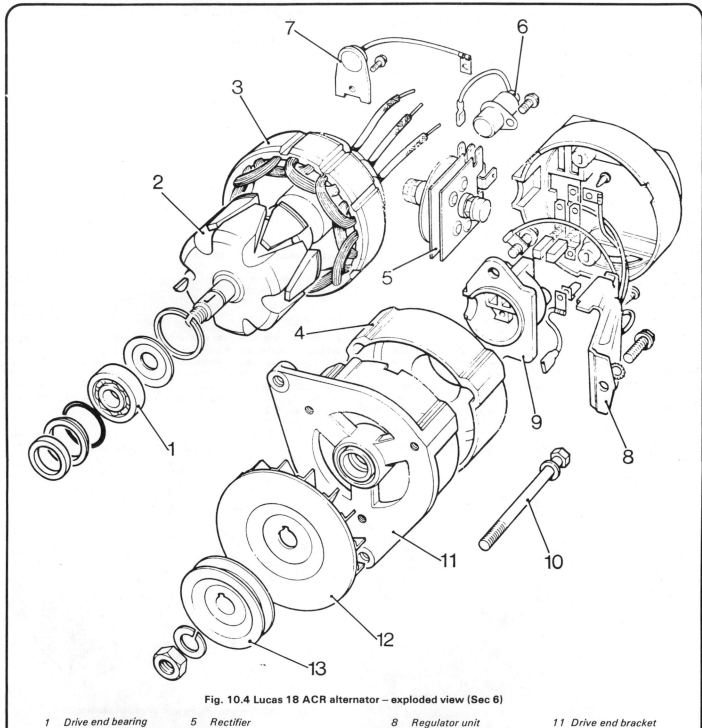

**Fig. 10.4 Lucas 18 ACR alternator – exploded view (Sec 6)**

| | | | |
|---|---|---|---|
| 1  Drive end bearing | 5  Rectifier | 8   Regulator unit | 11  Drive end bracket |
| 2  Rotor and slip ring | 6  Suppressor | 9   Brush box | 12  Fan |
| 3  Stator | 7  Surge protection device | 10  Through-bolt | 13  Pulley |
| 4  Slip ring bracket | | | |

setscrews retaining the plastic end cover.

2 Remove the end cover and disconnect, where applicable, the radio interference suppressor (capacitor) lead.

3 Remove the four small setscrews positioned in the centre of the brush box. When removing the setscrews, take a note of the exact positions of the various wires located by the screws.

4 Remove the single setscrew retaining the regulator unit and lift away the flat metal connector strip coupling the regulator to one of the smaller setscrews (referred to in paragraph 3).

5 The brushes can be lifted out of their locations in the brush box.

6 Examine the slip rings for discolouration before fitting the new brushes.

7 Where necessary the slip rings can be cleaned by polishing them with fine glass paper, crocus paper or metal polish. Ensure that no residue is left afterwards.

8 Better access to the slip rings can be achieved after removing the brush box which is retained by two setscrews. Note that the black wire from the regulator unit is located under the head of one of these setscrews.

9 Reassemble the alternator by reversing the dismantling procedure.

## 10 Starter motor – general description

When the ignition switch is turned, current flows through the solenoid pull-in winding on the starter motor, moving the solenoid armature. At the same time a much smaller current flows through the solenoid hold-in winding directly to earth.

The movement of the solenoid armature causes the drive pinion to move and engage with the starter ring gear on the flywheel. At the same time the main contacts close and energise the motor circuit. The pull-in winding now becomes ineffective and the solenoid remains in the operated condition by the action of the hold-in winding only.

A special one-way clutch is fitted to the starter drive pinion, so that when the engine commences to fire there is no possibility of it driving the starter motor.

When the ignition key is released, the solenoid is de-energised and returns to its original position. This breaks the supply to the motor and returns the drive pinion to the disengaged position.

## 11 Starter motor – removal and refitting

1 Detach the battery earth lead and raise the front of the vehicle to a suitable working height for access to the starter motor. A pit or ramp is best.

2 Remove the nut and spring washer, then disconnect the heavy battery feed cable to the starter motor solenoid.

3 Disconnect the two smaller wires at the solenoid by removing the two cross-head screws. Note the locations of the wires. Some have spade connector fittings.

4 Using a socket extension and ratchet spanner, remove the starter motor mounting flange bolts, and the exhaust heat shield on later models.

5 Lift the starter motor out and downwards from the engine (photo).

6 Refitting is the reverse of removal, but check that the solenoid wires are connected correctly.

7 Tighten the starter motor mounting bolts to the specified torque.

## 12 Starter motor – overhaul

### 3M100PE type

1 Slacken the nut which secures the connecting link to the solenoid terminal 'STA'.

2 Remove the two screws which secure the solenoid to the drive end bracket.

3 Lift the solenoid plunger upwards and separate it from the engagement level. Extract the return spring seat and dust excluder from the plunger body.

4 Withdraw the block from between the drive end bracket and the starter motor yoke.

5 Remove the armature end cap from the commutator end bracket.

6 Chisel off some of the claws from the armature shaft spire nut so that the nut can be withdrawn from the shaft.

7 Remove the two tie-bolts and then withdraw the commutator end cover and starter motor yoke from the drive end bracket.

8 Separate the commutator end cover from the starter motor yoke, at the same time disengaging the field coil brushes from the brush box to facilitate separation.

9 Withdraw the thrust washer from the armature shaft.

10 Remove the spire nut from the engagement lever pivot pin and then extract the pin from the drive end bracket.

11 Withdraw the armature and roller clutch drive assembly from the drive end bracket.

12 Using a piece of tubing, drive back the thrust collar to expose the jump ring on the armature shaft. Remove the jump ring and withdraw the thrust collar and roller clutch.

13 Remove the spring ring and release the engagement lever, thrust washers and spring from the roller-clutch drive.

14 Remove the dust-excluding seal from the bore of the drive end bracket.

15 Inspect all components for wear. If the armature shaft bushes require renewal, press them out or screw in a $\frac{1}{2}$ in tap to withdraw them. Before inserting the new bushes, soak them in engine oil for 24 hours.

16 If the brushes have worn below the minimum specified length, renew them by cutting the end bracket brush leads from the terminal post. File a groove in the head of the terminal post and solder the new

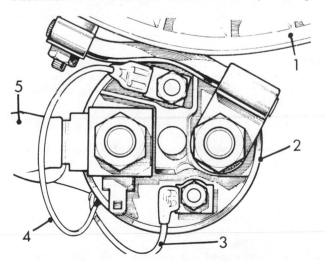

**Fig. 10.5 Starter motor solenoid wiring (Sec 11)**

1  Starter motor
2  Solenoid
3  Small lead
4  Small lead
5  Battery feed cable

11.5 Withdrawing the starter motor (engine removed from vehicle)

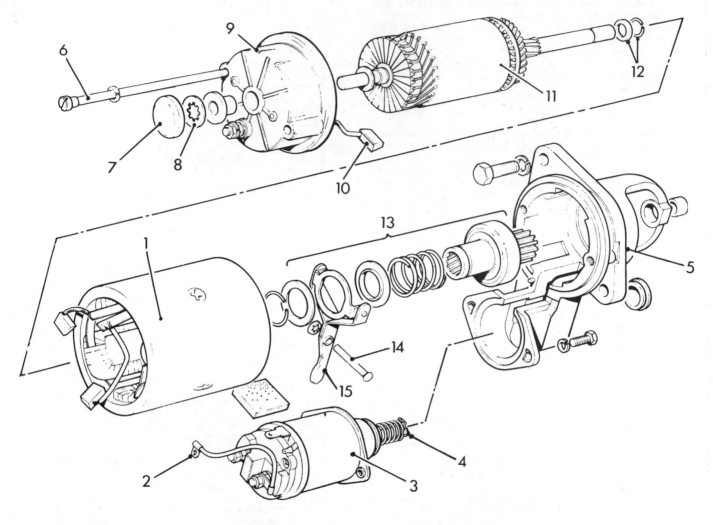

**Fig. 10.6 3M100PE type starter motor – exploded view (Sec 12)**

| | | | |
|---|---|---|---|
| 1 | Yoke | 5 | Drive end bracket |
| 2 | Connecting link | 6 | Through-bolt |
| 3 | Solenoid | 7 | End cap |
| 4 | Solenoid plunger | 8 | Spire nut |

| | | | |
|---|---|---|---|
| 9 | Commutator end cover | 13 | Engagement lever, thrust |
| 10 | Field coil brush | | collar and roller clutch |
| 11 | Armature | 14 | Pivot pin |
| 12 | Collar and circlip | 15 | Engagement lever |

brush leads in to the groove. Cut the field winding brush leads about ¼ in (6 mm) from the joint of the field winding. Solder the new brush leads to the ends of the old ones. Localise the heat to prevent damage to the field windings.

17  Check the field windings for continuity using a torch battery and test bulb. If the windings are faulty, removal of the pole shoe screws should be left to a service station having a pressure screwdriver, as they are very tight.

18  Check the insulation of the armature by connecting a test bulb and torch battery. Use probes placed on the armature shaft and each commutator section in turn. If the test bulb lights at any position then the insulation has broken down, and the armature must be renewed. Discolouration of the commutator should be removed by polishing it with a piece of glass paper (not emery cloth). Do not undercut the insulation.

19  Reassembly is a reversal of dismantling, but apply grease to the moving parts of the engagement lever, the outer surface of the roller clutch housing and to the lips of the drive end bracket dust seal. Fit a new spire nut to the armature shaft, positioning it to give the specified shaft endfloat. Measure this endfloat by inserting feeler blades between the face of the spire nut and the flange of the commutator end bush.

### M45 type

20  With the starter motor on the bench unscrew and remove the nut that secures the solenoid link wire or tag to the terminal on the starter motor body. lift off the link.

21  Mark the relative positions of the solenoid and drive end bracket, then undo and remove the two securing nuts (bolts on early models) and spring washers.

22  Withdraw the solenoid rearwards and disengage the solenoid plunger from the operating lever. Remove the solenoid from the starter motor.

23  Remove the rubber sealing grommet from the slot in the drive end bracket.

24  On later models, undo and remove the two nuts and rubber seals and lift off the commutator end cover and cover band. On early models, slacken the clamp screw and slide the cover band off the rear of the starter motor.

25  Using a hook-shaped length of wire, lift off the brush springs and withdraw the brushes from their holders.

26  Unscrew and withdraw the two long through-bolts that secure the commutator end bracket and lift off the end bracket from the starter body and armature.

27  Remove the drive end bracket complete with armature from the

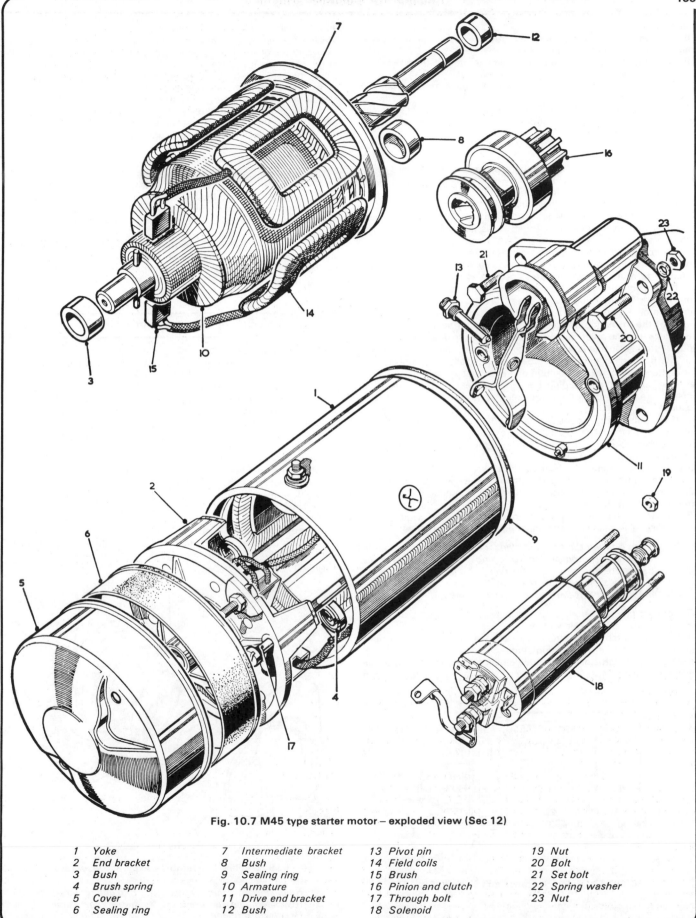

**Fig. 10.7 M45 type starter motor – exploded view (Sec 12)**

| | | | | | | |
|---|---|---|---|---|---|---|
| 1 | Yoke | 7 | Intermediate bracket | 13 | Pivot pin | 19 Nut |
| 2 | End bracket | 8 | Bush | 14 | Field coils | 20 Bolt |
| 3 | Bush | 9 | Sealing ring | 15 | Brush | 21 Set bolt |
| 4 | Brush spring | 10 | Armature | 16 | Pinion and clutch | 22 Spring washer |
| 5 | Cover | 11 | Drive end bracket | 17 | Through bolt | 23 Nut |
| 6 | Sealing ring | 12 | Bush | 18 | Solenoid | |

starter body.

28  Slacken the locknut and undo and remove the eccentric engagement lever pivot pin from the end bracket.

29  Withdraw the armature and intermediate bracket from the drive end bracket and lift off the engagement lever.

30  Push back the lockring cover on the end of the armature shaft and prise off the lockring.

31  Withdraw the drive assembly and intermediate bracket from the armature shaft. Note any shims that may be fitted behind the intermediate bracket.

32  On later models, remove the brake ring, steel and tufnol washers from the commutator end bracket.

33  With the starter motor dismantled, check that the brushes move freely in their holders. If necessary, they may be cleaned with a petrol moistened cloth or by very light rubbing with a smooth file.

34  If the brushes are worn they should be renewed.

35  The brush wires are soldered or crimped to terminal tags and must be unsoldered to remove. New brush wires may then be resoldered onto the tags.

36  Clean the commutator with a petrol-moistened rag, and if necessary wrap a piece of glass paper around the commutator and rotate the armature to remove any burnt areas or high spots.

37  If the commutator is badly worn, mount the armature in a lathe and with the lathe turning at high speed, take a very fine cut out of the commutator. Finish the surface by polishing with glass paper. Do not undercut the insulation between the commutator segments.

38  Check that the roller clutch rotates freely in one direction and locks up in the other. If this is not the case, the clutch must be renewed.

39  The field coil continuity may be tested as follows: Connect a 12 volt battery with a 12 volt bulb in one of the leads between the field terminal post and the tapping point of the field coils to which the brushes are connected. An open-circuit is proved by the bulb not lighting.

40  If the bulb lights, it does not necessarily mean that the field coils are in order, as there is a possibility that one of the coils will be earthed to the starter yoke or pole shoes. To check this, remove the lead from the brush connector and place it against a clean portion of the starter yoke. If the bulb lights, the field coils are earthing.

41  If the armature is damaged, this will be evident on inspection. Look for signs of burning, discolouration and for conductors that have lifted away from the commutator.

42  To reassemble the starter motor is the reverse sequence of dismantling. The following additional points should be noted:

   *(a)  When refitting the solenoid plunger to the engagement lever, turn the eccentric pin until the engagement lever is in its lowest and most forward position*

   *(b)  With the starter motor reassembled, reset the drive pinion engagement positions as described below.*

43  Connect one lead from a 12 volt battery to the small unmarked terminal on the starter solenoid.

44  Using a switch in the circuit, connect the other battery terminal lead to one of the solenoid fixing studs.

45  With the switch closed, the drive pinion will move forward to the engaged position. Measure the distance between the end of the pinion

and the lockring cover on the end of the armature shaft (Fig. 10.8).

46  A clearance within the limits given in the Specifications should exist with the drive pinion pushed gently back to take up any free play in the operating linkage.

47  If the clearance is incorrect, slacken the locknut and rotate the engagement arm fulcrum one way or the other until the correct clearance is obtained. Note that the adjustment arc is 180° and the arrow marked on the head of the fulcrum pin must be within 90° of either side of the cast arrow on the end casing.

48  When the clearance is correct, tighten the locknut.

*Testing the solenoid (all models)*

49  To test the solenoid contacts for correct opening and closing, connect a 12 volt battery and a 60 watt test lamp between the main battery feed terminal and the 'STA' terminal. The lamp should not light.

50  Energize the solenoid with a separate 12 volt supply connected to the small unmarked Lucar terminal and a good earth on the solenoid body.

51  As the coil is energized the solenoid should be heard to operate and the test lamp should light with full brilliance.

52  No attempt should be made to repair a faulty solenoid. If it is faulty it must be renewed as a complete unit.

### 13  Headlamp unit – removal and refitting

*Tungsten filament type*

1  The headlamp is of the sealed beam type and has no separate bulb.

2  Disconnect the battery negative lead as a safety precaution.

3  Open the bonnet and prop it securely.

4  Undo and remove the four cross-head screws which secure the headlamp retainer to the body (photo).

5  If the headlamp washers and wipers are fitted, disconnect the washer tubing to the jet and withdraw the wiper rack and the motor as described in Sections 37 and 40.

6  Withdraw the headlamp unit and retainer and disconnect the wiring at the rear of the unit (photo).

7  Remove the two adjusting screws to separate the lamp unit from the retainer. Later models have a clamp in addition to the adjusting screws (photo).

8  Remove the rubber seal.

9  Slacken the three rim retaining screws, turn the rim anti-clockwise and lift it away. The headlamp unit can now be separated from the mounting ring (photos).

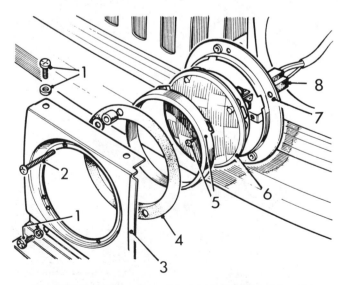

Fig. 10.9 Headlamp assembly – exploded view (Sec 13)

| | | | |
|---|---|---|---|
| 1 | *Headlamp retaining screws* | 5 | *Rim and retaining screw* |
| 2 | *Headlamp adjuster screw* | 6 | *Sealed beam unit* |
| 3 | *Headlamp retainer* | 7 | *Mounting ring* |
| 4 | *Seal* | 8 | *Wiring connectors* |

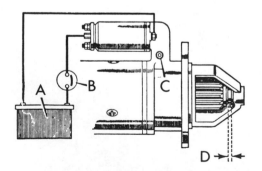

Fig. 10.8 Drive pinion clearance adjustment (Sec 12)

| | | | | | |
|---|---|---|---|---|---|
| *A* | *Battery* | *B* | *Switch* | *C* | *Pivot pin* |
| *D* | *Clearance = 0.005 to 0.015 in (0.12 to 0.40 mm)* | | | | |

13.4 Removing one of the headlamp retainer screws

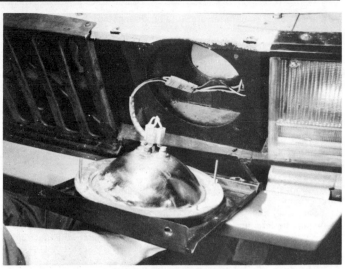

13.6 Withdrawing the complete headlamp unit

13.7 One of the headlamp adjusting screws almost removed

13.9a Slackening a rim retaining screw so that ...

13.9b ... the headlamp unit, rim, and mounting ring can be separated

10 Refitting is the reverse of the removal procedure.
11 The headlamps should be checked for alignment as soon as possible after refitting (Section 14).

### Quartz halogen type

12 Bulb renewal can be achieved without removing the headlamp unit provided that access can be gained from the rear.
13 Unplug the connector from the bulb and remove the bulb from the rear of the reflector unit. Take care if the bulb is hot.
14 Refitting is the reverse of the removal procedure. Do not touch the bulb envelope with bare fingers, or it will become blackened in use where it has been touched. If a bulb is accidentally touched, clean it using methylated spirit and a lint-free cloth.
15 Note that headlamp wipe/wash systems cannot be fitted in conjunction with quartz halogen headlamps, due to the high temperature at which the lamps run.

### 14 Headlamp beam alignment

1 Each headlamp is equipped with two adjusting screws. By screwing these two screws in or out, the alignment of the headlamps can be altered.
2 The owner or driver of the vehicle who wants to alter the beam

alignment must remember that it is an offence not to have the vehicle lights set correctly.
3  Any setting that is carried out without the correct beam setting equipment should only be regarded as a temporary measure.
4  If, after headlamp renewal, or after an accident, the beam alignment has to be reset, then the vehicle should be taken to a Range Rover dealer to have the headlamp beams correctly set as soon as possible.

### 15 Front side and flasher lamps – bulb renewal, removal and refitting

#### Bulb renewal
1  Remove the four cross-head screws which secure the combined lens cover.
2  Lift away the lens cover and seal. Recover the rubber washers between the lens and lamp unit screw holes (photo).
3  Remove the bulb. The top bulb is the flasher, the bottom is

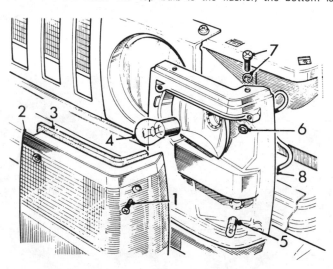

**Fig. 10.10 Front side and flasher lamp unit – exploded view (Sec 15)**

1  Lens retaining screw
2  Lens
3  Seal
4  Flasher bulb
5  Sidelamp bulb
6  Washer between lens and lamp unit at screw hole
7  Lamp unit retaining screw and washer
8  Wiring to lamp unit

15.2 Removing the front lamp lens cover and seal

sidelight. Both bulbs have a bayonet 'push-and-twist' type fitting.
4  Ensure that the new bulb is of the correct wattage.
5  Refit the lens and seal. Make sure the seal fits correctly so that water cannot enter the lamp unit.
6  Refit the four screws but do not overtighten them.

#### Removal and refitting
7  Remove the bulbs as described above.
8  Open the bonnet and prop it securely.
9  Remove the two screws in the top of the lamp unit which secure the unit to the front panel.
10  Lift the lamp unit up and forwards to clear the mounting pegs at the bottom.
11  Disconnect the wiring at the rear of the lamp unit and lift it away.
12  Refitting is the reverse of the removal procedure.

### 16 Rear lamp assembly – bulb renewal, removal and refitting

#### Bulb renewal
1  Remove the six lens retaining screws (photo).
2  Lift the lens and seal away (photo).
3  The bulbs are identified as follows: Top – flasher, centre – reversing lamp, bottom – tail/stop-lamp.
4  All bolts are of the bayonet 'push-and-twist' type.
5  Remove the required bulb.
6  Fit another bulb of the correct wattage and type.
7  Refit the lens and seal.
8  Refit the six screws; do not overtighten them.

#### Removal and refitting
9  Remove the lens and bulbs only if necessary (see below).
10  Remove the four cross-head screws which retain the lamp unit to the body. (It is possible to remove the nut without removing the lens and bulbs as the screws are accessible through the lens cover).
11  Remove the top and bottom screws in the side reflector unit.
12  Withdraw the lamp unit and disconnect the leads at the connectors.
13  The reflector can be removed from the lamp unit by removing the five screws which retain it. Note that there is a rubber seal behind it.
14  Refitting is the reverse of the removal procedure.

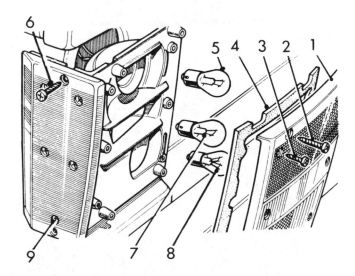

**10.11 Rear lamp assembly – exploded view (Sec 16)**

1  Lens
2  Lamp unit retaining screw
3  Lens retaining screw
4  Seal
5  Flasher bulb
6  Lamp unit retaining screw
7  Reversing bolt
8  Stop/fail bulb
9  Side reflector retaining screw

16.1 Removing the lens retaining screws (rear combination light)

16.2 Lifting the lens and seal away (rear combination light)

17.1 Removing the number plate light lens cover

## 17 Number plate lamp – bulb renewal, removal and refitting

### Bulb renewal
1   Remove the two lens cover retaining screws and lower the cover, lens and seal (photo).
2   The bulb is a bayonet 'push-and-twist' fitting.
3   Renew the bulb with one of the correct type and wattage.
4   Refit the seal, lens and cover and secure it with the two screws.

### Removal and refitting
5   Remove the bulb as directed.
6   Remove the two screws and nuts which secure the lamp base to the number plate. Lift the number plate up to reach the nuts more easily.
7   Disconnect the leads from the lamp base as it is withdrawn.
8   Refitting is the reverse procedure.

## 18 Interior lamp (roof-mounted) – bulb renewal, removal and refitting

1   The interior roof-mounted lamp(s) may have one or two festoon bulbs. The lamp is operated by switches on both door pillars and also by a switch on the steering column.

### Bulb renewal
2   To remove the lens cover, press and rotate it anti-clockwise (photo).

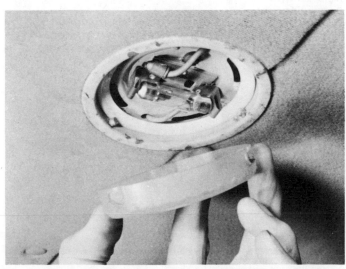

18.2 Removing the interior lamp lens cover (single bulb type lamp)

3   Remove the bulb(s) from the holder.
4   Fit a new bulb of the correct wattage.
5   Refit the lens cover.

### Removal and refitting
6   Remove the bulb(s) as directed. Disconnect the battery earth lead.
7   Prise the cable ends from the connectors.
8   Remove the screws which secure the lamp holder to the roof panel.
9   Withdraw the lamp holder, feeding the cables through the lamp holder base.
10  Refitting is the reverse of the removal procedure.

## 19 Cigar lighter – bulb renewal, removal and refitting

### Bulb renewal
1   The cigar lighter is illuminated only when the sidelights are switched on.
2   From behind the centre console pull out the bulb and holder from the mounting position.
3   Prise the bulb and socket from the holder.
4   The bulb is of the bayonet 'push-and-twist' fit type.
5   Renew the bulb with one of the correct type and wattage.
6   Fit the bulb and socket into the holder.
7   Refit the holder to the cigar lighter.

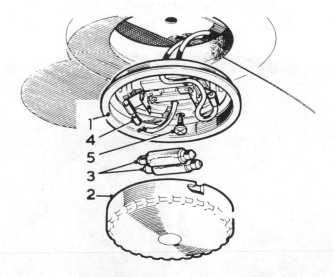

Fig. 10.12 Interior roof-mounted courtesy lamp (Sec 18)

1   Lamp holder        4   Cable end
2   Cover              5   Screw
3   Bulbs

## Removal and refitting
8    Remove the console unit as described in Section 29.
9    With the wiring disconnected, hold the back of the lighter using a pair of pliers. Unscrew the centre barrel and pull it out of the front of the console complete with chromed ring (Fig. 10.13).
10   Refitting is the reverse of the removal procedure.

### 20  Instrument panel – illumination and warning lamp renewal

1    All the illumination and warning lamp bulbs are housed in the instrument panel binnacle, on top of the dashboard in front of the steering wheel.
2    To remove the instrument binnacle rear cover, press in the bottom rear edge (towards the windscreen) and lift it off the mounting clips,

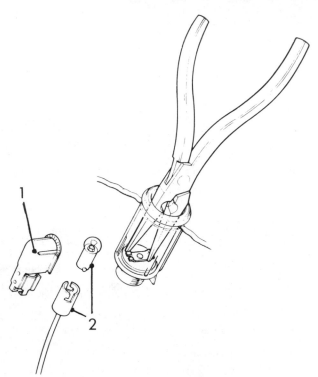

**Fig. 10.13 Cigar lighter removal (Sec 19)**

1    Bulb holder                    2    Bulb and socket

20.4  Bulb and holder removed from instrument panel

but do not disconnect any wiring to it.
3    Separate the binnacle from the instrument panel; there is no need to detach the speedo trip cable from the binnacle to do this.
4    All the warning and illumination lamp bulbs are of the capless type, held in position in small plastic holders (photo).
5    Identify the bulb, pull the holder and bulb out of the panel and renew the bulb. Ensure it is of the same type and wattage as that specified.
6    Refit the bulb and holder to the panel.
7    Refit the rear binnacle cover to the instrument panel and secure it on the clips.

### 21  Hazard flasher and heated rear screen switches – bulb renewal, removal and refitting

#### Bulb renewal
1    Unscrew the knob from the end of the switch.
2    Be careful not to lose the spring inside the knob.
3    Withdraw the bulb from the switch body.
4    Renew the bulb with one of the same type and wattage.
5    Refit the spring and knob. Note that the spring fits with the large diameter end towards the knob.

#### Removal and refitting
6    Remove the bulb as directed. Disconnect the battery earth lead.
7    Undo the locking ring which retains the switch to the facia or console.
8    To remove the hazard flasher switch, remove the facia panel below the steering column to which the switch is attached.
9    Withdraw the switch from the rear of the facia.
10   Note the wiring connectors and remove them.
11   To remove the heated rear screen switch remove the centre console, as described in Section 29.
12   Withdraw the switch, note the wiring connections and remove them.
13   Refitting of both switches is the reverse of the removal procedure.

### 22  Differential lock valve and warning light – bulb renewal, removal and refitting

1    The differential lock control valve is located on the floor to the right of the main gear lever. On early models the warning light is incorporated in the top of the knob itself, but from October 1973 onwards the warning light has been fitted to the bottom of the instrument panel. To remove the differential lock actuator switch refer to Section 27.

#### Bulb renewal
##### Early models
2    Undo the chrome locking ring in the top of the knob.
3    Remove the ring and lens and then withdraw the spring and bulb assembly.
4    Unscrew the spring and seat from the bulb.

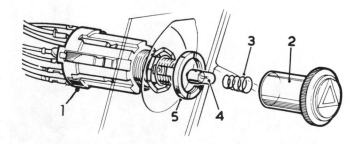

**Fig. 10.14 Hazard flasher switch – exploded view (Sec 21)**

1    Switch                          4    Bulb
2    Knob                            5    Locking ring
3    Spring

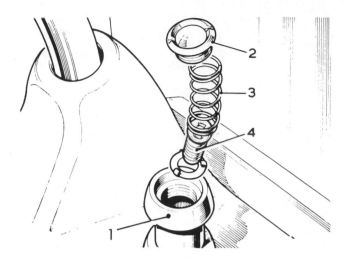

**Fig. 10.15 Early differential lock warning light assembly (Sec 22)**

1  *Knob*                          3  *Spring*
2  *Locking ring and lens*         4  *Bulb*

**Fig. 10.16 Later type differential lock warning light (Sec 22)**

1  *Lens cover*                    3  *Bulb*
2  *Bulb holder*

5  Fit the spring and seat to a new bulb of the correct type and wattage.
6  Refit the bulb spring and seat assembly to the knob, and screw in the lens and locking ring.
**Later models**
7  Prise the warning light holder, lens and bulb from the facia.
8  Pull the bulb holder out of the lens cover and remove the bulb.
9  Fit a new bulb of the correct wattage to the holder and refit the holder to the lens.
10  Refit the lens to the facia and locate the two pins on the lens to the holes in the facia.

*Control valve – removal and refitting*
11  Remove the rubber boot surrounding the main gear lever and differential lock control valve.
12  Undo the two bolts which retain the differential lock control valve to the top of the gearbox (photo).
13  Disconnect the vacuum tubing from the control valve, noting which tube fits onto which connector.
14  Disconnect the wiring from the warning light connectors, noting which wire fits where.
15  Remove the complete valve assembly.
16  Refitting is the reverse of the removal procedure.

---

**23  Relays and flasher units – removal and refitting**

---

*Hazard flasher unit/Direction indicator flasher unit*
1  The hazard flasher unit is located with the twin signal flasher unit on the steering column support bracket. The hazard flasher is the right-hand unit (photo).
2  Disconnect the battery earth lead and remove the lower facia panel. Pull the flasher unit from its spring mounting clip and disconnect the electrical leads, noting the locations of the leads for refitting.
3  Fit a new unit and reconnect the leads to the flasher, ensuring that they are correctly located.
4  Refit the flasher to the spring clip.
5  Refit the lower facia panel and reconnect the battery earth lead.

*Starter motor relay*
6  Disconnect the battery as a safety precaution.
7  The starter motor relay is located on the left-hand side of the rear engine compartment bulkhead, next to the windscreen washer reservoir on early models.
8  Disconnect the wiring from the relay, noting the wiring positions.
9  Remove the two self-tapping screws and lift the relay away.
10  Refitting is the reverse of the removal procedure. Do not forget the earthing wires.

22.12 Undo the differential lock valve retaining bolts (gear lever removed)

23.1 The hazard flasher can be seen (arrowed) below the round heavy duty flasher fitted for towing

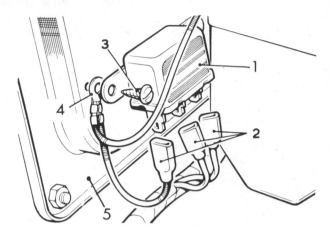

**Fig. 10.17 Starter relay (Sec 23)**

| | |
|---|---|
| 1   Relay | 4   Earth wires |
| 2   Wiring connectors | 5   Bulkhead panel |
| 3   Mounting screw | |

24.1 Fuse box location on rear bulkhead

25.4 Lower the bottom half shroud and switches away from the steering column

## 24 Fuses – general

1   The main fuse box is located in the engine compartment on the left-hand side of the bulkhead (photo).

2   The fuse box has a plastic push-on cover and the protected circuits are shown on it. Normally two spare fuses are located inside the fuse box.

3   All the fuses are of the 35 amp rating.

4   Some of the circuits such as the heater and heated rear screen are protected by in-line fuses in the appropriate circuit. Other auxiliary circuits such as the radio (where fitted) are protected in the same way.

5   If any item of electrical equipment fails to operate, first check the appropriate fuse. If the fuse has blown the first thing to do is to find the cause, otherwise it will merely blow again – (fuses can blow through age fatigue, but this is the exception rather than the rule). Having found the faulty fuse, switch off the electrical equipment and then fit a new fuse. From the wiring diagrams note which circuits are served by the blown fuse and then start to switch each one on separately in turn. (It may be necessary to have the ignition circuit switched on at the same time). The fuse should blow again when the faulty item is switched on. It the fuse does not blow immediately, start again, but this time leave the circuits switched on and build up the cumulative total lead on the fuse. If and when it blows you will have an indication of which circuits may be causing the problem. If a new fuse does not blow until the car is moving then look for a loose, chafed or pinched wire.

6   When fitting a new fuse always use a fuse of the correct rating. Do not, under any circumstances, fit a fuse of a higher rating or use a piece of tin foil as a substitute. It should be clearly understood that fuses are the weakest link in a circuit. Any fault causing shorting or an overload of a particular circuit will cause the fuse wire to melt and thus break the circuit.   A higher rated fuse or a piece of tin foil will not break the circuit and in such cases overheating and the risk of fire at the fault source, could easily occur.

7   If a fault occurs in one accessory or component and its rectification defies all efforts, always remember that it could be a relay at fault. Relays cannot be repaired or adjusted and, if faulty, should be renewed as a unit.

## 25   Column-mounted switches – removal and refitting

1   Disconnect the battery as a safety precaution.

2   Undo the four screws which retain the bottom half of the steering column shroud to the top half.

3   Remove the single screw which retains the top half of the shroud to the column bracket, and lift it away.

4   Lower the bottom half of the shroud and switches away from the steering column (photo).

### Ignition/starter switch

5   Remove the two self-tapping screws which retain the ignition/starter switch to the left-hand end of the steering column lock bracket.

6   Pull the switch out of its mounting and disconnect the wiring at the plug-in connector block.

7   Refitting is the reverse procedure to removal. Note that there is a lug on the side of the switch body which has to locate in the groove in the mounting bracket.

8   Should the steering column lock require renewal, this task must be undertaken by a Range Rover dealer with the necessary equipment.

### Main lighting switch

9   This is located on the right-hand side of the steering column and is the front stalk switch.

10   With the lower shroud away from the column, undo the locking ring on the switch and free it from the bracket.

11   Disconnect the wiring from the switch at the snap connectors, noting the wiring locations.

12   Refitting is the reverse of the removal procedure.

### Combination dipswitch, direction indicator, horn and flasher switch

13   This is located on the right-hand side of the steering column and

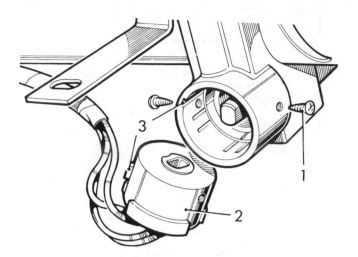

**Fig. 10.18 Ignition starter switch (Sec 25)**

1   Self-tapping screw           3   Lug and groove
2   Switch

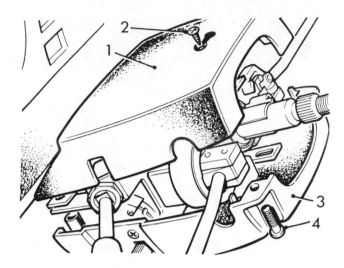

**Fig. 10.19 Steering column shrouds (Sec 25)**

1   Top half                     4   Bottom half retaining
2   Top half retaining screw         screw
3   Bottom half shroud

**Fig. 10.20 Bottom half shroud – switch mounting (Sec 25)**

1   Mounting bracket             3   Switch
2   Locking ring

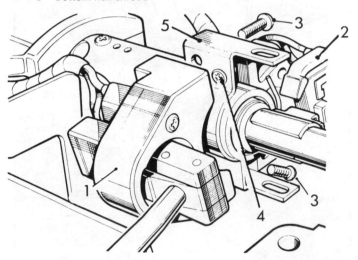

**Fig. 10.21 Rear column-mounted switches (Sec 25)**

1   Windscreen wiper/washer          left-hand switch
    switch                       4   Retaining screw for
2   Dip, indicator, horn             right-hand switch
    and flasher switch           5   Mounting bracket
3   Retaining screws for

is the rear stalk switch.

14  Remove the column shrouds as already described.

15  Remove the wiper/washer switch as described below.

16  Undo the two screws which retain the column switch to the mounting bracket.

17  Disconnect the wiring to the switch, noting the wiring colours and locations.

18  Refitting is the reverse of the removal procedure.

### Auxiliary driving lamps/foglamps switch

19  This is located on the left-hand side of the steering column and is the front stalk switch.

20  With the lower half of the column shroud lowered as already described, undo the locking ring and remove the switch from its mounting bracket.

21  Disconnect the switch wiring at the snap connectors, noting the wiring colours and locations.

22  Refitting is the reverse of the removal procedure.

### Windscreen wiper/washer switch

23  This is located on the left-hand side of the steering column and is the rear stalk switch. If headlamp wash/wipe facilities are fitted, this

switch operates them at the same time as the main windscreen wash/wipe system. However, this only operates when the headlamps are switched on.

24  Remove the steering column shrouds as described above.

25  Remove the two cross-head screws which retain the switch to the column bracket.

26  Lift the switch away and disconnect the wiring. Note the colours and locations of the wires.

27  Refitting is the reverse of the removal procedure.

### Panel light switch

28  The panel and instrument lighting switch is the front switch located in the lower half of the steering column shroud on the left-hand side of the column.

29  Remove the lower half shroud retaining screws and lower the shroud.

30  Disconnect the wiring from the switch, noting the wiring colours and locations.

31  Undo and remove the two screws and cup washers that retain the switch, and remove the switch from the shroud.

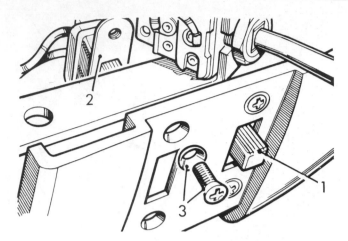

**Fig. 10.22 Panel light and interior light switches (Sec 25)**

1   *Interior light switch*        3   *Retaining screw and cup*
2   *Panel light switch*                *washer*
    *removed*

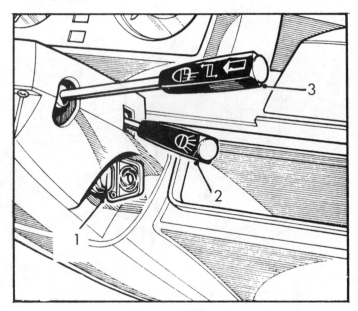

**Fig. 10.23 Switch identification – right-hand side of column**
**(Sec 25)**

1   *Ignition/starter*              3   *Dip, indicator, horn*
2   *Headlamp/sidelamp main*            *and flasher switch*
    *switch*

32   Refitting is the the reverse of the removal procedure.

## Interior light switch

33   This is located next to the panel lighting switch on the left-hand side of the lower half shroud, and is the rearmost of the two toggle switches.
34   Removal and refitting is identical to the procedure given above for the panel light switch.

## 26  Tailgate wiper/washer switch – removal and refitting

1   The tailgate wiper/washer switch (on models so equipped) is located on the facia to the right of the instrument binnacle.
2   Prise the rocker type switch out of the facia.
3   Disconnect the wiring from the rear of the switch, noting colours and locations.
4   Remove the switch.
5   Refitting is the reverse of the removal procedure..

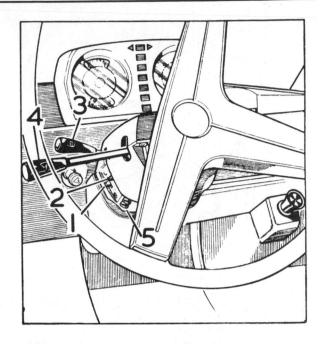

**Fig. 10.24 Switch identification – left-hand side column (Sec 25)**

1   *Panel lights switch*          4   *Wiper/washer for windscreen*
2   *Interior light switch*             *(and headlamps if fitted)*
3   *Auxiliary lamps switch*       5   *Plug-in sockets*

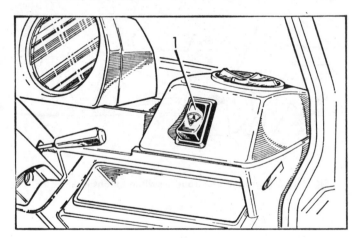

**Fig. 10.25 Tailgate wash/wipe switch location (1) (Sec 26)**

## 27  Automatically operated switches and coolant temperature transmitter – removal and refitting

### Door switch (courtesy lights)

1   With the door open, remove the single screw, withdraw the switch and detach the wiring connector.
2   Refitting is the reverse of the removal procedure.

### Reversing light switch

3   Disconnect the battery earth lead.
4   Remove the main gear lever rubber cover to gain access to the switch.
5   Disconnect the electrical leads from the switch and note their positions.
6   Unscrew and remove the switch and shim washer (photo).
7   Refitting is the reverse of the removal procedure.

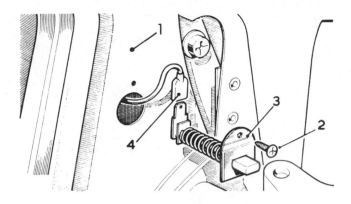

**Fig. 10.26 Door-operated courtesy light switch (Sec 27)**

| 1 | Door pillar | 3 | Switch |
|---|---|---|---|
| 2 | Screw | 4 | Wiring connector |

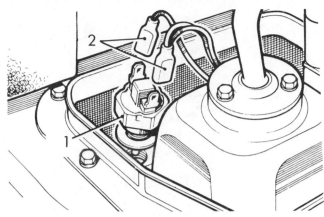

**Fig. 10.27 Reversing light switch (Sec 27)**

| 1 | Switch | 2 | Wiring connectors |
|---|---|---|---|

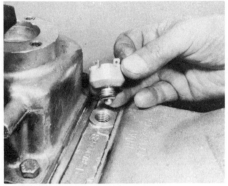

27.6 Removing the reversing light switch (gearbox removed)

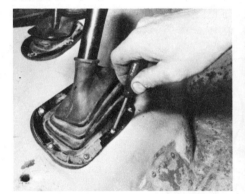

27.9 Removing the handbrake rubber boot and retaining plate

27.11 Handbrake warning light switch (gearbox removed)

### Handbrake warning light switch

8   Disconnect the battery earth lead.
9   Remove the retaining screws and lift off the handbrake rubber boot and retaining plate (photo).
10  Pull the handbrake fully on.
11  Remove the hexagonal nut which retains the switch to its mounting bracket (photo).
12  Withdraw the switch and disconnect the leads as it is removed.
13  Refitting is the reverse of the removal procedure.

### Differential lock actuator switch

14  Remove the front floor of the vehicle as described in Chapter 12.
15  Disconnect the wiring from the switch (photo).
16  Unscrew the switch and remove the switch and shim washers.
17  Refitting the switch is the reverse procedure to removal. Do not forget the shim washers. Refer to Chapter 6, Section 18 for details of the switch setting adjustment.

### Oil pressure warning light switch

18  Disconnect the battery as a safety precaution.
19  Disconnect the lead from the switch on the oil filter housing.
20  Unscrew the switch unit and remove it and the washer.
21  Refitting is the reverse of the removal procedure.

### Coolant temperature transmitter

22  Disconnect the battery as a safety precaution.
23  Drain the coolant from the inlet manifold as described in Chapter 2.
24  Disconnect the electrical wiring from the transmitter in the front end of the manifold (photo).
25  Unscrew the transmitter from the manifold and remove it and the washer.
26  Refitting is the reverse procedure, but use a new washer. Refill the

cooling system as described in Chapter 2.

### Choke warning light switch

27  Remove the switch cover, which is retained by one screw on later models.
28  Disconnect the wiring from the switch.
29  Remove the screw and clip which retain the switch to the choke cable, and remove the switch.

27.15 View of differential lock actuator switch (gearbox removed)

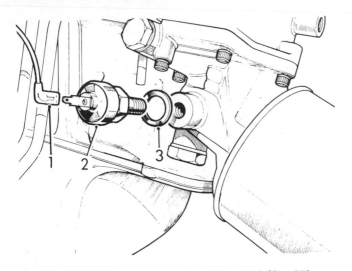

Fig. 10.28 Oil pressure warning light switch (Sec 27)

1   Head                    3   Washer
2   Switch

27.24 Coolant temperature transmitter (arrowed)

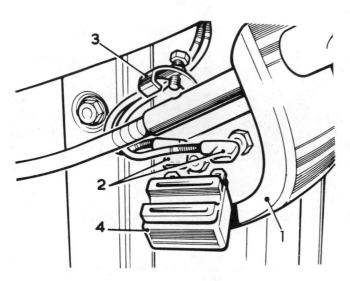

Fig. 10.29 Choke warning light switch (Sec 27)

1   Choke mounting bracket    3   Screw and retaining clip
2   Wiring connectors         4   Switch

30  Refitting is the reverse of the removal procedure.

### Stop-light switch

31  Disconnect the battery as a safety precaution.
32  Remove the lower facia panel beneath the steering column.
33  Depress the footbrake and remove the rubber cover (if fitted) from the operating end of the switch.
34  Undo the locking nut and withdraw the switch from the pedal box.
35  Disconnect the wiring and remove the switch.
36  Refitting is the reverse of the removal procedure. Check the correct operation of the switch on completion.

## 28  Instrument panel housing – removal and refitting

**Note**: *To remove the instrument panel illuminating bulbs and the warning light bulbs it is not necessary to remove the instrument panel housing completely. The rear of the binnacle can be removed by pressing inwards on the rear lower edge of the housing and releasing it from the mounting clips.*

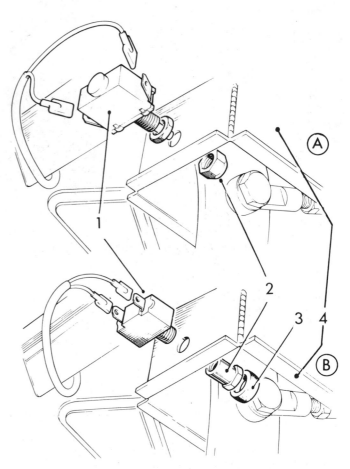

Fig 10.30 Stop-light switch (different types fitted) (Sec 27)

1   Switch          4   Pedal box
2   Locking nut     A   Early type
3   Rubber cover    B   Later type

1   Disconnect the battery negative lead.
2   Remove the binnacle rear casing.
3   Disconnect the speedometer cable from the speedometer as described in Section 31.
4   Unplug the electrical connector from the rear of the printed circuit (photo).
5   Remove the facia panel below the steering column.

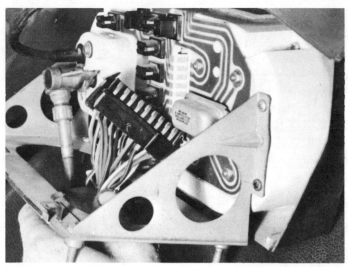

28.4 Unplug the electrical connector from the printed circuit

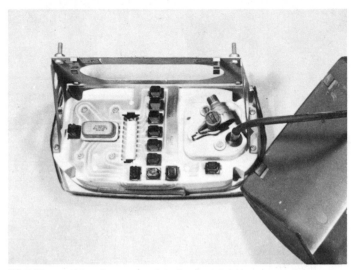

28.7 The complete instrument housing removed

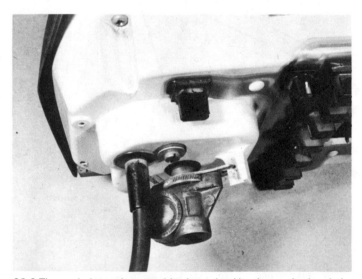

29.6 The angled speedometer drive is retained by the captive knurled nut

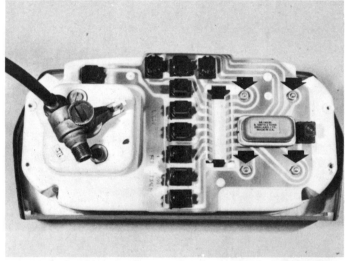

29.10 Fuel and water temperature gauge retaining nuts (arrowed)

6   Remove the four nuts and washers which secure the instrument panel housing to the dashboard.
7   Lift the instrument housing away complete with instruments (photo).
8   Refitting is the reverse of the removal procedure.

## 29 Instruments – removal and refitting

### Instruments mounted in the instrument panel

1   Remove the instrument panel housing as described in Section 28.
2   Unscrew the knurled nut which secures the speedometer trip reset control to the left-hand side of the binnacle rear cover.
3   Undo the four screws which retain the mounting bracket to the instrument panel, and remove it.
4   Remove the screws which retain the front of the instrument panel to the panel itself.
5   Separate the panel from the front cover.
**Speedometer**
6   Remove the angle drive from the rear of the speedometer by undoing the captive knurled nut (photo).
7   Remove the two screws, washers and bushes from the rear of the speedometer.
8   Withdraw the speedometer from the front of the panel.

9   Refitting is the reverse of the removal procedure.
**Fuel gauge**
10   Remove the two nuts and washers from the rear of the fuel gauge whilst holding the fuel gauge in the instrument panel (photo).
11   Withdraw the gauge, taking care that the pins do not damage the printed circuit as they are withdrawn.
12   Refitting is the reverse of the removal procedure.
**Coolant temperature gauge**
13   Hold the gauge and undo the two retaining nuts on the rear of the printed circuit panel.
14   Withdraw the temperature gauge, taking care not to damage the printed circuit with the mounting bolts.
15   Refitting is the reverse procedure.

### Instruments mounted in the facia

16   The same basic procedures apply to all the facia-mounted instruments.
17   Disconnect the battery negative lead.
18   Undo the grub screws and remove the heater control lever knobs.
19   Undo the screws and remove the heater control plate.
20   Undo the four heater console upper retaining screws.
21   Remove the centre face level louvre.
22   From inside the glovebox remove the lower centre console retaining screw.

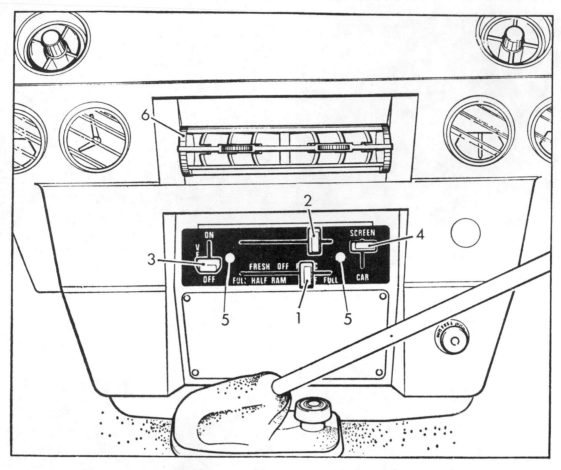

**Fig. 10.31 Heater panel/console removal (Sec 29)**

| | | |
|---|---|---|
| 1   Main air control | 3   Vent control | 5   Plate securing screws |
| 2   Temperature control | 4   Screen/car control | 6   Centre face level louvre |

29.23 Pull the console forward to reach the instruments

23 Move the console forwards to gain access to the instruments (photo).
24 Disconnect the wiring from the appropriate instrument.
25 Remove the illuminating bulb holder and bulb from the rear of the instrument.

26 Remove the knurled nut(s) from the mounting arm(s) for the instrument. Some have one, others have two.
27 Withdraw the instrument from the console.
28 Refitting is the reverse of the removal procedure.

## 30 Voltage stabiliser (instruments) – removal and refitting

1 Disconnect the battery as a safety precaution.
2 Remove the rear of the instrument binnacle.
3 Withdraw the instrument voltage stabilizer from the rear of the printed circuit panel.
4 Plug in the new stabilizer unit.
5 Refit the rear of the instrument binnacle and reconnect the battery.

## 31 Speedometer cable – removal and refitting

1 Disconnect the battery earth lead. Remove the rear of the instrument binnacle by pressing in on the rear lower edge to free it from the mounting clips.
2 Undo the knurled collar and free the cable from the speedometer angle drive.
3 From underneath the vehicle at the rear of the gearbox remove the cable retainer and nut.
4 Pull the cable from the speedo drive housing.
5 Release the cable retaining clips from the rear of the gearbox and the chassis side-member.
6 Withdraw the cable and grommet through the bulkhead.
7 Refit the cable from the top, as it is easier to feed it downwards.

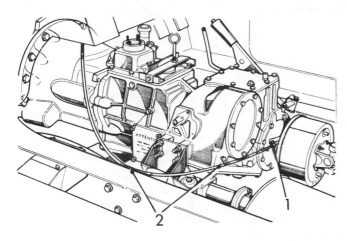

**Fig. 10.32 Speedometer cable location at gearbox (Sec 31)**

*1   Cable retainer and nut*          *2   Cable clips*

32.3 Left-hand horn location

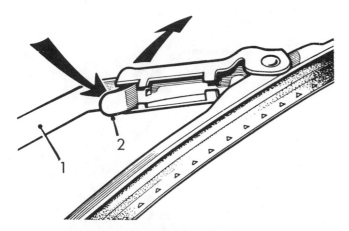

**Fig. 10.33 Wiper blade removal (Sec 33)**

*1   Arm*                         *2   Clip*

8   Reconnect the ends of the cable and secure it with the clips.
9   Refit the rear of the instrument binnacle and reconnect the battery earth lead.

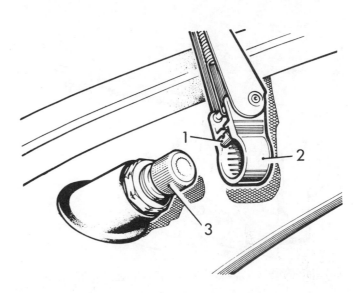

**Fig. 10.34 Wiper arm removal (Sec 33)**

*1   Retaining clip*          *3   Splined spindle*
*2   Wiper arm boss*

shoulder of the splined spindle.
5   Pull the wiper arm off the spindle.
6   To refit the wiper arm, first make sure the wiper motor is in the 'off' or parked position.
7   Push the boss of the wiper arm onto the spindle so that the wiper arm is correctly aligned.
8   Push the boss home so that the spring clip engages behind the shoulder of the spindle.

## 32 Horns – removal and refitting

1   Disconnect the battery.
2   Remove the radiator grille.
3   Undo the two nuts and bolts securing the horn to its mounting bracket. One horn is fitted to either side of the grille opening (photo).
4   Withdraw the horn, disconnecting the wiring.
5   Identify the horn if it is to be renewed. An identification letter is stamped on the front outer rim. The high note horn has a letter 'H', the low note 'L'.
6   Refitting is the reverse of the removal procedure.

## 33 Windscreen and tailgate wiper arms and blades – removal and refitting

### Wiper blade
1   Pull the wiper away from the windscreen.
2   Lift up the spring clip and withdraw the blade from the arm.
3   Refitting is the reverse of the removal procedure.

### Wiper arm
4   Prise the retaining clip on the wiper arm boss away from the

## 34 Windscreen wiper motor and drive assembly – removal and refitting

1   Remove both wiper arms as described in Section 33.
2   Remove the locknuts and washers from the wiper spindles.
3   Remove the rubber grommets from the spindle bases.
4   Remove the bonnet and front decker panel as described in Chapters 12 and 13 respectively.
5   Prise off the spring clips and separate the main link arms from the spindle link arms.
6   Prise off the spring clips and separate the main link arms from the

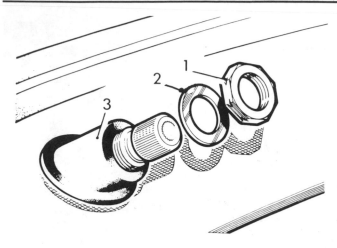

**Fig. 10.35 Wiper spindle assembly (Sec 34)**

1   Locknut              3   Grommet
2   Washer

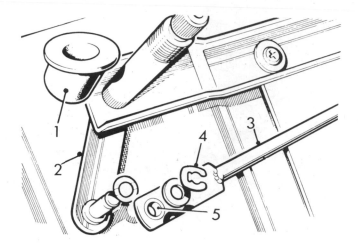

**Fig. 10.36 Spindle and linkage assembly (Sec 34)**

1   Grommet              4   Circlip
2   Spindle link arm     5   Bush
3   Main link arm

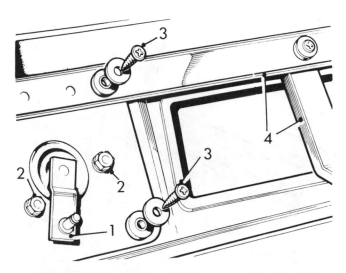

**Fig. 10.37 Wiper motor and linkage mounting (Sec 34)**

1   Wiper motor crank        3   Linkage mounting screws
2   Wiper motor mounting     4   Linkage assembly
    bolts

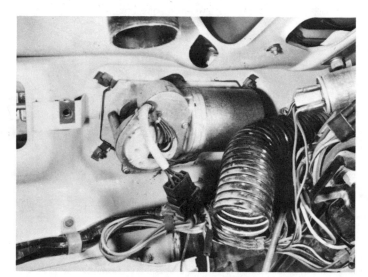

34.9 Disconnect the wiper motor plug-in connector

wiper motor crank. Note which way the bushes fit.
7   Remove the inner wiper spindle grommets.
8   Undo the screws which secure the wiper motor and linkage to the bulkhead.
9   From underneath the dashboard above the steering column withdraw the wiper motor. Disconnect the electrical plug-in connector (photo).
10  Refitting is the reverse of the removal procedure. Remember that the shorter link fits on the driver's side.

### 35 Windscreen wiper motor – overhaul

1   Remove the wiper motor as described in Section 34.
2   Remove the three bolts which secure the motor to its mounting plate.
3   Withdraw the motor crank through the grommet to separate the motor from the mounting plate.
4   Mark the gearbox cover adjacent to the arrowhead on the limit switch cover.
5   Undo the screws that retain the gearbox cover and lift it off.
6   Make sure that the end of the wiper motor shaft is free from burrs, then withdraw it and extract the dished washer.

7   Remove the thrust screw, or thrust screw and locknut, from the side of the wiper body.
8   Remove the through-bolts and slowly withdraw the cover and armature. The brushes will drop clear of the commutator, but do not allow them to become contaminated with grease from the worm gear.
9   Pull the armature out of the cover.
10  Undo the three screws that retain the brush assembly.
11  Lift and slide the limit switch sideways, to release it from the spring clip.
12  The brush assembly and limit switch can now be lifted away together.
13  Examine the various components for wear and renew as necessary.
14  Commence the reassembly procedure by sliding the limit switch in position and securing it with the clip.
15  Refit the brush assembly and secure it with the three screws.
16  Lubricate the cover bearing and soak the cover bearing felt washer with Shell Turbo 41 oil.
17  Refit the armature to the cover, lubricate the self-aligning bearing with Shell Turbo 41 oil, then insert the armature shaft through the bearing whilst restraining the brushes. Take care when inserting the armature shaft to prevent the brushes from becoming contaminated with grease.

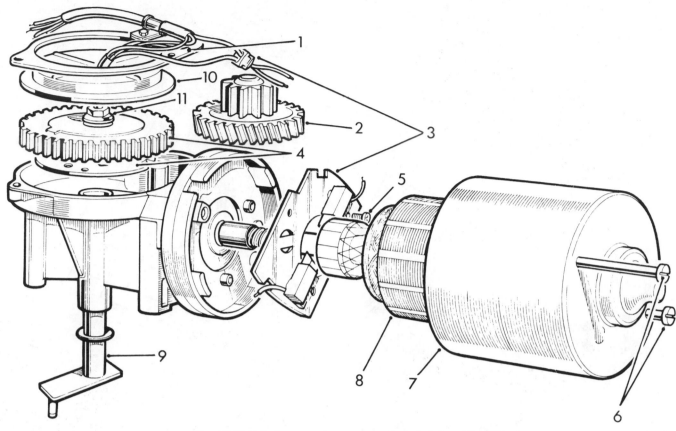

**Fig. 10.38 Windscreen wiper motor – exploded view (Sec 35)**

| | | | |
|---|---|---|---|
| 1 | Gearbox cover | 4 | Gear wheel and driving plate |
| 2 | Intermediate gear wheel | 5 | Brush assembly retaining |
| 3 | Wiring - to brush assembly | | screws |

| | | | |
|---|---|---|---|
| 6 | Through-bolts | 9 | Wiper motor crank |
| 7 | Yoke | 10 | Limit switch |
| 8 | Armature | 11 | Locknut |

18 Position the cover against the gearbox casing so that the datum lines are correctly aligned.

19 Insert the cover through-bolts and tighten them.

20 Refit the thrust screw, or the thrust screw and locknut, and then check the armature endfloat.

21 On types with an adjustable thrust screw, loosen the locknut and screw the adjustment screw inwards until resistance is felt. Turn the screw back by a quarter of a turn and tighten the locknut.

22 On types with a non-adjustable thrust screw, push the armature towards the cover and place a feeler gauge between the armature shaft and thrust screw. The endfloat at this point should be within the limits given in the Specifications. Where the endfloat is insufficient, the only solution is to place a packing washer under the head of the thrust screw. If the endfloat is excessive, then have metal machined from under the head of the thrust screw.

23 Lubricate the final gear bushes with Shell Turbo 41 oil and apply Ragosine Listate grease to the final gear cam.

24 Fit the dished washer with its concave surface facing the final drive gear then insert the shaft.

25 Pack the area around the worm and final gear with Ragosine Listate grease.

26 Reposition the gearbox cover and fit the rubber seal.

27 The wiper motor can now be refitted to the mounting plate by reversing the removal procedure.

## 36 Tailgate wiper motor and drive assembly – removal and refitting

**Note:** *Two different wiper systems have been fitted. On early models the wiper motor is located behind the right-hand rear quarter trim panel, and is secured to the body by a two-bolt mounting. On later models the wiper motor is located high up behind the left-hand rear quarter panel. This motor is retained to the body by a split bracket with a bolt and captive nut.*

1    Remove the appropriate quarter panel.

2    Pull the rear headlining away in order to reach the wiper wheelbox.

3    Remove the wiper arm complete as described in Section 33.

4    Remove the nut and spacer from the wiper spindle.

5    Disconnect the wiper rack tube clips from the body.

6    Disconnect the wiring plug connector at the wiper motor.

7    Remove the wiper motor retaining bolt(s) and support the unit.

8    Remove the wiper motor, withdrawing the rack tube and wheel-box with it as one assembly.

9    The wheelbox and end tube assembly can be removed by slackening the two bolts and nuts which retain it. Then slide it off the end.

10    The tube can be slid off the rack by undoing the nut at the wheelbox.

11    Refitting is the reverse procedure. Ensure that the wheelbox is correctly aligned on the rack before tightening the nuts.

## 37 Headlamp wiper motor and drive racks – removal and refitting

1    Unplug the wiring connector from the headlamp wiper motor, which is located on the right-hand inner front wing.

2    Undo the rack tube collar nuts at the motor.

3    Support the wiper motor, undo the two nuts and remove the clamp.

4    The wiper motor is now free.

5    With the help of an assistant to gently rotate the wiper blades, free

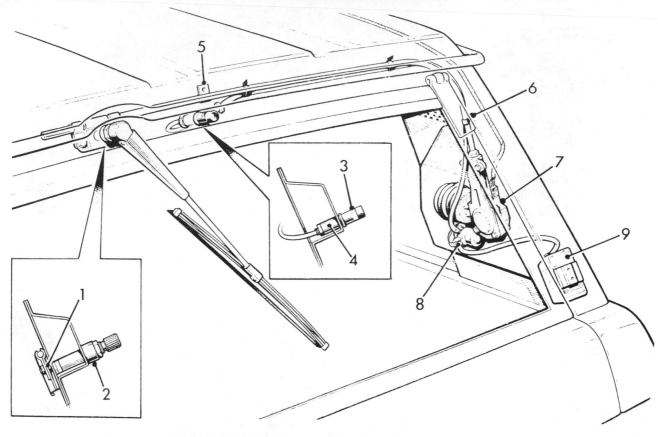

**Fig. 10.39 Tailgate wiper/washer layout (early type) (Sec 36)**

| | | | | | | |
|---|---|---|---|---|---|---|
| 1 | Wiper wheelbox | 4 | Sleeve | 6 | Wiper rack | 8 | Washer motor |
| 2 | Nut and spacer | 5 | Wiper rack clip | 7 | Wiper motor | 9 | Washer reservoir |
| 3 | Washer jet | | | | | |

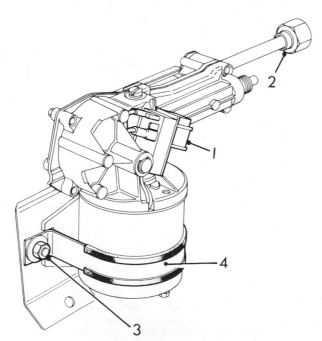

**Fig. 10.40 Headlamp wiper motor mounting (Sec 37)**

| | | | |
|---|---|---|---|
| 1 | Electrical connector socket | 3 | Mounting nut |
| 2 | Rack tube retaining nut | 4 | Clamp |

the wiper racks from the wheelboxes.
6   Withdraw the motor and racks from the flexible rack tubes.
7   Do not move the wiper blades on the headlamps, or refitting is made more difficult.
8   Refitting is the reverse of the removal procedure. When refitted, the headlamp wiper blades must be aligned with the centre frame when the rack has been fully engaged.

## 38  Headlamp wiper arm and blade – removal and refitting

**Note**: *The headlamp wiper arm and blade are serviced as one unit.*
1   Using only finger pressure to prevent the wiper arm from rotating, undo the centre screw.
2   Ease the centre frame away from the headlamp. The wiper arm and blades can then be withdrawn.
3   Refitting is the reverse of the removal procedure. Ensure that the arm is aligned with the centre frame.

## 39  Tailgate and headlamp wiper motors – overhaul

### Brush renewal

1   Unscrew the through-bolts and remove the yoke and armature assembly. Keep the yoke in a clean area, away from any metallic dust or swarf.
2   Note the position and colour coding of the wiring and disconnect it at the switch.
3   Withdraw the brush and plate assembly.
4   Remove the brushes from the insulating plate.
5   Renew the brushes if they are worn below the specified minimum.
6   Reassembly is the reverse of the dismantling procedure.

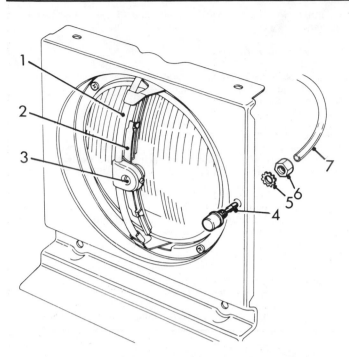

**Fig. 10.41 Headlamp wiper/washer jet assembly (Sec 38)**

| | | | |
|---|---|---|---|
| 1 | Centre frame | 5 | Washer |
| 2 | Wiper blade | 6 | Nut |
| 3 | Centre screw | 7 | Tubing |
| 4 | Jet | | |

*Dismantling*

7   Unscrew the gearbox cover screws and remove the cover.

**Headlamp motor**

8   Remove the circlip and washer in order to disconnect the racks from the driving gear. Then remove the racks from the motor.

**Tailgate motor**

9   Remove the circlip and washer which secure the connecting rod to the crankpin.

10  Lift away the connecting rod. Note the flat washer fitted beneath it.

11  Lift out the cable rack with the cross-head and outer casing threaded connector.

**All motors**

12  Remove the circlip and washer which retain the drivegear and shaft.

13  Make sure the gear shaft is free from burrs and withdraw it. Do not lose the dished washer underneath it.

14  Pull downwards and outwards to release the switch retaining clip.

*Inspection*

15  The resistance between adjacent commutator segments should be 0.34 to 0.41 ohms.

16  Carefully examine the internal wiring for signs of breaks or chafing which would lead to a short-circuit. Insulate or renew any damaged wiring.

17  Measure the value of the field resistance which should be between 12.8 and 14 ohms. If a lower reading than this is obtained it is likely that there is a short-circuit and a new field coil should be fitted.

18  Renew the gearbox gear if the teeth are damaged, chipped or worn.

*Reassembly*

19  Reassembly is a straightforward reversal of the dismantling sequence, but ensure the following items are lubricated:

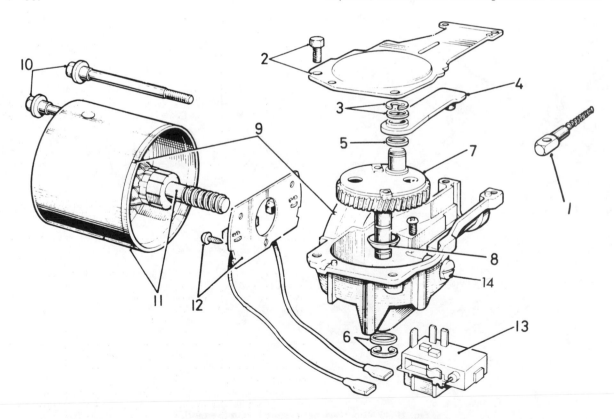

**Fig. 10.42 Tailgate and headlamp wiper motors (exploded view) (Sec 39)**

| | | | | | | | |
|---|---|---|---|---|---|---|---|
| 1 | Drive cable | 5 | Washer | 9 | Yoke and gearbox | 12 | Brush gear |
| 2 | Cover and securing bolt | 6 | Circlip and washer | 10 | Retaining bolts | 13 | Limit switch |
| 3 | Circlip and washer | 7 | Drive gear | 11 | Yoke and armature | 14 | Adjuster screw |
| 4 | Connecting rod | 8 | Dished washer | | | | |

(a) *Immerse the self-aligning armature bearing in engine oil for 24 hours before assembly*
(b) *Oil the armature bearings with engine oil*
(c) *Soak the felt lubricator in the gearbox with engine oil*
(d) *Grease generously the wormwheel bearings, crosshead, guide channel, connecting rod, crankpin, worm, cable rack and wheelboxes and the final gear shaft, using Ragosine Listate grease*

20 To set the armature endfloat, hold the yoke vertically with the adjuster screw uppermost. Screw the adjuster in very carefully until resistance is just felt. Then unscrew it one quarter of a turn.

### 40 Windscreen, tailgate and headlamp washer systems – description, component removal and refitting

#### Description

1   On early vehicles, only the windscreen washer is standard equipment. The reservoir is located in the engine compartment on the left-hand side. Where a tailgate washer is fitted, this may have a separate reservoir and pump mounted behind the right-hand rear quarter panel, or it may be fed via a second cap on the screen washer reservoir.
2   On later models a combined reservoir unit is mounted on the right-hand side of the engine compartment. Separate caps and pump units

are fitted for the windscreen, tailgate and (if applicable) headlamp washers.

#### Removal and refitting
##### Reservoirs
3   On models with pump integral with the cap, disconnect the electrical leads and hose connections (photo).
4   Remove the cap(s) from the reservoir.
5   Lift the reservoir out of its bracket.
6   Refitting is the reverse of the removal procedure.
##### Pump units
7   The early type pump unit is removed with the reservoir cap.
8   The later type pump units are each secured by two mounting screws. Remove the screws and disconnect the tubes to remove the pump.
9   Refitting is the reverse of the removal procedure.
##### Windscreen washer jet
10 Pull off the pipe, then remove the nut and anti-vibration washer, taking care that they are not dropped.
11 Remove the jet and sealing washer.
12 Refitting is the reverse of this procedure. If necessary, rotate the jet using a screwdriver to direct the jet satisfactorily.
##### Tailgate washer jet and sleeve
13 Pull the rear headlining away sufficiently to reach the jet securing nut and tube connection.
14 Disconnect the washer jet feed tubing from the pump, and drain

**Fig. 10.43 Wiper/washer system layout (Sec 40)**

| | | | |
|---|---|---|---|
| 1   *Early windscreen washer reservoir* | 4   *Tailgate wiper motor - later type* | 7   *Headlamp wiper motor* | 9   *Headlamp washer jets* |
| 2   *Later type reservoir for all washers* | 5   *Tailgate washer jet* | 8   *Headlamp wiper rack/tube* | 10   *Windscreen washer jets* |
| 3   *3 separate pump units* | 6   *Windscreen wiper motor* | | |

40.3 The early type of windscreen washer reservoir with integral pump

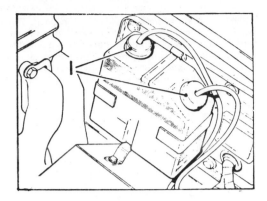

Fig. 10.44 Early type of combined screen and tailgate reservoir (Sec 40)

1   Reservoir caps

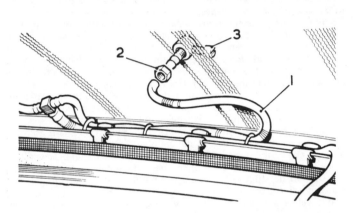

Fig. 10.45 Windscreen washer jet assembly (Sec 40)

1   Tubing                         3   Jet
2   Retaining nut

any water in the tubing to avoid damaging the trim.
15  Hold the jet sleeve and undo the retaining nut.
16  Remove the nut and distance piece.
17  Detach the jet and remove it from the sleeve.
18  Disconnect the tubing from the jet.
19  Withdraw the sleeve and washer from the tubing.
20  Withdraw the tubing inside the vehicle and remove the distance piece, seal and nut.
21  Refitting is the reverse of the removal procedure.
**Headlamp washer jet**
22  Remove the headlamp and holder from the body for access.
23  Disconnect the washer tubing from the jet.
24  Undo the nut and lockwasher and withdraw the jet from the front of the headlamp assembly.
25  Refitting is the reverse of the removal procedure.

## 41  Split charging facility – description

1   The purpose of having a split charging facility is to provide a separate source of 12 volt current to power auxiliary equipment, without discharging the vehicle main battery.
2   To achieve this a diode is located between the alternator and auxiliary terminal bracket. A second battery can then be fitted and connected to the terminals. This will be charged by the alternator when the engine is running.
3   When this battery is being used without the engine in use, it is

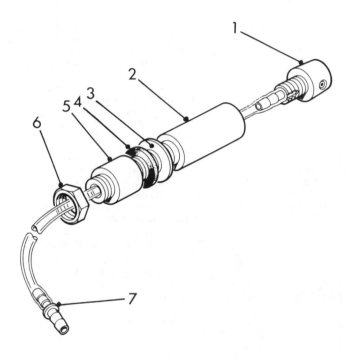

Fig. 10.46 Tailgate washer jet assembly (Sec 40)

1   Jet                           5   Distance piece
2   Sleeve                        6   Nut
3   Washer                        7   Tubing end
4   Seal

effectively isolated from the main vehicle electrical system.
4   A wiring diagram for this facility is provided at the end of the Chapter.

## 42  Radios and tape players – fitting (general)

A radio or tape player is expensive, and will only give its best performance if fitted properly. Do not expect concert hall performance from a unit that is badly installed.

There are in-car entertainment specialists who will do the fitting for you, if you wish. Make sure the unit is of the same polarity as the vehicle (ie negative earth), and that the units with adjustable polarity are correctly set before installation.

Final positioning of the radio/tape player, speakers and aerial is a matter of personal preference. However, the following paragraphs give guidelines, relevant to all installations.

## Radios

Most radios are a standard 7 in wide by 2 in deep. This ensures that they will fit into the radio aperture provided in most cars. If your car does not have such an aperture, fit the radio in a suitable position either in, or beneath the dashpanel. Alternatively, a console can be purchased which will fit between the dashpanel and the floor, or on the transmission tunnel. These consoles can also be used for additional switches and instrumentation.

Where no aperture is provided, the following points should be borne in mind before deciding exactly where to fit the unit:

(a)  *The unit must be within easy reach of the driver wearing a seat belt*

(b)  *The unit must not be mounted close to an electric tachometer, the ignition switch and its wiring, or the flasher unit and associated wiring*

(c)  *The unit must be mounted within reach of the aerial lead, and in such a place that the aerial lead will not have to be routed near the components detailed in paragraph b*

(d)  *The unit should not be positioned in a place where it might cause injury to the car occupants in an accident; for instance under the dashpanel above the driver's or passenger's legs*

(e)  *The unit must be fitted securely*

Some radios will have mounting brackets provided, together with instructions; others will need to be fitted using drilled and slotted metal strips, bent to form mounting brackets. These strips are available from most accessory stores. The unit must be properly earthed by fitting a separate earthing lead between the casing of the radio and the vehicle frame.

Use the radio manufacturer's instructions when wiring into the vehicle's electrical system. If no instructions are available, refer to the relevant wiring diagram to find the location of the radio feed connection in the vehicle's wiring circuit. A 1-2 amp in-line fuse must be fitted in the feed wire, and a choke may also be necessary (see next Section).

The type of aerial used and its position, is a matter of personal preference. In general, the taller the aerial, the better the reception. It is best to fit a fully retractable aerial; especially if a car-wash is used or if you live where cars tend to be vandalised. In this respect, electric aerials which are raised and lowered automatically when switching the radio on or off are convenient, but are more likely to give trouble than the manual type.

When choosing a site for the aerial, the following points should be considered:

(a)  *The aerial lead should be as short as possible; this means that the aerial should be mounted at the front of the vehicle*

(b)  *The aerial must be mounted as far away from the distributor and HT leads as possible*

(c)  *The part of the aerial which protrudes beneath the mounting point must not foul the roadwheels, or anything else*

(d)  *If possible, the aerial should be positioned so that the coaxial lead does not have to be routed through the engine compartment*

(e)  *The plane of the panel on which the aerial is mounted should not be so steeply angled that the aerial cannot be mounted vertically (in relation to the end-on aspect of the vehicle). Most aerials have a small amount of adjustment available*

Having decided on a mounting position, a hole will have to be made in the panel. The size of the hole will depend upon the aerial being fitted, although, generally, the hole required is of $\frac{3}{4}$ in (19 mm) diameter. When the hole has been made the raw edges should be de-burred with a file and then painted to prevent corrosion.

Fit the aerial according to the manufacturer's instructions. If the aerial is very tall, or if it protrudes beneath the mounting panel for a considerable distance, it is a good idea to fit a stay between the aerial and the vehicle frame. This can be manufactured from the slotted and drilled metal strips previously mentioned. The stay should be securely screwed or bolted in place. For best reception it is advisable to fit an earth lead between the aerial and the vehicle frame — this is essential on fibreglass bodied vehicles.

It will probably be necessary to drill one or two holes through bodywork panels in order to feed the aerial lead into the interior of the car. Ensure that the holes are fitted with rubber grommets to protect the cable and to prevent the entry of water.

Positioning and fitting of the speaker depends mainly on the type.

Generally, the speaker is designed to fit in the aperture provided in the car in the top of the dashpanel. Where this is the case, fitting the speaker is just a matter of removing the protective grille from the aperture and securing the speaker. Take care not to damage the speaker diaphragm whilst doing this. It is a good idea to fit a gasket beneath the speaker frame and the mounting panel to prevent vibration. Some speakers will already have such a gasket fitted.

When connecting a rear mounted speaker to the radio, the wires should be routed through the vehicle beneath the carpets or floor mats, preferably through the middle, or along the side of the floorpan where they will not be trodden on.

There will now be several yards of additional wiring in the car, use PVC tape to secure this out of the way. Do not leave the electrical leads dangling. Ensure that new connections are properly made (wires twisted together will not do) and secure.

The radio should now be working, but it will be necessary to trim the radio to the aerial. Follow the manufacturer's instructions in this respect.

## Tape players

Fitting instructions for both cartridge and cassette stereo tape players are the same, and in general the same rules apply as when fitting a radio. Tape players are not prone to electrical interference like radios – although it can occur, so positioning is not so critical. If possible, the player should be mounted on an even-keel. Also, it must be possible for a driver wearing a seat belt to reach the unit in order to change, or turn over, tapes.

For the best results from speakers recessed into a panel, mount them so that the back of the speaker protrudes into an enclosed chamber within the vehicle (eg door interiors).

To fit recessed type speakers in the front doors, check that there is room to mount the speaker in each door without it fouling the latch or window winding mechanism. Hold the speaker against the skin of the door and draw a line around the periphery. With the speaker removed, draw a second cutting line, within the first, to allow enough room for the entry of the speaker back but providing a broad seat for the speaker flange. When you are sure that the cutting-line is correct, drill a series of holes around its periphery. Pass a hacksaw blade through one of the holes and then cut through the metal between the holes until the centre section of the panel falls out.

De-burr the edges of the hole and paint the raw metal to prevent corrosion. Cut a corresponding hole in the door trim panel – ensuring that it will be completely covered by the speaker grille. Now drill a hole in the door edge and a corresponding hole in the door surround. These holes are to feed the speaker leads through – so fit grommets. Pass the speaker leads through the door trim, door skin and out through the holes in the side of the door and surround. Refit the trim panel and then secure the speaker to the door using self-tapping screws. **Note:** *If the speaker is fitted with a shield to prevent water dripping on it, ensure that this shield is at the top.*

## 43 Radios and tape players – suppression of interference (general)

To eliminate buzzes and other unwanted noises, costs very little and is not as difficult as sometimes thought. With common sense and patience, and following the instructions in the following paragraphs, interference can be virtually eliminated.

The first cause for concern is the alternator. The noise this makes over the radio is like an electric mixer and speeds up when you rev the engine (if you wish to prove the point, remove the fanbelt and try it). The remedy for this is simple; connect a 1.0 to 3.0 mf capacitor between earth, probably the bolt that holds down the alternator base and the large terminal on the alternator. If you connect it to the small terminal, you will probably damage the alternator permanently.

A second common cause of electrical interference is the ignition system. Here on non-electronic systems a 1.0 mf capacitor must be connected between earth and the SW or + terminal on the coil. This may stop the tick-tick-tick sound that comes over the speaker. Next comes the spark itself.

There are several ways of curing interference from the ignition HT system. One is the use of carbon-cored HT leads as original equipment. Where copper cable is substituted then use resistive spark plug caps. An alternative is to use in-line suppressors. If the interference is not too bad, you may get away with only one suppressor in the coil to

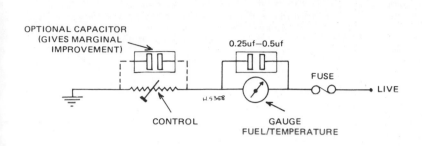

Fig. 10.47 Gauge and control unit interference suppression
(Sec 43)

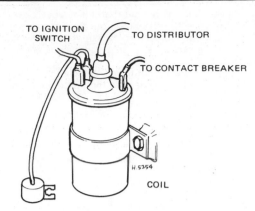

Fig. 10.48 The correct method of connecting a
capacitor to the ignition coil (Sec 43)

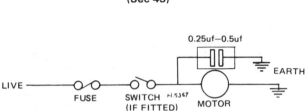

Fig. 10.49 Electric motor interference suppression (Sec 43)

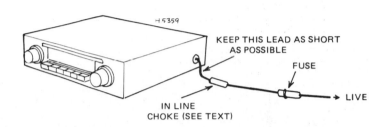

Fig. 10.50 Location of in-line choke and fuse (Sec 43)

distributor line. If the intererence does continue (a clacking noise), modify all HT leads.

At this stage it is advisable to check that the radio and aerial are well earthed, that the aerial plug is pushed well into the set and that the radio is properly trimmed (see preceding Section). Check that the wire which supplies the power to the set is as short as possible and does not wander all over the car. Check that the fuse is of the correct rating. For most sets this will be about 1 to 2 amps.

At this point, the more usual causes of interference have been suppressed. If the problem still exists, a look at the cause of interference may help to pinpoint the component generating the stray electrical discharges.

The radio picks up electromagnetic waves in the air, some made by regular broadcasters and some, which we do not want, are made by the car itself. The home made signals are produced by stray electrical discharges floating around in the car. Common producers of these signals are electric motors, ie the windscreen wipers, electric screen washers, heater fan or an electric aerial if fitted. Other sources of interference are flashing turn signals and instruments. The remedy for these cases is shown in Fig. 10.49 for an electric motor whose interference is not too bad and Fig. 10.47 for instrument suppression. Turn signals are not normally suppressed. In recent years, radio manufacturers have included in the line (live) of the radio, in addition to the fuse, an in-line choke. If your circuit lacks one of these, put one in as shown in Fig. 10.50.

All the foregoing components are available from radio or accessory stores. If an electric clock is fitted, this should be suppressed by connecting a 0.5 mf capacitor directly across it as shown for a motor.

If after all this you are still experiencing radio interference, first assess how bad it is, for the human ear can filter out unobtrusive unwanted noises quite easily. But if you are still adamant about eradicating the noise, then continue.

As a first step, a few experts seem to favour a screen between the radio and the engine. However, the whole set is screened anyway and if interference can get past that, then a small piece of aluminium is not going to stop it.

A more sensible way of screening is to discover if interference is coming down the wires. First, take the live lead; interference can get between the set and the choke (hence the reason for keeping the wires short). One remedy here is to screen the wire and this is done by buying screened wire and fitting that. The loudspeaker lead could be screened also to prevent pick-up getting back to the radio although this is unlikely.

Without doubt, the worst source of radio interference comes from the ignition HT leads, even if they have been suppressed. The ideal way of suppressing these is to slide screening tubes over the leads themselves. As this is impractical, we can place an aluminium shield over the majority of the lead areas. In a vee or twin-cam engine this is relatively easy but for a straight engine, the results are not particularly good.

Now for the really impossible cases, here are a few tips to try out. Where metal comes into contact with metal, an electrical disturbance is caused which is why good clean connections are essential. To remove interference due to overlapping or butting panels, you must bridge the join with a wide braided earth strap (like that from the frame to the engine/transmission). The most common moving parts that could create noise and should be strapped are, in order of importance:

(a)  Silencer-to-frame
(b)  Exhaust pipe-to-engine block and frame
(c)  Air cleaner-to-frame
(d)  Front and rear bumpers-to-frame
(e)  Steering column-to-frame
(f)  Bonnet lids-to-frame

These faults are most pronounced when (1) the engine is idling, (2) labouring under load. Although the moving parts are already connected with nuts, bolts, etc, these do corrode, thus creating a high resistance interference source.

If you have a ragged sounding pulse when mobile, this could be wheel or tyre static. This can be cured by buying some anti-static powder and sprinkling liberally inside the tyres.

If the interference takes the shape of a high pitched screeching noise that changes its note when the car is in motion and only comes now and then, this could be related to the aerial, especially if it is of the telescopic or whip type. This source can be cured quite simply by pushing a small rubber ball on top of the aerial as this breaks the electric field before it can form; but it would be much better to buy yourself a new aerial of a reputable brand. If a loud rushing sound occurs every time you brake, then this is brake static. This effect is most prominent on hot dry days and is cured only by fitting a special kit, which is quite expensive.

In conclusion, it is pointed out that it is relatively easy and cheap to eliminate 95 per cent of all noise, but to eliminate the final 5 per cent is time and money consuming. It is up to the individual to decide if it is worth it. Remember also, that you cannot get a concert hall performance out of a cheap radio.

Finally, tape players are not usually affected by car noise but in a very bad case, the best remedies are the first three suggestions plus using a 3 to 5 amp choke in the live line and in exceptionable cases, screening the live and speaker wires.

**Note**: *If your car is fitted with electronic ignition, then it is not recommended that either the spark plug resistors or the ignition coil capacitor be fitted as these may damage the system. Most electronic ignition units have built in suppression and should, therefore, not cause interference.*

## 44 Fault diagnosis – electrical system

| Symptom | Reason(s) |
|---|---|
| Starter motor fails to turn engine | Battery discharged<br>Battery defective internally<br>Battery terminal leads loose or earth lead not securely attached to body<br>Loose or broken connections in starter motor circuit<br>Starter motor switch or solenoid faulty<br>Starter brushes badly worn, or brush wire loose<br>Commutator dirty, worn or burnt<br>Starter motor armature faulty<br>Field coils earthed |
| Starter motor turns engine very slowly | Battery in discharged condition<br>Starter brushes badly worn, sticking, or brush wires loose<br>Loose wires in starter motor circuit |
| Starter motor operates without turning engine | Pinion or flywheel gear teeth broken or worn |
| Starter motor noisy or excessively rough engagement | Pinion or flywheel gear teeth broken or worn<br>Starter motor retaining bolts loose |
| Battery will not hold charge for more than a few days | Battery defective internally<br>Electrolyte level too low or electrolyte too weak due to leakage<br>Plate separators no longer fully effective<br>Battery plates severely sulphated<br>Fanbelt slipping<br>Battery terminal connections loose or corroded<br>Alternator regulator unit not working correctly<br>Short in lighting circuit causing continual battery drain |
| No charge light fails to go out, battery runs flat in a few days | Fanbelt loose and slipping, or broken<br>Brushes worn, sticking, broken or dirty<br>Brush springs weak or broken<br>Slip rings dirty, greasy, worn or burnt<br>Alternator stator coils burnt, open, or shorted |
| Horn operates all the time | Horn switch either earthed or stuck<br>Horn cable to horn switch earthed |
| Horn fails to operate | Blown fuse<br>Cable or cable connection loose, broken or disconnected<br>Horn has an internal fault |
| Horn emits intermittent or unsatisfactory noise | Cable connections loose or horn needs adjusting |
| Lights do not come on | If engine not running, battery disaharged<br>Light bulb filament burnt out or bulbs broken<br>Wire connections loose, disconnected or broken<br>Light switch shorting or otherwise faulty |
| Lights come on but fade out | If engine not running, battery discharged |
| Lights work erratically – flashing on and off, especially over bumps | Battery terminals or earth connection loose<br>Lights not earthing properly<br>Contacts in light switch faulty |
| Wiper motor fails to work | Blown fuse<br>Wire connections loose, disconnected or broken<br>Brushes badly worn<br>Armature worn or faulty<br>Field coils faulty |
| Wiper motor works very slowly and takes excessive current | Commutator dirty, greasy or burnt<br>Armature bearings dirty or unaligned<br>Armature badly worn or faulty |
| Wiper motor works slowly and takes little current | Brushes badly worn<br>Commutator dirty, greasy or burnt<br>Armature badly worn or faulty |
| Wiper motor works but wiper blades remain static | Wiper motor gearbox parts badly worn |

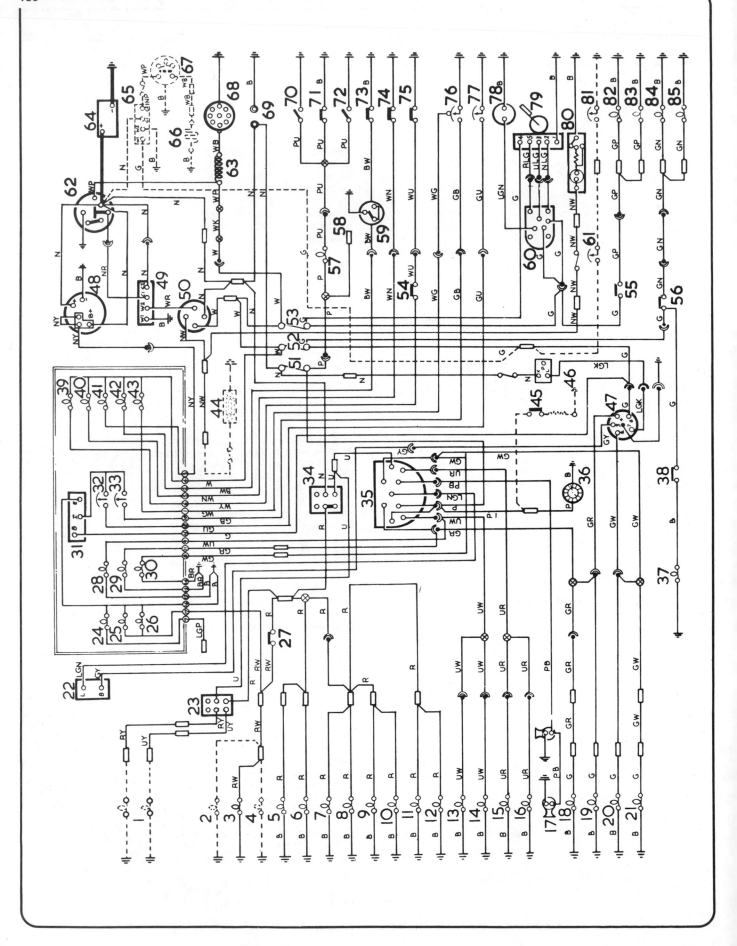

**Fig. 10.51 Wiring diagram for Models prior to 1974. Optional equipment shown dotted**

1 Auxiliary driving lamps
2 Cigar lighter illumination
3 Clock illumination
4 Auxiliary instrument illumination feed
5 LH front side lamp
6 RH front side lamp
7 LH rear marker lamp (NADA only)
8 LH rear tail lamp
9 Number plate illumination lamp
10 Number plate illumination lamp
11 RH rear tail lamp
12 RH rear marker lamp (NADA only)
13 RH headlamp, main
14 LH headlamp, main
15 RH headlamp, dip
16 LH headlamp, dip
17 Horns
18 LH rear indicator
19 LH front indicator

20 RH front indicator
21 RH rear indicator
22 Indicator unit
23 Auxiliary driving lamp switch
24 Trailer warning light
25 Instrument illumination
26 Instrument illumination
27 Panel light switch
28 Main beam warning light
29 LH indicator warning light
30 RH indicator warning light
31 Voltage stabiliser
32 Water temperature gauge
33 Fuel gauge
34 Lighting switch
35 Indicator, headlamp dip and horn switch
36 Clock
37 Differential lock warning light

38 Differential lock warning light switch
39 Choke warning light switch
40 Oil pressure warning light
41 Ignition warning light
42 Brake warning light
43 Fuel level warning light
44 Radio
45 Cigar lighter
46 Hazard warning unit
47 Hazard warning switch
48 Alternator
49 Starting relay
50 Ignition switch and steering lock
51 Fuse (1)
52 Fuse (2)
53 Fuse (3)
54 Choke switch

55 Stop-lamp switch
56 Reversing light switch
57 Interior light
58 Trailer socket connection
59 Shuttle valve (brake warning)
60 Windscreen wiper and washer switch
61 Oil pressure gauge
62 Pre-engaged starter
63 Coil
64 Battery
65 Relay
66 Heated rear screen
67 Heated rear screen switch
68 Distributor
69 Inspection sockets
70 Courtesy light switch

71 Interior light switch
72 Courtesy light switch
73 Handbrake switch
74 Oil pressure switch
75 Choke thermostat
76 Fuel gauge unit
77 Water temperature transmitter
78 Screen washer motor
79 Windscreen wiper motor
80 Heater motor
81 Oil pressure transmitter
82 Stop-light, RH
83 Stop-light, LH
84 Reversing light RH
85 Reversing light LH

**Cable colour code**

G Green       U Blue
P Purple      N Brown
L Light       Y Yellow
O Orange      B Black
S Slate       R Red
K Pink        W White

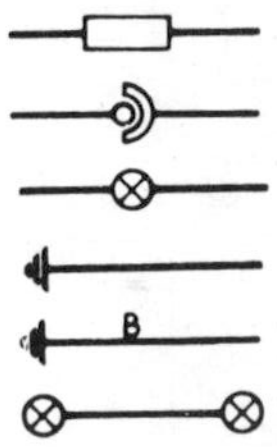

SNAP CONNECTORS

CONNECTIONS VIA PLUG & SOCKET

PERMANENT IN-LINE CONNECTIONS

EARTH CONNECTIONS VIA FIXING BOLTS

EARTH CONNECTIONS VIA CABLES

EUREKA RESISTANCE WIRE

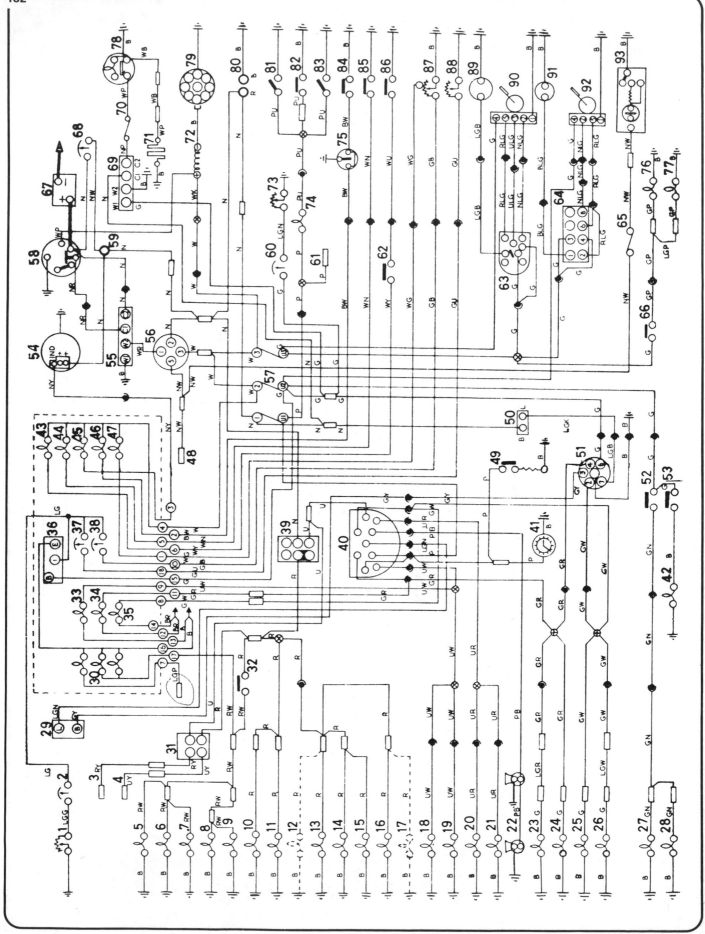

**Fig. 10.52 Wiring diagram – vehicles with auxiliary instruments (Pre-1975)**

1 Oil temperature transmitter
2 Oil temperature gauge
3 Pick-up point for auxiliary driving lamps
4 Pick-up point for auxiliary driving lamps
5 Ammeter illumination
6 Oil temperature gauge illumination
7 Cigar lighter illumination
8 Oil pressure gauge illumination
9 Clock illumination
10 Sidelamp, LH
11 Sidelamp, RH
12 Side marker lamp, tail, LH, as applicable
13 Tail lamp, LH
14 Number plate illumination
15 Number plate illumination
16 Tail lamp, RH
17 Side marker lamp, tail, RH, as applicable

18 Headlamp main beam, RH
19 Headlamp main beam, LH
20 Headlamp dip, RH
21 Headlamp dip, LH
22 Horns
23 Indicator lamp, rear LH
24 Indicator lamp, front LH
25 Indicator lamp, front RH
26 Indicator lamp, rear RH
27 Reversing lamp
28 Reversing lamp
29 Indicator unit
30 Trailer illumination
31 Auxiliary driving lamps switch
32 Panel lights switch
33 Warning light, headlamp main beam
34 Warning light, indicator, LH
35 Warning light, indicator, RH
36 Voltage stabiliser
37 Water temperature gauge

38 Fuel gauge
39 Main light switch
40 Headlamps, direction indicators and horn switch
41 Clock
42 Warning light, differential lock switch
43 Warning light, choke
44 Warning light, oil pressure
45 Warning light, ignition
46 Warning light, brake
47 Warning light, fuel level
48 Pick-up point for radio
49 Cigar lighter
50 Hazard warning unit
51 Hazard warning switch
52 Reversing lights switch
53 Differential lock switch
54 Alternator
55 Relay for starter motor
56 Ignition/starter switch

57 Fuses
58 Starter motor
59 Terminal post
60 Oil pressure gauge
61 Pick-up point for seven-pin trailer socket
62 Choke switch
63 Front wiper and washer switch
64 Rear wiper and washer switch
65 In-line fuse for heater
66 Stop-lamps switch
67 Battery
68 Ammeter
69 Relay for heated rearscreen
70 In-line fuse for heated rear screen
71 Heated rear screen
72 Ignition coil
73 Oil pressure transmitter
74 Interior light
75 Shuttle valve for brake switch

76 Stop-lamp, LH
77 Stop-lamp, RH
78 Heated rear screen switch
79 Distributor
80 Inspection light sockets
81 Courtesy light switch
82 Interior light switch
83 Courtesy light switch
84 Handbrake switch
85 Oil pressure switch
86 Choke control pick-up point switch
87 Fuel gauge, tank unit
88 Water temperature transmitter
89 Windscreen washer motor
90 Windscreen wiper motor
91 Rear screen washer motor
92 Rear screen wiper motor
93 Heater motor

*Refer to Fig. 10.51 for the cable colour code*

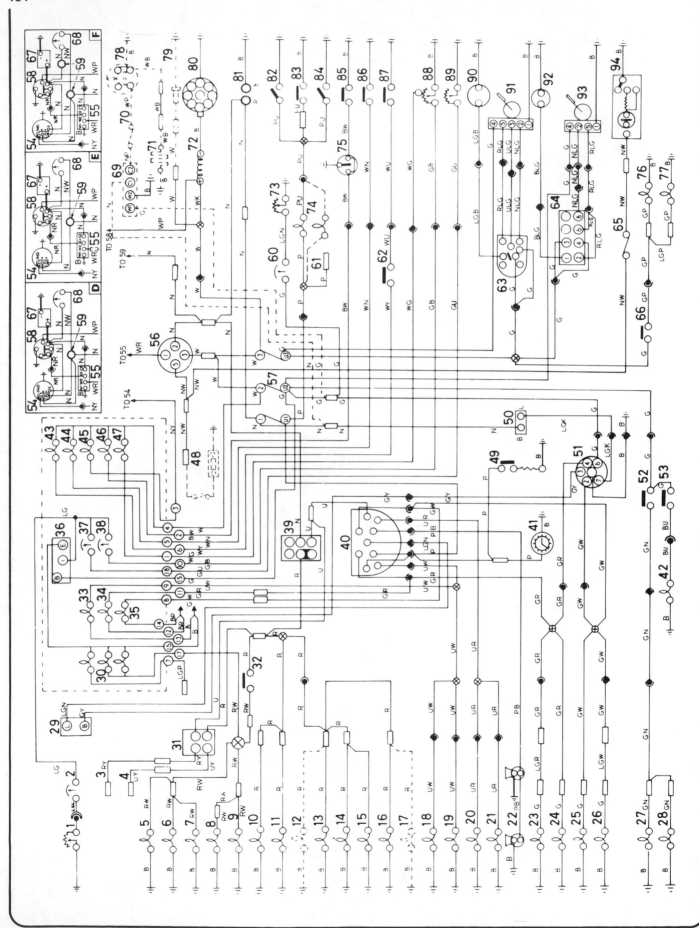

**Fig. 10.53 Wiring diagram — vehicles fitted with 16ACR or 18ACR alternator, 1975 onwards. Optional equipment shown dotted**

1 Oil temperature transmitter
2 Oil temperature gauge
3 Pick-up point for auxiliary driving lamps
4 Pick-up point for auxiliary driving lamps
5 Ammeter (or battery voltmeter) illumination
6 Oil temperature gauge illumination
7 Cigar lighter illumination
8 Oil pressure gauge illumination
9 Clock illumination
10 Sidelamp, LH
11 Sidelamp, RH
12 Side marker lamp, tail, LH, as applicable
13 Tail lamp, LH
14 Number plate illumination
15 Number plate illumination
16 Tail lamp, RH

17 Side marker lamp, tail, RH, as applicable
18 Headlamp main beam, RH
19 Headlamp main beam, LH
20 Headlamp dip, RH
21 Headlamp dip, LH
22 Horns
23 Indicator lamp, rear LH
24 Indicator lamp, front LH
25 Indicator lamp, front RH
26 Indicator lamp, rear RH
27 Reversing lamp
28 Reversing lamp
29 Indicator unit
30 Trailer illumination
31 Auxiliary driving lamps switch
32 Panel lights switch
33 Warning light, headlamp main beam
34 Warning light, indicator, LH
35 Warning light, indicator, RH
36 Voltage stabiliser
37 Water temperature gauge

38 Fuel gauge
39 Main light switch
40 Headlamps, direction indicators and horn switch
41 Clock
42 Warning light, differential lock switch
43 Warning light, choke
44 Warning light, oil pressure
45 Warning light, ignition
46 Warning light, brake
47 Warning light, fuel level
48 Pick-up point for radio
49 Cigar lighter
50 Hazard warning unit
51 Hazard warning switch
52 Reversing lights switch
53 Differential lock switch
54 Alternator
55 Relay for starter motor
56 Ignition/starter switch
57 Fuses

58 Starter motor
59 Terminal post
60 Oil pressure gauge
61 Pick-up point for seven-pin trailer socket
62 Choke switch
63 Front wiper and washer switch
64 Rear wiper and washer switch
65 In-line fuse for heater
66 Stop-lamps switch
67 Battery
68 Ammeter (or battery voltmeter)
69 Relay for heated rearscreen
70 In-line fuse for heated rear screen
71 Heated rear screen
72 Ignition coil
73 Oil pressure transmitter
74 Interior light
75 Shuttle valve for brake switch

76 Stop-lamp, LH
77 Stop-lamp, RH
78 Heated rear screen switch
79 Fuel pump
80 Distributor
81 Inspection light sockets
82 Courtesy light switch
83 Interior light switch
84 Courtesy light switch
85 Handbrake switch
86 Oil pressure switch
87 Choke control pick-up point switch
88 Fuel gauge, tank unit
89 Water temperature transmitter
90 Windscreen washer motor
91 Windscreen wiper motor
92 Rear screen washer motor
93 Rear screen wiper motor
94 Heater motor

*Refer to Fig. 10.51 for the cable colour code*
*Later vehicles may be fitted with air cord 12 volt oil pressure gauges not wired via the voltage stabiliser or 10 volt gauges in circuit with it.*

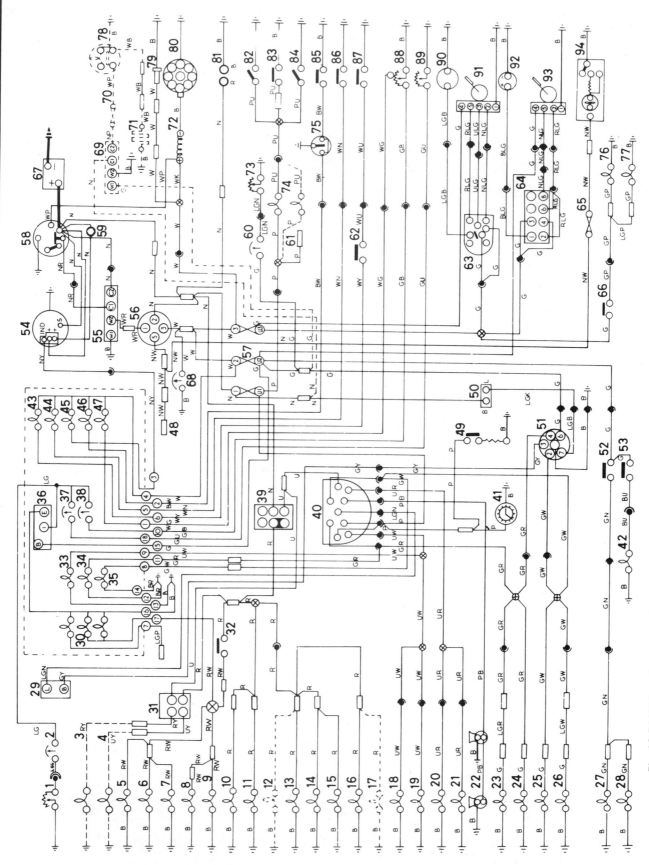

Fig. 10.54 Wiring diagram – vehicles fitted with voltmeter instead of ammeter. Optional equipment shown dotted. For key see Fig. 10.53

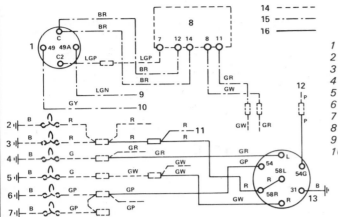

Fig. 10.55 Wiring diagram for trailer lighting circuit

1 Replacement flasher unit
2 Side marker lamp, LH
3 Tail lamp, LH
4 Indicator lamp, LH
5 Indicator lamp, RH
6 Stop-lamp, LH
7 Stop-lamp, RH
8 Instrument binnacle
9 From indicator switch
10 From hazard warning switch

11 To number plate illumination
12 Feed from fuse A2
13 Seven-pin vehicle socket
14 Dotted lines indicate vehicle wiring
15 Chain dotted lines indicate vehicle wiring repositioned
16 Unbroken lines indicate the conversion harness

Refer to Fig. 10.51 for the cable colour code

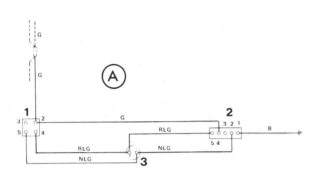
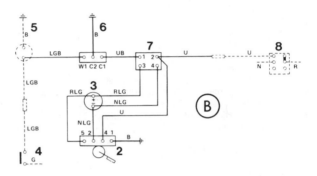

Fig. 10.56 Circuit diagram for headlamp wipers and washers

A Earlier vehicles
B Later vehicles
1 Headlamp wiper washer switch
2 Headlamp wiper motor
3 Headlamp washer pump
4 Windscreen washer switch
5 Windscreen washer pump
6 Headlamp wiper relay
7 Headlamp wiper relay unit
8 Vehicle lighting switch
Refer to Fig. 10.51 for the cable colour code

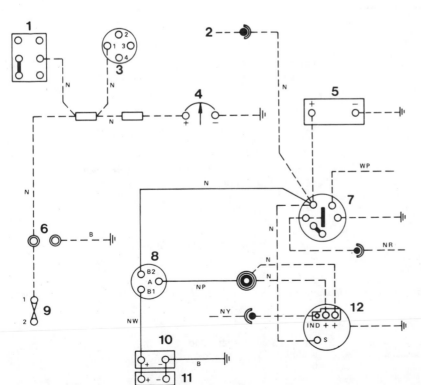

Fig. 10.57 Circuit diagram – split charging facility

1 Lighting switch
2 Connection to starter relay
3 Steering lock and ignition switch
4 Voltmeter
5 Vehicle battery
6 Inspection lamp sockets
7 Starter motor
8 Split charge diode
9 Fuse unit
10 Terminal bracket, for second battery
11 Second bracket
12 Alternator
Circuits shown dotted are existing and contained in the basic vehicle
Circuits shown in full are additional
Refer to Fig. 10.51 for the cable colour code

# Chapter 11 Suspension and steering

*For modifications, and information applicable to later models, see Supplement at end of manual*

## Contents

## Specifications

### Suspension

| | |
|---|---|
| Front suspension | Coil springs with hydraulic telescopic shock absorbers. Axle located by radius arms and Panhard rod |
| Rear suspension | Coil springs with hydraulic telescopic shock absorbers and Boge self-levelling ride unit. Axle located by radius arms |

### Steering

Type:

| | |
|---|---|
| Early models (up to 1980) | Burman, recirculating ball, manual |
| Optional from 1973 | Power-assisted steering |
| Standard fitting, 1980 models | Adwest Varamatic, power-assisted steering |

| | **Manual** | **Power-assisted** |
|---|---|---|
| Number of turns, lock to lock | $4\frac{3}{4}$ (early), $5\frac{1}{2}$ (later) | $3\frac{1}{2}$ |
| Ratio – straight-ahead | 18.2 : 1 | 17.5 : 1 |
| Steering wheel diameter | 17 in (431.8 mm) | |

### Steering/front suspension geometry

| | |
|---|---|
| Front wheel alignment | 0.046 to 0.094 (1.2 to 2.4 mm) toe-out |
| Camber angle – unladen* | 0° |
| Castor angle – unladen* | 3° |
| Swivel pin inclination – unladen* | 7° |

*Unladen condition means vehicle empty but with water, oil and 5 gallons (25 litres) of fuel. Rock the vehicle up and down at the front to allow it to assume a static position

### Wheels

| | |
|---|---|
| Type | Pressed steel – enamelled |
| Fixing type | 5 stud |
| Size | 600 JK x 16 |

### Tyres

| | |
|---|---|
| Size | 205 x 16 (tubed) radial ply |

| Tyre pressures (cold) in lbf/in² (kgf/cm²) | Front | Rear |
|---|---|---|
| Normal use – on and off-road | | |
| All speeds – loads up to 500 lb (226 kg) .......................... | 25 (1.8) | 25 (1.8) |
| All speeds – loads above 500 lb (226 kg) .......................... | 25 (1.8) | 35 (2.5) |
| Off-road – emergency soft use: | | |
| Max speed 40 mph – up to 500 lb (226 kg) loads ................. | 15 (1.1) | 15 (1.1) |
| Max speed 40 mph (64 kph) – loads in excess of 500 lbs (226 kg) .......................... | 15 (1.1) | 25 (1.8) |

**Power steering pump drivebelt tension** ........................ 0.4 to 0.5 in (11 to 14 mm) deflection at midpoint of longest run

## Torque wrench settings

| | lbf ft | kgf m |
|---|---|---|
| Balljoint nuts .......................... | 30 | 4 |
| Steering joint pinch-bolt .......................... | 25 | 3.5 |
| Drop arm nut .......................... | 125 | 17.9 |
| Steering box cover bolts (manual) .......................... | 17 | 2.3 |
| Track rod clamp bolts .......................... | 10 | 1.4 |
| Steering wheel nut .......................... | 28 | 3.8 |
| Power steering pulley bolt .......................... | 12 | 1.6 |
| Self-levelling unit balljoint collar .......................... | 50 | 7.0 |
| Rear radius arm – stem end .......................... | 90 | 12.4 |
| Self-levelling unit-to-axle bracket .......................... | 130 | 17.9 |
| Power steering sector cover bolts .......................... | 16 to 20 | 2.2 to 2.8 |
| Steering pump valve cap .......................... | 30 to 35 | 4.0 to 4.9 |

## 1 General description

The live front and rear axles are both located by radius arms and in addition the front axle has the benefit of a Panhard rod. The heavy duty coil springs and double-acting hydraulic shock absorbers allow the suspension amazingly long vertical travel which enables it to give a smooth ride even over rough terrain. At the rear there is also a centrally mounted A-frame incorporating a Boge gas-filled self-levelling unit. This keeps the vehicle level when it is fully loaded or when towing a trailer.

Steering in early models was by a manual recirculating ball, worm and nut system with a safety steering column. Power steering by Adwest was not available until 1973, but even then only as an optional extra. From the advent of the 1980 model, in September 1979, power steering has been fitted as standard equipment. The power steering pump is belt-driven from the crankshaft.

In manual steering models the system is aided by a steering damper unit fitted between the track rod mounting bracket and the front axle casing.

The steering and suspension is relatively maintenance-free apart from (on models so equipped) periodically checking the tension of the steering pump drivebelt, power steering fluid level and renewing the power steering fluid reservoir filter. It is advisable to periodically inspect the entire steering and suspension systems.

## 2 Panhard rod – removal and refitting

1 The Panhard rod locates the front axle laterally. It is mounted onto a bracket on the axle casing at the left-hand end and onto a bracket below the right-hand chassis side-member.
2 Undo the nuts on the end of both bolts.
3 Drive out the left-hand bolt and then the right-hand bolt and remove the rod.
4 Bushes are fitted to both ends of the Panhard rod and these can be pressed out and renewed if required.
5 Ensure if new bushes are fitted that they are centrally located in the eyes at the end of the rod.
6 Refitting is the reverse of the removal procedure. Make sure the rod is fitted with the cranked section in front of the front axle differential case, facing forwards (Fig. 11.1).

## 3 Front radius arm – removal and refitting

1 Jack up the front of the vehicle on the appropriate side and support it securely with axle stands under the front axle. Chock the other wheels.
2 Remove the roadwheel on the side being worked on.
3 Undo the nut and remove the washer and bush on the rear end of the radius arm (Fig. 11.2).
4 Disconnect the track rod balljoint, at the side of the vehicle being worked on, as described in Section 14.

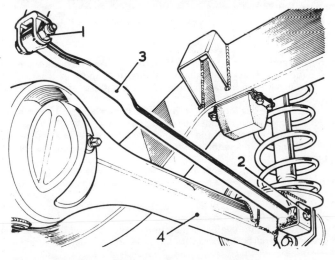

Fig. 11.1 Panhard rod assembly (Sec 2)

| 1 | Chassis mounting | 3 | Panhard rod |
|---|---|---|---|
| 2 | Axle mounting | 4 | Front axle |

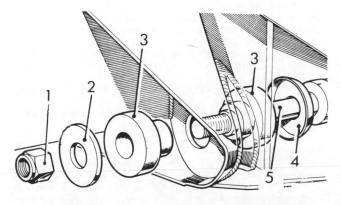

Fig. 11.2 Front radius arm – rear mounting (exploded view) (Sec 3)

| 1 | Nut | 4 | Cup washer |
|---|---|---|---|
| 2 | Washer | 5 | Radius arm |
| 3 | Bushes | | |

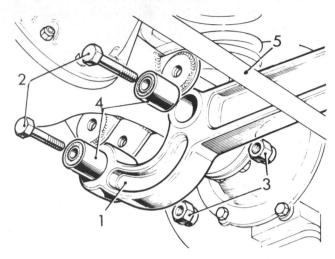

Fig. 11.3 Front radius arm – axle mounting (exploded view)
(Sec 3)

| | | | |
|---|---|---|---|
| 1 | Radius arm | 4 | Bushes |
| 2 | Bolts | 5 | Track rod |
| 3 | Nuts | | |

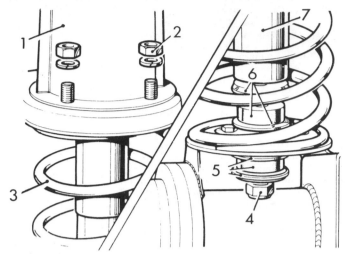

Fig. 11.4 Front shock absorber mountings (Sec 4)

| | | | |
|---|---|---|---|
| 1 | Shock absorber carrier | 5 | Washer, bush and seating |
| 2 | Retaining nut | | washer |
| 3 | Coil spring | 6 | Washer, bush and cup |
| 4 | Shock absorber lower | | washer |
| | retaining nut | 7 | Shock absorber |

4.4 Front shock absorber carrier location – left-hand side

4.7 On some models the shock absorber is retained by a single locknut

5   Undo the nuts on the ends of both bolts which retain the radius arm to the axle mounting bracket.
6   Drive out the bolts while supporting the arm.
7   Lower the radius arm from the axle and withdraw the rear end from the chassis mounting bracket.
8   The bushes can be pressed out of the front end of the radius arm and renewed if required. When fitting new bushes, ensure that they are centrally located in the eyes.
9   Renew the bushes on the rear end of the radius arm also if required.
10  Refitting is the reverse of the removal procedure. Tighten the track rod balljoint nut to the specified torque.

## 4   Front shock absorber – removal, refitting and bush renewal

1   Jack up the front of the vehicle and support it on axle stands under the chassis side-members and under the front axle. Chock the roadwheels and open the bonnet.
2   Remove the roadwheel on the appropriate side.
3   Undo the shock absorber lower retaining nut, and remove the washer, seating bush and seating washer.
4   Undo and remove the nuts which retain the shock absorber carrier

to the coil spring housing. Note that on the left-hand side unit there are two petrol pipe brackets beneath the inner nuts (photo).
5   The shock absorber and carrier can now be lifted straight out and removed from the car.
6   Recover the sealing washer, rubber bush and cup washer from the lower mounting point inside the coil spring.
7   Undo the locknut(s) and retaining nut from the top end of the shock absorber and withdraw the shock absorber from the carrier (photo).
8   Recover the cup washer, flat washer and top bush from the carrier, and withdraw the lower bush, flat washer and cup washer from the top of the shock absorber.
9   Check the condition of all four bushes, which are the same top and bottom. Renew them if necessary.
10  Refitting is the reverse of the removal procedure. Make sure that the washers and bushes are fitted in the correct order.

## 5   Front coil spring – removal and refitting

1   Remove the front shock absorber as described in Section 4, then

refit the nuts to the carrier mounting bolts.

2   With the chassis securely supported, carefully lower the jack beneath the front axle just enough to allow the coil spring to be withdrawn. Take care that the brake hoses are not stretched during this operation.

3   Refitting is the reverse of the removal procedure. Ensure the bottom of the coil spring is securely seated on its mounting plate, and that the top locates correctly under the carrier retainer as the axle is raised (Fig. 11.5).

## 6  Bump stops – removal and refitting

1   Bump stops are fitted front and rear beneath the chassis side-members directly above the axle location. At the front they are each retained by two bolts and nuts front and rear of the bump stop, while at the rear each bump stop is retained by single bolt and nut front and rear.

2   Jack up the vehicle and remove the appropriate roadwheel. Support the chassis side-member with axle stands, leaving the weight of the axle unsupported.

3   Undo the bump stop nuts and bolts and remove it.

4   Fit a new bump stop in position and secure it with the appropriate nuts and bolts.

5   Refit the roadwheel and lower the vehicle to the ground.

## 7  Rear shock absorber – removal, refitting and bush renewal

1   The rear shock absorbers are fitted to opposite sides of the rear axle casing, but the procedure is the same for both sides (photo).

2   Jack up the rear of the vehicle on the appropriate side.

3   Remove the roadwheel.

4   Place a jack under the rear axle to support it.

5   Undo the lower mounting nut and withdraw the cup washer, bush and flat washer (photo).

6   Undo the split pin in the upper mounting and remove the flat washer (Fig. 11.8).

7   Draw the shock absorber off the upper mounting. The inner bush may stay behind on the mounting pin. Pull it off as well for inspection.

8   Lift the shock absorber up to withdraw the bottom mounting from the axle bracket. Then withdraw the complete unit from the vehicle.

9   Recover the lower washer and bush if they become separated as the unit is removed.

10  Inspect the rubber bushes and renew them if cracked, damaged, worn or hard.

11  Refitting is the reverse of the removal procedure.

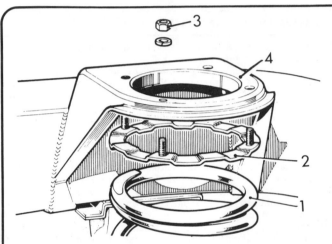

**Fig. 11.5 Front coil spring upper mounting point (Sec 5)**

| 1 | Coil spring | 3 | Retainer nut |
|---|---|---|---|
| 2 | Carrier retainer | 4 | Mounting bracket |

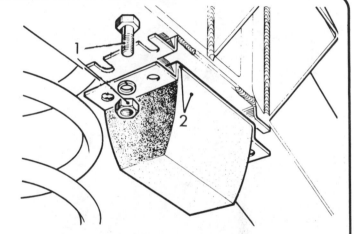

**Fig. 11.6 Front bump stop (Sec 6)**

| 1 | Nut and bolt | 2 | Bump stop rubber and carrier |
|---|---|---|---|

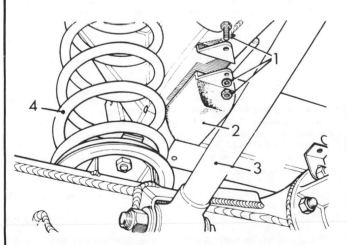

**Fig. 11.7 Rear bump stop and suspension layout (Sec 6)**

| 1 | Nut, bolt and washer | 3 | Radius arm |
|---|---|---|---|
| 2 | Bump stop | 4 | Coil spring |

7.1 The right-hand rear shock absorber is located to the rear of the axle

7.5 The rear shock absorber lower mounting point, showing its bushes

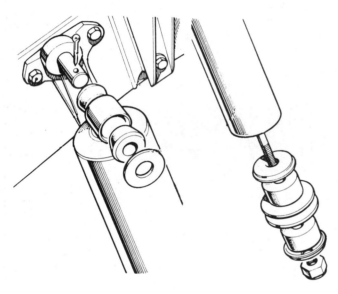

Fig. 11.8 Rear shock absorber assembly (Sec 7)

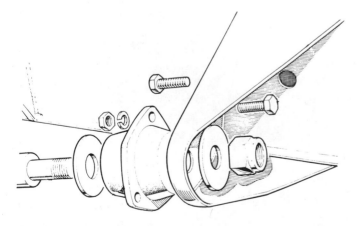

Fig. 11.9 Rear radius arm-to-bracket mounting. Either nuts and washers or self-locking nuts may be found (Sec 9)

## 8  Rear coil springs – removal and refitting

1    This operation is designed to replace both coil springs together. The operation has to be performed on the complete axle. It is not advisable to attempt one end of the axle only, due to the difficult angles that would be involved and uneven pressure on the springs and axle.

2    Jack up the rear of the vehicle and support it securely on axle stands under the chassis. Place a support jack under the axle casing.

3    Remove the rear roadwheels and chock the front ones.

4    Disconnect the lower ends of both rear shock absorbers as described in Section 7.

5    Undo the retaining nut on the A-frame pivot balljoint. Use a balljoint separator to free it from the axle mounting bracket.

6    Lower the axle carefully, avoiding strain on the rear flexible brake hose above the axle. The axle only needs to be lowered far enough to free the coil springs from their upper seats.

7    Undo the bolts and withdraw the lower spring retainer plates from the axle casing brackets.

8    Lift the coil springs away from the lower seats.

9    Remove the seats.

10   Refitting is the reverse procedure. Tighten the A-frame pivot balljoint retaining nut to its specified torque.

## 9  Rear radius arm – removal and refitting

1    Jack up the rear of the vehicle on the appropriate side. Place axle stands beneath the rear axle.

2    Remove the roadwheel, and chock the other wheels.

3    On the left-hand side, where the shock absorber is mounted in front of the rear axle casing, undo the lower mounting from the shock absorber and free it from the mounting bracket.

4    Undo the radius arm front end retaining nut and remove the washer.

5    Undo the rear retaining nut and withdraw the bolt.

6    Lower the radius arm from the rear bracket on the underneath of the axle casing and withdraw it from the front mounting bush. If difficulty is experienced, unbolt the front bush from the bracket and remove it with the arm (Fig. 11.9).

7    If the front bush is to be removed or renewed, undo the three nuts and bolts which retain it to the forward mounting point on the chassis side-member.

8    If the rear mounting bush is worn, press it out of the arm and fit a new bush, ensuring that it is located centrally.

9    If the front mounting bush has been removed, refit it to the front end of the radius arm before fitting the assembly to the vehicle. Do not tighten the front locknut.

10   Refit the front end of the radius arm and secure it lightly with one bolt, then refit and secure the rear end with its bolt and nut.

11   Fit the remaining front bolts and nuts and tighten them.

12   If applicable, refit the left-hand shock absorber lower mounting.

13   Refit the roadwheel and lower the vehicle.

14   Finally tighten the front locknut on the radius arm to its specified torque.

## 10  Self-levelling unit – removal and refitting

**Warning**: *Do not attempt to strip the self-levelling unit in any way as it contains pressurised gas.*

1    Jack up the rear of the vehicle and support the chassis side-member using axle stands.

2    Take the weight of the rear axle on a jack.

3    Remove the two bolts and nuts that retain the lower ends of the A-frame suspension unit to the lower pivot.

4    Pull up the rubber boot on the bottom of the self-levelling unit (photo).

5    Unscrew the lower balljoint from the levelling unit pushrod.

6    Undo the four mounting bolts and nuts which retain the upper mounting bracket to the chassis crossmember.

7    The self-levelling unit and upper mounting bracket may be withdrawn from the vehicle as one unit.

8    To separate the self-levelling unit from the upper mounting bracket, pull back the rubber boot and use a spanner to unscrew the

10.4 The self-levelling unit

upper balljoint from the unit.
9    Undo the retaining clips and remove the rubber boots at either end of the unit.
10   Refitting is the reverse procedure. Tighten all mounting bolts to their specified torque. Use thread sealant on both balljoint threads before screwing them into the self-levelling unit.

## 11 Self-levelling unit balljoints – renewal

1    Remove the self-levelling unit as described in Section 10.
2    Each balljoint is retained by a hexagonal collar. Undo the collar and withdraw the balljoint and seat.
3    Clean the balljoints and inspect them. If obviously worn they must be renewed. If however they are serviceable they may be re-used.
4    Clean out the balljoint seat and housing (Fig. 11.10).
5    Fit the seat and ensure that it is square.
6    Fill the housing with multi-purpose lithium-based grease.
7    Refit the balljoint and screw in the collar. Tighten the collar to the specified torque.
8    Wipe off any excess grease.
9    Refit the self-levelling unit as described in Section 10.

## 12 Upper suspension A-frame and pivot – removal and refitting

1    Jack up and support the rear of the vehicle securely. Place axle stands beneath the chassis side-members.
2    Take the weight of the axle on another jack.
3    Disconnect the lower end of the self-levelling unit from its bottom balljoint, as described in Section 10.
4    Remove the split pin and nut which retain the rear A-frame pivot balljoint to the mounting bracket on top of the rear axle casing.
5    Lower the axle on the jack and if necessary use a balljoint extractor wedge to separate the rear pivot from the bracket. Do not strain the brake hoses.
6    Undo the nuts and bolts which retain the front ends of the A-frame arms. Withdraw the bolts.
7    Lift the whole A-frame and pivot assembly from beneath the vehicle.
8    The pivot assembly and A-frame arms may now be separated. Undo the two nuts and bolts and withdraw them.
9    If required, the bushes in the front ends of the arms may be renewed. Press out the old bushes and fit new ones, ensuring that they are centrally located in the mountings.
10   Refitting is the reverse procedure. Do not fully tighten all mounting bolts and nuts until the complete assembly is refitted. Then tighten all nuts and bolts to their specified torques.

## 13 A-frame rear pivot balljoint – renewal

1    Follow the procedure given in the previous Section from paragraphs 1 to 5.
2    Undo the two bolts and nuts which retain the pivot bracket between the A-frame arms.
3    Remove the pivot bracket complete with A-frame pivot balljoint and the lower self-levelling unit balljoint.
4    Undo the two nuts and bolts and remove the rear pivot balljoint from the pivot bracket.
5    The balljoint assembly must not be dismantled. A replacement comes as a complete unit, pre-packed with grease.
6    Press the new balljoint into the pivot bracket.
7    Refit the two bolts and nuts.
8    Refit the pivot bracket complete assembly to the A-frame arms, fit the rear pivot balljoint to the axle bracket and reconnect the lower ends of the self-levelling unit.
9    Tighten all nuts and bolts to their specified torques.

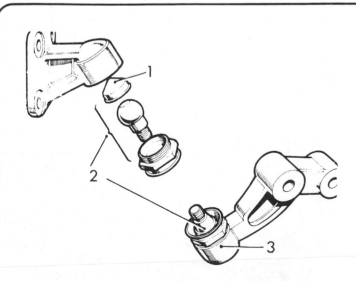

Fig. 11.10 Levelling unit balljoint components (Sec 11)

1    Joint seat               3    Levelling unit
2    Joint assembly

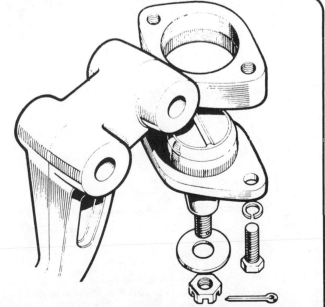

Fig. 11.11 Pivot bracket balljoint unit. Do not dismantle the joint (Sec 13)

## 14 Steering track rod and drag link balljoints – removal and refitting

1    Excessive play in the steering or a tendency for the vehicle to wander or follow undulations in the road surface, often indicates wear in the track rod or drag link balljoints. This may be confirmed by observing the balljoints from beneath the front of the vehicle whilst an assistant turns the steering wheel rapidly half a turn either way from the straight-ahead position. If there is any visible side-to-side movement of the balljoint it must be removed.

2    Slacken the front wheel nuts, jack up the front of the vehicle and support it on heavy duty stands. Chock the rear wheels and remove the appropriate front wheel.

3    Withdraw the split pin and undo and remove the castellated nut

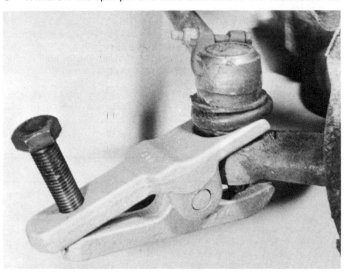

14.4 Balljoint separation method using a universal separator

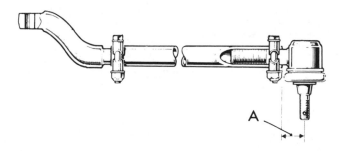

**Fig. 11.12 Set the balljoint-to-drag link dimension (A) to 1.25 in (28.5 mm) (Sec 14)**

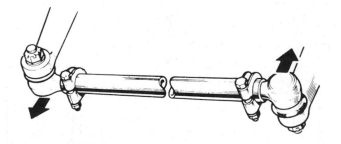

**Fig. 11.13 Tap the balljoints in the direction of the arrows (Sec 14)**

that secures the balljoint to the steering arm.

4    Using a universal balljoint separator, detach the balljoint shaft from the steering arm (photo). If a separator is not available, refit the castellated nut one or two turns to protect the threads and using a medium hammer, strike the end of the steering arm with a few sharp blows until the joint separates from the steering arm. Remove the castellated nut and lift off the balljoint.

5    Make a note of the number of threads on the shank of the balljoint protruding from the track rod or drag link. Slacken the nut and bolt that secure the clamp to the track rod or drag link and unscrew the balljoint. Note that the balljoints on one end of the track rod and drag link have left-hand threads.

6    Refitting the balljoint is the reverse sequence to removal, bearing in mind the following points:

(a)  Refit the balljoint to the track rod or drag link with the same number of threads exposed as were previously noted. Adjust the link-to-balljoint so that it is dimensionally as shown in Fig. 11.12

(b)  Referring to Fig. 11.13, tap each balljoint in the direction indicated so that the angular plane of each ball-pin is identical

(c)  Tighten the securing castellated nut to the torque setting given in the Specifications and secure with a new split pin

(d)  Turn the steering from lock to lock and check that full travel is available. If necessary adjust the lock stops as given in Section 33

(e)  If a balljoint on the track-rod has been renewed or its position altered, the front wheel alignment must be reset. Refer to Section 32

## 15 Track rod and steering damper – removal and refitting

1    Jack up the front of the vehicle and use axle stands to support the chassis.

2    Chock the rear and remove the front roadwheels.

3    Undo the steering damper locknuts and retaining nuts at the track rod and axle casing mounting brackets and withdraw the outer bush assembly from either end (Fig. 11.14).

4    Compress the damper and withdraw one end from one of the mounting brackets. Then lift the unit away.

5    Refit the outer bush assemblies to each end temporarily.

6    Undo the balljoints on either end of the track rod as described in the previous Section.

7    Lift the complete track rod away.

8    Refit the track rod and tighten the balljoint retaining nuts to the specified torque. Make sure that both balljoint pins are in the same plane.

9    Check the front wheel alignment as described in Section 32.

10   Before refitting the steering damper, check the condition of the bushes at either end. If they are cracked, hard or if a lot of play was noticed on removal, they should be renewed.

11   Fit new bushes, if necessary, to the inner ends of the damper mounting bolts.

12   Refit the damper to the track rod and axle casing brackets.

13   Fit new bushes and washers to the outer ends of the mounting bolts and refit the retaining and locknuts.

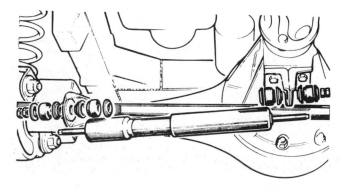

**Fig. 11.14 The steering damper and mounting bushes (Sec 15)**

## 16 Drag link – removal and refitting

1    The drag link is the rod that connects the front steering arm on the passenger side front wheel swivel to the drop arm from the steering box.
2    Jack up the front of the vehicle and support it securely on axle stands.
3    Remove the front passengers side roadwheel. Chock the rear wheels.
4    Disconnect the drag link balljoint from the front steering arm and the drag link from the drop arm balljoint as described in Section 14.
5    Remove the drag link from beneath the vehicle.
6    Refitting is the reverse procedure. Check that the balljoint pins are in the same plane before tightening them.

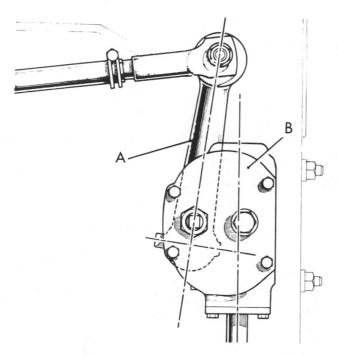

**Fig. 11.15 Drop arm fitting position (A) to steering box (B) (Sec 17)**

## 17 Drop arm – removal and refitting

1    Jack up the front of the vehicle and support it securely on axle stands.
2    Separate the drag link from the drop arm balljoint as directed in Section 14.
3    Undo the drop arm retaining nut and washer.
4    Use a puller to remove the drop arm from the splines on the steering box rocker shaft.
5    To refit the drop arm set the steering box so that it is in the mid-travel position (Fig. 11.15).
6    Refit the drop arm and align the blank splines.
7    Refit the drop arm retaining washer and nut and tighten the nut to the specified torque.
8    Refit the drag link to the drop arm and tighten the retaining nut to the specified torque. Refit the split pin.

## 18 Manual steering box – removal and refitting

1    Jack up the front of the vehicle and support it securely using axle stands.
2    Chock the rear wheels and remove the driver's side front road-wheel.
3    Open the bonnet and prop it securely.
4    Disconnect the drag link from the steering drop arm as described in the previous Section.
5    Slacken the pinch-bolt on the steering column lower universal joint (photo).
6    Undo the four bolts and nuts which retain the steering box to the chassis sidemember (photo).
7    Lift the steering box and drop arm off its mounting bolts and disengage the splined shaft from the bottom universal joint on the steering column as it is lifted away.
8    To refit the steering box, align the steering wheel centre spoke so that it points downwards to the 6 o'clock position.
9    Set the steering box in the mid-travel position.
10   Offer up the steering box to its mounting position and engage the shaft splined end into the lower universal joint.
11   Refit the steering box mounting bolts and nuts.
12   Check the steering wheel and drop arm alignment, then tighten the pinch-bolt on the universal joint to the specified torque.
13   Tighten the steering box mounting nuts and bolts.
14   Refit the drag link to the drop arm and tighten it to the specified torque.

18.5 The steering column lower (A) and upper (B) joint clamps

18.6 The steering box-to-chassis retaining nuts (arrowed)

### 19 Manual steering box – overhaul

1   Remove the drop arm using a puller as described in Section 17.
2   Remove the top cover and gasket and drain the oil into a suitable container.
3   Lift out the rocker shaft.
4   Slide the roller from the main nut assembly.
5   Undo the four bolts and remove the wormshaft end cover, seal plate and shims.
6   Withdraw the wormshaft by rotating it, and lift out the main nut. Recover any balls that fall out.
7   Remove the bearing balls and outer bearing race.
8   Tap the casing to free the inner bearing race.
9   Examine the rocker shaft and bush for wear and if necessary, remove the washer and oil seal. Press the bush out of the steering box and fit a new one. A new oil seal should be fitted as a matter of course.
10  Examine the inner track on the main nut and the wormshaft for

signs of pitting or scaling and renew them where necessary. Check the upper and lower ball-bearings and races for similar signs of wear.
11  If the wormshaft, main nut and bearings are all worn, the most sensible solution is to obtain a replacement steering box assembly.
12  Fit a new oil seal, lipped side first, to the wormshaft end cover.
13  To reassemble the steering box first fit the wormshaft inner bearing race to the casing and coat it with grease. Refit the ten ball-bearings (smaller size) to the race.
14  Reassemble the main nut bearing assembly. There should be 28 larger ball-bearings. Hold them in place with grease.
15  Position the main nut assembly in the casing and refit the wormshaft. Ensure that it fits correctly into the bearing race.
16  Grease the outer race and fit thirteen of the smaller ball-bearings to it. Then offer it up to the wormshaft.
17  Refit the shims, seal and end cover and check that there is no wormshaft endfloat. It should be loaded by 0.003 in (0.07 mm) but should still be free to rotate. Remove or fit shims as necessary.
18  Tighten the end cover bolts to the specified torque and check that

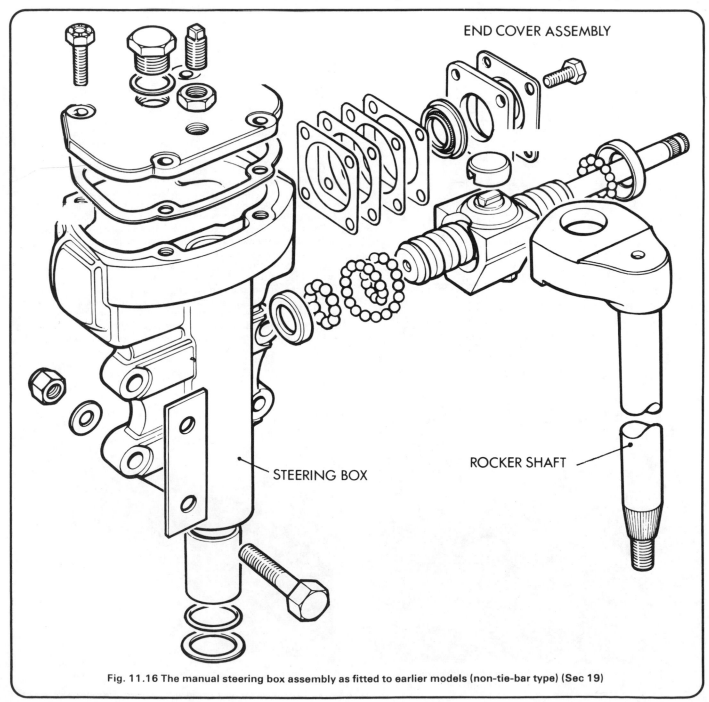

END COVER ASSEMBLY

STEERING BOX

ROCKER SHAFT

Fig. 11.16 The manual steering box assembly as fitted to earlier models (non-tie-bar type) (Sec 19)

the shaft is still free to rotate.

19  Fit a new O-ring to the rocker shaft bore.

20  Rotate the wormshaft so that the main nut is central, then refit the roller.

21  Insert the rocker shaft and engage it in the roller.

22  Smear both mating faces of the top cover and steering box with non-hardening sealant, fit a new gasket and refit the top cover.

23  Set the adjusting screw with the gear in the 'straight-ahead' driving position so that the gear is free to rotate with no backlash between the worm and rocker shafts. There should be no endfloat on the rocker shaft either.

24  On later models fitted with the tie-bar type steering box, see Fig. 11.17, the rocker shaft is spring-loaded and the spring pressure (and thus the endfloat) is adjusted by means of selected shims which are fitted between the cover and its top plate. When the plate retaining bolts are tightened, the shims fitted affect the plate-to-spring (and its top plug) pressure, which in turn bears onto the sector end.

25  Refit the drop arm and secure it as described in Section 17.

26  Refit the steering box to the vehicle as described in the previous Section.

27  Fill the steering box with the correct type of oil to the bottom of the filler plug hole in the cover plate. Refit the filler plug.

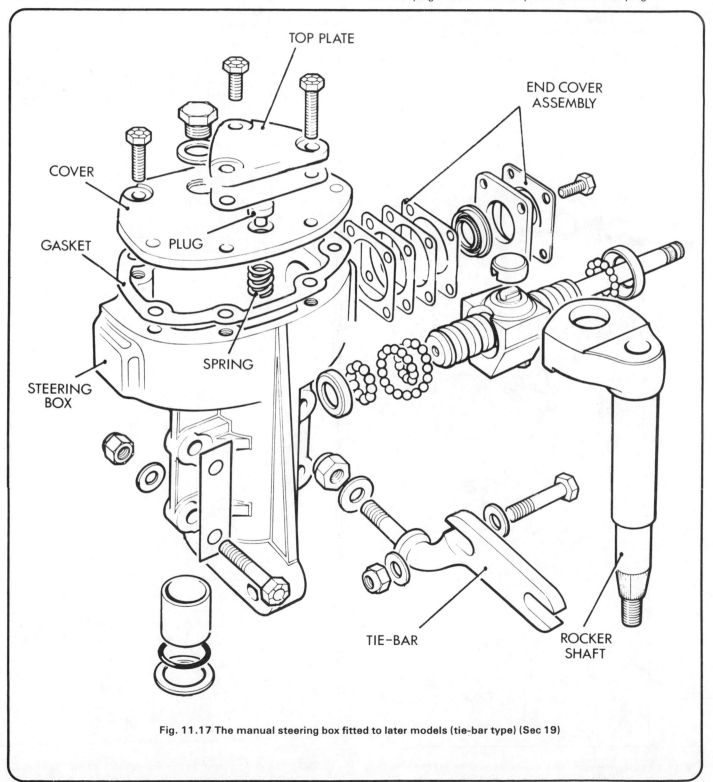

Fig. 11.17 The manual steering box fitted to later models (tie-bar type) (Sec 19)

## 20 Manual steering box – adjustment

1   Jack up the front of the vehicle and support it so that the front wheels are clear of the ground. Open the bonnet.

2   Set the roadwheels straight-ahead.

3   On early models fitted with the non-tie-bar steering box, slacken the adjuster locknut on the steering box and then loosen the adjuster screw (Fig. 11.18). Retighten the adjuster screw until there is a minimum amount of backlash between the steering shaft and drop arm. Return the screw in this set position and retighten the locknut. Recheck the backlash.

4   On later models the adjustment is made in inserting or extracting shims as required under the top plate. The plate is secured to the steering box cover by three bolts (Fig. 11.19). Shims are available in a number of thicknesses as required.

5   On completion of adjustment on both steering box types, turn the steering from lock to lock to check for tight spots or excessive slack. If satisfactory, lower the vehicle and close the bonnet to complete.

## 21 Power steering system – special precautions

1   Whenever any repairs are carried out or the flexible hoses are

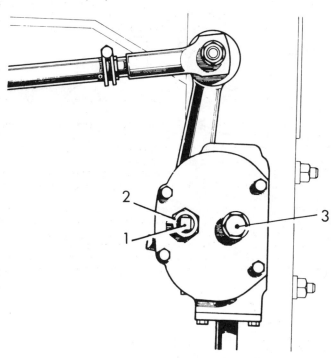

**Fig. 11.18 Early steering box adjuster screw (1), locknut (2) and filler plugs (3) (Sec 20)**

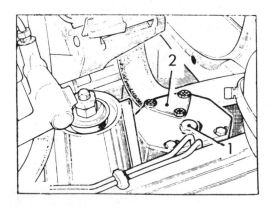

**Fig. 11.19 Later model manual steering box showing the filler plug (1) and top plate (2) (Sec 20)**

disconnected in the power steering system, particular care must be taken to ensure utmost cleanliness.

2   Clean components externally before detaching and when disconnected, seal off to prevent the entry of dirt. If any part of the system contains metallic sediment it must be completely checked, the defective part(s) renewed, and the system thoroughly cleaned out.

3   Do not start the engine until the power steering reservoir has been refilled to the correct level as given in Section 31. If the power steering pump is operated 'dry' it will be damaged.

## 22 Power steering box – removal and refitting

1   Jack up the front of the vehicle and support it securely on axle stands, and chock the rear wheels. Open the bonnet and prop it securely.

2   Separate the drag link from the drop arm balljoint as described in Section 16.

3   Remove the drop arm as described in Section 17.

4   Slacken the pinch-bolt on the lower universal joint on the steering column.

5   Remove the filler cap from the power steering fluid reservoir. Disconnect the fluid pipes from the pump and drain the fluid into a suitable container.

6   Disconnect the fluid pipes from the steering box and drain any fluid left in them. Refit the power steering reservoir cap. Cover the ends of the hoses to protect them.

7   The fluid which has been drained off must not be re-used under any circumstances.

8   Slacken the nut which secures the tie-bar to the chassis.

9   Undo the nuts which secure the steering box to the tie-bar and move the tie-bar to one side.

10  Remove the power steering box mounting bolts from the chassis side-member.

11  Remove the steering box disengaging the splined end of the wormshaft from the universal joint.

12  Refitting is basically the reverse procedure to removal. Note that the steering wheel must be set in the straight-ahead position before the universal joint is reconnected to the steering box.

13  Fill and bleed the power steering system as described in Section 31.

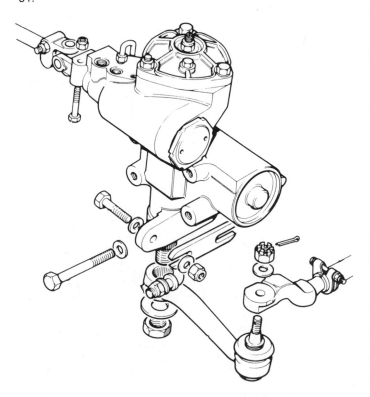

**Fig. 11.20 The power steering box and associated fittings (Sec 22)**

14 Check the system and if necessary adjust the steering box as described in Section 24.

15 Test the system for leaks. With the engine running, hold the steering wheel on full lock in both directions. **Do not** exceed this pressure for more than 30 seconds in any one minute or the oil will overheat and seal damage will result.

16 Check the front wheel alignment as described in Section 32.

## 23 Power steering box – overhaul

*Before starting to dismantle the power steering box, it should be noted that you will need the use of a suitable spring balance and special Rover tool number RO1016 with which to check and make adjustments during assembly. Other special tools required include a C-spanner (606600), peg spanner (606601), circlip pliers and some suitable tube drifts. You will also need to have a modicum of general engineering practice to access the setting adjustments on reassembly. With this in mind you should first read through the various overhaul procedures before starting, to fully assess what is required.*

*If all the tools required are available and you decide to carry out the overhaul, prepare a suitable work area and as the components are*

dismantled, lay them out in order of appearance for inspection and reassembly.

1 Remove the steering box as described in Section 22.

2 Mark the steering drop arm position on the splined shaft and then withdraw it, using a puller if necessary.

3 Turn the retaining ring to locate one end approximately 0.5 in (12 mm) from the extractor hole in the housing. Insert a suitable pin punch or similar through the hole to lift the retaining ring clear of its groove and then prise it free using a screwdriver as shown in Fig. 11.21.

4 Turn to right lock (RHD) or left lock (LHD) to enable the piston to be pushed out of the end cover.

5 Loosen the rack pad adjuster retaining screw (in the side of the boss) and unscrew and remove the pad adjuster.

6 Unscrew and remove the sector shaft locknut.

7 Remove the sector shaft cover retaining bolts and then tighten the sector shaft adjuster to remove the cover. Withdraw the sector shaft.

8 The piston is extracted by inserting a $\frac{1}{2}$ in UNC bolt into the tapped hole in the end face of the piston, and pulling it out.

9 Using a C-spanner, unscrew and remove the worm adjusting screw locknut.

10 You now need the use of Rover special tool number 606601 which is a peg spanner for removing the worm adjuster screw (Fig. 11.22). It should not be too difficult to fabricate a suitable spanner for this purpose if the Rover tool is not available.

11 To free the bearing, tap the splined end of the shaft using a soft hide mallet and withdraw the bearing.

12 Extract the valve and worm, but **do not** loosen or remove the trim screw (Fig. 11.23) or the calibration will be upset.

13 Extract the inner bearing and shims.

14 Prise free and remove the circlip and then withdraw the oil seal from the sector shaft housing.

15 Remove the input shaft circlip and oil seals in a similar manner.

16 If the sector shaft bush is to be renewed, extract the old one with a suitable tube drift.

17 If the input shaft needle bearing is to be renewed, remove it from its location housing.

18 With the main assemblies dismantled, they can be cleaned and examined for signs of wear and damage.

19 Check the steering box inlet tube seat, piston bore and feed pipe for signs of damage, wear or score marks in the bore and seat. Renew or repair as necessary.

20 Inspect the sector shaft unit. Check for side play in the rollers and the adjuster screw retainer, which should be secured by staking to the shaft. The endfloat of the adjuster screw must not exceed 0.005 in (0.12 mm); if it does, relieve the staking, rotate the adjuster retainer to suit and then restake to secure. Inspect the sector shaft gear teeth for signs of wear or damage and also look for signs of wear caused by the

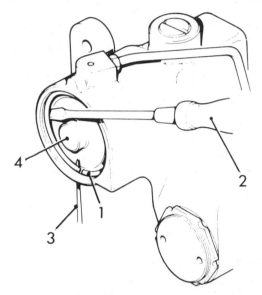

Fig. 11.21 Remove the retaining ring (1) with screwdriver (2) and pin punch (3) to extract the end cover (4) (Sec 23)

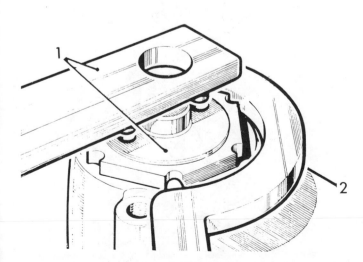

Fig. 11.22 Peg spanner (1) and C-spanner (2) used to remove the worm adjuster screw and locknut (Sec 23)

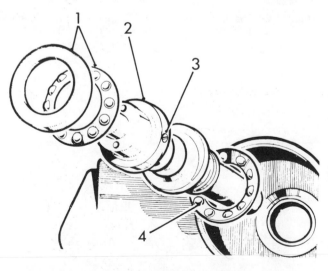

Fig. 11.23 Valve and worm unit components (Sec 23)

1  Bearing cup and caged ball-bearing
2  Valve and worm assembly
3  Trim screw - do not disturb it!
4  Inner bearing assembly

bearings on the shaft. Renew as necessary.

21 Examine the valve and worm unit. If the valve rings are scratched, damaged or loose in their grooves, they must be renewed. This is a task best entrusted to your Range Rover dealer as the fitting method is critical and requires the use of special tools. Check the bearings and worm for excessive wear and renew if necessary. Check the worm-to-valve sleeve endfloat which must not exceed 0.005 in (0.12 mm). Check that there is no free movement between the worm and the input shaft. If excessive endfloat or wear exists the valve and worm assembly complete must be renewed.

22 Inspect the bearing assemblies and if worn or damaged renew them, but don't lose the shim washers.

23 Examine the rack thrust pad and adjuster for wear or damage and renew if necessary.

24 Check the rack and piston, and if damaged or excessively worn, renew. A new rubber ring must be fitted to the piston. The white nylon seal should be warmed before fitment to the piston. When in position, slide the piston into the cylinder (rack tube outwards) and let it cool off.

25 If the input needle bearing is being renewed, insert the new bearing with its numbered face upwards. It must be flush with the top of the bore and just clear of the bottom of the bore.

26 All oil seals, and this includes the rubber seal at the rear of the plastic ring on the rack piston, must be renewed on reassembly. The plastic ring must also be renewed.

27 Lubricate the bearings and seals with petroleum jelly prior to fitment.

28 Start reassembly by inserting the input shaft oil seal into its housing with its lipped side inwards. When fitted, the seal backing must be flat on the bore shoulder. Locate the washer and retaining circlip to secure.

29 Refit the sector shaft seal with its wide flange inwards, followed by the washer and second seal, which has its lipped side facing outwards. Insert the circlip to secure (Fig. 11.26).

30 Where the valve and worm unit inner bearing was removed, refit together with the shims which were removed on dismantling. If the original shims cannot be fitted, insert shims of a nominal thickness of 0.030 in (0.76 mm).

31 Refit the valve and worm unit, taking special care not to damage the seal lips as it is pushed through.

32 Locate the outer bearings and cup, then locate the new worm adjuster seal ring and tighten the screw into the housing. Fit but do not tighten the locknut.

33 Tighten the worm adjuster to take up most of the endfloat. The shaft rolling resistance must now be checked and this can only be achieved using a spring balance, cord and special torque setting tool number RO1016. If these tools are not available, entrust the checking and setting to your Range Rover dealer. If the tools are available, coil the cord around the torque setting tool which should be located on the shaft, and measure and record the rolling resistance by pulling the balance and uncoiling the cord (Fig. 11.27). Rotate the adjuster to increase the recorded amount by 4 to 5 lb (1.8 to 2.2 kg) at 1.25 in (31.75 mm) radius in order to settle the bearings, then unscrew the adjuster so that the originally recorded figure is increased by 2 to 3 lb (0.9 to 1.3 kg). Tighten the locknut using the peg spanner and C-spanner to retain the setting.

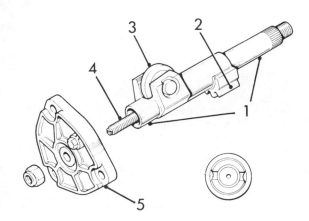

Fig. 11.24 Check the sector shaft (1), gear teeth (2), rollers (3), adjusting screw retainer (4) and end cover (5) (Sec 23)

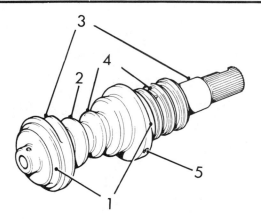

Fig. 11.25 Check the bearings (1), worm track (2) and torsion bar pins (3) for wear. Check worm-to-sleeve endfloat (4). Note the trim pin (5) (Sec 23)

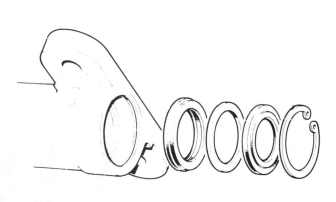

Fig. 11.26 Sector shaft seal assembly (Sec 23)

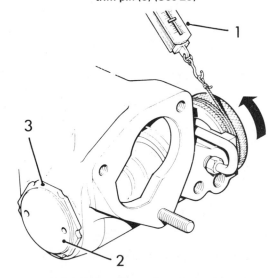

Fig. 11.27 Check the valve and worm setting using a spring balance (1). Adjust worm (2) and lock with nut (3) (Sec 23)

34 Reassemble the piston and rack and locate the piston 2.5 in (63.5 mm) from the bore outer end (use the ½ in UNC slave bolt). Carefully insert the sector shaft, aligning the central gear pitch of the rack with the centre tooth of the sector shaft (Fig. 11.28). Push the sector shaft in whilst rotating the input shaft slightly to allow the roller to engage with the worm.

35 Locate the seal ring on the rack adjuster and insert the adjuster and thrust pad to the point where they touch the rack, then unscrew by a half turn. Insert the nylon pad and the grub screw but do not fully tighten it yet, simply engage it with the rack adjuster.

36 The selector shaft cover is now fitted. Locate the seal ring onto the cover and then screw the cover onto the sector shaft adjustment screw so that it is flush with the casing. Tap the cover fully home, and if necessary loosen the adjustment screw to enable the cover joint to be fully flush with the case. Before tightening the cover retaining bolts, turn the input shaft through a small arc to ensure that the sector roller

is free. Tighten the retaining bolts to the specified torque.

37 Locate the square sectional seal into the groove in the cylinder cover, extract the slave bolt and then press the cover into the cylinder just enough to clear the retainer ring groove. The retainer ring can then be fitted and located so that one end of the ring is approximately 0.5 in (12 mm) from the extractor hole.

38 With the steering box assembled, the sector shaft adjustment must be checked and rack adjustment made. To adjust the sector shaft, centrally position the worm by turning it 1.5 rotations from either full lock position. Turn the sector shaft adjuster screw anti-clockwise to get backlash between the sector shaft and the input shaft, then turn the screw clockwise until the backlash in taken up (Fig. 11.29).

39 The input shaft maximum rolling resistance must now be measured using the spring balance, cord and torque tool RO1016 previously mentioned. Locate a new locknut whilst retaining the sector shaft adjuster screw in position, but do not tighten the nut yet. Now turn the adjuster screw to provide 2 to 3 lb (0.9 to 1.3 kg) additional resistance to the maximum figure previously noted. Under no circumstances must the final torque figure exceed 16 lb (7.25 kg). When set, tighten the grub screw to set the adjuster in the selected position.

40 The final check to be made before refitting the steering box is a torque peak check. When the input shaft is turned from lock to lock, a greater torque resistance should be found equally disposed across the centre of travel. This torque resistance depends on the amount of shims fitted between the casing and bearing of the valve and worm unit. The original shim or nominal shim (paragraph 30) should give the required torque peak but if major components have been renewed, further adjustment may be necessary.

41 To make this check, point the input shaft towards you and turn it fully anti-clockwise. Now use the previously mentioned spring balance, cord and torque tool (RO1016) to check the torque figures (Fig. 11.30). If the highest torque figure readings are not in the centre of travel, adjust as follows. If the torque peak occurs *before* the central position, a thinner washer must be fitted between the casing and the valve and worm unit, whilst a greater torque figure *after* the central position necessitates fitting a thicker washer. As a guide to adjustment, a 0.003 in (0.07 mm) washer difference will move the torque peak area by about a quarter of a turn on the shaft.

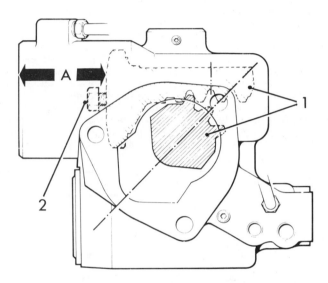

**Fig. 11.28 View showing piston fitting position (A) which is about 2.5 in (65 mm) from end of bore. Note correct rack-to-sector shaft engagement position (1) and slave bolt (2) (Sec 23)**

## 24 Power steering box – backlash adjustment

1    Jack up the front of the vehicle and support it securely, with the wheels clear of the ground. Check the rear wheels.

2    Set the wheels to the straight-ahead position.

3    Rock the steering wheel to get the 'feel' of the backlash that is present. It should not be more than 0.375 in (9.5 mm) measured at the rim of the steering wheel.

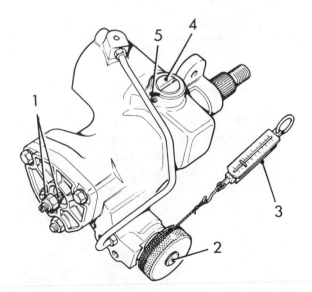

**Fig. 11.29 Sector shaft adjustment (Sec 23)**

| | | | |
|---|---|---|---|
| 1 | Sector shaft adjustment screw and locknut | 3 | Spring balance |
| 2 | Worm | 4 | Rack adjuster |
| | | 5 | Rack adjuster grub screw |

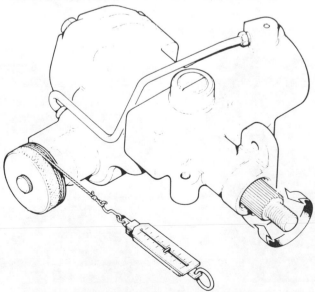

**Fig. 11.30 Method of checking the torque peak (Sec 23)**

4    With the help of an assistant, unlock the steering box adjuster nut and slacken off the adjuster screw whilst still rocking the steering wheel gently.
5    Screw the adjuster in until the backlash is reduced to the correct amount (Fig. 11.31).
6    Tighten the locknut and then turn the steering wheel from lock to lock, checking for any tight spots.
7    Close the bonnet, lower the vehicle to the ground and remove the rear wheel chocks.

## 25  Steering wheel – removal and refitting

1    Set the steering wheel in the straight-ahead position with the spokes at 9, 3 and 6 o'clock, or on 1980 models with the centre pad lettering horizontal.
2    Remove the central motif from the three-spoke steering wheel (photo) or remove the centre safety pad from the later type of steering wheel. It is retained by a single screw underneath and at the rear of the steering wheel.
3    Undo the retaining nut and washer from the top of the steering column.
4    Remove the steering wheel with a suitable puller. **Do not** hammer on the steering wheel to remove it, or the shear pins in the steering column may be broken.

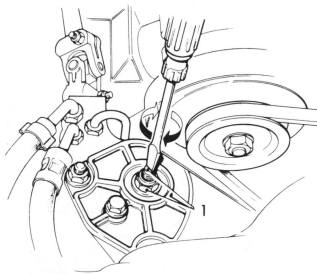

**Fig. 11.31 Power steering box backlash adjuster and locknut (1) (Sec 24)**

25.2 Remove the central motif to expose the retaining nut – early models

5    Refitting is the reverse of the removal procedure. Ensure that the front roadwheels are correctly set in the straight-ahead position before offering up the steering wheel, correctly aligned.
6    Tighten the retaining nut to the specified torque, and refit the central motif or centre pad.

## 26  Steering column – removal and refitting

1    Open the bonnet and disconnect the battery negative lead.
2    Remove the steering wheel as described in the previous Section.
3    Remove the lower facia panel below the steering column, as described in Chapter 12.
4    Disconnect the electrical multi-plug connectors beneath the dashboard for the steering column switches, noting their locations.
5    Undo and remove the lower univeral joint pinch-bolt at the steering box wormshaft.
6    Undo and remove the two bolts which secure the steering column to the interior floor of the vehicle (Fig. 11.32).
7    Undo the steering column support bracket nuts and free the steering column from the bracket.
8    Withdraw the steering column through the bulkhead into the interior of the vehicle, with the help of an assistant to guide the lower jointed end. Ensure that it does not snag any cables or brake pipes.
9    Recover the gasket from the column lower flange.
10   Refitting is the reverse procedure. Fit all the couplings and retaining nuts and bolts loosely to start with, then when the whole assembly is located correctly, tighten the mounting nuts and bolts. Leave the lower pinch-bolt till last. Retighten it to the specified torque.

## 27  Power steering pump – removal and refitting

1    Open the bonnet and remove the filler cap of the power steering reservoir.
2    Place a suitable receptacle underneath the power steering pump. Detach the inlet hose from the pump and drain the fluid.
3    After draining the fluid, seal the end of the hose to prevent the ingress of dirt and refit the reservoir cap.
4    Disconnect the outlet hose from the pump and seal its end to prevent the ingress of dirt.
5    Slacken and remove the adjustment and pivot nuts and bolts. Undo the two bolts securing the front bracket to the water pump.
6    Lift the drivebelt forward from the pulley and lift the pump away.
7    Refitting is the reverse of the removal procedure, but before installing the drivebelt carry out the initial bleeding operation (as described in Section 31) after refilling the hydraulic reservoir. The drivebelt adjustment procedure is described in Section 29 and the remainder of the bleeding operation is covered in Section 31.

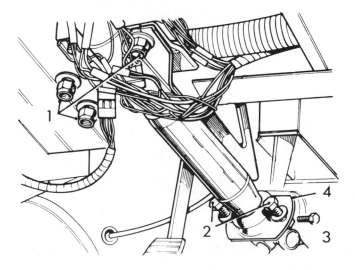

**Fig. 11.32 Steering column upper (1) and lower (2) mountings, clamp bolt (3) and gasket (4) (Sec 26)**

## 28 Power steering pump – servicing

1 Thoroughly clean the pump exterior surfaces.
2 Remove the pulley by removing its centre bolt, spring washers and plain washers.
3 Remove the front mounting bracket and body endplate, also the rear bracket.
4 Secure the pump body in a vice and remove the adaptor screw, adaptor, fibre washer and rubber seal. Do not remove the venturi flow director which is pressed into the cover.
5 Remove the six Allen screws which secure the cover to the pump body and remove the pump from the vice, holding it vertically as the cover is removed so that the internal components do not fall out.
6 Remove the O-ring seals from the groove in the pump body and discard them.
7 Tilt the pump and extract the six rollers.
8 Draw the carrier off the shaft and remove the drive pin. Withdraw the shaft, the cam and the cam lock peg. If essential, remove the shaft key and draw off the sealed bearings.
9 Extract the shaft seal from the pump body and then withdraw the valve cap, valve and valve spring.
10 Wash all components in methylated spirit or clean pump hydraulic fluid and renew all seals.

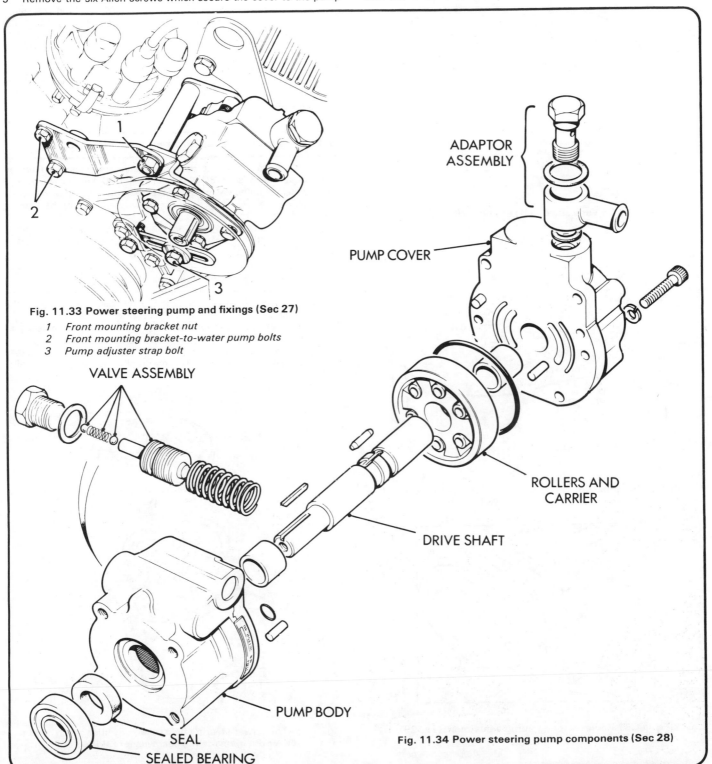

**Fig. 11.33 Power steering pump and fixings (Sec 27)**

1 Front mounting bracket nut
2 Front mounting bracket-to-water pump bolts
3 Pump adjuster strap bolt

VALVE ASSEMBLY

ADAPTOR ASSEMBLY

PUMP COVER

ROLLERS AND CARRIER

DRIVE SHAFT

PUMP BODY

SEAL

SEALED BEARING

**Fig. 11.34 Power steering pump components (Sec 28)**

11 Examine all components for wear or damage and renew as appropriate.

12 Reassembly is a reversal of dismantling, but observe the following points. The shaft seal is fitted to the pump body so that its lip is towards the carrier pocket. The vane carrier is fitted to the shaft so that the greater vane angle is as shown in Fig. 11.35.

13 Check the end clearance of the carrier and rollers in the pump body using a straight-edge and feeler gauges. If it is more than 0.002 in (0.05 mm), renew carrier and rollers.

14 Tighten the valve cap to the specified torque.

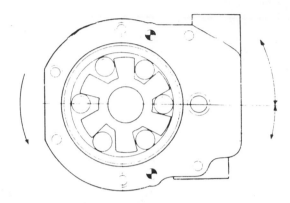

**Fig. 11.35 Vane angle to be as shown (Sec 28)**

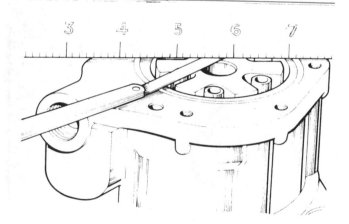

**Fig. 11.36 Check the carrier and roller endfloat clearance with rule and feeler gauges as shown (Sec 28)**

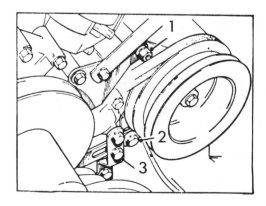

**Fig. 11.37 Power steering pump adjustment (Sec 29)**

| | |
|---|---|
| *1*   *Pivot bolt* | *3*   *Adjuster link bolt* |
| *2*   *Pump lower bracket bolt* | |

## 29 Power steering pump drivebelt – removal, refitting and adjusting

1 Remove the fan and alternator drivebelt as described in Chapter 2.

2 Slacken the power steering pump pivot bolt and adjuster nut and bolt (Fig. 11.37).

3 Push downwards on the pump and free the belt from the pulley.

4 Remove the belt over the crankshaft pulley.

5 Refitting of the drivebelt is basically the reverse of the removal procedure, but it will be necessary to adjust the drivebelt before tightening the pivot and adjuster nuts and bolts.

6 Check the deflection at a point midway between the crankshaft and pump pulleys. The total deflection should be as given in the Specifications. Adjust by carefully levering the pump towards or away from the engine until the belt deflection is correct, then tighten the adjuster and pivot nuts and bolts.

7 When a new drivebelt has been fitted it will be necessary to check its adjustment and tension after approximately 1000 miles (1500 km) of motoring, unless squealing is heard when the steering is operated at low speeds, in which case adjust it at once.

## 30 Power steering reservoir filter element – renewal

1 Rover recommend that the power steering reservoir filter be renewed at intervals of 20 000 miles (32 000 km) or where the steering rack or pump assemblies have been overhauled or renewed.

2 Unscrew the reservoir cap and remove the retaining bar, spring and filter from the reservoir.

3 Withdraw and discard the filter and reassemble using a new filter.

4 After installation check the fluid level and top up as necessary.

## 31 Power steering system – filling and bleeding

1 Turn the steering wheel so that the roadwheels are pointing in the straight-ahead position.

2 Before filling the fluid reservoir check the system completely to ensure that all the pipes, hoses and unions are satisfactory.

3 Fill the hydraulic reservoir with the recommended type of fluid (see Specifications) to a point 1 in (25 mm) below the base of the filler neck.

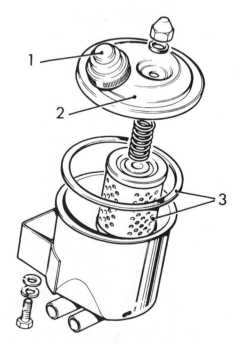

**Fig. 11.38 The power steering fluid reservoir, filler cap (1) and top cover (2), element and seal washer (3) (Sec 30)**

4    Loosen the pump adjuster/pivot bolts and nuts and relieve the drivebelt tension.
5    Rotate the hydraulic pump pulley, by hand, several times in a clockwise direction to prime the system.
6    Retension the drivebelt as described in Section 29, recheck the fluid level and top up as necessary.
7    Start the engine and whilst allowing it to idle, turn the steering wheel so that the roadwheels are deflected, from the straight-ahead position, to the full left-hand lock position. Return the roadwheels to the straight-ahead position and recheck the fluid level.
8    Repeat paragraph 7 but this time turn the steering to the right-hand lock position and then return it to the straight-ahead position. Recheck the fluid level and top up as necessary.
9    Repeat paragraphs 7 and 8 until all air is expelled. Finally recheck and top up the fluid level.

## 32  Front wheel alignment – checking and adjusting

1    In order to minimize tyre wear, and retain the correct steering and roadholding characteristics, it is essential that the front wheels are correctly aligned. Ideally, the alignment should be checked using special gauges. It is, therefore, recommended that the job is done by a Rover dealer. However, it is possible to do the check with a reasonable amount of accuracy if care is taken. Proprietary tracking gauges are available at car accessory stores.
2    The front wheels are correctly aligned when they are turning outwards at the front by the specified amount; this is the toe-out. This measurement is made with the wheels in the straight-ahead position, with the steering box in the mid-position of its travel, the ball centres of the tie-rod equal and the steering wheel correctly aligned as for steering wheel removal (Section 25).
3    Push the vehicle backwards and then forwards a short distance in order to settle the linkage. The vehicle must be on level ground.
4    Measure the distance between the insides of the wheel rims at hub height at the front and rear of the wheels. The distance at the front should be greater than the distance at the rear by the amount given in Specifications for toe-out.
5    To adjust the toe-out, jack up the front of the vehicle and support the chassis using axle stands. Chock the rear wheels.
6    Slacken the adjuster sleeve clamp bolts on both the track rod and the drag link.
7    Rotate the adjusters as necessary to shorten or lengthen the track rod or drag link, then re-check the toe-out.
8    When the setting is correct, clamp the sleeve bolts and tap the balljoints lightly in the directions shown in Fig. 11.39 as far as they will go to ensure that their travel is unrestricted.
9    Lower the front of the vehicle and remove the chocks.

## 33  Steering lock stop – checking and adjustment

1    Steering lock stops are fitted to the steering swivels to stop the swivels over-rotating and straining the main swivel-to-housing oil seals.
2    The bolts should protrude 1.59 in (40.5 mm) as shown (photo).
3    To adjust the lock stop, slacken the locknut on the rear of the bolt.
4    Screw the bolt in or out as required, then re-tighten the locknut.
5    Check the wheel positions at full lock.

## 34  Roadwheels and tyres

1    Whenever the roadwheels are removed it is a good idea to clean the insides to remove accumulations of mud and disc pad dust.
2    Check the condition of the wheel for rust and repaint if necessary.
3    Examine the wheel stud holes. If these are tending to become elongated or the dished recesses, in which the nuts seat, have worn or become overcompressed, then the wheel will have to be renewed.
4    With a roadwheel removed, pick out any embedded flints from the tread and check for splits in the sidewalls or damage to the tyre carcass generally.
5    Where the depth of tread pattern is 1 mm or less, the tyre must

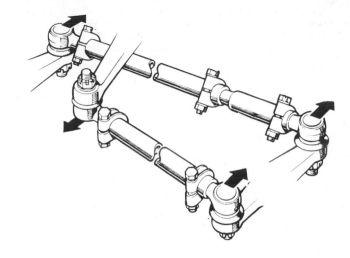

Fig. 11.39 Tap the balljoints in the direction of the arrows (Sec 32)

33.2 Measure the stop bolt protrusion between the points shown

be renewed.
6    Rotation of the roadwheels to even out wear may be a worthwhile idea if the wheels have been balanced off the car. Include the spare wheel in the rotational pattern. Do not move wheels from side to side, only from front to rear.
7    Wheel balancing should only be carried out with the wheels off the vehicle. **Warning**: *If the wheels have to be balanced on the vehicle, the differential lock must be engaged and the propeller shaft to the stationary wheels (axle) must be disconnected.*
8    If the wheels have been balanced on the car then they cannot be moved round the car as the balance of the wheel, tyre and hub will be upset. In fact their exact fitting positions must be marked before removing a roadwheel so that it can be returned to its original 'in-balance' state.
9    It is recommended that wheels are re-balanced halfway through the life of the tyres to compensate for the loss of tread rubber due to wear.
10    Finally, always keep the tyres (including the spare) inflated to the recommended pressures and always refit the dust caps on the tyre valves. Tyre pressures are best checked first thing in the morning when the tyres are cold.

## 35 Fault diagnosis – suspension and steering

| Symptom | Reason(s) |
| --- | --- |
| Steering feels vague, car wanders and 'floats' at speed | Tyre pressures incorrect<br>Dampers (shock absorbers) worn<br>Steering gear balljoints badly worn<br>Steering mechanism free play excessive<br>Front/rear suspension pick-up points out of alignment |
| Stiff and heavy steering | Tyre pressures too low<br>No grease in steering gear<br>Front wheel toe-out incorrect<br>Steering gear incorrectly adjusted<br>Steering column badly misaligned<br>Power steering pump defective<br>Power steering drivebelt slack or missing |
| Wheel wobble and vibration | Wheel nuts loose<br>Front wheels and tyres out of balance<br>Steering balljoints badly worn<br>Hub bearings badly worn<br>Steering gear free play excessive<br>Front springs weak or broken |

# Chapter 12  Bodywork and fittings

*For modifications, and information applicable to later models, see Supplement at end of manual*

## Contents

## 1  General description

The backbone of the Range Rover is the box section chassis frame. Although the base and main body structural points are manufactured in steel, the majority of body panels are of magnesium-aluminium alloy known as 'Birmabright'. This alloy has the advantage of being stronger than pure aluminium and it will not corrode or rust under normal operating conditions.

The station wagon style body has a single wide door at each side, hinged at the front. Wind-down windows and quarter vents are fitted to them.

At the rear the lower tailgate is manufactured in steel for additional strength whilst the rear body floor is corrugated aluminium. The rear seat can be folded forward for greater load area when required.

The information given in this Chapter refers to Range Rover models fitted with the standard body style and not to the various specialised bodies which can be fitted to suit individual requirements.

## 2  Maintenance – body and chassis

1  Because most of the bodywork on the Range Rover is constructed from an aluminium alloy, rust is not a great problem. However, if the vehicle is being used in wet, muddy conditions, the worst of the dirt should be washed off at least once a month using a hosepipe and brush. The hidden portions of the body, such as the wheel arches, the chassis and the engine compartment are equally important, though obviously not requiring such frequent attention as the immediately visible paintwork.
2  Once a year or every 12 000 miles, it is sound advice to visit your local main agent and have the underside of the body steam cleaned. All traces of dirt and oil will be removed and the underside can then be inspected carefully for rust, damaged hydraulic pipes, frayed electrical wiring and other faults.
3  At the same time, the engine compartment should be cleaned in the same manner. If steam cleaning facilities are not available brush a grease solvent over the whole engine and engine compartment with a stiff paintbrush, working it well in where there is an accumulation of oil and dirt. As the solvent is washed away it will take with it all traces of dirt, leaving the engine looking clean and bright.

## 3  Minor body damage – repair

### Repair of minor scratches in the vehicle's bodywork

If the scratch is very superficial, and does not penetrate to the metal of the bodywork, repair is very simple. Lightly rub the area of the scratch with a paintwork renovator or a very fine cutting paste to remove loose paint from the scratch and to clear the surrounding bodywork of wax polish. Rinse the area with clean water.

Apply touch-up paint to the scratch using a thin paint brush, continue to apply thin layers of paint until the surface of the paint in the scratch is level with the surrounding paintwork. Allow the new paint at least two weeks to harden; then, blend it into the surrounding paintwork by rubbing the paintwork in the scratch area with a paintwork renovator or a very fine cutting paste. Finally apply wax polish.

Where the scratch has penetrated right through to the metal of the bodywork, a different repair technique is required. Remove any loose paint, etc from the bottom of the scratch with a penknife. Using a rubber or nylon applicator, fill the scratch with bodystopper paste. If required, this paste can be mixed with cellulose thinners to provide a very thin paste which is ideal for filling narrow scratches. Before the stopper-paste in the scratch hardens, wrap a piece of smooth cotton rag around the top of a finger. Dip the finger in cellulose thinners and then quickly sweep it across the surface of the stopper-paste in the scratch; this will ensure that the surface of the stopper-paste is lightly hollowed. The scratch can now be painted over as described earlier in this Section.

### Repair of dents in the vehicle's bodywork

The alloy body panels on the Range Rover are easier to work on than steel, and minor dents or creases can be beaten out fairly easily. However, if the damaged area is quite large, prolonged hammering will cause the metal to harden and to avoid the possibility of cracking, it must be softened or 'annealed'. This can be done easily with a gas blowlamp but great care is required to avoid actually melting the metal. The blowlamp must always be kept moving in a circular pattern whilst being held a respectable distance from the metal.

One method of checking when the alloy is hot enough is to rub down the surface to be annealed and then apply a thin film of oil over it. The blowlamp should be played over the rear side of the oiled surface until the oil evaporates and the surface is dry. Turn off the blowlamp and allow the metal to cool naturally, the treated areas will now be softened and it will be possible to work it with a hammer or mallet. After panel beating, the damaged section should be rubbed down and painted as described later in this Section.

When deep denting of the vehicle's bodywork has taken place, the first task is to pull the dent out until the affected bodywork almost attains its original shape. There is little point in trying to restore the original shape completely, as the metal in the damaged area will have stretched on impact and cannot be reshaped to its original contour. It is better to bring the level of the dent up to a point which is about $\frac{1}{8}$ in (3 mm) below the level of the surrounding bodywork. In cases where the dent is very shallow anyway, it is not worth trying to pull it out at all.

If the underside of the dent is accessible, it can be hammered out gently from behind using the method described earlier.

Should the dent be in a section of the bodywork which has a double skin or some other factor making it inaccessible from behind, a different technique is called for. Drill several small holes through the metal inside the dent area, particularly in the deeper sections. Then screw long self-tapping screws into the holes just sufficiently for them to gain a good purchase in the metal. Now the dent can be pulled out by pulling on the protruding heads of the screws with a pair of pliers.

The next stage of the repair is the removal of the paint from the damaged area and from an inch or so of the surrounding 'sound' bodywork.

**Note:** *On no account should coarse abrasives be used on aluminium panels in order to remove paint. The use of a wire brush or abrasive on a power drill for example, will cause deep scoring of the metal and in extreme cases, penetrate the thickness of the relatively soft aluminium alloy.*

Removal of paint is best achieved by applying paint remover to the area, allowing it to act on the paintwork for the specified time and then removing the softened paint with a wood or nylon scraper. This method may have to be repeated in order to remove all traces of paint. A good method of removing small stubborn traces of paint is to rub the area with a nylon scouring pad soaked in thinners or paint remover.

**Note:** *If it is necessary to use this method, always wear rubber gloves to protect the hands from burns from the paint remover. It is also advisable to wear protection over the eyes as any paint remover that gets into the eyes will cause severe inflammation, or worse.*

Finally, remove all traces of paint and remover by washing the area with plenty of clean fresh water.

To complete the preparations for filling, score the surface of the bare metal with a screwdriver or the tang of a file, or alternatively, drill small holes in the affected area. This will provide a really good 'key' for the filler paste.

To complete the repair, see the Section on filling and respraying.

## Repair of holes or gashes in the vehicle's bodywork

Remove all the paint from the affected area and from an inch or so of the surrounding 'sound' bodywork, using the method described in the previous Section. With the paint removed you will be able to gauge the severity of the damage and therefore decide whether to replace the whole panel (if this is possible) or to repair the affected area. It is often quicker and more satisfactory to fit a new panel than to attempt to repair large areas of damage.

Remove all fittings from the affected area except those which will act as a guide to the original shape of the damaged bodywork (eg. headlamp shells etc). Then, using tin snips or a hacksaw blade remove all loose metal and other metal badly affected by damage. Hammer the edges of the hole inwards in order to create a slight depression for the filler paste.

Before filling can take place it will be necessary to block the hole in some way. This can be achieved by the use of zinc gauze or aluminium tape.

Zinc gauze is probably the best material to use for a large hole. Cut a piece to the approximate size and shape of the hole to be filled, then position it in the hole so that its edges are below the level of the surrounding bodywork. It can be retained in position by several blobs of filler paste around its periphery.

Aluminium tape should be used for small or very narrow holes. Pull a piece off the roll and trim it to the approximate size and shape required, then pull off the backing paper (if used) and stick the tape over the hole; it can be overlapped if the thickness of one piece is insufficient. Burnish down the edges of the tape with the handle of a screwdriver or similar, to ensure that the tape is securely attached to the metal underneath.

## Bodywork repairs – filling and respraying

Before using this Section, see the Section on dent, deep scratch, hole and gash repairs.

Many types of bodyfiller are available, but generally speaking those proprietary kits which contain a tin of filler paste and a tube of resin hardener are best for this type of repair. A wide, flexible plastic or nylon applicator will be found invaluable for imparting a smooth and well contoured finish to the surface of the filler.

Mix up a little filler on a clean piece of card or board. Use the hardener sparingly (follow the maker's instructions on the packet) otherwise the filler will set rapidly.

Using the applicator, apply the filler paste to the prepared area; draw the applicator across the surface of the filler to achieve the correct contour and to level the filler surfaces. As soon as a contour that approximates the correct one is achieved, stop working the paste; if you carry on too long the paste will become sticky and begin to 'pick-up' on the applicator. Continue to add thin layers of filler paste at twenty-minute intervals until the level of the filler is just 'proud' of the surrounding bodywork.

Once the filler has hardened, excess can be removed using a metal plane or file. From then on, progressively finer grades of abrasive paper should be used, starting with a 40 grade production paper and finishing with a 400 grade 'wet or dry' paper. Always wrap the abrasive paper around a flat rubber, cork, or wooden block, otherwise the surface of the filler will not be completely flat. During the smoothing of the filler surface, the 'wet-or-dry' paper should be periodically rinsed in water. This will ensure that a very fine smooth finish is imparted to the filler at the final stage.

At this stage, the 'dent' should be surrounded by a ring of bare metal, which in turn should be encircled by the finely 'feathered' edge of the good paintwork. Rinse and repair with clean water, until all the dust produced by the rubbing-down operation is gone.

Spray the whole area with a light coat of grey primer, this will show up any imperfections in the surface of the filler. If at all possible, it is recommended that an etch-primer is used on untreated alloy surfaces, otherwise the primer may not be keyed sufficiently and may subsequently flake off. Repair imperfections with fresh filler paste or bodystopper and once more, smooth the surface with abrasive paper. If bodystopper is used, it can be mixed with cellulose thinners to form a really thin paste which is ideal for filling small holes. Repeat the spray and repair procedures until you are satisfied that the surface of the filler, and the feathered edge of the paintwork are perfect. Clean the repair area with clean water and allow it to dry fully.

The repair area is now ready for spraying. Paint spraying must be carried out in a warm dry, windless and dust free atmosphere. This condition can be created artificially if you have access to a large indoor working area, but if you are forced to work in the open, you will have to pick your day very carefully. If you are working indoors, dousing the floor in the work area with water will 'lay' the dust which would otherwise be in the atmosphere. If the repair is confined to one body panel, mask off the surrounding panels; this will help to minimise the effects of a slight mis-match in paint colours. Bodywork fittings will also need to be masked off. Use genuine masking tape and several thickness of newspaper for the masking operation.

Before commencing to spray, agitate the aerosol can thoroughly, then spray a test area (an old tin, or similar) until the technique is mastered. Cover the repair area with a thick coat of primer; the thickness should be built up using several thin layers of paint rather than one thick one. Using 400 grade 'wet or dry' paper, rub down the surface of the primer until it is really smooth. Whilst doing this the work area should be thoroughly doused with water, and the 'wet-or-dry' paper periodically rinsed in water. Allow to dry before spraying on more paint.

Spray on the top coat, again building up the thickness by using several thin layers of paint. Start spraying in the centre of the repair area and then, using a circular motion, work outwards until the whole repair area and about 2 in of the surrounding original paintwork is covered. Remove all masking material 10 to 15 minutes after spraying on the final coat of paint.

## 4   Major chassis and body damage – repair

Major chassis and body repair work cannot successfully be

undertaken by the average owner. Work of this nature should be entrusted to a competent body repair specialist who should have the necessary jigs, welding and hydraulic straightening equipment as well as skilled panel beaters to ensure that a proper job is done.

If the damage is severe, it is vital that on completion of repair the chassis is in the correct alignment. Less severe damage may also have twisted or distorted the chassis although this may not be visible immediately. It is therefore always best on completion of the repair to check for twist and squareness to ensure that all is correct.

If distortion of the chassis is suspected, the chassis dimensions must be checked. Again, this is something that must be done by a specialist.

## 5 Maintenance – hinges and locks

1 Periodically oil the hinges of the bonnet, tailgate and doors with a drop or two of light oil. A good time is after the vehicle has been washed.
2 Periodically oil the bonnet release catch pivot pin and the safety catch pivot pin.
3 Do not over-lubricate door latches and strikers. Normally a little oil on the catch alone is sufficient.

## 6 Door rattles – tracing and rectification

1 Check first that the door is not loose at the hinges and that the latch is holding the door firmly in position. Check also that the door lines up with the aperture in the body.
2 If the hinges are loose or the door is out of alignment, it will be necessary to reset the hinge positions as described in Section 10.
3 If the latch is holding the door properly, it should hold the door tightly when fully latched and the door should line up with the body. If it is out of alignment it needs adjustment as described in Section 10. If loose, some part of the lock mechanism must be worn out and requiring renewal.

## 7 Bonnet – removal and refitting

1 Open and support the bonnet.
2 Detach the windscreen washer feed pipe at the reservoir.
3 Mark an outline around the bonnet hinge positions, then unscrew the retaining bolts whilst an assistant helps to support the bonnet in the raised position. With the bolts removed, lift the bonnet clear.
4 Refit in the reverse order of removal, checking bonnet alignment before fully tightening the retaining bolts.

## 8 Front wing – removal and refitting

1 Remove the bonnet as described in the previous Section.
2 Referring to Chapter 3, remove the air cleaner unit.
3 Refer to Chapter 10 and remove the windscreen wiper arms.
4 Unbolt and remove the decker panel, the retaining bolt and screw positions of which are shown in Fig. 12.1.
5 Refer to Chapter 10 and remove the front side and indicator light unit from the wing to be removed.
6 The wing panel on the side concerned can now be removed after its retaining bolts and screws are removed. Their positions are shown in Fig. 12.2.
7 Refitting the wing is a direct reversal of the removal procedure. Before fully tightening its fastenings, check the panel alignment. When refitting the decker panel, engage it fully under the top of the windscreen rubber surround.
8 On completion ensure that the lights, indicators, windscreen wipers and washers are fully operational.

## 9 Rear wing panel – removal and refitting

1 The rear wing panels are attached on their rear corner edge by means of pop rivets and therefore unless you have a pop rivet gun this task must be left to your Rover dealer or local body repair shop. If you intend to remove a panel yourself, proceed as follows.
2 On the right-hand panel only, refer to Chapter 3 and remove the fuel tank filler cap and neck.
3 Remove the spare wheel if necessary.
4 Refer to Chapter 10 and remove the rear combination light unit on the side concerned.
5 The pop rivets securing the wing panel at its rear and front edges must now be drilled through to detach it.
6 Unbolt or unscrew the other fastenings shown in Fig.12.3 from the locations indicated and withdraw the complete panel. Detach the rear corner panel from the wing.
7 Refitting is a reversal of the removal procedure. Apply a suitable body sealant at the corner panel-to-rear wing joint. Ensure that the panel is correctly aligned before retightening the retainers and inserting the pop rivets.
8 On completion, check the operation of the rear combination lights.

## 10 Doors – removal, refitting and adjustment

1 Open the door concerned and get an assistant to hold it for

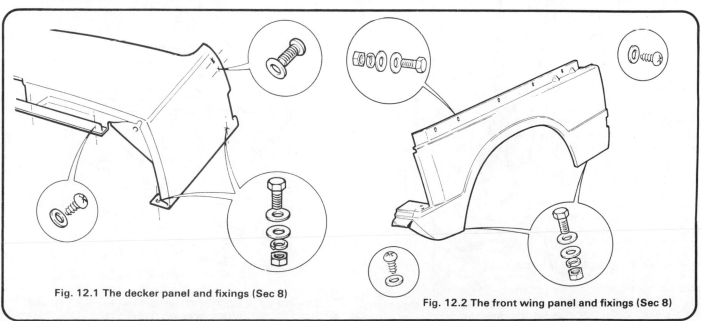

Fig. 12.1 The decker panel and fixings (Sec 8)

Fig. 12.2 The front wing panel and fixings (Sec 8)

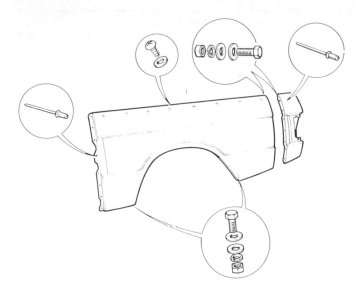

Fig. 12.3 The rear wing panel and fixings (Sec 9)

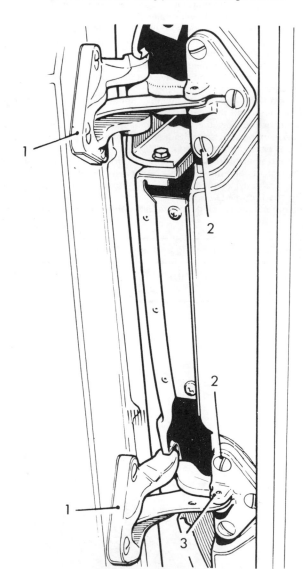

Fig. 12.4 The door hinges (1), retaining screws (2) and check strap
retaining pin (3) (Sec 10)

support during its removal.

2   Use a pin punch and drive out the check strap retaining pin.

3   Mark an outline around the door hinges so that you have an alignment guide when refitting, then unscrew and remove the hinge screws. Lift the door clear and temporarily reinsert the retaining screws, together with any shims fitted between the hinge and door (or door pillar as applicable), so that they do not get mislaid.

4   Refit the door in the reverse order to removal, positioning the hinges to the alignment marks during removal. If adjustment is necessary proceed as follows.

*Adjustment*

5   The doors can be adjusted by any of three methods.

6   To move the door in or out, add or subtract shims as required to the door hinge at the door pillar.

7   To adjust the door forwards or rearwards, add or subtract shims as necessary between the door hinge and the body pillar.

8   Door vertical adjustment is made by loosening the hinge-to-door screws and lifting or lowering the door as required.

9   The lock striker can be adjusted by adding or subtracting packing shims as required.

### 11   Upper tailgate – removal and refitting

1   Raise the tailgate and detach the support stay at one end. On early models prise free the retaining cap at the stay pivot, remove the plain washer and detach the stay (Fig. 12.6). On later models simply prise the stay itself from the pivot.

2   Get an assistant to support the tailgate and then unscrew and remove the hinge-to-tailgate screws.

3   On later models disconnect the heated rear window lead at its connector and also the rear screen wiper before lifting the tailgate clear.

Fig. 12.5 Lock striker and packing shims (Sec 10)

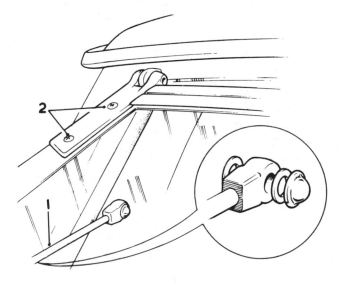

Fig. 12.6 The early model tailgate stay rod fixing (1) and
hinge screws (2) (Sec 11)

4   Refitting is a reversal of the removal procedure, but on later models check that the hinge fixing sealing washers are located correctly.

## 12  Lower tailgate – removal and refitting

1   Detach the rear number plate light wires at the connector.
2   Support the tailgate and then disconnect the check straps from the tailgate by prising free the retaining clip and removing the washers (Fig. 12.7).
3   Unscrew the tailgate hinge bolts and lift the tailgate clear.
4   Refit in reverse order to removal.

## 13  Lower tailgate lock – removal, refitting and adjustment

1   Remove the lock cover plate retaining screws and detach the plate.
2   Remove the retaining screws of the lock mounting plate.
3   Extract the split pin, withdraw the clevis pin and detach one of the bolt arms. The lock can now be withdrawn complete with the bolt arm still attached and this can be detached on removal.

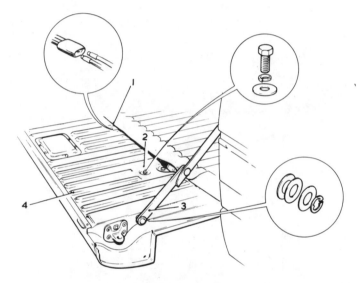

**Fig. 12.7 The lower tailgate (4), stay rod fixing (3), hinge bolts (2) and number plate light leads (1) (Sec 12)**

13.6 The lower tailgate lock mounting plate and adjusters

4   Refitting of the lock is in the reversal of the removal process but on completion close the tailgate and check the lock operation. If adjustment is required, proceed as follows.

### Adjustment
5   If the cover plate is in position, remove it.
6   Loosen the lock end adjuster locknuts off and also the locknuts at the bolt end of the adjuster (photo). The latter nuts have a *left-hand thread*.
7   Rotate the adjuster in the required direction to move the bolt outwards or inwards the necessary amount. Tighten the locknuts and recheck the operation before refitting the cover plate.
8   If the eye brackets on each side of the tailgate need adjusting, simply loosen the retaining screws and move the bracket accordingly. Retighten the screw to secure.

## 14  Upper tailgate lock – removal, refitting and adjustment

1   On earlier models, remove the rear cover from the lock. On later models, remove the side covers from the lock.
2   Detach the bolt arms (early models) or free the centre lock (later models).
3   Remove the lock retaining screws each side and remove the lock with bolt arms.
4   Refit in the reverse order to removal.
5   If adjustment is required, screw the bolt arms in or out as required. The striker plate(s) can be adjusted by loosening the retaining screws, repositioning the plate as necessary and then retightening the screws.

## 15  Door glass – removal and refitting

1   Remove the retaining screws and withdraw the window regulator handle (photo).
2   Remove the armrest retaining screws and lift the armrest clear, disengaging its upper location pegs from the door pull handle brackets (photo).
3   Remove the door handles, which are retained by a screw on the trim side (photo).
4   Remove the door pull handle retaining bolt and rotate the handle 90° to detach it (photos). Repeat the procedure with the other handle.
5   Carefully prise free the upper and lower trim panels from the door.
6   Remove the door top edge seals.
7   Unbolt and remove the glass frame channel. The frame securing bolts and screws are shown in Fig. 12.9.
8   The door glass can now be carefully lifted out of the door. On later models fitted with a door-mounted mirror, you may find removal and

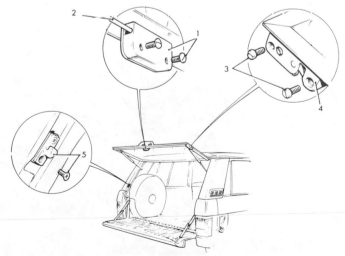

**Fig. 12.8 The upper tailgate lock cover screws (1), bolt arms (2), side lock mechanism and retaining screws (3 and 4) and striker plate location (5) (Sec 14)**

15.1 Remove the window regulator handle

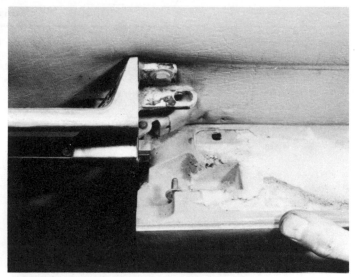

15.2 Disengage the armrest location peg to remove

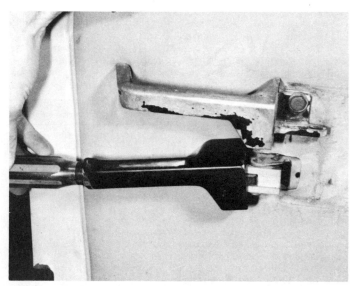

15.3 Remove the door handle retaining screw

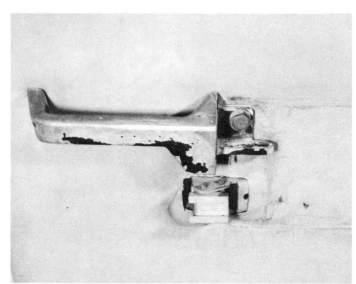

15.4a Remove the pull handle retaining bolt ...

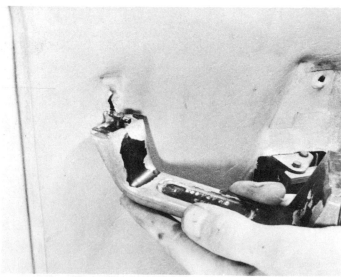

15.4b ... then twist handle to disengage

17.2 Window regulator retaining bolt positions

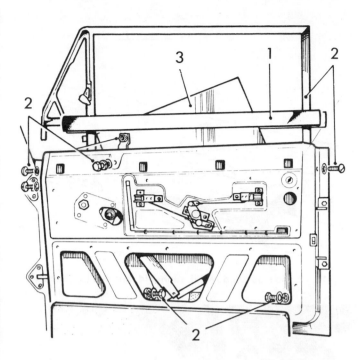

**Fig. 12.9 Door glass removal showing top seal (1), glass frame channel and retainers (2) and glass (3) (Sec 15)**

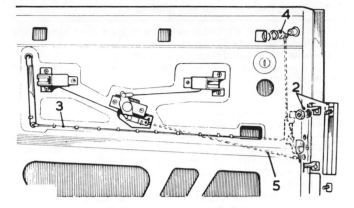

**Fig. 12.10 Door lock operating mechanism components (Sec 18)**

2   *Door handle retaining nuts*      4   *Key lock*
3   *Operating rod (lever-to-lock)*    5   *Inner handle operating rod*

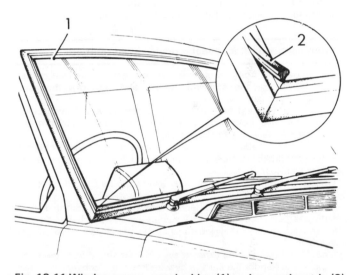

**Fig. 12.11 Windscreen surround rubber (1) and expander strip (2) (Sec 19)**

installation of the glass easier if the mirror is removed.
9   Refit the glass and assemble the various components in the reverse order to removal. Before reassembling the trim panels and fittings, check that the window winds up and down in a satisfactory manner. Minor frame adjustment may be required. Renew the upper seals if they are perished or damaged.

## 16   Door quarter vent – removal and refitting

1   Refer to the previous Section and remove the door glass.
2   Unscrew and remove the quarter vent lower pivot nut and withdraw the spring and washers.
3   The vent can now be pivoted, slightly tilted and lifted clear of the door.
4   Refit in the reverse order to removal. Check the operation of the vent before refitting the door glass and trim assembly.

## 17   Door glass regulator – removal and refitting

1   Refer to Section 15 and remove the door glass.
2   Unbolt and remove the regulator retaining bolts (photo) and then withdraw the regulator through the lower aperture.
3   Refitting is a direct reversal of the removal procedure. Lubricate the assembly prior to fitting and when the window is refitted, check that the winding mechanism is satisfactory before assembling the trim.

## 18   Door lock unit – removal and refitting

1   Refer to Section 15 and remove the door glass.
2   Unbolt and detach the door external handle, then remove the lever-to-lock operating rod (Fig. 12.10).
3   Detach the operating rod from the private (key) lock.
4   Detach the rod from the internal door handle relay at the lock end and then withdraw the lock.
5   Refit in the reverse order to removal.

## 19   Windscreen – removal and refitting

*Windscreen renewal is one job which the average owner is advised to leave to a specialist. The fitting charge is insignificant compared with the expense which will be incurred if a new screen is accidentally broken. For the owner who wishes to attempt the work himself, the following instructions are given.*
1   Referring to Chapter 10, remove the windscreen wiper arms and blades.
2   Prise free and remove the expander strip from the channel in the screen surround moulding (Fig. 12.11).
3   Gently ease the windscreen lower edge from the moulding and carefully lift it clear.
4   To refit the windscreen first smear the moulding screen location channel with wet soap to ease refitting.
5   Fit the windscreen bottom edge into the lower moulding channel, then using some suitable wood or plastic levers (with a tapered edge), progressively prise free the moulding and gradually insert the windscreen.
6   With the windscreen fully located into the moulding, refit the expander strip into the outer channel of the moulding and then refit the windscreen wiper arms and blades.
7   Any leakage around the screen can be repaired by squeezing some suitable waterproof 'screen sealant' between the glass and moulding or body and moulding as required.

## 20  Tailgate glass – removal and refitting

1   Refer to Section 11 and remove the tailgate, then remove the tailgate lock as described in Section 14.
2   Remove the tailgate lift handle and trim.
3   The glass and frame are now renewed as a unit – they are not supplied separately.
4   Refit in the reverse order to removal.

## 21  Body side glass – removal and refitting

1   Refer to Section 18 in Chapter 10 and remove the interior light.
2   Detach and remove the rear quarter trim panels.
3   Disconnect the gear handles each side at their rear end, or at the central fixings in later models.
4   Prise free the headlining at the rear so that it is clear of the rear location bracket and withdraw it to the rear, taking special care not to damage or tear it.
5   Prise free the expander strip from the moulding channel of the glass surround (Fig. 12.12).
6   Raise the front glass runner spring clip tongue and slide the runners clear of the glass.
7   Lift out the front then the rear side windows.
8   Refitting is a reversal of the removal procedure.

## 22  Front seats and floor panel – removal and refitting

1   To remove the front seats, unscrew and remove the seat runner check bolt, release the stop mechanism and withdraw the seat. Remove the floor carpets.
2   To remove the seat base unscrew the respective retaining bolts, disengage the eye bolts and detach the seat base unit from the chassis. Lift the base out of the vehicle.
3   Remove the retaining screws and release the grommet retainers from the handbrake, transfer and main gear levers, then remove the grommets (photos).
4   Unbolt and remove the main gear lever from its turret location in the main gearbox cover.
5   Unbolt and remove the differential lock vacuum control switch from its gearbox mounting. If the vacuum tubes are being disconnected make a note of their locations at the switch to ensure correct reassembly.
6   Unbolt and remove the exhaust system heat shield from the floor.
7   Detach the handbrake linkage by withdrawing a convenient clevis pin so that full lever movement is available.
8   Unscrew and remove the respective floor retaining bolts and screws. Two of the retaining bolt nuts are only accessible from the engine compartment side. You will need to remove the air filter assembly (see Chapter 3) to gain access to these two nuts/bolts.
9   The floor pan can now be removed. As it is withdrawn, move the handbrake lever upwards to enable the panel to clear it.
10  Refitting of the panel is a reversal of the removal process. As the panel is relocated apply some suitable waterproof sealant to the seal lip.
11  When relocating the main gear lever unit, tighten the retaining bolts to the specified torque setting of 11 lbf ft (1.5 kgf m).

## 23  Console unit – removal and refitting

1   Disconnect the battery earth lead.
2   Unscrew and remove the lower facia panel retaining screws, the positions of which are shown in Fig. 12.13.
3   Lower the facia panel just enough to enable the hazard warning switch wires to be detached from the multi-connector, then lift the panel clear.
4   Open the glovebox and detach the glovebox check strap (as given in Section 25).
5   Remove the facia finisher.
6   Unscrew and remove the respective heater knob retaining screws, then pull the knobs free. Remove the panel retaining screws and then withdraw the panel (photos).
7   Remove the console unit retaining screws, withdraw the unit far enough to enable the console instrument wire connections to be

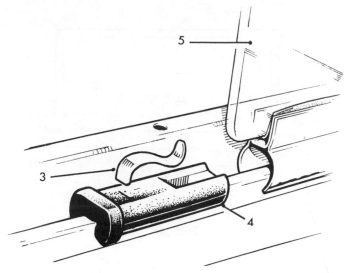

Fig. 12.12 The side window (5), runner (4) and clip (3) (Sec 21)

22.3a Remove the grommet retaining plate screws (handbrake shown)

22.3b Remove the retaining plates (main gear lever shown)

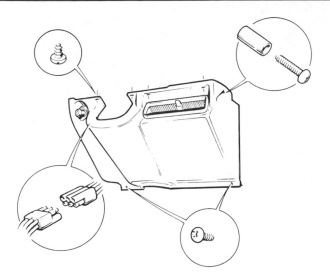

Fig. 12.13 Lower facia panel and fixings (Sec 23)

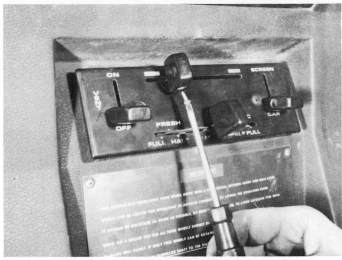

23.6a Remove the heater control knob screws ...

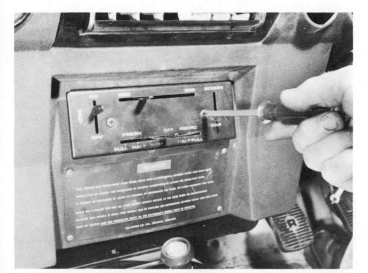

23.6b ... and panel screws to ...

23.6c ... remove the panel

detached, then withdraw the console unit.

8    Refitting the console unit is a direct reversal of the removal procedure. Ensure that the wiring connections are securely made.

## 24  Top facia panel – removal and refitting

1    Disconnect the battery earth lead.
2    Refer to the previous Section and remove the console unit.
3    Refer to Chapter 10, Section 28, and remove the instrument panel housing.
4    Unscrew and remove the top facia panel retaining nut and screws from underneath the panel and lift the panel clear, disconnecting the heater trunking and fresh air ducts as it is withdrawn.
5    Refit in the reverse order to removal.

## 25  Glovebox – removal and refitting

1    Unscrew and remove the glovebox hinge screws on each side underneath.
2    Open and withdraw the glovebox sufficiently to detach the check strap. Remove the glove box.
3    Refit in the reverse order to removal.

## 26  Heater controls – removal and refitting

1    Disconnect the battery earth lead.
2    Remove the lower facia panel, the glovebox and the console unit, referring to Sections 23 and 25 for the removal details.
3    Detach the switch wires.
4    Detach the relay rods from the 'Screen-Car' and 'Vent' levers.
5    Detach the control cables on each side of the heater unit then remove the controls, which are secured by a retaining bolt and nut on each side (Fig. 12.15).
6    Refitting the controls is a reversal of the removal procedure, but when attaching the unit, do not forget to locate the earth lead to the right-hand fixing stud before fitting the retaining nut and washer.
7    When retracting the control rods, adjust them to allow the flaps full movement.
8    Ensure that the control switch leads are connected correctly with the black/white lead to the front terminal.

## 27  Heater unit – removal and refitting

1    Disconnect the battery earth lead.
2    Refer to Section 2 in Chapter 2 and drain the cooling system.

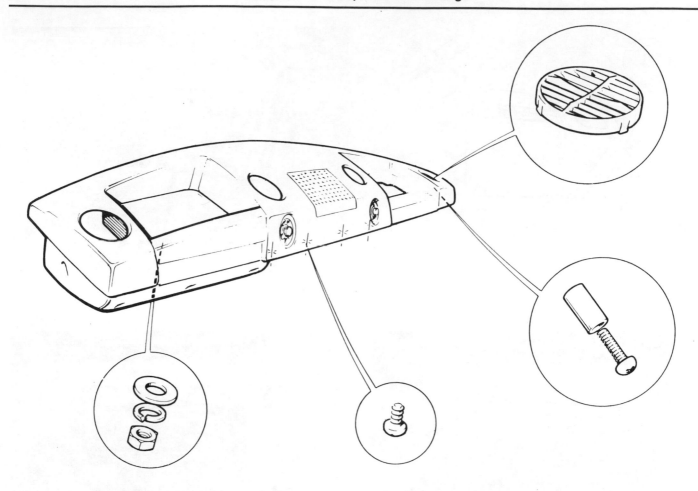

**Fig. 12.14 Top facia panel and fixing points (Sec 24)**

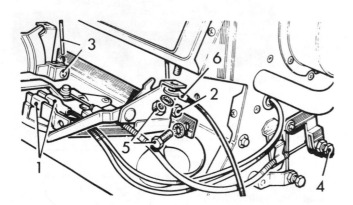

**Fig. 12.15 The heater control connections (Sec 26)**

| | | | |
|---|---|---|---|
| *1* | *Wire connectors* | *4* | *Control cable connection* |
| *2* | *Relay rod (Screen/Car lever)* | *5* | *Control unit fixings* |
| *3* | *Relay rod (Vent lever)* | *6* | *Earth wire connection* |

3    Remove the carburettor air cleaner unit as given in Section 3 of Chapter 3.
4    Unscrew the inlet and outlet hose retaining clips on the heater unit pipes protruding through the engine compartment bulkhead and detach the pipes (Fig. 12.16).
5    Remove the lower facia panel, the glovebox and the console unit, referring to Sections 23 and 25 for details.
6    Detach the four demister hoses from their heater unit connections

(two on each side) (photo).
7    Detach and remove the fresh air duct facia panel (photo).
8    Loosen the top facia panel retaining screws and lift the panel sufficiently to allow the fresh air duct to be withdrawn (photo).
9    Detach the heater unit wires at their connectors.
10   Unscrew and remove the heater unit retaining bolts (photo) and withdraw the unit (photo). Be prepared for some loss of coolant.
11   Refitting of the heater unit is a direct reversal of the removal procedure. Ensure that the fresh air intake seal is in position at the back of the unit and also the heater radiator seal on the pipes. Refill the cooling system as described in Chapter 2.

## 28  Heater radiator – removal and refitting

1    Refer to the previous Section and remove the heater unit.
2    Unscrew and remove the fresh air flap cam control bracket retaining screws. Detach the bracket.
3    Prise free the lockwashers from the four flap spindles.
4    Unscrew and remove the remaining left side cover retaining screws and withdraw the cover complete with the air flap.
5    Extract the radiator together with its seals from the heater unit.
6    Refit in the reverse order to removal, but when locating the left-hand side cover, seal its edge with a suitable sealing compound.

## 29  Heater fan motor – removal and refitting

### Early models
1    Refer to Section 27 and remove the heater unit.
2    Detach the wiring and air cooling hoses from the unit, noting their connections.
3    Unscrew and remove the fan unit retaining bolts, pull the motor and fan out sufficiently to enable the fan-to-motor grub screw to be

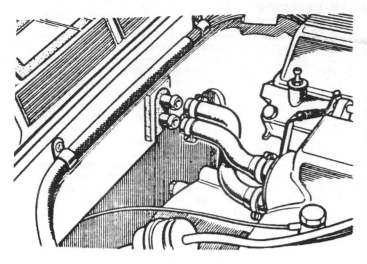

Fig. 12.16 The heater inlet and outlet coolant hose connections (Sec 27)

27.6 Detach the demister hoses

27.7 Remove the facia panel ...

27.8 ... and fresh air ducting

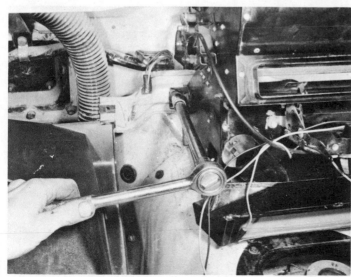

27.10a Unscrew the heater unit retaining bolts ..

27.10b ... and remove the unit

loosened, then extract the fan motor.

4    Refit in the reverse order to removal. When locating the fan motor, engage its spindle in the fan bearing then holding the unit in position, spin the motor to ensure that the fan can rotate freely. It may be necessary to readjust the fan-to-motor position to suit.

5    When reconnecting the wires, the green wire must be attached to the terminal next to the air hose.

## Later models

6    Remove and dismantle the heater fan motor unit as given in paragraphs 1 to 3. When the motor retaining bolts have been removed, drill out the pop rivets to remove the motor unit itself from the fan assembly.

7    Refit in the reverse order to removal, using new pop rivets to secure the fan.

## 30  Heater fan motor resistance – removal and refitting

1    Refer to Section 27 and remove the heater unit.

2    Detach the wires from the fan motor, noting their locations.

3    Detach the air hose.

4    Referring to the previous Section, remove the heater fan motor and fan assembly and detach the electrical leads from the control switch.

5    The resistance unit retaining pop rivets can now be drilled out and the unit withdrawn together with its leads.

6    Refit in the reverse order to removal. The black/white resistance lead must be attached to the control switch front terminal and the green fan motor lead attached to the terminal next to the air hose. Use new pop rivets where necessary.

# Chapter 13 Supplement:
# Revisions and information on later models

## Contents

## 1 Introduction

Since its introduction in 1970, the Range Rover has had a number of modifications and improvements made to it. Most of the modifications made up to 1980 will already be covered in the original text of Chapters 1 to 12 of this Manual. This Chapter covers modifications made from 1980 on, but in some instances items applicable to earlier models not covered in the previously mentioned Chapters are also included.

A brief resume of the principal model changes and improvements made since 1980 is as follows:

| | |
|---|---|
| August 1980 | Fleetline Special introduced |
| February 1981 | Vogue Estate, Two-door limited edition introduced: fitted with a centre console, walnut door cappings, stainless steel rear tailgate cappings and air conditioning |
| September 1981 | Four-door Station Wagon introduced |
| December 1981 | Monteverdi four-door limited edition introduced: having leather seats and air conditioning |
| August 1982 | Automatic transmission became an optional fitting |
| July 1983 | Five-speed manual transmission introduced |
| August 1983 | '325 In Vogue' special edition introduced with central door locking and other refinements |
| June 1984 | Electronic ignition, revised facia and instrument display, improved heating/ventilation system |

Optional items (standard on Vogue) include electrically-operated windows, heated door mirrors and a four speaker audio system.

In order to use this Supplement to the best advantage, particularly with later models, it is suggested that it is referred to before the main Chapter(s) of the Manual. This will ensure that any relevant information can be collected and accommodated into the procedures given in Chapters 1 to 12. Time and cost will therefore be saved and the particular job will be completed correctly.

## 2 Specifications

*The specifications listed here are revised or supplementary to the main specifications given at the beginning of each Chapter*

### *Engine*
### High compression engine (9.35 : 1)
| | |
|---|---|
| Power output (DIN) | 126 BHP (92.6 kW) at 4000 rpm |
| Maximum torque | 26.3 kgf m (190 lbf ft) |

### In Vogue models (limited edition)
| | | |
|---|---|---|
| Compression ratio | 9.35 to 1 | |
| Valve timing: | **Inlet** | **Exhaust** |
|   Valve opens | 36° BTDC | 74° BBDC |
|   Valve closes | 64° ABDC | 26° ATDC |

### *Cooling system*
### Thermostat
| | |
|---|---|
| Opening temperature: | |
|   High compression engine | 190°F (88°C) |
|   Non-emission engine and automatic transmission models | 180°F (82°C) |

### *Fuel system*
### In Vogue models
| | |
|---|---|
| Carburettors: | |
|   Number | Two |
|   Make | Zenith/Stromberg |
|   Type | 175 CDSE (4104) |
|   Needle | BIFH or IEL (non-emission) |
|   Idle speed | 700 to 750 rpm |
|   Fast idle speed | 1150 to 1250 rpm |
|   CO content (at idle) | 2 to 3.5% |

## High compression (9.35 : 1) engine with electronic ignition
Engine idle speed:

| | |
|---|---|
| Manual gearbox model | 700 to 750 rpm |
| Automatic transmission model | 650 to 750 rpm |
| Non-emission model | 550 to 650 rpm |

## Fuel octane rating

| | |
|---|---|
| 9.35 : 1 compression ratio engine | 97 RON (4-star) |
| 8.13 : 1 compression ratio engine | 91 to 93 RON (2-star) |

*Ignition system*
## High compression engine

| | |
|---|---|
| Distributor | Lucas 35 D8 |
| Serial number | 41872 |

Ignition timing:

| | |
|---|---|
| Static (and at idle speed with vacuum retard pipe detached) | 5 to 7° BTDC |
| Retard pipe position | Rear of vacuum capsule (nearest distributor) |
| Dynamic timing (at idle with vacuum retard pipe attached) | 4 to 8° ATDC |

Dwell:

| | |
|---|---|
| Angle | 24 to 30° |
| Percentage | 53 to 66% |

## Electronic ignition system
Distributor:

| | |
|---|---|
| Pick-up air gap | 0.008 to 0.014 in (0.20 to 0.35 mm) |
| Pick-up winding resistance | 2 K to 5 K ohms |

Ignition timing:

| | |
|---|---|
| Static | 6° BTDC |
| Dynamic (vacuum pipes detached) at 700 rpm | 6° BTDC |

*Manual transmission (four-speed)*
## In Vogue models
Transfer gearbox:

| | |
|---|---|
| High range ratios (direct) | 1.1 : 1 |

Overall ratios (final drive high transfer):

| | |
|---|---|
| 4th | 3.54 : 1 |
| 3rd | 5.33 : 1 |
| 2nd | 8.67 : 1 |
| 1st | 14.44 : 1 |
| Reverse | 13.00 : 1 |

## Later models – general

| | | |
|---|---|---|
| Transfer gearbox – standard compression engines: | | |
| High ratio – from gearbox number 35594060 C | 1.1227 : 1 | |
| Transfer gearbox – high compression engines: | | |
| High ratio – from gearbox number 12C 01061A | 0.9962 : 1 | |
| Overall ratios – high transfer: | **Standard compression** | **High compression** |
| 4th | 3.97 : 1 | 3.53 : 1 |
| 3rd | 5.98 : 1 | 5.30 : 1 |
| 2nd | 9.72 : 1 | 8.63 : 1 |
| 1st | 16.16 : 1 | 14.34 : 1 |
| Reverse | 14.56 : 1 | 12.91 : 1 |

*Five-speed gearbox*
## General

| | |
|---|---|
| Type | Five forward speeds and one reverse with synchromesh on all forward gears |
| Model | LT 77 |

## Ratios

| | |
|---|---|
| 5th | 0.770 : 1 |
| 4th | 1.00 : 1 |
| 3rd | 1.397 : 1 |
| 2nd | 2.132 : 1 |
| 1st | 3.321 : 1 |
| Reverse | 3.429 : 1 |

## Transfer gearbox

| | |
|---|---|
| Type | Two-speed on main gearbox output (high or low ratio) |

Ratios:
    High ................................................................. 1.192 : 1
    Low .................................................................. 3.320 : 1

## Overall ratios

|  | High transfer | Low transfer |
|---|---|---|
| 5th | 3.25 : 1 | 9.05 : 1 |
| 4th | 4.22 : 1 | 11.75 : 1 |
| 3rd | 5.89 : 1 | 16.41 : 1 |
| 2nd | 8.99 : 1 | 25.04 : 1 |
| 1st | 14.01 : 1 | 39.02 : 1 |
| Reverse | 14.46 : 1 | 40.26 : 1 |

## Main gearbox

Synchromesh hub unit:
    Synchro cone-to-gear hub minimum clearance ........................ 0.025 in (0.64 mm)
1st gear bush sizes available ........................................ 1.579 to 1.581 in (40.11 to 40.16 mm)
                                                                       1.581 to 1.583 in (40.16 to 40.21 mm)
                                                                       1.583 to 1.585 in (40.21 to 40.26 mm)
                                                                       1.585 to 1.587 in (40.26 to 40.31 mm)
                                                                       1.587 to 1.588 in (40.31 to 40.36 mm)
1st gear bush endfloat ............................................... 0.0002 to 0.0020 in (0.005 to 0.051 mm)
Mainshaft endfloat ................................................... 0.0004 to 0.0020 in (0.010 to 0.051 mm)
Layshaft endfloat .................................................... 0.0010 in (0.025 mm)
Layshaft preload ..................................................... 0.0010 in (0.025 mm)
5th gear-to-spacer clearance ......................................... 0.0002 to 0.0020 in (0.005 to 0.051 mm)

## Transfer gearbox

Input gear bearing preload ........................................... 0.001 to 0.003 in (0.03 to 0.08 mm)
Intermediate gear cluster endfloat ................................... 0.003 to 0.014 in (0.08 to 0.36 mm)
Front output shaft bearing preload ................................... 0.001 to 0.003 in (0.03 to 0.08 mm)
Centre differential pinion backlash .................................. Zero to 0.003 in (Zero to 0.08 mm)

## Lubrication

Main gearbox ......................................................... Dexron IID
Transfer gearbox ..................................................... 20W/50 engine oil, SAE 90 EP or Dexron IID
Capacities:
    Main gearbox ..................................................... 3.9 Imp pints (2.2 litres)
    Transfer gearbox ................................................. 5.0 Imp pints (2.80 litres)

## Torque wrench settings

*Main gearbox*

|  | lbf ft | kgf m |
|---|---|---|
| Oil drain plug | 23 | 3.1 |
| Oil filter plug | 23 | 3.1 |
| Oil filler plug (remote housing) | 23 | 3.1 |
| Oil level plug | 23 | 3.1 |
| Breather | 7 | 0.9 |
| Reverse switch hole blanking plug | 17 | 2.3 |
| Clutch housing-to-gearbox bolts | 55 | 7.6 |
| Front cover to gearcase | 17 | 2.3 |
| Attachment plate to gearcase | 6 | 0.8 |
| Attachment plate to remote housing | 6 | 0.8 |
| Clutch release lever clip | 6 | 0.8 |
| Extension case to gearbox | 17 | 2.3 |
| Remote selector housing to extension case | 17 | 2.3 |
| Gear lever housing to remote housing | 17 | 2.3 |
| Remote selector housing to extension case | 17 | 2.3 |
| Plunger housing to remote housing | 17 | 2.3 |
| Extension case blanking plug | 6 | 0.8 |
| Pivot plate | 17 | 2.3 |
| Oil pump to extension case | 6 | 0.8 |
| 5th support bracket | 17 | 2.3 |
| Gear lever retainer | 6 | 0.8 |
| Selector shaft yoke | 17 | 2.3 |
| Gear lever unit retaining nut | 37 | 5.1 |
| Reverse pin-to-centre plate nut | 37 | 5.1 |
| Detent spring plug | 17 | 2.3 |
| Clutch release sleeve guide | 17 | 2.3 |
| Slave cylinder to clutch housing | 17 | 2.3 |
| Layshaft fifth driven gear retaining nut (late models) | 160 | 22.0 |

| *Transfer gearbox* | lbf ft | kgf m |
|---|---|---|
| Gear change housing | 18 | 2.4 |
| End cover | 6 | 0.8 |
| Gear change housing locating plate | 5 | 0.7 |
| Transfer case bottom cover | 18 | 2.4 |
| Front output housing to transfer case | 18 | 2.4 |
| Cross shaft housing to front output housing | 18 | 2.4 |
| Front output housing cover | 18 | 2.4 |
| Extension housing bracket | 18 | 2.4 |
| Finger housing to front output housing | 18 | 2.4 |
| Mainshaft bearing housing | 18 | 2.4 |
| Operating arm pinch bolt | 6 | 0.8 |
| Gate plate to grommet plate | 6 | 0.8 |
| Pivot shaft | 18 | 2.4 |
| Connecting rod | 18 | 2.4 |
| Retaining plate intermediate shaft | 18 | 2.4 |
| Speedometer cable retainer | 6 | 0.8 |
| Speedometer housing/rear output | 6 | 0.8 |
| Gearbox to transfer box | 34 | 4.7 |
| Bearing housing to transfer gearbox | 34 | 4.7 |
| Drain plug | 23 | 3.1 |
| Oil filler/level plug | 23 | 3.1 |
| Transfer breather | 7 | 0.9 |
| Gearbox to transfer case | 34 | 4.7 |
| Differential case | 43 | 5.9 |
| Output flange | 120 | 16.6 |
| Link arm and crossshaft lever to balljoint | 8 | 1.1 |
| Transmission brake | 55 | 7.6 |
| Brake drum | 18 | 2.4 |
| Selector shaft high/low yoke | 18 | 2.4 |
| Selector fork high/low to shaft | 18 | 2.4 |
| Operating arm high/low | 18 | 2.4 |
| Speedometer housing to transfer case | 34 | 4.7 |
| Selector fork to cross-shaft | 34 | 4.7 |
| | | |
| *Gearbox/transfer box* | | |
| Bellhousing to engine | 30 | 4.1 |
| Gearbox housing to bellhousing | 120 | 16.6 |
| Gearbox housing to bellhousing | 70 | 9.6 |
| Gearbox housing to bellhousing nuts | 70 | 9.6 |
| Gearbox housing-to-bellhousing stud and nuts | 120 | 16.6 |
| Output flange nuts and bolts (rear) | 35 | 4.9 |
| Output shaft nut (rear) | 120 | 16.6 |
| Output shaft nut (front) | 120 | 16.6 |
| Gear selector spherical seat belts | 11 | 1.5 |
| Propeller shaft/flange bolts | 35 | 4.9 |
| Other nuts and bolts: | | |
|    M6 | 8 | 1.1 |
|    M8 | 20 | 2.7 |
|    M10 | 39 | 5.3 |

## *Automatic transmission*
## General

| | |
|---|---|
| Type number | A 727 |
| Type | Fully automatic with three forward speeds and one reverse. Epicyclic type with fluid torque converter |
| Lubrication method | Rotor pump |

## Gear ratios

| | | |
|---|---|---|
| Top | 1.00 : 1 | |
| 2nd | 1.45 : 1 | |
| 1st | 2.45 : 1 | |
| Reverse | 2.20 : 1 | |
| Transfer gearbox: | | |
|    High | 1.003 : 1 | |
|    Low | 3.320 : 1 | |
| Overall ratios: | **High transfer** | **Low transfer** |
|    Top | 3.55 : 1 | 11.75 : 1 |
|    2nd | 5.15 : 1 | 17.04 : 1 |
|    1st | 8.70 : 1 | 28.79 : 1 |
|    Reverse | 7.81 : 1 | 25.86 : 1 |

## Lubrication

Lubrication type:
| | |
|---|---|
| Automatic gearbox .................................................... | Dexron IID |
| Transfer gearbox ..................................................... | 20W/50 engine oil, SAE 90 EP or Dexron IID |

Capacity:
| | |
|---|---|
| Automatic gearbox .................................................... | 15 Imp pints (8.52 litres) |
| Transfer gearbox ..................................................... | 5 Imp pints (2.80 litres) |
| Automatic gearbox – refill after draining ........................ | 8 Imp pints (4.5 litres) |

## Torque wrench settings

| | lbf ft | kgf m |
|---|---|---|
| Breather tube banjo bolt ............................................. | 7 | 0.9 |
| Torque converter-to-driveplate bolts ............................. | 22.5 | 3.1 |
| Throttle lever clamp bolt ............................................ | 4.5 | 0.6 |
| Gearchange pivot self-locking nut ................................ | 18 | 2.4 |
| Tie plate to gearbox sump .......................................... | 18 | 2.4 |
| Tie plate to engine sump ............................................ | 18 | 2.4 |
| Gearbox sump .......................................................... | 17.5 | 2.3 |
| Lower bracket to gearbox ........................................... | 27.5 | 3.8 |
| Adaptor housing to gearbox ........................................ | 33 | 4.5 |
| Coupling shaft to mainshaft nut ................................... | 54 | 7.4 |
| Mainshaft special nut ................................................ | 100 | 13.8 |
| Drain plug .............................................................. | 22 | 3.0 |
| Oil filter to spacer .................................................... | 3 | 0.4 |
| Oil filter extension ................................................... | 3 | 0.4 |
| Starter ring to driveplate ........................................... | 25 | 3.4 |
| Spigot aligner to spacer ............................................ | 35 | 4.8 |
| Spacer to crankshaft ................................................ | 60 | 8.2 |
| Lower gearchange housing adaptor housing ................... | 18 | 2.4 |
| Kickdown pivot bracket adaptor ring ............................. | 18 | 2.4 |
| Cover plate to adaptor ring ........................................ | 6 | 0.8 |
| Torque converter housing packing ............................... | 5 | 0.7 |
| Oil cooler bridge pipe sleeve nuts ............................... | 6 | 0.8 |
| Oil cooler adaptors .................................................. | 8 | 1.1 |
| Oil cooler elbow to adaptors ...................................... | 8 | 1.1 |
| Valve body nuts ...................................................... | 8 | 1.1 |
| Kickdown band adjuster screw locknut .......................... | 30 | 4.1 |
| Low and reverse band adjuster screw locknut ................. | 30 | 4.1 |

## *Braking system*
## Torque wrench setting

| | lbf in | kgf cm |
|---|---|---|
| Brake pressure warning switch .................................... | 16 | 18 |

## *Electrical system*
## Main fusebox – later models (facia mounted)

| Fuse number | Circuit | Rating | Colour |
|---|---|---|---|
| 1 | RH headlamp – dipped ..................................... | 7.5 amp | Brown |
| 2 | LH headlamp – dipped ..................................... | 7.5 amp | Brown |
| 3 | RH headlamp – main ....................................... | 7.5 amp | Brown |
| 4 | LH headlamp – main ....................................... | 7.5 amp | Brown |
| 5 | RH sidelights and panel lights ........................... | 5 amp | Tan |
| 6 | LH sidelights ................................................ | 5 amp | Tan |
| 7 | Front and rear wiper motors .............................. | 15 amp | Light blue |
| 8 | Heater motor ................................................ | 20 amp | Yellow |
| 9 | Heated rear windows ....................................... | 15 amp | Light blue |
| 10 | Electric mirror heater elements* ......................... | 3 amp | Violet |
| 11 | Interior lights, clock, horns, cigar lighter, headlamp flasher, engine compartment light ............ | 15 amp | Light blue |
| 12 | Rear foglights (from headlamp dip) ..................... | 10 amp | Red |
| 13 | Indicators, stop-lights, reverse lights, electric mirror motors ................................................. | 15 amp | Light blue |
| 14 | Trailer auxiliary circuit ................................... | 15 amp | Light blue |
| 15 | Air conditioning fan* ...................................... | 20 amp | Yellow |
| 16 | Air conditioning fan* ...................................... | 20 amp | Yellow |
| 17 | Air conditioning compressor clutch* ................... | 5 amp | Tan |
| 18 | Air conditioning blower motor* .......................... | 20 amp | Yellow |
| 19 | Central door locking system* ............................ | 10 amp | Red |
| 20 | Electric window lifts* ...................................... | 25 amp | White |

*Optional fittings

**Note:** In addition to the above fuses, an in-line fuse of 7 amp rating protects the radio/cassette circuit (where fitted)

## Bulbs

| | |
|---|---|
| Rear foglamps | 21W |
| Side repeater lamps | 6W |
| Differential lock warning lamp | 2.2W |
| Engine compartment lamp | 5W |

## *Suspension and steering*
### Road springs

| Colour code | Rating – lb/in (kg/m) | Free length – in (mm) | No of coils |
|---|---|---|---|
| Yellow stripe | 130 (2321.5) | 16.34 (414.29) | 7.11 |
| Yellow stripe | 170 (3035.86) | 16.95 (430.53) | 8.85 |
| Green stripe | 150 (2678.7) | 16.13 (409.70) | 7.63 |
| Blue stripe | 133 (2375.1) | 15.4 (391.16) | 7.18 |
| Red/white stripe | 170 (3035.86) | 16.95 (430.53) | 7.00 |
| Red/yellow stripe | 150 (2678.7) | 17.18 (436.40) | 7.65 |
| Blue/white stripe | 133 (2375.1) | 16.44 (417.57) | 7.55 |
| Green/yellow stripe | 170 (3035.86) | 16.20 (411.48) | 7.00 |

Maximum allowable spring free length contraction (under that specified)  0.787 in (20 mm)
Rear axle bump stop-to-pad clearance (measured to front corner of pad):
    Average minimum allowable ... 2.8 in (67 mm)

### Tyre pressures
Michelin 205 R 16 M + S – all loads under normal conditions:
    Front (cold) ... 25 lbf/in² (1.8 kgf/cm²)
    Rear (cold) ... 35 lbf/in² (2.5 kgf/cm²)
Michelin 205 R 16 M + S – sustained high speed above 60 mph (100 kph) or
when checked above ambient temperature of 77°F (25°C):
    Front ... 28 lbf/in² (2.0 kgf/cm²)
    Rear ... 38 lbf/in² (2.7 kgf/cm²)
All models from July 1979*
  Normal use:
    Front ... 25 lbf/in² (1.8 kgf/cm²)
    Rear ... 35 lbf/in² (2.5 kgf/cm²)
  Emergency soft use:
    Front ... 15 lbf/in² (1.1 kgf/cm²)
    Rear ... 25 lbf/in² (1.8 kgf/cm²)
*Also suitable for earlier models fitted with heavy duty suspension

### Torque wrench settings

| | lbf ft | kgf m |
|---|---|---|
| Alloy roadwheel nuts | 90 to 95 | 12.5 to 13.1 |

## *General dimensions, weights and capacities – later models (where different from early models):*
### Heights

| | |
|---|---|
| Overall height | 70 in (1.78 m) |
| Maximum cargo height | 40 in (1.01 m) |
| Rear opening height | 40 in (1.01 m) |

### Weights

EEC kerb weight: **Total**
  Four-door ... 4248 lb (1927 kg)
  Two-door ... 4178 lb (1895 kg)
Maximum allowable towing weights (on road):
  Non-braked trailer ... 1100 lb (500 kg)
  Braked trailer ... 4400 lb (2000 kg)
  Four wheel trailer with continuous or semi-continuous
  (coupled) brakes ... 8800 lb (4000 kg)
Maximum allowable towed weights (off road):
  Non-braked trailer ... 1100 lb (500 kg)
  Braked trailer ... 2200 lb (1000 kg)
  Four wheel trailer with continuous or semi-continuous
  (coupled) brakes ... 2200 lb (1000 kg)
Maximum allowable roof rack load ... 165 lb (75 kg)

### Capacities
Luggage capacity:
  Rear seat in position – four door ... 36.18 cu ft (1.02 cu m)
  Rear seat in position – two-door ... 41.48 cu ft (1.17 cu m)
  Rear seat folded ... 70.8 cu ft (2.00 cu m)

## 3 Engine

### Inlet valve oil seals

1 On later models the inlet valves are fitted with an oil seal. These seals can be used on earlier models not previously having seals fitted.

2 When fitting the seals onto the valves, press the seal down until it abuts with the valve guide. When the engine is started the seal will automatically position itself on the valve stem (Fig. 13.1).

### Engine (automatic transmission models) – removal and refitting

3 The engine removal and refitting details for automatic transmission models are basically the same as described for the manual transmission models in Chapter 1. As with the manual gearbox models, the engine must be removed separately from the transmission (see Section 4 in Chapter 1).

4 In addition to those items detailed in Chapter 1 for engine removal, it will also be necessary to disconnect the oil cooler lines where they are attached to the side of the engine. These and other items which differ when disconnecting the engine from the automatic transmission are described in Section 7 of this Chapter.

### Engine and associated components – air conditioned models

5 When removing the engine or any of its ancillary components which will necessitate disconnecting the air conditioning system hoses or

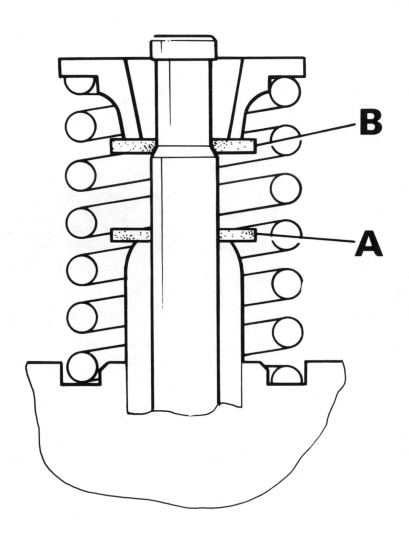

H14487

**Fig. 13.1 Inlet valve oil seal – fitment to early models (Sec 3)**

A   Abut oil seal with valve guide        B   Oil seal operating position

components, reference should first be made to the special precautions concerning the air conditioning system in Section 12 of this Chapter.

## 4 Fuel system

### Air cleaner baffle

1  Some models may have a baffle fitted to the end of the air intake unit. The baffle will have been fitted to prevent backfiring on the overrun and can be fitted to models not so equipped to prevent this problem. Before fitting the baffle, first check that the vacuum pipes to the air intake temperature control unit are correctly located, are in good condition and securely fitted. The baffle is fitted to the intake, as shown in Fig. 13.2, and is secured by self-tapping screws.

### Carburettors – idle speed adjustment

2  The idle speed adjustment screw on later models is secured by a locking ring which is housed in a protective cover, and a special tool (Zenith part number B25243) is necessary when making adjustments to the idle speed. The special tool is shown in Fig. 13.3. A similar tool would be easy to fabricate using a length of suitable diameter tube, shaped at one end. This would enable it to engage with the locking slots so that the ring can be held while adjustment is made using a screwdriver passed down through the tubing to turn the adjuster screw.

3  Any attempt to adjust the idle speed without this tool will result in damage to the adjuster screw and possibly the carburettor.

### Carburettors – mixture adjustment

4  The carburettor mixture adjustment on later models (from 1979) differs from the earlier types described in Chapter 3 in that the later CD type carburettors have a raised blade type mixture needle adjuster instead of the Allen key socket.

5  Mixture adjustment on the later carburettor types will require the use of Zenith special tool B25860 (shown in Fig. 13.4). The central socket engages over the tongue in the reservoir base and the external barrel locks into the air valve guide rod. When fitted in position to make any adjustments, ensure that the external barrel is correctly located to prevent the air valve from turning during adjustment which could damage the main diaphragm.

6  Turn the central socket clockwise to richen the mixture or anti-clockwise to weaken it.

### Exhaust system

7  On some models an insulation pad may be found clipped to the exhaust downpipe adjacent to the clutch slave cylinder. The insulation is fitted to prevent the heat from the exhaust shortening the life of the slave cylinder seals.

8  When renewing the exhaust system, or the left-hand downpipe, the insulation pad must be fitted to the new system to act as a heat shield adjacent to the clutch slave cylinder. The insulation pad is secured by three retaining clips.

9  The exhaust system fitted to models produced from 1980 was modified, but the downpipes and intermediate pipe sections on each side are interchangeable on earlier models.

### Pulsair air injection system

10  This emission control feature was introduced in 1981. The system operates by drawing air from the air cleaner unit under manifold depression, passing the air through gulp valves and pipes, and then injects the air into the exhaust manifold. The injected air mixes with the exhaust gases and reduces the CO (carbon monoxide) emission to atmosphere.

11  Very little in the way of maintenance to the system is required, apart from checking the condition and security of the hoses, pipes and air valves at 12 000 mile (20 000 km) intervals.

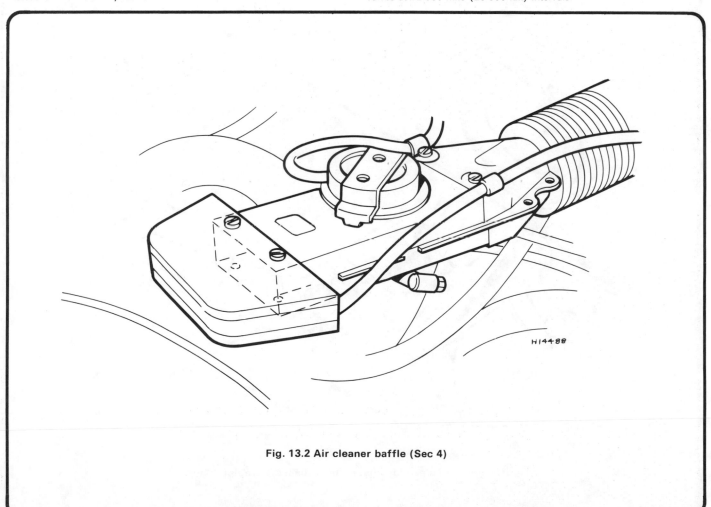

H14488

**Fig. 13.2 Air cleaner baffle (Sec 4)**

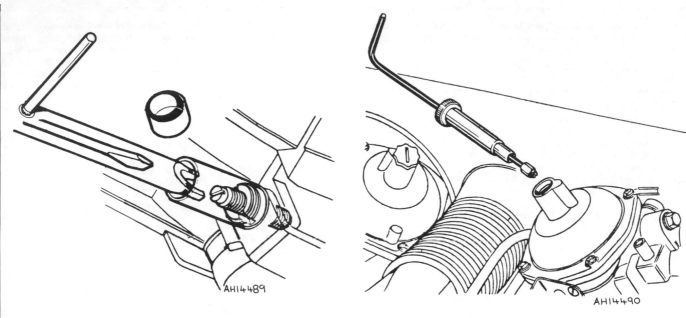

Fig. 13.3 Idle speed adjustment tool for later models (Sec 4)

Fig. 13.4 Mixture adjustment tool for later models (Sec 4)

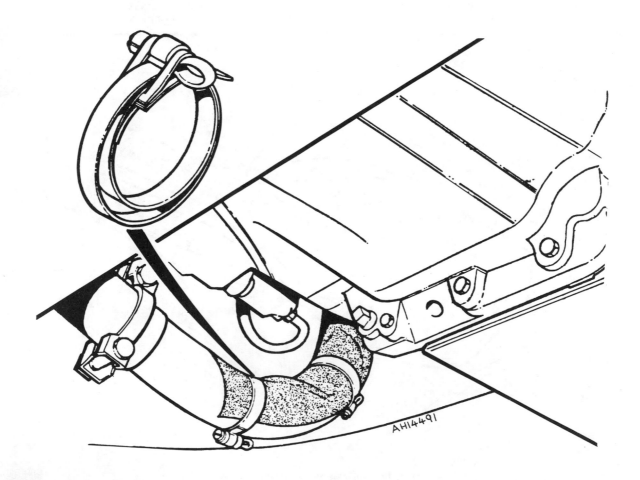

Fig. 13.5 Insulation pad location on the exhaust downpipe (Sec 4)

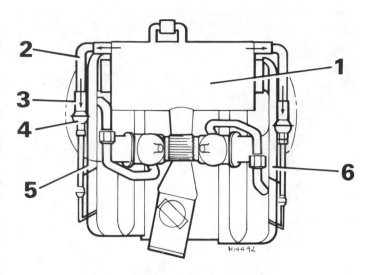

**Fig. 13.6 Pulsair injection system layout (Sec 4)**

| | |
|---|---|
| 1  Air cleaner unit | 4  Gulp valves |
| 2  Connecting pipes | 5  Air manifold (right-hand) |
| 3  Connecting hoses | 6  Air manifold (left-hand) |

## 5  Ignition system

### Lucas 35 D8 distributor with sliding contact braker points

1  The Lucas 35 D8 distributor fitted to models produced from 1981 differs in that it has sliding contact type breaker points fitted. These have the advantages of increased reliability and longer contact life, renewal being necessary at 24 000 mile (40 000 km) intervals rather than at 12 000 mile (20 000 km) intervals with the earlier type.

2  In all other respects, the distributor is the same as that fitted to earlier models; the removal, cleaning and refitting details being identical to that described in Section 4 of Chapter 4. However, the following special points must be noted.

(a)  Only sliding contact type breaker points must be fitted
(b)  When removing the contact breaker points, clean the contact faces with petrol to remove the protective coating
(c)  When fitting the contact points, lubricate the actuator ramps,

the contact breaker heel ribs, the heel actuator base and the fixed pin and actuator fork with grease (Fig. 13.8)
(d)  On fitting the contact points into position, the sliding actuator fork must engage over the baseplate pin and the pegs on the underside of the contact set engage with holes in the moveable plate
(e)  When new contact breaker points have been fitted, check the dwell angle after 1000 miles (1500 km) has been covered

### Ignition timing – 8.13:1 and 9.5:1 compression ratio engines

3  In addition to those details mentioned in Sections 3 and 8 in Chapter 4 the following items should be noted for these engine types.

4  Prior to checking the ignition timing, it is essential that the contact breaker points are correctly adjusted. If adjustment is necessary due to the gap being too small, the adjuster screw should be unscrewed beyond that required, then retightened to set the clearance specified. This method will avoid the possibility of backlash in the screw mechanism.

5  Run the engine up to its normal operating temperature.

6  On 8.13:1 compression ratio engines set the engine idle speed at 600 to 650 rpm, leaving the vacuum lines connected.

7  On 9.35:1 compression ratio engines set the idle speed at 550 to 650 rpm with both vacuum pipes connected. With the idle speed adjusted, detach both vacuum pipes from the distributor vacuum unit, the engine idle speed will then increase and must be reduced to 750 rpm by disconnecting a breather pipe from one of the carburettors. Further equal adjustment of the idle speed setting screws of the carburettors may be required to achieve this speed.

8  On both engine types the dwell angle can then be checked and adjusted, as described in Section 3 of Chapter 4.

9  After the dwell angle check is completed, the ignition timing should be checked dynamically, as described in Section 8 of Chapter 4.

10  On 9.35:1 compression ratio engines, complete the timing checks by reconnecting the vacuum retard pipes and the carburettor breather pipe, then recheck the engine idle speed.

11  If necessary readjust the idle speed to that specified, then recheck the dynamic timing which should be between 4 and 8° ATDC. If not then the vacuum system is at fault.

12  To check the vacuum unit, detach the vacuum retard pipe at the distributor. The idle speed should increase and the timing advance to between 6 and 14° BTDC.

### Electronic ignition system – general

13  From June 1984, all models are fitted with an electronic ignition system; a Lucas 35 DM 8 distributor being fitted instead of the Lucas 35 D8 previously (which had the mechanical contact breaker points).

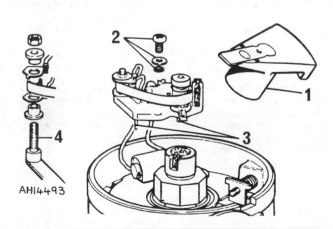

**Fig. 13.7 Sliding contact breaker points (Sec 5)**

| | |
|---|---|
| 1  Rotor arm | 4  Terminal post connections |
| 2  Retaining screw and washers | (red lead fits over bottom |
| 3  Moveable plate pegs | plastic bush) |

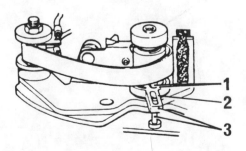

**Fig. 13.8 Sliding contact breaker points lubrication points (Sec 5)**

| | |
|---|---|
| 1  Actuator ramps and breaker heel ribs | 2  Heel actuator base |
| | 3  Fixed pin and fork |

5.14 Ignition coil and control unit – electronic ignition

5.26 Plastic insulation cover retaining screws (arrowed)
*Do not remove the cover unless absolutely necessary*

5.38 Checking the air gap

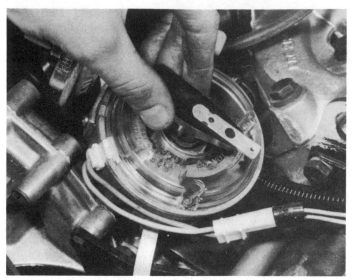

5.40 Refitting the rotor arm

14 The electronic system functions in a similar manner to a conventional system, but the contact points and condenser are replaced by a magnetic sensor in the distributor and a control unit (amplifier) mounted separately. As the distributor driveshaft rotates, the magnetic impulses are fed to the control unit which switches the primary circuit on and off. No condenser is necessary as the circuit is switched electronically with semiconductor components. The control unit is located directly under the ignition coil on top of the left-hand front wing valance (photo).

15 The ignition advance is controlled mechanically by centrifugal weights and by a vacuum capsule mounted on the side of the distributor.

16 To prevent damage to the system or personal injury observe the following precautions.

### Electronic ignition system – precautions

17 To prevent personal injury and damage to the ignition system, the following precautions must be observed when working on the ignition system.

18 Do not attempt to disconnect any plug lead or touch any of the high tension cables when the engine is running, or being turned by the starter motor.

19 Ensure that the ignition is turned OFF before disconnecting any of the ignition wiring.

20 Ensure that the ignition is switched OFF before connecting or disconnecting any ignition testing equipment such as a timing light.

21 If the HT cable is disconnected from the distributor the cable must immediately be connected to earth and remain earthed if the engine is to be rotated by the starter motor, for example if a compression test is to be done.

22 If an electric arc welder is to be used on any part of the vehicle, the vehicle battery must be disconnected while welding is being done.

### Electronic ignition system – maintenance

23 Every 48 000 miles (80 000 km) remove the distributor cap, withdraw the rotor arm and wipe clean the inner components using a clean wool-free cloth, but do not remove the plastic insulating cover protecting the magnetic pick-up module.

24 Wipe clean the ignition HT and LT leads and check that their respective connections are secure.

### Electronic ignition distributor – removal, dismantling and reassembly

25 The distributor can be removed and refitted in the same manner as that described for the conventional type in Section 5 of Chapter 4.

26 Commence dismantling by withdrawing the rotor arm then undo the three retaining screws (photo) and lift clear the plastic insulation cover (flash shield).

27 Undo the two screws securing the vacuum unit and withdraw the unit, disengage the connecting rod from the pick-up baseplate peg as it is removed.

28 Using a pair of circlip pliers, release the circlip securing the reluctor on the driveshaft, then withdraw the reluctor complete with the flat

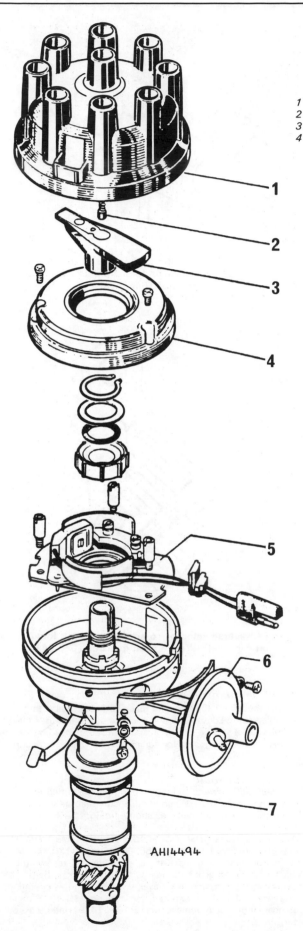

**Fig. 13.9 Electronic ignition distributor components (Sec 5)**

1  Cap
2  HT brush & spring
3  Rotor arm
4  Insulation cover (flash shield)
5  Pick-up and base-plate assembly
6  Vacuum unit
7  O-ring oil seal

washer and O-ring. To assist with the removal of the reluctor, insert a small screwdriver blade under it and prise it up the shaft. Note the coupling ring located underneath the reluctor.

29 To remove the pick-up, module and baseplate unit, unscrew and remove the three support pillars, but take care not to undo the two barrel nuts. These retain the pick-up module and if disturbed the air gap will have to be reset. Do not dismantle the distributor any further.

30 Clean and renew as necessary any items which are worn or suspected of malfunction.

31 Reassembly is a reversal of the removal procedure, but note the following special points.

32 When refitting the pick-up and baseplate unit locate the pick-up leads in the plastic channel (Fig. 13.10).

33 When refitting the reluctor, slide it down the shaft as far as possible then turn the reluctor so that it engages with the coupling ring underneath the baseplate.

34 Lubricate the following items during assembly:

(a) Three drops of clean engine oil to the felt pad in the top end of the rotor shaft

(b) Grease the vacuum unit connecting rod seal (within the unit) using Rocal MHT or an equivalent grease

(c) Lubricate the automatic advance mechanism, the pick-up plate centre bearing, pre-tilt spring and contact area, the vacuum unit connecting peg and corresponding connecting rod hole with a small amount of Chevron SR1 or equivalent grease.

35 Prior to refitting the insulation cover, check and, if necessary, adjust the pick-up air gap.

36 When the distributor is refitted it must be timed statically before starting the engine.

*Electronic ignition distributor – air gap adjustment*

37 The air gap should only need checking and adjusting when the distributor has been dismantled and either the original or a new pick-up and baseplate assembly have been fitted.

38 The air gap is checked by inserting a non-ferrous feeler gauge of the specified thickness between the pick-up limb and a reluctor tooth (photo).

39 Where adjustment is necessary, loosen the two barrel nuts retaining the pick-up module (these will already be loosened on a new unit) and move the module/pick-up to adjust the gap. Retighten the nuts.

40 Refit the plastic cover, rotor arm and distributor cap (photo).

*Ignition timing – electronic ignition*

41 The ignition timing and adjustment methods on models fitted with electronic ignition are the same as those described for the contact breaker type. When making a dynamic timing check, disconnect the vacuum pipes at the distributor and check that the idle speed does not exceed 750 rpm. Disconnect a carburettor breather hose to achieve this speed, as the speed must not be regulated by adjusting the carburettor idle speed screws. Do not allow the engine speed to exceed 3000 rpm during the check. Refer to the Specifications in this Chapter for the static and dynamic ignition timing.

*Ignition system – HT leads*

42 Further to the information given concerning HT leads in Chapter 4, it is important to note that if the leads are detached for any reason, they must be refitted and arranged as shown in Fig. 13.11. This arrangement ensures that there is no cross firing (arcing) between the leads which will cause misfiring.

AHI4494

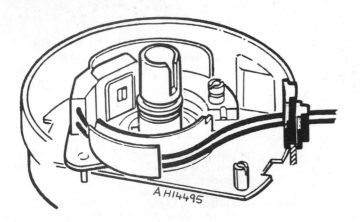

Fig. 13.10 Electronic ignition distributor pick-up leads arrangement (Sec 5)

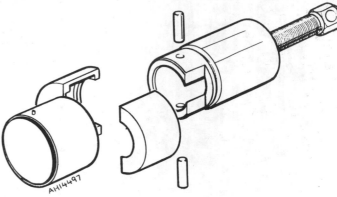

Fig. 13.12 Special tool 18G 1388 required to remove the transfer gear and spacer on later models – four-speed gearbox (Sec 6A)

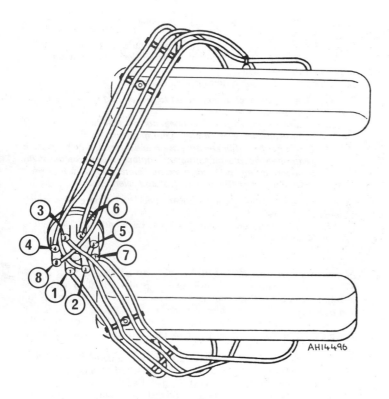

Fig. 13.11 HT leads arrangement (Sec 5)

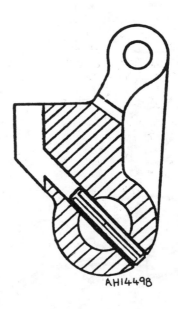

Fig. 13.13 Reverse selector-to-shaft spring pin location on later models – four-speed gearbox (Sec 6A)

## 6   Manual transmission

### Part A: Four-speed transmission – modifications

#### Gearbox mainshaft bearing

1   From 1979 the gearbox mainshaft bearing arrangement was modified by having a semi-circular groove machined in the periphery of the bearing outer race. A spring pin driven through a hole in the gearbox bearing housing engages with the groove in the bearing to prevent any possible lateral movement of the bearing in the housing. It therefore follows that when removing this bearing (fitted from gearbox number 35574323) it will first be necessary to withdraw the spring pin.

2   When fitting the bearing, align the peripheral groove with the pin hole in the housing, then drive a new roll pin in to secure.

#### Mainshaft and transfer gear

3   On later models (1983 on), the mainshaft spacer and transfer gear are assembled using Loctite 275 and because of this it is essential to use a later type special service tool number 18G 1388, instead of the special extractor RO 1004 suggested for earlier gearbox types in Section 5 of Chapter 6.

#### Reverse selector shaft

4   From late 1980 onwards, a longer spring pin was fitted to secure the reverse selector to the shaft. When fitted, ensure that the roll pin is driven fully into position and is located as shown in Fig. 13.13.

#### Main gearbox-to-transfer gearbox oil seal – renewal

5   From gearbox type numbers 35600623C and 12C15923A (later 9.35:1 compression engines), it is possible to renew the main gearbox-to-transfer gearbox oil seal without removing the gearbox or the selector lever cross-shaft. However, if attempting this operation, two Rover service tools will be required, these being 18G 1388 (mainshaft output gear and spacer remover) and 18G 1426 (inter box oil seal replacer).

6 Remove the drain plug and drain the oil from the transfer gearbox into a suitable container.

7 Refer to Section 10 in Chapter 6 and remove the speedometer drive housing.

8 Unbolt and remove the transfer gearbox bottom cover. It may be necessary to remove the intermediate exhaust pipe section to allow bottom cover removal.

9 Unbolt and remove the mainshaft rear bearing cover and gasket. Withdraw the roller bearing (see Fig. 6.4).

10 Screw a suitable (8 mm) bolt into the end of the intermediate gear shaft. Support the intermediate gear cluster from underneath and withdraw the shaft.

11 Keep the intermediate gears together during removal by inserting a suitable slave shaft through them – use Rover special tool number RO 1003 if available. Withdraw the intermediate gear cluster.

12 If dismantling of the gear cluster is necessary, this is dealt with in Section 12 of Chapter 6.

13 Before removing the mainshaft output (transfer) gear it should be noted that the gear, selective washer and snap-ring control the mainshaft endfloat.

14 If during the removal of these items the mainshaft is allowed to move forward, the 1st gear needle roller bearing thrust washer will become dislodged. To prevent this it is necessary to engage 3rd gear and then secure the main gearlever in this position during the subsequent operations until the output gear assembly is refitted.

15 With 3rd gear securely engaged, and the gear lever held under tension, release the snap-ring and remove it, together with the selective washer and the mainshaft output gear. Remove the output gear using Rover special tool 18G 1388.

16 Use this tool to remove the mainshaft spacer sleeve, but check that the extractor pins are fully engaged prior to withdrawal.

17 The interbox oil seal can now be levered out, but take care not to damage the housing bore.

18 Clean the mainshaft, output gear and spacer sleeve; ensuring that no traces of the old Loctite are present on them.

19 Wind some plastic insulation tape over the splined sections of the mainshaft so that the oil seal lip is protected from damage as it is located over the shaft.

20 Carefully locate the oil seal over the shaft and beyond the cross-shaft, then fit it into the housing using Rover special tool 18G 1426. When the seal is fully fitted into the housing bore, remove the special tool and unwind the protective tape from the shaft. Smear the oil seal lip with clean oil to provide initial lubrication.

21 Temporarily refit the spacer sleeve, output (transfer) gear and selective washer. Locate the snap-ring then measure the endfloat clearance between the snap-ring and the washer. If necessary obtain a selective thrust washer to adjust the clearance to that specified (Chapter 6).

22 Remove the washer, gear and spacer sleeve.

23 Smear the inner bores of the spacer sleeve and gear with Loctite 275 (paying attention to the manufacturer's instructions), but ensure that no sealant is allowed to contact the external surfaces and the spacer sleeve seal track.

24 Refit the spacer sleeve, gear and selected washer, and secure in position with the snap-ring, ensuring that it is fully engaged in its groove (without forcing it). Third gear can now be disengaged. If the washer and snap-ring prove difficult to fit it is probable that the 1st gear needle roller thrust washer is dislodged, in which case pull and simultaneously rotate the mainshaft until the thrust washer is correctly relocated and the shim washer and snap-ring can be fitted.

25 Refit the intermediate gears and shaft; reversing the removal procedure and referring to Section 12 in Chapter 6.

26 When refitting the speedometer drive housing, coat the gasket with Hylomar PL32 sealant or equivalent.

27 On completion top up the transfer gearbox with the recommended quality and quantity of oil.

### Top cover

28 From gearbox numbers 35596645L (standard compression engine) and 12C04252A (high compression engine), the top cover has an adjustable stop and locknut to provide a positive stop position for the reserve selector hinge unit.

### Selector jaw roll pin

29 From gearbox number 35589427C, the selector jaw roll pin fitted is both larger in diameter and longer than the roll pin fitted to earlier gearbox types. This modification was made to improve the 1st/2nd and reverse selector jaw location on the selector shafts.

## Part B: Five-speed transmission and transfer gearbox – removal and refitting

### Special notes

Before any attempt is made to remove the transmission unit, reference should be made to the Special notes in Section 2 of Chapter 6.

The five-speed transmission unit complete (main gearbox and transfer gearbox) is best removed upwards through the vehicle in circumstances where limited workshop tools and facilities are available. This method is described in this Chapter.

If for any reason a different removal method is used, whereby the transmission unit is disconnected and then lowered on a jack for removal underneath the vehicle, it will be necessary to suitably support the gearbox. To do this you will need to make up a special transmission support cradle to the dimensions shown in Fig. 13.14. Alternatively you may be able to borrow this tool from your local Range Rover dealer. An industrial trolley jack will also be required to support, lower and manoeuvre the transmission unit clear of the vehicle, when using this method. Any attempt to remove the transmission from underneath without using the recommended cradle and a suitable jack could result in both personal injury and damage to the transmission; therefore this method is not recommended for the DIY mechanic.

### Removal and refitting

1 Disconnect the battery earth lead.

2 Select the low range transfer gear then remove the high/low and main gear lever knobs.

3 Remove the main gear lever and the high/low gear lever gaiters.

4 Unclip and withdraw the ashtrays from their holders, then unscrew and remove the four self-tapping screws to release the holders (photo).

5 Peel back the base cover in the cubby box to expose its retaining bolts. Undo the bolts and lift the box clear (photo).

6 Loosen the two screws retaining the console at the front end then carefully withdraw the console rearwards and upwards. Disconnect the console switch wires as it is withdrawn.

7 Remove the rear compartment heater duct (photo).

8 Undo the retaining nut securing the main gear lever onto its splined shaft (photo), note and mark their relative alignment positions then pull the lever from the selector shaft.

9 Remove the transmission tunnel carpet and floor carpets.

10 Undo the retaining screws and remove the high/low gear lever rubber gaiter and retaining plate, then repeat this procedure and remove the main gearlever/top cover rubber gaiter from the top of the transmission tunnel (photo).

11 Lift the insulation moulding from the transmission top cover, then undo the retaining bolts and remove the aluminium top cover (photos).

12 Unbolt the front seat support frames and remove them, together with the seats. For access to the frame outer edge bolts, first detach the plastic covers which are secured by screws. Refer to the photos for bolt positions.

13 Undo the retaining screws and remove the handbrake lever gaiter (photo).

14 Remove the retaining bolts and lift clear the main gearlever housing (photo).

15 Unscrew the handbrake lever pivot bolt retaining nut and withdraw the bolt. Disconnect the handbrake link plate by extracting the split pin, withdrawing the clevis pin and collecting the flat washer and Thackeray washer; noting their location. Withdraw the lever and detach the handbrake warning switch leads (photos).

16 Unscrew and remove the front and rear (passenger compartment) floorpan retaining screws and bolts. Two bolts are particularly difficult to reach; these being located at the front end of the transmission cover section of the front floor section (above the bellhousing, near the bulkhead). Access to these bolts can be gained by removing the air filter unit (see Chapter 3) and reaching down under the bulkhead from the engine compartment side. An alternative method is to remove the chassis crossmember beneath the transmission. The crossmember is secured to the chassis member each side by four bolts and nuts (photo). Support the crossmember and lever or tap it downwards from the chassis, noting which way round it is fitted. With the crossmember removed, the two bolts are just accessible from underneath by reaching up between the

234

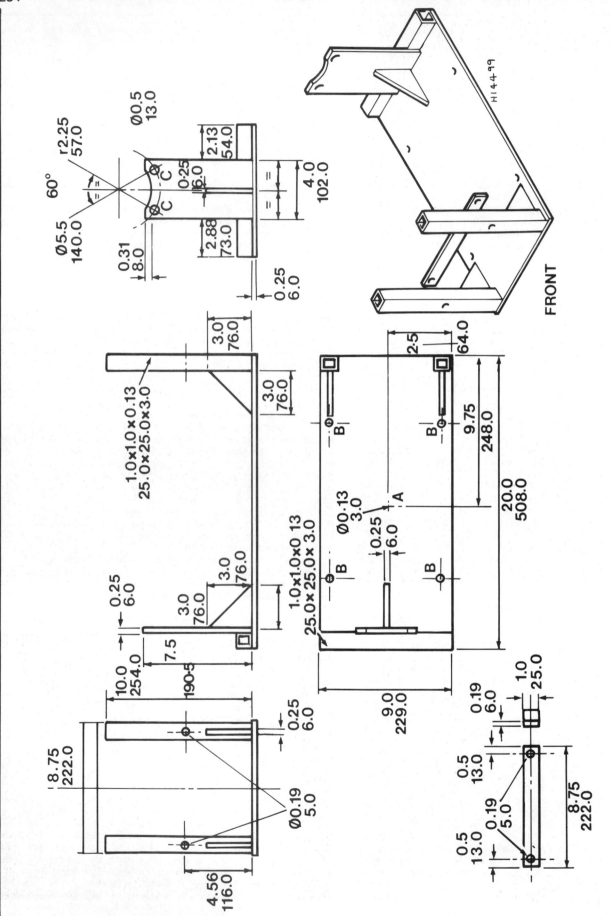

FRONT

HI4499

Fig. 13.14 Special cradle required when removing/refitting the five-speed transmission from underneath the vehicle (Sec 6B)

*Measurements in inches and millimetres*

6B.4 Remove the ashtray holder retaining screws (arrowed)

6B.5 Remove the cubby box retaining bolts (arrowed)

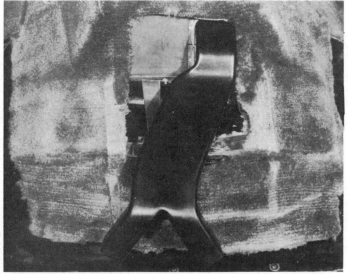

6B.7 Rear compartment heater duct

6B.8 Main gear lever retaining nut (arrowed)

6B.10 High/low gear lever and main gear lever gaiters

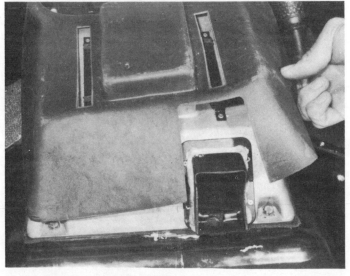

6B.11A Remove the insulation cover ...

6B.11B ... and the aluminium top cover

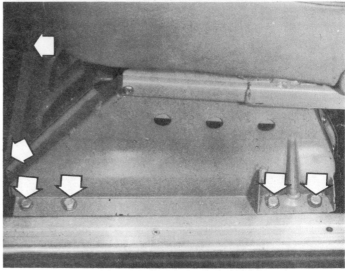
6B.12A Seat retaining bolts (arrowed) – leading and outer edges

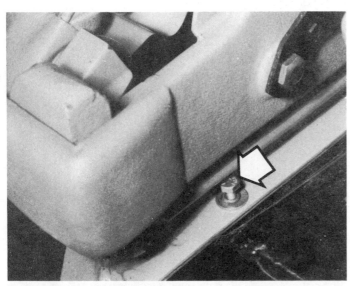
6B.12B Seat retaining bolt (arrowed) – inner edge at rear

6B.12C Seat retaining bolt (arrowed) – underside

6B.13 Handbrake lever gaiter, clamp plate and retaining screws

6B.14 Removing the main gear lever housing

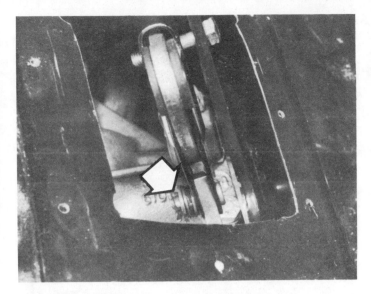

6B.15A Remove the handbrake lever pivot bolt and link plate clevis pin (arrowed)

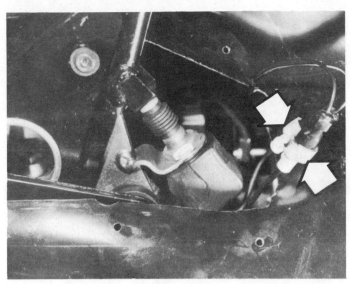

6B.15B Disconnect the handbrake warning switch leads (arrowed)

6B.16 Chassis crossmember retaining bolts (arrowed)

6B.17 Floorpan-to-chassis adjustable mounting

6B.18 Unbolt the exhaust heat shield from the floorpan

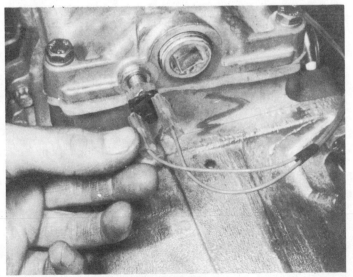

6B.20 Disconnect the reverse light switch leads

floor panel and the transmission. Note that if the transmission is to be lowered and removed from undeneath the vehicle, then the crossmember will have to be removed anyway, so try this method first.
17 Working underneath the vehicle, disconnect the floorpan rear adjustable mounting each side by extracting the split pin and withdrawing the clevis pin (photo). Loosen the adjuster nut to allow withdrawal of the clevis pin if necessary.
18 Unbolt and release the exhaust heat shield plate from the floorpan (photo).
19 Prise free and remove the floorpan from the rear passenger compartment, then repeat the procedure with the front floorpan/transmision cover; pulling it to the rear for removal. Note that the electric fuel pump wiring is secured to the underside of the transmission cover floorpan on the left-hand side, so prise back the clip and release the leads as the pan is removed.
20 Disconnect the leads to the reverse light switch (green and green/brown) (photo).
21 Disconnect the leads to the differential lock switch (green and black/blue) (photo).
22 Undo the retaining bolts and detach the breather hoses from the main and transfer gearboxes. Refit the bolts and fibre washers to the gearboxes to avoid losing them (photo).
23 Disconnect the wiring and the breather hoses from their location clips on the transmission and fold them back out of the way, but note their retaining clips and locations.
24 Disconnect the speedometer cable from the transmission and fold it back out of the way (photo).
25 Referring to Chapter 7, unbolt and detach the front and rear propeller shafts from the drive flanges on the transfer gearbox. Tie them up out of the way.
26 Position a suitable container under the transmission and drain the oil from the main gearbox and the transfer gearbox by removing their respective drain plugs (photo).
27 Unbolt and detach the front exhaust pipes from the manifolds and at their single pipe connection to the silencer and steady mounting (photo).
28 Unbolt and detach the clutch slave cylinder from the bellhousing. Leave the hydraulic line connected to the cylinder, and position the cylinder out of the way (photo).
29 Undo and remove the inspection plate bolts from the clutch bellhousing and note the position of the special retaining bolt each side. Remove the inspection plate (photo).
30 Undo and remove the clutch bellhousing-to-engine bolts and note the location of the harness locating clip.
31 The engine will now need to be supported, so position a suitable jack or safety stand under the engine and raise to support (not lift) the engine. Between the jack/stand and engine sump position a piece of wood to avoid damaging the sump.
32 The lifting sling must now be arranged around the main gearbox and the transfer gearbox so that, when lifted as a unit, the weight is equally distributed and they are kept level.
33 Wheel the gantry hoist into position over the gearbox, connect up the sling and take the weight. The hoist and sling must be as close to the transmission as possible to allow sufficient lift height clearance within the vehicle.
34 Remove the bolts from the transmission mountings on each side and detach from the chassis numbers (photo).
35 Unbolt and remove the upper bellhousing retaining bolts. Tilt the transmission downwards at the rear to enable the upper housing bolts to be withdrawn, but check that the engine mountings are not over-distorted.
36 Check that all of the transmission mounting and ancillary items are disconnected, then pull the transmission rearwards to detach it from the engine. As it disengages from the clutch unit, watch out for any imbalance in the lift sling arrangement which may cause the transmission to tilt appreciably. At least one assistant should be at hand to help steady the transmission and to guide it clear of surrounding fittings when lifting it clear (photo). Unless the steering wheel is removed, withdraw the transmission from the passenger side.
37 If the transmission is to be lowered and removed from under the vehicle using the jack and cradle method mentioned earlier, unscrew the two bottom bolts from the rear cover of the transfer gearbox then locate the rear of the cradle into position and reinsert the bolts. Check that the cradle is securely located under the transmission, raise the jack to support the assembly then withdraw the transmission rearwards and lower it once the transmission is clear of the engine. Get an assistant to

6B.21 Disconnect the differential lock switch leads

6B.22 Disconnect the breather hoses (main gearbox hose shown)

6B.24 Disconnect the speedometer cable

6B.26 Main gearbox (A) and transfer gearbox (B) drain plugs

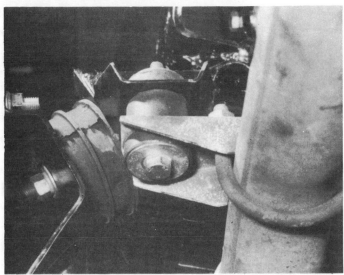

6B.27 Exhaust pipe steady mounting

6B.28 Unbolt and remove the clutch slave cylinder from the bellhousing

6B.29 Bellhousing retaining bolts/nuts – special bolt is arrowed

6B.34 Transmission-to-chassis mounting – note slotted holes to provide positional adjustment

6B.36 Transmission removal from within the vehicle – note lifting sling arrangement.

6B.49A Main gearbox filler/level plug (arrowed)

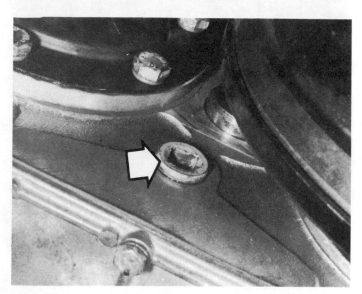

6B.49B Transfer gearbox filler/level plug (arrowed)

help steady the transmission as it is lowered and withdrawn from under the vehicle.

38 If the vehicle is to be moved whilst the transmission is out of the vehicle, locate a long bar through the clutch unit and into the flywheel pilot hole. Rest the rear of the bar on a support timber mounted transversely across and resting on top of the chassis. The engine support jack/stand can then be removed.

39 Refitting the transmission unit is a reversal of the removal sequence. In order to engage the primary pinion with the clutch splines it will probably be necessary to select a gear and then turn the transmission brake drum whilst pushing on the rear face of the gearbox. When the splines are in alignment the gearbox will slide forwards over the shafts.

40 Smear the vertical joint face of the bellhousing cover plate with jointing compound before fitting. The cover plate and clutch slave cylinder spacing plate must also be treated with jointing compound when refitting (Loctite 290 or similar).

41 Remove all self-locking (Nyloc) nuts and split pins.

42 Do not refit the chassis crossmember until after the exhaust pipe front section and the two upper retaining bolts at the top of the transmission bellhousing (unless the air cleaner unit was removed) are in position.

43 When reconnecting the wiring to the reverse switch and differential switch, route the wires through their retaining clips so that they do not interfere with the high/low gearchange linkage assembly.

44 The same applies when reconnecting the ventilation tubes to the

main gearbox and transfer gearbox. Use new fibre washers each side of the tube unions and do not overtighten the retaining bolts.

45 When refitting the clutch housing lower cover plate the special taper bolts must be correctly located in the second hole down each side. These bolts are tightened first to ensure correct positioning of the cover plate.

46 Do not fully tighten the mounting and retaining bolts until the transmission unit is fully located, then tighten them to the special torque wrench setting.

47 When refitting the floor panels, loosely locate the retaining screws with flat washers. In some instances it may be necessary to realign the captive nuts on the underside. When all of the retaining screws and bolts are located they can be fully tightened.

48 Lubricate the handbrake linkages when reconnecting. Check that the handbrake warning switch leads are securely connected.

49 Check that the drain plugs are secured in position then top up the oil levels: referring to the Specifications in this Chapter for the lubricant types and quantity. Apply sealant to the filler/level plugs before securing them in position (photo).

50 Before refitting the aluminium top cover, refit the gear lever housing and check the bias spring adjustment, as described in Part H of this Section. Check the main gearbox and the high/low gear selection and, if necessary, adjust as described in Part H.

## Part C: Five-speed main gearbox and transfer gearbox – separation and reassembly

### Separation

1 Extract the split pin and withdraw the clevis pin from the transmission brake link-to-handbrake link rod clevis (photo).

2 Undo the four retaining bolts and remove the handbrake lever mounting bracket from the side of the transfer gearbox (photo).

3 Unscrew and remove the two countersunk screws securing the transmission brake drum in position (photo). Withdraw the brake drum, then undo the four bolts securing the brake unit/backplate assembly in position (photo). Withdraw the brake assembly, complete with the backplate.

4 Undo the mounting bolts and remove the right-hand mounting plate.

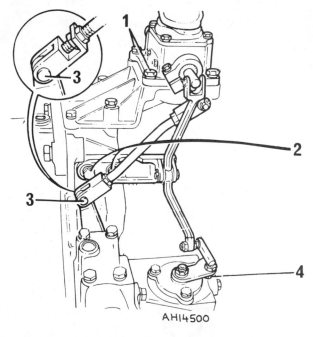

AH14500

Fig. 13.15 Gearchange housing and associated connections – early five-speed gearbox (Sec 6C)

1  Gearchange housing retaining bolts
2  Differential lock cross-shaft lever pivot bracket
3  High/low connecting rod-to-arm attachment
4  Differential lock lever assembly (early type)

6C.1 Handbrake link rod connection and mounting plate

6C.2 Handbrake lever mounting to the transfer gearbox

6C.3A Transmission brake drum retaining screws (arrowed)

6C.3B Undoing the transmission brake/backplate unit retaining bolts

6C.6 Tubular short cranked connecting link (as fitted to later models)

6C.7 Differential cross-shaft lever pivot bracket (A) and the high/low connecting rod to arm attachment (B) (later models)

5  On early models, detach the differential cross-shaft lever at the bottom end from the differential lock lever by undoing the self-locking nut and disconnecting the short connecting link (Fig. 13.15).
6  On later models a tubular short cranked connecting link is fitted and this can be detached by extracting the split pin and removing the flat washer (photo).
7  Unscrew the two differential cross-shaft lever pivot bracket retaining bolts (photo).
8  Extract the split pin and withdraw the clevis pin to detach the bottom end of the high/low operating arm link rod. Remove the plastic bushes.
9  Undo the four bolts retaining the gear lever housing then lift the housing clear.
10  Undo the four bolts and two nuts and remove the extension housing and main gearbox from the transfer gearbox (photo). It may be necessary to loosen the six bolts securing the high/low selector housing to allow the separation of the transfer gearbox from the extension housing.

### Reassembly
11  Reassembly of the transfer gearbox to the main gearbox assembly is a reversal of the removal procedure, but the following points should be noted.
12  The mating faces of the transfer gearbox and the extension housing should be cleaned of old sealant and new sealant applied (photo).
13  Engage a gear in the main gearbox then get an assistant to lift and align the transfer gearbox with it. Carefully guide the transfer gearbox

6C.10 Main gearbox and extension housing separation from the transfer gearbox

6C.12 Applying sealant to the extension housing mating face

into position against the main gearbox face, taking care not to damage the oil seal. Turn the mainshaft to align it with the input gear splines in the transfer gearbox. Refit and tighten the four bolts and two nuts retaining the two assemblies together. Tighten them to the specified torque wrench setting given at the start of this Chapter.
14  When reassembling the handbrake and differential lock lever and linkages, smear the pivots with grease and use new split pins.
15  Refit the high/low gearchange connecting rod, the differential lock switch and the main gear selector lever assembly; check their adjustments as described in Part H of this Section.

## Part D: Five-speed main gearbox – dismantling and inspection

### Special notes
Before deciding to dismantle the transmission, reference should be made to Section 4 of Chapter 6.

### Five-speed main gearbox – dismantling
1  Proceed as described in paragraphs 1 to 3 inclusive in Section 5 of Chapter 6 and remove the clutch release bearing assembly and the bellhousing.
2  Undo the three bolts and remove the gear selector housing from the 5th gear extension case. Remove the gasket and note that this must be renewed when reassembling.
3  Use a suitable pin punch and drive out the roll pin securing the selector yoke in position on the shaft (photo). Push the selector shaft forward and engage a gear (rotate the mainshaft if necessary). The selector yoke can now be withdrawn from the shaft, then the selector shaft returned to the neutral position.
4  Unclip and release the circlip securing the mainshaft oil seal collar on the rear of the gearbox, then use a suitable puller to withdraw the collar (photos).
5  Unscrew and remove the ten bolts (with spring washers) securing the extension housing (photo), then remove the housing and gasket. Renew the gasket during reassembly.
6  Fit two 8 x 35 mm slave bolts to the casing to secure the centre plate to the main case.
7  Remove the O-ring from the mainshaft and withdraw the oil pump driveshaft.
8  On later models a nut retains the 5th driven gear on the layshaft (photo) and it is advisable to loosen the nut at this stage. Engage the gears so that the shafts are locked, relieve the nut stake peening from the layshaft groove, then undo the nut so that it is loose on the shaft. Unlock the gears.
9  Remove the two bolts securing the 5th gear selector fork and bracket, then withdraw the 5th gear selector spool, fork and bracket (photo).
10  Remove the circlip retaining the 5th gear synchromesh unit to the mainshaft, withdraw the selective washer and then remove the synchromesh unit, together with 5th gear and spacer; withdrawing them from the mainshaft using a suitable puller.
11  Remove the split roller bearing from the mainshaft.
12  On early five-speed transmission models the 5th driven gear is retained on the layshaft by a collar and circlip. Remove the circlip and collar.
13  On later five-speed transmission models, unscrew and remove the layshaft 5th driven gear retaining nut (previously loosened in paragraph 8).
14  Remove the 5th driven gear from the layshaft using a suitable puller.
15  Release and remove the selector shaft circlip.
16  Undo the six retaining bolts and withdraw the front cover and gasket.
17  Withdraw the selective washers from the front end of the layshaft and mainshaft. Keep them in their housings in the front cover.
18  Undo and remove the two bolts with washers retaining the selector shaft front spool location boss. Withdraw the boss.
19  Undo the selector plug then extract the detent ball and spring from the centre plate.
20  Undo and remove the previously fitted slave bolts, then separate the gearcase from the centre plate and gear assemblies. Remove and renew the gasket.
21  Support the centre plate, then remove the circlip, pivot pin, reverse lever and the slipper pad (photo).

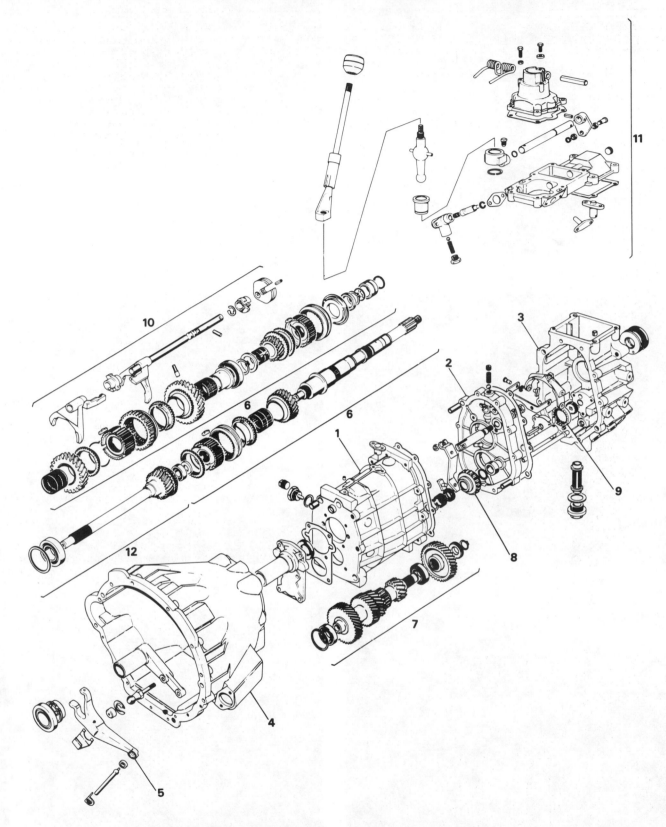

**Fig. 13.16 Exploded view of the five-speed main gearbox (Sec 6D)**

| | | | |
|---|---|---|---|
| 1 | Gearbox main casing | 5 | Clutch release arm |
| 2 | Centre plate | 6 | Mainshaft assembly |
| 3 | Extension case | 7 | Layshaft assembly |
| 4 | Bellhousing | | |

| | | | |
|---|---|---|---|
| 8 | Reverse idler gear assembly | 11 | Gearchange housing assembly |
| 9 | Oil pump | 12 | Input (primary) shaft |
| 10 | Gear selector assembly | | |

6D.3 Removing the selector yoke roll pin

6D.4A Remove the circlip and ...

6D.4B ... withdraw the collar from the rear of the mainshaft

6D.5 Undo the retaining bolts and remove the extension housing

6D.8 Fifth driven gear retaining nut on the layshaft (later models)

*Note the 8 x 35 mm centre plate to main case retaining bolt (arrowed)*

6D.9 Remove the fifth gear selector fork, spool and bracket

Fig. 13.17 Removing the main gearcasing (Sec 6D)

6D.25A Align the 5th gear selector pin with the centre plate slot ...

6D.25B ... and withdraw the mainshaft and selector shaft

6D.21 Reverse lever (A), slipper pad (B), pivot pin (C) and circlip (D)

6D.27 Remove the centre bearing circlip

22 Slide the reverse shaft to the rear and remove the thrust wahser, reverse gear and gear spacer.
23 Remove the layshaft cluster.
24 Remove the input (primary) shaft, and 4th gear synchromesh cone from the front end of the mainshaft by lifting clear.

6D.28 1st gear and bearing assembly removal using a puller

6D.32 Input shaft pilot bearing track removal using an extractor tool

6D.35 Oil trough location in the main gearbox

6D.36 Oil pump housing and retaining bolts – extension case

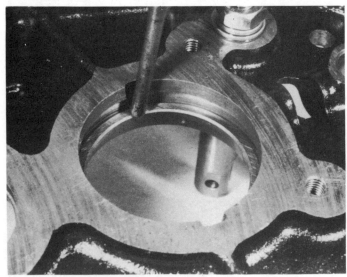

6D.39 Bearing track removal from the centre plate

6D.40 Selector housing showing the 5th gear spool retainer (A), selector yoke (B), roll pin (C) and yoke rollers (D)

25 Align the 5th gear selector retaining pin with the slot in the centre plate by turning the selector shaft clockwise (viewed from the top) (photo). The mainshaft, complete with the selector fork assemblies, can then be withdrawn from the centre plate (photo).

26 Withdraw the selector fork assembly from the mainshaft gear cluster unit.

## Mainshaft

27 Release and remove the circlip securing the centre bearing on the mainshaft (photo).

28 Using a suitable puller, withdraw the 1st gear, together with its bush, needle bearing and synchromesh cone (photo).

29 Remove the 1st/2nd gear synchromesh hub unit, 2nd gear and its needle bearing. Again, use a suitable puller or support the underside of 2nd gear and press or drift the shaft through the 1st/2nd gear assembly.

30 From the front end of the mainshaft, remove the pilot bearing spacer, 3rd/4th gear synchromesh hub, cone (3rd) and 3rd gear with its needle roller bearing using a suitable puller or, if possible, Rover press tool MS47 and extension located on the rear face of 3rd gear.

## Input shaft

31 To dismantle the input shaft, use a suitable puller and withdraw the bearing from the front of the shaft.

32 The pilot bearing track can be removed using a suitable extractor tool (photo).

## Layshaft bearings

33 The bearing cones can be removed using a suitable puller.

## Main gearbox casing

34 Using a suitable drift, drive the mainshaft and layshaft bearing tracks from their housings whilst supporting the casing underneath on wooden blocks to prevent damaging the casing face.

35 Withdraw the plastic oil trough from the casing end face (photo).

## Extension casing and oil pump

36 Unscrew the three oil pump housing retaining bolts and withdraw the housing and gears (photo). Pull free the oil pick-up pipe.

37 Unscrew the plug and withdraw the oil filter.

38 Prise free the oil seal (noting direction of fitting), then press or drift out the ferrobestos bush from the extension case.

## Centre plate

39 Unless the bearing tracks (cones) or the centre plate are being renewed the bearing tracks are best left in position. To remove the tracks, support the centre plate on blocks of wood and carefully drive out the bearing tracks using a suitable drift (photo).

## Selector housing

40 Unbolt and remove the 5th gear spool retainer (photo).

41 Unscrew and remove the large blanking plug and the reverse switch or small blanking plug from the rear of the housing.

42 Support the housing and, using a suitable pin punch, drive out the roll pin securing the selector yoke. Slide the yoke rearwards from the shaft, moving the shaft forwards to allow the yoke to be detached from it.

43 Release the circlip and remove the selector yoke rollers and pin.

44 Withdraw the selector shaft through the large blanking plug hole and then remove the O-ring from the shaft. Renew the O-ring on reassembly.

45 To dismantle the reverse gear plunger unit, unscrew the retaining plug and withdraw the spring and detent ball. Unbolt and remove the plunger unit from the housing, together with the adjustment shims. Release the circlip and remove the plunger and short spring.

## Inspection of components

46 Refer to Section 6 in Chapter 6 and renew any damaged, suspect or excessively worn components.

47 The synchromesh gear hub-to-cone clearances should be checked using a feeler gauge (photo). Push the cone towards the hub when

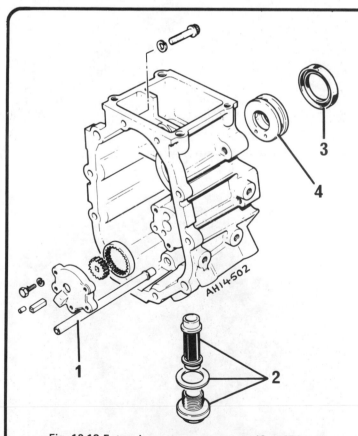

**Fig. 13.18 Extension case components (Sec 6D)**

1   *Oil pump and oil pick-up tube*     3   *Oil seal*
2   *Drain plug and filter*              4   *Ferrobestos bush*

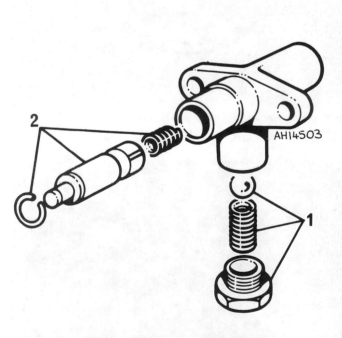

**Fig. 13.19 Reverse gear plunger unit (Sec 6D)**

1   *Detent plunger assembly (long spring)*
2   *Reverse gear plunger assembly (short spring)*

6D.47 Synchromesh hub-to-cone clearance check

6D.48 Synchromesh unit

6D.50 Check the oil pump for excessive wear

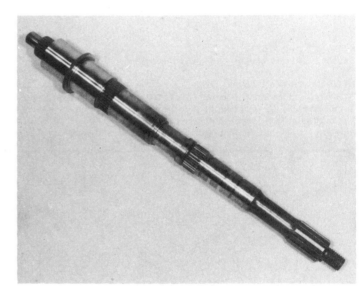

6E.1A Mainshaft ready for reassembly

6E.1B Fit the 2nd gear needle bearing ...

6E.1C ... 2nd gear ...

checking. If the clearance measured is under the specified minimum clearance allowed, renew the cone.
48  If dismantling the synchromesh unit (photo), note the positions of the slipper retaining rings then extract the rings and remove the slippers and hub from the sleeve. Keep the components of each unit together and lay them out in order and orientation of fitting to avoid possible confusion on reassembly. The backing plate on the fifth gear synchromesh unit can be levered free. Note that the slipper slots in the second gear synchromesh cone are larger than the slots in the other cones.
49  During reassembly of the mainshaft you will need to assess the 1st gear bush requirement to set the 1st gear endfloat. To do this make up or have a spacer made to the dimensions shown in Fig. 13.20. It may be possible to borrow the spacer from your local dealer. The spacer represents the bearing during the initial assessment when selecting the 1st gear bush.
50  Check the oil pump unit for excessive wear or damage (photo).

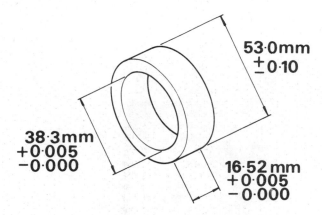

Fig. 13.20 Spacer required to assess 1st gear endfloat (Sec 6D)

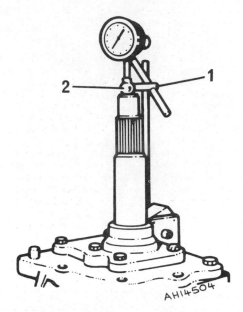

Fig. 13.21 Mainshaft endfloat check method showing dial gauge mounting (1) and ball-bearing location (2) (Sec 6E)

## Part E: Five-speed main gearbox – reassembly

### Mainshaft

1  Locate the 2nd gear needle bearing onto the mainshaft and lubricate the bearing with a light oil. Fit the 2nd gear and the synchromesh cone (with larger slipper slots) (photos).
2  Locate the 1st/2nd synchromesh hub unit onto the shaft (photos). The selector fork ring groove must face to the rear.
3  Fit the original 1st gear bush and the slave bearing spacer (see paragraph 53 in the previous sub-section). Secure them in position with a new circlip, but do not distort the clip when fitting it. Using feeler gauges, measure the clearance between the 1st gear bush rear face and the slave bearing front face. Push the slave bearing back against the circlip when measuring. The clearance requirement is 0.0002 to 0.0020 in (0.005 to 0.051 mm). If necessary select an alternative bush to obtain this clearance, the bush sizes available being given in the Specifications at the start of this Chapter. When fitted, the selected bush must rotate freely as well as giving the specified endfloat clearance.
4  Having selected the 1st gear bush, remove the circlip, slave bearing spacer and bush.
5  Lubricate the needle bearing and fit it to the 1st gear, together with the selected bush. Locate the assembled 1st gear unit onto the mainshaft (photo).
6  Support the mainshaft then, using a suitable tube drift which will bear on the bearing inner track, drive the centre bearing into position on the mainshaft and secure in position with the new circlip (photos).
7  Lubricate the 3rd gear needle roller bearing and locate it in position (photo).
8  Locate the 3rd gear and its synchromesh cone, followed by the 3rd/4th synchromesh unit (photos).
9  Fit the spacer and bearing onto the front end of the mainshaft to complete its assembly (photo).

### Input shaft

10  If being renewed, drive the new pilot bearing track into position in the input shaft using a suitable tube drift.
11  Drive the new input bearing into position using a suitable diameter tube drift (photo).

### Reverse gear

12  Locate a new circlip into position at the rear of the reverse idler gear (on the reverse gear shaft). Do not distort the circlip when fitting.
13  Lubricate the needle roller bearings with light oil and fit them into position with the short bearing to the rear (photo).
14  Fit the reverse gear and then the front end circlip.

### Extension case

15  Drift or press the new ferrobestos bush into position in the case using a suitable tube drift, positioning the drain holes at the bottom (photo).
16  Drive the new oil seal into position using a suitable tube drift. The oil seal lips must face towards the ferrobestos bush. The seal lips should be lubricated with an SAE 140 oil (photo).
17  Assemble the oil pump gears to the cover. The centre rotor square

6E.1D ... and its synchromesh cone (large slipper slots)

6E.2A Fit the 1st/2nd synchromesh hub ...

6E.2B ... and cone (1st gear)

6E.5 Fit the 1st gear, bearing and selected bush

6E.6A Locate the centre bearing cone ...

6E.6B ... drive it into position ...

6E.6C ... flush to the bush flange ...

6E.6D ... and secure with a circlip

6E.7 Locate the 3rd gear needle roller bearing

6E.8A Fit the 3rd gear ...

6E.8B ... and synchromesh cone ...

6E.8C ... then the synchromesh unit

6E.9A Locate the spacer ...

6E.9B ... then fit the bearing cone

6E.11 Input shaft with bearing cone fitted

6E.13 Reverse idler gear showing bearings and circlip

6E.15 Fit the Ferrobestos bush with the drain holes at the bottom

6E.16 Oil seal location in the extension case

6E.20 Fit the bearing tracks into the centre plate

drive must face towards the layshaft. Relocate the oil pump unit, fit the three retaining bolts and tighten them to the specified torque setting.

18 Check that the oil pick-up pipe is not blocked, then refit it to the extension case sealing it with Loctite 290.

19 Locate the new oil filter into its aperture in the extension case then refit the retaining plug (fitted with a new fibre washer) and tighten the plug to the specified torque.

### Centre plate and gear assemblies

20 Fit the new layshaft and mainshaft bearing tracks into position in the centre plate (photo).

21 Lubricate the selector shaft with a little light oil then align and engage the 1st/2nd and 3rd/4th selector forks with their corresponding synchromesh sleeve grooves on the mainshaft (photo). Engage the selector forks with the synchromesh hubs then refit the mainshaft, together with the selector shaft, into position in the centre plate. As they are assembled, rotate the 5th gear selector pin into alignment with the centre plate slot.

22 Refit the layshaft to the centre plate (photo).

23 Align the reverse crossover lever forks with the reverse pivot shaft by twisting the selector shaft and spool. Relocate the selection shaft to reposition the lever within the reverse gear pivot shaft fork. Fit the pivot pin and locate a new E clip to secure. Take care when fitting the E clip not to distort it (photos).

24 Refit the slipper pad to the reverse lever. Where a new reverse lever shaft is fitted, note that it will be necessary to ensure that its radial position is consistent with the reverse pad slippr engagement/clearance during initial reassembly (photo).

25 Locate the reverse gear spacer and gear unit, engaging the slipper pad with the reverse gear groove (photo). Fit the reverse gear shaft from the centre plate underside with the roll pin aligned with the casing slot.

26 Lubricate the detent ball and spring with light oil then insert them into the bore in the top of the centre plate. Smear the plug threads with a suitable sealant (Loctite 290 or similar) then fit the plug and screw it in until it is flush with the casing. Stake punch the plug and case to secure the plug in position (photos).

27 Locate the reverse gear spacer washer onto the reverse gear shaft (photo).

28 Position the 4th gear synchromesh cone into position on the 3rd/4th synchro-hub.

29 Assemble the input (primary) shaft to the mainshaft (photo).

30 Locate the new gasket into position on the centre plate.

31 Fit the new plastic trough into position on the rear face of the main gearbox with the trough opening towards the top.

32 Lubricate the gear assemblies with light oil, check that the gasket is correctly positioned on the centre plate then carefully refit the main gearcase over the gear assemblies (photo). As the case is being fitted ensure that the centre plate dowels and the selector shaft correctly engage with it, but do not use excessive force when fitting the case.

33 Refit the layshaft and input shaft bearing outer tracks (photo). The gearcase and centre plate can now be fully drawn together using the two 8 x 35 mm bolts used during dismantling. Tighten the bolts in stages to draw the two assemblies together in an even manner.

34 On early models, press or drive the fifth gear and collar into position on the rear end of the layshaft and secure with a new circlip.

35 On later models where the layshaft 5th gear is retained by a nut only (no collar), fit the gear onto the rear end of the layshaft and loosely fit the nut (photo).

36 Refit the locating shaft front spool to the top of the gearcase. Seal the area between the spool and casing with sealant.

37 Smear the bolt threads with sealant then refit the bolts with spring washers and tighten them to the specified torque setting (photo).

### Mainshaft endfloat assessment

38 To check the mainshaft endfloat a dial gauge will be required, also some masking tape.

39 Wind the masking tape ten full turns around the plain section of the input shaft elbow (below the splines). By fitting the tape in this manner any side movement of the shaft will be taken up so that an accurate endfloat check can be made. Locate the new front cover gasket and cover, then fit the six retaining bolts with spring washers. Tighten the bolts to a torque wrench setting of 16 lbf ft (2.2 kgf m) then check that the rise and fall of the input shaft is not restricted by the masking tape.

40 Position a ball-bearing into the end of the input shaft to provide an accurate datum point when checking the endfloat.

41 Position the dial gauge on the end face of the gearbox housing and

rest the gauge stylus on the centre of the ball-bearing. Zero the gauge, then push and pull the input shaft to measure the endfloat and check it against the specified requirement. The difference equals the spacer thickness required.

42 Spacers are available in thickness ranging from 0.058 in (1.48 mm) in increments of 0.00118 in (0.03 mm) to a maximum thickness of 0.0110 in (2.80 mm).

43 Select and fit the spacer thickness required to meet the specified endfloat requirement. With the selected spacer fitted, recheck the endfloat and if satisfactory remove the dial gauge and the ball-bearing. Unbolt the front cover and remove the tape from the input shaft.

### Layshaft endfloat assessment

44 Obtain and fit a nominal thickness spacer measuring 0.040 in (1.02 mm) in thickness. Locate the front cover and tighten the retaining bolts with spring washers to a torque seting of 16 lbf ft (2.2 kgf m).

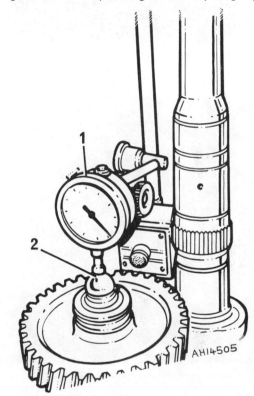

**Fig. 13.22 Layshaft endfloat check method showing dial gauge mounting (1) and ball-bearing location (2) (Sec 6E)**

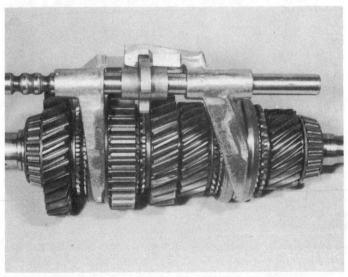

6E.21 Engage the selector shaft with the mainshaft assembly

6E.22 Layshaft and mainshaft assemblies fitted to the centre plate

6E.23A Locate the reverse crossover lever ...

6E.23B ... and secure the pin with E clip (arrowed)

6E.24 Locate the reverse gear slipper pad to the crossover lever and the gear spacer onto the centre plate. Note offset position of the slot in the slipper pad

6E.25 Refit the reverse gear shaft and gear. Note engagement of gear with slipper pad.

6E.26A Insert the detent ball, spring and plug ...

6E.26B ... stake the plug to secure it

6E.27 Fit the reverse gear spacer washer

6E.29 Fit the input shaft onto the mainshaft

6E.32 Refit the gearcase

6E.33 Fit the layshaft and input shaft bearing tracks

6E.35 Fifth driven gear on the layshaft – later models

6E.37 Refit the locating shaft front spool

6E.50 Locate the front cover gasket

6E.51 Locate the mainshaft and layshaft endfloat shims and fit the front cover

6E.52A Fit the spacer ...

6E.52B ... and roller bearing onto the mainshaft ...

6E.53A ... followed by 5th gear ...

45 Position a ball-bearing into the end of the layshaft to provide an accurate datum point when checking the endfloat.
46 Position the dial gauge on the end face of the gearbox housing and rest the gauge stylus on the centre of the ball-bearing. Zero the gauge then push and pull the layshaft to measure the amount of endfloat. Compare the endfloat reading with requirement specified then add the difference to the nominal spacer thickness to assess the spacer thickness required.
47 Layshaft endfloat spacers are available in thicknesses ranging from 0.063 in (1.60 mm) in increments of 0.00118 in (0.03 mm) to a maximum thickness of 0.103 in (2.62 mm).
48 Remove the dial gauge, ballbearing and front cover and fit the selected spacer of the appropriate thickness.
49 Support the front cover and carefully drive the new oil seal into position in it, with the lips of the seal facing towards the gearbox. Smear the lips of the oil seal with SAE 140 gear oil.
50 Smear the cover gasket with a little light grease then locate it in position (photo). Wind some insulation tape around the splines of the input shaft to protect the oil seal lips when fitting the front cover.
51 Check that the respective endfloat spacer shims are in position (photo) then refit the front cover into position. Smear the bolt threads with Loctite 290 sealant (or equivalent) then fit the bolts with spring washers and tighten them evenly to the specified torque wrench setting. Remove the insulation tape from the shaft.

### Fifth gear, selector fork and extension case

52 Fit the spacer and the 5th gear needle roller bearing onto the mainshaft and lubricate them with light oil (photos).
53 Locate 5th gear and its synchromesh cone (photo).
54 Use a suitable tube drift and carefully drive the 5th gear synchromesh unit into position on the mainshaft just enough to allow fitment of the selective spacer and the circlip.
55 Locate the selective spacer and the new circlip onto the mainshaft (photo).
56 Measure the clearance between the 5th gear and the front spacer using feeler gauges (photo). The correct clearance requirement is 0.0002 to 0.0020 in (0.005 to 0.051 mm). If necessary, remove the circlip and change the selective spacer washer for one which will provide the correct clearance. If a thicker washer is to be fitted carefully drive the 5th gear unit further onto the mainshaft to just allow fitment of the new selective washer and circlip. If a thinner spacer is to be fitted, draw the 5th gear unit back along the shaft to butt against the spacer and circlip. Spacers are available in thickness ranging from 0.2114 in (5.37 mm) in increments of 0.00118 in (0.03 mm) to a maximum thickness of 0.2125 in (5.40 mm).
57 Select two gears to lock the shafts, then tighten the layshaft 3rd driven gear retaining nut to the specified torque setting (late models). Stake punch the nut into the shaft groove to secure (photos). Disengage the gears.
58 Fit 5th gear selector fork and bracket, engaging with the synchrohub so that the large groove is to the rear (photo).
59 Locate the 5th gear spool onto the selector shaft then turn and locate the selector fork into its groove. The spool must be fitted with the long shoulder towards the front.
60 Fit the selector fork bracket bolts and tighten them to the specified torque.
61 Check that the circlip is in its groove on the spool shaft.
62 Unscrew the centre plate-to-main case slave bolts. Smear the centre plate-to-extension case mating face with a liberal amount of light grease, then locate the gasket into position on the centre plate.
63 Locate the oil pump driveshaft into the end of the layshaft (photo). Align the shaft with the oil pump so that when the extension case is fitted, the shaft will engage with the pump (photo).
64 Fit a new O-ring into its groove on the mainshaft (photo) and lubricate it with grease.
65 Carefully refit the extension case (photo) and check the oil pump driveshaft engagement as it is fitted. Fit and tighten the retaining bolts to the specified torque.
66 Move the selector shaft forwards to select a gear. Rotate the mainshaft if necessary to allow gear engagement then refit the gear selector yoke onto the rear end of the shaft and align the roll pin holes. Drive a new roll pin into position to secure the yoke (photo).
67 Pull the selector shaft rearwards to the neutral position.
68 Fit the oil seal collar onto the mainshaft so that it is positioned just clear of the circlip groove. Fit the retaining circlip and ensure that it is fully located in the groove in the mainshaft.

69 If it is assembled and ready for fitting, the remote control selector housing unit can now be fitted to the main gearbox using a new gasket and the three retaining bolts. If the remote control selector housing is still to be checked and assembled refer to paragraphs 73 to 81 inclusive.

### Final assembly

70 Refit the bellhousing, engaging it onto the dowels. When fitting the retaining bolts, the two long bolts are fitted together with spring washers and flat washers to the dowel locations. The other four bolts have spring washers only. Tighten the bolts to the specified torque setting.
71 Refit the clutch release bearing assembly, referring to Chapter 5.
72 Refit the oil drain plug with the filter (and use a new seal washer) to the main gearbox. The filler/level plug can be loosely fitted at the moment and fully tightened later, after the gearbox oil level has been topped up.

### Selector housing

73 Reassemble the reverse gear plunger unit by reversing the dismantling procedure. The short spring and plunger should be lubricated with grease when fitting and a new circlip used to secure them. Lubricate the detent ball with oil and insert it, followed by the spring. Take care not to get oil onto the plug threads when fitting them. Smear the plug threads with a locking sealant (Loctite 290) and tighten the plug to the specified torque setting. Refit the plunger unit, together with the adjuster shims.
74 Smear the selector shaft with oil before fitting the O-ring onto it.
75 Fit the gear selector rollers and pin and fit a new circlip to secure.
76 Slide the selector shaft into the selector housing through the large blanking plug orifice. The indent in the shaft must face the top when fitted.
77 Support the selector housing in a vice fitted with protective jaws, then refit the selector yoke onto the shaft-aligning the roll pin hole. Drive a new roll pin into position to secure the yoke.
78 Smear the threads of the reverse switch and the large blanking plug with a locking sealant then fit them and tighten to the specified torque.
79 Fit the new nylon insert into the transmission housing and secure it with a new circlip.
80 Fit the trunnion housing to the selector shaft ensuring that the locating bolt bore aligns with the indent in the shaft. Smear the bolt thread with locking sealant then fit the bolt and tighten it to the specified torque.
81 Locate the new gasket into position on the extension case then refit the selector housing and secure it with the three bolts and washers (photo).
82 The high/low gearchange housing unit can now be refitted to the selector housing. Use a new gasket and bolt the housing into position. When reconnecting the high/low connecting rod, check its adjustment, as described in Part H.
83 The gearbox is now ready for reconnecting to the transfer gearbox.
84 Refitting of the upper gear lever housing is best left until after the gearbox unit is refitted to the vehicle.

6E.53B ... and its synchromesh cone

6E55 Fit the spacer and circlip

6E.56 Check the 5th gear-to-spacer clearance

6E.57A Tighten the 5th driven gear retaining nut (later models) ...

6E.57B ... then stake punch the shoulder into the shaft groove

6E.58 Fit the 5th gear selector fork and bracket

6E.63A Locate the gasket and oil pump driveshaft (arrowed)

6E.63B Align the driveshaft to suit the pump

6E.64 O-ring position on the mainshaft (arrowed)

6E.65 Refit the extension case

6E.66A Move the selector shaft forwards ...

6E.66B ... and refit the selector yoke

6E.81 Refit the remote control gearchange housing to the extension case

## Part F: Transfer gearbox (five-speed transmission) – dismantling and overhaul

### Dismantling

1 Undo the securing bolts and remove the bottom cover from the transfer gearbox (photo).

2 A preliminary inspection can now be made of the transfer gears. If it is apparent that the gears are excessively worn or are damaged, consideration should be made whether to change the transfer gearbox complete for an exchange unit. The cost of renewing the individual gear assemblies and associated components could well exceed the cost of an exchange unit. Check this with your Range Rover dealer before dismantling.

3 Undo the intermediate shaft lockplate bolt on the rear face of the transfer gearbox and withdraw the lockplate. Use a soft drift to tap the intermediate shaft out rearwards. As the shaft is withdrawn, lift out the intermediate gear cluster and remove the thrust washer at the front and rear within the casing.

4 Extract the O-ring seal from the intermediate shaft bore.

5 Undo the six retaining bolts and remove the power take-off cover with its gasket from the rear face of the transfer gearbox.

6 Undo the two countersunk retaining screws and remove the mainshaft bearing housing and gasket. Remove the input gear unit.

7 Undo the six bolts and remove the high/low selector housing and gasket.

8 Loosen the high/low selector shaft yoke bolt then slide the shaft rearwards and remove the yoke (photo).

9 Undo the eight retaining bolts and remove the front output shaft housing. Note that the top bolt is longer than the other seven. Do not remove the radial dowel from the transfer gearbox face unless necessary (photo), see paragraph 14.

10 Unscrew the high/low selector shaft detent plug and extract the spring and ball. If preferred, the ball can be removed when the selector shaft is removed.

11 Withdraw the centre differential unit, together with the selector shaft and fork.

12 Undo the six screws securing the rear output shaft housing and remove the housing and gasket. Note that the upper screw is longer than the other five.

13 The transfer gearbox is now dismantled into its various sub-assemblies and can be cleaned, inspected and dismantled further, as required.

14 If the centre differential rear bearing track is to be removed from the transfer gearbox, support the gearbox on its front face on wooden blocks to avoid damaging the two protruding studs and the radial dowel. Alternatively, unscrew the studs and dowel to remove them, but note the exact orientation of the dowel as it is essential that it is refitted in its exact original position. The bearing track can be removed by drifting it from its housing using a suitable soft drift.

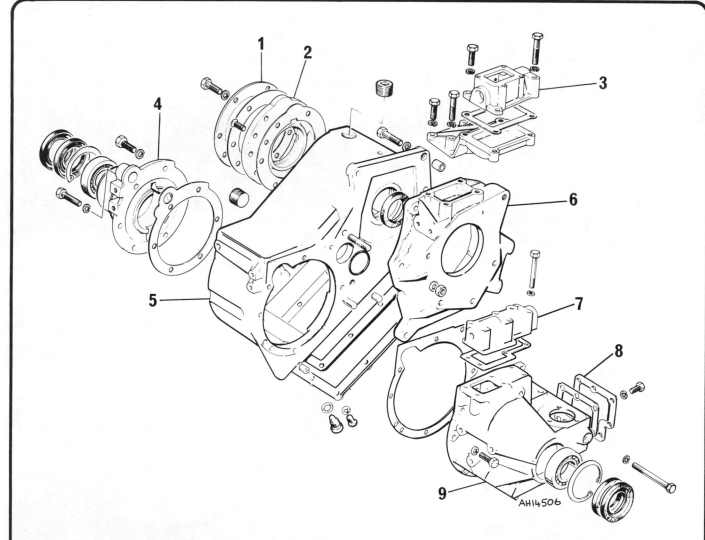

**Fig. 13.23 Exploded view of the transfer gearbox assemblies (Sec 6F)**

| | | |
|---|---|---|
| 1   Power take-off cover | 3   Transfer gearchange housing | 5   Transfer gearbox |
| 2   Rear bearing housing (mainshaft) | 4   Rear output shaft/ speedometer drive housing | 6   Extension housing |
| | | 7   High/low selector housing |
| 8   Differential lock selector side cover | | |
| 9   Front output shaft housing | | |

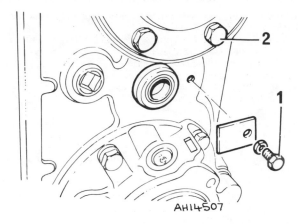

Fig. 13.24 Remove the intermediate shaft lockplate (1) and the power take-off cover (2) (Sec 6F)

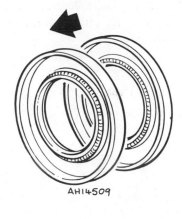

Fig. 13.26 Orientation of output shaft housing oil seals. The seals must be driven into position in direction of arrow (from the rear) (Sec 6F)

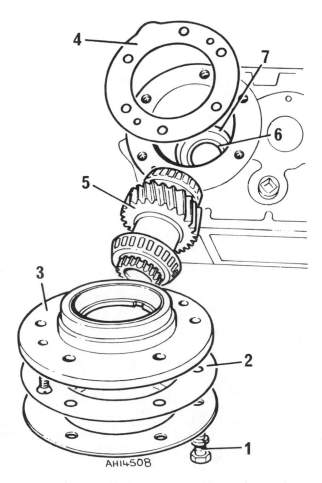

Fig. 13.25 Bearing housing and input shaft assembly (Sec 6F)

1  Power take-off cover/bolts
2  Gasket
3  Mainshaft bearing housing
4  Gasket
5  Input gear unit
6  Oil seal
7  Bearing track (front)

6F.1 Transfer gearbox bottom cover

6F.8 Loosen the high/low selector shaft yoke location bolt (or Allen screw)

6F.9 Do not remove the radial dowel (arrowed) unless absolutely necessary

6F.27 Differential lock selector side cover and retaining bolts

6F.25A Centre differential unit – showing front bearing cone

6F.25B Centre differential unit – showing rear bearing cone

### Rear output shaft housing – dismantling and overhaul

15 Support the output shaft housing then locate a suitable bar diagonally across two output flange bolts to prevent it from turning and undo the central flange nut. Remove the nut together with the steel and felt washers. Withdraw the output flange.
16 Prise free the speedometer spindle housing using a suitable screwdriver.
17 Using a suitable drift, drive the rear output shaft forwards through the housing to remove it.
18 Prise free the two oil seals (early models) or single dual-lipped seal (later models) from the housing.
19 If required, the oil catcher can be removed by prising free with a screwdriver inserted in the slot.
20 To remove the bearing, remove the circlip then drive the bearing out of its aperture from the rear of the housing.
21 Withdraw the speedometer driven gear and spindle then prise out the O-ring and oil seal.
22 The spacer and speedometer drive gear can be withdrawn along the output shaft.
23 Inspect and renew any parts which are excessively worn or damaged. Always renew the oil seal(s) and the O-ring.
24 Reassembly of the rear output shaft housing is a reversal of the dismantling procedure, but note the following special points:

(a) Ensure that the oil seal(s) are fitted with the lips facing inwards
(b) Lubricate the lips of the oil seal(s) with grease before refitting the output shaft
(c) Fit a new Nyloc nut to secure the output flange and tighten it to the specified torque wrench setting
(d) The centre differential rear bearing track must be in position in the transfer case before refitting the output shaft housing. This bearing track is set for position during assembly and should not be moved unless renewing it. Where a new bearing track is fitted, check that it is initially positioned 0.118 (3 mm) beneath the outer face of the casing. The bearing track will then be pressed fully into position when the rear output housing is tightened into position.

### Centre differential unit – dismantling and overhaul

25 The dismantling, overhaul and reassembly of the transmission differential unit is a specialised operation and is therefore not recommended as a DIY task. If the differential is known to be faulty, or is suspected of malfunction, have it checked and if possible repaired by your Range Rover dealer, or renew the unit complete (photos).
26 If renewing the rear taper roller bearing, the bearing track can be removed from the transfer gearbox, as described in Paragraph 14.

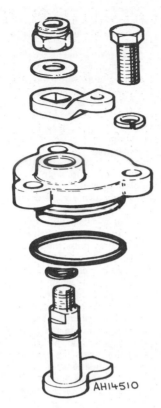

Fig. 13.27 Differential lock finger housing assembly
(Sec 6F)

*Front output shaft housing – dismantling and overhaul*

27 Undo the seven bolts securing the differential lock selector side cover then pull free the cover and remove it, together with its gasket (photo).

28 Undo the three bolts securing the differential lock finger housing and withdraw the housing. Remove the O-ring.

29 Loosen the locknut then unscrew and remove the differential lock switch.

30 Unscrew and remove the detent plug from the housing at the top then withdraw the spring and ball. Compress the selector fork spring and extract the spring location cap at each end (photo). The selector shaft

6F.30 Compress the spring to remove the location cap at each end

can then be withdrawn from the housing at the rear end, and the selector fork and spring removed through the aperture in the side.

31 Remove the dog sleeve from the rear of the output shaft housing.

32 Support the output shaft housing then locate a suitable bar diagonally across two flange bolts to prevent it from turning and undo the central flange retaining nut. Remove the nut with the steel and felt washers. Withdraw the output flange and oil seal shield.

33 Drive the output shaft at the front end using a suitable soft drift and withdraw the shaft rearwards from the housing. Remove the collar from the shaft.

34 Support the housing and prise free the two oil seals from it; noting their orientation. Later models are fitted with a dual lip seal.

35 To remove the output shaft bearing, release the circlip then drift the bearing out of its housing from the inside.

36 If the differential bearing front track is to be removed, use the same method, but collect the preload shim.

37 Clean and inspect the various components and renew any which are worn excessively or are damaged.

38 If new differential unit bearings, differential unit or output shaft bearings are being fitted then the bearing preload will have to be assessed and if necessary an alternative selective adjustment shim be fitted behind the differential front bearing track. In this instance proceed as described below in paragraphs 39 to 42 inclusive or have the assessment made by your Range Rover dealer before reassembly.

39 To check the bearing preload shim requirement you will need a dial gauge, Rover bracket RO 530106 and a mounting bracket to locate the gauge on the housing as shown in Fig. 13.28. Also required will be a 'trial' shim of slightly thinner thickness to that originally fitted.

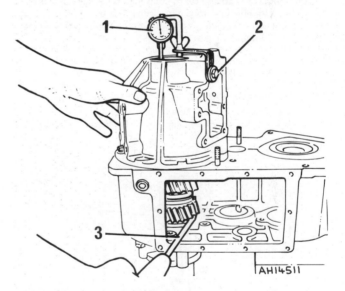

Fig. 13.28 Centre differential bearing preload assessment
(Sec 6F)

| | |
|---|---|
| 1  Dial gauge | 3  Leverage point |
| 2  Mounting bracket | |

40 Locate the trial shim into position in the bearing housing then carefully drive the new bearing track into position so that it is in contact with the shim.

41 Locate the rear output shaft housing and the differential unit into position in the transfer housing. Lubricate the output shaft housing gasket with grease before fitting and tighten the retaining bolts to the specified torque setting.

42 Lubricate the front output shaft housing gasket with grease and fit it together with the housing to the transfer gearbox; securing with four (of the seven) retaining bolts tightened to the specified torque.

43 Mount the dial gauge unit onto the housing and zero the stylus on the end of the output shaft. Insert a screwdriver between the gear assembly and the transfer case inner wall and lever the gear assembly upwards to assess the endfloat. Check the endfloat reading, compare this with the 'trial' shim thickness and select a shim to provide the specified preload endfloat requirement of 0.001 to 0.003 in (0.02 to 0.07 mm).

44 Remove the dial gauge, rear output shaft housing and differential/
gear assembly from the transfer gearbox. Remove the four retaining bolts
and withdraw the front output shaft housing. Drift out the bearing track
from the housing and extract the 'trial' shim. Locate the selected shim of
the correct thickness into the front output shaft housing, then support
the housing and drive the bearing track into position against the shim.
45 Complete the reassembly of the front output shaft housing by
suitably supporting it and drifting the new front bearing into its aperture
in the bearing and secure by installing the retaining circlip.
46 Fit the two oil seals (early models) or single double lip oil seal into
position with the seal lips facing inwards. Smear the seal lips with
grease.
47 Slide the collar (with its chamferred edge forwards) into position on
the output shaft then insert the shaft into the housing from the rear.
48 Locate the flange/oil seal shield onto the shaft followed by the felt
washer, plain washer and a new self-locking (Nyloc) nut. Support the
housing and tighten the nut to the specified torque; reversing the
removal procedure.
49 Locate the dog sleeve onto the rear end of the output shaft (with the
sleeve groove facing the front).
50 Compress the spring and fit it into position between the selector fork
legs, then fit the selector fork into position in the housing (through the
side cover aperture) and engage the groove with the output shaft dog
sleeve.
51 Slide the differential lock selector shaft into the housing from the
rear. The detent groove end of the shaft must be at the rear. Guide the
shaft through the selector fork lugs and coil spring and into the housing
at the front.
52 Twist the selector shaft so that the two flats are at the top, compress
the coil spring and refit the two C caps, one at each end of the spring.
53 Insert the detent ball, spring and plug. Smear the plug threads with
Loctite Driloc 290 before fitting.
54 To complete the reassembly of the front output shaft housing, screw
the differential lock switch into position, but do not fully tighten it yet as
its position has to be adjusted.

*Input gear – overhaul and bearing preload adjustment*

55 The front and rear taper roller bearing cones can be removed from the
input gear unit using a suitable puller, but take care not to damage the
gears.

56 To fit the new bearing cones, support the input gear unit and carefully
drive or press the bearings into position using a tube of suitable
diameter and thickness to bear against the end face of the bearing inner
track only (not on the cage).
57 The taper bearing cups (tracks) must also be renewed and these can
be removed by drifting them from their housings.
58 On removing the bearing cup from the mainshaft rear bearing
housing, retrieve the selective shim fitted at the rear of the bearing. This
shim was fitted to provide the correct input gear endfloat adjustment.
When the bearings and, if applicable, the input gear are being renewed,
the bearing preload adjustment will have to be re-assessed and if
necessary, adjusted by fitting an alternative shim of the appropriate
thickness behind the rear bearing.
59 Check that the bearing housings are clean then drive the new front
bearing cap fully into position in its housing.
60 Lubricate the bearing cones on the input gear and then fit the input
gear into position in the transfer gearbox; ensuring that the larger gear is
to the front.
61 Measure the thickness of the selective shim originally fitted, then
obtain a 'trial' shim that is slightly thinner than the original and locate it
into the bearing housing. Drift or press the new rear bearing cup fully
into the rear main bearing housing.
62 Smear the new gasket with grease and locate it onto the bearing
housing. Fit the bearing housing into position, locate the two securing
screws and tighten them to the specified torque.
63 Mount a dial gauge into position on the outer face of the rear main
bearing housing and rest the gauge stylus (pointer) on the end of the
input gear. Zero the gauge then, lifting the gear by hand through the
bottom cover aperture, measure the amount of endfloat present.
Compare the endfloat reading with the input gear bearing preload
adjustment given in the Specifications at the start of this Chapter.
Calculate the selective shim thickness required which, when fitted in
place of the 'trial' shim, will provide the specified bearing preload
adjustment.
64 Remove the dial gauge and the mainshaft bearing housing.
65 Drive the bearing cup out of the mainshaft bearing housing and
remove the 'trial' shim.
66 Insert the selected shim into the housing, then drive the bearing cup
fully into position in the housing against the shim.
67 Remove the input gear unit from the transfer gearbox.

*Intermediate gear unit – dismantling and overhaul*

68 Extract the first needle roller bearing unit, the central spacer and the
second needle roller bearing unit from the gear cluster bore (photo).

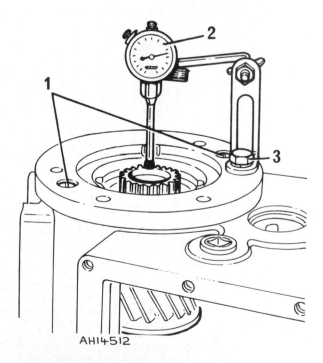

**Fig. 13.29 Input gear unit endfloat check method (Sec 6F)**

1  *Main bearing housing*      2  *Dial gauge*
   *retaining screws*          3  *Dial gauge mounting bracket*

6F.68 Removal of needle roller bearings and centre spacer from
intermediate gear cluster

69 Clean and inspect the bearings, the gear cluster and the intermediate
shaft itself. Renew any damaged or excessively worn components.
70 The intermediate shaft O-ring seal must always be renewed, as must
the O-ring seal within the shaft bore in the transfer case (front end).

71 It is also advisable to renew the thrust washer at each end, irrespective of condition.

72 Lubricate the respective components and reassemble them in the reverse order of dismantling, then place them to one side ready for installation into the transfer gearbox. Note that the bearings must be fitted so that their plain edges are facing outwards.

### High/low selector housing – overhaul

73 Using an Allen key, unscrew and remove the selector fork grub screw (photo).

74 Release and remove the cross-shaft circlip, then withdraw the cross-shaft from the selector housing and retrieve the selector fork.

75 Unscrew and remove the setscrew securing the operating arm to the cross-shaft and then withdraw the arm.

76 Renew any worn components and the two O-ring seals on the cross-shaft. Clean all traces of Loctite from the operating arm setscrew and the selector fork grub screw.

77 Reassembly is a reversal of the removal procedure. Lubricate the O-ring seals with oil to ease assembly.

78 Smear the threads of the operating arm setscrew and the selector fork grub screw with Loctite 290 or similar prior to fitting. Check that the arm and selector fork are correctly positioned on the shaft when fitting the setscrew and grub screw.

6F.73 Selector fork and grub screw – high/low selector housing

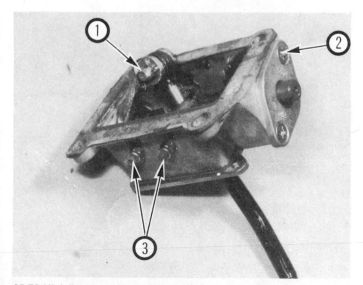

6F.79 High/low gearchange housing

1  Crank arm-to-lever clevis pin      3  Detent plate nuts
2  End cover

### High/low gearchange housing – overhaul

79 Invert and support the gearchange unit then extract the split pin and withdraw the clevis pin from the crank arm (photo).

80 Release and remove the circlip securing the lever bush, then withdraw the gearchange lever, complete with ball and bush.

81 To remove the cross-shaft, unscrew the two countersunk screws retaining the end cover, remove the cover and withdraw the cross-shaft. Note the O-ring seals on the cover. These should be renewed.

82 Remove the gearchange arm from the housing by depressing the detent spring. The crank arm O-rings must be renewed also.

83 Undo the two retaining nuts and withdraw the detent plate and spring.

84 Renew any excessively worn or damaged components.

85 Reassembly is a reversal of the removal procedure. Lubricate the O-ring seals and the gear lever, ball and bush with grease and renew the detent plate retaining nuts.

## Part G: Transfer gearbox (five-speed transmission) – reassembly

1  Check that the mating faces of the output shaft housings and the transfer gearbox are clean of old gaskets and sealant.

2  If the centre differential rear bearing track was removed for renewal, check that the new track is fitted in the set position in the transfer gearbox as described in paragraph 24 of Part F.

3  Smear the new rear output shaft housing gasket with grease, locate it and refit the rear output shaft housing into position on the transfer gearbox (photo). Smear the threads of the retaining bolts with sealant then fit them, together with their spring washers and tighten them evenly to the specified torque setting (photo). As the housing is tightened into position it will press the new bearing track into position in the transfer gearbox..

4  Lubricate the speedometer spindle housing O-ring and oil seal with oil then refit the speedometer driven gear and spindle (photo).

5  Locate the high/low selector shaft and fork unit into position in the centre differential, engaging the selector fork with the synchromesh groove and lubricate with oil.

6  Refit the centre differential unit, complete with selector fork/shaft assembly, into the transfer gearbox (photo).

7  The front output shaft and housing unit is next to be fitted. First engage the differential lock by moving the selector fork accordingly. Smear the housing gasket with grease and locate it into position. Carefully refit the front output shaft housing unit aligning the selector shaft as the housing is assembled to the transfer case.

8  Smear the threads of the eight retaining bolts with locking sealant then fit them, together with their spring washers, to secure the front

6G.3A Refit the rear output shaft housing unit ...

6G.3B ... and tighten the retaining bolts (longer bolt arrowed)

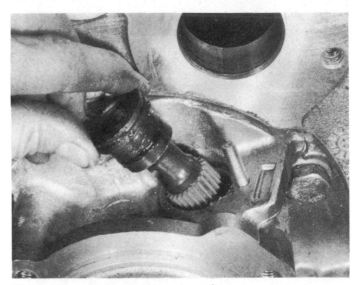

6G.4 Refit the speedometer driven gear unit

6G.6 Refit the centre differential unit complete with selector fork and shaft

6G.8 Refit the front output shaft housing unit to the transfer gearbox

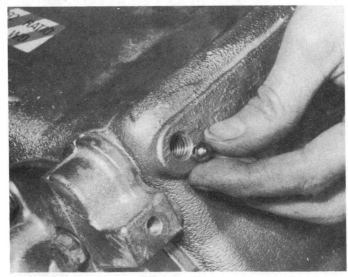

6G.10A Insert the selector detent ball ...

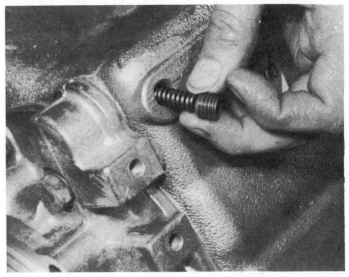

6G.10B ... spring and retaining plug

output shaft housing unit. When fitting the bolts, note that the upper centre bolt is longer than the others. Tighten them evenly to the specified torque wrench setting (photo).

9   Slide the high/low selector shaft to the rear (high range position) then slide the selector shaft yoke onto the shaft and align its set screw hole with the indent on the shaft. Smear the threads of the lock screw with locking sealant, then fit and tighten the screw to the specified torque setting.

10  Insert the selector detent ball and spring into their bore in the casing (photos). Smear the retaining plug threads with locking sealant, then fit and tighten it to the point where the selector shaft has satisfactory movement with positive engagement.

11  Smear the high/low selector housing gasket with grease then locate it into position on the front output shaft housing.

12  Refit the high/low selector housing (photo). As it is fitted into position engage the selector fork with the yoke side pins within the housing. Fit, but do not fully tighten at this stage, the six retaining bolts with plain washers.

13  Refit the input gear unit into position in the transfer gearbox (with the large gear to the front) (photo). If the gear unit or its bearings have been renewed, the bearing preload adjustment must have been assessed and adjusted, as described in Part F.

14  Locate the new gasket (lubricated with grease) onto the transfer gearbox face then refit the main bearing housing. Fit and tighten the two retaining screws to the specified torque setting (photos).

15  Lubricate the power take-off (PTO) cover gasket with grease, locate the gasket and refit the cover. Fit the six retaining bolts with spring washers and tighten them to the specified torque setting (photo).

16  Smear a light film of grease over the intermediate gear thrust washers then locate them into position within the transfer gearbox. The washers must be fitted so that their plain face is towards the casing, and the lug engages in the casing slot (photo).

17  Fit the assembled intermediate gear cluster and roller bearings into position in the transfer case so that the cluster gears are in mesh with the corresponding gears, and the intermediate shaft bores are in alignment (photo).

18  Refit the intermediate shaft; pushing it into position from the rear (photo). Smear the threads of the lockplate bolt with a locking sealant then refit the locking plate with retaining bolt and spring washers (photo).

19  Check the endfloat of the intermediate gear cluster using feeler gauges (photo). Lever the gear cluster using a suitable screwdriver to move the gears fully to one side for the reading which should be as given in the Specifications at the start of this Chapter.

20  Lubricate the bottom cover gasket with grease then locate it and refit the bottom cover to the transfer case. Smear a locking sealant onto the threads of the ten cover securing bolts as they are fitted.

21  If removed, refit the differential lock switch and adjust it, as described in Part H.

22  Refit the transmission brake unit reversing the removal procedure. Take care not to get any oil or grease onto the brake linings or the drum

6G.13 Refit the input shaft unit

6G.14A Locate the main bearing housing ...

6G.12 Refit the high/low selector housing

6G.14B ... and secure with retaining screws (arrowed)

6G.15 Refit the power take-off (PTO) cover and gasket

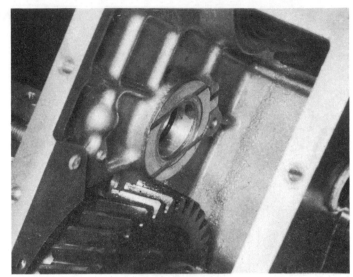
6G.16A Intermediate gear thrust washer location (front)

6G.16B Intermediate gear thrust washer location (rear)

6G.17 Locate the intermediate gear unit ...

6G.18A ... and insert the intermediate gear shaft with new O-ring fitted to the shaft at the rear ...

6G.18B ... and a new O-ring in the housing bore groove at the front

6G.18C Refit the intermediate shaft lockplate

6G.19 Check the intermediate gear endfloat

braking surface as they are fitted. Note that the two lower bolts which secure the brake backplate unit also secure the oil drip plate within the transfer casing. Tighten the retaining bolts to the specified torque setting.
23 Refit the handbrake linkage and lever mounting plate reversing the removal procedure.

## Part H: Five-speed transmission – selector adjustments

### Main gearbox gear selection bias spring adjustment

1   The gear selector bias springs are located externally on the main gear lever housing. For access, remove the main gear lever and the top covering from the transmission tunnel as described in Part B, paragraphs 1 to 6 inclusive.
2   Engage 3rd or 4th gear, loosen the two adjustment bolt locknuts and undo the bolts so that the spring leg on each side is clear of the cross pin in the lever. This should provide the gear lever with a slack radial movement (Fig. 13.30).
3   Move the gear lever to the left to take up any slack then tighten the adjustment bolt on the right-hand side to the point where the right-hand spring leg is just in contact with the gear lever cross pin on that side.

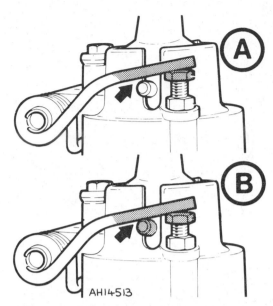

Fig. 13.30 Gear selection bias spring adjustment (Sec 6H)

A   Unscrew adjuster bolts to give clearance between the spring legs and the lever cross pin (arrow)
B   Tighten adjuster bolts so that the spring legs just make contact with the lever cross pin (arrow)

4   Move the gear lever to the right and repeat the procedure for the left-hand spring leg.
5   Now tighten each adjuster bolt progressively in equal amounts to the point where any slack radial movement of the lever is eliminated. Hold the gear lever at the lower end when making this adjustment for a more accurate assessment of the point where the slack is taken up.
6   Further tighten each adjuster bolt by two flats to set the spring tension.
7   Move the gear lever back to the neutral position, then move it backwards and forwards across the gate a few times and then release it. The lever should settle in the 3rd/4th gear selector gate position. Secure the setting by retaining the adjuster bolts in the set position and tighten the locknuts.

### Reverse plunger unit

8   If the gear selection in 1st and 2nd gears still proves difficult after making the bias spring adjustment, it may be that the shim adjustment of the reverse plunger unit is incorrect. The reverse plunger also acts as a stop when these gears are selected and if incorrectly set will cause the selector shaft to foul the reverse lever or 3rd/4th selector fork.
9   Unbolt and remove the reverse plunger unit from the selector housing. Remove the detent plunger cap and extract the spring and ball. Extract the circlip and remove the plunger from its bore.
10  Clean the plunger housing and components thoroughly, ensuring that the threads are cleaned of Loctite sealant.
11  Smear the plunger with a light coating of oil, refit it into its bore and secure with the circlip. Do not let any oil get onto the housing threads.
12  Refit the detent ball and spring and cap. If a washer was fitted under the cap refit this also (the washer should be about 1 mm thick and was fitted to ease reverse gear selection).
13  Select 1st or 2nd gear, turning the mainshaft if necessary to obtain engagement. Insert the reverse plunger unit to the point where it is felt to contact the gear lever yoke. Apply a light finger pressure to the plunger unit to maintain it in this position and measure the clearance between the plunger and selector housing mating faces using feeler gauges.
14  The shims required must equal the clearance measured plus 0.006 to 0.020 in (0.15 to 0.51 mm). Refit the reverse plunger unit ensuring that the detent cap faces upwards.
15  Move the gear lever through the 1st/2nd gate to check for satisfactory selection.
16  Remove the detent cap and smear the threads with a locking sealant, but not too much or the sealant may work its way into the housing bore when the cap is fitted.

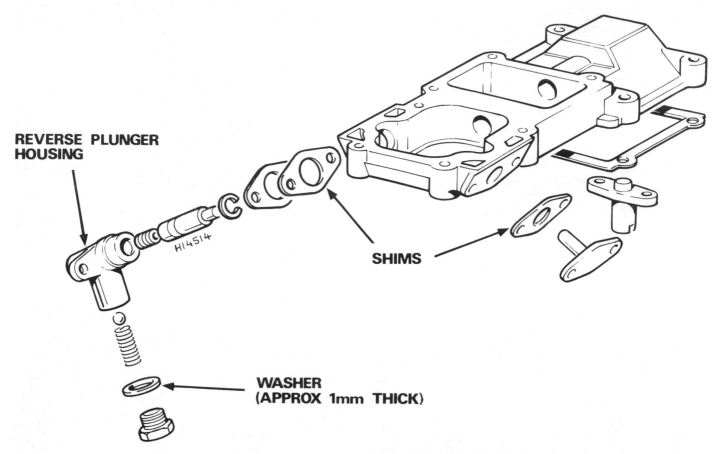

**Fig. 13.31 Reverse plunger unit and adjustment shims (Sec 6H)**

*Also shown is the 5th gear stop and shims*

17 Lightly screw the cap back into the plunger housing then move the gear lever through the reverse knock a minimum of ten times then connect a suitable spring balance to the gear lever directly underneath the knob. Pull on the spring balance and observe the loading required to pull the gear lever over. The correct loading should be between 30 to 35 lbs (13.6 to 15.8 kgs). Tighten the housing cap until the correct loading is achieved. This should be within two full turns of the cap. Leave the cap in the set position for the time specified by the locking sealant manufacturer to allow the sealant to harden and secure the cap (about 60 minutes normally).

**Fifth gear stop adjustment**
18 Check that the bias springs are correctly adjusted before making any checks or adjustments to the gear stop.
19 Unbolt and remove the 5th gear stop (photo).
20 Move the gear lever into the 5th gear engagement position turning the mainshaft if required to obtain full engagement.
21 Remove any shims from the stop unit, then refit it to the point where it is in light contact with the gear lever yoke. Hold it in this position under light finger pressure and measure the clearance between the 5th gear stop and selector housing using feeler gauges.
22 Select shims to equal the thickness of the gap measured plus 0.012 to 0.035 in (0.3 to 0.9 mm). Refit the 5th gear stop, together with the selected shims and check the 5th gear selection. Add or subtract further shims as required to obtain the satisfactory selector action.
23 Shims for both the reverse gear stop and 5th gear stop adjustment are available in two thicknesses: 0.02 and 0.03 in (0.51 and 0.76 mm).

*High/low gearchange connecting rod – adjustment*
**Early models**
24 To check if adjustment is required, select the high then low range gears and observe if the gear lever fouls the gate plate. If it does then adjustment is necessary.

6H.19 Fifth gear stop plate and adjustment shims

25 Loosen the operating arm fork locknut and remove the clevis pin securing the operating arm to the high/low connecting rod (Fig. 13.32).
26 Lift the operating arm fork clear of the connecting rod and rotate the fork as required, then temporarily reconnect the fork to the rod by inserting the clevis pin only.
27 Move the gearchange lever rearwards into the high range position and the selector housing operating arm on the cross-shaft forwards into

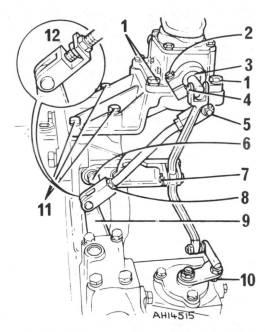

Fig. 13.32 High-low gearchange assembly (Sec 6H)

1  Gearchange housing bolts
2  Clamp bolt
3  Splined shaft and operating arm
4  Cross-shaft lever fork
5  Operating arm-to-high/low connecting rod clevis
6  Pivot bracket
7  Cross-shaft lever middle pivot
8  Operating arm fork locknut (early models)
9  High/low gearchange operating arm
10  Differential lock connecting link (short)
11  Gearchange housing (lower)-to-extension housing bolts
12  Connecting rod to operating arm (later models)

6H.34 Differential lock switch (1) and locknut (2)

6H.37 Differential lock switch adjustment using a multi-meter

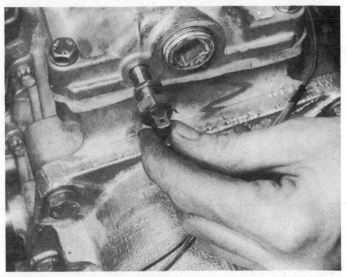

6H.39 Reverse light switch location

the high range position. Check that the gearchange lever does not foul the gate plate. Repeat this procedure for the low range engagement. Further adjustment of the fork may be necessary.

28 When the setting is satisfactory, move the gear lever back to the high range position, then tighten the locknut against the clevis fork. Refit the flat washer and split pin to secure the clevis pin in the connecting rod-to-operating arm connection.

29 If removal or refitting of the connecting rod-to-operating arm clevis pin is found to be difficult due to the closeness of the transfer gearbox casing an alternative adjustment method can be used.

30 Disconnect the differential lock cross-shaft lever from the gearchange cross-shaft then unscrew the gearchange housing retaining bolts and lift the housing clear.

31 Loosen the connecting rod fork locknut and then rotate the gearchange housing to rotate the fork on the rod and adjust its length accordingly.

32 Refit the housing and check the lever adjustment as described earlier.

**Later models**

33 The checking and adjustment procedure is similar to that described for automatic transmission models except that the grommet and grommet plate are not fitted, and the gate plate housing is secured by two screws to the housing. The four main bolts are fitted *in situ* via the floor-mounted gaiter assembly.

*Differential lock switch – removal, refitting and adjustment*

34 Located on the front output shaft housing, the switch is removed by detaching the wires, loosening the switch locknut and unscrewing the switch unit (photo).

35 Correct setting is important when refitting and the following procedure should be taken.

36 Move the differential lock lever to the right to select the differential lock.

37 Connect up a test light or multi-meter to the switch lead terminals then screw the switch in until the bulb lights up or a positive meter reading is given (photo). From this point tighten the switch a further half turn then retighten the locknut against the output shaft housing.
38 Detach the test equipment and return the differential lever to the left to disengage the differential lock.

### Reverse light switch – removal, refitting and adjustment
39 This is located in the rear end of the gear selector housing. The removal, refitting and adjustment procedures are similar to those described for the differential lock switch, but engage reverse gear when screwing the switch unit in for adjustment (photo).

## 7 Automatic transmission

### Part A: Automatic transmission and transfer gearbox – description, precautions and maintenance
1   The automatic transmission system comprises a torque converter and a fully automatic three-speed gearbox unit.
2   The torque converter enables the engine torque to be transmitted to the input shaft and thence to the gearbox multi disc clutches. It is a sealed unit type converter and cannot be repaired.
3   The automatic gearbox unit has two multiple disc clutches, an overrun clutch, two servos and bands and two planetary gear sets. These give three forward and one reverse gear. An internal oil pump and valve body provide the integral hydraulic system and the gearbox is vented by a passage in the top of the oil pump. The transmission fluid is cooled by a separate oil cooler.
4   The transfer gearbox is mounted to the automatic transmission extension housing in much the same manner as that for the manual transmission. The transfer gearbox fitted is the same type as that fitted to the five-speed manual gearbox type and can be overhauled by referring to the appropriate Section in this Chapter; only the ratios differ.
5   In view of the specialised knowledge and equipment required to test and overhaul the automatic transmission, such tasks should be entrusted to your Range Rover dealer.

### Special precautions
**Transmission fluid**
6   When topping-up the transmission fluid level or renewing the transmission fluid, use only the correct fluid specified. **Do not** use Dexron IIC, or damage to the transmission could result.

**Engine idling**
7   **Do not** allow the engine to run at idle speed with the gear selector in the P (Park) position for longer than ten minutes, or damage to the gearbox could result due to low lubricating pressure.
8   On models fitted with air conditioning equipment which is being used in high ambient temperatures where extended periods of stationary idling are necessary, N (Neutral) position must be selected with the handbrake fully applied.
**Converter housing drain plug**
9   A threaded drain hole is located in the base of the converter housing to allow any excess oil to be drained from the converter housing.
10   Where the vehicle is to be used in wading or very muddy conditions, the converter housing must be sealed by inserting the deep wading plug with the drain hole. This plug is normally located in the base of the tie plate between the engine and transmission when not required. When it is to be used, remove the plug from the tie plate and screw it into the drain hole in the converter housing. During use the plug must be periodically removed to allow any oil collected to drain from the converter housing and the plug then refitted.

### Routine maintenance
**Oil level – checking and topping-up**
11   The automatic transmission oil level must be checked at the specified intervals of 6000 miles (10 000 km) or every 6 months. However, where the vehicle is used in deep wading conditions, the oil level must be checked daily.
12   With the vehicle standing on level ground, fully apply footbrake and handbrake and select N (Neutral). Start the engine and run it up to its normal operating temperature then move the gear lever through the range of gears. As each gear is selected pause momentarily before selecting the next gear, and finally reselect N (Neutral).
13   With the engine still running at idle speed, withdraw the dipstick and wipe it clean using a non-fluffy cloth, then fully reinsert it and then withdraw it to check the oil level reading. The level must be maintained between the maximum (Full) mark and the minimum (Add 1 pint) mark on the dipstick.
14   If required, top up the oil level with the specified lubricant through the oil filler tube (Fig. 13.34), but take care not to overfill the transmission. When refitting the dipstick ensure that it is fully located.
**Oil and filter renewal**
15   The automatic transmission oil and oil filter must be renewed at the specified intervals of 24 000 miles (40 000 km) when in normal use or on a monthly basis when the vehicle is used in arduous conditions such as severe wading.

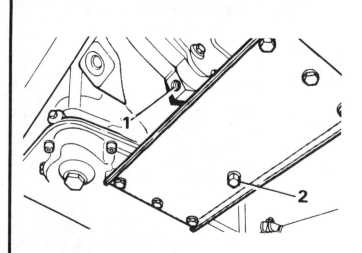

Fig. 13.33 Deep wading drain plug (Sec 7A)

1   Threaded torque converter    2   Plug location when nut in
    drain hole                           use

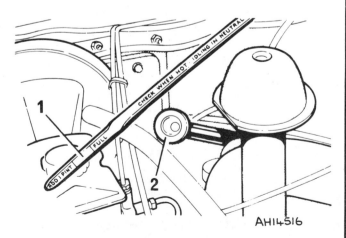

Fig. 13.34 Automatic transmission oil level dipstick (1) and filler tube (2) (Sec 7A)

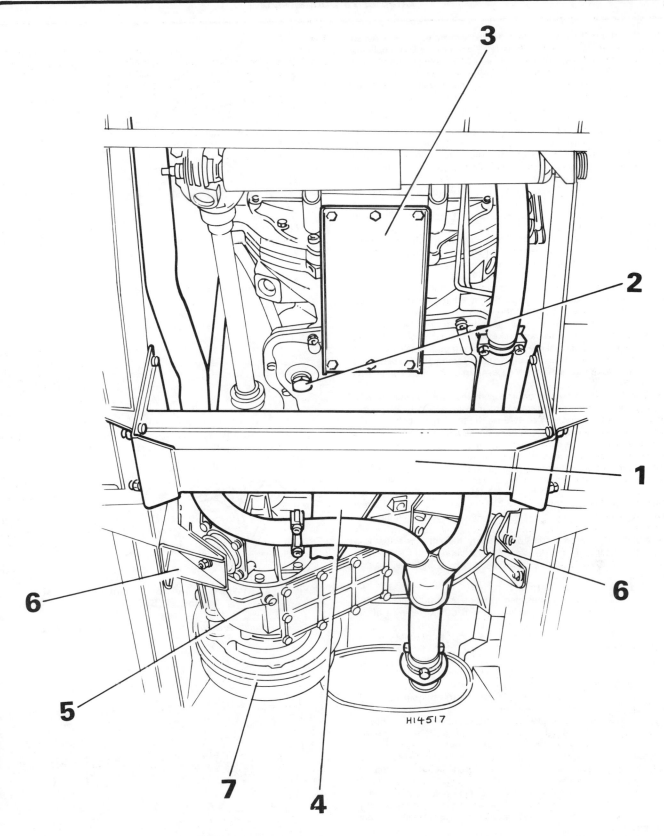

**Fig. 13.35 Underside of the automatic transmission (Sec 7A)**

1 Crossmember
2 Automatic transmission drain plug in sump
3 Engine to gearbox steady plate
4 Gearbox-to-transfer gearbox steady plate
5 Transfer gearbox drain plug
6 Transmission mountings
7 Transmission brake

16 The oil should be drained directly after the vehicle has been used so that the oil is warm. Park the vehicle on level ground and fully apply the handbrake. Undo the transmission drain plug and allow the oil to drain into a suitable container for disposal.

17 Undo the eight retaining bolts and remove the chassis crossmember.

18 Unbolt and remove the steady (tie) plates between the engine and transmission and the transfer gearbox and transmission (Fig. 13.35).

19 Detach the fluid temperature sensor lead.

20 Unbolt and detach the exhaust pipe front section from the manifolds and the flange connection forward of the front silencer. Remove the U-bolt securing the front system to the left-hand transmission mountings then lower the pipe a sufficient amount to allow the transmission sump removal.

21 Undo the sump bolts then tap the sump downwards at one corner to remove it, together with its gasket.

22 Unscrew and discard the valve body filter. Fit the new filter and tighten to the specified torque.

23 Thoroughly clean the sump, refit the drain plug with a new washer then refit the sump using a new gasket. Tighten the retaining bolts to the specified torque, also the drain plug. Reconnect the sensor lead.

24 Refit the exhaust front section, the tie plates and the chassis crossmember. Tighten the retaining bolts to the specified torque settings.

25 Top up the transmission oil level by initially adding about one gallon (five litres) of the specified lubricant through the filler tube. Restart the engine and run it at idle speed for a minimum period of two minutes, then fully apply the foot and handbrake and move the selector lever through each gear position. Allow a pause as each gear is selected, then reposition in N (Neutral). With the engine still running at idle speed, add further transmission fluid to bring the oil level up to the 'Add 1 pint' level mark on the dipstick.

26 Allow the engine to continue idling with the gear selector lever in neutral, then when the transmission fluid is warmed up to its normal operating temperature, recheck the level. It should be between the minimum and full markings. On completion check that the dipstick is fully located.

**Kickdown band adjustment**

27 The kickdown band adjustment is made at 24 000 mile (40 000 km) intervals and is a task normally undertaken when renewing the transmission oil. The kickdown band adjuster screw is located on the left-hand side of the gearbox (Fig. 13.37). Loosen the adjuster screw locknut and unscrew it five full turns. The adjuster screw should now turn freely.

28 The adjustment is now made by tightening the adjuster screw to a torque wrench setting of 72 lbf in (83 kgf cm), then undo the screw from this point two and a half turns. Retain the screw in this position and tighten the locknut.

**Low and reverse band adjustment**

29 The low and reverse band adjustment is made at 24 000 mile (40 000 km) intervals and is a task normally undertaken during renewal of the transmission oil.

30 Drain the transmission oil and remove the sump, as described earlier. The low and reverse band adjustment screw is then accessible from within the transmission case at the lower end (Fig. 13.38).

31 The adjustment procedure now follows that described for the kickdown band.

32 On completion, refit the sump and top up the transmission oil level.

**Transfer gearbox oil level – checking**

33 When the vehicle is being used under severe or wading conditions, the transfer gearbox oil level should be checked daily, or weekly, depending on the severity of conditions and usage.

34 With the vehicle parked on level ground, unscrew and remove the oil level/filler plug from the side of the transfer gearbox. The transfer gearbox oil should be level with the bottom of the level/filler plug hole. If required, top up the oil level through the level/filler plug hole using only the specified oil type. Refit the plug. If a significant amount of oil is required, or consistent topping-up is necessary, check for oil leaks and repair as necessary.

**Transfer gearbox – oil renewal**

35 The transfer gearbox oil must be renewed at 24 000 mile (40 000 km) intervals under normal operating conditions, but when the vehicle is used in severe wading conditions renew the oil monthly.

36 The oil is best renewed directly after the vehicle has been used when the oil is still hot. Park the vehicle on level ground, then unscrew and remove the drain plug from the base of the transfer gearbox and drain the old oil into a suitable container for disposal.

37 When draining is complete, refit the drain plug with its washer. Undo

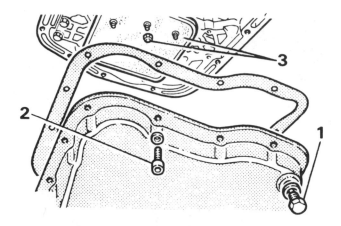

Fig. 13.36 Transmission sump drain plug and washer (1) retaining bolts (2) and filter (3) (Sec 7A)

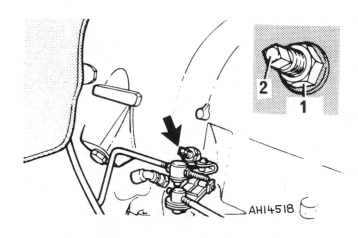

Fig. 13.37 Kickdown band adjustment screw location – arrowed (Sec 7A)

1   Adjuster locknut                    2   Adjuster screw

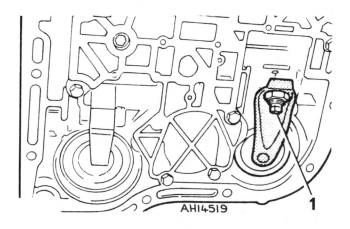

Fig. 13.38 Low and reverse band adjustment screw location (1) (Sec 7A)

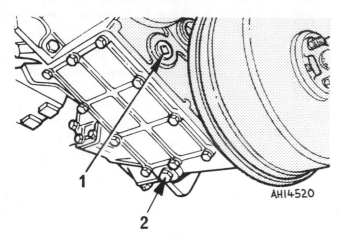

**Fig. 13.39 Transfer gearbox oil level/filler plug (1) and drain plug (2) (Sec 7A)**

the filler level plug on the side of the transfer gearbox and top up the oil level through the filler plug hole with the specified oil. When the oil is level with the bottom of the filler plug hole, refit the plug.

**Parking pawl engagement check**
38 The automatic transmission parking pawl engagement should be checked every 6000 mile (10 000 km). To carry out this check the vehicle must be standing on level ground with the engine switched off.
39 Move the gear lever to the P (Park) position and release the handbrake. Try to push the vehicle forwards and rearwards. If the parking pawl does not hold consult your Range Rover dealer.

## Part B: Automatic transmission and transfer gear-box – removal and refitting

*Removal methods*
1 The automatic transmission can be removed with the transfer gearbox or separately, after the removal of the transfer gearbox. Whichever method is employed, the main consideration to take into account is the considerable weight of each unit and, in addition, once freed from their mountings, they will need to be carefully supported during removal in order to overcome their imbalance.
2 The removal method described is for the transmission removal from underneath the vehicle, although it may be possible to remove them from above (within the vehicle) once they are free of their mountings and connections, in a similar manner to that described for the five-speed manual transmission (described elsewhere in this Chapter).
3 When removing the transmission from underneath you will need to make up a suitable adaptor plate with which to support the transmission during removal and refitting. It may be possible to borrow or hire this adaptor plate from your Range Rover dealer so check this first (see Fig. 13.40).
4 In addition you will need a trolley jack of sufficient capacity to support the transmission assembly during its removal and refitting.

*Automatic transmission (and transfer gearbox) – removal and refitting*
5 Disconnect the battery earth lead.
6 Remove the air cleaner unit, referring to Chapter 3.
7 Undo the mounting peg on the air cleaner left-hand side mounting and remove the coupling shaft support bracket. Detach the throttle return spring and the throttle coupling shaft (Fig. 13.41).
8 Loosen the outer two nuts which secure the cooling fan cowl. Rotate the inner cowl nuts anti-clockwise to lift the cowl so that it will not foul when the engine is lowered in subsequent operations.

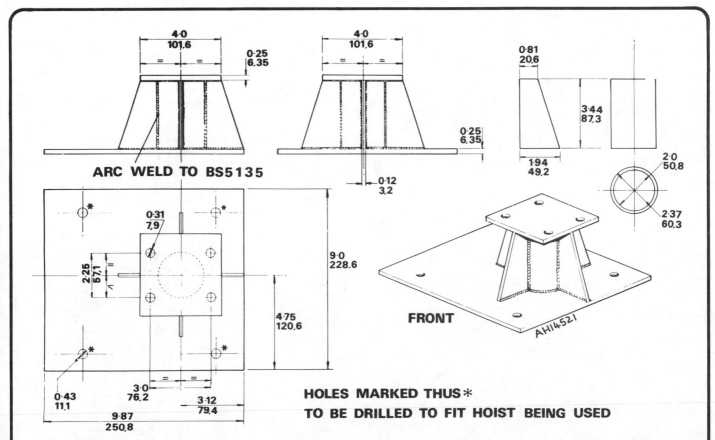

**Fig. 13.40 Special cradle required when removing the automatic transmission and transfer gearbox from underneath the vehicle (Sec 7B)**

*Measurements in inches and millimetres*

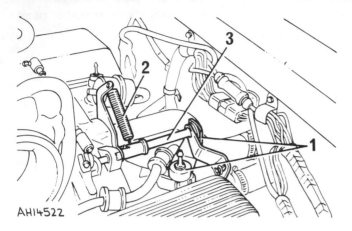

Fig. 13.41 The air cleaner left-hand mounting peg and support bracket (1), throttle return spring (2) and the coupling shaft (3) (Sec 7B)

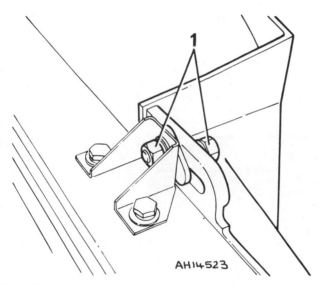

Fig. 13.42 Cooling fan cowl nuts to be loosened (1) (Sec 7B)

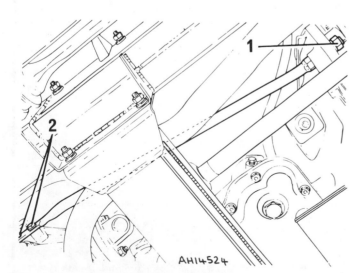

Fig. 13.43 Tie-bar to bellhousing (1) and transfer gearbox (2) mountings (Sec 7B)

9   Unclip and release the hose from the alternator mounting bracket.
10  Working inside the vehicle, remove the ashtrays and their holders from the transmission tunnel.
11  Remove the transmission tunnel carpet and insulation then undo and remove the ten screws retaining the handbrake gaiter. Withdraw the gaiter from the handbrake.
12  Unscrew and remove the high/low transfer gear lever knob, undo the four screws and withdraw the gaiter from the gear lever.
13  The vehicle will now need to be raised and supported on suitable safety stands to provide suitable working clearance and clearance for the transmission removal. Alternatively, if an inspection pit is available, position the verhicle over it.
14  Remove the drain plugs and drain the gearbox and transfer gearbox oils into a suitable container for disposal. Refit the drain plugs on completion.
15  Undo the four retaining bolts and nuts each side securing the chassis crossmember. Withdraw the bolts to allow the crossmember to be removed. It should be possible to tap it down and free using a suitable mallet, but if may be necessary to use a suitable chassis spreader to free it. Support the crossmember when removing it as it is heavy.
16  Detach and remove the starter motor solenoid.
17  Referring to Chapter 3, detach and remove the front exhaust pipe system complete.
18  Remove the tie plate located between the gearbox and the engine.
19  Disconnect the front propeller shaft from the transfer gearbox front drive flange (having marked them for alignment). Refer to Chapter 7 for further details.
20  Disconnect the rear propeller shaft from the transmission brake (referring to Chapter 7 if necessary) and then tie up the front and rear propeller shafts out of the way.
21  Unbolt and disconnect the bellhousing-to-transfer gearbox tie-bar at each end.
22  Detach the speedometer drive cable from the transfer gearbox connection and the retaining clip.
23  Undo the nut securing the gear selector cable to the fulcrum arm and the cable from its location clamp, then position the cable to one side out of the way.
24  Disconnect the upper and lower throttle links by extracting the split pin, then undo the bellhousing nut and bolt retaining the throttle valve linkage bracket. Position the assembly to one side out of the way.
25  Position a container beneath the oil cooler pipe connections forward of the engine sump of the left-hand side and undo and detach the pipes at the connectors. Loosen the retaining clamps securing the steel pipes on the left side of the engine.
26  Detach the oil cooler pipes from the transmission unions and remove the pipes. Plug the pipe ends to prevent the ingress of dirt and further leakage.
27  Unscrew the nine bellhousing cover plate retaining bolts and withdraw the cover plate.
28  Undo the four torque converter-to-driveplate retaining bolts. As the

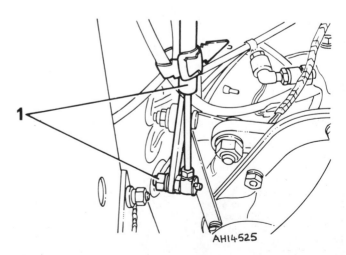

Fig. 13.44 Gear selector cable and fulcrum arm connection (1) (Sec 7B)

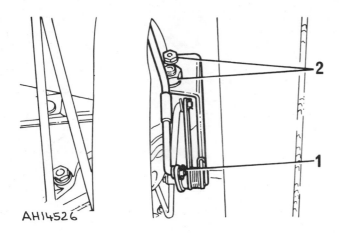

AHI4526

**Fig. 13.45 Vertical rod to upper and lower throttle valve linkage (1) and linkage bracket to bellhousing (2) (Sec 7B)**

AHI4527

**Fig. 13.46 Oil cooler pipe pipes and connections – arrowed (Sec 7B)**

last bolt is removed mark the relative positions of the driveplate and torque converter and bellhousing. This will ensure correct reassembly.

29 Remove the gearbox-to-transfer gearbox tie-bar.

30 The adaptor plate mentioned in paragraph 3 must now be bolted into position on the underside of the gearbox.

31 Locate the trolley jack and attach it to the adaptor plate. Raise the jack to take the weight of the transmission.

32 Unbolt and detach the transmission mounting bracket on each side.

33 Slowly lower the jack supporting the transmission just enough to allow the following items to be disconnected. As the engine will tilt with the transmission, get an assistant to keep a watchful eye on the engine ancillary items and connections to ensure that they are not damaged or distorted.

34 Disconnect the transmission selector light leads at the snap connectors, and also the inhibitor switch and reversing light switch leads multi-connector.

35 Unbolt and detach the breather tube banjo connector from the transfer gearbox. Refit the banjo bolt and the two washers to the transfer gearbox and move the breather tube out of the way.

36 Detach the differential lock wiring from the clips on the transfer gearbox, also the warning light lead connectors. Note the various wiring connections then move the wires out of the way.

37 Detach the breather tube from the automatic transmission, then refit the bolt with washers. Move the breather tube out of the way.

38 Undo and remove the bellhousing bolt which retains the gearbox filler tube. Detach the filler tube from the gearbox and cover hole.

39 Position a jack under the engine and raise it to support the weight of the engine.

40 Undo and remove the three remaining bellhousing-to-engine bolts.

41 The transmission is now ready to be removed from the vehicle. Check that all connections and ancillary items are detached and positioned out of the way then carefully withdraw the transmission from the engine whilst simultaneously lowering its supporting jack under the adaptor plate. An assistant will be helpful here to help guide the unit clear from under the vehicle.

42 If the vehicle is to be moved whilst the transmission is removed, an alternative method of supporting the engine will have to be made before removing the support jack.

43 Refitting is a reversal of the removal procedure, but the following special points should be noted.

44 Do not fully tighten the respective retaining and mounting bolts until all of the bolts and fastenings of the items concerned are located, then tighten the bolts to the specified torque settings.

45 Where the old torque converter is being used, align the previously made marks of the torque converter, driveplate and bellhousing when fitting the first retaining bolt.

46 When the engine and transmission are being bolted together the bolt retaining the throttle valve linkage is fitted with its lead to the rear.

47 Reconnect the wiring and breather tubes before raising the gearbox. Ensure correct connections and routing.

48 When refitting the transmission mounting bolts, fit the speedometer cable locating clip to the top front bolt on the left-hand side. The gear selector outer cable and locating clip is fitted to the left-hand mounting bracket.

49 When reconnecting the propeller shaft joint flanges align with the marks made during removal.

50 Refit the steady plates and exhaust system before refitting the chassis crossmember.

51 On completion, remove the jacks and top up the transmission and, if applicable, the transfer gearbox oil levels with the specified lubricant.

52 **Note:** If the old transmission fluid was badly discoloured and contaminated when drained it is advisable to flush out the oil cooler and tubes prior to reconnecting them and topping-up the transmission oil level with new fluid. Flush the old oil from the cooler by connecting a flexible pipe (hose) to the oil cooler inlet connection and then blow through the outlet connection with short sharp blasts of clean compressed air. Direct the old fluid into a container for disposal. On completing the flushing of the cooler, pump 1 pint (0.6 litre) of the specified new lubricant into the cooler before reconnecting the hoses to the transmission.

*Automatic transmission and transfer gearbox – separation and reassembly*

53 Undo the five bolts securing the automatic transmission to the transfer gearbox.

54 The transfer gearbox can now be withdrawn from the automatic transmission unit. If they prove difficult to separate, undo the six bolts securing the cover plate, withdraw the cover plate and unscrew and remove the coupling shaft bolt. The transfer gearbox, together with the extension case, can now be withdrawn from the automatic transmission unit.

55 Reassembly is a reversal of the separation procedure.

56 Ensure that the respective mating faces are clean.

57 To ensure correct alignment of the two units and also to avoid damaging the oil seal during reassembly, fit three guide studs into position in the transfer gearbox extension case as shown (Fig. 13.47).

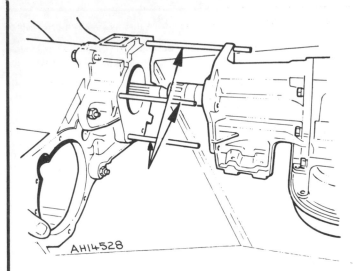

Fig. 13.47 Insert guide studs (arrowed) when reconnecting the automatic transmission to the transfer gearbox (Sec 7B)

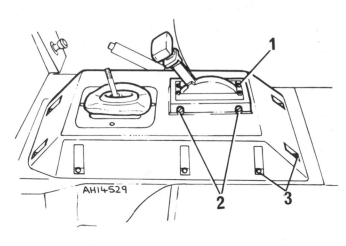

Fig. 13.48 Automatic transmission selector bezel retaining screws (1), selector-to-top cover screws (2) and top cover bolts (3) (Sec 7C)

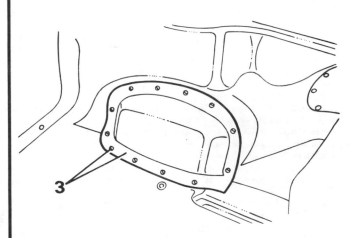

Fig. 13.49 Automatic transmission side cover (Sec 7C)

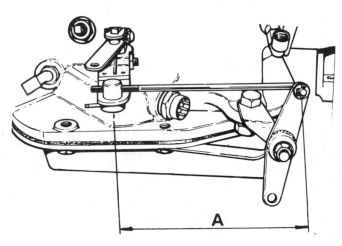

Fig. 13.50 Selector rod/cable adjustment check (Sec 7C)

*A = 6.26 to 6.34 in (159 to 161 mm)*

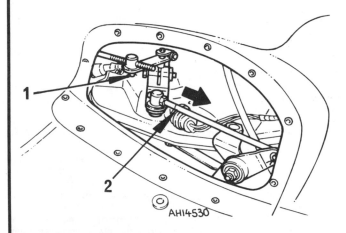

Fig. 13.51 Throttle valve lever-to-trunnion connection (1) and throttle valve lever (2) (Sec 7C)

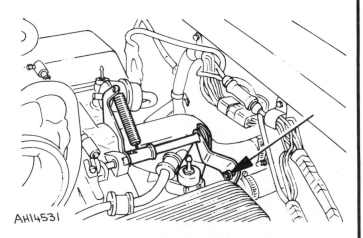

Fig. 13.52 Check the down link position at full throttle – arrowed (Sec 7C)

The stud fitted to the left side will need to be longer than the other two.
58 The automatic gearbox should be set in P (Park), then the transfer gearbox aligned with the studs and slid into position. When the two units are assembled together, remove the studs and refit the retaining bolts and tighten them to the specified torque.

## Part C: Automatic transmission/transfer gearbox selector and associated components – removal and adjustments

### Transmission tunnel top and side covers – removal and refitting

**Top cover**
1 Unscrew and remove the high/low transfer differential lock lever knob.
2 Prise the ashtrays from their holders then remove the screws securing the ashtray holders.
3 Remove the cubby box base cover then undo the three screws securing the cubby box to the transmission tunnel. Remove the cubby box.
4 Remove the carpet and sound insulation covering from the transmission tunnel.
5 Undo the four screws securing the gear selector bezel. Lift away the plate and trim.
6 Undo and remove the four gear selector unit retaining bolts then push the unit downwards and detach it from the top cover. Undo the bolts and remove the top cover.
7 Refitting is a reversal of the removal procedure. When refitting the cover, check that the sealant is evenly dispersed around the aperture of the tunnel.

**Side cover**
8 Unfold the footwell cover on the left-hand side, then unscrew and remove the twelve retaining bolts and remove the cover.
9 Refit in the reverse order of removal. Loosely fit all the bolts before fully tightening them and ensure that the sealant is evenly dispersed around the cover aperture.

### Automatic transmission gear selector unit – removal and refitting
10 Remove the transmission top cover, as described in paras 1 to 6.
11 Unscrew and remove the cable clamp-to-selector unit quadrant retaining nuts and bolts.
12 Detach the selector inner cable from the cross-shaft lever by extracting the split pin and removing the washer.
13 Disconnect the selector illumination bulb lead at the bullet connector, then withdraw the selector unit.
14 Refit in the reverse order of removal.

### Automatic transmission selector rod/cable – adjustment
15 Detach and remove the transfer gear lever knob and the lever gaiter.
16 Select N (Neutral) and keep it in this position throughout the adjustment.
17 Undo and remove the transmission tunnel cover retaining screws, then lift the cover just enough to allow access to the cable-to-gear selector quadrant connection.
18 Release the spring clip securing the cable trunnion to the quadrant then detach the trunnion from the quadrant.
19 Detach the transmission tunnel side cover plate (paragraph 8).
20 Check that the gear lever is still engaged in N (Neutral) then, referring to Fig. 13.50, measure the distance A, from the centre of the selector rod to the centre of the trunnion. If the adjustment is not as specified disconnect the selector rod from the arm (extract the split pin), then rotate the rod in the trunnion to give the correct adjustment. Reconnect the selector rod to the arm, fit the flat washer and split pin.
21 Before refitting the transmission covers check the selector cable adjustment, leaving the gear lever engaged in N (Neutral).
22 Check that the trunnion fits centrally into the corresponding gear selector quadrant hole and if required adjust its position on the cable thread.
23 Temporarily insert the trunnion retaining circlip and the gearbox top cover.
24 Operate the gear lever through the full range of selector positions and simultaneously check if the cable-to-link arm attachment interferes with the support bracket.
25 With the handbrake fully applied, check that the engine can be restarted when the lever is set in the P (Park) and N (Neutral) positions.
26 If the above checks are not satisfactory remove the transmission cover and make further adjustments to the selector rod and cable as necessary.
27 On completion, refit the transmission top and side covers and the transfer gear lever gaiter and knob.

### Automatic transmission throttle valve linkage – adjustment
28 Disconnect and remove the air cleaner unit, referring to Chapter 3 for further details.
29 Remove the ashtrays and floor covering from the transmission tunnel.
30 Undo the retaining screws and withdraw the transmission tunnel side cover for access to the throttle valve linkage at the transmission.
31 Extract the split pin, remove the washers and detach the throttle valve lever from the trunnion (Fig. 13.51).
32 Get an assistant to depress the accelerator pedal to the full throttle position and then check that the down link is at the bottom of the coupling shaft lever slot (Fig. 13.52).
33 Still with the accelerator pedal in the full throttle position, move the gearbox throttle valve lever to the rear and adjust the trunnion position on the rod so that it drops into the hole in the throttle valve lever.
34 Refit the trunnion temporarily to the throttle valve lever then get the assistant to release the accelerator pedal and then fully depress it again. The adjustment is correct if the throttle valve lever remains fully rearward with no further movement to the rear possible. Repeat the adjustment if not satisfactory.
35 Release the accelerator pedal then reconnect the trunnion and fit the washer with a new split pin.
36 Refit the cover and check that it is fully sealed.
37 Refit the air cleaner unit.
38 Refit the transmission coverings.

### High/low gearchange connecting rod – adjustment
39 Unbolt and remove the gearchange housing and remove the gearchange grommet plate and the lever grommet. Refit the four bolts to temporarily secure the gate plate in position.
40 Move the gear lever into high and then low range and observe if it fouls the gate plate. If it does then adjustment is necessary.
41 Loosen the connecting rod locknuts, move the change lever rearwards to select high range and the selector housing operating arm forwards into high range position.
42 Retighten the locknuts and check if the lever fouls the gate plate in the high range position. Now using the same method, engage and check the lever in the low range position.
43 When adjustment is made, move the lever back to the high range position, undo the bolts securing the gate plate, refit the grommet and plate and refit the retaining bolts.

### Reverse starter switch – testing, removal and refitting
44 Remove the transmission tunnel side cover (see paragraph 8).
45 Detach the lead connector from the switch then connect up a test meter or light. If using a test light and battery, connect the earth (negative) terminal to the transmission case.
46 Connect the positive test probe to the switch centre pin, then move the selector lever to the P (Park) position and check for continuity, then move the lever to N (Neutral) position and repeat the check. In each case a continuity reading should be given or, if using a test lamp, the bulb should illuminate.
47 To check the reverse light function of the switch, connect the earth lead to an outer pin on the switch and the test probe to the other pin. Select reverse and check for continuity.
48 If the switch is found to be defective it must be removed and renewed. Unscrew the switch to remove it.
49 Screw the new switch into position and connect up the lead multi-connector, but before refitting the side cover, check that the switch functions are satisfactory.

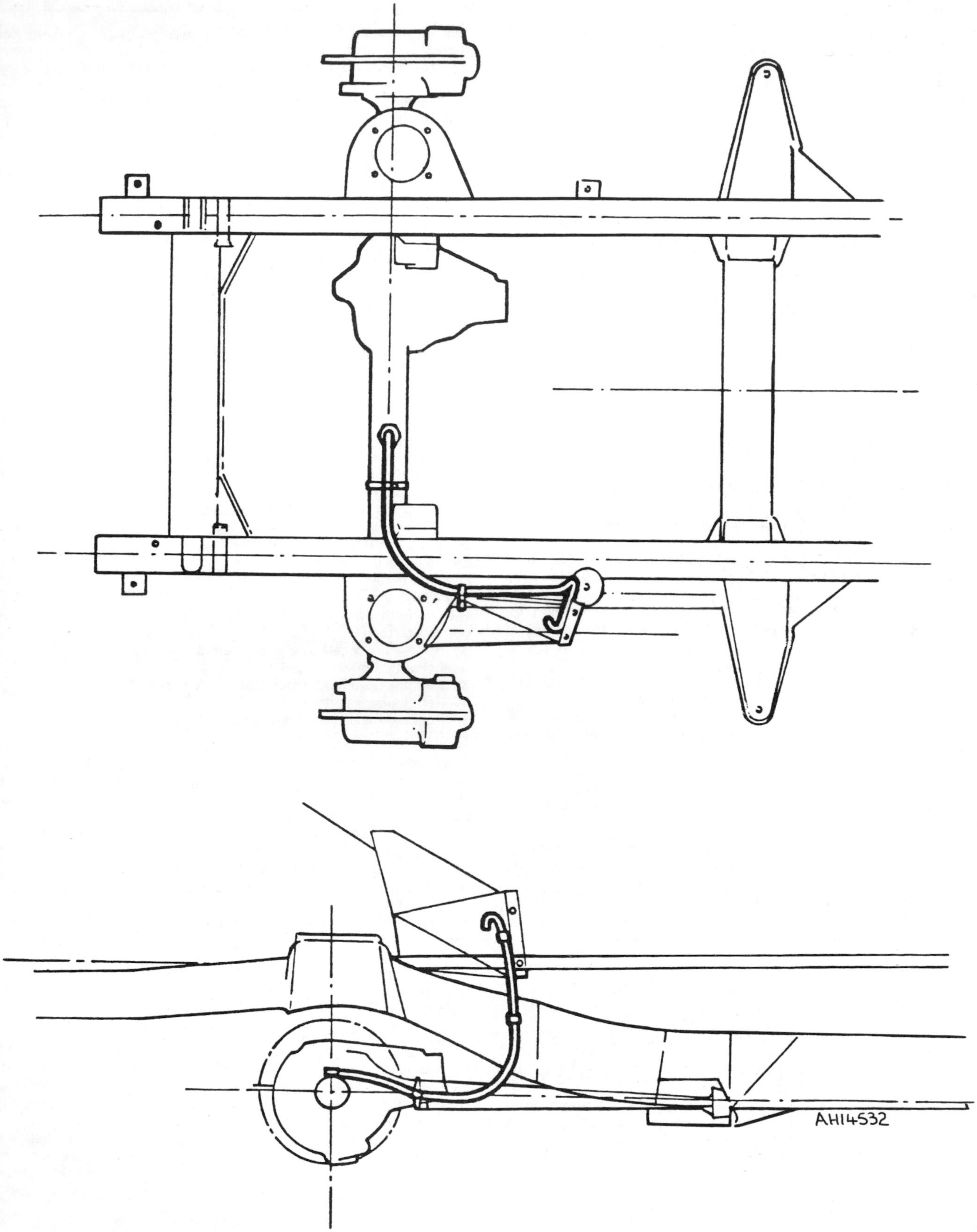

Fig. 13.53 Front axle breather location – later models (Sec 8)

AHI4532

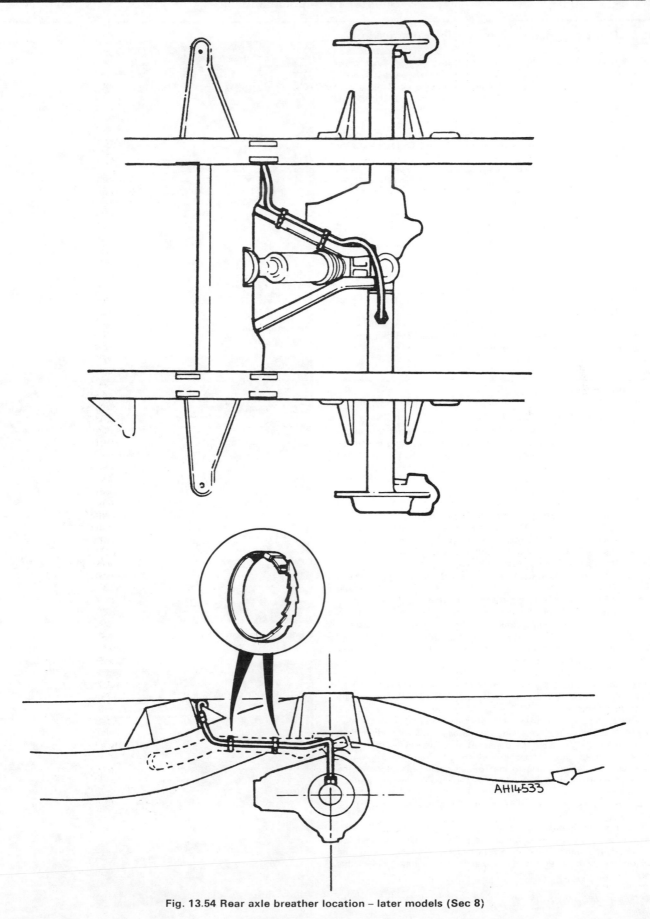

Fig. 13.54 Rear axle breather location – later models (Sec 8)

AHl4533

## Part D: Fault diagnosis – automatic transmission

1  As has been mentioned elsewhere in this Section, no service repair work should be considered by anyone without the specialist know-ledge and equipment required to undertake this work. This is also relevant to fault diagnosis. If a fault is evident, carry out the various adjustments previously described, and if the fault still exists consult the local garage or specialist.

2  Before removing the automatic transmission for repair, make sure that the repairer does not require to perform diagnostic tests with the transmission installed.

3  Most minor faults will be due to incorrect fluid level, incorrectly adjusted selector control or throttle cables and the internal brake band being out of adjustment.

## 8  Front and rear axles

### Axle breathers
1  To prevent the possibility of oil leakage past the axle seals caused by pressure within the casing, later models have axle breathers fitted.
2  The location and layout of the breathers and tubes are shown in Figs. 13.53 and 13.54.
3  If the breathers and tubes are removed at any time it is essential when refitting them to check that they are correctly relocated and that they are not blocked by excessive bending or damage.

## 9  Braking system

### Brake pad and lining renewal
1  whenever new brake pads and linings have been fitted a suitable running-in period should be observed; when heavy braking should be avoided wherever possible. The running-in period allows the new brake pads, linings, discs or drums to wear themselves in so that a full friction surface contact area is achieved. The suggested running-in period by the manufacturers is 350 miles (600 km).

### Brake hydraulic system components – modifications
2  In order to comply with EEC brake regulations, the brake pipes and connections were changed from non-metric (UNF) to metric connec-tions. At the same time the master cylinder was fitted with an integral pressure differential warning actuator (photo).
3  The metric brake line system can be identified by a yellow label attached to the brake servo hose. The pressure differential warning actuator (PDWA) can be seen in the end of the master cylinder.
4  It is important when renewing any part of the brake system not to mix non-metric with metric components. The threads and fittings can be identified by external markings and also by hose and colour codes (Fig. 13.55). Note that, unlike non-metric thread hoses, the metric thread hoses do not use sealing washers.

### Brake pressure reducing valve – removal and refitting
5  This unit is located beneath the master cylinder in the engine compartment (photo).
6  To remove the unit, first place a film of clean polythene over the filler neck of the brake fluid reservoir and refit the cap. This will reduce fluid loss when the brake pipes are disconnected from the valve unit.
7  Clean the brake pipe connections at the pressure reducing valve, then loosen and detach the inlet and outlet pipe connections at the valve. Plug the pipes and the valve ports to prevent fluid leakage and the ingress of dirt.
8  Unscrew and remove the valve unit retaining bolt and remove the valve.
9  Refit in the reverse order of removal.
10  Ensure that the brake line connections are clean when reconnecting them. Bleed the brakes on completion in accordance with the instructions given in Section 2 of Chapter 9 and paragraph 14 in this Section.

### Master cylinder and brake pressure warning switch – later models
11  On later models the brake master cylinder differs to that fitted to earlier variants in having the brake pressure warning switch and the

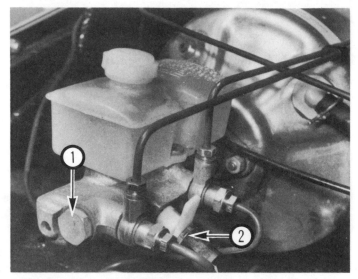

9.2 Brake master cylinder fitted to late models showing the pressure differential warning actuator PDWA (1) and  pressure warning switch (2)

9.5 Brake pressure reducing valve

9.16A Transmission brake adjuster – late models

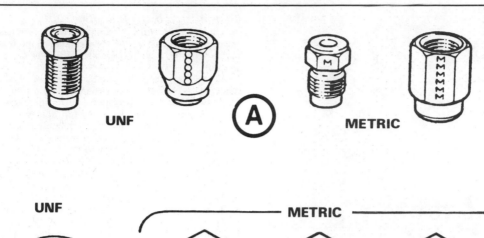

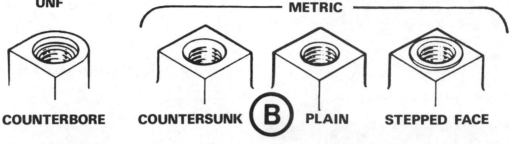

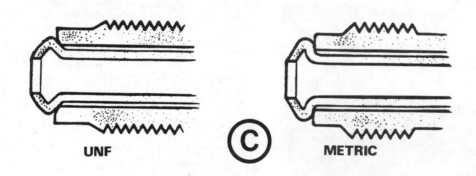

Fig. 13.55 Brake hydraulic system tube nuts and fittings identification (Sec 9)

A   Tube nut types          C   Flare types
B   Port types              D   Hose types

pressure differential warning actuator fitted as an integral part of the cylinders.

12 The master cylinder removal and overhaul procedure remains the same as that described in Section 10 of Chapter 9 except that the leads to the brake pressure warning switch will need to be disconnected and the switch removed by unscrewing it from the master cylinder body.

13 When refitting the brake pressure warning switch, tighten it to the specified torque given at the start of this Chapter.

*Brake hydraulic system – bleeding*

14 When bleeding the brake hydraulic system on later models with the brake pressure warning switch fitted in the side of the master cylinder, disconnect the switch leads then unscrew the switch four complete turns. The procedure is then as described in Section 2 of Chapter 9.

15 On completion retighten the switch to the specified torque and reconnect the leads.

9.16B General view of transmission brake – late models

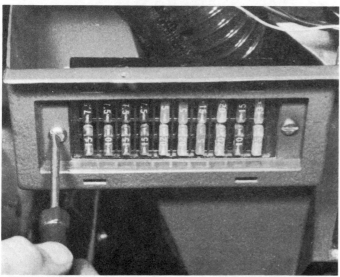

10.7 Removing a fusebox retaining screw

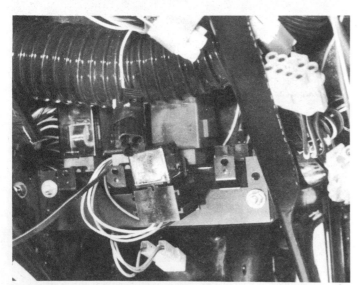

10.8 Relay panel unit – late models

## Transmission brake (handbrake)

16 On later models the transmission handbrake has an external adjuster fitted, being located on the forward side of the brake backplate. Access to the adjuster is from underneath the vehicle on the left-hand side (photos).

17 To take up the brake adjustment, first chock the front and rear roadwheels. The vehicle must be standing on level ground.

18 Fully release the handbrake. Turn the adjuster in a clockwise direction until the brake shoes are in contact with the drum. At each quarter turn of the adjuster a click will be heard and felt from it.

19 Turn the adjuster anti-clockwise half a turn (two clicks) then fully apply the handbrake to centralise the shoes.

20 Remove the roadwheel chocks then release and fully apply the handbrake to check that its operation is satisfactory.

## Brake testing on a rolling road – special precautions

21 Where the efficiency of the front or rear roadwheel brakes are to be tested using a two-wheel self-powered rolling road (such as for the MOT certificate) it is essential that the following conditions are met:

    (a)  *Disengage the centre differential*
    (b)  *The transfer gearbox must be in neutral*
    (c)  *The axle speed must not exceed 3 mph (5 kph)*

22 The following conditions must be met where a self-powered four-wheel rolling road is to be used:

    (a)  *All rollers must turn at the same speed*
    (b)  *Disengage the centre differential*

23 If the vehicle is to be checked on a free running four-wheel rolling road then the centre differential must be engaged. For high speed testing consult your Range Rover dealer as special tyres may need to be fitted to suit the rolling road type.

24 If the vehicle is to be checked on a free running two-wheel rolling road under high speed conditions then the propeller shaft to the stationary axle must be detached, the stationary wheels chocked and the centre differential engaged.

25 The tyres may also need to be changed according to the rolling road type – consult your dealer to check this point. Do not make extended high speed tests on a rolling road unless provision has been made for the vehicle to be adequately cooled.

## 10 Electrical system

### 25 ACR alternator

1 On later models the wiring connections to the 25 ACR alternator differ in that they are attached by stud and nut fixings instead of the moulded multi-connector previously used.

2 Whilst the later type alternator is directly replaceable with the earlier type, the wiring connections will have to be changed to suit.

### Alternator wiring harness

3 The alternator wiring harness has a spare brown lead taped to the cable assembly. This lead is for use with a split charge system or battery-sensed alternator system only. Care must be taken never to allow this lead to be attached to the spare Lucar connection on current machine-sensed alternators.

### Fuses

4 On later models the main fusebox is accessible from within the vehicle – being located next to the heater/ventilation control panel on the lower facia.

5 Prise free and unclip the cover for access to the fuses.

6 It will be noted that the cover inner face retains spare 10 amp and 20 amp fuses and also has a label for fuse identification and value for the various circuits. Whenever a spare fuse is used it should be replaced with an 'Autofuse' of the correct value.

7 To remove the fusebox unit, disconnect the battery earth lead then undo the two retaining screws and release the fuse holder unit from the facia (photo). The wiring to the rear of the fuse holder can then be inspected and detached as required.

### Relays

8 On later models, further circuit relays have been added and these are located under the lower facia panel on the driver's side (photo).

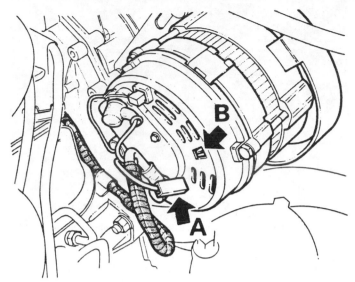

Fig. 13.56 Alternator wiring harness showing the spare brown lead (A) and the spare Lucar connection (B) (Sec 10)

*Do not connect A and B together*

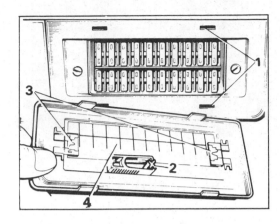

Fig. 13.57 The fusebox fitted to later models (Sec 10)

1  Cover retaining clip     3  Spare fuses
2  Fuse extractor           4  Fuse identification label

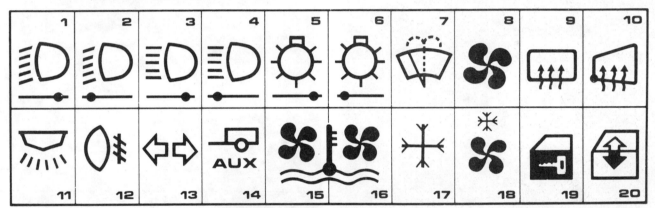

Fig. 13.58 Fuse circuits identification label (Sec 10)

*For circuits protected and fuse ratings refer to the Specifications*

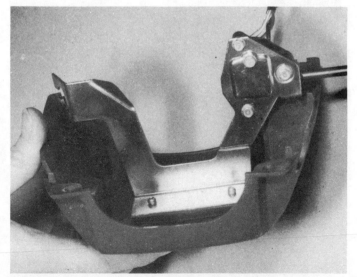

10.10 Steering column lower shroud showing the rear screen wiper washer switch attachment. The main lighting switch retaining bracket is on the left

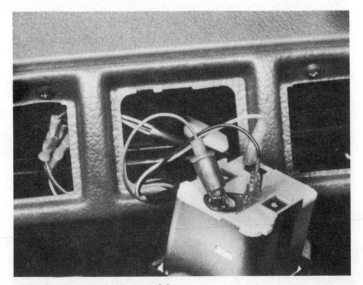

10.24 Clock removal – late models

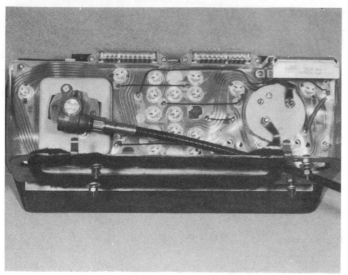

10.27 Instrument panel rear face layout – late models

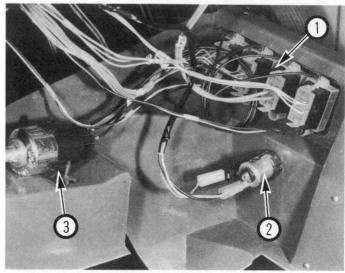

10.29 Underside view of the lower facia panel

1  Auxiliary switches      3  Fibre optic light unit
2  Cigar lighter

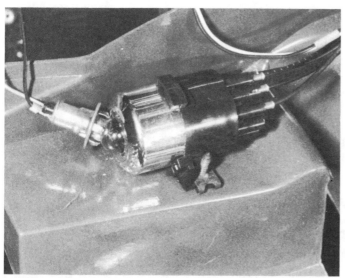

10.30 Bulb and holder removal from the fibre optic unit

10.33 Remove the lower facia panel on the right-hand side ...

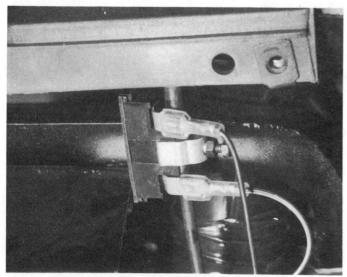

10.34 ... for access to the choke control and warning light unit

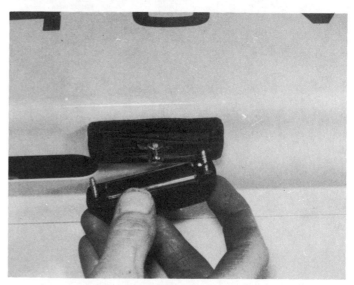

10.36 Number plate lamp lens and cover removal – late models

9   Remove the lower facia panel for access then remove the two bolts and nuts securing the relay panel unit, withdraw it and detach the relay concerned.

### Column-mounted switches – later models

10   Whilst the individual functions and removal procedures of the column-mounted stalk switches are similar to the earlier models, their positions have changed and are as follows:

(a)   **Main lighting switch:** *This is located on the left-hand side of the steering column and is the front stalk switch*

(b)   **Combination dipswitch, direction indicator horn and flasher switch:** *This is located on the left-hand side of the steering column and is the rear stalk switch*

(c)   **Rear screen wiper/washer switch:** *This is located on the right-hand side of the steering column and is the front stalk switch*

(d)   **Windscreen wiper/washer switch:** *This is located on the right-hand side of the steering column and is the rear stalk switch*

(e)   **The rear foglamp switch** *is now located on the auxiliary switch panel*

(f)   **The rear screen wiper/washer switch** *is connected to the mounting bracket attached to the lower shroud by retaining bolts. Undo the bolts to remove the switch from the mounting bracket (photo)*

### Auxiliary switch panel – later models

11   The auxiliary switch panel can be prised free from the lower facia and partially withdrawn to allow the switches or their warning bulbs (where applicable) to be removed.

12   With the panel withdrawn from the facia, unclip and release the switch lead connector, pull free the switch symbol fibre optic leads (at the top) and, where applicable, withdraw the warning light bulb holder. The switch can then be unclipped and removed from the panel.

13   Refit in reverse and check the switch concerned for satisfactory operation

### Clock (early models) – removal and refitting

14   Disconnect the battery earth leads.

**Fig. 13.59 Clock removal – early models (Sec 10)**

| | |
|---|---|
| 1   Console | |
| 2   Feed (+) wire | 4   Clock illumination wire |
| 3   Earth (–) wire | 5   Nut and bracket |

15   Undo the heater control knob grub screws and pull the knobs free.

16   Undo the two heater escutcheon plate retaining screws and then withdraw the plate.

17   Unscrew and remove the heater console-to-facia panel retaining screws (four at the top edge).

18   Remove the central louvre.

19   Open the glovebox lid on the passenger side then remove the heater console bottom retaining screw.

20   The console can now be eased away to allow access to the clock. Detach the connecting wires; noting respective connections. Unscrew the knurled retaining nut and remove the clock retaining bracket. Withdraw the clock.

21   The bulb and holder can be pulled from the clock and the bulb extracted for renewal.

22   Refit in the reverse order of removal and reset the clock.

### Clock (later models) – removal and refitting

23   Disconnect the battery earth lead.

24   The clock is secured in its aperture in the facia by spring clips and it may be possible to carefully prise it free from its aperture. Failing this, remove the face level vent on one or both sides of the clock and, reading through the vent aperture, push the clock out of the facia from the rear (photo).

25   Disconnect the wiring and pull free the bulb holder to remove the clock completely.

26   Refit in the reverse order of removal, then reset the clock.

### Instrument panel – later models

27   The removal and refitting of the instrument panel unit and its associated fittings on later models is similar to that for early models, but the layout differs slightly (photo).

### Fibre optic light unit

28   This unit is attached to the lower facia panel directly beneath the auxiliary switch panel unit. The fibre optic leads from the unit illuminate the auxiliary switches, but not their warning lights (where applicable).

29   Detach and withdraw the lower facia panel so that access can be gained to the switch (photo). Leave the switch leads attached.

30   Pull free the bulb holder from the base of the light unit then withdraw the bulb from its holder for renewal (photo).

31   To remove the unit, pull free the fibre optic leads, remove the bulb holder then undo the two retaining screws and remove the unit from the panel.

32   Refit in the reverse order of removal.

### Choke cable warning light switch

33   The choke cable warning light switch is located on the underside of the choke cable knob attachment to the facia panel. For access, undo the retaining screws and withdraw the lower facia panel on the right-hand side (photo).

34   Disconnect the wiring connections from the switch (photo), then loosen the locknut and unscrew the switch retaining strap bolt. Remove the switch.

35   Refit in the reverse order of removal and check operation before refitting the lower facia panel.

### Number plate lamp – later models

36   Although different in design to the early models, the rear number plate lamp unit and its bulb can be removed and refitted in the same manner as that of the earlier type (photo).

**Wiring diagrams commence overleaf**

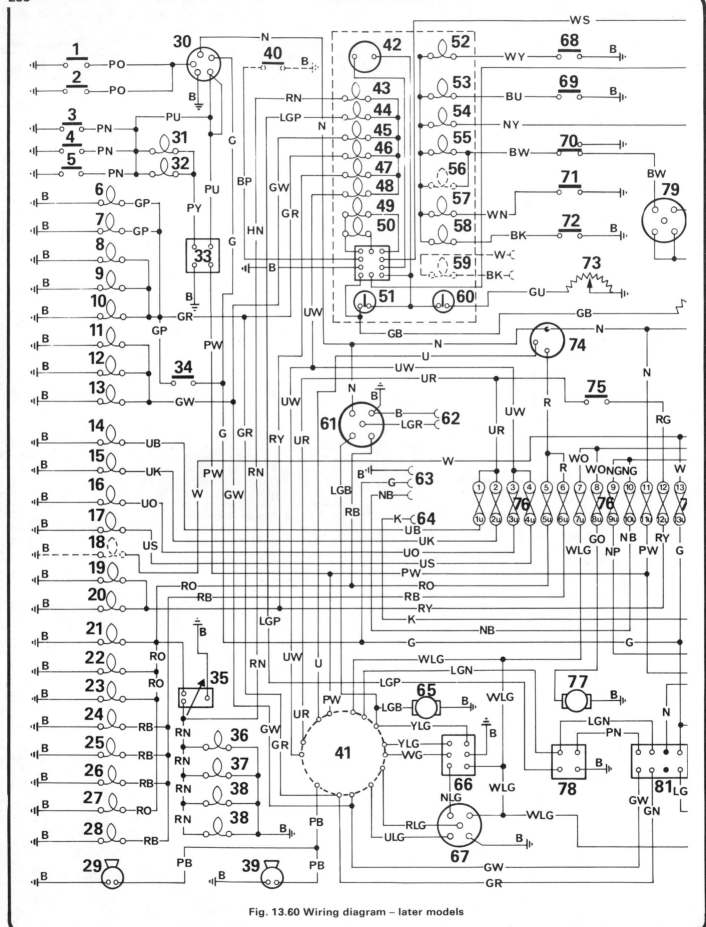

Fig. 13.60 Wiring diagram – later models

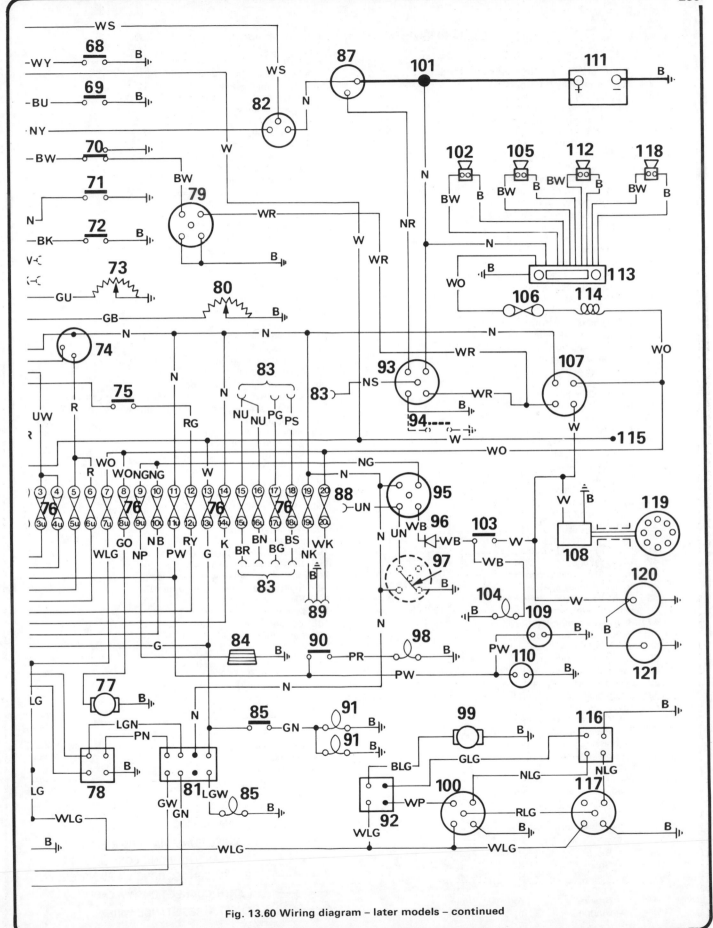

Fig. 13.60 Wiring diagram – later models – continued

**Fig. 13.60 Key to wiring diagram for later models**

1   Front door switch (left-hand)
2   Front door switch (right-hand)
3   Tailgate switch
4   Rear door switch (left-hand)
5   Rear door switch (right-hand)
6   Stop-lamp (right-hand)
7   Stop-lamp (left-hand)
8   Left-hand front indicator lamp
9   Left-hand rear indicator lamp
10  Left-hand side repeater lamp
11  Right-hand front indicator lamp
12  Right-hand rear indicator lamp
13  Right-hand side repeater lamp
14  Right-hand headlamp dip
15  Left-hand headlamp dip
16  Right-hand headlamp main
17  Left-hand headlamp main
18  Automatic gear selector graphics illumination
19  Right-hand rear foglamp
20  Left-hand rear foglamp
21  Right-hand number plate lamp
22  Right-hand side-lamp
23  Right-hand tail-lamp
24  Left-hand number plate lamp
25  Left-hand sidelamp
26  Left-hand tail-lamp
27  Radio illumination
28  Switch illumination
29  Right-hand horn
30  Interior lamp delay
31  Front interior lamp
32  Rear interior lamp
33  Interior lamp switch
34  Stop-lamp switch
35  Rheostat
36  Cigar lighter illumination
37  Clock illumination
38  Heater illumination
39  Left-hand horn
40  Automatic transmission oil cooler temperature switch
41  Steering column switches
42  Tachometer
43  Instrument illumination
44  Trailer warning light
45  Right-hand indicator
46  Left-hand indicator
47  Rear fog warning light
48  Headlamp warning light
49  Oil cooler temperature warning light
50  Low fuel warning light
51  Fuel indicator warning light
52  Cold start warning light
53  Differential lock warning light
54  Ignition warning light
55  Brake failure warning light
56  Brake failure warning light (Australia)
57  Oil pressure warning light
58  Park brake warning light
59  Park brake warning light (Australia)
60  Water temperature gauge
61  Headlamp wash timer (option)

62  Headlamp wash pump (option)
63  Heated electric mirrors (option)
64  Trailer socket (option)
65  Front screen wash
66  Wiper delay
67  Wiper motor
68  Cold start warning lamp switch
69  Differential lock switch
70  Brake failure switch
71  Oil pressure switch
72  Park brake switch
73  Water temperature transducer
74  Light switch
75  Rear foglamp switch
76  Fuses
77  Heater motor switch
78  Flasher unit
79  Brake failure warning lamp check relay
80  Fuel tank unit
81  Hazard switch
82  Alternator
83  Air conditioning (option)
84  Heated rear screen
85  Reverse lamp switch
86  Hazard warning lamp
87  Starter solenoid
88  Split charge relay (option)
89  Electric windows and central door locking (options)
90  Engine compartment (bonnet) light switch
91  Reverse lamps
92  Rear wipe/wash switch
93  Starter solenoid relay
94  Start inhibitor switch (automatic)
95  Heated rear window relay
96  Diode
97  Voltage switch (option)
98  Bonnet lamp
99  Rear screen wash motor
100 Rear wiper relay
101 Terminal post
102 Left-hand rear speaker (option)
103 Heated rear window switch
104 Heated rear window warning lamp
105 Right-hand rear speaker (option)
106 Radio fuse
107 Ignition switch
108 Constant energy ignition unit
109 Cigar lighter
110 Clock
111 Battery
112 Left-hand front speaker
113 Radio (option)
114 Radio choke
115 Split charge relay (option)
116 Rear wiper delay
117 Rear wiper motor
118 Right-hand front speaker
119 Distributor
120 Fuel pump
121 Fuel pump capacitor

### Colour code

| B | Black  | P | Purple |
|---|--------|---|--------|
| G | Green  | R | Red    |
| K | Pink   | S | Slate  |
| L | Light  | U | Blue   |
| N | Brown  | W | White  |
| O | Orange | Y | Yellow |

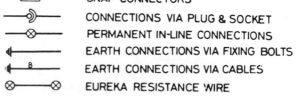

SNAP CONNECTORS
CONNECTIONS VIA PLUG & SOCKET
PERMANENT IN-LINE CONNECTIONS
EARTH CONNECTIONS VIA FIXING BOLTS
EARTH CONNECTIONS VIA CABLES
EUREKA RESISTANCE WIRE

## Fig. 13.61 Key to wiring diagram for later models with manual gearbox

1 Oil temperature transmitter
2 Front foglamp pick-up point
3 Front foglamp pick-up point
4 Battery voltmeter illumination
5 Oil temperature gauge illumination
6 Cigar lighter illumination
7 Oil pressure gauge
8 Clock illumination
9 LH Front side-lamp
10 RH Front sidelamp
11 Number plate illumination
12 Number plate illumination
13 LH Rear tail-lamp
14 RH Rear tail-lamp
15 Underbonnet illumination
16 Direction indicator side repeater
17 LH Front indicator lamp
18 Horns
19 RH Headlamp main beam
20 LH Headlamp main beam
21 RH Headlamp dipped beam
22 LH Headlamp dipped beam
23 LH Rear indicator
24 Direction indicator side repeater
25 RH Front indicator lamp
26 RH Rear indicator lamp
27 Reverse lamp LH
28 Reverse lamp LH
29 Oil temperature gauge
30 Underbonnet lamps
31 Direction indicator switch
32 Trailer warning light
33 Panel illumination
34 Panel illumination
35 Panel lighting switch
36 Differential lock warning light
37 Main beam warning light
38 LH Indicator warning light
39 RH Indicator warning light
40 Voltage stabiliser
41 Water temperature gauge
42 Fuel gauge
43 Rear fog lighting switch
44 Differential lock switch
45 Rear fog warning light
46 Sidelight warning light
47 Lighting switch
48 Indicator, headlamps, dipped beam and horn switch
49 Clock
50 Reverse lamp switch
51 Choke warning lamp
52 Oil warning lamp
53 Ignition warning lamp

54 Brake warning lamp
55 Fuel warning lamp
56 Cigar lighter
57 Hazard warning switch
58 Radio speakers
59 Fuse unit
60 Hazard unit
61 Ignition switch
62 Battery voltmeter
63 Brake fluid pressure switch
64 Choke switch
65 Alternator
66 Starter relay
67 Interior lights
68 Heater fuse
69 Stop-lamp switch
70 Oil pressure gauge
71 Starter motor
72 Resistive wire
73 Oil pressure transmitter
74 Courtesy lighting delay unit
75 Heated rear screen switch
76 Front wiper washer switch
77 Rear wiper washer switch
78 Heater motor
79 Coil
80 Fuse
81 Battery
82 Electric fuel pump
83 Distributor
84 Inspection sockets
85 Courtesy lighting switches
86 Interior lighting switch
87 Courtesy lighting switches
88 Brake circuit check relay
89 Oil pressure switch
90 Choke thermocoupling switch
91 Park brake warning light (optional)
92 Fuel gauge unit
93 Water temperature transmitter
94 Relay (heated rear screen)
95 Heated rear screen
96 Front screen washer motor
97 Two speed front wiper motor
98 Rear screen washer motor
99 Single speed rear wiper motor
100 LH stop-lamp
101 RH stop-lamp
102 LH rear foglamp
103 RH rear foglamp
104 Trailer socket connection
105 Programmed wash/wipe unit

*For colour code see key to Fig. 13.60*

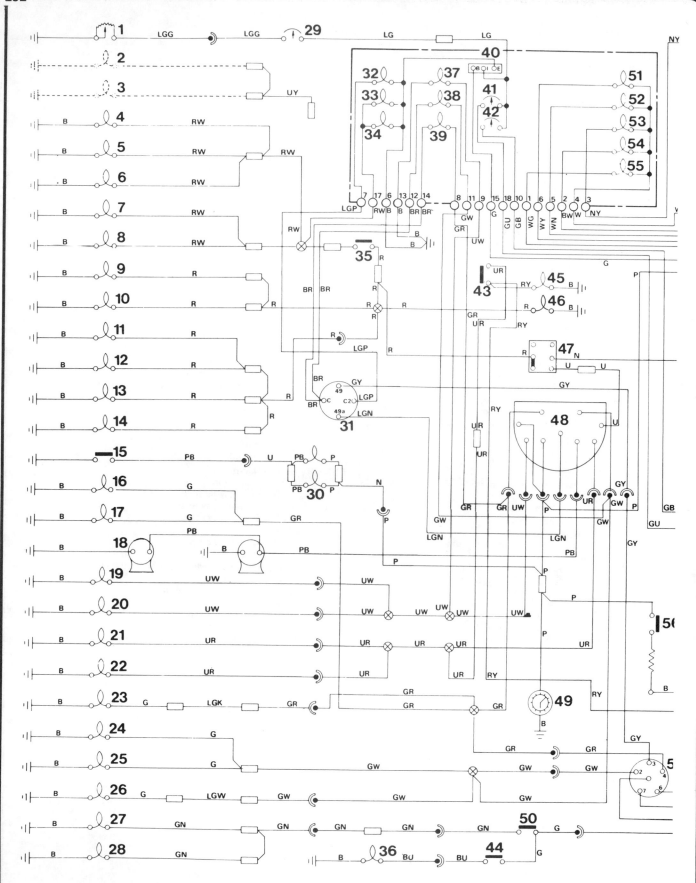

Fig. 13.61 Wiring diagram – later models with manual gearbox

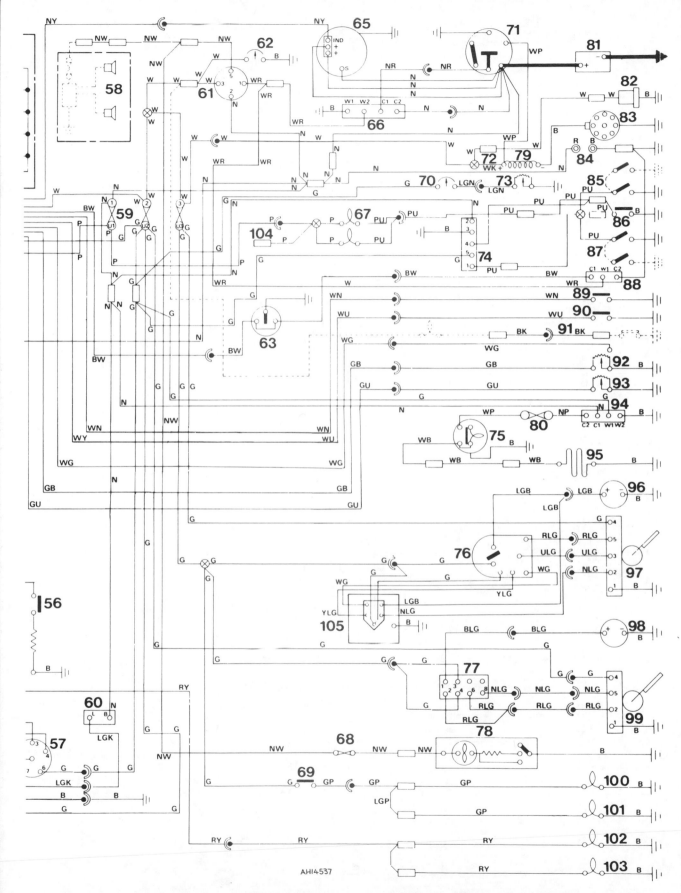

**Fig. 13.61 Wiring diagram – later models with manual gearbox – continued**

AHI4537

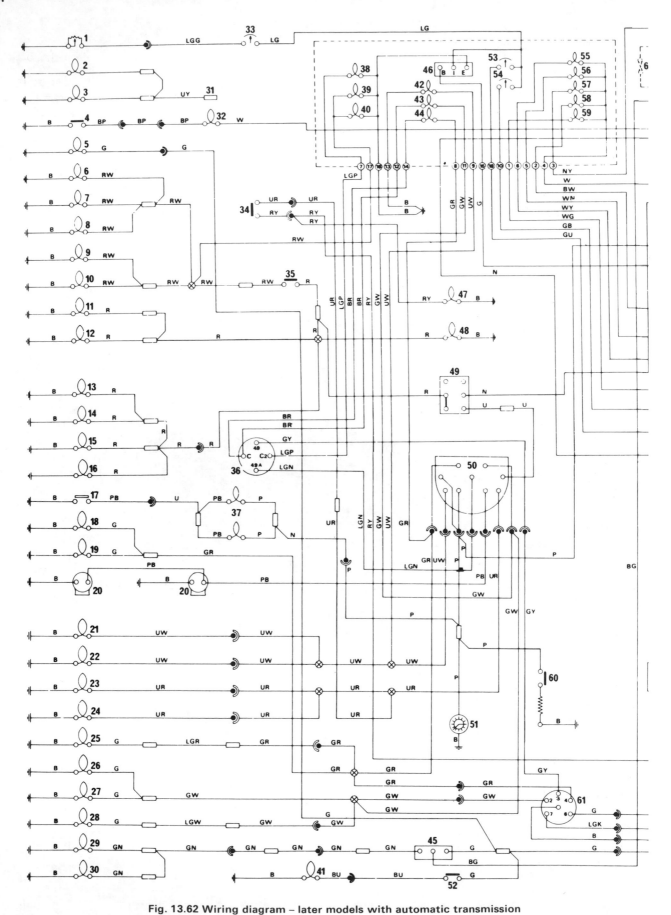

Fig. 13.62 Wiring diagram – later models with automatic transmission

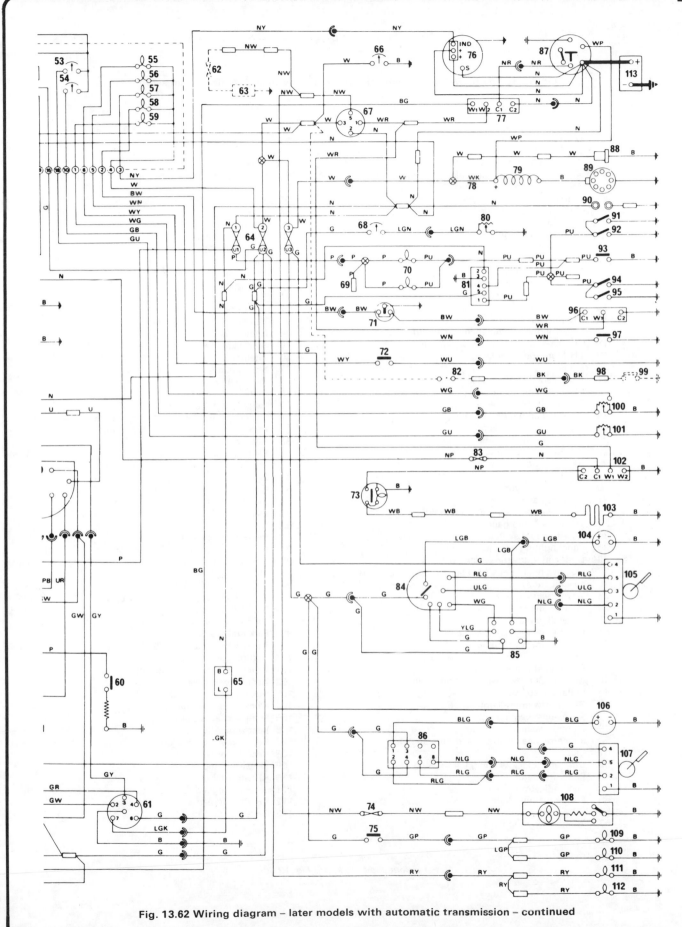

Fig. 13.62 Wiring diagram – later models with automatic transmission – continued

## Fig. 13.62 Key to wiring diagram for later models with automatic transmission

| | | | |
|---|---|---|---|
| 1 | Oil temperature transmitter | 58 | Brake warning light |
| 2 | LH Front foglamp | 59 | Fuel warning light |
| 3 | RH Front foglamp | 60 | Cigar lighter |
| 4 | Automatic gearbox oil cooler temperature switch | 61 | Hazard warning switch |
| 5 | Automatic gearbox graphics illumination | 62 | Radio fuse (when fitted) |
| 6 | Battery voltmeter illumination | 63 | Radio (when fitted) |
| 7 | Oil temperature gauge illumination | 64 | Fuse unit |
| 8 | Cigar lighter illumination | 65 | Hazard unit |
| 9 | Clock illumination | 66 | Battery voltmeter |
| 10 | Oil pressure indicator | 67 | Ignition switch |
| 11 | LH Front sidelamp | 68 | Oil pressure indicator |
| 12 | RH Front sidelamp | 69 | Trailer socket connection |
| 13 | Number plate illumination | 70 | Interior lights |
| 14 | Number plate illumination | 71 | Brake fluid check switch |
| 15 | LH Rear tail lamp | 72 | Choke switch |
| 16 | RH Rear tail lamp | 73 | Heater rear screen switch |
| 17 | Underbonnet illumination (where fitted) | 74 | Heater fuse |
| 18 | LH Direction indicator side repeater | 75 | Stop-lamp switch |
| 19 | LH Front indicator lamp | 76 | Alternator |
| 20 | Horns | 77 | Starter relay |
| 21 | RH Headlamp main beam | 78 | Resistive wire |
| 22 | LH Headlamp main beam | 79 | Coil |
| 23 | RH Headlamp dipped beam | 80 | Oil pressure transmitter |
| 24 | LH Headlamp dipped beam | 81 | Courtesy light delay unit (when fitted) |
| 25 | LH Rear indicator lamp | 82 | Park brake warning light (when fitted) |
| 26 | RH Direction indicator side repeater | 83 | Rear screen fuse |
| 27 | RH Front indicator lamp | 84 | Front wash/wiper switch |
| 28 | RH Rear indicator lamp | 85 | Programmed wash/wipe control unit |
| 29 | LH Reverse lamp | 86 | Rear wash/wipe control unit |
| 30 | RH Reverse lamp | 86 | Rear wash/wiper switch |
| 31 | Front foglamps pick-up point | 87 | Starter motor |
| 32 | Oil cooler temperature warning light | 88 | Electric fuel pump |
| 33 | Oil temperature gauge | 89 | Distributor |
| 34 | Rear foglamp switch | 90 | Inspection sockets |
| 35 | Panel lighting switch | 91 | Courtesy light switch (4-door only) |
| 36 | Direction indicator switch | 92 | Courtesy light switch |
| 37 | Underbonnet lamps (one lamp or two according to specification) | 93 | Interior light switch |
| 38 | Trailer warning light | 94 | Courtesy light switch |
| 39 | Panel illumination | 95 | Courtesy light switch (4-door only) |
| 40 | Panel illumination | 96 | Brake circuit check relay |
| 41 | Differential lock warning light | 97 | Oil pressure switch |
| 42 | Main beam warning light | 98 | Park brake pick-up point |
| 43 | LH Indicator warning light | 99 | Park brake switch (if fitted) |
| 44 | RH Indicator warning light | 100 | Fuel gauge transmitter |
| 45 | Neutral, Start & Reverse lighting switch | 101 | Water temperature transmitter |
| 46 | Voltage stabiliser | 102 | Heated rear screen relay |
| 47 | Rear fog warning light | 103 | Heated rear screen element |
| 48 | Sidelamps warning light | 104 | Front screen washer motor |
| 49 | Lighting switch | 105 | Front screen wiper motor |
| 50 | Indicator, headlamp dip and horn switch | 106 | Rear screen washer motor |
| 51 | Clock | 107 | Rear screen wiper motor |
| 52 | Differential lock warning light switch | 108 | Heater motor |
| 53 | Water indicator | 109 | LH Stop-lamp |
| 54 | Fuel indicator | 110 | RH Stop-lamp |
| 55 | Choke warning light | 111 | LH Rear foglamp |
| 56 | Oil warning light | 112 | RH Rear foglamp |
| 57 | Ignition warning light | 113 | Battery |

*For colour code see key to Fig. 13.60*

## 11 Suspension and steering

### Steering lock stop
1 When checking and adjusting the steering lock stop, as described in Section 33 of Chapter 11, it is important that the prescribed setting adjustment is adhered to. Any attempt to improve the steering lock by altering the setting beyond that specified will cause the steering rocker arm to foul with the steering box lock stops and place excessive loading on the rocker arm when under full lock. Any deviation from the specified setting is not permissible.

### Power steering pump reservoir – fluid level checking
2 The power steering system fluid reservoir filler cap on some models incorporates a dipstick. When checking the fluid level on such models ensure that the filler cap and the dipstick are cleaned then refitted and fully tightened down before removal to check the fluid level. If the cap is not fully tightened a false reading will be given and the reservoir will then be overfilled as a consequence.
3 When the filler cap is removed (either type), also check that the cap seal is in good condition. Renew the seal if necessary (photo).

11.3 Checking the fluid level in the power steering reservoir (non-dipstick type). Check the cap seal (arrowed)

### Alloy roadwheels
4 On later models, optional alloy roadwheels became available in place of the standard pressed-steel type normally fitted. At the same time the roadwheel hubs and fixing studs were modified to suit, the studs being

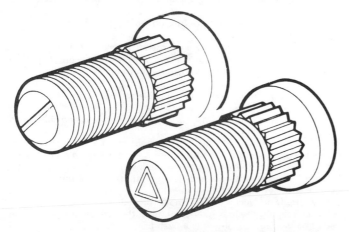

Fig. 13.63 Alloy roadwheel studs showing identification slot or triangle (Sec 11)

identified by a slot or triangle stamped into the outer endface.
5 It is important to note that alloy roadwheels **must not** be fitted to earlier models unless they have have had the later hub/stud assemblies changed to suit. Consult your Range Rover dealer before fitting the alloy roadwheels to earlier models to check for suitability.
6 Whenever an alloy roadwheel is removed, it is advisable to spray the wheel location face with an anti-seize compound. The manufacturers suggest 'Rocol' or an equivalent compound. **Do not** allow the compound to be sprayed on the brake discs or wheel studs.
7 With regard to maintenance, alloy roadwheels should be checked regularly for signs of damage and for corrosion. If a wheel is damaged, it must be renewed. Regular cleaning with a proprietary wheel cleaner and an annual protective coating of a suitable compound will prevent severe corrosion and keep them looking smart. If the wheels are allowed to become severely corroded have them checked by your Range Rover dealer for advice on their safety and possible renovation.
8 Special roadwheel nuts are fitted with alloy wheels. These nuts have a rotating washer located under the bolt head. Although the washer is staked to prevent it from being separated from the nut it is advisable, whenever they are removed, to check that the washer is in position on each nut and that it is free to rotate, but not loose enough to be separated from the nut. If any nuts are found to be defective, renew as necessary.

### Under ride protection bar
9 An under ride protection bar becomes available as an optional fitting to the new models from 1982; but, where required, it can be fitted to earlier models. The protection bar is mounted transversely under the chassis at the front and provides protection to the steering gear and associated components against damage when travelling over rough terrain.

## 12 Bodywork and fittings

### Decker panel – removal and refitting
1 The decker panel is located at the rear of the bonnet.
2 Unbolt and remove the bonnet (Section 7 in Chapter 12).
3 Detach and remove the air cleaner unit (Section 3 in Chapter 3).
4 Remove the windscreen wiper arms and blades, as described in Chapter 10, Section 33.
5 Unscrew and remove the decker panel retaining screws along the top leading edge (refer to Fig. 12.1).
6 Unscrew and remove the retaining screw each side at the top rear edge (open the doors for access).
7 Unscrew and remove the two side bolts from within the cavity.
8 Withdraw the decker panel forwards from under the windscreen lower rubber moulding and remove it. On some models it will also be necessary to disconnect the engine compartment light switch lead and, where applicable, the radio aerial.
9 Refit in the reverse order of removal. Slide the panel under the windscreen lower rubber moulding and locate all of the retaining screws and bolts prior to fully tightening them.

### Rear door glass (four-door models) – removal and refitting
10 Remove the rear door trim panel, as described in paragraphs 45 to 50 in this Section.
11 Temporarily refit the window regulator handle and adjust the window so that the lift arm stud is visible in the glass lifting channel. Support the glass in this position with a block of wood.
12 Unscrew and remove the four bolts securing the window regulator, to the door inner panel, then disconnect the lift arm stud from the glass channel and withdraw the regulator through the aperture in the inner door panel.
13 Detach the control rod from the door release handle by pulling it free from the plastic connector.
14 Raise the glass to the closed position and tape it to the door frame at the top for support. Remove the wooden support block.
15 Unscrew and remove the bolt (with spring and flat washer) retaining the short rear glass run channel at the bottom.
16 Undo the two screws (with shakeproof and flat washers) retaining the front door frame at the hinge face of the door.
17 Undo the two screws (with shakeproof and flat washers) retaining the rear door frame at the trailing (lock) end of the door.
18 Detach and remove the waist rail finisher which is secured in position by two self-tapping screws or pop rivets. If pop rivets are used they will have to be drilled through to release them.

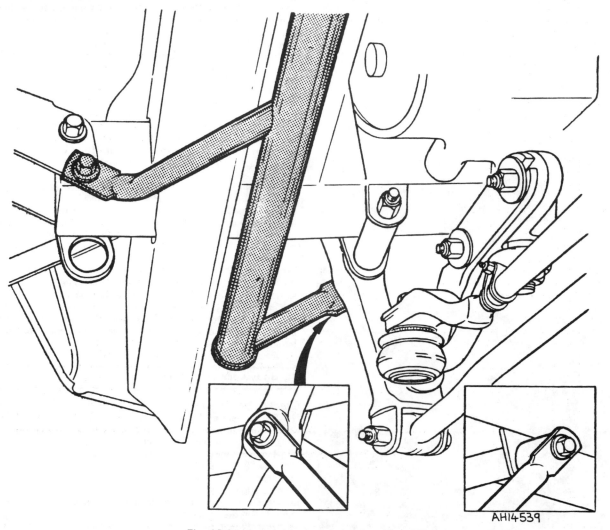

Fig. 13.64 Under ride protection bar (Sec 11)

19 Unclip and remove the weather strip from the outer door panel.
20 Unclip and remove the inner seals from the inner door panel.
21 The door frame and glass can now be lifted from the door. Untape and remove the glass from the frame.
22 Refitting is a reversal of the removal procedure.

### Front door lock (four-door models) – removal and refitting
23 Remove the front door trim panel (Section 15 in Chapter 12).
24 Detach the leads to the door loudspeaker then remove the thin pad and speaker unit.
25 Peel back the insulation sheet from the inner door panel.
26 Remove the door glass (referring to Section 15 in Chapter 12).
27 Detach the control rod from the key lock by releasing the metal securing clip.
28 Pull free the control rod from the door outer release handle, then detach the control rod from the inner door release handle by pulling it from the plastic connector block. Note that the control rod is also located in a guide bracket on the outboard side of the inner panel (within the cavity).
29 Undo and remove the two countersunk screws retaining the lock unit on the outside of the single screw with its shakeproof washer on the inside, and then withdraw the lock unit from the door.
30 The door inner and outer release handles can be removed in the same manner as that described for the rear door handles (described in the following sub-section).
31 Refit in the reverse order of removal.

### Rear door lock (four-door models) – removal and refitting
32 Remove the rear door trim panel, as described in paragraphs 45 to 50 in this Section.
33 Detach the control knob from the connector block within the door.
34 Release the metal retaining clip and release the manual lock control rod from the door lock.
35 Pull free and detach the control rod from the plastic ferrule of the outer door release handle.
36 Unscrew and remove the two countersunk screws securing the lock unit to the outer face and the single screw with shakeproof washers securing on the inside. Withdraw the lock unit, complete with the control rods.
37 If required, the inner door release handle can be removed by undoing the four retaining screws and flat washers.
38 The outer door release handle is secured by two nuts and shakeproof washers on the inside.
39 To remove the manual (sill) lock quadrant, insert a rod or screwdriver of suitable diameter into the square insert and press the plastic lock pin through to release it. When loosened the insert can be pushed into the door and the quadrant unit withdrawn, with its control rods, from the lower aperture in the inner door panel.
40 Refitting is a reversal of the removal procedure.
41 When refitting the lock quandrant, push the lock pin into the square insert from the outside until it is a flush fit.
42 When refitting the inner door handle, the front centre screw must be fitted first.
43 Although adjustment to the door lock release mechanism should not

normally be necessary, the outer door handle connecting rod length can be varied to suit and the inner handle position can be adjusted by loosening its retaining screws, When the position is adjusted retighten the front centre screw first.

44  On completion check that the door lock releases before the total handle movement is used up to allow for a minimal amount of over-throw movement.

### Rear door (four-door models) – removal and refitting

45  Disconnect the battery earth lead.

46  Open the door concerned and then unscrew the locking knob.

47  Fully close the door window then undo the retaining screw and withdraw the window regulator handle.

48  Undo the two armrest securing screws and remove the armrest.

49  Prise free the door release handle bezel which comprises an upper and lower section.

50  The door trim pad can now be removed by carefully prising it away from the door using a flat implement inserted around the periphery of the trim. The trim is secured by eighteen plastic clips which should pop free as leverage is applied. With the trim panel removed, peel back and remove the plastic insulation sheet.

51  Extract the circlip from the check strap clevis pin then withdraw the pin with its spacers.

52  Get an assistant to support the door during its removal and mark an outline around the door hinges to provide an alignment guide when refitting. Undo the lower hinge bolts then the upper hinge bolts and remove the door. Note any adjustment shims which may be fitted between the hinge and door pillar.

53  Refit in the reverse order of removal. If adjustment is required adjust the door in the same manner as that described for the front doors in Chapter 12.

### Central door locking system – general

54  This system is fitted to four-door models only. The four doors (but not the tailgate) are locked atomatically by means of the external door key or by the internal lock button.

55  The system is operated electrically and comprises a control unit fitted to the steering column support bracket under the lower facia panel, and a lock actuator unit in each door.

### Central door locking system control unit – removal and refitting

56  Disconnect the battery earth lead.

57  Undo the five retaining screws and remove the lower facia panel.

58  Detach the wiring multi-plug connector from the base of the control unit.

59  Unscrew and remove the two screws securing the control unit to the steering column support bracket and remove the unit. The unit is not repairable and if defective must be renewed.

60  Refit in the reverse order of removal.

### Control door locking system actuator unit – removal and refitting

61  Remove the door trim panel. For front door trim panel removal, refer to Section 15 in Chapter 12. For rear door trim panel removal refer to the Rear door (four-door models) – removal and refitting sub-section in this Chapter.

62  If removing a front door actuator, detach the leads to the door loud-speaker then remove the trim pad and speaker unit.

63  Peel back the insulation sheet at the top rear corner to gain access to the actuator unit within the door.

64  On front doors, undo the four actuator unit mounting plate retaining screws. On rear doors undo the two unit-to-door mounting screws.

65  Disconnect the wiring connection to the actuator unit by releasing the securing clip. On rear doors the wiring and connector plug are secured to the door inner panel by two spring clips; access to which is gained through the aperture in the inner panel.

66  Withdraw the actuator unit, manoeuvring it so that the operating rod can be detached from the actuator link of the door lock.

67  When the actuator unit is withdrawn the wiring connectors will be

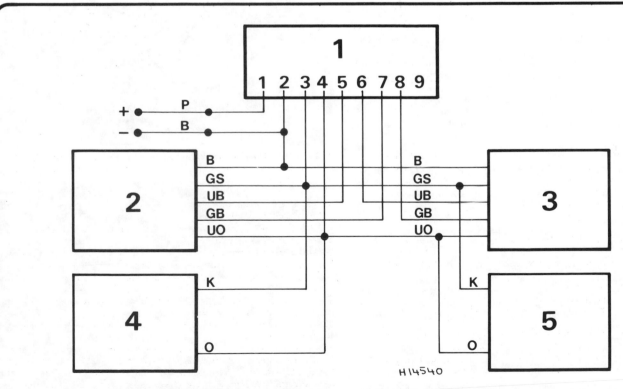

Fig. 13.65 Wiring diagram for the central door locking system (Sec 12)

1   Control unit
2   Lock actuator – driver's door
3   Lock actuator – front passenger door
4   Lock actuator – rear door
5   Lock actuator – rear door

*For colour code see key to Fig. 13.60*

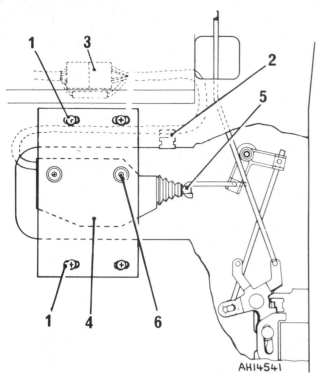

AH14541

**Fig. 13.66 Central door locking actuator unit (Sec 12)**

| | |
|---|---|
| 1 Retaining screws | 5 Operating rod/eye |
| 2 Cable clips | 6 Actuator unit-to-mounting |
| 3 Cable connectors | plate screws (rubber |
| 4 Actuator unit | mounted) |

exposed as they are pulled from their channel and can be disconnected and the actuator fully removed.

68 The actuator units are not repairable and, if defective, must be renewed. Disconnect the front door actuator unit from its mounting plate by undoing the two rubber mounted screws.

69 Refit the actuator unit in the reverse order of removal.

70 When attaching the actuator mounting plate to the inner door panel (front door units), adjust the mounting plate so that it is in the centre of the slotted holes.

71 Do not refit the door trim panel until the locking action is checked as follows.

72 Check the lock actuation manually and electrically to ensure that the actuator operating rod does not restrict the operation of either locking method. If necessary adjust the mounting position of the actuator to suit.

73 On the front doors, move the manual lock to the halfway position of its total movement then hold in this position and check that the door locks electrically. Further adjustment of the mounting plate may be necessary to achieve this.

*Facia panels (later models) – removal and refitting*
**Lower facia panel – driver's side**

74 Undo and remove the five retaining screws and withdraw the lower facia panel, together with the driver's side glovebox. Note the spacer fitted on the right-hand end between the facia panels (upper and lower).

75 Refit in the reverse order to removal.

**Steering column lower facia panel**

76 Remove the eight retaining screws, lower the panel sufficiently far to allow the light rheostat wiring connections to be detached, then remove the panel.

77 To remove the rheostat switch, undo the two retaining screws and withdraw the unit from the panel (photo).

78 Refit in the reverse order to removal.

**Lower centre facia panel**

79 Undo the retaining screws and pull free the heater/ventilation control knobs (photo).

80 Undo the two heater/ventilation control panel retaining screws then remove the panel (photo).

12.77 Rheostat (light dimmer) switch and retaining screws on the steering column lower facia panel

12.79 Undoing the control knob retaining screw

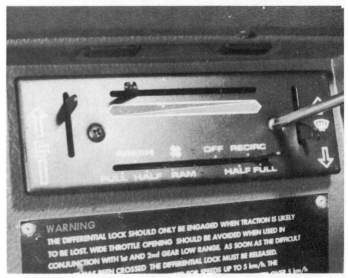

12.80 Undoing the heater/ventilation control panel retaining screws

81 Undo and remove three retaining screws from the lower edge of the panel and two screws each side (facing). Partially withdraw the panel so that the auxiliary switch panel and cigar lighter can be disconnected or removed from the heater/ventilation panel. Pull free the heater control illumination bulb holders (photo) and withdraw the panel.

82 Refit in the reverse order of removal.

**Glovebox – passenger side**

83 This is secured by screws at the side and rear, the rear screws being shown in the photo.

**Clock/vent facia panel**

84 Remove the glovebox and the lower centre facia panel as described previously.

85 Remove the clock and the fresh air louvre vents each side.

86 Undo the retaining screw and remove the side trim piece (photo).

87 Undo and remove the four screws at the front via the vent apertures.

88 Unscrew and remove the nearside retaining screw (photo).

89 Undo and remove the single screw from the underside on the left.

90 Undo the two screws from the underside near the grab handle.

91 The panel can then be withdrawn.

92 If required, the grab handle can be removed by undoing the three nuts and washers from the underside of the upper facia panel.

93 Refit the clock/centre vents facia panel by reversing the removal procedure.

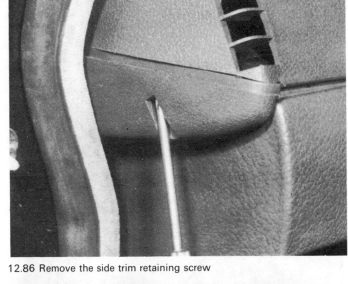

12.86 Remove the side trim retaining screw

12.81 Heater/ventilation control illumination bulb and holder

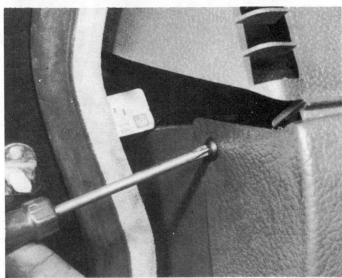

12.88 Lower facia side retaining screw removal

12.83 Glovebox inner retaining screws

### Air conditioning system – precautions and maintenance

*Where fitted, the following special precautions should be noted concerning the air conditioning system*

94 **Never** disconnect any part of the air conditioning refrigeration circuit unless the system has first been discharged by your dealer or a qualified refrigeration engineer.

95 Where the compressor or condenser obstruct other mechanical operations such as engine removal, then it is permissible to unbolt their mountings and move them to the limit of their flexible hose deflection, but not to disconnect the hoses. If there is still insufficient room to carry out the required work then the system must be discharged before disconnecting and removing the assemblies. The system will, of course, have to be recharged on completion.

96 Regularly check the condenser for clogging with flies or dirt. Hose clean with water or compressed air.

97 Regularly check the tension of the compressor drivebelt. The belt deflection should be 0.2 in (5.0 mm) at the centre point between the idler puller and the compressor. If adjustment is necessary, loosen the compressor pivot and mounting bolts to allow the compressor to be swung in the desired direction; adjust the drivebelt then retighten the bolts.

98 If any part of the wiring harness of the air conditioning system is disconnected or disturbed at any time, ensure that they are reconnected

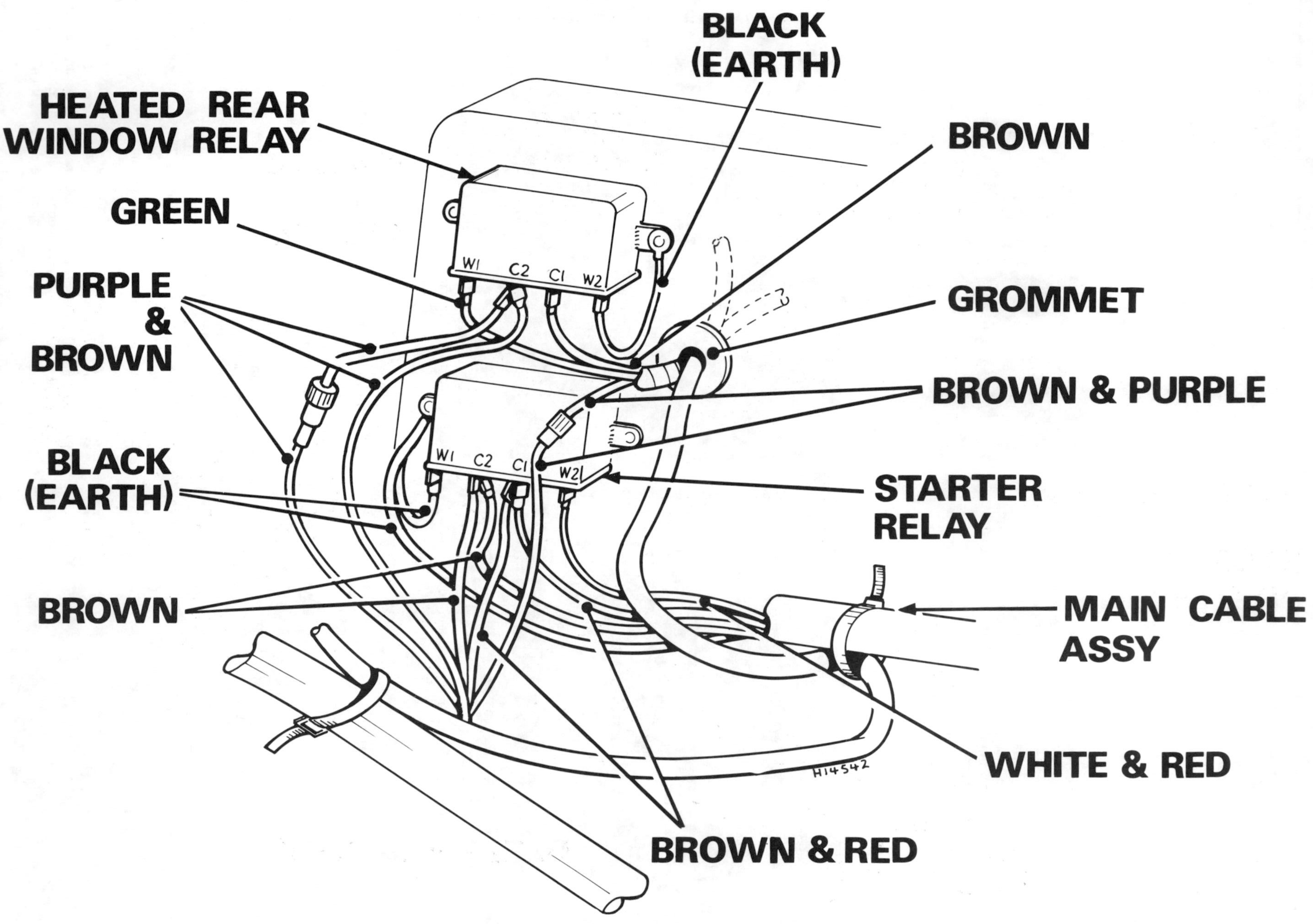

BLACK
(EARTH)

BROWN

GROMMET

BROWN & PURPLE

STARTER
RELAY

MAIN CABLE
ASSY

WHITE & RED

BROWN & RED

HEATED REAR
WINDOW RELAY

GREEN

PURPLE
&
BROWN

BLACK
(EARTH)

BROWN

W2

C1

C2

W1

W2

C1

C2

W1

Fig. 13.67 Air conditioning system wiring connections to the heated rear window relay and starter relay (Sec 12)

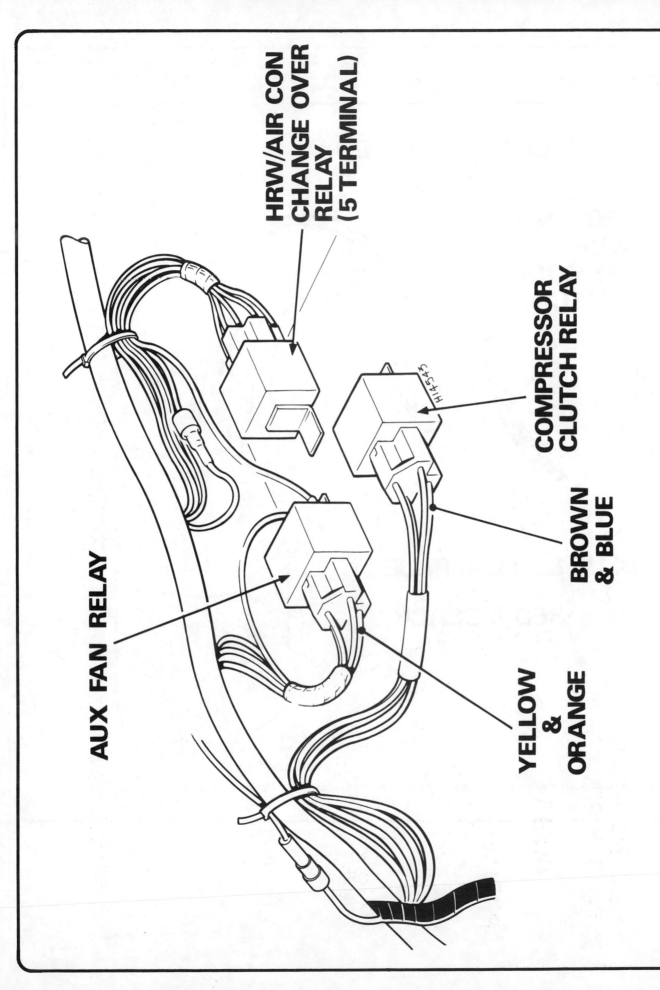

**HRW/AIR CON CHANGE OVER RELAY (5 TERMINAL)**

**COMPRESSOR CLUTCH RELAY**

H14543

**AUX FAN RELAY**

**BROWN & BLUE**

**YELLOW & ORANGE**

Fig. 13.68 Air conditioning system relays (Sec 12)

correctly, securely and are kept well clear of the exhaust manifold system. To avoid confusion when reconnecting the system wiring, refer to Figs. 13.67, 13.68 and 13.69. These illustrations show the basic system diagrams for right-hand drive models; some variations from those shown are possible on right and left-hand drive vehicles. If in doubt, check with your Range Rover dealer.

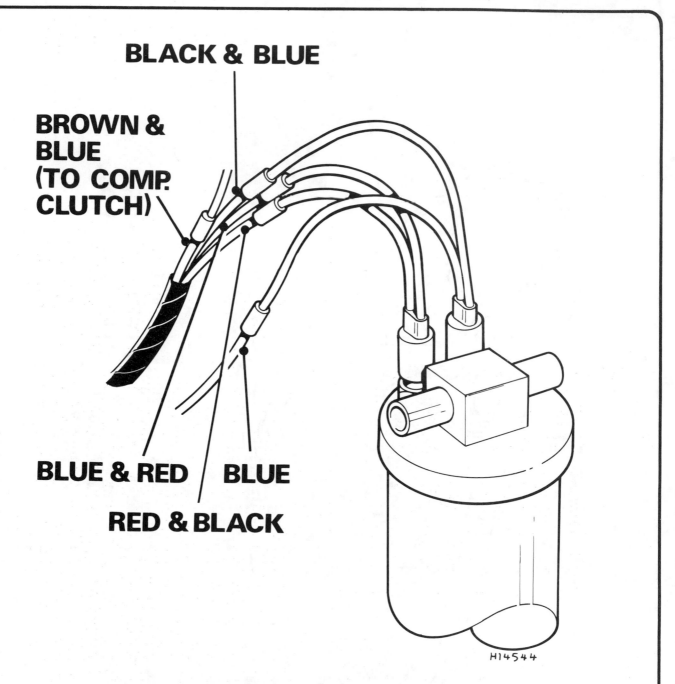

**BLACK & BLUE**

**BROWN & BLUE (TO COMP. CLUTCH)**

**BLUE & RED**      **BLUE**

**RED & BLACK**

H14544

Fig. 13.69 Air conditioning system wiring connections – compressor clutch and pressure switches (viewed from the front) (Sec 12)

# General repair procedures

Whenever servicing, repair or overhaul work is carried out on the car or its components, it is necessary to observe the following procedures and instructions. This will assist in carrying out the operation efficiently and to a professional standard of workmanship.

## Joint mating faces and gaskets

Where a gasket is used between the mating faces of two components, ensure that it is renewed on reassembly, and fit it dry unless otherwise stated in the repair procedure. Make sure that the mating faces are clean and dry with all traces of old gasket removed. When cleaning a joint face, use a tool which is not likely to score or damage the face, and remove any burrs or nicks with an oilstone or fine file.

Make sure that tapped holes are cleaned, and keep them free of jointing compound if this is being used unless specifically instructed otherwise.

Ensure that all orifices, channels or pipes are clear and blow through them, preferably using compressed air.

## Oil seals

Whenever an oil seal is removed from its working location, either individually or as part of an assembly, it should be renewed.

The very fine sealing lip of the seal is easily damaged and will not seal if the surface it contacts is not completely clean and free from scratches, nicks or grooves. If the original sealing surface of the component cannot be restored, the component should be renewed.

Protect the lips of the seal from any surface which may damage them in the course of fitting. Use tape or a conical sleeve where possible. Lubricate the seal lips with oil before fitting and, on dual lipped seals, fill the space between the lips with grease.

Unless otherwise stated, oil seals must be fitted with their sealing lips toward the lubricant to be sealed.

Use a tubular drift or block of wood of the appropriate size to install the seal and, if the seal housing is shouldered, drive the seal down to the shoulder. If the seal housing is unshouldered, the seal should be fitted with its face flush with the housing top face.

## Screw threads and fastenings

Always ensure that a blind tapped hole is completely free from oil, grease, water or other fluid before installing the bolt or stud. Failure to do this could cause the housing to crack due to the hydraulic action of the bolt or stud as it is screwed in.

When tightening a castellated nut to accept a split pin, tighten the nut to the specified torque, where applicable, and then tighten further to the next split pin hole. Never slacken the nut to align a split pin hole unless stated in the repair procedure.

When checking or retightening a nut or bolt to a specified torque setting, slacken the nut or bolt by a quarter of a turn, and then retighten to the specified setting.

## Locknuts, locktabs and washers

Any fastening which will rotate against a component or housing in the course of tightening should always have a washer between it and the relevant component or housing.

Spring or split washers should always be renewed when they are used to lock a critical component such as a big-end bearing retaining nut or bolt.

Locktabs which are folded over to retain a nut or bolt should always be renewed.

Self-locking nuts can be reused in non-critical areas, providing resistance can be felt when the locking portion passes over the bolt or stud thread.

Split pins must always be replaced with new ones of the correct size for the hole.

## Special tools

Some repair procedures in this manual entail the use of special tools such as a press, two or three-legged pullers, spring compressors etc. Wherever possible, suitable readily available alternatives to the manufacturer's special tools are described, and are shown in use. In some instances, where no alternative is possible, it has been necessary to resort to the use of a manufacturer's tool and this has been done for reasons of safety as well as the efficient completion of the repair operation. Unless you are highly skilled and have a thorough understanding of the procedure described, never attempt to bypass the use of any special tool when the procedure described specifies its use. Not only is there a very great risk of personal injury, but expensive damage could be caused to the components involved.

# Conversion factors

**Length (distance)**

| | | | | | |
|---|---|---|---|---|---|
| Inches (in) | X | 25.4 | = Millimetres (mm) | X 0.0394 | = Inches (in) |
| Feet (ft) | X | 0.305 | = Metres (m) | X 3.281 | = Feet (ft) |
| Miles | X | 1.609 | = Kilometres (km) | X 0.621 | = Miles |

**Volume (capacity)**

| | | | | | |
|---|---|---|---|---|---|
| Cubic inches (cu in; in$^3$) | X | 16.387 | = Cubic centimetres (cc; cm$^3$) | X 0.061 | = Cubic inches (cu in; in$^3$) |
| Imperial pints (Imp pt) | X | 0.568 | = Litres (l) | X 1.76 | = Imperial pints (Imp pt) |
| Imperial quarts (Imp qt) | X | 1.137 | = Litres (l) | X 0.88 | = Imperial quarts (Imp qt) |
| Imperial quarts (Imp qt) | X | 1.201 | = US quarts (US qt) | X 0.833 | = Imperial quarts (Imp qt) |
| US quarts (US qt) | X | 0.946 | = Litres (l) | X 1.057 | = US quarts (US qt) |
| Imperial gallons (Imp gal) | X | 4.546 | = Litres (l) | X 0.22 | = Imperial gallons (Imp gal) |
| Imperial gallons (Imp gal) | X | 1.201 | = US gallons (US gal) | X 0.833 | = Imperial gallons (Imp gal) |
| US gallons (US gal) | X | 3.785 | = Litres (l) | X 0.264 | = US gallons (US gal) |

**Mass (weight)**

| | | | | | |
|---|---|---|---|---|---|
| Ounces (oz) | X | 28.35 | = Grams (g) | X 0.035 | = Ounces (oz) |
| Pounds (lb) | X | 0.454 | = Kilograms (kg) | X 2.205 | = Pounds (lb) |

**Force**

| | | | | | |
|---|---|---|---|---|---|
| Ounces-force (ozf; oz) | X | 0.278 | = Newtons (N) | X 3.6 | = Ounces-force (ozf; oz) |
| Pounds-force (lbf; lb) | X | 4.448 | = Newtons (N) | X 0.225 | = Pounds-force (lbf; lb) |
| Newtons (N) | X | 0.1 | = Kilograms-force (kgf; kg) | X 9.81 | = Newtons (N) |

**Pressure**

| | | | | | |
|---|---|---|---|---|---|
| Pounds-force per square inch (psi; lbf/in$^2$; lb/in$^2$) | X | 0.070 | = Kilograms-force per square centimetre (kgf/cm$^2$; kg/cm$^2$) | X 14.223 | = Pounds-force per square inch (psi; lbf/in$^2$; lb/in$^2$) |
| Pounds-force per square inch (psi; lbf/in$^2$; lb/in$^2$) | X | 0.068 | = Atmospheres (atm) | X 14.696 | = Pounds-force per square inch (psi; lbf/in$^2$; lb/in$^2$) |
| Pounds-force per square inch (psi; lbf/in$^2$; lb/in$^2$) | X | 0.069 | = Bars | X 14.5 | = Pounds-force per square inch (psi; lbf/in$^2$; lb/in$^2$) |
| Pounds-force per square inch (psi; lbf/in$^2$; lb/in$^2$) | X | 6.895 | = Kilopascals (kPa) | X 0.145 | = Pounds-force per square inch (psi; lbf/in$^2$; lb/in$^2$) |
| Kilopascals (kPa) | X | 0.01 | = Kilograms-force per square centimetre (kgf/cm$^2$; kg/cm$^2$) | X 98.1 | = Kilopascals (kPa) |

**Torque (moment of force)**

| | | | | | |
|---|---|---|---|---|---|
| Pounds-force inches (lbf in; lb in) | X | 1.152 | = Kilograms-force centimetre (kgf cm; kg cm) | X 0.868 | = Pounds-force inches (lbf in; lb in) |
| Pounds-force inches (lbf in; lb in) | X | 0.113 | = Newton metres (Nm) | X 8.85 | = Pounds-force inches (lbf in; lb in) |
| Pounds-force inches (lbf in; lb in) | X | 0.083 | = Pounds-force feet (lbf ft; lb ft) | X 12 | = Pounds-force inches (lbf in; lb in) |
| Pounds-force feet (lbf ft; lb ft) | X | 0.138 | = Kilograms-force metres (kgf m; kg m) | X 7.233 | = Pounds-force feet (lbf ft; lb ft) |
| Pounds-force feet (lbf ft; lb ft) | X | 1.356 | = Newton metres (Nm) | X 0.738 | = Pounds-force feet (lbf ft; lb ft) |
| Newton metres (Nm) | X | 0.102 | = Kilograms-force metres (kgf m; kg m) | X 9.804 | = Newton metres (Nm) |

**Power**

| | | | | | |
|---|---|---|---|---|---|
| Horsepower (hp) | X | 745.7 | = Watts (W) | X 0.0013 | = Horsepower (hp) |

**Velocity (speed)**

| | | | | | |
|---|---|---|---|---|---|
| Miles per hour (miles/hr; mph) | X | 1.609 | = Kilometres per hour (km/hr; kph) | X 0.621 | = Miles per hour (miles/hr; mph) |

**Fuel consumption***

| | | | | | |
|---|---|---|---|---|---|
| Miles per gallon, Imperial (mpg) | X | 0.354 | = Kilometres per litre (km/l) | X 2.825 | = Miles per gallon, Imperial (mpg) |
| Miles per gallon, US (mpg) | X | 0.425 | = Kilometres per litre (km/l) | X 2.352 | = Miles per gallon, US (mpg) |

**Temperature**

Degrees Fahrenheit = (°C x 1.8) + 32

Degrees Celsius (Degrees Centigrade; °C) = (°F − 32) x 0.56

*It is common practice to convert from miles per gallon (mpg) to litres/100 kilometres (l/100km), where mpg (Imperial) x l/100 km = 282 and mpg (US) x l/100 km = 235

# Index

## A

**Air cleaner baffle** – 227
**Air cleaners** – 60
**Air conditioning system**
   precautions and maintenance – 301
**Air filter elements renewal** – 61
**Air intake temperature control system**
   description – 62
   flap valve – 63
   operational check – 62
   temperature sensor – 63
**Alternator**
   brush renewal – 152
   description – 150
   drivebelt adjustment – 151
   maintenance – 150
   precautions – 150
   removal and refitting – 151
   testing in situ – 150
   wiring harness – 284
   25 ACR alternator – 284
**Automatic choke** – 70
**Automatic transmission** – 272 et seq
   automatic transmission and transfer gearbox
     precautions and maintenance – 272
   fault diagnosis – 282
   routine maintenance – 272
   special precautions – 272
**Automatic transmission and transfer gearbox**
   removal and refitting – 275
   removal methods – 275
   separation and reassembly – 277
**Automatic transmission/transfer gearbox selector and associated components**
   automatic transmission gear selector unit removal and refitting – 279
   automatic transmission selector rod/cable, adjustment – 279
   automatic transmission throttle valve linkage, adjustment – 279
   high/low gearchange connecting rod, adjustment – 279
   reverse starter switch, testing, removal and refitting – 279
   transmission tunnel top and side covers, removal and refitting – 279

## B

**Battery**
   charging – 150
   electrolyte replenishment – 150
   maintenance – 149
   removal and refitting – 148
   split charging facility – 175
**Big-end bearing clearances** – 37

**Bodywork and fittings** – 297 et seq
   air conditioning system, precautions and maintenance – 301
   central door locking system, general – 299
   central door locking system actuator unit, removal and refitting – 299
   central door locking system control unit, removal and refitting – 299
   console – 214
   decker panel, removal and refitting – 297
   description – 207
   facia panel, top – 215
   facia panels (later models) removal and refitting – 300
   floor panel – 214
   front door lock (four-door models), removal and refitting – 298
   glass, side – 214
   glovebox – 215
   glovebox, passenger side – 301
   hinges – 209
   locks – 209
   maintenance – 207, 209
   rear door (four-door models), removal and refitting – 299
   rear door glass (four-door models), removal and refitting – 297
   rear door lock (four-door models), removal and refitting – 298
   repair, major damage – 208
   repair, minor damage – 207
   se ts, front – 214
   w ng, front – 209
   wing, rear – 209
**Bonnet** – 209
**Braking system** – 134 et seq
   bleeding the hydraulic system – 135, 283
   brake hydraulic system components, modifications – 282
   brake pads and linings, renewal – 136, 282
   brake pressure reducing valve, removal and refitting – 282
   brake testing on a rolling road, special precautions – 284
   caliper, overhaul – 138
   caliper, removal and refitting – 137
   description – 134
   disc – 139
   failure warning valve and switch – 139
   fault diagnosis – 146
   master cylinder – 140
   master cylinder and brake pressure warning light switch, later models – 282
   pedal – 142
   pipes and hoses – 142
   servo unit
     filter renewal – 141
     general – 140
     removal and refitting – 141
   specifications – 134
   torque wrench settings – 134
   transmission brake (handbrake) – 284
     adjustment – 145
     lever and linkage – 142
     overhaul – 143

Printed by
**J H Haynes & Co Ltd**
Sparkford  Nr Yeovil
Somerset  BA22 7JJ England